ENCYCLOPEDIA OF

DRUGS, ALCOHOL & ADDICTIVE BEHAVIOR

EDITORIAL BOARD

ENCYCLOPEDIA OF

DRUGS, ALCOHOL & ADDICTIVE BEHAVIOR

THIRD EDITION

Volume 2

D–L

Pamela Korsmeyer and Henry R. Kranzler

EDITORS IN CHIEF

MACMILLAN REFERENCE USA
A part of Gale, Cengage Learning

Detroit • New York • San Francisco • New Haven, Conn • Waterville, Maine • London

Encyclopedia of Drugs, Alcohol, & Addictive Behavior, 3rd edition

Pamela Korsmeyer and Henry R. Kranzler, Editors in Chief

For product information and technology assistance, contact us at
Gale Customer Support, 1-800-877-4253.
For permission to use material from this text or product,
submit all requests online at **www.cengage.com/permissions.**
Further permissions questions can be emailed to
permissionrequest@cengage.com

Since this page cannot legibly accommodate all copyright notices, the acknowledgments constitute an extension of the copyright notice.

While every effort has been made to ensure the reliability of the information presented in this publication, Gale, a part of Cengage Learning, does not guarantee the accuracy of the data contained herein. Gale accepts no payment for listing; and inclusion in the publication of any organization, agency, institution, publication, service, or individual does not imply endorsement of the editors or publisher. Errors brought to the attention of the publisher and verified to the satisfaction of the publisher will be corrected in future editions.

Library of Congress Cataloging-in-Publication Data

Encyclopedia of drugs, alcohol & addictive behavior / Pamela Korsmeyer and Henry R. Kranzler. -- 3rd ed.
    p. cm.
  Includes bibliographical references and index.
  ISBN 978-0-02-866064-6 (set) -- ISBN 978-0-02-866065-3 (vol. 1) -- ISBN 978-0-02-866066-0 (vol. 2) -- ISBN 978-0-02-866067-7 (vol. 3) -- ISBN 978-0-02-866068-4 (vol. 4)
    1. Drug abuse--Encyclopedias. 2. Substance abuse--Encyclopedias. 3. Alcoholism--Encyclopedias. 4. Drinking of alcoholic beverages--Encyclopedias. I. Korsmeyer, Pamela, 1945- II. Kranzler, Henry R., 1950-

HV5804.E53 2009
362.2903--dc22   2008012719

Gale
27500 Drake Rd.
Farmington Hills, MI 48331-3535

ISBN-13: 978-0-02-866064-6 (set)   ISBN-10: 0-02-866064-1 (set)
ISBN-13: 978-0-02-866065-3 (vol. 1)   ISBN-10: 0-02-866065-X (vol. 1)
ISBN-13: 978-0-02-866066-0 (vol. 2)   ISBN-10: 0-02-866066-8 (vol. 2)
ISBN-13: 978-0-02-866067-7 (vol. 3)   ISBN-10: 0-02-866067-6 (vol. 3)
ISBN-13: 978-0-02-866068-4 (vol. 4)   ISBN-10: 0-02-866068-4 (vol. 4)

This title is also available as an e-book.
ISBN-13: 978-0-02-866114-8; ISBN-10: 0-02-866114-1
Contact your Gale sales representative for ordering information.

Printed in the United States of America
1 2 3 4 5 6 7 12 11 10 09 08

CONTENTS

v

DAST. *See* **Drug Abuse Screening Test (DAST).**

DELIRIUM. The primary clinical feature of delirium is the disturbance of consciousness and/or attention. Associated symptoms are disorientation, memory deficits, and language or perceptual disturbances. Any cognitive function may be affected. Fleeting false beliefs, including paranoid ideas, are common but usually short-lived. Additional clinical symptoms include sleep/wake cycle disturbances (insomnia, daytime drowsiness, sleep/wake cycle reversal, nocturnal worsening of symptoms), increased or decreased psychomotor activity, increased or decreased flow of speech, increased startle reaction, and emotional disturbances (irritability, depression, euphoria, anxiety, apathy). Delirium develops within hours to days, and its symptoms fluctuate over time. Although many cases of delirium resolve promptly with the treatment of the underlying cause, symptoms may persist for months after treatment, especially in the elderly. Sometimes an episode of delirium establishes a new, lower cognitive baseline.

Regarding epidemiology, the community prevalence of delirium is age-dependent: 0.4 percent in those over 18, 1.1 percent in those over 55 and 13.6 percent in those over 85 (Folstein, Bassett, Romanowsk, et al., 1993). Delirium is common in the hospital setting: 11 to 42 percent. Among the elderly presenting for hospital admission, 24 percent of community dwelling and 64 percent of nursing home residents are delirious. Delirium is associated with increased morbidity and mortality. For example, 25 percent of elderly patients with delirium during hospitalization die within six months after discharge (American Psychiatric Association, 2000).

Risk factors associated with delirium are as follows: age over sixty-five, physical frailty, severe illness, multiple diseases, dementia, visual or hearing impairment, polypharmacy, sustained heavy drinking, renal impairment, and malnutrition. Precipitants are acute infections, electrolyte disturbances, drugs (especially anticholinergics), alcohol withdrawal, pain, constipation, neurological disorder, hypoxia, sleep deprivation, surgery, and environmental factors (Young & Inouye, 2007).

Delirium is an acute dysfunction of arousal and/or attentional brain networks. Since arousal and attention are the bases for higher cognitive functions, most cognitive functions are affected. Neurochemically, delirium is characterized by disturbances in acetylcholine, dopamine, norepinephrine, glutamate, gamma aminobutyric acid, and serotonin systems. Cytokines and blood-brain barrier abnormalities may also play a role (Alagiakrishnan & Wiens, 2004; Van Der Mast, 1998).

Treatments for delirium target the underlying cause(s), as well as the associated behavioral problems and neuropsychiatric symptoms. Modifiable risk factors or precipitants should be addressed (e.g., by treating the underlying medical condition, withdrawing of possible offending medications, correcting sensory deficits by using hearing aids and eyeglasses). Behaviors that put an individual at risk should be managed by changing the environment (e.g., providing access to familiar people and objects, protecting the individual on a locked treatment unit when there is a risk of wandering) and through behavioral interventions (e.g., reorientation, de-escalation techniques), possibly in combination with medications. Neuropsychiatric symptoms (e.g., perceptual disturbances, agitation, aggression) are managed with antipsychotics, mood stabilizers, or antiepileptics. Benzodiazepines may be useful in treating withdrawal from alcohol.

See also **Complications.**

BIBLIOGRAPHY

Alagiakrishnan, K., & Wiens, C. A. (2004). An approach to drug induced delirium in the elderly. *Postgraduate Medical Journal, 80,* 388–393.

American Psychiatric Association. (2000). *Diagnostic and Statistical Manual of Mental Disorders* (4th rev. ed.). Washington, DC: Author.

Folstein, M. F., Bassett, S. S., Romanowsk, A. J., et al. (1993). The epidemiology of delirium in the community: The Eastern Baltimore Mental Health Survey. *International Psychogeriatrics, 3,* 169–179.

Van Der Mast, R. C. (1998). Pathophysiology of delirium. *Journal of Geriatric Psychiatry and Neurology, 11*(3), 138–45.

Young, J., & Inouye, S. (2007). Delirium in older people. *British Medical Journal, 334,* 842–846.

KALOYAN TANEV

DELIRIUM TREMENS (DTS). *Delirium tremens* (DTs) refers to the most severe form of the alcohol withdrawal syndrome, occurring with the abrupt cessation of, or reduction in, alcohol consumption in an individual who has been a heavy drinker for many years. It is associated with a significant mortality rate of an estimated 1 to 5 percent, which is likely higher (perhaps up to 15 percent) if untreated.

DTs usually begin at seventy-two to ninety-six hours after the cessation of drinking and usually last two to three days but can occasionally last considerably longer. Early treatment of withdrawal symptoms is thought to prevent the risk of developing DTs and its related mortality. Risk factors for DTs include infection, a history of epileptic seizures, tachycardia (rapid heart rate) upon admission to hospital, withdrawal symptoms with a blood alcohol concentration 1 g/L, and a prior history of DTs. Concurrent medical conditions such as infection, trauma, and liver failure may increase the mortality of DTs.

Symptoms of DTs include those typically seen in delirium, including disorientation, confusion, fluctuating levels of consciousness and attention, vivid hallucinations, delusions, agitation, and also include those found in alcohol withdrawal; fever, elevated blood pressure, rapid pulse, sweating, and tremor. Delirium is the hallmark and defining feature of DTs and differentiates the syndrome from uncomplicated alcohol withdrawal. The delirium may at times be preceded by a withdrawal seizure, although a seizure neither defines nor is its presence required to diagnose DTs, and not all patients that experience withdrawal seizures develop DTs. The treatment of DTs necessitates close monitoring in the hospital setting.

For patients in alcohol withdrawal but without DTs, as the severity of withdrawal increases, patients may experience transient mild hallucinations that are auditory, visual, or tactile in nature. Loss of insight into hallucinations or development of more severe and persistent hallucinations may suggest that the syndrome has progressed or is progressing to DTs. Delirium tremens is differentiated from the syndromes of *alcoholic hallucinosis* and *chronic alcoholic hallucinosis*, which are terms used inconsistently in the literature to refer to the transient hallucinosis experienced during alcohol withdrawal and/or the subsequent development of a state of psychosis accompanied by hallucinations and/or delusions (particularly persecutory) that persists beyond the period of detoxification. There is controversy as to whether chronic alcoholic hallucinosis syndrome exists.

See also **Delirium; Withdrawal.**

BIBLIOGRAPHY

Debellis, R., Smith, B. S., Choi, S., & Malloy, M. (2005). Management of delirium tremens. *Journal of Intensive Care Medicine, 20* (3), 164–173.

De Millas, W., & Haasen, C. (2007). Treatment of alcohol hallucinosis with risperidone. *American Journal of Addictions, 16* (3), 249–250.

Graham, A. W., Schultz, T. K., Mayo-Smith, M., & Ries, R. K. (Eds.). (2003). *Principles of addiction medicine, third edition*. Chevy Chase, MD: American Society of Addiction Medicine.

MYROSLAVA ROMACH
KAREN PARKER
REVISED BY ALBERT J. ARIAS (2009)

DENMARK. *See* **Nordic Countries (Denmark, Finland, Iceland, Norway, and Sweden).**

DEPRESSION. The term *depression* refers to both a mood and a group of psychiatric disorders. In the *Diagnostic and Statistical Manual of Mental Disorders* (*DSM-IV-TR*, 2000) depressed mood occurs as part of major depressive disorder (MDD), dysthymic disorder (chronic, less severe depression), and schizoaffective disorder (psychosis co-occurring with depressed or manic mood), and can also occur in bipolar disorder (periods of mania that can alternate with periods of depression) and during intoxication or withdrawal from certain substances.

Many people experience brief periods of depressed mood that are often responses to stressful life events or negative experiences. However, when depression-related symptoms cluster, persist, and ultimately cause impairment in functioning, the person is considered to be experiencing a depressive syndrome. The *DSM-IV* classifies this syndrome as a major depressive episode and requires the following criteria: a period of low mood (or loss of interest or pleasure in usual activities) lasting at least two weeks; four or more out of eight additional symptoms (significant change in weight or appetite, poor or increased sleep nearly every day, psychomotor agitation or retardation that is noticeable to others nearly every day, fatigue or low energy nearly every day, feelings of worthlessness or inappropriate guilt nearly every day, difficulty concentrating or making decisions nearly every day, and recurring thoughts of death, suicide, or suicidal attempt); and functional impairment or clinically significant distress.

If the symptoms of depression are the direct physiological effects of heavy consumption of alcohol or another psychoactive substance and are greater than the expected effects of intoxication or withdrawal, the depression is considered to be substance-induced. In *DSM-IV*, normal bereavement is not present if inappropriate guilt, thoughts of death unrelated to the deceased person, a preoccupation with worthlessness, marked psychomotor retardation, and hallucinations that are not a phenomenon shared by others in one's cultural group are present, signaling the presence of a major depressive episode. Major depressive disorder is also distinguished from low mood resulting from a medical condition and mood changes that are due to exposure to a toxin or chemical substance.

Major Depression is one of the most common psychiatric disorders experienced by adults. One study of data drawn from the 2001–2002 National Epidemiologic Survey on Alcohol and Related Conditions indicated that approximately 13 percent of the U.S. population has experienced a major depressive episode (Hasin et al., 2005). Women have higher rates of lifetime depression than men (17.10 percent vs. 9.01 percent), Native Americans are at greater risk for depression than other ethnic groups, and individuals who are middle-aged or widowed, separated, or divorced, and those with lower income levels are at increased risk. Depression is associated with substantial impairment (Weissman et al., 1991; Kessler et al., 1994; Kessler et al., 2003), psychiatric comorbidity (Weissman et al., 1991; Kessler et al., 1994; Kessler et al., 2003; Hasin et al., 2005), poor health (Dentino et al., 1999), and mortality (Insel & Charney, 2003).

The cause of depression is multi-systemic. Imaging studies have shown abnormal neurochemical activity and changes in volume in specific areas of the brain of depressed people. These biological changes, combined with genetic and psychosocial factors (e.g., life events, learned behaviors, and cognitions) all interact to varying degrees. Depression is a highly recurrent but treatable illness. Effective treatment options are available (e.g., psychotherapy, pharmacotherapy, psychoeducation, and, generally as a last option, electroconvulsive therapy), and the choice of treatment depends on multiple factors such as the individual's psychiatric history, the severity of the current episode, family and social support, general medical health, the patient's level of motivation, and the compatibility of the treatment with the patient's current circumstances.

See also **Complications: Mental Disorders; Risk Factors for Substance Use, Abuse, and Dependence: An Overview.**

BIBLIOGRAPHY

American Psychiatric Association. (2000). *Diagnostic and statistical manual of mental disorders* (4th rev. ed.). Washington, DC: Author.

Dentino, A. N., Pieper, C. F., Rao, M. K., Currie, M. S., Harris, T., Blazer, D. G., et al. (1999). Association of interleukin-6 and other biologic variables with depression in older people living in the community. *Journal of the American Geriatric Society, 47,* 6–11.

Hasin, D., Goodwin, R., Stinson, F. S., & Grant, B. F. (2005). Epidemiology of major depressive disorder: Results from the national epidemiologic survey on alcoholism and related conditions. *Archives of General Psychiatry, 62,* 1097–1106.

Insel, T. R., & Charney, D. S. (2003). Research on major depression: Strategies and priorities. *Journal of American Medical Association, 289,* 3167–3168.

Kessler, R. C., Berglund, P., Demler, O., Jin, R., Koretz, D., Merikangas, K. R., et al. (2003). National Comorbidity Survey Replication: The epidemiology of major depressive disorder: Results from the National Comorbidity Survey Replication (NCS-R). *Journal of American Medical Association, 289,* 3095–3105.

Kessler, R. C., McGonagle, K. A., Zhao, S., Nelson, C., Hughes, M., Eshleman, S., et al. (1994). Lifetime and 12-month prevalence of *DSM-III-R* psychiatric disorders in the United States: Results from the National Comorbidity Survey. *Archives of General Psychiatry, 51,* 8–19.

Weissman, M. M., Bruce, L. M., Leaf, P. J., Florio, L. P., & Holzer, C., III. (1991). Affective disorders. In L. N. Robins & D. A. Regier (Eds.), *Psychiatric disorders in America: The Epidemiologic Catchment Area Study* (pp. 53–80). New York: Free Press.

SHARON SAMET

DESIGNER DRUGS. "Designer drugs" are synthetic chemical analogs of abused substances that are designed to produce pharmacological effects similar to the substances they mimic. In the pharmaceutical industry, the design of new drugs often utilizes principles of basic chemistry, so that the structure of a drug molecule is slightly altered in order to change its pharmacological activity. This strategy has a long and successful history in medical pharmaceutics, and many useful new drugs or modifications of older drugs have clearly resulted in improved health care for many people throughout the world. The principles of structure-activity relationships have been applied to many medically approved drugs, especially in the search for a nonaddicting opioid analgesic for the treatment of pain. However, the clandestine production of "designer" street drugs is intended to avoid federal regulation and control. This practice can often result in the appearance of new and unknown substances with wide-ranging variations in purity. The quality of personnel involved in clandestine designer-drug synthesis can range from "cookbook" amateurs to highly skilled chemists, which means that these substances have the potential to cause dangerous toxicity with serious health consequences for the unwitting drug user.

A resurgence in the popularity of a relatively old drug, methamphetamine, was observed during the first decade of the twenty-first century. Although methamphetamine is manufactured in foreign or domestic "superlabs," the drug is also easily made in small clandestine laboratories with relatively inexpensive over-the-counter ingredients. This practice can lead to wide variations in the purity of the methamphetamine available for illicit distribution. Methamphetamine is a highly addictive central nervous system stimulant that was developed early in the twentieth century and initially used in nasal decongestants and bronchial inhalers. Like amphetamine, methamphetamine produces increased activity and talkativeness, anorexia, and a general sense of well-being. However, methamphetamine differs from amphetamine in that much higher levels of methamphetamine get into the brain when comparable doses are administered, making it a more potent stimulant drug. And while methamphetamine blocks the reuptake of dopamine at low doses, in a manner similar to cocaine, it also increases the release of dopamine, leading to much higher concentrations of this neurotransmitter. Although the pleasurable effects of methamphetamine most likely result from the release of dopamine, the elevated release of this neurotransmitter also contributes to the drug's deleterious effects on nerve terminals. Specifically, brain-imaging studies have demonstrated alterations in the activity of the dopamine system that are due to methamphetamine use. Recent studies of chronic methamphetamine users have revealed structural and functional changes in areas of the brain associated with emotion and memory, which may account for many of the emotional and cognitive problems experienced by chronic users.

Addicts typically exhibit anxiety, confusion, insomnia, mood disturbances, and violent behavior, and they can also display a number of psychotic features, including paranoia, visual and auditory hallucinations, and delusions. These psychotic symptoms can last for months or years after methamphetamine use has ceased, and stress has been shown to precipitate the spontaneous recurrence of methamphetamine psychoses. Methamphetamine can also produce a variety of cardiovascular effects, including rapid heart rate, irregular heartbeat, and increased blood pressure. Hyperthermia (elevated body temperature) and convulsions may occur during a methamphetamine overdose, and, if not treated immediately, this can result in death. Tolerance to methamphetamine's pleasurable effects develops with chronic use, and abusers may take higher doses of the drug, take it more frequently, or change their method of drug intake in an effort to intensify the desired effects. Methamphetamine has also become associated with a culture of risky sexual behavior, both among men who have sex with men and heterosexual populations, because methamphetamine and related psychomotor stimulants can increase libido. Paradoxically, however, long-term methamphetamine abuse may be associated with decreased sexual functioning.

Other hallucinogenic designer drugs that are amphetamine analogs—such as methylenedioxyamphetamine (MDA), methylenedioxymethamphetamine (MDMA or "Ecstasy") and methylenedioxyethamphetamine (MDEA or "Eve")—can also produce acute and chronic toxicity. Acute toxicity from these drugs is usually manifested as restlessness, agitation, sweating, high blood pressure, tachycardia, and other cardiovascular effects, all of which are suggestive of excessive central nervous system stimulation. Following chronic administration, MDA produces a

degeneration of serotonergic nerve terminals in rats, implying that it might induce chronic neurological damage in humans as well.

Newer designer drugs of abuse that have recently emerged on the black market include amphetamine-derived drugs such as para-methoxyamphetamine (PMA), para-methoxymethamphetamine (PMMA) and 4-methylthioamphetamine (4-MTA). In addition, newer designer drugs of the benzyl or phenyl piperazine type, and of the pyrrolidinophenone type, have gained popularity and notoriety as party or "rave" drugs. These include N-benzylpiperazine (BZP); 1-(3, 4-methylenedioxybenzyl)piperazine (MDBP); 1-(3-chlorophenyl)piperazine (mCPP); 1-(3-trifluoromethylphenyl)piperazine (TFMPP); 1-(4-methoxyphenyl)piperazine (MeOPP); alpha-pyrrolidinopropiophenone (PPP); 4'-methoxy-alpha-pyrrolidinopropiophenone (MOPPP); 3', 4'-methylenedioxy-alpha-pyrrolidinopropiophenone (MDPPP); 4'-methyl-alpha-pyrrolidinopropiophenone (MPPP); and 4'-methyl-alpha-pyrrolidinoexanophenone (MPHP). These drugs produce feelings of euphoria and energy and a desire to socialize. While "word on the street" suggests that these designer drugs are safe, studies in rats and primates have suggested that they present risks to humans. In fact, a variety of adverse effects have been associated with the use of this class of drugs in humans, including a life-threatening serotonin syndrome (due to an excess of this neurotransmitter), and toxic effects on the liver and brain that result in behavioral changes.

An opioid that has resulted in serious health hazards on the street is fentanyl (Sublimaze), a potent and extremely fast-acting narcotic analgesic with a high abuse liability. This drug has also served as a template for many look-alike drugs in the clandestine chemical laboratory. Very slight modifications in the chemical structure of fentanyl can result in analogs such as para-fluoro-, 3-methyl-, or alpha-methyl-fentanyl, with relative potencies that are 100, 900, and 1,100 times that of morphine, respectively. Unfortunately, a steady increase in deaths from drug overdoses associated with fentanyl-like designer drugs has been reported.

Designer drugs already on the street, such as methamphetamine and related stimulants, can produce significant brain damage following long-term use, and analogs of the opioid fentanyl can produce fatal overdoses. Taken to the extreme, the widespread illicit manufacture and use of designer drugs with unknown toxicity could result in millions of people ingesting the drug before the toxic effects are known, potentially producing an epidemic of neurodegenerative disorders and fatalities.

See also **Controlled Substances Act of 1970; MDMA; MPTP.**

BIBLIOGRAPHY

Barnett, G., & Rapaka, R. S. (1989). Designer drugs: An overview. In K. K. Redda, C. A. Walker, & G. Barnett (Eds.), *Cocaine, marijuana, designer drugs: Chemistry, pharmacology, and behavior* (pp. 163–174). Boca Raton, FL: CRC Press.

Beebe, D. K., & Walley, E. (1991). Substance abuse: The designer drugs. *American Family Physician, 43*(5), 1689–1698.

Christophersen, A. S. (2000). Amphetamine designer drugs: An overview and epidemiology. *Toxicology Letters, 112–113*, 127–131.

de Boer, D., Bosman, I. J., Hidvégi, E., Manzoni, C., Benkö, A. A., dos Reys, L. J., et al. (2001). Piperazine-like compounds: A new group of designer drugs-of-abuse on the European market. *Forensic Science International, 121*(1–2), 47–56.

Klein, M., & Kramer, F. (2004). Rave drugs: Pharmacological considerations. *AANA Journal, 72*(1), 61–67.

Maurer, H. H., Kraemer, T., Springer, D., & Staack, R. F. (2004). Chemistry, pharmacology, toxicology, and hepatic metabolism of designer drugs of the amphetamine (ecstasy), piperazine, and pyrrolidinophenone types: A synopsis. *Therapeutic Drug Monitoring, 26*(2), 127–131.

Nichols, D. E. (1989). Substituted amphetamine controlled substance analogues. In K. K. Redda, C. A. Walker & G. Barnett (Eds.), *Cocaine, marijuana, designer drugs: Chemistry, pharmacology, and behavior* (pp. 175–185). Boca Raton, FL: CRC Press.

Soine, W. H. (1986). Clandestine drug synthesis. *Medicinal Research Reviews, 6*(1), 41–47.

Staack, R. F., & Maurer, H. H. (2005). Metabolism of designer drugs of abuse. *Currents in Drug Metabolism, 6*(3), 259–274.

Trevor, A., Castagnoli, N., Jr., & Singer, T. P. (1989). Pharmacology and toxicology of MPTP: A neurotoxic by-product of illicit designer drug chemistry. In K. K. Redda, C. A. Walker & G. Barnett (Eds.), *Cocaine, marijuana, designer drugs: Chemistry, pharmacology, and behavior* (pp. 187–200). Boca Raton, FL: CRC Press.

Ziporyn, T. (1986). A growing industry and menace: Makeshift laboratory's designer drugs. *Journal of the American Medical Association, 256*(22), 3061–3063.

NICHOLAS E. GOEDERS

DEXTROAMPHETAMINE. This is the *d*-isomer of amphetamine. It is classified as a psychomotor stimulant drug and is three to four times as potent as the *l*-isomer in eliciting central nervous system (CNS) excitatory effects. It is also more potent than the *l*-isomer in its anorectic (appetite suppressant) activity, but slightly less potent in its cardiovascular actions. It is prescribed in the treatment of narcolepsy and obesity, although care must be taken in such prescribing because of the substantial abuse liability.

High-dose chronic use of dextroamphetamine can lead to the development of a toxic psychosis as well as to other physiological and behavioral problems. This toxicity became a problem in the United States in the 1960s, when substantial amounts of the drug were being taken for nonmedical reasons. Although still abused by some, dextroamphetamine is no longer the stimulant of choice for most psychomotor stimulant abusers.

See also **Amphetamine Epidemics, International; Coca/ Cocaine, International.**

BIBLIOGRAPHY

de Wit, H., et al (2002). Acute administration of d-amphetamine decreases impulsivity in healthy volunteers. *Neuropsychopharmacology, 27*, 813–825.

Schmetzer, A. D. (2004). The psychostimulants. *Annals of the American Psychotherapy Association, 7*, 31–32.

MARIAN W. FISCHMAN

DIAGNOSIS OF SUBSTANCE USE DISORDERS: DIAGNOSTIC CRITERIA. *Diagnosis* is the process of identifying and labeling specific disease conditions. The signs and symptoms used to classify a sick person as having a disease are called *diagnostic criteria*. Diagnostic criteria and classification systems are useful for making clinical decisions, estimating disease prevalence, understanding the causes of disease, and facilitating scientific communication.

Diagnostic classification provides the treating clinician with a basis for retrieving information about a patient's probable symptoms, the likely course of an illness, and the biological or psychological processes that underlie the disorder. For example, the *Diagnostic and Statistical Manual* (*DSM*) of the American Psychiatric Association is a classification of mental disorders that provides the clinician with a systematic description of each disorder in terms of essential features, age of onset, probable course, predisposing factors, associated features, and differential diagnosis. Mental health professionals can use this system to diagnose substance use disorders in terms of the following categories: acute intoxication, abuse, dependence, withdrawal, delirium, and other disorders. In contrast to screening, diagnosis typically involves a broader evaluation of signs, symptoms, and laboratory data as these relate to the patient's illness. The purpose of diagnosis is to provide the clinician with a logical basis for planning treatment and estimating prognosis.

Another purpose of classification is the collection of statistical information on a national and international scale. The primary purpose of the *World Health Organization's International Classification of Diseases* (*ICD*), for example, is the enumeration of morbidity and mortality data for public health planning. In addition, a good classification will facilitate communication among scientists and provide the basic concepts needed for theory development. Both the *DSM* and *ICD* have also been used extensively to classify persons for scientific research. Classification thus provides a common frame of reference in communicating scientific findings.

Diagnosis may also serve a variety of administrative purposes. When a patient is suspected of having a substance use disorder, diagnostic procedures are needed to exclude "false positives" (i.e., people who appear to have the disorder but who really do not) and borderline cases. Insurance reimbursement for medical treatment increasingly demands that a formal diagnosis be confirmed according to standard procedures or criteria. The need for uniform reporting of statistical data, as well as the generation of prevalence estimates for epidemiological research, often requires a diagnostic classification of the patient.

CLASSIFICATION SYSTEMS

Alcoholism and drug addiction have been variously defined as medical diseases, mental disorders, social problems, and behavioral conditions. In some cases, they are considered the symptom of an underlying mental disorder (Babor, 1992). Some of these definitions permit the classification of alcoholism and drug dependence within standard nomenclatures such as the *DSM* and *ICD*. The most recent revisions of both of these diagnostic systems—*DSM-IV* (1994) and *ICD-10* (1992)—have resulted in a high degree of compatibility between the classification criteria used in the United States and those used internationally. Both systems now diagnose dependence according to the elements first proposed by Edwards and Gross (1976). They also include a residual category (harmful alcohol use [*ICD-10*]; alcohol abuse [*DSM-IV*]) that allows classification of psychological, social, and medical consequences directly related to substance use.

HISTORY TAKING

Obtaining accurate information from patients with alcohol and drug problems is often difficult because of the stigma associated with substance abuse and the fear of legal consequences. At times, these individuals want help for the medical complications of substance use (such as injuries or depression) but are ambivalent about giving up alcohol or drug use entirely. It is often the case that these patients are evasive and attempt to conceal or minimize the extent of their alcohol or drug use. Acquiring accurate information about the presence, severity, duration, and effects of alcohol and drug use therefore requires a considerable amount of clinical skill.

The medical model for history taking is the most widely used approach to diagnostic evaluation. This model consists of identifying the chief complaint, evaluating the present illness, reviewing past history, conducting a review of biological systems (e.g., gastrointestinal, cardiovascular), asking about family history of similar disorders, and discussing the patient's psychological and social functioning. A history of the present illness begins with questions on the use of alcohol, drugs, and tobacco. The questions should cover prescription drugs as well as illicit drugs, with additional elaboration of the kinds of drugs, the amount used, and the mode of administration (e.g., smoking, injection). Questions about alcohol use should refer specifically to the amount and frequency of using the major beverage types (wine, spirits, and beer). A thorough physical examination is important because each substance has specific pathological effects on certain organs and body systems. For example, alcohol commonly affects the liver, stomach, cardiovascular system, and nervous system, while drugs often produce abnormalities in "vital signs" such as temperature, pulse, and blood pressure.

A mental status examination frequently gives evidence of substance use disorders, which can be signaled by poor personal hygiene, inappropriate affect (e.g., sad, euphoric, irritable, anxious), illogical or delusional thought processes, and memory problems. The physical examination can be supplemented by laboratory tests, which sometimes aid in early diagnosis before severe or irreversible damage has taken place. Laboratory tests are useful in two ways: (1) alcohol and drugs can be measured directly in blood, urine, or exhaled air; (2) biochemical and psychological functions known to be affected by substance use can be assessed. Many drugs can be detected in the urine for 12 to 48 hours after their consumption. An estimate of blood alcohol concentration (BAC) can be made directly by blood test or indirectly by means of a breath or saliva test. Elevations of the liver enzyme gamma-glutamyl transpeptidase (GGTP) or the protein carbohydrate-deficient transferrin (CDT) are sensitive indicators of chronic and heavy alcohol intake. However, while these tests can detect recent use of a wide variety of psychoactive substances (e.g., opioids, cannabis, stimulants, barbiturates), they are not able to detect alcohol or drug dependence.

In addition to the physical examination and laboratory tests, a variety of diagnostic interview procedures have been developed to provide objective, empirically based, reliable diagnoses of substance use disorders in various clinical populations. One type, exemplified by the Diagnostic Interview Schedule (DIS; see Robins et al., 1981) and the Composite International Diagnostic Interview (CIDI; see Robins et al., 1988), is highly structured and requires a minimum of clinical judgment by the interviewer. These interviews provide information not only about

substance use disorders, but also about physical conditions and psychiatric disorders that are commonly associated with substance abuse. Because of its standardized questioning procedures, the CIDI has been used by the World Health Organization to estimate the prevalence of mental disorders, including substance use disorders, in the general populations of countries throughout the world (Haro et al., 2006). In the United States, the Alcohol Use Disorder and Associated Disabilities Interview Schedule-IV (AUDADIS-IV) has been used extensively in population surveys, including the National Epidemiologic Survey on Alcohol and Related Conditions (Grant et al., 2003). It covers alcohol consumption, tobacco use, family history of depression, and selected *DSM-IV* Axis I and II psychiatric disorders.

A second type of diagnostic interview is exemplified by the Structured Clinical Interview for *DSM-IV* (SCID), which is designed for use by mental health professionals (Spitzer et al., 1992; First et al., 2002). The SCID assesses the most commonly occurring psychiatric disorders described in *DSM-IV*, including mood disorders, schizophrenia, and substance use disorders. A similar clinical interview designed for international use is the Schedules for Clinical Assessment in Neuropsychiatry (SCAN; see Wing et al., 1990). The SCID and SCAN interviews allow the experienced clinician to tailor questions to fit the patient's understanding, to ask additional questions that clarify ambiguities, to challenge inconsistencies, and to make clinical judgments about the seriousness of symptoms. Both are modeled on the standard medical history practiced by many mental health professionals. Questions about the chief complaint, past episodes of psychiatric disturbance, treatment history, and current functioning all contribute to a thorough and orderly psychiatric history that is extremely useful for diagnosing substance use disorders. The Psychiatric Research Interview for Substance and Mental Disorders (PRISM; Hasin et al., 2006) is another semistructured diagnostic interview. It is designed to deal with the problems of psychiatric diagnosis when subjects or patients drink heavily or use drugs. The PRISM is used for making a number of *DSM-IV* Axis I and Axis II diagnoses, including alcohol and drug use disorders, in a way that allows differentiation of psychiatric disorders from substance-induced disorders and from the expected effects of intoxication and withdrawal.

In recent years, there has been interest in developing better methods to obtain accurate information from patients with substance use disorders, both for diagnostic purposes and for the measurement of treatment outcomes. It has been assumed that information obtained from alcohol and drug users cannot be trusted, because they often unconsciously deny that they have a problem or deliberately lie about their substance use to avoid the embarrassment of being labeled as an alcoholic or a drug addict. Another factor is clinical suspicion that individuals with substance use disorders often are not capable of reporting their symptoms accurately, due to the cognitive effects of chronic substance use.

With advances in the technology of psychiatric interviewing, questionnaire design, and psychological measurement, it is now possible to obtain valid measurement at the symptom level and to improve classification accuracy at the syndrome level (Haro et al., 2006). According to one systematic review of methodological studies, self-report measures using questionnaires and interviews tend to be valid and reliable in the aggregate under most circumstances (Del Boca & Noll, 2000). Nevertheless, patients may bias their responses in a socially desirable direction when they do not understand the purpose of the questions, feel threatened by the possible outcome of the diagnostic evaluation (e.g., being labeled as having a psychiatric disorder), have cognitive disabilities that affect memory and recall, or have personality characteristics (e.g., psychopathy) that increase the chances of deliberate lying.

DIAGNOSIS OF ABUSE AND HARMFUL USE

A major diagnostic category that has received increasing attention in research and clinical practice is substance abuse—in contrast to dependence. This category permits the classification of maladaptive patterns of alcohol or drug use that do not meet criteria for dependence. The diagnosis of abuse is designed primarily for persons who have recently begun to experience alcohol or drug problems, as well as for chronic users whose substance-related consequences develop in the absence of marked dependence symptoms. Examples of situations in which this category would be appropriate include: (1) a pregnant woman who keeps drinking alcohol even though her physician has told her that it could cause fetal damage; (2) a college student whose weekend binges result in missed classes, poor grades, and alcohol-related traffic accidents; (3) a middle-aged beer drinker regularly consuming a six-pack each day who develops high blood pressure and fatty liver in the absence of alcohol-dependence symptoms; and (4) an occasional marijuana smoker who has an accidental injury while intoxicated.

In the fourth revision of the *Diagnostic and Statistical Manual* (American Psychiatric Association, 1994), *substance abuse* is defined as a maladaptive pattern of alcohol or drug use leading to clinically significant impairment or distress, as manifested by one or more of the symptoms listed in Table 1. (For comparative purposes, the table also lists the criteria for harmful use in *ICD-10*.) To assure that the diagnosis is based on clinically meaningful symptoms, rather than the results of an occasional excess, the duration criterion specifies how long the symptoms must be present to qualify for a diagnosis.

In *ICD-10*, the term *harmful use* refers to a pattern of using one or more psychoactive substances that causes damage to health. The damage may be: (1) physical (physiological)—such as pancreatitis from alcohol or hepatitis from needle-injected drugs; or (2) mental (psychological)—such as depression related to heavy drinking or drug use. Adverse social consequences often accompany substance use, but they are not in themselves sufficient to result in a diagnosis of harmful use. The key issue in the definition of this term is the distinction between perceptions of adverse effects (e.g., wife complaining about husband's drinking) and actual health consequences (e.g., trauma due to accidents during drug intoxication). Since the purpose of *ICD* is to classify diseases, injuries, and causes of death, *harmful use* is defined as a pattern of use already causing damage to health.

Harmful patterns of use are often criticized by others, and they are sometimes legally prohibited by governments. However, the fact that alcohol or drug intoxication is disapproved by another person or by the user's culture is not in itself evidence of harmful use, unless socially negative consequences have actually occurred at dosage levels that also result in psychological and physical consequences. This is the major difference that distinguishes

	ICD-10 Criteria for Harmful Use	DSM-IV Criteria for Abuse
Symptom Criteria	Clear evidence that alcohol or drug use is responsible for causing actual psychological or physical harm to the user	A maladaptive pattern of alcohol or drug use indicated by at least one of the following: (1) failure to fulfill major role obligations at work, school, or home (e.g., neglect of children or household); (2) use in situations in which it is physically hazardous (e.g., driving an automobile); (3) recurrent substance-related legal problems (e.g., arrests for substance-related disorderly conduct); (4) continued substance use despite having recurrent social or interpersonal problems
Duration Criterion	The pattern of use has persisted for at least 1 month or has occurred repeatedly over the previous 12 months	One or more symptoms has occurred during the same 12-month period

Table 1. Diagnostic Criteria for Harmful Use (IDC-10) and Substance Abuse (DSM-III-R, DSM-IV). ILLUSTRATION BY GGS INFORMATION SERVICES. GALE, CENGAGE LEARNING

ICD-10's harmful use from *DSM-IV*'s substance abuse—the latter category includes social consequences in the diagnosis of abuse.

THE DEPENDENCE SYNDROME CONCEPT
The diagnosis of substance use disorders in *ICD-10* and *DSM-IV* is based on the concept of a "dependence syndrome," which is distinguished from disabilities caused by substance use (Edwards, Arif, & Hodgson, 1981). An important diagnostic issue is the extent to which dependence is sufficiently distinct from abuse or harmful use to be considered a separate condition. In *DSM-IV*, *substance abuse* is a residual category that allows the clinician to classify clinically meaningful aspects of a patient's behavior when that behavior is not clearly associated with a dependence syndrome. In *ICD-10*, *harmful substance use* implies identifiable substance-induced medical or psychiatric consequences that occur in the absence of a dependence syndrome. In both classification systems, dependence is conceived as an underlying condition that has much greater clinical significance because of its implications for understanding etiology, predicting course, and planning treatment.

The dependence syndrome is seen as an interrelated cluster of cognitive, behavioral, and physiological symptoms. Table 2 summarizes the criteria used to diagnose dependence in *ICD-10* and *DSM-IV*. A diagnosis of dependence in all systems is made if three or more of the criteria have been experienced at some time in the previous twelve months.

The dependence syndrome may be present for a specific substance (e.g., tobacco, alcohol, or diazepam), for a class of substances (e.g., opioid drugs), or for a wider range of various substances. A diagnosis of dependence does not necessarily imply the presence of physical, psychological, or social consequences, although some form of harm is usually present. There are some differences among these classification systems, but the criteria are very similar, making it unlikely that a patient diagnosed in one system would be diagnosed differently in the other.

The syndrome concept implicit in the diagnosis of alcohol and drug dependence in *ICD* and *DSM* is a way of describing the nature and severity of addiction (Babor, 1992). Table 2 describes four dependence syndrome elements (salience, impaired control, tolerance, withdrawal, and withdrawal relief) in relation to the criteria for *DSM-IV*, and *ICD-10*. The same elements apply to the diagnosis of dependence on all psychoactive substances, including alcohol, marijuana, opioids, cocaine, sedatives, phencyclidine, other hallucinogens, and tobacco. The elements represent biological, psychological (cognitive), and behavioral processes. This helps to explain the linkages and interrelationships that account for the coherence of signs and symptoms. The co-occurrence of signs and symptoms is the essential feature of a syndrome. If three or more criteria occur repeatedly during the same period, it is likely that dependence is responsible for the amount, frequency, and pattern of the person's substance use.

Salience. Salience means that drinking or drug use is given a higher priority than other activities in spite of its negative consequences. This is reflected in the emergence of substance use as the preferred activity from a set of available alternative activities. In addition, the individual does not respond well to the

Dependence element	Diagnostic level	ICD-10 symptoms	DSM-IV symptoms
Salience	Cognitive, behavioral	Progressive neglect of alternative activities in favor of substance use	Important social, occupational, or recreational activities given up
	Behavioral	Persistence with substance use despite harmful consequences	Continued use despite psychological or physical problems
Impaired control	Behavioral, cognitive	A strong desire or sense of compulsion to drink or use drugs	Substance often taken in larger amounts or over a longer period than intended
	Behavioral	Evidence of impaired capacity to control substance use in terms of its onset, termination, or levels of use	Any unsuccessful effort or a persistent desire to cut down or control substance use
Tolerance	Biological, behavioral	Increased doses of substance are required to achieve effects originally produced by lower doses	Either (a) increased amounts needed to achieve desired effect; or (b) markedly diminished effect with continued use
Withdrawal and withdrawal relief	Behavioral, biological, cognitive	A physiological withdrawal state Use to relieve or avoid withdrawal symptoms and subjective awareness that this strategy is effective	Either (a) characteristic withdrawal syndrome for substance; or (b) the same substance taken to relieve or avoid symptoms

Table 2. ICD and DSM Diagnostic Criteria for Dependence (labeled according to diagnostic level—physiological, cognitive, and behavioral—and underlying dependence elements). ILLUSTRATION BY GGS INFORMATION SERVICES. GALE, CENGAGE LEARNING

normal processes of social control. For example, when drinking to intoxication goes against the tacit social rules governing the time, place, or amount typically expected by the user's family or friends, this may indicate increased salience.

One indication of salience is the amount of time or effort devoted to obtaining, using, or recovering from substance use. For example, people who spend a great deal of time at parties, bars, or business lunches give evidence of the increased salience of drinking over nondrinking activities.

Chronic drinking and drug intoxication interfere with the person's ability to conform to tacit social rules governing daily activities—such as keeping appointments, caring for children, or performing a job properly—that are typically expected by the person's reference group. Substance use also results in mental and medical consequences. Thus, a key aspect of the dependence syndrome is the persistence of substance use in spite of social, psychological, or physical harm—such as loss of employment, marital problems, depressive symptoms, accidents, and liver disease. This indicates that substance use is given a higher priority than other activities, in spite of its negative consequences.

One explanation for the salience of drug- and alcohol-seeking behaviors despite negative consequences is the relative reinforcement value of immediate and long-term consequences. For many alcoholics and drug abusers, the immediate positive reinforcing effects of the substance, such as euphoria or stimulation, far outweigh any delayed negative consequences, which may occur either infrequently or inconsistently.

Impaired Control. The main characteristic of impaired control is the lack of success in limiting the amount or frequency of substance use. For example, the alcoholic wants to stop drinking, but repeated attempts to do so have been unsuccessful. Typically, rules and other stratagems are used to avoid alcohol entirely or to limit the frequency of drinking. A resumption of heavy drinking after receiving professional help for a drinking problem is evidence of lack of success. The symptom is considered present if the drinker has repeatedly failed to abstain or has only been able to control drinking with the help of treatment, mutual-help groups, or removal to a controlled environment (e.g., prison).

In addition to an inability to abstain, impaired control is also reflected in the failure to regulate the amount of alcohol or drug consumed on a given occasion. The cocaine addict vows to snort only a small amount but then continues until the entire supply is used up. For the alcoholic, impaired control includes an inability to prevent the spontaneous onset of drinking bouts, as well as a failure to stop

Symptom	Alcohol	Amphetamine	Caffeine	Cocaine	Opioids	Nicotine
Craving					X	X
Tremor	X					
Sweating, fever	X				X	
Nausea or vomiting	X				X	
Malaise, fatigue	X	X		X		
Hyperactivity, restlessness	X	X	X	X		X
Headache	X					
Insomnia	X	X	X		X	
Hallucinations	X					
Convulsions	X					
Delirium	X					
Irritability	X	X		X		X
Anxiety	X		X	X		X
Depression	X			X		
Difficulty concentrating						X
Gastrointestinal disturbance			X			
Increased appetite						X
Diarrhea					X	

Table 3. Withdrawal symptoms associated with different psychoactive substances. ILLUSTRATION BY GGS INFORMATION SERVICES. GALE, CENGAGE LEARNING

drinking before intoxication. This behavior should be distinguished from situations in which the drinker's "control" over the onset or amount of drinking is regulated by social or cultural factors, such as during college beer parties or fiesta drinking occasions. One way to judge the degree of impaired control is to determine whether the drinker or drug user has made repeated attempts to limit the quantity of substance use by making rules or imposing limits on his or her access to alcohol or drugs. The more these attempts have failed, the more the impaired control is present.

Tolerance. *Tolerance* is a decrease in response to a psychoactive substance that occurs with continued use. For example, increased doses of heroin are required to achieve effects originally produced by lower doses. Tolerance may be physical, behavioral, or psychological. Physical tolerance is a change in cellular functioning. The effects of a dependence-producing substance are reduced, even though the cells normally affected by the substance are subjected to the same concentration. A clear example is the finding that alcoholics can drink amounts of alcohol (e.g., a quart of vodka) that would be sufficient to incapacitate or kill nontolerant drinkers.

Tolerance may also develop at the psychological and behavioral levels, independent of the biological adaptation that takes place. Psychological tolerance occurs when a marijuana smoker or heroin user no longer experiences a "high" after the initial dose of the substance. Behavioral tolerance is a change in the effect of a substance because the person has learned to compensate for the impairment caused by a substance. Some alcoholics, for example, can operate machinery at moderate doses of alcohol without impairment.

Withdrawal Signs and Symptoms. A "withdrawal state" is a group of symptoms occurring after cessation of substance use. It usually occurs after repeated, and usually prolonged, drinking or drug use. Both the onset of and course of withdrawal symptoms are related to the type of substance and the dose being used immediately prior to abstinence. Table 3 lists some common withdrawal symptoms associated with different psychoactive substances. Some drugs, such as hallucinogens, do not typically produce a withdrawal syndrome after cessation of use. Although generally thought of as not being characterized by withdrawal symptoms, recent evidence supports the existence of a cannabis (marijuana) withdrawal syndrome (Agrawal et al., 2008).

Alcohol withdrawal symptoms follow within hours of the cessation or reduction of prolonged heavy drinking. These symptoms include tremor, hyperactive reflexes, rapid heartbeat, hypertension, general malaise, nausea, and vomiting. Seizures and convulsions may occur, particularly in people with a preexisting seizure disorder. Patients may have hallucinations, illusions, or vivid nightmares, and sleep is usually disturbed. In addition to physical withdrawal symptoms, anxiety and depression are also common. Some chronic drinkers never have a long enough period of abstinence to permit withdrawal to occur.

The use of a substance with the intention of relieving withdrawal symptoms and with awareness that this strategy is effective are cardinal symptoms of dependence. Morning drinking to relieve nausea or the "shakes" is one of the most common manifestations of physical dependence in alcoholics.

Other Features of Dependence. To be labeled dependence, symptoms must have persisted for at least one month or must have occurred repeatedly (two or more times) over a longer period of time. The patient does not need to be using the substance continually to have recurrent or persistent problems. Some symptoms (e.g., craving) may occur repeatedly whether the person is using the substance or not.

Many patients with a history of dependence experience a rapid reinstatement of the syndrome following resumption of substance use after a period of abstinence. Rapid reinstatement is a powerful diagnostic indicator of dependence. It points to the impairment of control over substance use, the rapid development of tolerance, and frequently, physical withdrawal symptoms.

Patients who receive opiates or other drugs for pain relief following surgery (or for a malignant disease such as cancer) sometimes show signs of a withdrawal state when the use of these drugs is terminated. The great majority of these individuals have no desire to continue taking such drugs, and they therefore do not fulfill the criteria for dependence. The presence of a physical withdrawal syndrome in these patients does not necessarily indicate dependence, but rather a state of neuro-adaptation to the drug that was being administered. It is commonly assumed that severe dependence is not reversible, and this assumption is supported by the rapid reinstatement of dependence symptoms when drinking or drug use is resumed after a period of detoxification.

CATEGORICAL VERSUS DIMENSIONAL APPROACHES TO DIAGNOSIS

Clinical decision-making often requires the classification of a patient's condition into discrete categories reflecting whether a disorder such as alcohol dependence is present or absent. This kind of categorical thinking is convenient for the diagnostician and consistent with the way in which physical diseases are diagnosed, but it may not fit the way in which substance use disorders are manifested in clinical practice. Typically, people with substance use disorders vary widely in the severity of their symptoms, with no clear demarcation between mild, moderate, and severe cases. This makes it difficult to diagnose patients whose problems with substance use are at the threshold between mild and moderate severity. For this reason, it has been proposed that the fifth revision of the *Diagnostic and Statistical Manual* (*DSM-V*) include the option of rating patients' substance use disorders along a continuum that reflects the actual severity of their dependence or abuse (Helzer et al., 2006). The concept of a continuum of alcohol dependence with various levels of severity is consistent with the original formulation of the dependence syndrome (Edwards et al., 1981), and it has been supported empirically by psychometric studies (Hasin, Liu, et al., 2006).

MAKING A DISTINCTION BETWEEN ABUSE AND DEPENDENCE

Questions have been raised about whether two diagnoses are needed for substance use disorders, or whether one diagnosis that combines abuse and dependence criteria in some form could be more efficient while still being reliable and valid. A number of studies using factor analysis have shown that two factors are generally found to fit existing data better than a single factor, but that the two factors are very highly correlated (Hasin, Hatzenbuehler, et al., 2006). In the first decade of the twenty-first century, investigators have used Item Response Theory (IRT) analysis to examine alcohol abuse and dependence criteria in general population data (Saha et al., 2006). These investigators found that alcohol abuse and dependence criteria appear to combine well into a single continuum of severity, with some abuse criteria (e.g., interpersonal problems related to drinking, failure to perform in major roles) actually indicating more severe aspects of dependence than some of the currently used dependence criteria (e.g., drinking more or longer than intended). However, whether these findings will extend to other substances remains a question to be answered by further research.

See also **Addiction: Concepts and Definitions; Alcoholism: Origin of the Term; Blood Alcohol Concentration; Computerized Diagnostic Interview Schedule for DSM-IV (C DIS-IV); Diagnostic and Statistical Manual (DSM); International Classification of Diseases (ICD); Models of Alcoholism and Drug Abuse; Physical Dependence; Risk Factors for Substance Use, Abuse, and Dependence: An Overview; Structured Clinical Interview for DSM-IV (SCID); Tolerance and Physical Dependence; Wikler's Conditioning Theory of Drug Addiction.**

BIBLIOGRAPHY

Agrawal, A., Pergadia, M. L., & Lynskey, M. T. (2008). Is there evidence for symptoms of cannabis withdrawal in the national epidemiologic survey of alcohol and related conditions? *American Journal on Addictions, 17*(3), 199–208.

American Psychiatric Association. (1987). *Diagnostic and statistical manual of mental disorders* (3rd ed., Rev.). Washington, DC: Author.

American Psychiatric Association. (1994). *Diagnostic and statistical manual of mental disorders* (4th ed). Washington, DC: Author.

Babor, T. F. (1992). Nosological considerations in the diagnosis of substance use disorders. In M. Glantz & R. Pickens (Eds.), *Vulnerability to drug abuse*. Washington DC: American Psychological Association.

Babor, T. F. (2007). We shape our tools, and thereafter our tools shape us: Psychiatric epidemiology and the alcohol dependence syndrome. *Addiction, 102*(10), 1534–1535.

Del Boca, F. K., & Noll, J. A. (2000). Truth or consequences: The validity of self-report data in health services research on addictions. *Addiction, 95*(Suppl. 3), S347–S360.

Edwards, G., Arif, A., & Hodgson, R. (1981). Nomenclature and classification of drug- and alcohol-related problems: A WHO memorandum. *Bulletin of the World Health Organization, 59*(2), 225–242.

Edwards, G., & Gross, M. M. (1976). Alcohol dependence: Provisional description of a clinical syndrome. *British Medical Journal, 1*(6017), 1058–1061.

First, M. B., Spitzer, R. L., Gibbon, M., & Williams, J. B. W. (2002). Structured Clinical Interview for DSM-IV axis I disorders, research version, non-patient edition (SCID-I/NP). New York: Biometrics Research, New York State Psychiatric Institute.

Grant, B. F., Dawson, D. A., Stinson, F. S., Chou, P. S., Kay, W., & Pickering, R. (2003). The Alcohol Use Disorder and Associated Disabilities Interview Schedule-IV (AUDADIS-IV): Reliability of alcohol consumption, tobacco use, family history of depression, and psychiatric diagnostic modules in a general population sample. *Drug and Alcohol Dependence, 71*(1), 7–16.

Haro, J. M., Arbabzadeh-Bouchez, S., Brugha, T. S., de Girolamo, G., Guyer, M. E., Jin, R., Lepine, J. P., (2006). Concordance of the Composite International Diagnostic Interview Version 3.0 (CIDI 3.0) with standardized clinical assessments in the WHO World Mental Health Surveys. *International Journal of Methods in Psychiatric Research, 15*(4), 167–180.

Hasin, D., Hatzenbuehler, M. L., Keyes, K., & Ogburn, E. (2006). Substance use disorders: Diagnostic and Statistical Manual of Mental Disorders, fourth edition (DSM-IV) and International Classification of Diseases, tenth edition (ICD-10). *Addiction, 101*(Suppl. 1), 59–75.

Hasin, D. S., Liu, X., Alderson, D., & Grant, B. F. (2006). DSM-IV alcohol dependence: A categorical or dimensional phenotype? *Psychological Medicine, 36*(12), 1695–1705.

Hasin, D. S., Samet, S., Nunes, E., Meydan, J., Matseoane, K., & Waxman, R. (2006). Diagnosis of comorbid disorders in substance users assessed with the Psychiatric Research Interview for Substance and Mental Disorders for DSM-IV. *American Journal of Psychiatry, 163*(4), 689–696.

Helzer, J. E., Van den Brink, W., & Guth, S. E. (2006). Should there be both categorical and dimensional criteria for the substance use disorders in DSM V? In J. B. Saunders et al. (Eds.), *Diagnostic issues in substance use disorders: Refining the research agenda for DSM-V*, (pp. 21–30). Arlington, VA: American Psychiatric Association, 2006.

Li, T. K., Hewitt, B. G., & Grant, B. F. (2007). The alcohol dependence syndrome, 30 years later: A commentary: The 2006 H. David Archibald Lecture. *Addiction 102*(10) 1522–1530.

Robins, L. (1981). The diagnosis of alcoholism after DSM III. In R. E. Meyer et al., (Eds.), *Evaluation of the* alcoholic: Implications for research, theory and treatment. NIAAA Research Monograph No. 5, DHHS Publication No. (ADM) 81–1033. Washington, DC: U.S. Government Printing Office.

Robins, L. N., Helzer, J. E., Croughan, K. S., & Ratcliff, K. S. (1981). National Institute of Mental Health Diagnostic Interview Schedule: Its history, characteristics, and validity. *Archives of General Psychiatry, 38*(4), 381–389.

Robins, L. N., Wing, J., Wittchen, H. U., Helzer, J. E., Babor, T. F., & Burke, J. (1988). The Composite International Diagnostic Interview: An epidemiological instrument suitable for use in conjunction with different diagnostic systems and in different cultures. *Archives of General Psychiatry, 45*(12), 1069–1077.

Saha, T. D., Chou, S. P., & Grant, B. F. (2006). Toward an alcohol use disorder continuum using item response theory: Results from the National Epidemiologic Survey on Alcohol and Related Conditions. *Psychological Medicine, 36*(7), 931–941.

Spitzer, R. L., Williams, J. B., Gibbon, M., & First, M. B. (1992). The structured clinical interview for DSM-III-R (SCID), I: History, rationale and description. *Archives of General Psychiatry, 49*(8), 624–629.

Tarter, R. E., & Kirisci, L. (1997). The drug use screening inventory for adults: Psychometric structure and discriminative survey. *American Journal of Drug and Alcohol Abuse, 23*(2), 207–220.

Wing, J. K., Babor, T., Brugha, J., Burke, J. E., Cooper, R., & Giel, A. (1990). SCAN: Schedules for Clinical Assessment in Neuropsychiatry. *Archives of General Psychiatry, 47*(6), 589–593.

Winters, K. C., Latimer, W., & Stinchfield, R. D. (1999). The DSM-IV criteria for adolescent alcohol and cannabis use disorders. *Journal of Studies on Alcohol, 60*(3), 337–344.

World Health Organization. (1992). *The ICD-10 classification of mental and behavioural disorders: Clinical descriptions and diagnostic guidelines.* Geneva: Author. Available from http://www.who.int/.

THOMAS F. BABOR

DIAGNOSTIC AND STATISTICAL MANUAL (DSM).

The *Diagnostic and Statistical Manual of Mental Disorders (DSM)* is the most widely accepted psychiatric diagnostic system in the United States, although psychiatric disorders are also included in the *International Classification of Diseases (ICD)*. First published by the American Psychiatric Association (APA) in 1952, the *DSM* is used by medical professionals, insurance companies, the pharmaceutical industry, and the court system to diagnose and define mental illnesses and disorders, including substance abuse and dependence. In fact, the diagnosis code assigned to a case often determines insurance reimbursement for treatment. The book is also an important indicator of societal mores: Until 1973 homosexuality was defined as a mental disorder. This suggests that at least some psychiatric disorders are experienced because of the way in which a society reacts to an individual's behavior, and what is considered deviant in some cultures may be normative in others.

The first tabulation of mental illness in the United States appeared in the 1840 census, when the categories *idiots* and *insane* were first counted. By the 1880 census seven types of mental illness were recognized, including epilepsy. In 1917 the American Medico-Psychological Association (now the APA), in conjunction with the National Commission on Mental Hygiene, further enlarged its categories of mental illness. This broader list, while certainly of greater clinical use, was still chiefly designed to count the numbers and types of patients in mental hospitals. Several years after this tabulation, the newly renamed APA released a compendium of nationally recognized psychiatric terms—most of which applied to psychotic disorders and severe neurological impairments—that would become part of the American Medical Association's standard classified nomenclature of disease.

After the end of World War II, the Veterans Administration (VA) added many more diagnoses to the APA inventory, incorporating the various psychological disorders exhibited by servicemen. This expanded compilation proved to be influential, for shortly after its publication, the World Health Organization (WHO) published the sixth edition of its *ICD*, which for the first time included information on mental disorders, much of it based on the VA classifications.

The first edition of the *DSM (DSM-I)* was little more than a pamphlet where symptoms were not specified in detail. Its importance, however, lay in its description and definition of the approximately 100 diagnostic categories then recognized by clinicians. The seventh and eighth editions of *ICD* heavily influenced *DSM-I*, like its successor, *DSM-II*. Until the publication of *DSM-III*, the American system for classifying psychiatric disorders was virtually identical to the *ICD*.

During the 1970s, however, researchers affiliated with the Washington University School of Medicine (Feighner et al., 1972) developed the *research diagnostic* approach to psychiatric diagnosis, which emphasized clearly formulated and observable signs and symptoms that could be used for both research and clinical practice. *DSM-III*, published in 1980, incorporated this approach, adding clear diagnostic standards and objective descriptions of symptoms and behaviors.

DSM-III also introduced a multiaxial system for diagnostic evaluation to ensure that all relevant clinical information was considered. Axis I describes syndromes such as major depression, schizophrenia, and substance use disorders. Axis II covers childhood and personality disorders that often persist into adult life. Axis III refers to physical disorders or conditions that are potentially relevant to the understanding or management of the patient. Axis IV rates the severity of psychosocial stressors that have occurred in the year preceding the current evaluation and that may have contributed to the patient's symptoms. Axis V is a global assessment of psychological, social, and occupational functioning, which should be taken into account in treatment planning.

DEFINING SUBSTANCE USE DISORDERS

For the first time, *DSM-III* listed substance use disorders as a separate diagnostic category, distinguishing them from personality disorders, which they had previously been considered. In addition, the term "dependence" replaced the more generic terms "alcoholism" or "addiction," and was distinguished from *abuse* by the presence of the symptoms of tolerance or withdrawal. Alcohol and drug abuse were assigned to separate subcategories, permitting a greater differentiation and range of severity for each.

A revised version of *DSM-III* was published in 1987, containing important changes in the section on substance use disorders (Rounsaville, Spitzer, & Williams, 1986). One modification was the adoption of a new dependence syndrome concept (Edwards, Arif, & Hodgson, 1981), in which dependence was defined as an interrelated cluster of psychological symptoms: a strong desire or craving for the substance; physiological signs, especially tolerance and withdrawal; and behavioral indicators, in particular using the substance to relieve withdrawal discomfort.

Significantly, the medical and social consequences of both acute intoxication and chronic substance use, such as accidents and liver damage, are not among the primary diagnostic criteria of dependence. They did, however, play a prominent role in defining the *substance abuse* category.

After the publication of the revised third edition in 1987 (*DSM-III-R*), a fourth edition (*DSM-IV*) was published in 1994, with a "Text Revision," known as the *DSM-IV-TR*, providing updated and revised information in 2000. *DSM-IV* contained further changes in the diagnosis of substance use disorders that were designed to assure compatibility between *DSM* and *ICD* (see Table 1). *DSM-IV* now defines substance dependence as a maladaptive pattern of substance use leading to clinically significant impairment or distress, as manifested by three or more of the following seven symptoms occurring in the same twelve-month period:

Tolerance—the need for markedly increased amounts of the substance to achieve intoxication or the desired effect, or a markedly diminished effect with continued use of the same amount of the substance;

Withdrawal—behavioral changes that occur when blood or tissue levels of the substance decline after a period of prolonged or heavy use; often accompanied by use of the substance to relieve withdrawal symptoms;

Impaired control—taking the substance in larger amounts or over a longer period than was intended;

Unsuccessful attempts (or a persistent desire) to cut down or control substance use;

Much time spent in activities related to procuring or using the substance or recovering from its effects;

Giving up or reducing important social, occupational, or recreational activities because of substance use;

Continued use despite knowledge of persistent or recurrent physical or psychological problems caused or worsened by use of the substance.

In *DSM-IV*, patients can be diagnosed as dependent on any of the following: alcohol, tobacco, sedatives and hypnotics, anxiolytics, cannabis (marijuana), stimulants, opioids, cocaine, hallucinogens, PCP (phencyclidine), or a combination

ICD-10 Dependence Syndrome	DSM-IV Substance Dependence

A cluster of physiological, behavioural, and cognitive phenomena in which the use of a substance or a class of substances takes a higher priority for an individual than other behaviours that once had greater value. A central characteristic of the syndrome is the desire (often strong, sometimes overpowering) to take psychoactive drugs (medically prescribed or not), alcohol, or tobacco. There may be evidence that return to substance use after a period of abstinence leads to a more rapid reappearance of other features of the syndrome than occurs with nondependent individuals.
 	
Diagnostic guidelines
A definite diagnosis of dependence should usually be made only if three or more of the following have been experienced or exhibited during the previous year:
 	
(a) a strong desire or sense of compulsion to take the substance;
(b) difficulties in controlling substance-taking behaviour in terms of its onset, termination, or levels of use;
(c) a physiological withdrawal state . . . when substance use has ceased or been reduced, as evidenced by: the characteristic withdrawal syndrome for the substance; or use of the same (or a closely related) substance with the intention of relieving or avoiding withdrawal symptoms;
(d) evidence of tolerance, such that increased doses of the substance are required to achieve effects originally produced by lower doses (examples are alcohol- and opiate-dependent individuals who may take doses sufficient to incapacitate or kill nontolerant users);
(e) progressive neglect of alternative pleasures or interests because of psychoactive substance use, increased amount of time necessary to obtain or take the substance or to recover from its effects;
(f) persisting with substance use despite clear evidence of overtly harmful consequences, such as harm to the liver through excessive drinking, depressive mood states consequent to periods of heavy substance use, or drug-related impairment of cognitive functioning; determination should be made of the user's actual or expected awareness of the nature and extent of the harm
 	
Narrowing of the personal repertoire of patterns of psychoactive substance use has also been described as a characteristic feature (e.g., a tendency to drink alcoholic drinks in the same way on weekdays and weekends, regardless of social constraints that determine appropriate drinking behaviour).
	A maladaptive pattern of substance use, leading to clinically significant impairment or distress, as manifested by three or more of the following occurring at any time in the same twelve-month period:
	
	(1) tolerance, as defined by either of the following:
	   (a) need for markedly increased amounts of the substance to achieve intoxication or desired effect
	   (b) markedly diminished effect with continued use of the same amount of the substance
	
	(2) withdrawal, as manifested by either of the following:
	   (a) the characteristic withdrawal syndrome for the substance . . .
	   (b) the same (or closely related) substance is taken to relieve or avoid withdrawal symptoms
	
	(3) the substance is often taken in larger amounts or over a longer period than was intended
	
	(4) a persistent desire or unsuccessful efforts to cut down or control substance use
	
	(5) a great deal of time is spent in activities necessary to obtain the substance (e.g., visiting multiple doctors or driving long distances), use the substance (e.g., chain-smoking), or recover from its effects.
	
	(6) important social, occupational, or recreational activities given up or reduced because of substance use
	
	(7) continued substance use despite knowledge of having had a persistent or recurrent physical or psychological problem that was likely to have been caused or exacerbated by the substance (e.g., current cocaine use despite recognition of cocaine-induced depression, or continued drinking despite recognition that an ulcer was made worse by alcohol consumption)
	
	Specify if:
	  with physiological dependence: Evidence of tolerance or withdrawal (i.e., either item [1] or [2] is present):
	  without physiological dependence: No evidence of tolerance or withdrawal (i.e., neither item [1] nor [2] is present).

Table 1. A comparison of *ICD-10* and *DSM-IV* criteria for dependence. ILLUSTRATION BY GGS INFORMATION SERVICES. GALE, CENGAGE LEARNING

of drugs, which is known as polysubstance dependence. The most important factor in determining dependence, according to the *DSM-IV*, is not simply the abuse of alcohol or drugs, but the patient's inability to stop using the substance(s) despite recognizing the serious problems this causes (i.e., impaired control over substance use).

FUTURE VERSIONS

The fifth version of the *DSM* is currently in the planning stage, with publication of the new criteria tentatively scheduled for 2012. As with the previous two versions, the revision process leading to DSM-V will be guided by a task force responsible for conducting literature reviews, independent data analyses, field trials of the new criteria, consensus conferences, and the publication of background monographs. One such monograph (Saunders et al., 2007) contains papers written by an international group of experts that are designed to stimulate research on critical diagnostic issues related to substance use disorders. Among the issues under consideration in the next revision to DSM are addictions that do not require substance use (e.g., pathological gambling, Internet addiction), the need for graded or continuous measures rather than yes-or-no diagnoses, whether to diagnose abuse independently from dependence, and whether to drop the category of abuse entirely.

See also **Addiction: Concepts and Definitions; Alcoholism: Origin of the Term; Diagnosis of Substance Use Disorders: Diagnostic Criteria; Models of Alcoholism and Drug Abuse; Personality Disorders.**

BIBLIOGRAPHY

American Psychiatric Association. (1980). *Diagnostic and statistical manual of mental disorders* (3rd. ed.). Washington, DC: Author.

American Psychiatric Association. (1987). *Diagnostic and statistical manual of mental disorders* (3rd. ed., Rev.). Washington, DC: Author.

American Psychiatric Association. (1994). *Diagnostic and statistical manual of mental disorders* (4th. ed.). Washington, DC: Author.

American Psychiatric Association. (2000). *Diagnostic and statistical manual of mental disorders* (4th. ed., text revision). Washington, DC: Author.

Edwards, G., Arif, A., & Hodgson, R. (1981). Nomenclature and classification of drug- and alcohol-related problems: A WHO memorandum. *Bulletin of the World Health Organization, 59*, 225–242.

Feighner, J., Robins, E., Guze, S., Woodruff, R., Winokur, G., & Muñoz, R. (1972). Diagnostic criteria for use in psychiatric research. *Archives of General Psychiatry, 26*, 57–63.

Rounsaville, B. J., Spitzer, R. L., & Williams, J. B. (1986). Proposed changes in DSM-III substance use disorders: Description and rationale. *American Journal of Psychiatry, 143*, 463–468.

Saunders, J. B., Schuckit, M. A., Sirovatka, P. J., & Regier, D. A. (Eds.). (2007). *Diagnostic issues in substance use disorders: Refining the research agenda for DSM-V.* Arlington, VA: American Psychiatric Association.

THOMAS F. BABOR

DIAGNOSTIC INTERVIEW FOR GENETIC STUDIES (DIGS).

The Diagnostic Interview for Genetic Studies (DIGS; Nurnberger et al., 1994) is a clinical interview developed by principal investigators in the National Institute of Mental Health (NIMH) Schizophrenia and Bipolar Disorder Genetics Initiatives and NIMH extramural program staff for the assessment and differential diagnosis of major mood and psychotic disorders and related "spectrum" conditions. It is a semi-structured interview designed for use by trained interviewers (ideally those with clinical experience). Training generally consists of observation of interviews done by experienced personnel followed by administration under observation by a clinical supervisor. This process continues until the supervisor certifies that the interviewer has mastered the skip-out pattern and has achieved sufficient expertise in follow-up questions to code accurately the critical sections for diagnosis. Major Axis I disorders are covered, and there are additional sections on demographics, medical history, self-injurious behavior, present symptoms, comorbidity, and the Axis II diagnosis of antisocial personality disorder. A graphic timeline is included for the documentation of the longitudinal course of illness. A narrative summary is prepared by the interviewer at the end of the session. The narrative summary should be 1 to 2 pages in length and should cover all positive diagnoses including relevant criterion items, pertinent negative diagnoses, and should include a summary of the interview venue and length, as well as a judgment regarding reliability. Administration may require several hours for a complicated case. As of 2008, 30 to 40 different groups were using this instrument; it had been translated into six languages and cited in 397 publications.

The DIGS has the following features: (a) diagnoses can be made in multiple systems that include the Research Diagnostic Criteria (RDC), the *Diagnostic and Statistical Manual of Mental Disorders* (*DSM-III*, *DSM-III-R*, and *DSM-IV*), Feighner et al. criteria (Feighner et al., 1972), and the *International Classification of Diseases, 10th Revision* (*ICD-10*); (b) a detailed assessment is made of the longitudinal course of illness, with particular attention to the co-occurrence of substance abuse and psychotic and mood symptoms; (c) detailed sections are included to assess current and past occurrences of episodes of substance abuse or dependence; and (d) a detailed psychosis section is included to collect data that allow a careful distinction to be drawn among schizophrenia, schizoaffective disorder, and other psychotic conditions. DIGS assessments of self-reported mental disturbance are organized into several domains of psychopathology: somatization, major depression, mania/hypomania, dysthymia/depressive personality/hyperthymic personality, alcohol abuse or dependence, other drug abuse or dependence, psychosis, schizotypal personality features, suicidal behavior, anxiety disorders, eating disorder, pathological gambling, and antisocial personality disorder. The DIGS collects self-reported demographic and medical history data, and ratings are also made on the Global Assessment Scale (GAS: Endicott et al.,

1976) and the Scales for the Assessment of Positive and Negative Symptoms (SANS, SAPS: Andreasen et al., 1990). Schizotypal and other Axis II Cluster A personality features are assessed by using a modified version of the Schedule for Schizotypy (SIS; Kendler et al., 1989). This combination in the DIGS of features (including both lifetime diagnoses in multiple systems and current mood state assessment) is unique among structured interviews for psychiatric disorders.

The DIGS is used in conjunction with information from family interviews and medical records to permit a final best estimate diagnosis by experienced clinicians. Typically, all available information is reviewed independently by two clinicians. If there is disagreement between them, they discuss the case together to reach a consensus. If a consensus cannot be reached (about 2% of cases), a third clinician reviews all information including the existing best estimate sheets and acts as a tiebreaker.

The development of the DIGS proceeded in parallel with a similar development of the SSAGA (Semi-Structured Assessment for the Genetics of Alcoholism). Some investigators participated in both processes. As a consequence, the structure and wording of some sections is similar between the two instruments, particularly with regard to substance abuse and mood disorders sections. Nevertheless, it should be noted that the DIGS is intended to allow more flexible use and scoring by interviewers with clinical experience.

The DIGS requires significant clinical judgment and summarizes information in narrative form as well as in ratings. The polydiagnostic approach involves recording clinical information in sufficient detail to allow differing criteria for diagnosis. This feature was incorporated because it creates the broadest possible dataset. Since the pathophysiologic characteristics of bipolar disorder and schizophrenia are unknown, valid definitions for these diagnoses are ambiguous. The polydiagnostic interview ensures maximum comparability of the data collected with other datasets.

The DIGS provides more details regarding the phenomenology of mood disorders and schizophrenia than many other available instruments. This is an inevitable consequence of its polydiagnostic aspect, since each diagnostic system requires some items not found in others. Many items have been included expressly for gathering descriptive information not required by any current diagnostic scheme, but which permit the construction of quantitative phenotypes or reconfiguration of the information gathered into new biologically based categories. For example, questions regarding mixed states of mania and depression, rapid cycling, suicidal behavior and comorbidity are included, as well as a timeline to help specify the course of illness.

As part of interview development, a two-phase reliability study was conducted with three major goals: (a) to determine the reliability of key diagnoses; (b) to determine the feasibility of automated scoring of the DIGS using external diagnostic algorithms; and (c) to assess diagnostic reliability among collaborating sites. Six weeks of independent interviewing at each site (phase 1) was followed by two weeks of cross-site interviewing (phase 2). Since there were no significant site differences in overall agreement in either phase of the reliability study, data were combined within each phase for the analysis of individual diagnoses (bipolar disorder, unipolar depression, schizophrenia, and schizoaffective disorder). For all target diagnoses except schizoaffective disorder, values of kappa (a chance corrected measure of diagnostic agreement) obtained for algorithmic and interviewer clinical diagnoses were in the excellent range: 0.73 to 0.96. For the entire sample, agreement on algorithmic criteria defining specific syndrome patterns was high: for example, *DSM-III-R* major depressive episode criterion A: 87%, kappa=0.78; manic episode criteria A and B: 71%, kappa=0.72; and schizophrenia criterion A: 74%, kappa=0.77.

The DIGS 2.0 was used in Genetics Initiative family studies starting in 1990. Version 3.0/B of the DIGS was created in 1998 to allow additional distinctions among diagnoses and other clinical features and to provide compatibility with *DSM-IV*.

Version 4.0/BP of the DIGS was developed in 2003. As part of the collaborative effort during the last funding period, the DIGS was reviewed and revised (DIGS 4.0) to allow collection of additional data on post-traumatic stress disorder and adult attention deficit disorder. A major change was made in the Best Estimate Diagnostic process, to incorporate clinician judgment of multiple phenotypic indicators including age of onset and number of episodes of depression, hypomania, and mania; temporal relationship of mood disorder to substance abuse and psychosis; evidence of mixed episodes and rapid cycling; and a summary of the family history information. All of these indicators are scored independently by a senior clinician (at most sites a psychiatrist) based on medical records and interview information.

The DIGS, version 4, is available as an electronic form for INFOTECH Soft's Aspect mental health assessment platform. Thus it may be administered by computer (e.g., by an interviewer using a laptop or tablet computer in the field), and the computerized version can later be used to support the best estimate process.

The DIGS is designed to be used along with the FIGS (Family Instrument for Genetic Studies), which allows a comprehensive assessment of a family pattern of illness. The FIGS begins with the construction of a pedigree, then moves to general screening questions: "Has any member of your family had psychiatric or emotional problems?", and finally asks about each first-degree relative in turn, including symptom assessment, treatment history, and impairment.

The DIGS and FIGS are both available through the NIMH Genetics Initiative Web site at zork.wustl.edu. This Web site also contains a manual for the 3.0/B version and a link to the data entry system for the 4.0 version. Additional information is available from the authors.

See also **Addictive Personality and Psychological Tests; Alcohol: Psychological Consequences of Chronic Abuse; Antisocial Personality Disorder; Computerized Diagnostic Interview Schedule for DSM-IV (C DIS-IV); Depression; International Classification of Diseases (ICD); Schizophrenia; Semi-Structured Assessment for the Genetics of Alcoholism (SSAGA); Structured Clinical Interview for DSM-IV (SCID).**

BIBLIOGRAPHY

Andreasen, N. C., Flaum, M., Swayze, V. W. II, Tyrrell, G., & Arndt, S. (1990). Positive and negative symptoms in schizophrenia. A critical reappraisal. *Archives of General Psychiatry, 47*(7), 615–621.

Endicott, J., Spitzer, R. L., Fleiss, J. L., & Cohen, J. (1976). The global assessment scale. A procedure for measuring overall severity of psychiatric disturbance. *Archives of General Psychiatry, 33*(6), 766–771.

Feighner, J. P., Robins, E., Guze, S. B., Woodruff, R. A. Jr., Winokur, G., & Muñoz, R. (1972). Diagnostic criteria for use in psychiatric research. *Archives of General Psychiatry, 26*(1), 57–63.

Kendler, K. S., Lieberman, J. A., & Walsh, D. (1989). The Structured Interview for Schizotypy (SIS), a preliminary report. *Schizophrenia Bulletin, 15*(4), 559–571.

Nurnberger, J. I. Jr., Blehar, M. C., Kaufmann, C. A., York-Cooler, C., Simpson, S. G., Harkavy-Friedman, J., et al. (1994). Diagnostic interview for genetic studies. Rationale, unique features, and training (DIGS). *Archives of General Psychiatry, 51,* 849–859, discussion 863–864.

Washington University in St. Louis, Center for Collaborative Genetic Studies on Mental Disorders. *Diagnostic Interviews for Genetic Studies (DIGS).* (versions 2.0, 3.0B, and 4.0/BP). Available from http://zork.wustl.edu.

Washington University in St. Louis, Center for Collaborative Genetic Studies on Mental Disorders. *Family Interview for Genetic Studies (FIGS).* Available from http://zork.wustl.edu/.

JOHN I. NURNBERGER JR.
CAROLYN YORK O'NEIL

DIAGNOSTIC INTERVIEW SCHEDULE FOR DSM-IV. *See* **Computerized Diagnostic Interview Schedule for DSM-IV (C DIS-IV).**

DIHYDROMORPHINE. Dihydromorphine is a semisynthetic opioid analgesic (painkiller) derived from morphine. Structurally, it is very similar to morphine—the only difference being the reduction of the double bond between positions 7 and 8 in morphine to a single bond. Although slightly more potent than morphine in relieving pain, it is not widely used clinically. At standard analgesic doses, it has a side-effect profile very similar to that of morphine. These include constipation and respiratory depression. Chronic use will produce tolerance and physical dependence.

See also **Addiction: Concepts and Definitions; Opiates/Opioids; Opioid Complications and Withdrawal.**

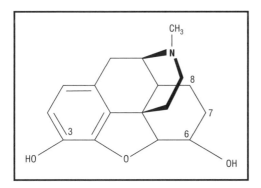

Figure 1. Chemical structure of dihydromorphine. ILLUSTRATION BY GGS INFORMATION SERVICES. GALE, CENGAGE LEARNING

BIBLIOGRAPHY

Reisine, T., & Pasternak, G. (1996). Opioid analgesics and antagonists. In A. G. Gilman et al. (Eds.), *Goodman and Gilman's the pharmacological basis of therapeutics* (9th ed.). New York: McGraw-Hill Medical. (2005, 11th ed.)

GAVRIL W. PASTERNAK

DIMETHYLTRYPTAMINE (DMT).
This drug is a member of the hallucinogenic substances known as indoleamines. These are compounds that are structurally similar to the neurotransmitter serotonin. Although found in certain plants and, according to some evidence, can be formed in the brain, DMT is synthesized for use. Its effects are similar to those produced by lysergic acid diethylamide (LSD), but unlike LSD, DMT is inactive after oral administration. It must be injected, sniffed, or smoked.

DMT has a rapid onset, usually within one minute, but the effects last for a much shorter period than those produced by LSD—with the user feeling "normal" within thirty to sixty minutes. This is because DMT is very rapidly destroyed by the enzyme monoamine oxidase, which metabolizes structurally related compounds, such as serotonin. The dose amount of DMT is critical, since larger doses produce slightly longer, much more intense, and sometimes very uncomfortable "trips" than do lower doses. The sudden and rapid onset of a period of altered perceptions that soon terminates is also disconcerting to some users. DMT was known briefly as the "businessman's LSD"—one could have a psychedelic experience during the lunch hour and be back at work in the afternoon. It has,

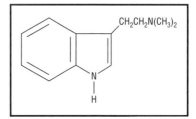

Figure 1. Chemical structure of dimethyltryptamine (DMT). ILLUSTRATION BY GGS INFORMATION SERVICES. GALE, CENGAGE LEARNING

however, in fact never been a widely available, steadily obtainable, or popular drug on the street.

See also **DOM; MDMA.**

BIBLIOGRAPHY

Gouzoulis-Mayfrank, E., et al. (20050). Psychological Effects of (S)-Ketamine and N,N-Dimethyltryptamine (DMT): A Double-Blind, Cross-Over Study in Healthy Volunteers. *Pharmacopsychiatry, 38,* 301–311.

Hollister, L. E. (1978). Psychotomimetic drugs in man. In *Handbook of Psychopharmacology,* Vol. 11. New York: Plenum Press.

Strassman, R. J., & Qualls, C. R. (1994). Dose-response study of N,N-Dimethyltryptamine in humans. I. neuroendocrine, autonomic and cardiovascular effects. *Archives of General Psychiatry, 51,* 2, 85–97.

DANIEL X. FREEDMAN
R. N. PECHNICK

DISTILLATION.
Distillation is the process of purifying liquid compounds on the basis of different boiling points or the process of separating liquids from compounds that do not vaporize. Since the actual process causes liquids to precipitate in a wet mist or drops that concentrate and drip, the word derives from the Latin *de* (from, down, away) + *stillare* (to drip).

In the simplest form of distillation, saltwater can be purified to yield freshwater by steam distillation, leaving a residue of salt. Distillation is also the process by which alcohol (ethanol, also called ethyl alcohol) as liquors or spirits, are separated from fermenting mashes of grains, fruits, or vegetables. When this process is used to distill alcohol, it is based on the following: Ethyl alcohol (C_2H_6O) has a lower boiling point than does water (78.5°C versus 100°C), so alcohol vapors rise first

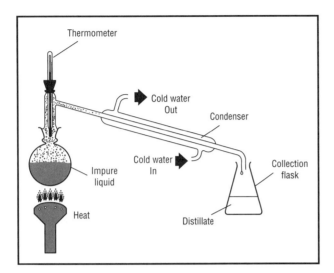

Figure 1. Simple distillation apparatus. ILLUSTRATION BY GGS INFORMATION SERVICES. GALE, CENGAGE LEARNING

into the condenser, where cool water circulates around the outside of the condenser, causing the alcohol vapors to return to liquid form and drop into the collection flask. The purity of the distillate can be increased by repeating the process several times.

About 800 CE, the process of distillation was evolved by the Arabian alchemist Jabir (or Geber) ibn Hayyah. He may also have named the distillate *alcohol*, since the word derives from an Arabic root, *al-kuhul*, which refers to powdered antimony (kohl) used as an eye cosmetic in the Mediterranean region; with time and use it came to mean any finely ground substance, then the "essence," and eventually, the essence of wine—its spirit, or alcohol. It came into English from Old Spanish, from the Arabic spoken by the Moors of the Iberian peninsula during their rule there (750–1492 CE).

See also **Beers and Brews; Distilled Spirits, Types of; Fermentation.**

BIBLIOGRAPHY

Blocker, J. S., Fahey, D. M., & Tyrrell, I. R. (Eds.). (2003). *Alcohol and temperance in modern history.* Oxford, U.K.: ABC-Clio.

Bryce, J. H., & Stewart, G. G. (2004). *Distilled spirits: Tradition and innovation.* Nottingham, U.K.: Nottingham University Press.

Lucía, S. P. (1963). *Alcohol and civilization.* New York: McGraw-Hill.

SCOTT E. LUKAS

DISTILLED SPIRITS, TYPES OF.

Distilled spirits (or, simply, spirits or liquors) are the alcohol-containing fluids (ethanol, also called ethyl alcohol) obtained via distillation of fermented juices from plants. These juices include wines, distillates of which are termed brandies. The most commonly used plants are sugarcane, potatoes, sugar beets, corn, rye, rice, and barley; various fruits such as grapes, peaches, and apples are also used. Flavors may be added to provide distinctive character.

All distilled spirits begin as a colorless liquid, pure ethyl alcohol (as it was called by 1869)—C_2H_6O. This had been called *aqua vitae* (Latin, water of life) by medieval alchemists; today it is often called grain alcohol, and the amount contained in distilled spirits ranges from 30 to 100 percent (60 to 200 proof)—the rest being mainly water.

Examples of distilled spirits include brandy, whiskey, rum, gin, and vodka. Brandy was called *brandewijn* by the Dutch of the 1600s—burned, or distilled, wine. It was originally produced as a means of saving space on trade ships, to increase the value of a cargo. The intent was to add water to the condensate to turn it back into wine, but customers soon preferred the strong brandy to the acidic wines it replaced. Cognac is a special brandy produced in the district around the Charente river towns of Cognac and Jarnac, in France, where wine is usually distilled twice, then put into oak barrels to age. The spirits draw color and flavor (tannins)

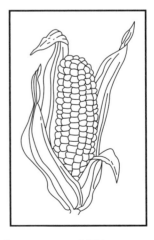

Figure 1. Corn. ILLUSTRATION BY GGS INFORMATION SERVICES. GALE, CENGAGE LEARNING

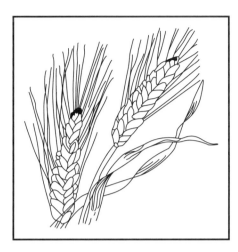

Figure 2. Wheat. ILLUSTRATION BY GGS INFORMATION SERVICES. GALE, CENGAGE LEARNING

Figure 3. Oat. ILLUSTRATION BY GGS INFORMATION SERVICES. GALE, CENGAGE LEARNING

from the wood during the required five-year aging process.

Beer and wine were the most popular drinks of the New World colonists. By the mid-1700s, whiskey (from *uisce beathadh* in Irish Gaelic; *uisge beatha* in Scots Gaelic) was introduced into the American colonies by Scottish and Irish settlers to Pennsylvania. Whiskey is distilled off grains—usually corn or rye, but millet, sorghum, and barley are also used. Traditional American whiskeys are bourbons (named after Bourbon county in Kentucky), which are made from a sour mash of rye and corn. Bourbons typically contain 40 to 50 percent ethyl alcohol (called 80 to 100 proof, doubled by the liquor industry). Canadian whiskey is very similar to bourbon and to rye whiskey, while Irish whiskey is dry (has less sugar), with a distinctive austere flavor gained by filtration. All these whiskeys lack the smoky taste of Scotch whiskeys, which get their unique flavor by using malt that had been heated over peat fires. By using less malt and by aging for only a few years in used sherry casks (traditionally), a light flavor is produced; by using more malt and long aging, heavy peaty smoky flavors are produced. Today, some scotches and other whiskeys are blended to achieve uniform taste from batch to batch.

The distillation of fermented sugarcane (*Saccarum officinarum*) results in rum. Of all distilled spirits, rum best retains the natural taste of its base, because (1) the step of turning starch into sugar is unnecessary; (2) it can be distilled at a lower proof; (3) chemical treatment is minimized; and (4) maturing can be done with used casks. The amount of added (sugar-based) caramel gives rum its distinctive flavor and color—which can vary from clear to amber to mahogany. The New England colonists made rum from molasses, which is the thick syrup separated from raw sugar during crystal sugar manufacture. Caribbean colonists grew sugarcane and shipped barrels of molasses to New England. New Englanders shipped back barrels of rum. Both substances were originally ballast for the barrels, which were made from New England's local forests to hold the sugar shipped from the Caribbean to the mother country, England.

Gin is a clear distillate of a grain (or beer) base that is then reprocessed; juniper berries and other herbs are added to give it its traditional taste. Vodka is also clear liquor, often the same as gin without the juniper flavor. Traditional vodkas, made in Russia, Ukraine, Poland, and other Eastern European countries, are made from grain or potatoes at a very high proof; typical ranges are 65 to 95 proof, or about 33 to 43 percent ethyl alcohol. Vodka has no special taste or aroma, although some are slightly flavored with immersed grasses, herbs, flowers, or fruits. The Scandinavian aquavit is clear, like vodka, distilled from either grain or potatoes, and flavored with caraway seed; it is similar to Germany's kümmelvasser (*kümmel* means caraway in German). When any clear liquor is added to fruit syrups, the product is called a cordial or a liqueur. Swiss kirschwasser is, however, a clear high-proof cherry-based brandy (*kirsche* means cherry in German); and slivovitz is a clear high-proof Slavic plum-based brandy.

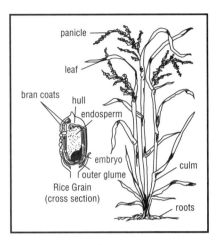

Figure 4. Rice. ILLUSTRATION BY GGS INFORMATION SERVICES. GALE, CENGAGE LEARNING

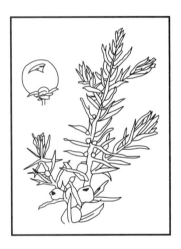

Figure 5. Juniper. ILLUSTRATION BY GGS INFORMATION SERVICES. GALE, CENGAGE LEARNING

The raw grain alcohol distilled in the American South and in Appalachia has been called *white lightning* since the early 1900s; this is also known as moonshine, corn whiskey, or corn liquor—illegally produced in private nonlicensed stills, in very high proofs, to avoid state and federal controls or taxation. The term *firewater* was used along the American frontier after about 1815, to indicate any strong alcoholic beverage; this was often traded, given, or sold to Native Americans, causing cultural disruptions and social problems that continue even today. These include a high rate of alcoholism and children born with fetal alcohol syndrome.

See also **Alcohol: History of Drinking (International); Alcohol: History of Drinking in the United States; Beers and Brews.**

BIBLIOGRAPHY

Brander, M. (1905). *The original scotch.* New York: Clarkson N. Potter.

Bryce, J. H., & Stewart, G. G. (2004). *Distilled spirits: Tradition and innovation.* Nottingham, U.K.: Nottingham University Press.

Lucía, S. P. (1963). *Alcohol and civilization.* New York: McGraw-Hill.

SCOTT E. LUKAS

DISTILLED SPIRITS COUNCIL. In 1974, the Distilled Spirits Council of the United States, Inc. (DISCUS) was formed by the merger of three organizations—the industrywide Licensed Beverage Industries, Inc. (LBI), the Distilled Spirits Institute (DSI), and the Bourbon Institute. DISCUS, headquartered in Washington, D.C., is supported by the distilled spirits producers, representing 90 percent of the liquor sold in the United States. In all major respects DISCUS is a trade association representing producers and marketers of distilled spirits sold in the United States.

DISCUS's primary functions are to maintain legislative relations with state and federal governments (lobbying); to conduct or support economic and statistical research; to promote export and standards of identity for American-made liquors; to maintain a voluntary code of advertising practices; and to represent the distilling industry on social issues of concern, such as teenage drinking, drunk driving, and other forms of alcohol abuse. State government relations activities are conducted by DISCUS regional representatives.

As a trade association, DISCUS seeks to inform the public about the importance of distilled spirits to the U.S. economy. By 1999, the distilled spirits industry generated $95 billion in U.S. economic activity annually and over 1.3 million people were employed in the United States through the manufacture, distribution, and sale of distilled spirits. Jobs within the distilled spirits industry account for more than $28 billion in U.S. wages.

As had its predecessor LBI, DISCUS has supported programs of alcohol abuse prevention and research conducted by independent groups and experts in education, traffic safety, and alcoholism. These projects have included the Grand Rapids,

Michigan, study of drunk driving (1961–1965) and the research led by Harburg and Gomburg (1978–1984) on how drinking may affect the off-spring of different types of drinkers.

In addition to supporting the Harvard Medical School course for diagnosis and treatment of alcoholism, now adopted by eighty medical schools, DISCUS has provided extensive support to national organizations in the alcoholism field since 1970. Its approach is based on the knowledge that alcoholism is an identifiable illness and can respond to intervention and treatment.

In 1978, DISCUS endorsed the "responsible decisions on alcohol" approach developed by the Education Commission of the States, and in 1982, it supported the National Association of State Boards of Education in its nationwide project based on this concept (which includes abstinence). In 1980, DISCUS cooperated with the U.S. Department of Health and Human Services and other sponsors in supporting the Friends of the Family parenting education program.

In 1979, DISCUS became a charter member of the Licensed Beverage Information Council (LBIC), an industrywide consortium (beer, wine, and spirits at the producer, wholesaler, and retailer levels), whose membership includes nine other associations. LBIC has supported varied prevention groups and specialists in conducting medical and public education programs devoted to alcoholism as a treatable illness; fetal alcohol syndrome (FAS); teenage drinking; and drunk driving. The consortium has conducted the nationwide Friends Don't Let Friends Drive Drunk campaign.

DISCUS member companies are the principal supporters of the Century Council, a nonprofit organization dedicated to reducing alcohol abuse across the United States. Through public/private partnerships, Century Council investigates, funds, and implements innovative approaches to address the problems of drunk driving and underage drinking.

In 1994, DISCUS developed and initiated the Drunk Driving Prevention Act (DDPA), model legislation that strengthens drunk driving laws. Its provisions, many of which are being considered and adopted by state legislatures around the country, include mandatory alcohol and drug education for drivers; a ban of open containers in motor vehicles; Administrative License Revocation (ALR) authorizing a police officer to confiscate the license of any driver who either fails a chemical test or refuses to submit to it; zero tolerance for drivers under age 21; mandatory license revocation for persons under age 21 who attempt to purchase, consume, or misrepresent their age for the purpose of buying or consuming beverage alcohol; and mandatory alcohol and drug testing in fatal crashes.

DISCUS has also developed BACCHUS (Boosting Alcohol Consciousness Concerning Health of University Students). BACCHUS is a college-based peer education program to reduce alcohol abuse. Its educational materials include Open Doors, a Guide to Alcohol and Residence Life for Resident Administrators; Community College Guide to Peer Education; Gamma Guide (Greeks Advocating Mature Management of Alcohol); Certified Peer Educator Training Program; and Student Athletes as Peer Educators.

DISCUS has discouraged drinking by underage youth; encouraged adults who choose to drink to do so responsibly; and emphasized significant distinctions between normal social drinking and alcohol abuse.

The organization's economic research includes annual compilations of "apparent consumption" data (i.e., distilled spirits entering channels of trade) and an assessment of the liquor industry's contributions to the economy. Total U.S. distilled spirits consumption has declined in recent years, a fact noted by DISCUS as one of the many refutations of the "control of alcohol availability" hypothesis.

The DISCUS Code of Good Practice provides for self-regulation of advertising practices by distillers. An unusually high degree of compliance has been achieved even with nonmembers. The code was applied to radio in 1936, when that was a major medium; it has voluntarily excluded the use of television as an advertising medium by distillers since 1947. Contrary to a widely held impression, spirits advertising on television is not prohibited by law.

Distilled spirits have been the most heavily taxed consumer commodity in the United States. DISCUS and its predecessors have claimed over the years that such taxes are discriminatory and excessive, and they do not reduce chronic alcohol-abuse problems.

DISCUS has consistently argued that the tax structure imposed on distilled spirits is unjust because the government taxes spirits at a higher rate than beer and wine. It contends that standard servings of beer, wine, and distilled spirits contain the same amount of alcohol, yet the federal tax rate on distilled spirits is almost three times the rate on wine and over two times the rate on beer.

In 1999, DISCUS continued to lobby Congress for a reduction in excise taxes. DISCUS pointed out that more than half of the price that consumers spend on a typical bottle of distilled spirits is taxes. Federal, state, and local governments receive more than $18 billion per year in tax revenue from the beverage alcohol industry and tax revenues from the distilled spirits industry alone account for more than $7.5 billion. DISCUS pointed out that federal, state, and local governments combined realize fourteen times more in spirits tax revenues than the distillers make in profits. However, Congress has remained unresponsive to the attempt by DISCUS to reduce excise taxes.

As a long-standing policy, DISCUS and its members do not encourage people to start drinking or to drink too much. DISCUS's review of the research literature indicates that there is no scientific evidence that brand advertising either influences or shapes those behaviors. The marketing purpose of product advertising is to build consumer acceptance of specific brands, according to DISCUS. In the late 1990s, DISCUS began publicizing the health benefits of alcohol consumption. It noted a growing body of scientific evidence reporting that moderate beverage alcohol consumption may reduce the risk of cardiovascular disease, the leading cause of death in the United States. This potential benefit is equally available from moderate consumption of any form of beverage alcohol—distilled spirits, beer, or wine. However, DISCUS does not promote the use of alcohol consumption for health reasons.

See also **Alcohol: History of Drinking (International); Alcohol: History of Drinking in the United States; Legal Regulation of Drugs and Alcohol; Minimum Drinking Age Laws; Prevention; Social Costs of Alcohol and Drug Abuse; Tax Laws and Alcohol.**

BIBLIOGRAPHY

Borkenstein, R. F. (1965). The role of the drinking driver in traffic accidents. Project of the Department of Police Administration, Indiana University, initiated November 10, 1961.

Distilled Spirits Council of the United States (DISCUS). Available from http://www.discus.org.

Harburg, E., & Gomberg, E. (1984). Alcohol use/abstinence among men and women in a small town setting. Project of the University of Michigan, initiated November 1, 1978.

PAUL F. GAVAGHAN
REVISED BY FREDERICK K. GRITTNER (2001)

DOGS IN DRUG DETECTION. In 1970 the U.S. Customs Service faced a shrinking inspectional staff, a flood of illegal narcotics, and an increasing load of vehicles and passengers entering the United States. In that same year a manager in the U.S. Customs Service thought that dogs could be used to detect illegal narcotics. The manager's name has been lost in the corporate history of the Customs Service, yet years later dogs are not only used to detect narcotics, but U.S. Customs and Border Protection (CBP) canines also detect explosives, currency, agriculture (fruits, vegetables, and meats), and concealed persons. CBP canines are also used for BORSTAR (Border Patrol Search, Trauma, and Rescue). Dogs could be trained to detect anything that produces an odor. Although the idea of narcotic detector dogs originated in the U.S. Customs Service, Customs' managers had to go to the U.S. Air Force for the technical expertise—not in narcotic detection, because it did not exist, but dog training in general. The air force loaned the Customs Service five instructors to develop the program. Those instructors, using the age-old method of trial and error, developed a training method for narcotic detection that was still used in the 1990s. Through the years, several key aspects of the training program were identified and became the basis for a very successful program—dog selection, development of a conditioned response, and odor integrity.

It became evident that to make the training program successful the instructors had to start with a dog that displayed certain natural traits. Those traits were retrieval motivation and self-confidence. The instructors soon realized that a dog displaying a natural desire to retrieve was the easiest to condition for response to the narcotic odor. They used

A narcotics detector dog, inspecting student lockers. AP IMAGES.

the retrieval method just as the Russian physiologist Ivan Pavlov (1849–1936) used a bell: In Pavlov's experiments, he had observed that dogs salivate when food is placed in their mouths. He would give the dogs food while providing another stimulus such as a bell ringing. After a few repetitions, the dogs would salivate when they heard the bell ring—even without the food being present. The dogs had learned to associate the bell ringing with food. This response was called a *conditioned response*.

The Customs' instructors used a similar method to create a conditioned response to a drug odor. A dog was subjected to a series of retrieval exercises using a specific drug's odor. After each retrieval, the dog played a game of tug-of-war with its handler and received physical praise. The dog soon associated the specific drug odor with the game and the physical praise.

Using a dog's natural desire to retrieve as a selection criterion limited the number of breeds that

could be considered for this type of training. It was obvious that most of the sporting breeds fit this criterion—golden retrievers, Labrador retrievers, German shorthair retrievers, and mixed breeds of these types. They have had the retrieval drive bred into them over the centuries. In addition, these breeds predominated in the dog shelters and humane societies used by U.S. Customs as the primary source for its dog procurement, which has not only benefited the Customs' program but the local dog shelters too. Local shelters must by law destroy stray dogs after a certain time period if no one selects or adopts the dog. The Customs' instructors select dogs scheduled to be put to sleep.

The Customs' training method is based on the natural behavior of these retriever breeds of dogs. By using a dog's natural behavior, the instructors can adjust certain aspects of their training program to deal with the individual personality of each dog. Although each dog that entered the training program possessed the same basic qualifications, each then displayed them in varying degrees of intensity because of personality differences.

During the training process, the other aspect of the program that has ensured success has been maintaining the integrity of the narcotic odor. During the development of the training program there were several incidents when the detector dog would respond to nondrug odors. In those incidents a common factor was identified: The same nondrug odor was also present during the training program. To the dog, the materials that were used in the scent-association process (a process by which the dog identifies the narcotic odor with the tug-of-war game) combined with the drug odor represented a completely different odor picture (a combination of odors that the dog associates with a positive reward). This problem was eliminated by ensuring that all materials used in the training process smelled like the specific drug in question. Additionally, nondrug odor materials are routinely available or added as distractors during many training, certification, and maintenance protocols to ensure that the dogs do not alert to nondrug odors.

In recent years scientific studies have expanded our understanding of the behavioral and chemical basis of canine alerts to specimens and have demonstrated the sensitivity and reliability of detector dog teams. For example, beginning in 1987, reports of cocaine residues on money shed doubts on the validity of using canines to indicate narcotics odor on currency and even the validity of such searches where innocently contaminated currency could illicit a conditioned response by a detector dog team. Detailed scientific studies of the specific chemicals and amounts have subsequently confirmed that most currency in circulation is contaminated with nanogram to microgram quantities of microscopic cocaine residues but that the levels of narcotic odor chemicals emanating from such currency is insufficient to illicit the conditioned response from a narcotic detector dog. These studies have demonstrated that a narcotic detector dog's conditioned response indicates significant recent contamination of the currency by narcotic odor and these responses have been used in courts of law as part of forfeiture proceedings.

Dog selection, the development of a conditioned response, and the integrity of the narcotic odor are all key elements in the employment of dogs as drug detectors. Further information about this type of dog training can be obtained through the U.S. Customs and Border Protection Canine Enforcement Program in Washington, D.C.

See also **Asset Forfeiture; Drug Interdiction; Seizures of Drugs; U.S. Government: Agencies in Drug Law Enforcement and Supply Control; U.S. Government Agencies: U.S. Customs and Border Protection (CBP).**

BIBLIOGRAPHY

Furton, K. G., Hong, Y. C, Hsu, Y.-L., Luo, T., Rose, S., & Walton, J. (2002). Identification of odor signature chemicals in cocaine using solid-phase microextraction-gas chromatography and detector-dog response to isolated compounds spiked on U.S. paper currency. *Journal of Chromatographic Science, 40,* 147–155.

U.S. Customs and Border Protection. (2007, May). *Canine programs,* available from http://www.cbp.gov/.

U.S. Customs Service (1978). *Detector dog training manual.* Washington, DC: U.S. Government Printing Office.

CARL A. NEWCOMBE
REVISED BY KENNETH G. FURTON (2009)

DOM. This drug's street name is STP. During the hippie drug culture of the Vietnam War period, its name referred to "serenity, tranquility, and peace." This was also a taunt and a spoof, since the initials were the same as a widely available oil additive that made an automobile engine run smoothly. The drug DOM is a member of a family of hallucinogenic substances based on molecular additions to phenethylamine. This is a group of compounds that have structural similarities to the catecholamine-type neurotransmitters, such as norepinephrine, epinephrine, and dopamine. While our bodies make these catecholamines from dietary amino acids, they do not make the chemical substitutions that produce a psychedelic compound. Mescaline is the best and longest known of this family of hallucinogens.

DOM is a synthesized compound that produces effects similar to mescaline and lysergic acid diethylamide (LSD), but the effects of DOM can last for fourteen to twenty hours, much longer than those of LSD. In addition, the effects of DOM have a very slow onset. Some of the initial street

Figure 1. Chemical structure of DOM (STP). ILLUSTRATION BY GGS INFORMATION SERVICES. GALE, CENGAGE LEARNING

users of DOM had previous experience with LSD, a drug with a much more rapid onset. When the typical LSD-type effects were not found soon after taking DOM, some users took more drug, which led to a very intense and long-lasting psychedelic experience. Ironically, DOM was originally manufactured in the hope of producing a shorter, less-intense trip than LSD, which, it was thought, might be more useful and manageable in producing a period of insight and self-reflection in psychotherapy. This hope was never achieved.

See also **Designer Drugs; Dimethyltryptamine (DMT).**

BIBLIOGRAPHY

Hanson, G. R., Venturelli, P. J., & Fleckenstein, A. E. (2005). *Drugs and Society.* Sudbury, MA: Jones & Bartlett Publishers.

Shulgin, A., & Shulgin, A. (1991). *PIHKAL: A chemical love story.* Berkeley, CA: Transform Press.

Williams, M. E. (Ed.). (2004). *Hallucinogens.* Farmington Hills, MI: Greenhaven Press.

DANIEL X. FREEDMAN
R. N. PECHNICK

DOPAMINE. Dopamine (DA) is a catecholamine according to its chemical structure and a neurotransmitter of special importance for drug addiction. DA is a decarboxylated form of dopa (an amino acid) found especially in the basal ganglia. Chemically known as 3,4 dihydroxyphenylethylamine, DA arises from dihydroxphenylacetic acid (dopa) by the action of the enzyme dopa decarboxylase. DA-containing neurons (nerve cells) are widespread in the brain and the body. DA is also found in minute amounts in other catecholamine neurons as a precursor to norepinephrine. Small

DA-containing interneurons are found in the autonomic ganglia, retina, hypothalamus, and medulla. Long axon neurons are found in two extensive circuits: (1) the nigrostriatal pathway, which links the substantia nigra neurons to the basal ganglia neurons and regulates locomotor events; (2) the mesocortical and mesolimbic circuits (i.e., mesocorticolimbic system), which arise in the ventral tegmental area and project to the neocortex, limbic cortices, nucleus accumbens, and amygdala, where they regulate emotional events, including several forms of drug addiction, reinforcement, or reward.

The DA system is important in responding to salient stimuli and facilitating conditioned learning. Stimuli, including non-drug rewards (such as food) and a variety of commonly abused drugs, can activate the mesocorticolimbic system. Acute administration of opioids, nicotine, alcohol, and cannabinoids all facilitate the release of DA in the nucleus accumbens through actions on the ventral tegmental area or the nucleus accumbens directly. Although a wide range of commonly abused drugs stimulate the release of DA, it is important to note that DA is not the sole neurotransmitter involved in reward. The reinforcing effects of the above-mentioned drugs have both DA-dependent and DA-independent mechanisms. This is shown by the fact that the rewarding effects of heroin, nicotine, and alcohol are still present in rodents following inactivation of the mesocorticolimbic DA system.

Psychostimulants, such as amphetamine, methamphetamine, and cocaine, have a direct effect on mesocorticolimbic dopamine by blocking the DA transporter. The DA transporter, which transports DA from outside the nerve terminal to inside the nerve terminal, functions to retrieve released DA and help terminate its actions at receptors. By preventing the reuptake of dopamine, psychostimulants increase the extracellular concentration of DA, thereby facilitating activation of DA receptors. Animal studies have shown that blockade of dopamine receptors with systemically administered receptor antagonists (blockers) reduces the reinforcing effects of psychostimulants. Human subjects, both drug abusers and non-drug abusers, show an increase in striatal extracellular DA when acutely administered a psychostimulant. The increases in DA were associated with increases in self-reported measures of euphoria by the subjects. Striatal DA is also increased in addicted subjects when exposed to a stimulus associated with the drug (videotaped scenes of subjects taking cocaine). Imaging studies have shown that long-term drug use can result in decreased striatal DA release and alterations in D2 dopamine receptors.

DA is also thought to be involved in schizophrenia and psychosis since DA-receptor-blocking drugs are clinically useful antipsychotic agents. Another disease, in which DA is lost due to the degeneration of DA-containing neurons, is Parkinson's disease, which can be treated by replacing DA with its precursor, dopa.

See also **Neuron.**

BIBLIOGRAPHY

Koob, G. F., & Le Moal, M. (2006). Neurobiological theories of addiction. In *Neurobiology of addiction* (pp. 379–428). Oxford, England: Academic Press, Elsevier.

Volkow, N. D., Fowler, J. S., Wang, G., Swanson, J. M., & Telang, F. T. (2007). Dopamine in drug abuse and addiction. *Archives of Neurology, 64*(11), 1575–1579.

FLOYD BLOOM
REVISED BY MARK MOFFETT (2009)

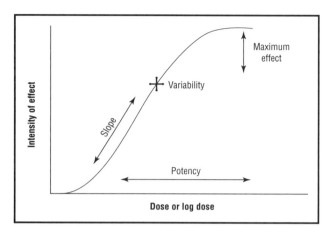

Figure 1. Representative dose-effect curve, with its four characteristics. ILLUSTRATION BY GGS INFORMATION SERVICES. GALE, CENGAGE LEARNING

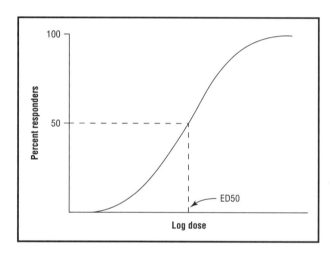

Figure 2. Representative dose-effect curve, showing a median effect dose (ED50). ILLUSTRATION BY GGS INFORMATION SERVICES. GALE, CENGAGE LEARNING

DOSE-RESPONSE RELATIONSHIP.

The relationship between the dose (amount) of a drug and the response observed can often be extremely complex, depending on a variety of factors including the absorption, metabolism, and elimination of the drug; the site of action of the drug in the body; and the presence of other drugs or disease. In general, however, at relatively low doses, the response to a drug generally increases in direct proportion to increases in the dose. At higher doses of the drug, the amount of change in response to an increase in the dose gradually decreases until a dose is reached that produces no further increase in the observed response (i.e., a plateau). The relationship between the concentration of the drug and the observed effect can therefore be graphically represented as a hyperbolic curve (see Figure 1).

Often, however, the response (ordinate) is plotted against the logarithm of the drug concentration (abscissa) to transform the dose-response relationship into a sigmoidal curve. This transformation makes it easier to compare different dose-response curves—since the scale of the drug concentration axis is expanded at low concentrations where the effect is rapidly changing, while compressing the scale at higher doses where the effect is changing more slowly (see Figure 2).

Finally, there are two basic types of dose-response relationships. A graded dose-response curve plots the degree of a given response against the concentration of the drug as described above. The second type of dose-response curve is the quantal dose-effect curve. In this case, a given quantal effect is chosen (e.g., a certain degree of cough suppression), and the concentration of the drug is plotted against the percentage of a specific population in which the drug produces the effect. The median effective dose (ED50 or the dose at which 50% of the individuals exhibit the specified quantal effect) and the median lethal dose (LD50 or the dose at which death is produced in 50% of the experimental animals in preclinical studies) can be estimated from quantal dose-effect curves. With this type of curve, the relative effectiveness of various drugs for producing a desired or undesired effect, as well as the relative safety between various drugs, can be determined. The ratio of the LD50 to the ED50 for a given effect indicates the therapeutic index of a drug for that effect and suggests how selective the drug is in producing its desired effects. In clinical studies, the concentration of the drug required to produce toxic effects can be compared to the concentration required for a specific therapeutic effect in the population to estimate the clinical therapeutic index.

See also **Drug Metabolism; ED50.**

BIBLIOGRAPHY

Gilman, A. G., et al. (Eds.). (1990). *Goodman and Gilman's the pharmacological basis of therapeutics* (8th ed.). New York: Pergamon. (2005, 11th ed. New York: McGraw-Hill Medical.)

Krishna, R. (Ed.). (2006). *Dose optimization in drug development.* New York: Informa Healthcare.

Ting, N. (Ed.). (2006). *Dose finding in drug development.* New York: Springer.

NICK E. GOEDERS

DOVER'S POWDER.

Dover's Powder, developed and described by the British physician Thomas Dover in 1732, was one of the more popular and enduring of the opium-based medications that were widely used in the United States and Europe prior to the twentieth century. The medication combined opium with what we know today as ipecac (ipecacuanha), a substance that induces vomiting. The result was a pain-reducing potion that might induce a sense of euphoria but could not be ingested in large quantities because of its emetic properties. Taken as a nonprescription medicine by the general public for over 200 years, it was also prescribed by physicians for home and hospital use. Versions of the preparation are still listed in pharmaceutical formularies in which "Dover's Powder" commonly denotes any opium-based mixture that includes ipecacuanha. The wide use of Dover's Powder declined in the early 1900s largely because of the addiction that resulted from the prolonged use of opiates, because of the introduction of other nonaddicting analgesics (painkillers), mainly aspirin, and because of laws regulating sales of opium products.

Thomas Dover (1662–1742) studied medicine at Oxford University in the 1680s. He claimed to have served an apprenticeship with Dr. Thomas Sydenham, the illustrious seventeenth-century practitioner and teacher, who originated the formula for laudanum, another early and popular opium-based medicine. Dover practiced medicine for over fifty years, although during his lifetime he was more famous for his exploits as an adventurer and privateer. His involvement in the early slave trade and in the plundering of Spanish settlements off the coast of South America brought him fortune and fame. On one of his voyages he found the shipwrecked Alexander Selkirk, who, on being returned to London, created a sensation and was to become the inspiration for Daniel Defoe's *Robinson Crusoe.* Dover retired from his merchant sailing career a wealthy man, but poor investments led him to resume his medical career first in Gloucestershire and later in London.

In 1732, probably to attract patients to his new practice in London, Dover published *An Ancient Physician's Legacy to His Country,* one of the earliest medical treatises written for the general public. The book listed forty-two ailments with successful treatments used by Dover, and included the testimonial letters of many "cured" patients. The book enjoyed popular success and was reprinted eight times, the last in 1771, nearly thirty years after his death. One remedy described in the book, the use of mercury, earned him the nickname during his lifetime of the Quicksilver Doctor, but the formula for Dover's Powder, which appears unchanged in all eight editions, has proven to be his most enduring legacy. Appearing on page 18 of the original edition as a treatment for gout, the directions read:

Take Opium one ounce, Salt-Petre and Tartar vitriolated each four ounces, Ipecacuana one ounce, Liquorish one ounce. Put the Salt Petre and Tartar into a red hot mortar, stirring them with a spoon until they have done flaming. Then powder them very fine; after that slice your opium, grind them into powder, and then mix the other powders with these. Dose from forty to sixty or seventy grains in a glass of white wine Posset going to bed, covering up warm and drinking a quart or three pints of the Posset—Drink while sweating.

Dover's familiarity with opium most probably resulted from his association with Thomas Sydenham and thereby his acquaintance with the benefits of laudanum (an alcoholic tincture of opium). Dover's ingenious use of opium with ipecacuanha seems to have been original. His unique formula, Pulvis Ipecacuanha Compositus, with its specificity of ingredients, produced a relatively reliable and consistent potion in an era when there was no regulation of medications and little standardization in their preparation. Medications could be purchased at apothecary shops with or without doctors' prescriptions or at back-street stores that sold drugs along with food, clothing, and other necessities of life. The major issue at the time in the use of opiate-based medications was not that they contained what we now know to be a narcotic, but whether the consistency of the formula or the misuse by the patient caused overdoses of what could be poisonous ingredients. Dover's Powder provided a stable product that, because of the ipecacuanha, could not be taken in excess at any one time. The powder came to be trusted by the general public and widely prescribed by physicians. It was considered such a safe remedy that it was even prescribed for children.

Although Dover originated his powder as treatment for gout, it was used throughout the eighteenth and nineteenth centuries along with many other opium-based patent and official preparations by large numbers of people for a wide variety of disorders. Opium, used as a healing plant for over 6,000 years, was an ingredient in countless formulas that were openly available and credited with curing the most common disorders of the time. Mixed in a tincture, it was found in laudanum; in a camphorated formula it became paregoric; and it was also included in preparations for lozenges, plasters, enemas, liniments, and other general medications.

Opium-based medicines were used for many disorders, including insomnia, diarrhea, bronchitis, tuberculosis, chronic headache, insanity, menstrual disorders, pain, malaria, syphilis, and smallpox. Often both physicians and patients mistook its narcotic properties, which relieved pain and created a sense of well-being, as curative rather than palliative, and little was understood of the darker side of opiate medications—the destructive nature of addiction—until well into the nineteenth century. By this time, it was common for middle- and upper-class people, especially women and those with chronic diseases, to be addicted to opiates that were frequently seen in innocuous health elixirs or in remedies that had been originally prescribed by physicians. Widespread prescribing by physicians and easy availability of the opiate medications made addiction a frequent result of medical therapeutics.

By the middle of the nineteenth century, the issue of opium addiction began to appear with more frequency in the medical literature, and in both the United States and England there were pressures to regulate both the pharmacy trade and the use of narcotic medications, especially the patent medicines containing opiates. Even then, it was not until the end of the century—as a result of better education of physicians and pharmacists, advances in diagnosis and therapeutics, and a growing understanding of the nature of addiction—that opium-based medications were supplanted by other curative treatments and by nonaddictive salicylate analgesics such as aspirin. Opium-based medicines used today, such as morphine and codeine, are government-regulated and can be purchased legally only by prescription.

Dover's Powder in its original form is now an obsolete medication. It should be recognized for its place in the history of pharmacology as a relatively reputable medicine used from 1732 until the 1930s, an era in which opium-based medications were one of the few remedies that brought relief to suffering patients. Many of these medications came to be misused by both patients and physicians who had little understanding of addiction and few options for pain relief. Thomas Dover, seen as an adventurer and opportunist by many during his lifetime, developed a preparation that allowed patients to use a narcotic while limiting its ingestion. More precise knowledge of the healing as well as the addictive properties of narcotics allows modern physicians and pharmacologists to deal specifically with the dosage of narcotic medications. Nevertheless, Dover's Powder, an ingenious and effective solution to a thorny problem, became a household name long after its originator's medical career had ended and his medical treatise had been published.

See also **Addiction: Concepts and Definitions; Britain; Opiates/Opioids.**

BIBLIOGRAPHY

Berridge, V., & Edwards, G. (1981). *Opium and the people: Opiate use in nineteenth century England.* London: Allen Lane.

Boyes, J. H. (1931). Dover's Powder and Robinson Crusoe. *New England Journal of Medicine, 204,* 440–443.

Cockayne, E. E., & Stow, N. J. (2005). *Stutter's casebook: A junior hospital doctor, 1839–1841.* Woodbridge, U.K.: Boydell Press.

Courtwright, D. T. (1982). *Dark paradise: Opiate addiction in America before 1940.* Cambridge, MA: Harvard University Press.

Duke, M. (1985). Thomas Dover—physician, pirate and powder, as seen through the looking glass of the 20th-century physician. *Connecticut Medicine, 49,* 179–182.

Osler, W. (1896). Thomas Dover, M. B. (of Dover's Powder), physician and buccaneer. *Bulletin of the Johns Hopkins Hospital, 7,* 1–6.

Thompson, C. J. S. (2003). *Mystery and art of the apothecary.* Whitefish, MT: Kessinger Publishing.

VERNER STILLNER

DRAMSHOP LIABILITY LAWS.

Dramshops are taverns, saloons, bars, and drinking establishments. All states impose fines and other punishments when alcohol is sold to visibly intoxicated customers or habitual drunkards. Although historically these laws aimed to preserve public order and morality, as of 2008 they were perceived primarily as tools to curtail drunk driving. Their effectiveness is a direct function of compliance and enforcement. Although compliance has rarely been studied, one study in Michigan found that an increase in police enforcement (through visits and warnings) resulted in a three-fold increase in the rates of service refusal to intoxicated patrons. In addition, service intervention training has been voluntarily implemented in many states and is required by law in some. Although the evidence is mixed, some research indicates that sustained server training can reduce the risk of drunk driving.

In addition to these statutory penalties, more than half the states also impose tort liability on tavern keepers for injuries caused to third parties by intoxicated patrons. Liability in such situations serves both compensatory and deterrent purposes. In the first comprehensive analysis of dramshop liability laws, Frank Sloan (2002) concludes that they are more effective than either administrative or criminal regulation in changing the behavior of those who serve alcohol. As a consequence, these laws reduce alcohol-related traffic fatalities. Vendors of alcohol must also balance the costs of liability insurance under a dramshop act by increasing drink prices. More than thirty states and many cities have extended the dramshop principle to private so-called social hosts who fail to take adequate precautions to prevent obviously intoxicated guests from getting behind the wheel.

The threat of liability for servers of alcohol appears to exert a deterrent effect. These laws also serve an important pedagogical effect. Together with other legal and cultural factors, dramshop laws help to shape social norms against driving while intoxicated.

See also **Alcohol: History of Drinking (International); Alcohol: History of Drinking in the United States; Driving, Alcohol, and Drugs; Driving Under the Influence (DUI); Drug Interactions and Alcohol; Drug Testing Methods and Clinical Interpretations of Test Results; Legal Regulation of Drugs and Alcohol; Mothers Against Drunk Driving (MADD); Students Against Destructive Decisions (SADD).**

BIBLIOGRAPHY

Edwards, G., Anderson, P., Babor, T. F., & Casswell, S. (1994). *Alcohol policy and the public good.* Oxford: Oxford University Press.

Sloan, F. (2002). *Drinkers, drivers and bartenders: Balancing private choices and public accountability.* Chicago: University of Chicago Press.

Stout, E. (2000). Reducing harmful alcohol-related behaviors: Effective regulatory methods. *Journal of Studies on Alcohol, 61,* 402–412.

Wagenaar, A. C., & Holder, H. D. (1991). Effects of alcoholic beverage server liability on traffic crash injuries. *Alcoholism: Clinical and Experimental Research 15,* 942–947.

CHRISTOPHER B. ANTHONY
REVISED BY RICHARD J. BONNIE (2001)
FREDERICK K. GRITTNER (2009)

DREAMS/DREAMING. *See* Sleep, Dreaming, and Drugs.

DRIVING, ALCOHOL, AND DRUGS.

Injuries, especially from motor vehicle collisions, are the leading cause of death for individuals under age 44. The presence of alcohol is the factor most frequently associated with fatalities in vehicle crashes, drownings, falls, and fire, according to the U.S. Department of Health and Human Services (1987). In the first report of the U.S. Department of Transportation to Congress on traffic safety and alcohol (in 1968), it was concluded that more than 50 percent of fatal traffic collisions and 33 percent of serious-injury traffic collisions were alcohol-related.

EARLY STUDIES AND SUCCESSES

Although the association between alcohol consumption and traffic accidents had been recognized by the beginning of the twentieth century, the magnitude of the problem did not capture public attention until the 1970s, when public tolerance of driving under the influence of alcohol (DUI) decreased sharply. This shift in attitude, combined with increased legal countermeasures, resulted in a significant decline in alcohol-related traffic fatalities (among drivers, passengers, pedestrians, etc.) from a high of 60 percent in 1982 to 40 percent by 1997 of traffic fatalities with victims who had alcohol present. Similarly, the proportion of alcohol-involved drivers in traffic fatalities declined from 41 percent in 1982 to 24 percent in 1997, according to the Department of Transportation's *Traffic Safety Facts 2005.*

Unfortunately, there has been a halt in this decline since 1997, and little progress in reducing alcohol-related accidents and fatalities occurred between the mid-1990s and the late 2000s. This has been reflected not only in the U.S. data but throughout the majority of industrialized nations. Thus, alcohol still remains the single largest factor in traffic fatalities and serious injuries.

BLOOD ALCOHOL CONCENTRATION AND DRIVING

Voas and colleagues (1998) compared the relative frequency of driving under the influence of alcohol in three U.S. nationwide surveys, done in 1973, 1986, and 1996 on weekend nights. Drivers were stopped at random and asked to provide breath samples for alcohol testing. The blood alcohol concentrations (BACs) from the three surveys were compared regarding time, day, gender, age, ethnicity, geographical region, and other factors. Across nearly all population subgroups, the presence of alcohol in nighttime weekend drivers dropped from 36 percent in 1973 to 26 percent in 1986, and then to 17 percent in 1996. However, although the percent of decline for drivers with BACs below 0.10 percent was 54 percent from 1973 to 1996, there was only a 45 percent decline in drivers with over 0.10 percent BAC.

Epidemiological studies have compared the BACs of collision-involved drivers with those of randomly selected drivers passing the collision site at similar times. These studies have demonstrated that the probability of a crash increases with any departure from zero BAC, and that it increases exponentially with increasing BAC levels. By the time BAC levels exceed 0.20 percent (200 mg/ 100 mL), the probability of a collision increases more than 100 times, or 10,000 percent.

Most areas of human behavior are eventually impaired by increasing alcohol levels. However, the examination of alcohol-related collision data from governmental investigations and police collision reports suggests that information-processing errors are common in the majority of alcohol-related traffic collisions. Information-processing deficits include impairment of attention, visual search, and perception. The second largest category of errors involves errors in judgment, such as speed selection. Failure to control a car because of decreasing motor skills remains a distant third cause of crashes, despite the popular assumption that links driving impairment with the appearance of intoxication and motor incapacitation.

The results observed in epidemiological survey studies are supported by numerous experimental studies in which driver behavior was examined under controlled conditions. Such studies may examine one or two driving relevant behaviors in laboratories, or they may be more complex studies of driving-related behavior using driving simulators or closed-course driving situations that preserve the safety of the driver.

AREAS OF IMPAIRMENT

Moskowitz and Robinson (1988) reviewed 177 experimental studies of alcohol's effects on driving-related behaviors that met criteria of scientific merit. The behavior found to be most affected by alcohol was divided attention, with impairment seen even at alcohol levels below 0.02 percent (20mg/100mL). Divided-attention tasks involve simultaneously monitoring and responding to more than one source of information, which is characteristic of many complex man-machine interactions, such as driving and flying. While operating a vehicle, drivers under the influence of alcohol frequently fail to detect significant potential threats in the environment.

Similarly, studies have indicated that information processing and perception are affected at low BAC levels. Tracking, which is analogous to car-control functions such as maintaining a heading and lane position, has been shown to be impaired at low BACs when performed simultaneously with other functions in divided-attention situations, though this ability is less impaired when the tracking task is performed by itself. Complex reaction-time tasks involving several competing stimuli and responses are impaired at low BACs, whereas simple reaction-time tasks requiring little information processing are more resistant to the effects of alcohol.

Studies of psychomotor skills in driving simulators and closed-course driving studies have shown considerable variation in the BAC levels at which impairment appears. These variations are likely explained by the differences in information-processing requirements among these varied tasks. The Moskowitz and Robinson review concluded that there is no minimum threshold for alcohol's impairment of complex human-machine tasks. Thus, any reliable measure of alcohol in the human system produces some impairment.

Other areas that have been suggested as leading to alcohol-related accidents include poor judgment and violent and aggressive behavior. Both laboratory studies and epidemiological data, such as the incidents of alcohol in violence, have provided evidence that the effects of alcohol on aggression are significant. On the other hand, because of the difficulties in modeling the behavior, few studies have been performed in the laboratory on the effect of alcohol on judgment. Nonetheless, laboratory studies have indicated significant impairment at low BAC levels, and epidemiological studies have shown increased crash frequency at BAC levels below those at which the majority of the population would exhibit symptoms of intoxication, such as slurred speech and unsteady gait. Thus, the absence of signs of intoxication is not evidence that a driver is capable of operating a motor vehicle or other machinery safely.

In 2000, Moskowitz and Fiorentino updated Moskowitz and Robinson's 1988 report with a review of an additional 112 studies published from 1981 to 1997. Although the main conclusions of the 1988 report were confirmed, this review found more frequent reports of impairments at very low alcohol levels, reflecting improvements in the sensitivity and reliability of scientific investigation. Moreover, new behavioral areas are being explored, such as the tendency to fall asleep at the wheel, which increases significantly even at low BAC levels.

OTHER DRUGS

The major involvement of alcohol in traffic accidents and other injuries is well documented. However, it is a bit more difficult to draw conclusions about the role of drugs other than alcohol in traffic safety. Although laboratory studies on the effects of many drugs are similar to alcohol in demonstrating the impairment of performance skills, there are difficulties in executing epidemiological studies on the effects of drugs in driving. For example, few non-crash-involved drivers volunteer to provide blood samples so that their drug levels can be compared with blood samples obtained from collision victims. This makes it difficult to perform studies comparing blood-drug levels.

While studies have been completed in hospitals comparing blood-drug levels in trauma patients involved in driving collisions with blood-drug samples from volunteers who were in the hospital for other reasons, serious questions arise regarding the representativeness of the control group. Another problem in relating drug use to vehicle crashes has been the difficulty of evaluating the behavioral significance of blood-drug levels. Unlike alcohol, where levels in venous blood samples or breath samples are essentially equivalent to those from blood in the brain (the site of drug action), for most other drugs there is a complex relationship between blood level and the magnitude of behavioral impairment. Many drugs remain present in the blood for weeks beyond any period in which behavioral effects may be observed. In other cases, drug levels in the blood drop extremely rapidly and become difficult to detect, while behavioral impairment remains. Thus, many epidemiological studies of drugs and driving report the presence of the drug rather than the level of drug concentration.

One technique to circumvent control-group problems has been to assign responsibility or non-responsibility to crash-involved drivers, and to then correlate the presence of drugs with the frequency of crash responsibility. Within the constraints of these epidemiological studies, researchers have often concluded that tranquilizers, antihistamines, and antidepressants are overrepresented in crash-involved drivers. Terhune and colleagues (1992) examined the presence of drugs in blood specimens from 1,882 fatally injured drivers. Both illicit and prescription drugs were found in 18 percent of the fatalities, while marijuana was found in 6.7 percent, cocaine in 5.3 percent, tranquilizers in 2.9 percent, and amphetamines in 1.9 percent.

When crash responsibility was assigned and correlated with drug use, the small number of individuals in each separate drug classification made statistical significance difficult to obtain, despite the fact that several drug categories were associated with increased crash responsibility. Crash-responsibility rates did increase significantly as the number of drugs in the driver increased. Many of the drug users in the Terhune study used several drugs simultaneously, and these drivers had the highest collision rates. Alcohol, meanwhile, was found in 52 percent of the fatalities, with more than 90 percent of the drivers with BACs over 0.08 percent considered responsible for the crash.

MARIJUANA

Since the 1950s, the most frequently used illicit drug in the United States has been marijuana. Epidemiological studies have demonstrated that it is also the drug most frequently consumed by drivers. Bates and Blakely (1999) reviewed the epidemiological literature for marijuana's role in motor vehicle crashes. They concluded that there is no evidence marijuana alone increased either fatal or serious-injury crashes. However, the evidence is inconclusive whether the presence of marijuana in combination with alcohol increases fatalities or serious injuries over the number produced by alcohol alone. Nor was it possible to determine whether marijuana increases the rate of less serious vehicle crashes.

Baldock's 2007 review of the literature on marijuana and crash risk reached similar conclusions. The many methodological problems involved in obtaining blood samples from crash-involved drivers and from a comparable representative sample of control drivers led the author to conclude that no existing study was conclusive, and that the driving risk associated with marijuana "remains to be determined."

SKILLS PERFORMANCE

In contrast to the ambiguity of scientific information available from epidemiological sources about the role of drugs in causing collisions, numerous experimental studies have been performed to evaluate the effects of drugs on skills performance. Regulatory agencies in many countries have frequently required an evaluation of the side effects of prescription drugs on the performance of various skills, and several governments have supported studies of the effects of illicit and abused drugs on skills performance in the laboratory.

Thus, the evaluation of the effects of drugs on driving and other human-machine interactions has depended primarily on experimental studies in which changes in behavior can be observed as a function of differences in administered doses and the time after administration. However, no other drug has been evaluated in as extensive a range of behaviors as has alcohol. Nevertheless, many drugs have been studied with respect to some important variables required for driving.

The emphasis in these drug studies has tended to be on the evaluation of vision, attention, vigilance, and psychomotor skills. Driving-simulator studies have also been done on occasion. The psychomotor skill most often examined has been some form of tracking. Reviewing this literature presents considerable difficulties, however, because there are so many differences between classes of drugs, as well as between individual drugs within the same drug classification. For example, many minor tranquilizers, especially benzodiazepines, have been shown to impair attention and tracking in a wide variety of studies. However, newer tranquilizers, such as buspirone, exhibit little evidence of impairment.

Conclusions about impairments in a drug category are likely to change due to the pressures exerted by the drug regulatory agencies on drug companies to develop medicines that do not impair skills performance. Most hypnotics exhibit residual skills impairment the day following use, but new drugs have been introduced whose duration of effects is shorter, so there will be less residual impairment after awakening.

Another class of psychoactive drugs, the antidepressants, especially amitriptyline, has long been known to impair performance in a variety of skills. Again, recently introduced types of antidepressants do not produce the same degree of impairment. Although narcotic analgesics derived from opium (opiates) have been shown experimentally to lead to decreased alertness, chronic use produces considerable tolerance to some side effects, which may explain why epidemiological studies have not found consistent evidence of differences in crash rates between narcotic users and control groups. Moreover, patients maintained on a stabilized dosage of methadone, a synthesized narcotic, have shown little evidence of impairment in a wide variety of experimental and epidemiological studies.

Another category of drug that shows evidence of impairing skills performance in laboratory studies is the antihistamines, many of which produce impairment of performance accompanied by complaints of drowsiness and lack of alertness. Again, recent pharmacological advancements have produced antihistamine drugs which maintain antihistamine actions but have difficulty crossing the blood-brain barrier and thus produce little impairment. One such drug is loratadine (Claritin).

Of all the illicit drugs, marijuana has had the largest number of experimental studies performed to examine its effects. Many of these studies indicate that marijuana impairs coordination, tracking, perception, and vigilance. It has also been shown to impair performance in driving simulators and on-the-road studies. Yet, epidemiological studies have been inconclusive in demonstrating increased crash risk, perhaps due to the relatively brief duration of elevated blood THC levels or perhaps due to compensatory behaviors as observed in several simulator studies.

Although there has been concern over an increased use of stimulants such as amphetamines and cocaine among drivers, there is little experimental evidence demonstrating driving impairment with these drugs. On the contrary, most studies of these stimulants, as well as of caffeine, indicate an improvement in skills performance. However, with the chronic (long-term) use of stimulants, an increased dose must be taken as tolerance develops. Thus, the dose levels examined in the laboratory may not reflect those found among drivers. In addition, after the stimulation phase, a subsequent depressed phase occurs (called the "crash"), with increased drowsiness and lack of alertness. The stimulant drugs have not been well studied in relation to driving and this needs to be remedied. Further study is needed, both for acute (one-time) use and chronic use.

See also **Alcohol: Chemistry and Pharmacology; Benzodiazepines; Blood Alcohol Concentration; Cocaine; Dose-Response Relationship; Dramshop Liability Laws; Driving Under the Influence (DUI); Marijuana (Cannabis); Minimum Drinking Age Laws; Mothers Against Drunk Driving (MADD); Opiates/Opioids; Psychomotor Effects of Alcohol and Drugs; Social Costs of Alcohol and Drug Abuse; Students Against Destructive Decisions (SADD).**

BIBLIOGRAPHY

Baldock, M. R. J. (2007). *Review of the literature on cannabis and crash risk* (Centre for Automotive Safety Research, Report No. CASR010). Adelaide, Australia: University of Adelaide.

Bates, M. N., & Blakely, T. A. (1999). Role of cannabis in motor vehicle crashes. *Epidemiological Reviews, 21*(2), 222–232.

Moskowitz, H., & Fiorentino, D. (2000). *A review of the literature on the effects of low doses of alcohol on driving-related skills* (Report No. DOT HS 809 028). Washington, DC: U.S. Department of Transportation.

Moskowitz, H., & Robinson, C. D. (1988). *Effects of low doses of alcohol on driving-related skills: A review of the evidence* (Report No. DOT HS 807 280). Washington, DC: U.S. Department of Transportation.

Terhune, K. W., Ippolito, C. A., Hendriks, D. L., & Michalovic, J. G. (1992). *The incidence and role of drugs in fatally injured drivers* (Report No. DOT 808 065). Washington, DC: U.S. Department of Transportation.

U.S. Department of Health and Human Services. (1987). *Sixth special report to the U.S. Congress on alcohol and health.* Rockville, MD: Author.

U.S. Department of Transportation. (1968). *Alcohol and highway safety: A report to the Congress.* Washington, DC: U.S. Government Printing Office.

U.S. Department of Transportation, National Highway Traffic Safety Administration. *Traffic safety facts 2005: A compilation of motor vehicle crash data from the Fatality Analysis Reporting System and the General Estimates System* (Report No. DOT HS 810 631). Washington, DC: Author.

Voas, R. B., Wells, J., Lestina, D., Williams, A., & Greene, M. (1998). Drinking and driving in the United States: The 1996 national roadside survey. *Accident, Analysis & Prevention, 30*(2), 267–275.

HERBERT MOSKOWITZ

DRIVING UNDER THE INFLUENCE (DUI).

Driving under the influence is defined in the statutes of fourteen states as incapacity, meaning that the influence of a drug leaves a driver incapable of driving safely. Specific blood-alcohol concentration (BAC) limits are associated with a DUI offense. As of 2008, all fifty states, the District of Columbia, and Puerto Rico have reduced the legal BAC limit from .10 percent to .08 percent.

The FBI reports that 1,460,498 people were arrested for DUI in 2006. The National Survey of Drug Use and Health, a household survey of approximately 30.5 million people aged twelve and older, indicates that an estimated one in ten (12.4%) reported driving under the influence at least once in the past year. Males were twice as likely as females to report drinking and driving and nearly half were aged eighteen to twenty-five.

An individual with a BAC of .08 percent or higher is eleven times more likely than an individual who has had nothing to drink to be involved in a fatal crash. An analysis of crash fatality data from the National Highway Traffic Safety Administration (NHTSA) shows that the number of persons killed in alcohol-related crashes jumps sharply when the highest BAC involved reaches .08 percent or higher.

The total number of fatalities in alcohol-related crashes decreased 33 percent from 26,173 in 1982 to 17,602 in 2006. NHTSA reports that nearly half (41%) of the total traffic fatalities that year were alcohol-related and an estimated three-fourths involved a driver with a BAC of .08 percent or greater. Drivers involved in fatal crashes with a BAC of .08 or higher in 2006 were most likely to be male and aged twenty-one to forty-four. One in four young drivers (fifteen to twenty years old) who died in motor vehicle crashes that year had a BAC of .08 or higher. NHTSA also projected that three out of ten Americans would be involved in an alcohol-related crash sometime in their lives.

See also **Breathalyzer; Dramshop Liability Laws; Driving, Alcohol, and Drugs; Drug Interactions and Alcohol; Mothers Against Drunk Driving (MADD); Remove Intoxicated Drivers (RID-USA, Inc.); Students Against Destructive Decisions (SADD).**

BIBLIOGRAPHY

Keall, M., Frith, W., & Patterson, T. (2004). The influence of alcohol, age, and number of passengers on the night-time risk of driver fatal injury in New Zealand. *Accident Analysis and Prevention 36,* 49–61.

National Highway Traffic Safety Administration. (2001). *The traffic stop and you: Improving communications between citizens and law enforcement* (DOT HS 809 212). Washington, DC: Author. Available from http://www.madd.org/.

National Highway Traffic Safety Administration. (2007). *2006 Traffic safety annual assessment: A preview* (DOT HS 810 791). Washington, DC: Author. Available from http://www.nrd.nhtsa.dot.gov/.

United States Department of Health and Human Services, Substance Abuse and Mental Health Services Administration, Office of Applied Studies. (2006). *Results from the 2006 national survey on drug use and health.* Available from http://oas.samhsa.gov/.

United States Department of Justice, Federal Bureau of Investigation. (2006). *Crime in the United States 2006:*

Persons arrested (Table 29). Available from http://www.fbi.gov/.

Zador, P., Krawchuk, S., & Voas, R. (2000). *Relative risk of fatal crash involvement by BAC, age, and gender* (DOT HS 809 050). Washington, DC: National Highway Traffic Safety Administration.

MYROSLAVA ROMACH
KAREN PARKER
REVISED BY FREDERICK K. GRITTNER (2001)
ERIN ARTIGIANI (2009)

DROPOUTS AND SUBSTANCE USE.

Governments and the international community view education as essential in reducing social inequities and poverty worldwide and promoting a more peaceful and sustainable future for all. Yet there is not a country in the world that does not experience the problem of young people dropping out of high school. Research, mostly conducted in the developed world, has attempted to investigate why so many young people drop out of high school by examining the relationship between this behavior and a number of factors that have been found to be associated with leaving school early. One of these factors is substance use.

A REVIEW OF THE LITERATURE

A 2007 review of 46 international research studies conducted by Loraine Townsend and others examined the link between substance use and dropping out of high school. The cross-sectional studies that were reviewed found that high school dropouts were more likely than high school graduates to report tobacco use (cigarette smoking), to report cigarette smoking at an early age, and to be heavy smokers. Furthermore, dropouts and students at risk for dropping out reported higher levels of alcohol consumption and more current and lifetime marijuana use than did in-school students and high school graduates. Compared to high school graduates, and in some cases to General Equivalency Diploma holders, dropouts were more likely to have injected a drug recently, and to have a history of injecting drug use.

Tobacco Use. The longitudinal studies in the review that followed high school dropouts and graduates into early adulthood provide evidence of the unique effect of tobacco use (cigarette smoking) on high school dropout rates, after taking into account a number of other factors that could possibly explain this effect. These factors were: age, gender, family structure, problem behavior, peer influence, and school-related factors such as poor school performance, poor commitment to school, and motivation to perform well at school. While some longitudinal studies in the review found that alcohol use was a factor in dropping out, other studies found that such factors as family and academic background, parental care, truancy, deviant behavior, and school environment had more to do with why some students drop out of school than alcohol use alone.

Studies conducted in Australia and the United States found a strong association between the frequency of early marijuana use and dropping out of school. Even when taking into account other possible explanations, such as other drug use and alcohol consumption, the use of marijuana remained a unique predictor of high school dropout. Furthermore, one study conducted by Helen E. Garnier, Judith A. Stein, and Jennifer K. Jacobs found that teenage drug use was among a number of predictors. However, other studies were able to demonstrate that dropping out of high school had more to do with adopting age-inappropriate roles—such as early marriage, pregnancy, and parenthood—than with drug use alone.

The Townsend review also found evidence that some high school dropouts continued to use tobacco as they got older, whereas the rates of tobacco use among high school graduates declined over time. Researchers in the United States found that dropping out of high school was strongly related to an increased risk of adult-onset alcohol abuse and dependence. This association persisted even when the early onset of alcohol problems was taken into account. Findings from one study conducted in Australia suggest that dropping out of high school does not lead to an increase in marijuana use soon after dropping out. On the other hand, findings from three studies conducted in the United States found that dropping out of high school leads to an increase in marijuana use in the long term (Ensminger et al., 1996; Green & Ensminger, 2006; Kogan et al., 2005).

Substance Abuse. The findings from the studies that were part of the review suggest that there is a strong link between substance use and dropping out of high school. Not only is it possible that substance use leads to dropping out of school, but also that dropping out of school leads to substance use or an increase in substance use. However, the problem with this overall conclusion is that it gives the impression that all dropouts resist conforming to the demands of educational systems and engage in (or begin to engage in) deviant behaviors. This picture is highly inaccurate, as it does not take into account the fact that a great many of the young people who drop out of high school do not use substances and do not engage in deviant behavior. The studies reviewed by Townsend and colleagues revealed that many more dropouts were not using substances than were. Evidently, there are protective factors that provide some high school dropouts with the ability to resist maladaptive behaviors, and indeed to succeed in their daily lives. Little research on these protective factors has been conducted to date, however.

THEORIES OF SUBSTANCE USE AMONG DROPOUTS

In addition to the evidence from research studies, a number of theories have been put forward to try to explain the role that substance use may play in the dropout phenomenon. Some of the more commonly cited theories are listed here.

Social control theory. This theory proposes that when the moral bonds that tie people together, and that tie people to accepted social norms, are broken, mechanisms that were customarily used to restrain antisocial behavior no longer operate. When this happens, people are more likely to deviate from societal norms by, for example, using illicit drugs or consuming excessive amounts of alcohol. They are also more likely to have a poor commitment to conventional social groups (such as families) and institutions (such as schools). From this perspective, the relationship between substance use and dropping out of high school would be explained by a weakening of the social controls that operate within families and schools to discourage antisocial behavior such as substance use and dropping out of school.

Problem-prone behavior and general deviancy theory. This theory describes dropping out of high school and substance use as just two of a number of nonconformist, deviant behaviors to which certain adolescents are prone. From this perspective, adolescents who hold nonconformist attitudes and values are also more likely to engage in a variety of other nonconformist behaviors, such as smoking, drug and alcohol use, and abandoning the student role. A number of studies in the Townsend review were able to demonstrate that substance-using adolescents are at risk for a variety of other problem behaviors, such as dropping out of school, truancy, perpetrating and being victims of violent behavior, early sexual involvement, and mental health problems.

Primary socialization theory. This theory proposes that adolescents are most at risk when ties to school and family are weak and ties to peers are strong, particularly when their peers use substances or are dropouts.

Social learning theory. This theory is similar to the primary socialization theory. The theory proposes that when social bonds are weak, learning processes occur within peer groups such that delinquent socialization becomes the strongest learning influence. This leads to deviant behaviors, including substance use and dropping out of high school.

Peer cluster theory. This theory proposes that problems at school are a dominant factor in creating deviant peer groups or clusters. Those students experiencing academic or disciplinary problems at school have a way of seeking each other out and forming peer groups. These peer groups encourage, support, and normalize a range of deviant behaviors and attitudes, such as substance use and dropping out of school, by means of social learning processes.

The theory of differential association. This theory is similar to peer cluster theory, except that it proposes substance use, rather than problems at school, as the mechanism that brings substance-using peers together. The newly found peers act as role models and reinforce behaviors that increase the likelihood of dropping out of school.

Deviant affiliation theory. This theory proposes that adolescents who have strong affiliations to delinquent and substance-using peers are encouraged to exhibit the same behaviors.

Strain theory. This theory explains how adolescents who are experiencing problems at school such as poor or failing grades, seek out alternative self-defining behaviors that are often deviant in nature, such as substance use. From this perspective, school failure, poor academic performance, dissatisfaction with school, and high rates of substance use should all be strongly related to dropping out.

While all these theories provide some explanation of the relationship between substance use and high school dropout, there is no one theory that provides us with a clear explanation of the link between dropping out and substance use alone. There are a number of possible reasons for this. First, the dropout phenomenon is highly complex and has many possible explanations, only one of which may have to do with substance use. Second, theories and research to date may not have accounted for all the possible explanations for the dropout–substance use relationship. For example, obvious biological explanations may account for the relationship between dropping out and alcohol use, marijuana use, and other illicit drug use (Lynskey & Hall, 2000). These explanations would include the effects of alcohol, marijuana, and illicit drug use on such phenomena as motivation and cognitive functioning. However, the same cannot be said for the relationship between tobacco use and high school dropout. It is likely that some as yet undetected factors may be associated with an increased risk of tobacco use and dropping out of school.

Third, the people who dropped out of the longitudinal studies over time, and for whom there was therefore no information, were often overrepresented by socially disadvantaged people, poor people, school dropouts, and drug users. These are the people most at risk for dropping out and substance use, and excluding their information from research findings may have resulted in incomplete or inaccurate explanations of the relationship between dropping out of high school and substance use. Finally, researchers in Australia have suggested that future studies should explore the experiences and opinions of those who drop out of school in searching out ways to address the problem

(Shacklock, Smyth, & Wilson, 1998; Smyth, 2005; Smyth & Hattam, 2001). These researchers suggest that research to date may have been focusing too much on factors that are not relevant to the dropouts themselves.

In spite of these limitations, the theories and research findings do suggest areas of focus for high school dropout and substance use prevention efforts. Many of the theories suggest weakened bonds to conventional society and institutions as reasons why students drop out of school or use illicit substances. Strengthening ties to and creating a commitment to conventional institutions such as school may go a long way to reducing the dropout and substance use problems. To this end, academic achievement programs may not only reduce school dropout rates, they may also reduce the rates and levels of teenage substance use. Several research groups have investigated whether intervention programs directed at first- and second-graders might change their risk for later drug use, conduct problems, and dropping out. Other research groups have targeted high-risk elementary and middle school students, giving them and their families special programs to promote learning and a sense of mastery over schoolwork.

Given that dropout rates are not declining, and are in fact increasing in some parts of the world, some researchers have suggested that student-focused programs have limited effectiveness. They suggest that research should shift its focus from students' life circumstances—such as their families, their attitudes towards school, and their motivations to perform well at school—and begin to examine schools themselves. What schools offer young people, the way in which it is done, and what students and dropouts themselves have to say about school are areas of possible research.

The range of unfortunate effects of dropping out of school makes it important to sustain stay-in-school programs as well as outreach programs for youth who are chronically absent from school or who have dropped out before graduation. At the same time, it is important for governments and the international community to investigate schools, and school systems themselves, as possibly contributing to the dropout phenomenon.

See also **Alcohol; Amotivational Syndrome; Marijuana (Cannabis); Tobacco.**

BIBLIOGRAPHY

Aloise-Young, P. A., & Chavez, E. L. (2002). Not all school dropouts are the same: Ethnic differences in the relation between reason for leaving school and adolescent substance use. *Psychology in the Schools, 39*(5), 539–547.

Aloise-Young, P. A., Cruikshank, C., & Chavez, E. L. (2002). Cigarette smoking and perceived health in school dropouts: A comparison of Mexican American and non-Hispanic white adolescents. *Journal of Pediatric Psychology, 27*(6), 497–507.

Arellano, C. M., Chavez, E. L., & Deffenbacher, J. L. (1998). Alcohol use and academic status among Mexican-American and white non-Hispanic adolescents. *Adolescence, 33*(32), 751–760.

Battin-Pearson, S., Newcomb, M. D., Abbott, R. D., Hill, K. G., Catalano, R. F., & Hawkins, D. (2000). Predictors of early high school dropout: A test of five theories. *Journal of Educational Psychology, 92*(3), 568–582.

Beauvais, F., Chavez, E. L., Oetting, E. R., Deffenbacher, J. L., & Cornell, G. R. (1996). Drug use, violence, and victimization among white American, Mexican American, and American Indian dropouts, students with academic problems, and students in good academic standing. *Journal of Counseling Psychology, 43*(3), 292–299.

Brook, J. S., Balka, E. B., & Whiteman, M. (1999). The risks for late adolescence of early adolescent marijuana use. *American Journal of Public Health, 89*(10), 1549–1554.

Crum, R. M., Ensminger, M. E., Ro, M. J., & McCord, J. (1998). The association of educational achievement and school dropout with risk of alcoholism: A twenty-five year prospective study of inner-city children. *Journal of Studies on Alcohol, 59*(3), 318–326.

Crum, R. M., Helzer, J. E., & Anthony, J. C. (1993). Level of education and alcohol abuse and dependence in adulthood: A further inquiry. *American Journal of Public Health, 83*(6), 830–837.

Dee, T. S., & Evans, W. N. (2003). Teen drinking and educational attainment: Evidence from two-sample instrumental variables estimates. *Journal of Labor Economics, 21*(1), 178–209.

Eggert, L. L., & Herting, J. R. (1993). Drug involvement among potential dropouts and "typical" youth. *Journal of Drug Education, 23*(1), 31–55.

Ellickson, P., Saner, H. S., & McGuigan, M. S. (1997). Profiles of violent youth: Substance use and other concurrent problems. *American Journal of Public Health, 87*(6), 985–991.

Ensminger, M. E., Lamkin, R. P., & Jacobson, N. (1996). School leaving: A longitudinal perspective including neighborhood effects. *Child Development, 67*(5), 2400–2416.

Escobedo, L. G., & Peddicord, J. P. (1996). Smoking prevalence in US birth cohorts: The influence of gender and education. *American Journal of Public Health, 86*(2), 231–236.

Fagan, J., & Pabon, E. (1990). Contributions of delinquency and substance use to school dropout among inner-city youths. *Youth & Society, 21*(3), 303–354.

Fergusson, D. M., & Horwood, L. J. (1997). Early onset cannabis use and psychosocial adjustment in young adults. *Addiction, 92*(3), 279–296.

Fergusson, D. M., Horwood, L. J., & Beautrais, A. L. (2003). Cannabis and educational achievement. *Addiction, 98*(12), 1681–1692.

Fergusson, D. M., Lynskey, M. T., & Horwood, L. J. (1996). The short-term consequences of early onset cannabis use. *Journal of Abnormal Child Psychology, 24*(4), 499–512.

Flischer, A. J., & Chalton, D. O. (1995). High-school dropouts in a working-class South African community: Selected characteristics and risk-taking behaviour. *Journal of Adolescence, 18*(1), 105–121.

Garnier, Helen E., Stein, Judith A., & Jacobs, Jennifer K. (1997). The process of dropping out of high school: A 19-year perspective. *American Educational Research Journal, 34*(2), 395–419.

Gfroerer, J. C., Greenblatt, J. C., & Wright, D. A. (1997). Substance use in the US college-age population: Differences according to educational status and living arrangement. *American Journal of Public Health, 87*(1), 62–65.

Green, K. M., & Ensminger, M. E. (2006). Adult social behavioral effects of heavy adolescent marijuana use among African Americans. *Developmental Psychology, 42*(6), 1168–1178.

Kaplan, H. B., & Liu, X. (1994). A longitudinal analysis of mediating variables in the drug use–dropping out relationship. *Criminology, 32*(3), 415–439.

Kogan, S. M., Luo, Z., Brody, G. H., & Murry, V. M. (2005). The influence of high school dropout on substance use among African American youth. *Journal of Ethnicity in Substance Abuse, 4*(1), 35–51.

Lynskey, M., & Hall, W. (2000). The effects of adolescent cannabis use on educational attainment: A review. *Addiction, 95*(11), 1621–1630.

Lynskey, M. T., Coffey, C., Degenhardt, L., Carlin, J. B., & Patton, G. (2003). A longitudinal study of the effects of adolescent cannabis use on high school completion. *Addiction, 98*(5), 685–692.

McCluskey, C. P., Krohn, M. D., Lizotte, A. J., & Rodriquez, M. L. (2002). Early substance use and school achievement: An examination of Latino, white, and African-American youth. *Journal of Drug Issues, 32*(3), 921–944.

Newcomb, M. D., Abbott, R. D., Catalano, R. F., Hawkins, D., Battin-Pearson, S., & Hill, K. (2002). Mediational and deviance theories of late high school failure: Process roles of structural strains, academic competence, and general versus specific problem behaviors. *Journal of Counseling Psychology, 49*(2), 172–186.

Obot, I. S., & Anthony, J. C. (1999). Association of school dropout with recent and past injecting drug use among African American adults. *Addictive Behaviors, 24*(5), 701–705.

Obot, I. S., & Anthony, J. C. (2000). School dropout and injecting drug use in a national sample of white non-Hispanic American adults. *Journal of Drug Education, 30*(2), 145–155.

Obot, I. S., Hubbard, S., & Anthony, J. C. (1999). Level of education and injecting drug use among African Americans. *Drug and Alcohol Dependence, 55*(1–2), 177–182.

Register, C. A., Williams, D. R., & Grimes, P. W. (2001). Adolescent drug use and educational attainment. *Education Economics, 9*(1), 1–18.

Roebuck, M. C., French, M. T., & Dennis, M. L. (2004). Adolescent marijuana use and school attendance. *Economics of Education Review, 23*(2), 133–141.

Rosenthal, B. S. (1998). Non-school correlates of dropout: An integrative review of the literature. *Children and Youth Services Review, 20*(5), 413–433.

Shacklock, G., Smyth, J., & Wilson, N. (1998). *Conceptualising and capturing voices in dropout research.* Paper presented to the annual meeting of the Australian Association for Research in Education, Adelaide, November–December, 1998. Available from http://www.aare.edu.au/.

Smyth, J. (2005). An argument for new understandings and explanations of early school leaving that go beyond the conventional. *London Review of Education, 3*(2), 117–130.

Smyth, J., & Hattam, R. (2001). "Voiced" research as a sociology for understanding "dropping out" of school. *British Journal of Sociology of Education, 22*(3), 401–415.

Townsend, L. J., Flisher, A. J., & King, G. (2007). A systematic review of the relationship between high school dropout and substance use. *Journal of Clinical Child and Family Psychology Review, 10*(4), 259–317.

UNESCO. (2002). *Education for All (EFA) global monitoring report, 2002: Is the world on track?* Available from http://portal.unesco.org/education/efa.

Wang, M. Q., Fitzhugh, E. C., Eddy, J. M., & Westerfield, R. C. (1998). School dropouts' attitudes and beliefs about smoking. *Psychological Reports, 82*(3), 984–986.

Wichstrøm, L. (1998). Alcohol intoxication and school dropout. *Drug & Alcohol Review, 17*(4), 413–421.

Yamada, T., Kendix, M., & Yamada, T. (1996). The impact of alcohol consumption and marijuana use on high school graduation. *Health Economics, 5*(1), 77–92.

Zimmerman, M. A., & Maton, K. I. (1992). Life-style and substance use among male African-American urban adolescents: A cluster analytic approach. *American Journal of Community Psychology, 20*(1), 121–138.

Loraine Townsend

DRUG. As a therapeutic agent, a drug is any substance, other than food, used in the prevention, diagnosis, alleviation, treatment, or cure of disease. It is also a general term for any substance, stimulating or depressing, that can be habituating. According to the U.S. Food, Drug, and Cosmetic Act, a drug is (1) a substance recognized in an official pharmacopoeia or formulary; (2) a substance intended for use in the diagnosis, cure, mitigation, treatment, or prevention of disease; (3) a substance other than food intended to affect the structure or function of the body; (4) a substance intended for use as a component of a medicine but not a device or a component, part, or accessory of a device.

Pharmacologists consider a drug to be any molecule that, when introduced into the body, affects living processes through interactions at the molecular level. Hormones can be considered to be drugs, whether they are administered from outside the body or their release is stimulated endogenously. Although drug molecules vary in size, the molecular weight of most drugs falls within the range of 100–1,000, since to be a drug it must be absorbed and distributed to a target organ. Efficient absorption and distribution may be more difficult when drugs have a molecular weight greater than 1,000. The drug's molecular shape is also important, since most drugs interact with specific receptors to produce their biological effects. The shape of the receptor determines which drug molecules are capable of binding. The shape of the drug molecule must be complementary to that of the receptor to produce an optimal fit and, therefore, a physiological response.

Within this general definition, most poisons would be considered to be drugs. Although water and oxygen technically fit this general definition and are used therapeutically and discussed in pharmacology textbooks, they are rarely considered to be drugs. Efforts have been made to develop a more restricted definition, but because so many molecules and substances can affect living tissue, it is difficult to draw a sharp line.

See also **Inhalants; Plants, Drugs From; Vitamins.**

BIBLIOGRAPHY

Hardman, J. G., et al. (Eds.). (1996). *The pharmacological basis of theraupeutics* (9th ed.). New York: McGraw-Hill Medical. (2005, 11th ed.)

Stedman's Medical Dictionary. (1992). (27th ed.). Baltimore, MD: Lippincott Williams & Wilkins. (2005, 28th ed.)

NICK E. GOEDERS

DRUG ABUSE REPORTING PROGRAM (DARP).

The Drug Abuse Reporting Program (DARP) began in 1969 as a comprehensive study that included intake and during-treatment information on individuals entering a drug treatment system established under the U.S. Narcotic Addict Rehabilitation Act of 1966. The DARP was the first national effectiveness evaluation of these new community-based treatments, conducted prospectively at Texas Christian University over a period of twenty years. The study strategy included four distinct phases of research: (1) describing major treatment modalities and the characteristics of drug abusers entering them in the early 1970s, (2) describing during-treatment performance measures and how they related to differences in treatments and clients, (3) describing post-treatment outcomes and how they related to differences in treatments and clients, and (4) describing important elements of long-term addiction careers.

The DARP data system contained records on almost 44,000 admissions during 1969 to 1973 at fifty-two federally supported treatment agencies located across the United States. The study population consisted of clients from major treatment modalities—methadone maintenance programs, therapeutic community, outpatient drug-free, and detoxification—as well as a comparison intake-only group.

THE EFFECTIVENESS OF DRUG-ABUSE TREATMENT

Initial research in this twenty-year project focused on ways of measuring characteristics of treatments, clients, and behavioral outcomes (see Sells, 1975). It was found that drug use and criminal activities decreased significantly during treatment, including outpatient as well as residential programs. More important, the effects continued after treatment ended. Some 6,402 clients located across the United States were selected for follow-up an average of three years after leaving DARP treatment (and 83 percent were relocated). Methadone maintenance, therapeutic communities, and outpatient drug-free programs were associated with more favorable outcomes among opioid addicts than outpatient detoxification and intake-only comparison groups; however, only clients who remained in treatment three months or longer showed significant improvements after treatment. Numerous studies of these data helped establish that treatment is effective and that the longer clients stay in treatment, the better they function afterwards (see Simpson & Sells, 1982).

LONG-TERM OPIOID ADDICTION CAREERS

To study long-term treatment outcomes, a sample of 697 daily opioid (primarily heroin) users were followed up with again, at twelve years after entering treatment (and 80 percent were relocated). It was found that about 25 percent of the sample was still addicted to daily opioid use in year twelve. Length of addiction (defined as the time between first and last daily opioid use) ranged from one to thirty-four years. Of the total sample, 50 percent was addicted nine-and-a-half years or longer, yet 59 percent never had a period of continuous daily use that exceeded two years. Only 27 percent reported continuous addiction periods that lasted more than three years.

Three-fourths of the addicts studied had experienced at least one relapse to daily opioid use. Among those who had ever temporarily quit daily opioid use, 85 percent had done so while in a drug-abuse treatment, 78 percent had quit while in a jail or prison, 69 percent had temporarily quit on their own (without treatment), and 41 percent had quit while in a hospital for medical treatment. The most frequent reasons cited for quitting addiction the last time involved psychological and emotional problems. Ex-addicts reported they had become tired of the hustle (rated as being important by 83 percent of the sample) and needed a change after hitting bottom (considered important by 80 percent). Other reasons cited as being important were personal or special events such as a marriage or the death of a friend (64 percent), fear of being sent to jail (56 percent), and the need to meet family responsibilities (54 percent) (see Simpson & Sells, 1990, for further details).

The DARP findings have been widely used to support continued public funding of drug-abuse treatments and to influence federal drug policy in the United States. Other similar national treatment evaluation studies were planned and undertaken in the 1980s (Treatment Outcome Prospective Study; TOPS) and in the 1990s (Drug Abuse Treatment Outcome Studies; DATOS) in the United States, as well as in the 1990s in England (National Treatment Outcome Research Study; NTORS). Subsequent research has advanced to increasing understanding of the particular elements of treatment that are most effective and how they can be improved.

See also **Drug Abuse Treatment Outcome Studies (DATOS); Narcotic Addict Rehabilitation Act (NARA); Treatment Outcome Prospective Study (TOPS).**

BIBLIOGRAPHY

Sells, S. B. (1975). The DARP research program and data system. *American Journal of Drug and Alcohol Abuse, 2,* 1–136.

Simpson, D. D., & Sells, S. B. (1982). Effectiveness of treatment for drug abuse: An overview of the DARP research program. *Advances in Alcohol and Substance Abuse, 2*(1), 7–29.

Simpson, D. D., & Sells, S. B. (1990). *Opioid addiction and treatment: A 12-year follow-up.* Malabar, FL: Krieger.

D. DWAYNE SIMPSON

DRUG ABUSE SCREENING TEST (DAST).

The assessment of drug use and related problems is important for both prevention and clinical care. Measures that are both reliable and valid provide tools for health education, for identifying problems (early if possible) in health care and community settings, and for evaluating the effectiveness of treatment. As well, this information is useful for matching individual needs and readiness for change with tailored interventions.

The Drug Abuse Screening Test (DAST) was designed to be used in a variety of settings to provide a quick index of drug-related problems. The DAST yields a *quantitative* index of the degree of consequences related to drug abuse. This instrument takes approximately 5 minutes to administer and may be given in questionnaire, interview, or computerized formats. The DAST provides a brief, self-report instrument for population screening, identifying drug problems in clinical settings and treatment evaluation.

DAST-20 and DAST-10 Versions. The DAST was modeled after the widely used Michigan Alcoholism Screening Test. Measurement properties of the DAST were initially evaluated using a clinical sample of 256 drug-alcohol-abuse clients (Skinner, 1982). The 20-item DAST has excellent internal consistency reliability (alpha) at 0.95 for total sample and 0.86 for the drug-abuse sample. Good discrimination is evident among clients classified by their reason for seeking treatment. Most clients with alcohol-related problems scored 5 or below, whereas the majority of clients with drug problems scored 6 or above on the 20-item DAST. The DAST-10 correlates very highly (r=0.98) with the longer DAST-20 and has high internal consistency reliability for a brief scale (0.92 for the total sample and 0.74 for the drug-abuse sample).

Subsequent research has evaluated the DAST with various populations and settings including psychiatric patients (Cocco & Carey, 1998; Maisto et al., 2000; Staley & El Guebaly, 1990), prison inmates (Peters et al., 2000), substance-abuse patients (Gavin et al., 1989), primary care (Maly, 1993), in the workplace (El-Bassel et al., 1997), and adapted for use with adolescents (Martino et al., 2004). Overall, these studies support the reliability and diagnostic validity of the DAST in diverse contexts.

Advantages

1. The DAST is brief and inexpensive to administer. Versions are being developed in different languages (French and Spanish).

2. It provides a quantitative index of the extent of problems related to drug abuse. Thus, one may

move beyond the identification of a drug problem and obtain a reliable estimate of the degree of problem severity.

3. The DAST has been evaluated and demonstrated excellent reliability and diagnostic validity in a variety of populations and settings.

4. Routine administration of the DAST would provide a convenient way of recording the extent of problems associated with drug abuse, ensuring that relevant questions are asked of all clients/patients.

5. The DAST can provide a reference standard for monitoring changes in the population over time, as well as for comparing individuals in different settings.

Limitations

1. Since the content of the DAST items is obvious, individuals may fake results.

2. Since any given assessment approach provides an incomplete picture, there is a danger that DAST scores may be given too much emphasis. Because the DAST yields a numerical score, this score may be misinterpreted.

Administration, Scoring and Interpretation.

The DAST may be administered in a questionnaire, interview, or computerized format. The questionnaire version allows the efficient assessment of large groups. The DAST should not be administered to individuals who are presently under the influence of drugs, or who are undergoing drug withdrawal. Under these conditions the reliability and validity of the DAST would be suspect. Respondents are instructed that "drug abuse" refers to (1) the use of prescribed or over-the-counter drugs in excess of the directions and (2) any nonmedical use of drugs. The various classes of drugs may include cannabis, (e.g., marijuana, hash), solvents or glue, tranquillizers (e.g., valium), barbiturates, cocaine, stimulants, hallucinogens (e.g., LSD), or narcotics (e.g., heroin). Remember that the questions do not refer to the use of alcoholic beverages.

The DAST total score is computed by summing all items that are endorsed in the direction of increased drug problems. Guidelines for interpreting DAST scores and recommended action are given in Table 1. A score of 3 or more on the DAST-10 and

	DAST-10	DAST-20	Action	ASAM*
None	0	0	Monitor	
Low	1–2	1–5	Brief counseling	Level I
Intermediate (likely meets DSM** criteria)	3–5	6–10	Outpatient (intensive)	Level I or II
Substantial	6–8	11–15	Intensive	Level II or III
Severe	9–10	16–20	Intensive	Level III or IV

*ASAM–American Society of Addiction Medicine Placement Criteria
**DSM-IV–American Psychiatric Association

Table 1. DAST Interpretation Guide. ILLUSTRATION BY GGS INFORMATION SERVICES. GALE, CENGAGE LEARNING

6 or more on the Dast-20 indicates the likelihood of substance abuse or dependence (e.g., *DSM-IV*, American Psychiatric Association). This diagnosis would need to be established by conducting a further diagnostic assessment.

Availability. Copies of the DAST may be obtained from the Centre for Addiction and Mental Health in Toronto, Ontario (http://www.camh.net).

See also **Treatment, Stages/Phases of: Screening and Brief Intervention.**

BIBLIOGRAPHY

Cocco, K. M., & Carey, K. B. (1998). Psychometric properties of the Drug Abuse Screening Test in psychiatric outpatients. *Psychological Assessment*, 10, 408–414.

El-Bassel, N., Schilling, R. F., Schinke, S., et al. (1997). Assessing the utility of the Drug Abuse Screening Test in the workplace. *Research on Social Work Practice*, 7, 99–114.

French, M. T., et al. (2001). Using the Drug Abuse Screening Test (DAST-10) to analyze health services utilization and cost for substance users in a community-based setting. *Substance Use and Misuse*, 36, 6/7, (927–946).

Gavin, D. R., Ross, H. E., & Skinner, H. A. (1989). Diagnostic validity of the DAST in the assessment of DSM-III drug disorders. *British Journal of Addiction*, 84, 301–307.

Maisto, S. A., Carey, M. P., & Carey, K. B., et al. (2000). Use of the Audit and the DAST-10 to identify alcohol and drug use disorders among adults with a severe and persistent mental illness. *Psychological Assessment, 12*, 186–192.

Maly, R. C. (1993). Early recognition of chemical dependence. *Primary Care, 20*, 33–50.

Martino, S., Grilo, C. M., & Fehon, D. C. (2004). Development of the Drug Abuse Screening Test for adolescents (DAST-A). *Addictive Behaviors, 25,* 57–70.

Peters, R. H., Greenbaum, P. E., Steinberg, M. L., et al. (2000). Effectiveness of screening instruments in detecting substance use disorders among prisoners. *Journal of Substance Abuse Treatment, 18,* 349–358.

Skinner, H. A. (1982). The Drug Abuse Screening Test. *Addictive Behaviors, 7,* 363–371.

Skinner, H. A. (1994). *Computerized lifestyle assessment manual.* Toronto: Multi-Health Systems.

Staley, D., & El Guebaly, N. (1990). Psychometric properties of the Drug Abuse Screening Test in a psychiatric patient population. *Addictive Behaviors, 15,* 257–264.

Yudko, E., Lozhkina, O., & Fouts, A. (2007). A comprehensive review of the psychometric properties of the Drug Abuse Screening Test. *Journal of Substance Abuse Treatment, 32,* 2, (189–198).

HARVEY A. SKINNER

DRUG ABUSE TREATMENT OUTCOME STUDIES (DATOS).

This family of studies is designed to provide comprehensive information on continuing and new questions about the effectiveness of the drug-abuse treatment that is available in a variety of publicly funded and private programs. These data update and augment the information available from earlier national studies, such as the Drug Abuse Reporting Program (DARP) study, which began in the late 1960s, and the Treatment Outcome Prospective Study (TOPS) of clients entering treatment in the 1970s. The work was sponsored by the National Institute on Drug Abuse (NIDA) and conducted by the National Development and Research Institute, Texas Christian University, and the University of California, Los Angeles.

The major objective of DATOS is to examine the effectiveness of drug-abuse treatment by conducting a multisite, prospective clinical and epidemiological longitudinal study of drug-abuse treatment. Effectiveness was examined by using data from 10,010 client interviews conducted from 1991 to 1993 at entry to treatment each three months, during treatment, and one year after leaving treatment. Interviews of clients at admission were supplemented with comprehensive clinical assessments of psychological, social, and physical impairments in addition to drug and alcohol dependence. Treatment outcomes were compared for clients who entered treatment with varied patterns of drug abuse and levels of psychosocial impairment.

A secondary objective was to investigate the process of drug-abuse treatment. A detailed examination was being conducted of the treatments and services available and provided to each client, how these treatments and services are delivered to the client, and how the client responds to treatment in terms of cognitive and behavioral changes.

The study population includes 1,540 clients from twenty-nine outpatient methadone programs; 2,774 clients from twenty-one long-term residential or therapeutic community programs; 2,574 clients from thirty-two outpatient drug-free programs; and 3,122 clients from fourteen short-term, inpatient, or chemical dependency programs. In addition, treatment programs from DATOS were compared with those for TOPS a decade earlier and for DARP two decades earlier in order to determine how drug-abuse treatment programs have changed and what the changes imply for the provision of effective treatment approaches and services.

The DATOS research builds and expands the knowledge generated from previous research on the effectiveness of treatment. Several events, however, have necessitated a continuing nationally based multisite study of drug-abuse treatment and treatment effectiveness. Major changes have occurred in the nation's drug-abusing population and treatment system. The OMNIBUS Recommendation Act of 1981 shifted the administration of treatment programs from the federal government to the states. The AIDS epidemic has intensified interest in drug-abuse treatment as a strategy to reduce exposure to the human immunodeficiency virus (HIV), which causes AIDS. Cocaine use rather than opioid use was the major drug problem of the late 1980s and early 1990s. Efforts to contain health-care costs may dramatically transform both the public and private treatment systems. It has therefore become necessary to update information so as to reexamine what we have learned about treatment effectiveness, and so as to augment the types of data that are available for exploring new issues about the nature, effectiveness, and costs of treatment approaches. The research based on DATOS has been organized into four areas: (1) treatment selection, access, and utilization, (2) treatment engagement and retention, (3) addiction and treatment, and (4) applications and policy development. Details of these studies can be found in the following references as well as at the URL http://www.DATOS.org.

The initial comparison of data from the DATOS and from the TOPS shows the following about the clients in DATOS: They are older, a greater percentage of them are women, they have more years of education, more of them are married, fewer are fully employed, and a lower percentage of them report that they have considered or attempted suicide. A higher proportion of the clients on methadone are entering treatment for the first time, and the proportion of criminal-justice referrals is higher in long-term residential and outpatient drug-free programs than they are in short-term inpatient programs.

In all types of programs, cocaine abuse predominated in the early 1990s, compared to heroin abuse in the past, but the cocaine use was usually combined with extensive use of alcohol. Multiple abuse of psychotherapeutic agents has decreased, so less than 10 percent of clients report that they regularly use these agents as opposed to treatment services. Outpatient programs have fewer early dropouts, but this may reflect better screening and longer, more extensive intake processes. The influence of cost-containment measures and managed care became evident with shortened durations of treatment for short-term inpatients. Short-term inpatient programs also admit more public sector patients than in the 1980s. Early analyses from the DATOS indicate that rates of drug use toward the start of outpatient treatment are two to three times higher than those that were found in TOPS.

The early results of DATOS also show that clients entering drug treatment are a diverse group who have multiple problems. Two-thirds of the clients are men, and approximately half have previously been in treatment. Those who have health insurance that covers treatment are, by far, in the minority. Although the clients entering short-term inpatient chemical-dependency programs appear to have a higher rate of private insurance coverage (40 percent) than any other classification of clients,

their rate is considerably lower than that observed among the same type of clients in the 1980s. Depending on the type of treatment, 25 to 50 percent of clients reported predatory criminal activity in the previous year, and less than 20 percent were fully employed. The clients have a variety of health problems, and many report significant psychiatric impairment. Few have received mental health services, however, and about one in every three clients report that they use emergency rooms as their primary health-care provider. Taken together, these data indicate that most clients have deficits in many areas of their lives and have multiple needs in addition to those directly related to their drug abuse (e.g., medical services and vocational needs).

Patterns of drug use vary markedly by type of treatment in DATOS clients. Although cocaine is the most frequently cited drug of abuse, most clients abuse multiple drugs and exhibit complex patterns of drug use. Frequent alcohol use is also common among many of the clients, as is weekly use of marijuana. Multiple abuse of psychotherapeutic agents is reported by less than 10 percent of clients.

Drug-treatment programs are focusing on providing drug-counseling services to meet the multiple problems of clients, but fewer specialized services, such as medical or psychological services, are being provided to meet clients' other needs. Only a third to a half of clients who report a need for medical services are receiving them, and the situation is much worse in regard to psychological, family, legal, employment, and financial services. Less than 10 percent of clients who report a need actually receive the service while they are in methadone and outpatient drug-free programs. The percentage of clients who receive specialized services other than drug counseling (e.g., medical or psychological attention) has declined dramatically since the mid-1980s. The impact of cost-containment measures and managed care is evident in the shorter stays of clients, particularly those enrolled in short-term inpatient programs.

Limited information on treatment outcomes has provided a mixed indication of the outcomes of treatment. The combination of more severe impairment and less extensive services suggests the potential for poorer outcomes. On the positive side, clients in treatment are being retained in treatment. However, compared to earlier findings, findings from the early 1990s indicated that a higher percentage of clients were actively using drugs during the first months of treatment.

Two other studies have been included under the DATOS program of research. The Drug Abuse Treatment Outcome Study–Adolescent (DATOS–Adolescent) research study is designed to examine the effectiveness of drug-abuse treatment for adolescents through a multisite prospective longitudinal study of youth entering treatment programs that focus on adolescents. Effectiveness will be examined by using interview data from youth under eighteen supplemented by interviews with parents or guardians conducted at entry to treatment, during treatment, and one year after leaving treatment. Treatment outcome will also be assessed by using such measures as changes in the use of the primary problem drug; the use of other drugs; antisocial, delinquent, or criminal behavior; school attendance and achievement; vocational training and employment; family and social functioning; and treatment retention. A secondary objective of DATOS–Adolescent is to investigate the drug-abuse treatment that adolescents receive. A sample of thirty long-term residential, outpatient drug-free, and short-term inpatient programs will be used to accomplish these objectives. The proposed sample design will include three thousand clients.

The Early Retrospective Study of Cocaine Treatment Outcomes is an accelerated retrospective study of clients with a primary diagnosis of cocaine dependence who had been admitted to DATOS–Adult programs prior to or in the early stages of DATOS. The research will provide data about outcomes for cocaine abusers during the first year of treatment, describe the treatment received by these clients through a study of treatment process, and establish a client data base for future follow-up studies. A sample of 2,000 records for cocaine-abusing clients discharged from residential, hospital-based, and outpatient nonmethadone programs will be abstracted to obtain baseline data. A sample of 1,200 face-to-face, follow-up interviews will be completed, after twelve months of treatment, with the discharged clients whose records were reviewed during the record-abstraction phase of the project.

Data analyses of the project will be targeted at describing the posttreatment outcomes for cocaine abusers by detailing their treatment experiences and investigating their posttreatment experiences. This description will include the type, intensity, and duration of services received and an examination of the interrelationships between client and treatment characteristics and posttreatment outcomes. Along with cocaine use, other outcomes that will be considered include the use of drugs other than cocaine, economic functioning, illegal activities, and psychological status. Analytic methods will include univariate and descriptive statistics as well as multivariate methods. The collection of follow-up data for this retrospective study will be conducted simultaneously with the collection of data for the twelve-month follow-up of DATOS clients. A close coordination with the DATOS–Adult is designed to permit comparison across studies.

See also **Drug Abuse Reporting Program (DARP); Methadone Maintenance Programs; Opioid Dependence: Course of the Disorder Over Time; Treatment: A History of Treatment in the United States; Treatment Outcome Prospective Study (TOPS).**

BIBLIOGRAPHY

Drug Abuse Outcome Studies (DATOS). (2008). Available from http://www.datos.org.

Friedmann, P., et al. (2003). Predictors of follow-up health status in the Drug Abuse Treatment Outcome Study (DATOS). *Drug and Alcohol Dependence, 69,* 3, 243–251.

Hubbard, R. L., Craddock, S. G., & Anderson, J. (2003). Overview of 5-year follow-up outcomes in the Drug Abuse Treatment Outcome Studies (DATOS). *Journal of Substance Abuse Treatment, 25,* 3, 125–134.

Simpson, D. D., & Brown, B. S. (Eds.). (1999). Special issue: Treatment processes and outcome studies from DATOS. *Drug and Alcohol Dependence, 57,* 2, 81–174.

Simpson, D. D., & Curry, S. J. (Eds.). (1997). Special issue: Drug abuse treatment outcome study (DATOS). *Psychology of Addictive Behavior, 11,* 4, 211–337.

Simpson, D. D., & Joe, G. W., Fletcher, B. W., et al. (1999). A national evaluation of treatment outcomes for cocaine dependence. *Archives of General Psychiatry, 56,* 507–514.

ROBERT HUBBARD
REVISED BY DWAYNE SIMPSON (2001)

DRUG ABUSE WARNING NETWORK (DAWN).

The Drug Abuse Warning Network (DAWN) provides information on some of the medical consequences of substance use, misuse, and abuse that manifest in visits to hospital emergency departments. DAWN records substances associated with drug-related emergency department visits; provides a means for monitoring drug misuse and abuse patterns, trends, and the emergence of new substances; assesses some of the morbidity associated with drug misuse and abuse; and generates information for national, state, and local drug policy and program planning. DAWN is also a tool that is increasingly being used for postmarketing surveillance and risk management for the pharmaceuticals regulated by the Food and Drug Administration (FDA). DAWN is the responsibility of the Office of Applied Studies, a federal statistical unit within the Substance Abuse and Mental Health Services Administration (SAMHSA).

DAWN was established in 1972 by the U. S. Department of Justice, Drug Enforcement Administration (DEA), primarily as a surveillance system for new drugs of abuse. In 1980 responsibility for DAWN was transferred to the U.S. Department of Health and Human Services (HHS). At HHS, DAWN was initially managed by the National Institute on Drug Abuse (NIDA) and, more recently, by the Office of Applied Studies at SAMHSA.

At its outset the DAWN system included inpatient units of non-federal, short-term, general hospitals; emergency departments of such hospitals; county medical examiners or coroners; student health centers; and crisis intervention centers not directly affiliated with colleges and universities. Initially, data were collected in selected metropolitan areas in each of thirteen DEA regions. Later in its development, DAWN concentrated its focus on emergency departments and medical examiners/coroners. Additionally, a probability sample of hospitals capable of producing estimates for 21 metropolitan areas and estimates for the coterminous United States was instituted for the first time after NIDA became responsible for DAWN operations. Statistical estimates of the number of hospital emergencies in the metropolitan areas or across the nation were not available from 1972 to 1987.

Beginning in 1988 DAWN data were collected from a representative sample of eligible hospitals in 21 metropolitan areas. A sample of hospitals from outside the 21 metropolitan areas was used to supplement the metropolitan areas and enabled the production of estimates for the coterminous United States as well as the 21 metropolitan areas.

Even with annual sample maintenance, such factors as changes in the hospital industry, the health care system as a whole, and major shifts in the population of the United States resulted in a need to consider changes to the sample and other features of DAWN that had remained static since its inception in 1972. As a result OAS/SAMHSA launched a two-year evaluation of DAWN's features, which resulted in a plan for a comprehensive new design.

The new data collection protocol was introduced for DAWN in 2003. This new design addressed many long-standing limitations associated with DAWN data. Because virtually every feature of DAWN changed with the redesign, data from 2004 and beyond are not comparable to data from 2002 and prior years. Data from 2003 represent a transition year that is not comparable to prior or subsequent years.

Today, DAWN relies on a national probability sample of non-federal, short-stay, general hospitals that operate 24-hour emergency departments. Hospitals are oversampled in selected metropolitan areas and divisions, and a remainder sample covers hospitals in the rest of the United States. Based on data from sampled units, national estimates of drug-related emergency department visits for the United States are produced annually.

DAWN estimates for 2006 are based on a sample of 544 eligible hospitals, with 160 (28% to 70%) responding in oversample areas and 45 (23%) responding in the remainder area. Estimates reflect adjustments for the stratified sample design, unit nonresponse, and nonresponse within a facility. Whether an oversample area stands alone in the national estimate depends on its response rate and the potential for nonresponse bias. At this time, comparisons over time are available only for 2004, 2005, and 2006.

In addition, authorized users in DAWN member hospitals; federal, state, and local public health agencies, including SAMHSA and the FDA; and

New DAWN (began 2003)	Old DAWN (ended 2002)
Cases reported to DAWN	
All types of drug-related ED visits	ED visits related to drug abuse only
Simple case criteria: Any ED visit related to recent drug use	Complex case criteria: ED visits related to drug abuse, defined as the use of an illicit drug or the non-medical use of a licit drug for one of the following purposes: • Suicide attempt or gesture • Dependence • To achieve psychic effects
Current or recent drug use	Drug abuse at any time • Current or recent drug abuse • Past (history of) drug abuse
Patient's intent is not considered	Patient's intent to abuse a drug was key
Patients of any age	Patients age 6 to 97
Eight case types: • Suicide attempt • Seeking detox • Alcohol only (age < 21) • Adverse reaction (to pharmaceuticals) • Overmedication • Malicious poisoning • Accidental ingestion • Other (any case not categorized above)	One case type with three subcategories: • Suicide attempt or gesture • Seeking detox • Other drug abuse
Drugs reported to DAWN	
Only those drugs related to the ED visit	Any drug
All types of drugs: • Illicit drugs • Prescription and over-the-counter medications • Dietary supplements • Non-phamaceutical inhalants	Same as new DAWN
Maximum of six drugs, plus alcohol	Maximum of four drugs, plus alcohol
"Alcohol-in-combination" for any case; "Alcohol only" for patients age < 21	"Alcohol-in-combination" (alcohol with another reportable drug) only
Current medications reported only if related to the visit	Current medications reported, even if unrelated to the visit
Other data items	
Whether each drug was confirmed by toxicology	No information about laboratory confirmation
Information about health: • Chief complaints • Diagnoses	No information about health
Expanded categories for patient disposition: • Three categories for treated and released • Five categories for patients admitted to the hospital	Limited categories for patient disposition: • One category for treated and released • One category for patients admitted to the hospital
Form and source of drug are not collected	Form and source of drug
Six categories for route of administration	Seven categories for route of administration

Table 1. Comparison of major features, new DAWN versus old DAWN. (Source: Drug Abguse Warning Network, Office of Applied Studies, Substance Abuse and Mental Health Services Administration, U.S. Department of Health and Human Services, 2004.) ILLUSTRATION BY GGS INFORMATION SERVICES. GALE, CENGAGE LEARNING

New DAWN (began 2003)	Old DAWN (ended 2002)
Other changes	
Case finding by retrospective review of medical charts for all patients treated in the ED	Screening methods with limited chart review
Rigorous reporter training and quality assurance	Limited oversight
Performance feedback to hospitals and reporters	Limited feedback
Sample of hospitals	
Sample of hospitals representing the complete United States	Sample of hospitals representing the coterminous United States (48 States)
Eligible hospitals: Short-term, general, non-Federal hospitals operating 24-hour EDs	Same as new DAWN
Complete National estimates based on: • Oversampling in designated metropolitan areas • "Supplementary sample" representing hospitals outside those areas in all 50 States and the District of Columbia	Estimates for coterminous United States based on: • Oversampling in 21 metropolitan areas • "National panel" sample representing hospitals outside those areas in the 48 States and the District of Columbia
Metropolitan areas represented: • Boundary definitions based on the 2000 census • Expansion to additional areas planned	Metropolitan areas represented: • Boundary definitions based on the 1980 census • Oversampling in 21 areas
ED = emergency department.	

Table 1 (continued). Comparison of major features, new DAWN versus old DAWN. (Source: Drug Abuse Warning Network, Office of Applied Studies, Substance Abuse and Mental Health Services Administration, U.S. Department of Health and Human Services, 2004.) ILLUSTRATION BY GGS INFORMATION SERVICES. GALE, CENGAGE LEARNING

pharmaceutical firms receive access to the raw DAWN case data, in de-identified form, as the DAWN cases are submitted. This surveillance of sentinel events is possible through a secure, Internet-based query system called DAWN *Live!*

To collect the data, each hospital emergency department that participates in DAWN has one or more reporters who review emergency department medical records retrospectively to find DAWN cases. Cases reported to DAWN include emergency department visits caused by or related to drug use for patients of any age. (From 1972 to 2002 DAWN used case criteria that depended on the patient's intent to abuse a drug. Upon evaluation, the case criteria and case finding methods were revamped with the redesign.) The drug use must be recent; chronic effects and history of drug abuse are not reportable. Visits related to drugs used for therapeutic purposes, as well as drug misuse and abuse, are all included.

For each reportable visit the demographic, visit, and drug characteristics are abstracted from the medical record. Each DAWN visit is classified into one of eight case types:

1. Drug-related suicide attempt
2. Seeker of detoxification or substance abuse treatment services
3. Underage alcohol use (with no other drug involved)
4. Adverse reactions to pharmaceuticals taken as prescribed
5. Overmedication when the dose of a prescription or over-the-counter medication or dietary supplement was exceeded
6. Malicious poisonings
7. Accidental ingestions when a drug was used accidentally or unknowingly
8. All others, including explicit drug abuse

This classification and the drugs reported to DAWN are used to derive analytic subgroups (e.g., for visits involving illicit drug use, alcohol use, or nonmedical use of pharmaceuticals) for a variety of purposes and audiences. Other data items characterize drug-related visits in terms of diagnoses or disposition.

DAWN captures very detailed drug information. As many as 16 drugs, plus alcohol, are reported for each DAWN case. Drug-related emergency department visits often include multiple drugs—on average 1.6 drugs per visit. For adults, alcohol is reportable only when present with another reportable drug; for minors, alcohol is always reportable. Drug information is captured at the level of detail present in the medical record. The same drug may be reported to DAWN by brand, generic, chemical, street, or nonspecific name, depending on the completeness and specificity of information in the medical record. Training and automated rules prompt DAWN reporters to use all available documentation in the medical chart to record drugs by their most specific names (e.g., OxyContin, when documented as such, instead of oxycodone), not to record the same drug by different names (e.g., heroin and opiates), and to exclude current medications unrelated to the visit. Estimates are published at the generic level (e.g., acetaminophen-hydrocodone), for specific ingredients (e.g., dextromethorphan), or by drug category (e.g., opiates/opioids, benzodiazepines). Estimates attributed to particular brand or trade names (e.g., Concerta) are generally not published.

Because data for DAWN are extracted from a retrospective review of medical records, no patients or health care providers are interviewed. Health care settings within the hospital but outside of the emergency department, or emergency facilities outside of hospitals, are not covered. Laboratory findings to detect the presence of a drug are not recorded for DAWN cases, although each drug report has an associated indicator for whether the drug was confirmed by toxicology testing. Only the patient's own drug use is considered; a patient's intent to misuse or abuse a drug is not a factor in the DAWN case determination, and source of the drug is not captured because it is so rarely available in medical records. Repeat visits by the same individual cannot be linked together. Visits due to chronic conditions associated with a history of drug abuse are explicitly excluded. While DAWN does not collect direct identifiers, such as patient name, the content of the case data does render the data

individually identifiable, and individually identifiable data are protected by federal law from disclosure without consent.

Drug-related emergency department visits may not accurately reflect the level or type of drug abuse in the population as a whole. Therefore, DAWN should not be interpreted as measuring the prevalence of drug abuse in the population. For example, the availability of health insurance and/or other sources of care may influence whether an individual seeks care in an emergency department. Purity of the drug, experience with a particular drug, or other factors related to the physiological effects of drugs may affect whether a condition gives rise to an emergency department visit.

DAWN also collects data on drug-related deaths reviewed by medical examiners and coroners (ME/Cs) in selected metropolitan areas and selected states. The death investigation jurisdictions that participate in DAWN do not constitute a statistical sample nor is every jurisdiction within a metropolitan area necessarily a participant. As a result, extrapolation of drug-related deaths to the nation as a whole is not possible, and metropolitan area totals are only possible if all jurisdictions within the area participate. The number of jurisdictions that participate in DAWN varies from year to year. In 2003, the last year for which mortality data were published, 122 jurisdictions in 35 metropolitan areas and 126 jurisdictions constituting six states participated in DAWN. The case criteria and data collection procedures for drug-related deaths mirror those used in emergency departments. Causes and manner of death are captured in lieu of case type and diagnoses.

See also **Abuse Liability of Drugs: Testing in Humans; Accidents and Injuries from Drugs; Drug Interactions and Alcohol; Epidemiology of Drug Abuse; National Survey on Drug Use and Health (NSDUH); U.S. Government Agencies: National Institute on Drug Abuse (NIDA); U.S. Government Agencies: Substance Abuse and Mental Health Services Administration (SAMHSA).**

BIBLIOGRAPHY

DAWN. (2002). *Publications (1994–2002)*. Available from http://dawninfo.samhsa.gov/.

Substance Abuse and Mental Health Services Administration, Office of Applied Studies. (2002). *Drug Abuse*

Warning Network: Development of a new design (methodology report). DAWN Series M-4, DHHS Publication No. (SMA) 02-3754, Rockville, MD: Author.

Substance Abuse and Mental Health Services Administration, Office of Applied Studies. (2005). *Drug Abuse Warning Network, 2003: Area Profiles of Drug-Related Mortality*. DAWN Series D-27, DHHS Publication No. (SMA) 05-4023. Rockville, MD: Author.

Substance Abuse and Mental Health Services Administration. (2006, October 4). Office of Applied Studies (OAS) help desk & mail room. Available from http://www.oas.samhsa.gov/.

Substance Abuse and Mental Health Services Administration, Office of Applied Studies. (2008). *Drug Abuse Warning Network, 2006: National estimates of drug-related emergency department visits*. Rockville, MD: Author.

CLARE MUNDELL
REVISED BY PATRICIA OHLENROTH (2001)
JUDY K. BALL (2009)

DRUG COURTS. Drug courts emerged as a method for responding to America's drug problems at a time when health, treatment, and justice systems were overwhelmed by the drug epidemics of the 1980s. The dramatic increase in the availability of cocaine and, later, crack cocaine, particularly in America's cities, translated into a new challenge for the criminal justice system that was already at its limits. The volume of court cases exploded, pushing the judicial process to its limits and threatening traditional modes of managing the criminal caseload. Worse, the huge wave of arrests of drug offenders beginning in and accelerating during the 1980s found a correctional system of local jails and state prisons in many locations in the nation that was already chronically overcrowded. With little room in prisons for the new arrestees, institutional crowding was exacerbated and the processing of criminal cases was slowed, causing backlogs in the courts and a wide range of problems for the justice system as a whole.

In 1989 drug courts began experimentally as an answer to mounting drug-related arrests and to the undeniable fact that incarceration alone did not halt the drug-crime cycle (Sanford & Arrigo, 2005). The first drug court in the United States went into operation in Miami under the supervision of Judge Stanley Goldstein, the nation's first drug court judge. Since the breakthrough efforts of the Miami justice leaders, the growth of drug courts in the United States has been extraordinary. In the Bureau of Justice Assistance [BJA] and National Drug Court Institute's annual report titled *Painting the Current Picture: A National Report Card on Drug Courts and Other Problem Solving Courts*, statistics indicate that in 2007 there were 2,147 problem solving-courts in operation in the United States. Of these, there were 1,174 adult drug courts, 455 juvenile drug courts, 301 family dependency courts, 110 DWI (Driving While Under the Influence) courts, 24 reentry courts (an approach to improving offenders returning to their communities from prison), 72 Tribal courts (a court administered through self-government of an American Indian tribe on a reservation and having federally prescribed jurisdiction over custody and adoption cases involving tribal children, criminal jurisdiction over offenses committed on tribal lands by members of the tribe, and broader civil jurisdiction over claims between tribe members and nonmembers), six campus drug courts, and five Federal District drug courts. Furthermore, in the early twenty-first century, England and Wales have introduced drug courts, community courts, and domestic-violence courts; and other countries such as South Africa, Canada, Scotland, New Zealand, Australia, Ireland, Bermuda, and Jamaica have erected other problem-solving courts.

Drug courts represent the coordinated efforts of justice and treatment professionals to actively intervene and break the cycle of substance abuse, addiction, and crime. As an alternative to less effective interventions, drug courts quickly identify substance-abusing offenders and place them under ongoing judicial monitoring and community supervision coupled with effective, long-term treatment services (Huddleston, Marlow, & Casebolt, 2008). The foundation of the drug court model lies in its underlying values, philosophical outlook, and the central role it assigns to the judge as it incorporates a mix of values with a decided shift toward treatment and restoration of offenders to the community. The mix also includes deterrent and desert values.

The therapeutic activities associated with the treatment-oriented drug court occur in a "theater in the square," the square representing not only the architectural features of the physical courtroom

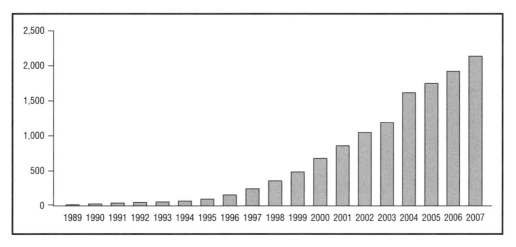

Figure 1. Number of drug courts in the United States, 1989–2007. (Adapted from National Drug Court Institute, January 2008.) ILLUSTRATION BY GGS INFORMATION SERVICES. GALE, CENGAGE LEARNING

but also the boundaries imposed by the criminal process. Led and closely supervised by the judge, the drug court operates in the context of the criminal process and, therefore, differs notably from substance abuse treatment provided to addicted citizens in civilian contexts outside of the justice system. Within those judge-enforced boundaries marking the criminal process, however, the drug court model created a new working relationship between the criminal court and health, treatment, and related services that adapts the criminal process to the needs of treatment and an understanding of addiction. The drug court seeks to resolve the apparently contradictory aims of the typically punitive justice process and the more supportive treatment process.

Prior to the implementation of drug courts, the criminal justice system did not have the capacity to identify offenders with serious drug problems. As a result, the likelihood of offenders being placed in treatment was poor and depended on their being convicted and, usually, sentenced to probation. (Only in rare cases would incarceration include drug treatment.) Before the inception of drug courts, drug treatment has also been available for less serious offenses but has not demonstrated significant impact. From a judicial perspective, however, the court's typical involvement in substance abuse treatment was to order or refer offenders to treatment, if such treatment was recommended by probation staff at the pre-sentence stage. The judge

in such cases would have little other involvement in the treatment process, except to set treatment as a condition of probation, and, later, to hear allegations of noncompliance at revocation hearings. By keeping a judicial distance from the treatment process, judges deferred to the expertise and practices of treatment providers and probation agencies whose responsibilities were to manage and monitor the treatment process.

Drug courts were established to reinvent a helping justice role, similar to the one formerly played by probation services, but this time entrusted to the authority of the criminal court judge and occurring at an earlier stage. The justice and treatment systems working together in drug courts can achieve the goal of providing an intensive regimen of substance abuse treatment, case management, drug testing, and probation supervision along with regularly scheduled status hearings before a judge with specialized expertise in the drug court model (Huddleston, Marlow & Casebolt, 2008; Fox & Huddleston, 2003). In addition to these general elements of the treatment-oriented philosophy, the central judicial role, and new criminal court-treatment relationship, drug courts are characterized by other distinguishing elements. The Drug Court Program Office of the U.S. Department of Justice sponsored an initiative by the National Association of Drug Court Professionals (NADCP) to identify key components of drug courts. The ten components identified by NADCP and adopted as a standard by the Justice Department in reviewing grant applications include integration of treatment and case processing; use of a non-adversarial approach that also respects due process and public safety; early identification and enrollment of participants; provision of a continuum of treatment services; provision of drug testing; inclusion of court responses to performance in treatment; hands-on judicial supervision of treatment; monitoring and evaluation; continuing interdisciplinary education; and, forging partnerships between the court and other criminal justice, health, social service agencies, and the community.

Prior to the NADCP identification of key components of drug courts for constructing standards, a working typology of drug courts identified eight critical dimensions of the drug court innovation mainly for the purposes of evaluation. These include addressing the target problems drug courts were designed to handle; targeting specific criminal justice populations to enroll in treatment; employing mechanisms to identify and evaluate court treatment candidates; modifying the traditional court process, structure, and content of the treatment delivered to substance abusing offenders; altering the methods employed in the drug courts to encourage positive and discourage negative behavior by participants (including the use of sanctions and incentives); measuring the productivity of the courts (in terms of outcomes such as reduced substance abuse and criminal behavior); and assessing the extent of system-wide support in and outside criminal justice and health systems.

ADULT DRUG AND DWI COURTS

Drug court evaluations boast some impressive outcomes (Sanford & Arrigo, 2005). Research verifies that no other justice intervention can rival the results produced by drug courts. According to more than a decade of research, drug courts significantly improve substance abuse treatment outcomes, substantially reduce crime, and produce greater cost benefits than any other justice strategy. As such, scientists from the Treatment Research Institute at the University of Pennsylvania reported in 2003, drug courts outperformed virtually all other strategies used with drug-involved offenders (Huddleston, Marlow & Casebolt, 2008; NADCP, 2008). In February 2005 the U.S. Government Accountability Office (GAO, 2005)

Drug courts combine the goals of justice and treatment in a pragmatic effort to curtail substance abuse, dependence and crime. AP IMAGES

issued its third comprehensive report on the effects of adult criminal drug courts. At the time results of 23 program evaluations confirmed that drug courts significantly reduced crime. In addition, although up-front costs were somewhat higher for drug courts than for standard probation, drug courts were determined to be more cost-effective because they avoided expenditures related to law enforcement efforts, judicial case-processing, and victimization resulting from future criminal activity. In the ensuing years researchers continued to uncover definitive evidence for the efficacy and cost-effectiveness of drug courts (NADCP, 2008). In 2005 Sanford & Arrigo reported the findings from a two-year follow-up that indicated the re-arrest rate for graduates was 19 percent compared to 53 percent for non-graduates. In another evaluation, findings indicated that 20 percent of the graduating participants recidivated, or relapsed, within 12 months, compared to 51 percent for non-participants. Drug-related arrest rates decreased, with drug court graduates being arrested significantly less (13%) than non-drug court participants (30%) within the same period.

The most rigorous and conservative measurement of the effect of any program is derived from what scientists call *meta-analysis*. This involves statistically averaging the effects of a program over dozens of research studies. Five independent meta-analyses concluded that adult drug courts significantly reduce crime by an average of 8 to 26 percent. Importantly, because these figures reflect *average* effects, they also include drug court programs that were new or were not well implemented. Well-administered drug courts reduced crime rates by as much as 35 percent (NADCP, 2008).

Numerous drug court and DWI court program evaluations have reported similar findings. In most instances, re-arrest rates for drug court and DWI court participants were approximately 15 percent lower than for comparable individuals on probation or adjudication as usual. In a nationally representative sample of more than 2,000 graduates from 95 different drug courts, the average re-arrest rate was only 16 percent in the first year after leaving the program and 27 percent after the second year (NADCP, 2008; Roman et al., 2003). This compares highly favorably to typical recidivism rates on conventional probation, in which roughly 46 percent of offenders commit a new offense, and more than 60 percent commit a probation violation one year after completing probation supervision (Langan & Cunniff, 1992). A recent study of nine drug courts in California found that re-arrest rates over a four-year period were 29 percent for drug court participants (and only 17% for drug court graduates) as compared to 41 percent for similar drug offenders who did not participate in drug court (NADCP 2008, Carey et al., 2006). Another study of four adult drug courts in Suffolk County, MA, found that drug court participants were 13 percent less likely to be re-arrested, 34 percent less likely to be re-convicted, and 24 percent less likely to be re-incarcerated than probationers who had been carefully matched to the drug court participants using sophisticated *propensity score* analyses (NADCP 2008; Rhodes et al., 2006). A 2007 three-county evaluation of courts in Michigan found that DWI court participants were substantially less likely than comparable DWI offenders sentenced to probation to be arrested for a new DWI offense or any new criminal offense within two years of entering the programs. Participants in the DWI courts also averaged fewer re-offenses and remained arrest-free for significantly longer periods of time after leaving the programs (NADCP, 2008; Michigan State Court Administrative Office & NPC Research, 2007).

JUVENILE DRUG COURTS

The total number of criminal offenses for both juveniles and adults decreased between 1994 and 2003, but drug abuse violations increased by about 22 percent (FBI, 2003). For juveniles, specifically, drug abuse violations increased by almost 19 percent (FBI, 2003). This occurred while incarceration of juvenile drug offenders declined. According to figures from the Office of Juvenile Justice and Delinquency Prevention (OJJDP) *Census of Juveniles in Residential Placement*, detention of juveniles for drug offenses decreased by 12 percent between 1997 and 2003. This decline in incarceration for drug offenses corresponds with the increase in drug courts and an increased focus on treatment and rehabilitation.

In the mid-1990s a number of innovative jurisdictions started drug court dockets in response to juvenile offenders' cycling through courts that were ill-equipped to intervene successfully (Bureau of Justice Assistance, 2003). Because the drug court model was consistent with the original intent of juvenile courts to rehabilitate offenders and strengthen families, the drug court model was adopted without hesitation.

Juvenile drug courts were designed using the core principles of the adult drug courts, which are to assess, to refer for treatment, to monitor closely treatment progress using judicial oversight, and to shape behaviors by responding swiftly and appropriately. The goals of the juvenile drug court were to: (a) provide immediate intervention, treatment, and structure in the lives of juveniles through ongoing, active oversight and monitoring by the drug court judge; (b) improve juveniles' level of functioning in their environment, address problems that may be contributing to their use of drugs, and develop/strengthen their ability to lead crime- and drug-free lives; (c) provide juveniles with skills to aid them in leading productive substance-free and crime-free lives—including skills that relate to their educational development, sense of self-worth, and capacity to develop positive attitudes; (d) strengthen families of drug-involved youth by improving their capability to provide structure and guidance to their children; and (e) promote accountability of both juvenile offenders and those who provide services to them (Bureau of Justice Assistance, 2003).

Since the early twenty-first century, the field has learned that drug court programs for youth must incorporate individually tailored and developmentally appropriate, comprehensive treatments that

Due process	Drug court
1. Event oriented, i.e., did a certain crime happen as alleged: Historically, this is the jurisprudential link between the criminal courts and the community.	1. Process oriented, i.e., does the offender have a drug/alcohol addiction and can treatment benefit the offender? This type of process is considered in far more limited types of criminal charges.
2. Offense-specific	2. Behavior-specific
3. The determination of guilt and imposition of sentence is essentially the end of the criminal law process.	3. The determination of addiction and referral to drug court is essentially the beginning of the process.
4. The process is identical for all equally accused persons. Quite often, punishment is mandated to be identical as well. The offender's family is rarely considered in this process.	4. The offender is central to the process and quite often the treatment is individualized. The offender's family is viewed as an ingredient in the overall treatment decisions.
5. Judicial interaction exists only with the representatives of the parties.	5. Judicial interaction exists directly with the offender.
6. Responsibility equals atonement and punishment. The relationship of the offender to the community is one where, as a result of adjudication of guilt, the offender is removed from or placed in a condition that protects or shields the community from the offender.	6. Responsibility equals behavioral changes leading to restoration of mental and spiritual health. The offender is viewed as a part of the community. As the offender will generally be treated while an outpatient in the community, behavioral change is designed to reduce conflict by reducing addictive behavior.
7. When there is post adjudication monitoring, it is generally designed to uncover violations and therefore done primarily for enforcement of probation terms.	7. There is always extensive post adjudication monitoring. It is always designed to reinforce treatment.
8. The judge is neutral agent among various competitors.	8. The judge is an active participant in a partnership between the offender, the treatment providers, and the court.
9. The legal history supporting this system is approximately 400–years old; change is difficult.	9. The legal history that supports this system is 10–years old; change is relatively easy.

Table 1. Comparison between drug court models and standard criminal law due process courts. (Source: Bureau of Justice Assistance, U.S. Department of Justice.) ILLUSTRATION BY GGS INFORMATION SERVICES. GALE, CENGAGE LEARNING

draw on strengths while simultaneously addressing the needs of participants and their families (Bureau of Justice Assistance, 2003). To formalize the program components and standardize measures of success of these courts across the nation, in 2003 the U.S. Department of Justice, Bureau of Justice Assistance [BJA] established 16 strategies for jurisdictions to use as a guide when planning and implementing their juvenile drug courts. They are (a) collaborative planning; (b) teamwork; (c) clearly defined target population and eligibility criteria; (d) judicial involvement and supervision; (e) monitoring and evaluation; (f) community partnerships; (g) comprehensive treatment planning; (h) developmentally appropriate services; (i) gender-appropriate services; (j) cultural competence; (k) focus on strengths; (l) family engagement; (m) educational linkages; (n) drug testing; (o) goal-oriented incentives and sanctions; and (p) confidentiality.

Although there are common elements shared by most drug courts, proliferation of the drug court model is not explained by the wholesale adoption of a fixed, cookie-cutter approach in the many jurisdictions across the nation. Therefore, to sustain continued outcome success, existing and new partners to the drug court and other problem-solving court efforts must maintain a clear vision of what they want to achieve by establishing defined goals that are tailored to unique jurisdictional characteristics.

See also **Adolescents and Drug Use; Crime and Drugs; Criminal Justice System, Treatment in the; Prevention, Education and; Treatment, Specialty Approaches to: Adolescents.**

BIBLIOGRAPHY

Bureau of Justice Assistance (2003). *Juvenile drug courts: Strategies in practice.* Washington, DC: U.S. Department of Justice, Office of Justice Programs.

Carey, S. M., Finigan, M., Crumpton, D., & Waller, M. (2006). California drug courts: Outcomes, costs, and promising practices: An overview of phase II in a statewide study. *Journal of Psychoactive Drugs, SARC Supplement 3,* 345–356.

Federal Bureau of Investigation. (2003). *Crime in the United States*. Washington, DC.: U.S. Government Printing Office.

Fox, C., & Huddleston, W. (2003). Drug courts in the U.S. *Issues of Democracy: The changing face of U.S. courts, 8*(1), 13–19.

Goldkamp, J. S. (1994). *Justice and treatment innovation: The drug court movement: A working paper of the first National Drug Court Conference*. Philadelphia: Crime and Justice Research Institute.

Goldkamp, J. S. (1999a). The origins of the treatment drug court in Miami. In C. Terry III (Ed.), *The early drug courts: Case studies in judicial innovation*. Beverly Hills: Sage Publications.

Goldkamp, J. S. (1999b). Challenges for research and innovation: When is a drug court not a drug court? In C. Terry III (Ed.), *Judicial change and drug treatment courts: Case studies in innovation*. Newbury Park: Sage Publications.

Goldkamp, J. S. (2000). The drug court response: Issues and implications for justice change. *Albany Law Review, 63*, 923–961.

Goldkamp, J. S., White, M. D., & Robinson, J. (2000). Retrospective evaluation of two pioneering drug courts: Phase I findings from Clark County, Nevada, and Multnomah County, Oregon. *An interim report of the national evaluation of drug courts*. Philadelphia: Crime and Justice Research Institute.

Hora, P. F., Schma, W. G., & Rosenthal, J. T. A. (1999). Therapeutic jurisprudence and the drug court movement: Revolutionizing the criminal justice system's response to drug abuse and crime in America. *Notre Dame Law Review, 74*, 439–537.

Huddleston, C. W., III, Marlowe, D. B., & Casebolt, R. (2008). *Painting the current picture: A national report card on drug courts and other problem-solving court programs in the United States*. (Vol. II, No. 1). Washington, DC: Bureau of Justice Assistance Office of Justice Programs. U.S. Department of Justice.

Langan, P. A., & Cunniff, M. A. (1992). *Recidivism of felons on probation*. Washington DC: Bureau of Justice Statistics.

MacCoun, R., Kilmer, B., & Reuter, P. (July 2003). Research on drugs-crime linkages: The next generation. In *NIJ special report: Toward a drugs and crime research agenda for the 21st century*. (pp. 65–96). Washington, DC: U.S. Department of Justice. Available from http://www.ncjrs.gov/.

Marlowe, Doug B. (2008) *Recent studies of drug courts and DWI courts: Crime reduction and cost savings*. National Association of Drug Court Professionals. Available from http://www.isc.idaho.gov/.

Michigan State Court Administrative Office, & NPC Research. (2007, October). *Michigan DUI courts outcome evaluation: Final report*. Lansing, MI: Authors. Available from http://www.npcresearch.com/.

National Association of Drug Court Professionals. (1997). *Defining drug courts: The key components*. Washington, DC: U.S. Department of Justice, Office of Justice Programs, Drug Courts Program Office.

Rhodes, W., Kling, R., & Shively, M. (2006). *Suffolk County Court Evaluation*. Cambridge, MA: Abt Associates.

Roman, J., Townsend, W., & Bhati, A. S. (2003). *Recidivism rates for drug court graduates: Nationally based estimate—Final report*. Washington, DC: The Urban Institute and Caliber.

Sanford, J. S., & Arrigo, B. A. (2005). Lifting the cover on drug courts: Evaluation findings and policy concerns. *International Journal of Offender Therapy and Comparative Criminology, 49*(3), 239–259. Available from http://ijo.sagepub.com/.

U.S. Government Accountability Office. (2005). Adult drug courts: Evidence indicates recidivism reductions and mixed results for other outcomes. (No. GAO-05-219). Washington, DC: Author.

JOHN S. GOLDKAMP
REVISED BY JAYME A. DELANO (2009)

DRUG INTERACTION AND THE BRAIN.

When two or more drugs are taken at the same time complex interactions may occur. Drugs can interact to change biological functions within the body through pharmacokinetic or pharmacodynamic mechanisms or through their combined toxic effects. Changes in the pharmacokinetic properties of a drug can include changes in absorption, distribution, metabolism, and excretion of the drug, and each of these can affect blood and plasma concentrations and, ultimately, brain levels of the drug. Although a change in the speed at which a drug reaches the bloodstream is rarely clinically relevant, a change in the amount of drug absorbed can be important, because this can lead to changes in the plasma levels of the drug, which can influence the amount of drug that reaches the brain.

The distribution of a drug throughout the body can be affected by changes in the binding of the drug to proteins in the bloodstream or by displacing the drug from tissue binding sites, both of which can affect the plasma concentration of the drug and potentially affect the amount of drug that reaches the brain. Drug metabolism can be either stimulated or inhibited, resulting in decreased or increased plasma concentrations of the drug, respectively. The stimulation (induction) of drug-metabolizing enzymes in the liver can be produced by drugs such as the barbiturates, but a week or more is often required before maximal effects on drug metabolism are observed. As drug metabolism increases, the amount of drug available to enter the brain decreases.

The inhibition of drug metabolism often occurs much more rapidly than the stimulation, usually as soon as a sufficient concentration of the metabolic inhibitor is achieved, which results in increased plasma and brain concentrations of the drug. The renal (kidney) excretion of drugs that are weak acids or weak bases can be influenced by drugs that alter urinary pH to change the reabsorption of the drug from urine into the kidney. The active secretion of the drug into the urine can also be affected. Both processes can ultimately affect the plasma and subsequent brain concentrations of the drug. Pharmacodynamic mechanisms can either enhance or reduce the response of a given drug. For example, if two drugs are agonists for the same receptor site—diazepam (Valium) and chlordiazepoxide (Librium) for benzodiazepine receptor-binding sites—then an additive biological response is likely to occur unless a maximum response is already present. If, however, an agonist competes with an antagonist for the same binding site (e.g., see morphine and naloxone in opioids, discussed below), then a decreased biological response is likely.

Enhanced or diminished biological responses can be observed even if the drugs do not interact with the same receptor-binding sites. In this case, the net effect is the sum of the pharmacological properties of the drugs. For example, if two drugs share a similar biological response (e.g., central nervous system depression) even though they produce their effects at different sites, then the concurrent ingestion of both drugs can result in an enhanced depression of the central nervous system (see the alcohol [ethanol] and Valium discussion below). Finally, the concurrent ingestion of two or more drugs, each with toxic effects on the same organ system, can increase the chance for extensive organ damage.

DEPRESSANTS

Alcohol (Ethanol) and Valium. Reactions that are additive (combined) or synergistic (cooperative effects greater than the sum of the independent effects of the drugs taken alone) are common side effects that result from the consumption of two or more drugs with similar pharmacological properties. For example, although alcohol (ethanol) is considered by many to be a stimulant drug because, typically, it releases an individual's latent behavioral inhibitions (i.e., it produces disinhibition), alcohol actually produces a powerful depression of the central nervous system similar to that seen with general anesthetics. The subsequent impairment of muscular coordination and judgment associated with alcohol intoxication can be enhanced by the concurrent administration of other central nervous system depressants. Often, Valium or Librium (benzodiazepines that are considered relatively safe drugs) may be purposely ingested along with ethanol in an attempt to "feel drunk" faster or more easily. Since ethanol actually increases the absorption of benzodiazepines, and also enhances the depression of the central nervous system, the potential toxic side effects of the two drugs are augmented. Ethanol is often a common contributor to benzodiazepine-induced coma as well as to benzodiazepine-related deaths, demonstrating that interactions of these drugs with alcohol can be especially serious. Furthermore, the combination of alcohol with the sedative-hypnotic barbiturates (e.g., pentobarbital, secobarbital) can also produce a severe depression of the central nervous system, with decreased respiration. The intentional ingestion of ethanol and secobarbital (or Valium) is a relatively common means of suicide.

Alcohol (Ethanol) and Opioids. Alcohol can also enhance the respiratory depression, sedation, and hypotensive effects of morphine and related opioid drugs. Therefore, the concurrent ingestion of the legal and socially acceptable drug ethanol with other sedatives, hypnotics, anticonvulsants, antidepressants, antianxiety drugs, or with an analgesic agent (such as morphine) can result in serious and potentially fatal drug interactions through a potentiation of the depressant effects of these drugs on the central nervous system. Since the 1960s, a significant number of musicians, actors, and other high-profile personalities have either accidentally or intentionally overdosed from a combination of alcohol and other central nervous system depressants. A few notable examples include actress Marilyn Monroe, musicians Jimi Hendrix, Janis Joplin, Jim Morrison, Keith Moon, and John Bonham.

STIMULANTS

Stimulants and Toxic Effects. Synergistic toxic effects are also often obscured with other classes of drugs. For example, the concurrent ingestion of central nervous system stimulants (e.g., amphetamine, cocaine, caffeine) can also produce additive side effects, especially with respect to toxic reactions involving the heart and cardiovascular system. These toxic reactions are often manifested as an irregular heartbeat, stroke, heart attack, or even death. Drugs with apparently different mechanisms of action can result in dangerous and unexpected synergistic side effects with fatal consequences. For example, some amphetamine and cocaine users often attempt to self-medicate their feelings of "overamp," or the excessive stimulant high resulting from prolonged central nervous system stimulation, through the concurrent administration of central nervous system depressants such as alcohol, barbiturates, or heroin (i.e., a "speedball"). The rationale behind this potentially dangerous practice is that a few beers, a Quaalude, or perhaps a shot of heroin will help the individual "mellow out" for a while before inducing a stimulant high again. High doses of cocaine or amphetamine can, however, result in respiratory depression from actions on the medullary respiratory center. Therefore, the concurrent ingestion of a central nervous system stimulant (e.g., cocaine) with a depressant (e.g., heroin) can result in increased toxicity or death from the enhanced respiratory depression produced by the combination of the two drugs. The most well-known casualty from this type of pharmacological practice was comedian John Belushi.

CLINICAL USES

The principles of drug interactions can be used clinically for the treatment of acute intoxication and for withdrawal—by transforming, reducing, or blocking the pharmacological properties and/or the toxic effects of drugs used and abused for nonmedical purposes. Although these interactions often involve a competition with the abused drug for similar central nervous system receptor sites, other mechanisms are also clinically relevant.

Disulfiram and Alcohol (Ethanol). One such nonreceptor-mediated interaction involves disulfiram (Antabuse) and ethanol (alcohol). Since an ethanol-receptor site has not yet been conclusively identified, specific receptor agonists and antagonists are not yet available for the treatment of ethanol intoxication, withdrawal, and abstinence (as they are for opioids). Disulfiram is sometimes used in the treatment of chronic alcoholism, although the drug does not cure alcoholism; rather, it interacts with ethanol in such a way that it helps to strengthen an individual's desire to stop drinking. Although disulfiram by itself is relatively nontoxic, it significantly alters the intermediate metabolism of ethanol, resulting in a five- to tenfold increase in plasma acetaldehyde concentrations. This acetaldehyde syndrome results in vasodilatation (dilation of blood vessels), headache, difficulty breathing, nausea, vomiting, sweating, faintness, weakness, and vertigo. All of these reactions are obviously unpleasant, especially at the same time, thus well worth avoiding. The acetaldehyde syndrome therefore helps to persuade alcoholics to remain abstinent, since they realize that they cannot drink ethanol for at least three or four days after taking disulfiram. The consumption of even small or moderate amounts of ethanol following disulfiram pretreatment can result in extremely unpleasant drug interactions through the acetaldehyde syndrome.

Opioids. Drug interactions involving opioids (morphine-like drugs) and opioid receptors are classic examples of how knowledge of the molecular mechanisms of the actions of a class of drugs can assist in the treatment of acute intoxication, withdrawal, and/or abstinence. Naloxone, the opioid-receptor antagonist, can be used as a diagnostic aid in emergency rooms. In the case of a comatose patient with unknown medical history, the intravenous administration of naloxone can provide information on whether or not the coma is the result of an opioid overdose. The antagonist competes with the agonist (usually heroin or morphine) for the opioid-receptor sites, displacing the agonist from the binding sites to reverse the symptoms of an overdose effectively and rapidly. Continued naloxone therapy and supportive treatment are often still necessary.

If, however, naloxone is administered to an individual dependent on opioids but not in a coma, a severe withdrawal syndrome develops within a few minutes and peaks after about thirty minutes. Depending on the individual, such precipitated withdrawal can be more severe than that following the abrupt withdrawal of the opioid-receptor agonist (e.g., heroin). In the former instance, the binding of the agonist to opioid receptors is suddenly inhibited by the presence of the antagonist (e.g., naloxone); even relatively large doses of the agonist (e.g., heroin) cannot effectively overcome the binding of the antagonist. Quite the contrary, respiratory depression can develop if higher doses of the agonist are administered. Therefore, opioid-receptor antagonists are not recommended for the pharmacological treatment of opioid withdrawal. Rather, longer acting, less potent, opioid receptor-agonists, such as methadone, are more commonly prescribed.

Methadone. The symptoms associated with methadone withdrawal are milder, although more protracted, than those observed with morphine or heroin. Therefore, methadone therapy can be gradually discontinued in some heroin-dependent people. If the patient refuses to withdraw from methadone, the person can be maintained on methadone relatively indefinitely. Tolerance develops to some of the pharmacological effects of methadone, including any reinforcing or rewarding effects (e.g., the euphoria or "high"). Therefore, the patient cannot attain the same magnitude of euphoria with continued methadone therapy, although the symptoms associated with opioid withdrawal will be prevented or attenuated. Cross-tolerance also develops to other opioid drugs, so the patient will not feel the same high if heroin is again used on the street.

This type of maintenance program makes those who are heroin dependent more likely to accept other psychiatric or rehabilitative therapy. It also reduces the possibility that methadone patients will continue to seek heroin or morphine outside the clinic. In this way, the principles of drug interactions involving opioid receptors in the central nervous system have helped to stabilize treatment strategies for opioid withdrawal and abstinence.

See also **Accidents and Injuries from Drugs; Complications: Neurological; Drug Abuse Warning Network (DAWN).**

BIBLIOGRAPHY

Cloninger, C. R., Dinwiddie, S. H., & Reich, T. (1989). Epidemiology and genetics of alcoholism. *Annual Review of Psychiatry, 8,* 331–346.

Cregler, L. L. (1989). Adverse consequences of cocaine abuse. *Journal of the National Medical Association, 81,* 27–38.

Griffin, J. P. & D'Arcy, P. F. (1997). *Manual of adverse drug interactions* (5th ed.). Oxford: Elsevier Science.

Hansten, P. D., & Horn, J. R. (2008). *The top 100 drug interactions: A guide to patient management, year 2008.* Freeland, WA: H&H Publications.

Hollinger, M. A. (2003). *Introduction to pharmacology.* Boca Raton, FL: CRC Press.

Karalliedde, L., & Henry, J. (Eds.). (1998). *Handbook of drug interactions.* New York: Oxford University Press.

Korsten, M. A., & Lieber, C. S. (1985). Medical complications of alcoholism. In J. H. Mendelson & N. K. Mello (Eds.), *The diagnosis and treatment of alcoholism.* New York: McGraw-Hill.

Liebowitz, N. R., Kranzler, H. R., & Meyer, R. E. (1990). Pharmacological approaches to alcoholism treatment. *Alcohol Health & Research World, 14,* 144–153.

Middleton, R. K. (2006). Drug interactions. In R. A. Helms (Ed.), *Textbook of therapeutics: Drug and disease management.* Philadelphia, PA: Lippincott Williams & Wilkins.

Mozayani, A., & Raymon, L. P. (Eds.). (2003). *Handbook of drug interactions: A clinical and forensic guide.* Totowa, NJ: Humana Press.

Redmond, D. E., Jr., & Krystal, J. H. (1984). Multiple mechanisms of withdrawal from opioid drugs. *Annual Review of Neuroscience, 7,* 443–478.

Sands, B. F., Knapp, C. M., & Domenic, A. (1993). Medical consequences of alcohol-drug interactions. *Alcohol Health & Research World, 17,* 316–320.

NICK E. GOEDERS
REVISED BY PUBLISHER (2001)

DRUG INTERACTIONS AND ALCOHOL.

The term *alcohol-drug interaction* refers to the possibility that alcohol may alter the intensity of the pharmacological effect of a drug, so that the overall actions of the combination of alcohol plus drug are additive, potentiated, or antagonistic. Such interactions can be divided into two broad categories—pharmacokinetic and pharmacodynamic. Pharmacokinetics are concerned with the extent and rate of absorption of the drugs, their distribution within the body, binding to tissues, biotransformation (metabolism), and excretion. Pharmacokinetic interactions refer to the ability of alcohol to alter the plasma and tissue concentration of the drug and/or the drug metabolites, such that the effective concentration of the drug at its target site of action is significantly decreased or increased. Pharmacodynamics are concerned with the biochemical and physiological effects of drugs and their mechanisms of action. Pharmacodynamic interactions refer to the combined actions of alcohol and the drug at the target site of action, for example, binding to enzyme, receptor, carrier, or macromolecules. Pharmacodynamic interactions may occur with or without a pharmacokinetic component. For many drugs acting on the central nervous system that exhibit cross-tolerance (a similar tolerance level) with alcohol, pharmacodynamic interactions with alcohol are especially important.

Most drugs are metabolized in the liver by an enzyme system usually designated as the cytochrome P450 mixed-function oxidase system, and the liver is the principal site of many alcohol-drug pharmacokinetic interactions. Two major factors—blood flow to the liver and the activity of drug-metabolizing enzymes—strongly influence the overall metabolism of drugs. Biotransformation of drugs that are actively metabolized by liver enzymes mainly depends on the rate of delivery of the drug to the liver. These may be flow-limited drugs, where the liver can transform as much drug as it receives, or capacity-limited drugs, which have a low liver-extraction ratio—their clearance (removal from the blood) primarily depends on the rate of their metabolism by the liver.

There are a number of factors other than the drugs themselves that influence the speed and intensity of alcohol/drug interactions in the human body. These include the patient's sex, weight, age, and race; the presence or absence of food in the stomach; and history of alcohol intake. For example, the levels of alcohol dehydrogenase (ADH), a stomach enzyme that oxidizes alcohol to acetaldehyde, are lower in women than in men; lower in Asians than in Western Caucasians; and lower in alcoholics than in nonalcoholics. Elderly persons are at greater risk of alcohol/drug interactions than younger adults, because they usually take more prescription medications, are more likely

to have a serious illness, and show age-related changes in the absorption and clearance of certain medications. With regard to stomach contents, food generally slows the rate of alcohol absorption. Consequently, medications that increase the rate of gastric emptying, such as erythromycin (Eryc, Ilotycin) or cisapride (Propulsid), enhance the rate of alcohol metabolism.

ALCOHOL-DRUG INTERACTIONS
Alcohol-drug interactions are complex. The consequences of using alcohol and drugs together vary with the dosage of the drug; the amount of alcohol consumed; the mode of administering the drug (oral, intravenous, intramuscular, etc.); and the nature of the drug (anticonvulsant, vasodilator, analgesic, etc.). The alcohol may alter the effects of the drug; the drug may change the effects of alcohol; or both may occur.

Alcohol-drug interactions are most important with drugs that have a steep dose-response curve and a small therapeutic ratio—so that small quantitative changes at the target site of action lead to significant changes in drug action. In alcoholics, changes in susceptibility to drugs are due to changes in their rates of metabolism (pharmacokinetics) and the adaptive and synergistic effects on their organs, such as the central nervous system (pharmacodynamics). The clinical interactions of alcohol and drugs often appear paradoxical: Sensitivity to many drugs, especially sedatives and tranquilizers, is strikingly increased when alcohol is present at the same time; however, alcoholics, when abstinent, are tolerant to many drugs. These acute and chronic actions of alcohol have been attributed, respectively, to additive and adaptive responses in the central nervous system (pharmacodynamic interactions).

It is now recognized that alcohol can also interact with the cytochrome P450 drug-metabolizing system, binding to P450, being oxidized to acetaldehyde by P450, increasing the content of P450, and inducing (causing an increase in the activity of) a unique isozyme of P450. Inhibition of drug oxidation when alcohol is present at the active site of P450 is due to displacement of the drug by alcohol and competition for metabolism; this increases the half-life and circulating concentration of drugs. Induction of P450 by chronic-alcohol treatment can result in the increased metabolism of drugs, as long as alcohol is not present to compete for oxidation. These pharmacokinetic interactions may contribute to either increased sensitivity or the tolerance observed with alcohol-drug interactions.

Alcohol can affect drug pharmacokinetics by altering drug absorption from the alimentary tract. For example, diazepam (Valium) absorption is enhanced by the effects of alcohol on gastric emptying. Alcohol placed in the stomach at concentrations of 1 percent to 10 percent increases the absorption of pentobarbital, phenobarbital, and theophylline, whereas drugs such as disulfiram and caffeine decrease alcohol absorption by decreasing gastric emptying. Cimetidine (Tagamet)—a drug used to treat stomach ulcers—increases blood alcohol concentrations by inhibiting ADH in the stomach and first-pass metabolism of alcohol. Binding of a drug to plasma proteins will change the effective therapeutic level of the drug, because when the drug is linked to the proteins, it is not available to act on the tissue. Alcohol itself and alcohol-induced liver disease cause a decreased synthesis and release of such plasma proteins as albumin. The resulting hypoproteinemia can result in decreased plasma-protein binding of such drugs as quinidine (Quinidex), dapsone (DDS), triamterene (Dyrenium), and fluorescein (Fluorescite). Alcohol may also directly displace drugs from plasma proteins.

The effects of alcohol on blood flow in the liver are controversial, although most recent reports suggest an increase; this could be significant with respect to metabolism of flow-limited drugs. At higher concentrations, alcohol can act as an organic solvent and "fluidize" cellular membranes, which may increase the uptake or diffusion of drugs into the cell.

METABOLISM

Many alcohol-drug interactions occur at the level of actual metabolism. Ethanol (ethyl alcohol—common in wines and liquors) will compete with such other alcohols as methanol (methyl alcohol—called wood alcohol) or ethylene glycol (antifreeze), for oxidation via alcohol dehydrogenase. In fact, treatment against poisoning by methanol or ethylene glycol involves the administration of ethanol—as the competitive inhibitor—or the

addition of inhibitors of alcohol dehydrogenase such as pyrazole or 4-methylpyrazole.

As discussed above, the presence of alcohol will inhibit the oxidation of drugs by cytochrome P450. Alcohol has been shown to inhibit oxidation of such representative drugs as aniline, pentobarbital (Nembutal), benzphetamine (Didrex), benzpyrene, aminopyrine, ethylmorphine, methadone, meprobamate (Equanil, Miltown), phenytoin (Dilantin), propranolol (Inderal), caffeine, tolbutamide (Orinase), warfarin (Coumadin), phenothiazine, benzodiazepine, chlordiazepoxide, amitriptyline (Elavil), chlormethiazole, chlorpromazine (Thorazine), isoniazid (INH), imipramine (Tofranil), dextropropoxyphene, triazolam (Halcion), industrial solvents, and acetaminophen (Tylenol). As this partial list indicates, oxidation of many classes of drugs can be inhibited in the presence of alcohol; these include hypnotics, opioids, psychotropic drugs, anticonvulsants, vasodilators, antidiabetics, anticoagulants, analgesics, and antibacterials. Chronic consumption of alcohol induces the P450 drug-metabolizing system, which could increase oxidation of drugs in sober or abstinent alcoholics. Among the drugs that may be more rapidly metabolized in abstinent alcoholics are ethoxycoumarin, ethylmorphine, aminopyrine, antipyrine, pentobarbital, meprobamate, methadone, theophylline (Bronkodyl, Theo-Dur), tolbutamide, propranolol, rifamycin, warfarin, acetaminophen, phenytoin, deoxycline, and ethanol itself. An important consequence of this ability of chronic ethanol intake to increase drug-clearance rates is that the effective therapeutic level of a drug will be different in an abstaining alcoholic than it is in a nondrinker. This metabolic drug tolerance can persist for several days to weeks after alcohol withdrawal.

PHARMACODYNAMIC IMPLICATIONS

These alcohol-drug pharmacokinetic interactions can have major pharmacodynamic implications. Some examples include the following: The concurrent administration of alcohol plus amitriptyline (Elavil) to healthy volunteers resulted in an increase in the plasma-free concentration of amitriptyline, since the alcohol inhibited drug clearance. Other pharmacodynamic interactions between alcohol and amitriptyline include decreased driving skills (and other psychomotor skills), greater than additive loss of righting reflex, unexpected blackouts, and even death. Laisi et al. (1979) showed that plasma levels of the tranquilizer diazepam (Valium—an antianxiety drug) were increased in the presence of beer and wine, so the combination of alcohol plus diazepam produced impaired tracking skills, increased nystagmus (nodding off), and impaired oculomotor (eye) coordination, as compared to diazepam alone. Therapeutic doses of the tranquilizers diazepam or chlordiazepoxide (Librium) plus alcohol have been consistently shown to produce impairment of many mental and psychomotor skills; EEG (electroencephalogram) abnormalities could still be detected sixteen hours after administration of fluorazepam in the presence of alcohol to volunteers. Alcohol also decreases the rates of elimination of several benzodiazepines in humans. Phenothiazines and alcohol compete for metabolism by P450, resulting in the decreased clearance of chlorpromazine (Thorazine), for example, and enhanced sedative effects, impaired coordination, and a severe potentially fatal respiratory depression. Alcohol inhibits the metabolism of barbiturates, prolonging the time and increasing the concentration of these drugs in the bloodstream, so that central nervous system interactions are intensified. In humans, alcohol doubles the half-life of pentobarbital; this is associated with a 10 to 50 percent lower concentration of barbiturate sufficient to cause death by respiratory depression, as compared to the lethal dose in the absence of alcohol. Striking pharmacokinetic and pharmacodynamic interactions occur between alcohol and the hypnotic drug chloral hydrate—the so-called Mickey Finn or knockout drops. Alcohol inhibition of morphine metabolism increases morphine accumulation, potentiates central nervous system actions, and increases the probability of death.

OTHER CONSEQUENCES

Pharmacokinetic interactions between alcohol and drugs also have important toxicological and carcinogenic consequences. The metabolism of certain drugs produces reactive metabolites; these are much more toxic than the parent compound. The induction of P450, especially the P4502E1 isozyme by alcohol, results in the increased activation of drugs and solvents to toxic reactive intermediates—such as carbon tetrachloride, acetaminophen, benzene, halothane, enflurane, cocaine, and isoniazid. In a similar manner, procarcinogens—such as aflatoxins, nitrosamines, and aniline dyes—are activated to

carcinogenic metabolites after alcohol induction of P4502E1. Since P4202E1 is localized largely in the perivenous zone of the liver cell, the increased activation of these toxins (and alcohol itself) after induction by alcohol may explain the preferential perivenous toxicity of several hepatotoxins, carcinogens, and alcohol itself.

See also **Drug Interaction and the Brain; Drug Metabolism; Psychomotor Effects of Alcohol and Drugs.**

BIBLIOGRAPHY

Beers, M. H., & Berkow, R. (Eds.). (1999). *The Merck manual of diagnosis and therapy* (17th ed.). Whitehouse Station, NJ: Merck Research Laboratories. (2006, 18th ed.)

Deitrich, R. A., & Petersen, D. R. (1981). Interaction of ethanol with other drugs. In B. Tabakoff, P. B. Sutker, and C. L. Randall (Eds.), *Medical and social aspects of alcohol abuse*. New York: Plenum Press.

Downie, G., Mackenzie, J., & Williams, A. (2003). *Pharmacology and medicines management for nurses* (3rd ed.). Philadelphia, PA: Elsevier Health Sciences.

Hardman, J. G., et al. (Eds.). (1996). *Goodman and Gilman's the pharmacological basis of therapeutics* (9th ed.). New York: McGraw-Hill Medical. (2005, 11th ed.)

Kinney, J. (2006). *Loosening the grip: a handbook of alcohol information*. New York: McGraw-Hill.

Laisi, U., et al. (1979). Pharmacokinetic and pharmacodynamic interactions of diazepam with different alcoholic beverages. *European Journal of Clinical Pharmacology, 16*, 263–270.

Leary, A., & MacDonald, T. (2000). *Interactions between alcohol and drugs*. Edinburgh, U.K.: Royal College of Physicians of Edinburgh.

Lieber, C. S. (1982). *Medical disorders of alcoholism: Pathogenesis and treatment*. Philadelphia, PA: W. B. Saunders.

Lieber, C. S. (1990). Interaction of ethanol with drugs, hepatotoxic agents, carcinogens and vitamins. *Alcohol and Alcholism, 25*, 157–176.

Medical Economics Company. (1999). *Physicians' desk reference* (53rd ed.). Montvale, NJ: Author.

Mozayani, A., & Raymon, L. P. (Eds.). (2003). *Handbook of drug interactions: A clinical and forensic guide*. Totowa, NJ: Humana Press.

Rubin, E., & Lieber, C. S. (1971). Alcoholism, alcohol and drugs. *Science, 172*, 1097–1102.

Wilson, B. A., Shannon, M. T., & Stang, C. L. (Eds.). (1995). *Nurse's drug guide* (3rd ed.). Norwalk, CT: Appleton & Lange.

ARTHUR I. CEDERBAUM
REVISED BY REBECCA J. FREY (2001)

DRUG INTERDICTION.

The *interdiction* of illicit drugs into the United States is the effort to seize them, together with the transport and/or persons that carry them on their way from the producing country to the importing country; many of the seizures occur just as the drugs are brought across the border. The principal drugs subject to U.S. interdiction are cocaine, marijuana, methamphetamine, precursor chemicals for synthetic drugs, and bogus prescription drugs. Unlike other modern nations, the United States has made interdiction, at least for cocaine and marijuana, a significant part of its effort to control the supply of drugs, since about 1975. Both U.S. federal agencies and the military have been involved in this effort. Though interdictors have seized large quantities of drugs, as of 2008 there remained numerous questions about the effectiveness of the program as a method of reducing the use of drugs, particularly cocaine.

Seizures by law enforcement officers are intended to make drug smuggling more risky and less profitable. AP IMAGES

TWO GOALS OF INTERDICTION

Interdiction has two general goals. First, it seeks to reduce the consumption of specific drugs within the nation by making it more expensive and risky for smugglers to conduct their business. Drug seizures raise costs by increasing the amount that has to be shipped in order to ensure that a given quantity will reach the market. An effective interdiction program seeks to raise the probability that a courier is arrested, thereby increasing the price smugglers have to pay to those who undertake the task. These higher fees raise smugglers' costs of doing business and thus the price they must charge their customers, the importers. The combined effect produces increased costs that lead to a higher retail price and serve to lower drug consumption.

At one time it was thought that interdiction could impose a physical limit on the quantity of drugs available in the United States. With a fixed supply available in the producing nations, each kilogram seized on its way to the United States would be one less kilogram available for consumption inside the country. However, this has not proven to be the case. In the early 2000s, it was generally believed that production is expandable and that increased seizures can be compensated for with increases in production, although farmers may have to receive higher prices to provide greater production.

The second, more modest, general goal is to increase the difficulty of smuggling itself and to provide suitable punishment. Smugglers, or at least the principals in smuggling organizations, are among the most highly rewarded participants in the illegal drug trade. Programs are promoted that make their lives more difficult and that subject these criminals to the risks of punishment.

TYPES OF ILLEGAL IMPORTED DRUGS

Three illegal drugs have traditionally dominated imports: heroin, cocaine, and marijuana. Heroin is subject to only modest interdiction efforts because it is usually smuggled in conventional commercial cargo, or it is carried on (or within) the person of the smugglers who travel by commercial traffic (in one method of smuggling heroin, couriers swallow heroin-filled latex balloons before boarding commercial airlines). Seizures are made only in the course of routine inspection of cargo and traffic. It is estimated that ten tons of heroin are smuggled into the United States each year, and seizures of more than ten kilograms are rare. The Drug Enforcement Administration (DEA) annual seizure reports reveal that heroin has a fairly stable market. A total of 805 kilograms of heroin were seized in 2006, about the same amount seized in 1995. Cocaine and marijuana have been the primary targets of interdiction; however, an effective program of interdiction against Colombian maritime smuggling led to a sharp rise in the share of the U.S. marijuana market served by domestic producers.

The rise in popularity of methamphetamine (meth) has led federal and state governments to impose restrictions on the sale of precursor chemicals needed to make meth. The federal Combat Meth Act of 2006 and laws enacted by over forty states have placed restrictions on the sale of products containing ephedrine and pseudoephedrine—ingredients essential to the production of methamphetamine. These restrictions contributed to a 29 percent reduction in domestic methamphetamine lab seizures in 2005. However, domestic restrictions have fueled the rise in smuggling methamphetamine and precursor chemicals into the United States. As of 2008, domestic production was in the hands of organizations headquartered in other countries with Mexico being a major source of methamphetamine. The United States has worked with Canada and Mexico to limit the amount of legal methamphetamine precursors coming into those countries, and it succeeded in having the United Nations pass a resolution in 2006 that requests governments to work harder against the diversion of chemicals for illicit manufacture. Regarding law enforcement, the United States monitors the shipment of precursor chemicals from Asia to North America and Central America.

The growth of the Internet has also spawned illicit online pharmacies that traffic in legitimate and bogus prescription drugs. Active drug cases involving the Internet rose 25 percent in 2006 over the previous year. The DEA, Federal Bureau of Investigation (FBI), and Immigration and Customs Enforcement (ICE) have increased investigations and asset seizures involving online sale of pharmaceuticals without a prescription. Between 2004 and 2006 the DEA seized more than $52 million in cash, property, and assets from online traffickers. The Food and Drug Administration (FDA) also investigates illicit online pharmacies.

TECHNIQUES

The techniques of interdiction inevitably mirror those of smugglers. Drugs enter the United States by air, land, and sea, by private vessel and commercial carrier. Interdiction must, if it is to have any substantial effect on the drug trade, act against all the modes of smuggling; otherwise smugglers will rely on the mode that is not subject to interdiction.

Interdiction has three separate elements: monitoring, detection and sorting, and pursuit and apprehension. For example, U.S. Coast Guard ships supported by an extensive radar system patrol the Caribbean, which constitutes the major thoroughfare for smuggling from Latin America. The Coast Guard patrol vessels attempt to see, either directly or through radar, all ships moving along certain routes, which constitutes the monitoring activity. The interdictors must then sort, from all that traffic, the relatively small number that are carrying illegal drugs. Finally, they must pursue the smugglers that have been detected, arrest the personnel, and seize the drugs and the ship itself. The interdiction system is as weak as its weakest component; for example, a system that has good pursuit capacities but is unable to sort smugglers from innocents effectively will waste much of that pursuit capacity in chasing nonsmugglers. Similarly, good detection will lead to few captures without effective monitoring capabilities.

The Coast Guard and the U.S. Customs and Border Protection, both part of the Department of Homeland Security (created in the aftermath of the terrorist attacks of September 11, 2001), share primary responsibility for marine and air interdiction. The Coast Guard patrols more distant routes, with U.S. Customs having a greater role in the U.S. coastal zone. Both agencies also conduct interdiction against private planes, with U.S. Customs having primary responsibility over the Mexican land border, a major trafficking area. The DEA has expanded its air surveillance and as of 2007 had a fleet of over one hundred aircraft. The Border Patrol, also a unit of the U.S. Customs and Border Protection, has primary responsibility for the interdiction of drugs carried in cars or on persons crossing the land border. In the late 1990s, new technology, such as x-ray machines that examine commercial vehicles, was installed at border stations in the Southwest. By 2007 more sophisticated electronic surveillance technology was employed along the southwest border. This effort targeted smuggling of both contraband and people.

Both U.S. Customs and the Border Patrol make many seizures and arrests in the course of routine inspection. For example, Customs may find a shipment of cocaine concealed inside a cargo container being unloaded in the Miami port; the Border Patrol, in the course of pursing illegal immigrants, might find a "mule" (a person) carrying a backpack full of cocaine or heroin. Drugs are shipped in an array of forms; for example, suspended in frozen fruit pulp being imported from Ecuador or in hollowed lumber from Brazil.

MILITARY INVOLVEMENT

For a variety of reasons, there was pressure throughout the 1980s to increase the extent of military involvement in drug interdiction. The drug problem was viewed as a national crisis with an important international element. The military was seen as having unique capabilities, both in its equipment and its training of personnel, to protect the borders.

Historically, the military was ambivalent about engaging in drug interdiction because it viewed this activity as a potential corruption of, and an inappropriate diversion from, its primary mission. With the collapse of its principal strategic enemy, the Soviet Union, the U.S. military became more willing to play a major interdiction role, which was reflected in large increases to the military budgets to handle these new responsibilities. Law in the early 2000s prohibits military personnel from making arrests. Accordingly, military participation has been confined to detection and monitoring rather than pursuit and apprehension. Despite the terrorist attacks of September 11, 2001, and the subsequent wars in Afghanistan and Iraq, military involvement in drug interdiction has continued.

The U.S. Navy provides a number of ships for interdiction patrols in both the Caribbean and the Pacific, combining training with a useful mission. The military runs the integrated radar and communication system that links U.S. Customs, the Coast Guard, the Border Patrol, and other agencies. As of 2008, no significant problems of corruption associated with the military role in drug interdiction had been reported, but relations between the military and the civilian law-enforcement agencies with primary jurisdiction have sometimes been strained, the result largely of differences in organizational cultures.

With the proliferation of U.S. government units involved in interdiction, the need arose for coordinated command. The government has two Joint Inter-Agency Task Forces, one based in Key West, Florida, the other in Alameda, California. These task forces coordinate transit zone activities, including the U.S.-Mexico land border and air and maritime traffic along the borders and sea coasts. The U.S. Interdiction coordinator is the commandant of the U.S. Coast Guard.

EVALUATION TECHNIQUES

Evaluation of the effectiveness of interdiction has been a vexed issue ever since the activity became prominent in the late 1970s. Very large quantities of drugs, particularly of cocaine, have been seized, but the size of such seizures has been cited both as evidence of success and of failure. Some wonder if more cocaine is being seized because interdictors are getting better at their job or because more cocaine is being shipped.

Measuring seizures as a fraction of total shipments (consumption plus seizures) would be helpful, but, unfortunately, consumption is difficult to estimate. Even expressed as a fraction of shipments, seizures are clearly an inadequate measure of the effectiveness of interdiction, since the program imposes two other costs on smugglers—namely, seizure of assets (e.g., boats, planes, real estate, and financial holdings) and the arrest and imprisonment of smuggling agents (e.g., crew members on ships, pilots, and couriers for financial transactions).

Reuter and colleagues (1988) suggest that the most appropriate measure is a price increase in the smuggling sector of drug distribution. Effective interdiction should cause increased smugglers' costs; the increase ought to appear in the difference between the price at which smugglers purchase drugs in the producer country (export price) and the sale price in the importing country (import price). However, the process cannot serve as an operational criterion for any individual component of interdiction, since prices are set in a national market served by all modes and routes of smuggling. Anderberg (1992) concluded that the available data supported only inappropriate and/or inadequate measures of effectiveness, and a more cogent measure requires data that are not available and are not likely to be readily obtained.

One negative consequence of interdiction identified by Reuter and colleagues (1988) has received little attention. By seizing drugs on their way from the source country, interdiction may actually increase export demand for those drugs.

As noted earlier, more stringent interdiction has two effects; it raises prices and thus reduces final demand in the United States, but it also increases the amount that must be shipped to meet a given consumption (because of a higher replacement rate). It appears that, based on reasonable assumptions about the cost structure of the cocaine trade, the second effect has proven greater than the first.

EFFECTIVENESS OF INTERDICTION

Interdiction clearly has had some important consequences for the U.S. drug trade. In contrast to the 1970s, little marijuana in the early 2000s was being imported from Colombia, though that nation remains a low-cost producer. Successful interdiction, particularly against marine traffic from Colombia, imposed such high costs on Columbian imports that both Mexican and U.S. producers came to dominate the U.S. market. Interdiction against Mexican-produced drugs is more difficult and thus the import price of Mexican marijuana is less than that of Colombian.

For cocaine there is much less evidence of success, though interdictors have certainly forced changes in modes of smuggling. In the early 1980s much of the cocaine was brought in by private plane directly from Colombia, but in the early 2000s most of it arrived either by transshipment through Mexico or by commercial cargo. However, though interdictors seize a large share of all shipments, they have not managed as of 2008 to prevent a massive decline in the landed price of the drug. Street prices of cocaine and heroin dropped dramatically between the early 1980s and the early 2000s.

The reasons for this limited success are not hard to identify. Smugglers defray the risks of getting caught by carrying across very large quantities, so that the risks per unit smuggled are low. A pilot who charges $250,000 for the risks (imprisonment, suffering injury or death in the course of landing) involved in bringing across a shipment of 250 kilograms is asking for only one dollar per gram, less than 1 percent of the retail price. Even if interdictors make smuggling much more risky, so that the pilot doubles the demand to $500,000, the higher fee still adds only another 1 percent to the retail price.

Moreover, it is difficult to make smuggling very risky when the United States is determined also to maintain the free flow of commerce and traffic. Hundreds of millions of people enter the country each year; cargo imports also amount to hundreds of millions of tons. Only a few hundred tons of cocaine need to be concealed in that mountain of goods and only a few thousand of those who enter need be in the smuggling business to ensure an adequate and modestly priced supply of cocaine.

Interdiction has accounted for a significant portion of federal government expenditures on drug control. Many critics of the interdiction effort have argued that these resources should be put into drug treatment programs and other programs that could reduce the demand for illegal drugs. Nevertheless, the U.S. government has remained committed to interdiction operations.

See also **Border Management; Dogs in Drug Detection; Foreign Policy and Drugs, United States; International Drug Supply Systems; Operation Intercept; U.S. Government: The Organization of U.S. Drug Policy.**

BIBLIOGRAPHY

Anderberg, M. (1992). *Measures of effectiveness in drug interdiction.* Santa Monica, CA: The Rand Corporation.

Office of National Drug Control Policy. (2007). *National drug control strategy: Annual report.* Washington, DC: U.S. Government Printing Office.

Office of National Drug Control Policy. (2007). *National southwest border counternarcotics strategy: Unclassified summary.* Washington, DC: U.S. Government Printing Office.

Reuter, P., Crawford, G., & Cave, J. (1988). *Sealing the borders: The effects of increased military participation in drug interdiction.* Santa Monica, CA: Rand.

Steffen, G. S., & Candelaria, S. (2002). *Drug interdiction.* Boca Raton, FL: CRC Press.

PETER REUTER
REVISED BY FREDERICK K. GRITTNER (2009)

DRUG LAWS: FINANCIAL ANALYSIS IN ENFORCEMENT.

Using financial investigative techniques to uncover sophisticated forms of crime began decades ago to bring organized crime bosses to justice. They were charged not with bootlegging or extortion, but for reaping financial windfalls from activities that either were not federal offenses at the time or that prosecutors could not prove. Beginning with the federal tax case against Al Capone in 1931, Department of Treasury investigators dealt with both the lack of federal laws proscribing racketeering activity and the difficulties in catching underworld bosses for their offenses. The approach was creative but simple: Internal Revenue Service (IRS) agents gathered evidence to prove that the racketeers spent more income than they reported on their tax returns. The difference between what they reported and what the government alleged they earned established that the IRS targets received substantial amounts of unreported income. In an underworld without pay stubs and annual wage statements, how did the government know what the racketeers earned? To tax investigators, it was straightforward: Show how much the person spent—or at least the portion of income spent that could be substantiated.

As Prohibition gave way to different forms of industrial racketeering, syndicated gambling, and drug trafficking, federal agents grew more frustrated over their inability to prosecute increasingly sophisticated criminals. Investigators turned more and more to financial analysis as a means of prosecution. They reasoned that what worked against Al Capone and his cohorts would probably work against other high-profile racketeers who were too insulated by their underlings to be implicated in syndicate transactions.

Proving that individuals—whether they were Mafia bosses or Colombian drug importers—received more income than they could substantiate was difficult. Typically, no records pointed directly to one large unreported sum of yearly income. Rather, evidence of unreported income was gathered by tracing documented purchases that left a paper trail of deposit slips, bank statements, advices, credit card receipts, and mortgages. Investigators soon learned that financial analyses frequently turned up large amounts of money in the possession of people who recently had approved plans for a lucrative drug deal or some other illegal transaction.

For investigators struggling to tie drug traffickers to crimes that had only been planned, finding the proceeds of those transactions was welcome evidence. Money connected the investigator's target to drug or other illegal transactions that other evidence showed they had planned or approved. Drug traffickers and other racketeers who never touched drugs did touch, or otherwise control, the money exchanged for the drugs. Hundreds of criminals have been sent to prison because financial analyses tied large sums to the defendants and their alleged criminal transactions.

As organized crime began to wane in national prominence in the 1970s, an amalgam of home-grown and foreign-based drug traffickers soon took its place. Often as smart and insulated as Mafia bosses, drug traffickers were surprised to find themselves equally vulnerable to cases built on financial evidence. Passage of a number of federal drug reform laws (in 1970, 1978, 1984, 1986, and 1988) added the remedy of asset forfeiture to the government's arsenal of weapons. In order to show that their targets had acquired assets with tainted funds that rendered them forfeitable, investigators resorted to the same financial investigative techniques that had helped build criminal tax cases against underworld leaders.

By the mid-1990s virtually all federal enforcement agencies provided some type of basic training in financial investigation, and several—such as the Drug Enforcement Administration (DEA), Federal Bureau of Investigation (FBI), and Internal Revenue Service (IRS)—have highly specialized programs at their academies. DEA and FBI expert investigators and financial analysts support major drug-trafficking cases by providing evidence of unexplained income to prove the drug charges and to tie the money to drug activity for the purpose of forfeiture.

The USA Patriot Act, enacted following the September 11, 2001, terrorist attacks, gave additional tools to law enforcement to combat money laundering and tax evasion. One provision requires anyone involved in a trade or business, except financial institutions, to report currency received for goods or services in excess of $10,000 on a federal tax form. This information is shared with both the IRS and the Financial Crimes Enforcement Network in the Treasury Department. In addition, a Bulk Cash Statute was passed that authorizes law enforcement to investigate and prosecute persons who transport or attempt to transport currency or other monetary instruments of more than $10,000 from within the United States to outside of the United States, or from outside the United States to within the United

States and knowingly conceal it with the intent to evade federal reporting requirements.

See also **International Drug Supply Systems; Money Laundering.**

BIBLIOGRAPHY

Lehman, J., & Phelps, S. (2004). *West's encyclopedia of American law* (2nd ed.). Farmington Hills, MI: Gale.

Office of the Inspector General, Audit Division, U.S. Dept. of Justice. (2007, January). *Assets Forfeiture Fund and Seized Asset Deposit Fund annual financial statement fiscal year 2006*. Washington, DC: Author.

U.S. Dept. of Treasury. (2007). *2007 National money laundering strategy*. Washington, DC: Author.

CLIFFORD L. KARCHMER
REVISED BY FREDERICK K. GRITTNER (2009)

DRUG LAWS, PROSECUTION OF.

Drug arrests in the United States involve a wide variety of controlled substances, including marijuana, cocaine, heroin, methamphetamine, phencyclidine (PCP), prescription medications, and others. An individual may be charged with a number of different offenses, including possession, dealing (selling), and conspiracy to sell. After arrest, the prosecutor exercises broad discretion, choosing from this range of offenses in deciding whether to bring a charge and for what activity. In 2005 the Uniform Crime Reports of the Federal Bureau of Investigation (FBI) estimated that there were about 1,846,400 state and local arrests for drug abuse violations in the United States. Four out of five of these arrests were for possession. In 1987 some 7.5 percent of arrests were for drugs; by 2005 drug arrests accounted for 13 percent of all arrests in the United States.

Drug offenses can violate either federal or state laws. Since the majority of arrests are made by local law-enforcement officials, most defendants are charged in state courts. The cases received by federal prosecutors, called U.S. attorneys, from such federal enforcement agencies as the FBI or the Drug Enforcement Administration (DEA), frequently involve more complex matters such as drug trafficking. However, the volume of federal drug prosecutions rose in the 1990s, as tougher federal drug laws and sentencing provisions led state prosecutors to refer these cases to federal jurisdiction. In addition, federal prosecutors have used the Racketeer Influenced and Corrupt Organizations Act (RICO) to prosecute drug traffickers and to confiscate property used in drug enterprises. The federalization of drug crimes has had a profound impact on the work of the federal courts and the budget of the federal prison system.

In determining what charges should be filed against the offender, the prosecutor examines many factors: the criminal history of the defendant, the seriousness of the drug involved, and the quality of the evidence. Most states give the prosecutor the discretion to charge an enhanced-penalty crime for a repeat offender.

The vast majority of the cases lead to guilty pleas, through some form of plea bargaining between the prosecutor and the defense attorney. In these agreements, which must be approved by the court, the defendant pleads guilty, often in return for a fine, court-ordered counseling, or a lessened prison term. Repeat offenders face tougher agreements.

In deciding what plea to accept, prosecutors consider many of the same factors they did when they brought the original charges. A critical factor is the quality of the evidence. Many drug cases are easy to prove because the defendant purchased or sold the drugs directly to a police officer or because a search warrant leads to the discovery of drugs in an area controlled by the defendant. Prosecutors face much more difficult challenges in convicting suspects involved in complicated conspiracy charges such as those associated with the shipment or distribution of drugs. In many drug prosecutions, motions to suppress evidence are filed by defense attorneys to determine whether the search that turned up the drugs violated the Search and Seizure Clause of the Fourth Amendment. During the 1990s and into the first decade of the twenty-first century, a more conservative U.S. Supreme Court has made it much more difficult to suppress drug evidence, whether seized with or without a search warrant.

Another important factor involves the level of cooperation provided by the defendant. The prosecutor often accepts a more lenient agreement for defendants who assist law-enforcement officers and/or testify in court concerning who sold them the drugs they possessed or resold. These plea agreements allow the police to target other offenders and also relieve the pressure on the courts. Plea bargaining does, however, raise serious questions in the public's mind about the dangers of leniency; it raises other questions, among defendants and their attorneys, about equity and fairness. Additionally, narcotics officers and prosecutors often disagree about the outcome or the handling of a case. These differences are often mediated by task forces in which prosecutors with specialized drug experience are assigned to work with a select group of narcotics officers.

Generally less than 10 percent of drug cases go to trial. In a trial the police officer is a witness in the case brought by the prosecutor. By questioning the officer, the prosecutor—as lawyer for the state—elicits evidence designed to show that the defendant possessed or sold drugs.

Ultimately, the judge determines the actual sentence. Beginning in the late 1980s, federal and state sentencing guidelines limited judicial discretion, requiring judges to impose sentences based on the severity of the criminal offense and the criminal history of the defendant. However, in 2005 the Supreme Court struck down the federal sentencing guidelines, ruling them a violation of the Sixth Amendment. Though the guidelines were subsequently viewed only as advisory, in a 2007 case the Supreme Court made clear that the guidelines must be consulted by the federal courts to determine whether a sentence is deemed reasonable. Many criminal statutes avoid the guidelines entirely by imposing mandatory minimum sentences for drug crimes. But commonly in a plea agreement or after trial, the prosecutor can modify the severity of the sentence by reducing the charge or by recommending that the court reduce the sentence. Across the United States, and even within large counties, great differences occur in sentencing and in sanction recommendations.

DRUG COURTS AND FORFEITURE LAWS

Participants in the criminal justice system recognized that drug-related crimes should be addressed in different ways. The emergence of drug courts in the 1990s signaled a new way of prosecuting drug offenders. Drug courts seek to reduce drug use and associated criminal behavior by retaining drug-involved offenders in treatment. Drug courts divert drug offenders from jail or prison by referring them to community treatment. Defendants who complete the program either have their charges dismissed or probation sentences reduced. A 1994 federal law authorized the U.S. attorney general to make grants to state and local governments to establish drug courts. These grants proved effective. By 1999, some 416 drug courts were operating in the United States, with over 270 more in the planning stages. By 2007 the numbers had jumped dramatically: 1,699 drug courts were in operation, with another 349 in the planning stage. These courts shift discretion from the prosecutor and place it with the judge, who has broad discretion in a drug court.

Federal and state prosecutors have also used asset forfeiture laws to attack drug traffickers. Forfeiture laws authorize prosecutors to file civil lawsuits asking a court for permission to take property from a criminal defendant that was either used in the crime or was the fruit of a criminal act. In 2005 over $1.25 billion in assets was seized by federal agencies.

Aside from civil forfeiture, prosecutors have also used tax and money laundering laws to prosecute drug traffickers. The USA Patriot Act, enacted following the September 11, 2001, terrorist attacks, sought in part to combat money laundering and tax evasion. One provision requires anyone involved in a trade or business, except financial institutions, to report currency received for goods or services in excess of $10,000 on a federal tax form (financial institutions have reported similar cash transactions to federal authorities since the 1990s.) Another provision, the Bulk Cash Statute, authorizes law enforcement to investigate and prosecute persons who transport or attempt to transport currency or other monetary instruments of more than $10,000 outside the United States or who bring large amounts of currency into the United States.

Prosecutors sometimes employ non-criminal statutes and ordinances to attack drug crimes. For example, prosecutors may use public nuisance laws, zoning laws, and public health laws to remove drug offenders from property where drugs are being used and sold. Though the legal action is addressed to the landlord or property owner, it has the effect of removing drug users and traffickers from apartments and houses. Increasingly, cities are condemning and destroying buildings that have been used as crack houses and meth labs.

See also **Exclusionary Rule; Mandatory Sentencing; Rockefeller Drug Laws.**

BIBLIOGRAPHY

Gray, M. (2007, August 17). Mandatory sentencing: Stalled reform. *Time.* Available from http://www.time.com/time/nation/.

Lehman, J., & Phelps, S. (Eds.). (2002). *West's encyclopedia of American law* (2nd ed.). Farmington Hills, MI: Gale.

U.S. Department of Justice. (2006). *Assets Forfeiture Fund and Seized Asset Deposit Fund annual financial statement fiscal year 2006.* Washington, DC: U.S. Department of Justice, Office of the Inspector General, Audit Division.

U.S. Department of Treasury. (2007.) *2007 National money laundering strategy.* Washington, DC: Author.

White House Office of National Drug Control Policy. (2006). *Drug courts: The second decade.* Washington, DC: U.S. Government Printing Office.

White House Office of National Drug Control Policy. (2007). *National drug control strategy: 2007 annual report.* Washington, DC: U.S. Government Printing Office.

STEPHEN GOLDSMITH
REVISED BY FREDERICK K. GRITTNER (2009)

DRUG METABOLISM.

Most drugs are taken by mouth and, in order to be absorbed through the stomach and intestine, they need to be lipid-soluble. This solubility permits them to easily cross the membrane barrier. After absorption, organs with plentiful blood-flow such as the brain, liver, lungs, and kidneys are first exposed to the drug. Only highly lipid-soluble drugs can enter the brain by crossing the blood-brain barrier.

Drug concentration at the target organ is an important index for therapy and generally has an optimal range. The drug level can be raised by increasing dose, or by more frequent administration, but too high a level could cause toxicity. The drug level at the target organ can also be lowered by elimination through the urine or by metabolic steps that convert the drug to more water-soluble forms. Water-soluble metabolites are eliminated quickly in the urine. Most drugs given orally are lipid-soluble enough to be reabsorbed in the kidneys and are eliminated only slowly in small amounts in the unchanged form in urine. Therefore drug metabolism is an important factor that controls drug levels in the body, because without the metabolic step the drug usually remains in the body or accumulates if it continues to be taken. Drug metabolism is a biochemical process and involves enzymes; drugs are metabolized sequentially or by parallel pathways to various products called metabolites. Many enzymes have been identified and some are very specific for drugs or substrates, whereas others have broad or less stringent structure requirements.

Many factors can modify drug metabolism. Genetic factors or inherited deficiency of an enzyme could cause accumulation of certain drugs. Increased levels and increased toxicity may be caused by inhibition of drug metabolism by other concurrently administered drugs. Decreased plasma levels of drugs after repeated administration have been observed and this is attributed to increased enzyme activity by a process called induction; auto-induction causes the increased metabolism of the inducing drug and cross-induction refers to the accelerated metabolism of other drugs.

DRUG-METABOLIZING ENZYMES

Drug-metabolizing enzymes change the chemical nature of drugs by inserting oxygen, hydrogen, water, or small molecules such as amino acids and sugar molecules. The resulting metabolites may thus contain hydroxyl (the univalent group or ion OH), or hydrogenated or hydrolysis products, or be conjugated with sugar or other functional groups. By far the most commonly occurring metabolic step is hydroxylation (the addition of oxygen) by the enzyme oxygenase—and this will be discussed in detail.

OXIDATION BY CYTOCHROME P450 MONOOXYGENASE

Oxygen is vital for living organisms, and enzymatic reactions involving this molecule for drug metabolism are numerous and well characterized. Lipid-solubility is an important factor for absorption across the stomach and intestinal wall, and the insertion of an oxygen atom to lipid-soluble compounds results in hydroxylated groups ($-OH$) that are more water-soluble than the parent compound. The pioneering work on the oxygenation reaction involved the metabolism of barbiturates, a class of centrally acting drugs very popular in the 1950s. A long-acting barbiturate, phenobarbital, very slowly hydroxylates compared to other barbiturates, such as hexobarbital, pentobarbital, and secobarbital. The oxygenation enzymes involved were named cytochrome P450 after the wavelength of light they absorbed in a spectrophotometer (peak at 450 nanometers [nm]). Subcellular fractionation by centrifugation yielded "microsome" pellets which contained the cytochrome P450 activity. Cytochrome P450 is most abundant in the liver and, before the full nature of cytochrome P450 was known, the microsomal oxygenase was often called mixed function oxidase. Cytochrome P450 consists of a superfamily of enzymes, with wide and sometimes overlapping substrate specificities.

Although phenobarbital is no longer widely used for therapeutic purposes, because of better alternatives with fewer side effects, it is an excellent inducer of certain forms of cytochrome P450 (e.g., the CYP2B family).

Other important drugs of abuse that are metabolized by cytochrome P450 include benzodiazepines (tranquilizers such as diazepam [Valium], chlordiazepoxide, alprazolam, triazolam) and opioids (codeine, oxycodone, dextromethorphan). The first group of drugs is hydroxylated and the second group is metabolized by loss of a carbon moiety (dealkylation). The dealkylation reactions are also mediated by cytochrome P450.

Many cytochrome P450 enzymes have been isolated and characterized. With molecular biology techniques, the genetic code DNA has been identified for many cytochrome P450 enzymes. Among these, two forms of cytochrome P450 are known to be deficient in certain individuals. In the mid-1970s, a deficiency of the specific cytochrome P450 called CYP2D6 was independently reported for sparteine (a labor-inducing or antiarrhythmic drug) and for debrisoquine (an antihypertensive agent). Since then, more than thirty clinically useful drugs have been shown to be metabolized by this enzyme. The presence of this cytochrome P450 in a population is polymorphic, that is, some people lack this enzyme. A simple urine test using dextromethorphan, a cough suppressant, is commonly used to identify the enzyme deficiency in a patient. Another cytochrome P450 deficiency involves metabolism of mephenytoin (CYP2C type) but not many drugs are metabolized by this enzyme. The frequency of both deficiencies were first established in Caucasians, and CYP2D6 deficiency was reported to be 7 percent while CYP2C deficiency was 3 percent. Because of the presence of deficient subjects, the population data do not show a bell-shaped normal distribution curve but rather a bimodal distribution indicating polymorphism.

ALCOHOL METABOLISM

Alcohol (ethanol) metabolism predominantly involves a type of oxidation called dehydrogenation (loss of hydrogen) and the subcellular fraction called the mitochondria is the major site. Alcohol is metabolized by successive dehydrogenation steps, first producing acetaldehyde and secondly acetic acid. The major organ for alcohol metabolism is the liver. In heavy drinkers, however, alcohol induces another enzyme, cytochrome P450, and the proportion of the metabolism by this route compared to dehydrogenation becomes significant. Because the amount of alcohol ingested must be relatively large to have pharmacological effects, the amount of alcohol exceeds the amount of enzyme, resulting in saturation. Acetaldehyde, in general, is toxic because it is reactive and forms a covalent bond with proteins. When the enzyme that metabolizes acetaldehyde to acetic acid is inhibited by an external agent, acetalaldehyde levels increase and produce a toxic syndrome. Inhibitions of this enzyme, such as disulfiram (Antabuse), have been used in the treatment of excessive drinking.

TRANSFERASES FOR CONJUGATION/ SYNTHETIC REACTIONS

Products formed by oxidation (e.g., by cytochrome P450) are often metabolized further with small molecules such as glucuronic acid (glucose metabolite) or sulphate. The enzymes involved are called transferases. Other conjugation reactions are carried out by transferases linking glutathione with reactive metabolic products, acetyl-CoA with an amino group on aromatic rings, and glycine (amino acid) with salicylate.

Glucuronic-acid conjugations are catalyzed by various forms of glucuronyl transferases, which appear to have broad substrate specificity. Glucuronide conjugates are very water-soluble and likely to be quickly eliminated via the kidneys. The plasma levels of glucuronide conjugates of oxazepam (a benzodiazepine antianxiety agent) are, however, several-fold higher than the parent drug. This can be explained by the relatively rapid process of conjugation reaction in the liver compared to the renal (kidney) clearance of its conjugate. Because glucuronidation involves a glucose metabolite, which is abundant, the transferase would not reach saturation easily, although sulfo-transferase utilizes the sulphate which is of limited supply via foods and can be saturated. For example, acetaminophen (Tylenol) forms both glucuronide and sulfate conjugates and the sulfation process can be easily saturated after a few tablets.

Glutathione conjugation is very important as a detoxification pathway. Unstable or reactive metabolites formed from other metabolic reactions may cause toxicity by reacting with so-called house-keeping enzymes in the body. Glutathione, because of its abundance, can react with these metabolites instead and acts as a scavenger; an epoxide whose formation is catalyzed by cytochrome P450 is detoxified, except in an overdose case, by glutathione transferase. Some epoxide intermediary metabolites have been shown to be ultimate carcinogens, and detoxification by gluthione would be beneficial.

Glycine is the smallest amino acid and the conjugation with salicylic acid (formed rapidly from aspirin) is the major metabolic pathway for salicylates. Salicylate poisoning, especially in children, was very common before the introduction of the child-proof cap for drug containers in the 1960s. The difficulty of treating the salicylate poisoning was due to saturable glycine conjugation; the higher the dose, the slower was the rate of elimination.

Acetylation is also important for the detoxification of carcinogens containing aromatic amines. One form of N-acetyltransferase is polymorphic (people have different forms of the enzyme). The frequency of slow acetylator types shows a large variation ranging from 5 to 10 percent in Oriental and Inuit (Eskimo) subjects to as high as 50 percent in Caucasians and Africans. Drugs affected by this genetic polymorphism are isoniazid (antituberculosis), procainamide (antiarrhythmic), sulfamethazole (antibiotic), and other amine-containing compounds.

CLINICAL CONSEQUENCES

Drug metabolites are often pharmacologically less active than the parent drug. Yet some biotransformation products are active—for example codeine is relatively inactive but is metabolized to the active drug morphine. Because the liver is the major site of drug metabolism, acute or chronic liver diseases would alter drug metabolism, resulting in prolonged drug half-lives and effects.

See also **Complications: Liver (Metabolic); Drug Interaction and the Brain; Drug Interactions and Alcohol.**

BIBLIOGRAPHY

Coleman, M. (2005). *Human drug metabolism: An introduction.* Hoboken, NJ: Wiley.

Ionescu, C., & Caira, M. R. (2006). *Drug metabolism: Current concepts.* New York: Springer.

Jakoby, W. B. (Ed.). (1980). *Enzymatic basis of detoxication.* New York: Academic Press.

Kalow, W. (Ed.). (1992). *Pharmacogenetics of drug metabolism.* New York: Pergamon.

Katsung, B. G. (Ed.). (1992). *Basic and clinical pharmacology* (5th ed.). Norwalk, CT: Appleton & Lange. (2005, 10th ed. New York: McGraw-Hill Medical.)

Uetrecht, J. P., & Trager, W. (2007). *Drug metabolism: Chemical and enzymatic aspects.* London: Informa Healthcare.

TED INABA
REVISED BY MARY CARVLIN (2001)

DRUG POLICY ALLIANCE (DPA).

The Drug Policy Alliance (DPA) is a not-for-profit organization established to advance those policies and attitudes that best reduce the harms of both drug misuse and drug prohibition and to promote the sovereignty of individuals over their minds and bodies. DPA envisions a just society in which the use and regulation of drugs are grounded in science, compassion, health, and human rights; in which people are no longer punished for what they put into their own bodies, but only for crimes committed against others; and in which the fears, prejudices, and punitive prohibitions are no more.

Headquartered in New York, DPA has eight offices, 50 staff, 25,000 dues-paying members, more than 50,000 online subscribers, and a growing track record of success at the local, state, and federal levels. DPA's New York-based Lindesmith Library contains more than 10,000 books, reports, government documents, periodicals, videos, and articles on drugs and drug policy; and its $1.5 million Advocacy Grants Program funds allied organizations and efforts.

BRIEF HISTORY

The Drug Policy Alliance was formed in July 2000 when the Lindesmith Center, an activist drug policy think tank established in 1994, merged with the Drug Policy Foundation, a membership and grant-making organization established in 1987, to create an umbrella organization working for drug policy reform. The Lindesmith Center (TLC) was founded in 1994 by Ethan Nadelmann, JD, PhD, a professor of politics at Princeton University, whose writings on drug policy had attracted international attention. The Lindesmith Center, named after Professor Alfred Lindesmith—an Indiana University professor who was the first prominent scholar in the United States to challenge conventional thinking about drugs, addiction, and drug policy—became the first domestic project of George Soros's Open Society Institute (OSI), an operating and grant-making foundation established in 1993 that promotes democratic institutions in Central and Eastern Europe and the former Soviet Union.

The Drug Policy Foundation (DPF) was founded in 1987 by Arnold S. Trebach, JD, PhD, a professor at American University, and Kevin B. Zeese, an attorney who had directed the National Organization for Reform of Marijuana Laws (NORML) in the early 1980s. They envisioned DPF as "the loyal opposition to the war on drugs" and introduced a number of initiatives that have defined the drug policy reform movement ever since. These included an annual drug policy reform conference (which shifted to a biennial conference in 2001), a regular publication series, and an awards program to recognize achievement in various fields of drug policy reform. DPF was also the first and most significant effort to build a membership organization around drug policy reform.

On July 1, 2000, these two organizations merged to create the Drug Policy Alliance with the objective of becoming a powerful advocacy organization nationally and internationally. DPA has worked in tandem with various 501(c)(4) affiliates, including the Drug Policy Alliance Network, the Center for Policy Reform, the Campaign for New Drug Policies, and Americans for Medical Rights.

DRUG POLICY REFORM MILESTONES

- The Lindesmith Center collaborated in 1995 with the OSI program on public health to create the International Harm Reduction and Development program, which has since advanced harm reduction in Central and Eastern Europe, the former Soviet Union, and Asia.

- DPA affiliates were primarily responsible in California (1996), Alaska (1998), Oregon (1998), Washington (1998), Maine (1999), Colorado (2000), Nevada (1998 and 2000), and New Mexico (2007) for making cannabis legally available to seriously ill patients and reducing criminal penalties for possession, objectives supported by roughly three out of four Americans.

- The Lindesmith Center published in 1997 *Marijuana Myths, Marijuana Facts: A Review of the Scientific Evidence*, by Lynn Zimmer, PhD and John P. Morgan, MD. Fifty-thousand copies have been sold and it is available in seven languages.

- The Safety First Project was launched in 1998 to provide parents, teens, and educators with information about marijuana and other drugs, as well as realistic options for dealing with drug use by promoting reality-based models based on comprehensive sex education. It has worked closely and affiliated with the California Parent-Teacher Association. DPA has distributed worldwide more than 225,000 copies (in nine languages) of *Safety First: A Reality-Based Approach to Teens, Drugs, and Drug Education* (2007) by Dr. Marsha Rosenbaum, who founded the Safety First program. DPA also publishes *Beyond Zero Tolerance: A Reality-Based Approach to Drug Education and School Discipline* (2007) by Dr. Rodney Skager and *Making Sense of Student Drug Testing: Why Educators Are Saying No* (Kern et al., 2004).

- The Lindesmith Center drafted an open letter to United Nations Secretary General Kofi Annan in anticipation of the 1998 U.N.

General Assembly Special Session on the World Drug Problem. The letter was signed by more than 500 prominent political leaders, scholars, academics, and scientists from around the world and appeared in the *New York Times*.

- In 2000 Ethan Nadelmann and the Lindesmith Center worked closely with Arianna Huffington's Shadow Conventions to host two four-day forums in Los Angeles (alongside the Democratic National Convention) and Philadelphia (alongside the Republican National Convention) to highlight bipartisan neglect of key social issues, including the drug war, income inequality, and campaign finance reform.

- DPA supported California's landmark treatment-not-incarceration law, Proposition 36, approved via ballot initiatives by 61 percent of California voters in November 2000. Proposition 36 allows first- and second-time nonviolent drug offenders the opportunity to receive substance abuse treatment instead of jail time. More than 84,000 people were diverted from jail or prison to drug treatment and graduated from the program in the first five years after Proposition 36 became law, saving taxpayers at least $1.5 billion.

- In 2005 DPA New Mexico assembled stakeholders from around the state to form the New Mexico Methamphetamine Working Group, co-chaired by the governor's drug czar and the director of DPA New Mexico. The working group produced the first statewide "four pillars" approach to methamphetamine in the United States that emphasizes the principles of harm reduction. DPA New Mexico subsequently received a $500,000 grant from the U.S. Justice Department to create a statewide methamphetamine education and prevention program.

- DPA New Jersey supported the "Bloodborne Pathogen Harm Reduction Act," which was signed into law in 2006. The law allows up to six cities to establish syringe access programs to help prevent the spread of HIV/AIDS, hepatitis C, and other blood-borne diseases. Previously, DPA played a pivotal role in successful efforts to make syringes legally available in New York (2000) and California (2004) and

supported successful efforts in Connecticut, Illinois, and other states.

- DPA has worked across the country to pass 911 Good Samaritan immunity laws. The first of these was enacted in New Mexico, where DPA wrote and led the successful campaign in 2007 to eliminate fear when calling 911 for help during an overdose. The law provides limited immunity from drug possession charges when a drug-related overdose victim or a witness to an overdose seeks medical assistance.

- DPA has built broad coalitions to eliminate mandatory minimum sentencing (in Alabama, New York, Maryland, and Wisconsin) and racially biased crack/cocaine sentencing at the state (in Connecticut and California) and federal levels.

See also **Legalization vs. Prohibition of Drugs: Policy Analysis.**

BIBLIOGRAPHY

Andreas, P., & Nadelmann, E. A. (2006). *Policing the globe: Criminalization and crime control in international relations*, with Peter Andreas. New York: Oxford University Press.

Drug Policy Alliance. (2008). Available from http://www.drugpolicy.org.

Kern, J., Gunja, F., Cox, A., Rosenbaum, M., Appel, J., & Verma, A. (2004). *Making sense of student drug testing: Why educators are saying no*. New York: Drug Policy Alliance. Available from http://www.aclu.org/.

Nadelmann, E. A. (1993). *Cops across borders: The internationalization of U.S. criminal law enforcement*. University Park: Pennsylvania State University Press.

Rosenbaum, M. (2007). *Safety first: A reality-based approach to teens, drugs, and drug education*. San Francisco: Studio Reflex. Available from http://www.safety1st.org/.

Safety 1st Project. (2008). Available from http://www.safety1st.org.

Skager, R. (2007). *Beyond zero tolerance: A reality-based approach to drug education and school discipline*. San Francisco: Studio Reflex. Available from http://www.safety1st.org/.

Zimmer, L., & Morgan, J. P. (1997). *Marijuana myths, marijuana facts: A review of the scientific evidence*. New York: Lindesmith Center.

ETHAN NADELMANN

DRUG TESTING METHODS AND CLINICAL INTERPRETATIONS OF TEST RESULTS.

As interest increases in employment-related drug testing, the technologies and the interpretive skills of analysts continue to evolve. Although recent literature indicates that significant refinements and modifications to drug testing technology have been made, the complexity of drug effects is so great that many problems exist in interpretation of the test results. The most frequent problems that confront the toxicology laboratory relate to developing technology that can determine how much and when the drug was taken, how long after use the tests are capable of showing positive results, the causes and rates of false positive and false negatives, and how tests can be "beaten" by employees. These problems will be discussed and the various laboratory procedures that are used to combat these problems will be examined.

DRUG PROPERTIES: ABSORPTION, DISTRIBUTION, AND ELIMINATION PHASES

Detection of a drug depends largely on its absorption, distribution, and elimination properties. There are various routes of drug administration; oral (e.g., drinking alcohol or swallowing pills), intravenous (e.g., heroin injected into a vein) and inhalation (e.g., smoking marijuana; snorting cocaine; sniffing glue). Drugs taken orally are usually the slowest to be absorbed (i.e. the speed at which the drug reaches the brain and other body organs) whereas intravenous and inhalation routes result in the fastest absorption. Once the absorbed drug enters the blood stream it is rapidly distributed to the various tissues in the body. The amount of drug stored depends on the nature of the drug, the quantity, duration of ingestion, the tissue holding the drug and the frequency of use.

Some drugs are fat-soluble and are deposited in fat tissues. For example, δ^9-tetrahydrocannabinol (THC), the active ingredient in marijuana, is highly fat-soluble, resulting in rapid reductions in blood levels as the drug is being distributed to the various tissues. Blood levels of δ^9-THC peak and start to decline in half the time it takes to smoke a marijuana "joint." Concentrations are known to fall by almost 90 per cent in the first hour. Depending on the amount of drug stored in the fat tissues, detection may be possible in the urine for many days after last use. There are cases where marijuana metabolites have been detected for as long as sixty days after last use, since small amounts from fat go back into blood and appear in the urine. Ethanol or ethyl alcohol (the beverage alcohol) is not fat-soluble but is distributed in the total body water. Since blood is mostly made up of water, the presence of alcohol is easier to detect than fat-soluble drugs like δ^9- THC.

The "absorption" and "distribution" phases are followed by an "elimination" phase. The liver is the major detoxification center in the body where the drugs are metabolized as blood circulates through this organ. The metabolites are then excreted into the urine through the kidneys. At the same time, drugs deposited in fat tissues are also slowly released into the blood stream and metabolized.

Drugs vary by their elimination half-life. An elimination half-life is the amount of time needed for the drug level to fall by 50 percent. Every half-life the drug level falls by 50 percent. Table 1 shows the impact of the half-life on the amount of drug left in the body. At the end of seven half-lives over 99 percent of the drug will be eliminated from the body. (See Table 2 for drug half-lives). The half-life of a drug is heavily influenced by a variety of factors including the individual's age, sex, physical condition as well as clinical status. A compromised liver and concurrent presence of another disease or drug have the potential of enhancing the toxic effects of the drug by slowing down the elimination process. Under different clinical conditions, however, this process may be speeded up. Therefore, great variation can be found in the half-lives of the same drug.

Approximately seven half-lives are required to eliminate 99 per cent of any drug. Because cocaine's half-life is relatively short, averaging one hour, only six hours are needed for elimination of 99 per cent of the drug. On the other hand, cocaine's metabolites have a longer half-life and can be detected for a considerably longer period of time through urine drug assays. Compared to cocaine, phenobarbital has a much longer half-life of 80–120 hours, so that at least 480 hours (or 20 days) are required to eliminate 99 per cent of the drug. Since there is much variation in the half-life of different drugs

	Amount of drug left in the body	Amount of drug eliminated
Start	100%	100%
End of 1st half-life	50.0%	50.0%
End of 2nd half-life	25.0%	75.0%
End of 3rd half-life	12.5%	87.5%
End of 4th half-life	6.25%	93.75%
End of 5th half-life	3.125%	96.87%
End of 6th half-life	1.56%	98.44%
End of 7th half-life	0.78%	99.22%

Table 1. Impact of half-life. ILLUSTRATION BY GGS INFORMATION SERVICES. GALE, CENGAGE LEARNING

and the absolute amount of drug present can be very small, it is crucial that the appropriate body fluid for analysis is selected for testing.

Ethanol is absorbed from the stomach by simple diffusion. Gastric absorption is fastest when strong drinks, distilled spirits containing 40 to 50 percent ethanol by volume, are consumed. Dilute beverages, such as beer (4–5% ethanol) or wine (11–12% ethanol) are absorbed slowly. Alcohol is absorbed very rapidly from the small intestines. The essential action of food is to delay gastric emptying and thus slow the absorption process. Typically, studies have shown that peak BAC is reached between 30 minutes and 90 minutes of consumption; earlier on an empty stomach and later on a full stomach. Once absorbed, ethanol rapidly diffuses throughout the aqueous compartments of the body, going wherever water goes.

Absorption, distribution into different tissues, and elimination are dynamic processes and take place simultaneously. The rate of removal of ethanol from the body is the sum of the rates of excretion in urine, breath, and sweat, and the rate of the metabolism in the liver and other tissues. In humans, alcohol metabolism follows a "zero" order kinetics, i.e., it is largely independent of alcohol concentration in the blood and its levels decline almost linearly over time. The implication of this is that BAC falls at a constant rate over time. In social drinkers it is from 0.015 to 0.018 percent (15 mg/100mL to 18 mg/100mL) per hour and in heavy drinkers it is typically between 0.018 and 0.025 percent (18mg/100mL to 25mg/100mL) per hour. In the alcoholic patient, the elimination rate is generally higher. In forensic calculations, a rate of 0.015 percent (15mg/100mL) per hour is usually used. In our studies we have found 0.018 percent (18mg/100mL) per hour to be the average rate of metabolism. The larger the dose of alcohol given, the longer the duration of the measurable blood alcohol concentration.

SELECTION OF DRUGS TO BE TESTED
A number of different criteria can be applied to the drug(s) or category of drugs that should be tested or monitored. Drug availability, clinical effects, and robustness of the analytical method(s) used for analysis are probably the most important.

Availability. Prescription patterns of psychoactive and other drugs vary from place to place and country to country. Abuse of benzodiazepine nitrazepam is common in Europe but almost unknown in North America, since it is not sold here. The psychoactive chemical cathinon (cathine), the active ingredient in the leaves of the khat plant, is chewed in northeast Africa, is not a problem in North America. Codeine, an opioid available in Canada as over-the-counter preparations, is sold only by prescription in the United States.

A wide availability of "legal" stimulants poses an interesting problem since they are a common finding in accident victims. A study carried out by the U.S. National Transportation Safety Board from October 1987 to September 1988 showed that over-the-counter stimulants—such as ephedrine, pseudoephedrine and phenylpropanolamine—were commonly found among drivers killed in heavy truck accidents. Amongst the eight States that participated in this safety study almost all amphetamine use was in the California region. Similar findings are also reported from emergency rooms over the past five years as well as from admissions in a trauma unit due to motor-vehicle accidents. All this suggests that drug use varies not only from place to place but also region to region within a given country.

Thus, the selection of a drug to be tested and monitored, appropriate for one country and place, may not necessarily be appropriate for another country.

Clinical Effects. Drugs that manifest abuse potential and impair behavior such that job performance can be affected are prime candidates for testing or monitoring in the workplace. Alcohol and cocaine are examples of this.

Analytical Methods. A false positive finding can have a serious impact on the livelihood of the person being tested. Therefore, special attention needs to be paid to the testing methods. Ideally the analytical method should be specific for the drug being tested (i.e., no false positive), easy, and inexpensive to perform. Confirmation methods should also be readily available. Availability of technical and scientific expertise to perform the tests is also essential.

Interpretation of the analytical results also needs to be carefully considered as even a normal diet can result in a positive drug identification. For example, poppy seed ingestion can result in a true positive *analytical* result (opiates, like heroin, are derived from the poppy plant *Papaver soniferum*) but it is a false positive for drug use. Some ethnic diets may also lead to these confounding problems, as when food containing poppy seeds is eaten during Ramadan.

What should be analyzed? Ideally the analysis should look for the parent drug rather than its metabolite, although this may not always be possible as some drugs are very rapidly metabolized (e.g., heroin metabolism to morphine). Sensitivity of the analytical procedure should be dictated by the drugs' psychoactive pharmacological properties. If the drug is shown to be devoid of abuse potential then its detection beyond the time of pharmacological activity, although important in the clinical management of the patient, does not necessarily serve a useful purpose for a workplace drug screening programme.

The guidelines developed by the National Institute on Drug Abuse in April 1988 address five "illegal" drugs: marijuana, phencyclidene, amphetamine, cocaine and heroin. Rapid screening methods that allowed for "mass screening" were available at that time, as were the confirmation methods for these five drugs. Mood altering substances such as benzodiazepines, barbiturates and some stimulants such as antihistamines are at present excluded from these regulations in the United States. This is probably due to the wide availability of these drugs as medications within the general population and the

technological requirements for screening and monitoring of these drugs.

TYPES OF TESTING: BLOOD, URINE, AND HAIR SPECIMENS

Blood and urine are the most commonly used biological fluids in the analysis for drugs other than alcohol. Blood, obtained by an invasive procedure, is available only in small quantities and drug concentration levels in blood are typically low. Urine is the preferred sample of choice as it is available in larger volumes, contains the metabolite and requires less invasive procedures in its collection. Both sampling procedures, however, are limited in their ability as they only determine the absolute amount of drug present in the fluid being examined. This quantity is dependent upon the amount of the drug used, when it was last used, as well as the half-life of the drug.

Recently, hair samples have been used to detect drug use. A number of technical problems must be overcome before hair can be used as a definitive proof of drug use. Hair treatment and environmental absorption are but two of the many concerns and problems that have been cited. An advisory committee of the Society of Forensic Toxicology has recently reported that "The committee concluded that, because of these deficiencies, results of hair analysis alone do not constitute sufficient evidence of drug use for application in the workplace."

Various body fluids such as sweat, saliva, blood, urine, and breath, have been used for alcohol analysis. Breath, though not a body fluid, is commonly used by law enforcement authorities. Although a number of variables can affect breath/blood ratio, a 2100:1 alveolar breath/blood conversion ratio has been used and accepted for use with breathalyzers. Breath-testing equipment calibrated with a blood:-breath conversion factor of 2100 consistently underestimate actual blood alcohol concentrations (BAC). Accuracy of breath analysis results is subject to various instruments and biological factors. Potential errors in breath analysis can also be caused by the presence of residual alcohol in the mouth. Immediately after drinking there is enough alcohol vapour in the mouth to give artificially high concentrations on breath analysis. Generally this effect disappears twenty minutes after drinking but high values for as long as forty-five minutes have been reported.

As of the early 1990s, all existing technologies are limited in terms of determining how much or when the drug was consumed.

Blood and saliva concentrations reflect the current blood alcohol concentration, but generally a blood sample is used in hospitals to access the patient in the casualty wards. In programs requiring monitoring of alcohol use, urine is probably the sample of choice. Urine alcohol concentration, which represents the average blood alcohol concentration between voiding, has the potential of being "positive" while the blood may be "negative."

MEASURING IMPAIRMENT

Except for alcohol, the degree to which a person is influenced or impaired by a drug at the time of the test cannot be determined from test results alone. Correlations between positive blood levels and degree of impairment are usually stronger than correlations between urine levels and degree of impairment; however, neither blood nor urine tests are sufficiently accurate to indicate impairment even at high levels of concentration. Human studies using marijuana and cocaine have shown that a "perceived high" is reached *after* the drug concentration has peaked in the blood. Generally, blood can only show positive results for a short time after drug consumption, whereas urine can be positive for a few days to weeks after last use. For example, metabolites of δ^9-THC (active ingredient in marijuana) that are lipid-soluble can be detected in the urine from a few days to many weeks, depending on the drug-habit of the user. Excretion of the drug in urine and its concentrations are also affected by several factors, such as dilution and pH (acidity) of the urine. There have been many cases where a strong, positive urine sample for cannabinoids was found in the morning, a borderline positive in the afternoon, followed by a strong positive the next morning; there have been similar cases with respect to phenobarbital.

A positive urine test cannot reveal the form in which the drug was originally taken—or when and how much was taken. For example, crack-cocaine, impure cocaine powder, or cocaine paste (which can be smoked, inhaled, injected, or chewed) all give the same result in the urine test. The consumption of poppy seeds has been reported to give positive results for opiate use, because some seeds contain traces of opiates and some have been known to be contaminated with opium derivatives. Similarly, consumption of herbal coca tea has resulted in positive results for cocaine use. These diverse incidences illustrate the difficulties involved in measuring impairment using urine results.

The problem of interpreting urine-test results is one of the major bases of concern for restricting their use in the employment setting. Even the effectiveness of preemployment drug-screening tests, due to the difficulties in interpretation is being questioned. Based on a study of 2,229 preemployment drug screening tests and follow-up, one group of researchers have come to the following conclusion: "our findings raise the possibility that a preemployment drug screening may be decreasingly effective in predicting adverse outcomes associated with marijuana use after the first year of employment." They make a similar comment about cocaine.

There is no threshold for alcohol effects on performance or motor-vehicle-accident risk. Although the effects of alcohol on impairment and crash risk appear more dramatically above 80mg/100mL, a review of literature would suggest that impairment may be observed at levels as low as 15mg/100mL. It is not possible to specify a blood alcohol concentration level above which all drivers are dangerous and below which they are safe or at "normal" risk. An author of a major literature review on the behavioral effects of alcohol concluded "that alcohol sensitivity can vary from time to time, person to person, and situation to situation, the setting of a "safe" BAC will always be arbitrary, being based on a low, but a non-zero, incidence of effects below that level" and "the most striking feature to emerge from any review of the effects of alcohol on behavior is the marked lack of agreement between authors, amounting, in many instances, to direct contradiction. This is especially true for the effects of smaller dose."

"Legal" BAC levels differ in different countries. Some even have more than one legal limit over which the driver of a vehicle is considered as "impaired." Some European countries have 50mg/100ml; others have 80mg/100ml as their legal limits. In the United States, the legal limits vary from 80mg/100mL to 100mg/100mL in different states, but employees who are regulated by the U. S. Department of Transportation have a BAC legal limit of

Drug	Half-life (t2)	Detection period
Methamphetamine	12–34 hours	2–3 days
Amphetamine (metabolite of methamphetamine)	7–34 hours	
Heroin	60–90 minutes	In minutes
Morphine (metabolite of heroin)	1.3—6.7 hours	Opiates positive for 2–4 days (EIA)
6-Mono-acetyl-morphine (MAM)	30 minutes	Few hours
Phencyclidine (PCP)	7–16 hours	2–3 days
Cocaine	0.5–1.5 hours	Few hours
Benzoylecgonine (metabolite of cocaine)	5–7 hours	3–5 days
δ -Tetrahydrocannabinol	14–38 hours	90% fall in 1 hour (blood)
δ -Tetrahydrocannabinoic acid (marijuana metabolite in urine)		Depending on use, few days to many weeks
Benzodiazepines	Few hours to days	days to weeks, depending on half-life
Diazepam	15–40 hours	2 weeks
Flunitrazepam (rohypnol)	9–25 hours	0.2% excreted unchanged!
Methadone	15–40 hours In chronic patient ~22–24 hours	
Barbiturate (phenobarbital)	35–120 hours	1–2 weeks after last use
Alcohol (ethanol)	Blood levels fall by an average of 4–5 mmol/L/hour (15–18 mg/ 100 mL)/hour	1.5 > 12 hours depending on the peak blood level. Urine typically positive for an additional 1–2 hours.
Gamma-hydroxybutyrate (GHB)	0.3–1.0 hour	Less than 12 hours

The detection period is very much dose-dependent. The larger the dose, the longer the period the drug/metabolite can be detected in the urine.

Table 2. Drug half-lives and approximate urine detection periods. ILLUSTRATION BY GGS INFORMATION SERVICES. GALE, CENGAGE LEARNING

40mg/100mL. In Canada there are also two limits: 50mg/100mL and 80mg/100mL. BAC levels between 50mg/100mL and 80mg/100mL call for suspension of driving privileges but above 80mg/100mL are subject to criminal charges.

URINE TESTING METHODS

Urine is the most commonly used fluid for drug screening. The methods most commonly used in toxicology laboratories are: *immunoassay, chromatographic* and *chromatography coupled with mass spectrometry.* These methods vary considerably with respect to their sensitivity and reliability. Thin-layer chromatography is least expensive, gas chromatography coupled with mass spectrometry (GC/MS), which is considered as nearly perfect or "gold standard," is the most expensive. Table 2 summarizes the various methods.

Immunoassays (EIA, EMIT, FPIA, CEDIA and KIMS). Immunoassay methods are used for preliminary screening (i.e., initial screening). Since these methods are based on an antibody-antigen reaction, small amounts of the drug or metabolite(s) can be detected. Antibodies specific to a particular drug are produced by injecting laboratory animals with the drug. These antibodies are then tagged with markers such as an enzyme (enzyme immunoassay, EIA), a radio isotope (radioimmunoassay, RIA) or a fluorescence (fluorescence polarization immunoassay, FPIA) label. Reagents containing these labelled antibodies can then be introduced into urine samples, and if the specific drug against which the antibody was made is present, a reaction will occur. RIA is the oldest immunoassay method used to detect drugs. The major drawback of this method is that it requires a separation step and generates radioactive waste. RIA also requires special equipment to measure radioactivity.

Typically, immunoassays are designed for a *class* of drugs. Thus, their specificity (the ability to detect the presence of a *specific* drug) is not very good, since substances that have similar chemical structures will "cross-react" and give a false positive reaction. For example, the immunoassay method for cannabinoids was developed to detect the carboxylic acid metabolite of δ^9-THC. Yet, there is a suggestion in the literature that some nonsteroidal anti-inflammatory drugs, such as ibuprofen (a nonprescription drug in the U. S. and Canada) and naproxyn give random or sporadic false positive results for cannabinoids. Cough-syrup codeine will also give a positive reaction for the morphine (a

1. *Immunoassays*
   Enzyme immunoassay (EIA)
   Enzyme-multiplied immunoassay technique (EMIT)
   Fluorescence polarization immunoassay (FPIA)
   Radio immunoassay (RIA)
   Kinetic interaction of microparticles in solution (KIMS)
   Cloned enzyme donor immunoassay (CEDIA)
   Rapid slide tests (point-of-care testing)
2. *Chromatographic Methods*
   Thin-layer chromatography (TLC)
   Liquid chromatography (HPLC)
   Gas chromatography (GC)
3. *Chromatography/Mass Spectrometry*
   Gas chromatography/mass spectrometry (GC/MS)
   Liquid chromatography/mass spectrometry (HPLC/MS)

Table 3. Common drug-testing methods. ILLUSTRATION BY GGS INFORMATION SERVICES. GALE, CENGAGE LEARNING

metabolic product of heroin use) immunoassay and many antihistamines that are available over-the-counter may yield positive reactions for amphetamines. While some reagent manufacturers claim to have overcome many of these cross-reactivity problems, confirmation by a nonimmunoassay method is very important.

Urine test kits, designed to detect drugs, have been available in North America for the past few years. More recently, single and multiple test immunoassay kits designed for home and on-site testing have also been introduced. These kits generally carry a cautionary disclaimer that positive test results must be confirmed by the reference GC/MS method. When used in the non-laboratory environment, they are prone to procedural inaccuracies, poor quality control, abuse and misinterpretations. Therefore, these kits should be used with great caution. The risk of labelling a person with a false positive is high without the accompanying confirmatory analysis. Table 3 summarizes the advantages and disadvantages of immunoassay testing.

Chromatographic Methods. Separation of a mixture is the main outcome of the chromatographic method. For illustrative purposes, if one were to put a drop of ink on a blotting paper and hold the tip of the paper in water, one would observe the water rise in the paper. After a period of time and under the right conditions, the single ink spot would separate into many different compounds (spots) of different colors (blue ink is a mixture of many dyes). This process, where a mixture of

substances is separated in a stationary medium (filter paper), is called chromatography. The types of chromatographic processes used in the analysis of drugs include thin-layer, gas, and liquid chromatography as well as a combination of gas or liquid chromatography with mass spectrometry.

Of the several chromatographic methods, thin layer chromatography (TLC) is the one most similar to the ink separation example mentioned previously. This method requires extensive sample preparation and technical expertise on the part of the analyst, but it is inexpensive and very powerful if used properly. With the exception of *Cannabis*, which requires separate sample preparation, a large number of drugs (e.g., cocaine, amphetamine, codeine, and morphine) can be screened at the same time. By combining different TLC systems, a high degree of specificity can be obtained, although the training of the analyst is crucial because of the subjectivity involved in interpreting the results. To identify positive TLC "spots," the technologist looks for the drugs and/or its metabolite pattern, often by spraying with reagents that react to form different colors with different drugs. The trained technologist can comfortably identify more than forty different drugs.

Similar to TLC, gas chromatography (GC) requires extensive sample preparation. In GC, the sample to be analyzed is introduced via a syringe into a narrow bore (capillary) column which sits in an oven. The column, which typically contains a liquid adsorbed onto an inert surface, is flushed with a carrier gas such as helium or nitrogen. (GC is also sometimes referred to as gas-liquid chromatography (GLC). In a properly set up GC system, a mixture of substances introduced into the carrier gas is volatilized, and the individual components of the mixture migrate through the column at different speeds. Detection takes place at the end of the heated column and is generally a destructive process. Very often the substance to be analyzed is "derivatized" to make it volatile or change its chromatographic characteristics.

In contrast to GC, high pressure liquid chromatography (HPLC), a liquid under high pressure, is used to flush the column rather than a gas. Typically, the column operates at room or slightly above room temperature. This method is generally used for

Advantages

1. Screening tests can be done quickly because automation and batch processing are possible.
2. Technologists doing routine clinical chemistry testing can be easily trained.
3. Detection limits are low and can be tailored to meet the program screening requirements. For example, lower detection thresholds can be raised to eliminate positives due to passive inhalation of marijuana smoke.
4. Immunoassays are relatively inexpensive, although the single-test kits can be very expensive when quality assurance and quality control samples are included.
5. Immunoassays do not require a specialized laboratory. Most clinical laboratories have automated instruments to do the procedures.

Disadvantages

1. Although the tests are useful for detecting classes of drugs, specificity for individual drugs is weak.
2. Since the antibody is generated from laboratory animals, there can be a lot-to-lot or batch-to-batch variation in the antibody reagents.
3. Results must be confirmed by another nonimmunoassay method.
4. A radioactive isotope is used in RIA that requires compliance with special licensing procedures, use of gamma counters to measure radioactivity, and disposal of the radioactive waste.
5. Only a single drug can be tested for at one time.

Table 4. Advantages and disadvantages of immunoassays. ILLUSTRATION BY GGS INFORMATION SERVICES. GALE, CENGAGE LEARNING

substances that are difficult to volatilize (e.g., steroids) or are heat labile (e.g., benzodiazepines).

Gas chromatography/mass spectrometry (GC/MS) is a combination of two sophisticated technologies. GC physically separates (chromatographs or purifies) the compound, and MS fragments it so that a fingerprint of the chemical (drug) can be obtained. Although sample preparation is extensive, when the methods are used together the combination is regarded as the "gold standard" by most authorities. This combination is sensitive, i.e., can detect low levels, is specific, and can identify all types of drugs in any body fluid. Furthermore, assay sensitivity can be enhanced by treating the test substance with reagents. When coupled with MS, HPLC/MS is the method of choice for substances that are difficult to volatilize (e.g. steroids).

Given the higher costs associated with CG/MS, urine samples are usually tested in batches for broad classes of drugs by immunoassays and positive screens are later subjected to confirmation by this more expensive technique.

Table 4 gives a summary of the advantages and disadvantages of each method of chromatographic drug testing and Table 5 compares all the methods of testing. The initial minimal immunoassay and GC/MS (cut-off) levels for five drugs or classes of drugs, as suggested by the U.S. National Institute of Drug Abuse, are listed in Table 6.

Procedures for Alcohol Testing. Since the introduction of the micro method for alcohol analysis in blood by Widmark in 1922, many new methods and modifications have been introduced. The distillation/oxidation methods are generally *non-specific* for alcohol (ethanol), whereas biochemical methods (spectrophotometric) using alcohol dehydrogenase (ADH) obtained from yeast and the gas chromatographic method that are currently used are specific for ethanol. The radiative attenuation energy technique and those using alcohol oxidase method are non-specific and will detect not only ethanol but also other alcohols. The recently introduced alcohol dipstick based on the ADH enzyme system is not only specific for ethanol, but also sensitive and does not require instrumentation. It can be used for the detection of ethanol in all body fluids and can provide semi-quantitative results in ranges of pharmacological-toxicological interest. Alcohol dipsticks are being used in a number of laboratories as a screening device.

Breath can be analyzed by using a variety of instruments. Most of the instruments used today detect ethanol by using thermal conductivity, colorimetry, fuel cell, infrared, or gas chromatography. Typically in most countries, local statutes define the instrument and method that can be used for evidenciary purposes. A variety of Breathalyser instruments ranging in costs from $100 to $1000 are available to do the test. These instruments are compact and portable. Canadian law enforcement authorities use the Breathalyser "Alert" which can give a "pass" or "fail" result as a roadside alcohol-screening device. The "failed" person is generally subjected to a "Borkenstein" Breathalyser to measure the BAC before any charges are brought. Many devices are available to preserve the breath sample for later analysis if a Breathalyser is not available

Advantages

All the chromatographic methods are specific and sensitive and can screen a large number of drugs at the same time.

TLC	Negligible capital outlay is needed.
GC	The procedure can be automated.
HPLC	Of the chromatographic procedures, this has the easiest sample preparation requirements. The procedure can be automated.
GC/MS	This is the "gold standard" test.
	Computerized identification of fingerprint patterns makes identification easy. The procedure can be automated.
	This is currently the preferred method for defense in the legal system.

Disadvantages

All chromatographic methods are labor-intensive and require highly trained staff. Although the chromatographic methods are specific, confirmation is still desirable.

TLC	Interpretation is subjective, hence, training and experience in interpretation capabilities of the technologist are crucial.
HPLC or GC	Equipment costs are high, ranging between $25,000 to $60,000, depending on the type of detector and automation selected (1994 $)
GC/MS	Equipment costs are the highest, ranging from $120,000 to $2000,000, depending on the degree of sophistication required (1994 $). Due to the complexity of the instrument, highly trained operators and technologists are required.

Table 5. Summary of chromatographic methods. ILLUSTRATION BY GGS INFORMATION SERVICES. GALE, CENGAGE LEARNING

immediately. In forensic laboratories, gas chromatography (North America) or biochemical procedures (many European countries) are used to analyze biological samples.

Blood samples that cannot be analyzed soon after collection should have sodium fluoride (NaF) added as a preservative. Alcohol dehydrogenase (ADH), the enzyme responsible for the oxidation of alcohol, is also present in the red blood cell and will slowly metabolise the alcohol, causing its concentration to drop if the preservative is not added. Large amounts of alcohol can be produced *in-vitro* in the urine samples of diabetic patients if samples are not processed immediately or properly preserved.

INTERPRETATIONS OF TEST RESULTS

False Negatives. A positive or negative result is highly dependent on the sensitivity of the drug detection method. A false negative occurs when the drug is present but is not found because the detection limit of the method used is too high or the absolute quantity of the drug in the specimen is too low.

Large amounts of fluids consumed prior to obtaining a sample for analysis can affect detection of drugs in urine samples. Under conditions of dilution, although the absolute amount of drug or metabolite excreted may be the same over a period of time, the final concentration per milliliter will be reduced and may give a false negative result. Acidity levels in the urine may also affect the excretion of the drug into the urine. In some cases elimination is enhanced, whereas in other cases, the drug is reabsorbed.

Several measures can be used to decrease the likelihood of obtaining a false negative result. First, sensitivity of the method can be enhanced by analyzing for the drugs' metabolites. Heroin use, for example, is determined by the presence of its metabolite, morphine. Increasing the specimen volume used for analysis or treating it with chemicals can also make laboratory methods more sensitive. Studies have shown that a 5-mg dose of Valium® is usually detected for three to four days; however, when these improved methods are utilized, sensitivity can be increased, such that, the same dose can be detected for up to 20 days. One important drawback of such high sensitivities is, that estimates of when the drug was taken are far less accurate.

False Positives. A false positive occurs when results show that the drug is present, when in fact it is not. False-positive tests are obtained if an interfering drug or substance is present in the biological fluid and it cross-reacts with the reagents. An example of this is Daypro (oxaprozin) will give a false positive for benzodiazepines. Other substances may have a metabolite that will give a positive reaction. An example of this is Selegiline, an anti-Parkinson drug, which has amphetamine as one of its metabolites. Although this would be analytically a true positive, it is a false positive from a drug abuse perspective. As discussed in the previous section on immunoassay, an initially positive test based on an immunoassay technique should always be confirmed with an nonimmunoassay method. A confirmed positive finding only implies that the urine sample contains the detected drug and nothing more.

Test	Initial test	Confirmatory test
Marijuana metabolite[1]	50 ng/mL	15 ng/mL
Cocaine metabolites[2]	300 ng/mL	150 ng/mL
Opiate metabolites	2,000 ng/mL	
Morphine		2,000 ng/mL
Codeine		2,000 ng/mL
6-Acetylmorphine[3]		10 ng/mL
Phencyclidine (PCP)	25 ng/mL	25 ng/mL
Amphetamines	1,000 ng/mL	
Amphetamine		500 ng/mL
Methamphetamine[4]		500 ng/mL

[1]Delta-9 THC carboxylic acid
[2]Benzoylecgonine
[3]Test for 6-AM when the morphine concentration is greater than or equal to 2,000 ng/mL
[4]Specimen must also contain amphetamine at a concentration greater than or equal to 200 ng/mL

Table 6. Cut-off levels for initial and confirmatory rests. (Source: HHS Mandatory Guidelines, November 1, 2004. Division of Workplace Programs, Substance Abuse and Mental Health Administration, U.S. Department of Health and Human Services.) ILLUSTRATION BY GGS INFORMATION SERVICES. GALE, CENGAGE LEARNING

	EMIT FPLA	RIA	TLC	GC HPLC	GC/MS
Ease of sample preparation	X	X		X	
Less highly trained technologists required	X	X			
Limited equipment required	X	X	X		
Low detection limits	X	X	X	X	X
Adjustable lower threshold	X	X			
Highly specific and sensitive			X	X	X
Computerized identification possible					X
Screen for several drugs at a time			X	X	X
Procedure can be automated	X	X		X	X
Special atomic energy license required		X			
Confirmation of results required	X	X	X	X	
Interpretation is subjective		X			

Table 7. Comparison of all testing methods. ILLUSTRATION BY GGS INFORMATION SERVICES. GALE, CENGAGE LEARNING

At times false positives are attributable to ingested substances such as allergy medications. Some authors have suggested that employees subject to drug screening refrain from using popular over-the-counter medications, such as Alka-Seltzer Plus and Sudafed, because they have caused false-positives. Some natural substances such as herbal teas and poppy seeds can also give positive responses to screens. These may be analytically true positives but need to be distinguished from those due to illegal drug use. In some instances, false-positives have been due to mistakes or sabotage of the chain of custody for urine samples.

COMMON ADULTERATION METHODS
The method of switching "clean" urine for "dirty" urine; resubmitting one's own or urine that is provided by someone else are the most common ways to fool the drug screening system. A number of entrepreneurs have attempted to bypass urine-specimen inspection by substituting clean urine. For example, a company in Florida sells lyophilized (freeze dried) clean urine samples through newspaper and magazine advertisements. Hiding condoms containing "clean" urine on the body or inside the vagina is another common trick.

Some have substituted apple juice and tea in samples for analysis. Patients are known to add everything from bleach, liquid soap, eye-drops, and many other household products, hoping that their drug use will be masked. Others may hide a masking substance under their fingernails and release it into the urine specimen. Another method is to poke a small hole into the container with a pin so that the sample leaks out by the time it reaches the laboratory.

Since addition of table salt (NaCl) or bleach to the urine is a common practice, many laboratories routinely test for Na and Cl in the urine. Liquid soap and crystalline drain cleaners that are strong alkaline products containing sodium hydroxide (NaOH) are also used to adulterate the urine sample. These contaminators can be detected by checking for high levels of pH in the urine sample. In-vivo alkalizing or acidifying the urine pH can also change the excretion pattern of some drugs including amphetamines, barbiturates and phencyclidine (PCP).

Water-loading (drinking large amounts of water prior to voiding) poses an interesting challenge to testing laboratories. Specific gravity has been used to detect dilution; however, the measurement range is limited so it is not yet useful. Creatinine levels on random urine samples appear to be a promising method for detection of water-loading. A number of adulteration methods are being advertised on the Internet. Invariably, one of the instructions for adulteration is to drink copious amounts of fluids to bring about in-vivo dilution or water-loading. Some Internet sites even sell adulterants that can be added to the urine.

Typically these products either try to oxidise the drug present or try to change the pH of the urine to interfere with the analytical method. Most of the laboratories involved in drug testing routinely test for the various adulterants. To detect resubmitted samples, a "urine fingerprinting" method using dietary components has been described.

Drug users are very resourceful and their ingenuity should not be underestimated. To reduce the opportunities for specimen contamination, some workplaces require that employees provide a urine sample under direct supervision. Another technique used to detect any sample adulteration is to take the temperature of the sample. In a study, Kapur et al. (1993) took the temperature of urine samples when taken within one minute of voiding; it fell between 36.5°C and 34 degrees Celsius, reflecting the inner body core temperature. It is very difficult to achieve this narrow temperature range by hiding a condom filled with urine under the armpit or adding water from a tap or toilet bowl to the urine sample. It is important that the temperature of the specimen be measured immediately after the sample is taken, since it can drop rapidly.

LABORATORY PROCEDURAL AND SECURITY STANDARDS

It is important that the laboratory drug testing facility has qualified individuals who follow a specific set of laboratory procedures and meet recommended security standards.

DRUG TESTING METHODS AND CLINICAL INTERPRETATIONS OF TEST RESULTS: SUMMARY AND CONCLUSION

In this paper, major issues related to drug testing are discussed. For example, drug-testing techniques measure drug presence but are not sophisticated enough to measure impairment from drug use. It is also very difficult to determine the route of drug administration, quantity, frequency, or when the drug was last taken.

Selection of the drug to be tested should depend on the local availability of the drug, its abuse potential, and clinical effects, as well as the available analytical technology and expertise in testing and interpretation of the laboratory results. The most sophisticated drug-testing approach, gas chromatography in combination with mass spectrometry, is considered as a gold standard and thus utilized in confirmatory testing. Typically GC/MS is preceded by a rapid immunoassay method to eliminate the majority of negative samples.

Despite the existence of sophisticated drug-testing methods, incorrect test results can still occur. These can be due to the presence of interfering substances or adulteration of the urine sample. Patients have been known to adulterate urine samples to avoid drug detection. A number of techniques can be employed to reduce the likelihood of obtaining erroneous results, as well as detect adulterated urine samples. "Positive" drug finding can have a serious impact on the livelihood of an individual, therefore the performance of these tests should adhere to the strictest laboratory standards of performance. Only qualified and experienced individuals with proper laboratory equipment should perform these analyses. Standards of laboratory performance must meet local legal and forensic requirements. Access to the patient samples as well as laboratory records must be restricted in order to prevent tampering with samples and results. To maintain confidentiality and assure proper interpretation of results, the results must be communicated only to the physician reviewing the case/patient. Chain of custody and all documents pertaining to the urine sample must be maintained so that they can be examined in case of a legal challenge. The laboratory must have a complete record on quality control. Finally, specific initial and confirmatory testing requirements should be met.

See also **Blood Alcohol Concentration; Breathalyzer; Hair Analysis as a Test for Drug Use.**

BIBLIOGRAPHY

Jenkins, A. J., & Goldberger, B. A. (Eds.). (2001). *On-site drug testing.* Totowa, NJ: Humana Press.

Kapur, B. M. (1993). Drug testing methods and clinical interpretations of test results. *Bulletin on Narcotics, 45,* 2, 115–154.

Kintz, P. (2006). *Analytical and practical aspects of drug testing in hair.* Boca Raton, FL: CRC Press.

Rom, W. N., & Markowitz, S. B. (2006). *Environmental and occupational medicine.* Philadelphia, PA: Lippincott, Williams & Wilkins.

Wong, R. C., & Tse, H. Y. (2005). *Drugs of abuse: Body fluid testing.* Totowa, NJ: Humana Press.

BHUSHAN M. KAPUR

DRUG TYPES

DRUG TYPES. The various types of drugs that are used and abused by humans for nonmedical purposes can be divided into several major categories, based upon their general pharmacological and subjective effects. These categories include: ethanol, nicotine and tobacco, central nervous system depressants, central nervous system stimulants, cannabinoids, opioids, psychedelics, inhalants, and arylcyclohexylamines. Although the mechanisms of action may vary among the drugs within a single category, the general effects of the drugs in each category are similar. The drugs in each category are described below in terms of their pharmacology, abuse, dependence, and withdrawal, as well as their toxicity. The legal and readily available drugs (i.e., alcohol and tobacco) are described first, because the use and abuse of these drugs is more widespread than that of all of the other categories of abused drugs combined. The health problems associated with the chronic use of alcohol and tobacco are, therefore, a far-reaching problem in modern society, not only because of the vast numbers of people who suffer and die each year due to the toxic effects of these substances, but also because of the financial drain they impose due to absenteeism from work and increased health-care costs.

Prescription drugs are covered next, and then the illegal drugs are discussed. Although the illicit use of heroin, cocaine and other drugs remains a major social, legal, financial, and health problem in the United States, the percentage of the population physically dependent on these drugs is relatively low when compared to legal drugs that are abused. Finally, it is important to take into consideration the fact that individuals often do not restrict their drug use to drugs within a single category. Alcoholics typically smoke cigarettes, and they often use benzodiazepines as well. Many heroin users also smoke, and they may consume alcohol and other sedatives, cannabis, or stimulants. Multiple drug use is, therefore, a relatively common occurrence among individuals who use drugs for their subjective, nonmedical effects.

ALCOHOL

Although alcohol has been used throughout recorded history, it is generally accepted that the therapeutic value of ethanol is extremely limited and that chronic alcoholism is a major social and medical problem. Approximately two-thirds of all adults in the United States use alcohol occasionally. Hundreds of thousands of individuals suffer and die each year from complications associated with chronic alcoholism, and tens of thousands of innocent individuals are injured or killed each year in alcohol-related traffic accidents. Thus, alcoholism is a far-reaching problem, affecting the lives of individuals who consume ethanol as well as those who do not.

Although alcohol is considered by many people to be a stimulant drug because it typically releases an individual's latent behavioral inhibitions, alcohol actually produces a powerful primary and continuous depression of the central nervous system, similar to that seen with general anesthetics. In general, the effects of alcohol on the central nervous system are proportional to the blood (and brain) concentrations of the drug. Initially, memory and the ability to concentrate decrease and mood swings become more evident. As the level of intoxication increases, so does the impairment of nervous function, until a condition of general anesthesia is reached. However, there is little margin of safety between an anesthetic dose of ethanol and severe respiratory depression.

In chronic alcoholism, brain damage, memory loss, sleep disturbances, psychoses, and increased seizure susceptibility often occur. Chronic alcoholism is also one of the major causes of cardiomyopathy (impaired function of the heart muscle) in the United States due to irreversible ethanol-induced damage to that tissue. Ethanol also stimulates the secretion of gastric acid in the stomach, and it can produce ulcers of the stomach and intestine. One of the primary metabolic products of ethanol is acetaldehyde, which is toxic. In chronic alcoholism, acetaldehyde can accumulate in the liver, resulting in hepatitis and cirrhosis of the liver. Finally, the long-term use of alcohol can result in a state of physical dependence.

With relatively low levels of dependence, withdrawal from alcohol may be associated with problems such as sleep disturbances, anxiety, weakness, and mild tremors. In more severe dependence, the alcohol withdrawal syndrome can include more pronounced tremors, seizures, and delirium, as well as a number of other physiological and psychological effects. In some cases, this withdrawal can be life threatening. Because alcohol has cross-tolerance with other central nervous system depressants, benzodiazepines or barbiturates can be successfully used to decrease the severity of the alcohol withdrawal syndrome. Longer-acting benzodiazepines and related drugs can be used as an ethanol substitute, and the dose of the benzodiazepine can then be gradually reduced over time to attenuate or prevent the occurrence of convulsions and other potentially life-threatening toxic reactions generally associated with alcohol withdrawal.

As outlined above, the chronic use of ethanol can result in a wide range of toxic effects on a variety of organ systems. However, the mechanisms through which ethanol produces its varied effects are not clearly understood. The anesthetic or central nervous system depressant effects may result, in part, from general changes in the function of ion channels that occur when ethanol dissolves in lipid membranes. Other research suggests that alcohol may interact with specific binding sites associated with the inhibitory neurotransmitter gamma-aminobutyric acid (GABA), in a manner somewhat analogous to other central nervous system depressants (e.g., benzodiazepines or barbiturates). However, because an ethanol receptor site has not yet been conclusively identified, specific receptor agonists and antagonists are not yet available for the treatment of ethanol intoxication or withdrawal, or for the maintenance of abstinence.

Disulfiram is sometimes used in the treatment of chronic alcoholism, although the drug does not cure alcoholism. Rather, disulfiram interacts with ethanol to alter the intermediate metabolism of ethanol, resulting in a five- to tenfold increase in plasma acetaldehyde concentrations. This acetaldehyde syndrome results in vasodilatation, headache, breathing difficulties, nausea, vomiting, sweating, faintness, weakness, and vertigo. Thus, it helps persuade alcoholics to remain abstinent, because they realize that they cannot drink ethanol for up to two weeks after taking disulfiram. More recently, naltrexone was approved as the first agent for the pathological reward and reinforcement effects of alcohol. Naltrexone is an opioid receptor antagonist that appears to reduce these responses in alcoholics via the endogenous opioid system. Oral naltrexone has demonstrated efficacy and safety in the treatment of alcohol dependence in controlled clinical trials. A long-acting injectable formulation of naltrexone has also been approved for use in the United States. Finally, acamprosate, a medication first evaluated in Europe, has also been approved for use in the United States. This medication acts on both GABA and glutamate (an excitatory neurotransmitter) to maintain abstinence in alcohol-dependent individuals.

TOBACCO

Tobacco was first introduced to Europe by the crews that accompanied Christopher Columbus to the "New World." By the middle of the nineteenth century, tobacco use had become widespread. Although tobacco use has declined dramatically in recent years, 18 to 24 percent of the adults in the United States are still regular tobacco smokers. This relatively high use of tobacco exists despite the large body of scientific evidence linking cigarette smoking to numerous life-threatening health disorders, including lung cancer and heart disease. The constituents of tobacco smoke that are most likely to contribute to these health problems include carbon monoxide, nicotine, and "tar."

Nicotine is the primary component of tobacco smoke that promotes smoking. Nicotine facilitates memory, reduces aggression, and decreases weight gain. Each of these effects could, by itself, provide a rationale for continued tobacco use, as most individuals find increased alertness and memory, decreased irritability, and decreased weight gain to be positive effects. However, these effects may actually be secondary to the primary reinforcing effects of nicotine itself. In laboratory settings, smokers report that the intravenous injection of nicotine produces a pleasant feeling on its own. However, nicotine causes unpleasant effects in nonsmokers, often resulting in dizziness, nausea, and vomiting. Tolerance to these unpleasant effects develops rapidly, however. Although nicotine obviously binds to nicotinic receptors associated with the neurotransmitter acetylcholine, there is evidence that the reinforcing or rewarding properties of nicotine may result from an activation of ascending limbic neurons that release the neurotransmitter dopamine (i.e., in the mesocorticolimbic dopaminergic system, which has been implicated in the reinforcing properties of a variety of drugs, including stimulants and opiates).

As stated above, tobacco smoking has been associated with a wide variety of serious health effects, including cancer and heart disease. However, the chances of developing these health problems decrease once smoking is terminated. Although some of the smoking-induced damage is irreversible, the incidence rates for cancer and heart disease gradually become more similar to that of nonsmokers the longer that the smoker refrains from smoking. However, those who quit smoking experience a withdrawal syndrome that varies in intensity from individual to individual and often leads to a relapse. This syndrome consists of a craving for tobacco, irritability, weight gain, difficulty concentrating, drowsiness, and sleep disturbances. The introduction of nicotine replacement therapy (in the form of chewing gum, transdermal patches, nasal spray, inhalers, tablets, or lozenges) has significantly helped to sustain abstinence from smoking in a number of individuals by delivering nicotine in a less toxic way. The orally administered medications varenicline and bupropion, which are not nicotine replacement therapies, are also regarded as first-line treatments, either used alone or as an adjunct to nicotine replacement therapy. Second-line treatments include clonidine and nortriptyline. Other treatment strategies that have been examined include monoamine oxidase inhibitors (MAOIs) and selective serotonin-reuptake inhibitors (SSRIs), but efficacy has yet to be proven definitively for these medications. A novel approach to treatment using the cannabinoid-1 receptor antagonist rimonabant is also under investigation.

CENTRAL NERVOUS SYSTEM DEPRESSANTS
Central nervous system depressants include barbiturates, benzodiazepines, and related drugs. Receptor binding sites for benzodiazepines and barbiturates are part of a macromolecular complex associated with chloride ion channels and the inhibitory neurotransmitter GABA. The interaction of these drugs with their distinct binding sites results in a facilitation of GABAergic neurotransmission, producing an inhibitory effect on neuronal impulse flow in the central nervous system. The shorter-acting barbiturates such as pentobarbital ("yellow jackets") or secobarbital ("red devils") are usually preferred to the longer-acting drugs such as phenobarbital. Nonbarbiturates such as meprobamate, glutethimide, methyprylon, and methaqualone (Quaalude) are also abused, though these medications are not as widely available as they were before the introduction of the benzodiazepines. Some of the shorter-acting benzodiazepines are also abused, providing evidence that the quicker the onset of action for a particular central nervous system depressant, the better the "high."

There is no general rule that can be used to predict the pattern of use of a central nervous system depressant for a given individual. There is often a fine line between the appropriate therapy for insomnia or anxiety and drug dependence. Some individuals exhibit cyclic patterns of abuse, with gross intoxication for a few days interspersed with periods of abstinence. Other barbiturate or benzodiazepine users maintain a chronic low level of intoxication without any observable signs of impairment. Such individuals have developed a tolerance to many of the side effects of these drugs. When higher doses are used, however, the intoxication may resemble alcohol intoxication, with slurred speech, difficulty thinking, memory impairment, sluggish behavior, and emotional instability. Withdrawal from chronic barbiturate or benzodiazepine use can also be manifested to varying degrees. In the mildest form, the individual may only experience mild anxiety or insomnia. With greater degrees of physical dependence, tremors and weakness may also occur. In severe withdrawal, delirium and tonic-clonic seizures may also be present. This severe withdrawal syndrome can be life threatening. The degree of severity of the withdrawal syndrome appears to be related to the pharmacokinetics of the drug used. For example, shorter-acting benzodiazepines and barbiturates produce much more severe cases of withdrawal than the longer-acting drugs. Therefore, in the case of severe withdrawal symptoms associated with the chronic use of a short-acting drug, a longer-acting drug should be substituted. The dose of this longer-acting drug can thus be gradually decreased so that the individual experiences a much milder and less threatening withdrawal.

CENTRAL NERVOUS SYSTEM STIMULANTS
Central nervous system stimulants include caffeine, cocaine, and amphetamine. Perhaps 80 percent of the world's population ingests caffeine in the form of tea, coffee, cola-flavored drinks, or chocolate. In the central nervous system, caffeine decreases drowsiness and fatigue and produces a more rapid and clearer flow of thought. With higher doses,

however, nervousness, restlessness, insomnia, and tremors may result. Cardiac and gastrointestinal disturbances may also be seen. Tolerance typically develops to the anxiety and dysphoria (negative mood) experienced by some individuals. However, some degree of physical dependence has been associated with the chronic consumption of caffeine. The most characteristic symptom of caffeine withdrawal is a headache, although fatigue, lethargy, and some degree of anxiety are also common. In general, the long-term consequences of chronic caffeine consumption are relatively minor. On the other hand, the problems associated with chronic cocaine and amphetamine use and withdrawal are much more serious.

More than 20 million people have used cocaine in the United States alone. Following the introduction of cocaine in the free alkaloid base ("freebase" or "crack") form, there was a significant increase in cocaine-related medical, economic, social, and legal problems. In the freebase form, cocaine can be smoked, resulting in blood levels and brain concentrations of the drug that compare to those observed when the drug is injected intravenously. In normal subjects in a laboratory setting, the administration of cocaine or amphetamine produces an elevation of mood, an increase in energy and alertness, and a decrease in fatigue and boredom. In some individuals, however, anxiety, irritability, and insomnia may be observed. In non-laboratory settings, heavy users of cocaine often take the drug in bouts or binges, only stopping when their supply runs out or they collapse from exhaustion. Immediately following the intravenous administration or inhalation of cocaine, the individual experiences an intense pleasurable sensation known as a "rush" or "flash," that is followed by a sense of euphoria. Cocaine rapidly penetrates into the brain to produce these effects, but it is then rapidly redistributed to other tissues. In many cases, the intense pleasure followed by the rapid decline in the cocaine-induced elevation of mood is sufficient for the individual to begin immediately to seek out, procure, and use more of the drug to prolong these pleasurable effects. With the intranasal administration of cocaine, the pleasure is less intense and the decline in brain concentrations is much slower, so that the craving for more of the drug is less pronounced.

Cocaine and amphetamine appear to produce their reinforcing or pleasurable effects through interactions with the neurotransmitter dopamine, especially in the limbic and cortical regions of the brain (i.e., within the mesocorticolimbic dopaminergic system). Both cocaine and amphetamine block the reabsorption of dopamine into the neurons where it was released, thereby prolonging the action of dopamine in the synapse (the space between nerve cells). Amphetamine can also cause the direct release of dopamine from nerve cells, and it can inhibit the metabolism of the neurotransmitter. It is important to note, however, that every drug that augments the action of dopamine does not produce pleasurable or rewarding subjective effects. Toxicity associated with cocaine or amphetamine use can be quite severe and is often unrelated to the duration of use or to any preexisting medical conditions in the individual. This potential for serious toxic side effects is amplified by the fact that tolerance usually develops to the subjective feelings of the cocaine-induced rush and euphoria, but not to some of the other central nervous system effects of the drug, especially seizure susceptibility.

Some of the more minor toxic reactions include dizziness, confusion, nausea, headache, sweating, and mild tremors. These symptoms are experienced by virtually all cocaine and amphetamine users to some degree as a result of the stimulation of the sympathetic nervous system. However, more serious reactions are also frequently observed, including irregular heartbeats, convulsions and seizures, heart attack, liver failure, kidney failure, heart failure, respiratory depression, stroke, coma, and death. The effects on the heart and vascular system can sometimes be treated with alpha- and beta-noradrenergic receptor antagonists or calcium channel blockers, although even prompt medical attention is not always successful. The convulsions can sometimes be controlled with diazepam, and ventilation may be required for the respiratory depression.

In addition to the effects described above for cocaine, amphetamine has been reported to produce direct and irreversible neuronal damage to dopaminergic and nondopaminergic neurons. A similar effect for cocaine has not yet been identified. Psychiatric abnormalities resulting from chronic central nervous system stimulant abuse can include anxiety, depression, hallucinations, and, in some cases, a paranoid psychosis that is virtually indistinguishable from a paranoid schizophrenic psychosis.

A withdrawal syndrome is also observed following the abrupt cessation of chronic cocaine or amphetamine use. This syndrome begins with exhaustion during the "crash" phase and is followed by prolonged periods of anxiety, depression, anhedonia (reduced capacity to experience pleasure), hyperphagia (voracious eating), and an intense craving for the drug that may persist for several weeks, depending on the individual. The administration of dopaminergic agonists or tricyclic antidepressants may have some utility in decreasing the severity of withdrawal symptoms, which could reduce the risk of relapse. More recently, however, a number of novel targets for cocaine pharmacotherapy have emerged. Disulfiram, a medication with dopaminergic effects, has been reported to reduce cocaine use in a number of clinical trials, as have GABA medications, such as tiagabine and topiramate. A beta-adrenergic blocker, propranolol, may also be effective, especially among cocaine-addicted individuals with high withdrawal severity. Treatment with modafinil, a stimulant medication, has also been reported to reduce cocaine use. Finally, a cocaine vaccine that slows entry of cocaine into the brain by binding cocaine in the bloodstream may eventually hold promise. However, there is no FDA-approved medication for the treatment of dependence on cocaine, amphetamine or related drugs.

CANNABINOIDS

Marijuana, or cannabis (commonly referred to as "grass," "weed," or "pot"), is still the most commonly used illicit drug in the United States, with about 55 percent of young adults reporting some experience with the drug during their lifetimes. The active ingredient in marijuana is δ^9-tetrahydrocannabinol (δ^9-THC), which exerts its most prominent effects on the central nervous system and the cardiovascular system. A marijuana cigarette containing approximately 2 percent δ^9-THC produces an increase in feelings of well-being or euphoria and relaxation. Short-term memory is impaired, however, as is the ability to carry out goal-directed behavior, such as driving or operating machinery, effects that often persist for much longer than the subjective effects. With higher doses, paranoia, hallucinations, and anxiety or panic may be

manifested. Chronic marijuana users sometimes exhibit what is called the "amotivational syndrome," which consists of apathy, impairment of judgment, and a loss of interest in personal appearance and the pursuit of conventional goals. However, it is not clear whether this syndrome results from the use of marijuana alone or from other factors. δ^9-THC also produces a dose-related increase in heart rate, although this is seldom severe. Tolerance develops to the effects of marijuana, and in some countries, regular users of hashish (a concentrated resin containing high levels of δ^9-THC) consume quantities of the drug that would be toxic to most marijuana users in the United States. The withdrawal associated with the cessation of marijuana smoking is relatively mild and consists of irritability, restlessness, nervousness, insomnia, weight loss, chills, and increased body temperature.

The endogenous cannabinoid system—called the endocannabinoid system—was discovered in the 1980s, and the compounds that modify this system are currently being reconsidered for their therapeutic potential. Thus, the term *cannabinoid* includes the numerous synthetic cannabinoids obtained by modifications of plant-derived cannabinoids or from the compounds that behave as endogenous ligands for the different cannabinoid receptor types. The term also refers to some prototypes of selective antagonists for these receptors. The explanation for this exponential growth in cannabinoid pharmacology is the discovery and characterization of the endocannabinoid signaling system (receptors, ligands, and inactivation system), which plays a modulatory role mainly in the brain, but also in the periphery. The endocannabinoid system is currently under investigation, not only for its role in marijuana dependence, but also for its ability to mediate dependence on other drugs, such as cocaine.

OPIOIDS

According to the 2005 Monitoring the Future Survey, the use of opioids in the United States is much less prevalent than the other drugs discussed above. Data suggest that less than 1.5 percent of young adults have reported trying heroin at some time during their lives, although the incidence of prescription opioid abuse is on the increase. There are three basic patterns of opioid use and dependence in the United States. The smallest percentage of opioid users includes those individuals who initially began using morphine-like drugs medically for the relief of pain. A second group began using these drugs through experimentation and then progressed to chronic use and dependence. A third group comprises physically addicted individuals who eventually switched to oral methadone obtained through organized treatment centers. Interestingly, the incidence of opioid addiction is greater among physicians, nurses, and related health-care professionals than among any other group with a comparable educational background. In many instances, individuals addicted either to heroin purchased illegally on the street or to methadone are able to hold jobs and raise a family. Opioids reduce pain, aggression, and sexual drives, so that the use of these drugs is unlikely to induce crime. Obviously, however, other individuals (e.g., "junkies") are unable or unwilling to hold a job and resort to crime to support their drug habit.

Opioid drugs produce their pharmacological effects by binding to opiate receptors. The euphoria associated with the use of opioids results from the interaction of these drugs with the μ-opiate (or mu-opiate) receptor, possibly resulting in the stimulation of mesocorticolimbic dopaminergic neuronal activity. The rapid intravenous injection of morphine (or heroin, which is converted to morphine once it enters the brain) results in a warm flushing of the skin and sensations in the lower abdomen that are often described as being similar in intensity and quality to sexual orgasm. This initial "rush" (or "kick" or "thrill") lasts for about 45 seconds and is followed by a "high" that has been described as a state of dreamy indifference. Depending on the individual, good health and productive work are not incompatible with the regular use of opioids. Tolerance can develop to the analgesic, respiratory depressant, sedative, and reinforcing properties of opioids, but the degree and extent of tolerance depends largely on the pattern of use. The desired analgesia can often be maintained through the intermittent use of morphine. Tolerance develops more rapidly with more continuous opioid administration.

The abrupt discontinuation of opioid use can lead to a withdrawal syndrome that varies in degree and severity, depending on both the individual and the particular opioid used. Watery eyes (lacrimation), a runny nose (rhinorrhea), yawning, and sweating occur within 12 hours of the last dose of the opioid. As the syndrome progresses, dilated pupils, anorexia, gooseflesh ("cold turkey"), restlessness, irritability, and tremors can develop. As the syndrome intensifies, weakness and depression are pronounced, and nausea, vomiting, diarrhea, and intestinal spasms are common. Muscle cramps and spasms, including involuntary kicking movements ("kicking the habit"), are also characteristic of opioid withdrawal. However, seizures do not occur and the withdrawal syndrome is rarely life threatening. Without treatment, the morphine-induced withdrawal syndrome usually runs its course within 7 to 10 days.

Opiate receptor antagonists (e.g., naloxone) are contraindicated in opioid withdrawal as these drugs can precipitate a more severe withdrawal on their own. Rather, longer-acting and less potent opiate receptor agonists such as methadone are more commonly prescribed. The symptoms associated with methadone withdrawal are milder, although more protracted, than those observed with morphine or heroin. Therefore, methadone therapy can be gradually discontinued in some heroin-dependent individuals. If the patient refuses to withdraw from methadone, the individual can be maintained on methadone more or less indefinitely. In addition, a high-affinity partial μ agonist, buprenorphine, has been demonstrated to be as effective as methadone in the treatment of heroin dependence, with significantly better opiate abuse control. This treatment may therefore allow for longer and more effective treatment programs with reduced relapse rates.

PSYCHEDELICS

The psychedelics include drugs related to the indolealkylamines, such as lysergic acid diethylamide (LSD), psilocybin, psilocin, dimethyltryptamine (DMT), and diethyltryptamine (DET); to the phenylethylamines (e.g., mescaline); or to the phenylisopropylamines, such as 2,5-dimethoxy-4-methylamphetamine (DOM, or "STP"), as well as 3,4-methylenedioxyamphetamine (MDA) and 3,4-methylenedioxymethamphetamine (MDMA, or "Ecstasy"). According to the National Institute on Drug Abuse, in 2004, 9.7 percent of Americans aged 12 and older reported using LSD at least once in their lifetimes, while 0.2 percent had used it in the past year, and 0.1 percent had used it in the past month. Lifetime use declined significantly from 2003 to 2004 among persons aged 12 to 17 and 18 to 25. Also according to the National Institute on Drug Abuse, an estimated 450,000 people in the United States aged 12 and older reported having used MDMA in the previous 30 days. MDMA use dropped significantly among persons 18 to 25—from 14.8 percent in 2003 to 13.8 percent in 2004 for lifetime use, and from 3.7 percent to 3.1 percent for past-year use. The feature that distinguishes these psychedelic agents from other classes of drugs is their capacity to reliably induce states of altered perception, thought, and feeling. There is a heightened awareness of sensory input accompanied by an enhanced sense of clarity, but there is also a diminished control over what is experienced. The effects of LSD and related psychedelic drugs appear to be mediated through a subclass of receptors associated with the inhibitory neurotransmitter serotonin (i.e., serotonin $5HT_2$ receptors). Immediately after the administration of LSD, somatic symptoms such as dizziness, weakness, and nausea are present, although euphoric effects usually predominate. Within two to three hours, visual perceptions become distorted; for example, colors are heard and sounds may be seen. Vivid visual hallucinations are also often present. Many times this loss of control is disconcerting to the individual, resulting in the need for structure in the form of experienced companions during the "trip." The entire syndrome begins to clear after about 12 hours. However, there is little evidence of long-term changes in personality, beliefs, values, or behavior produced by the drug. Tolerance rapidly develops to the behavioral effects of LSD after three or four daily doses of the drug. In general, however, the psychedelic drugs do not give rise to patterns of continued use over extended periods. The use of these drugs is generally restricted to the occasional "trip."

Withdrawal phenomena are not observed after the abrupt discontinuation of LSD-like drugs, and no deaths directly related to the pharmacological effects of LSD have been reported. However, other drugs chemically similar to MDMA, such as MDA (methylenedioxyamphetamine, the parent drug of MDMA) and PMA (paramethoxyamphetamine, which has been associated with fatalities in the United States and Australia) are sometimes sold as MDMA. These drugs can be neurotoxic or create additional health risks to the user. MDMA tablets may also contain other substances in addition to MDMA, such as ephedrine (a stimulant), dextromethorphan (DXM, a cough suppressant that has PCP-like effects at high doses), ketamine (an anesthetic used by veterinarians that also has PCP-like effects), caffeine, cocaine, and methamphetamine. While the combination of MDMA with one or more of these drugs may be inherently dangerous, users also combine them with substances such as marijuana and alcohol, putting themselves at further physical risk.

INHALANTS

The intoxicating and euphorigenic properties of nitrous oxide and ethyl ether were well known even before their potential as anesthetics was recognized. Physicians, nurses and other health-care professionals have been known to inhale anesthetic gases, even though they have access to a wide variety of other drugs. Adolescents with restricted access to alcohol often resort to "glue sniffing" or the inhalation of vapors from substances with marked toxicity such as gasoline, paint thinners, or other industrial solvents. The alkyl nitrites (butyl nitrite, isobutyl nitrite, and amyl nitrite) have been used as aphrodisiacs because the inhalation of these agents is thought to intensify and prolong orgasm. More than 17 percent of young adults have reported some experience with inhalants. However, fatal toxic reactions (usually due to cardiac arrhythmias) are often associated with the inhalation of many of these drugs. Inhalation from a plastic bag can result in hypoxia as well as an extremely high concentration of vapor; fluorinated hydrocarbons can produce cardiac arrhythmias and ischemia; chlorinated solvents depress myocardial contractility; and ketones can produce pulmonary hypertension. Neurological impairment can also occur with a variety of solvents.

ARYLCYCLOHEXYLAMINES

Arylcyclohexylamines include phencyclidine (PCP, or "angel dust") and related drugs that possess central nervous system stimulant and depressant effects and hallucinogenic and analgesic properties. These drugs (also known as dissociative anesthetics) are well absorbed using all methods of administration. Even small doses can produce an intoxication characterized by staggering gait, slurred speech, and numbness in the extremities. PCP users may also exhibit sweating, catatonia, and a blank stare, as well as hostile and bizarre behavior. Amnesia during the intoxication may also occur. In higher doses, anesthesia, stupor, convulsions, and coma may appear. The typical "high" from a single dose can last four to six hours and is followed by a prolonged period of "coming down." PCP and related compounds bind with high affinity to a number of distinct sites in the central nervous system, although it is not certain which site (or sites) is responsible for the primary pharmacological effects of these drugs. PCP binds to the sigma site, which also has a high affinity for opioids. PCP also blocks the cation channel (e.g., Ca^{2+}) that is regulated by N-methyl-D-aspartate (NMDA), one type of receptor for excitatory amino acid neurotransmitters such as glutamate or aspartate. PCP also blocks the reabsorption of the neurotransmitter dopamine into the neurons from which it was released, resulting in a prolonged action of the neurotransmitter, especially within the mesocorticolimbic dopaminergic neuronal system.

There appears to be some degree of tolerance to the effects of PCP, and some chronic users of PCP complain of cravings and difficulties with recent memory, thinking, and speech after discontinuing the use of the drug. Personality changes following repeated use can range from social withdrawal and isolation to severe anxiety, nervousness, and depression. Although the frequency is uncertain, deaths due to direct toxicity, violent behavior, and accidents have been reported following the use of PCP. The drug can also produce acute behavioral toxicity consisting of intoxication, aggression, and confusion, as well as coma, convulsions, and psychoses. A PCP-induced psychosis can persist for several weeks following a single dose of the drug.

See also **Addiction: Concepts and Definitions; Epidemiology of Drug Abuse; Gamma-Aminobutyric Acid (GABA); National Survey on Drug Use and Health (NSDUH); Treatment: An Overview of Drug Abuse/Dependence.**

BIBLIOGRAPHY

Baker, J. R. (2005). Psychedelic sacraments. *Journal of Psychoactive Drugs, 37*(2), 179–187.

Benowitz, N. L. (2008). Clinical pharmacology of nicotine: Implications for understanding, preventing, and treating tobacco addiction. *Clinical Pharmacology & Therapeutics, 83*(4), 531–541.

Bernschneider-Reif, S., Oxler, F., & Freudenmann, R. W. (2006). The origin of MDMA ("Ecstasy"): Separating the facts from the myth. *Pharmazie, 61*(11), 966–972.

Bonomo, Y., & Proimos, J. (2005). Substance misuse: Alcohol, tobacco, inhalants, and other drugs. *British Medical Journal, 330*(7494), 777–780.

Ciraulo, D. A., Dong, Q., Silverman, B. L., Gastfriend, D. R., & Pettinati, H. M. (2008). Early treatment response in alcohol dependence with extended-release naltrexone. *Journal of Clinical Psychiatry, 69*(2), 190–195.

Connock, M., Juarez-Garcia, A., Jowett, S., Frew, E., Liu, Z., Taylor, R. J., et al. (2007). Methadone and buprenorphine for the management of opioid dependence: A systematic review and economic evaluation. *Health Technology Assessment, 11*(9), 1–171.

Crocq, M. A. (2007). Historical and cultural aspects of man's relationship with addictive drugs. *Dialogues in Clinical Neuroscience, 9*(4), 355–361.

Deas, D. (2006). Adolescent substance abuse and psychiatric comorbidities. *Journal of Clinical Psychiatry, 67*(Suppl. 7), 18–23.

Doogue, M., & Barclay, M. (2005). Death due to butane abuse: The clinical pharmacology of inhalants. *New Zealand Medical Journal, 118*(1225), U1732.

Felder, C. C., Dickason-Chesterfield, A. K., & Moore, S. A. (2006). Cannabinoids biology: The search for new therapeutic targets. *Molecular Interventions, 6*(3), 149–161.

Frishman, W. H. (2007). Smoking cessation pharmacotherapy: Nicotine and non-nicotine preparations. *Preventive Cardiology, 10*(2 Suppl. 1), 10–22.

Gómez-Ruiz, M., Hernández, M., de Miguel, R., & Ramos, J. A. (2007). An overview on the biochemistry of the cannabinoid system. *Molecular Neurobiology 36*(1), 3–14.

Gray, R. W. (2005). Playing "Russian roulette" with inhalants, pt. 2. *Tennessee Medicine, 98*(8), 387.

Hanus, L. O. (2007). Discovery and isolation of anandamide and other endocannabinoids. *Chemistry & Biodiversity 4*(8), 1828–1841.

Kalivas, P. W. (2007). Neurobiology of cocaine addiction: implications for new pharmacotherapy. *American Journal on Addictions, 16*(2), 71–78.

Kleber, H. D., Weiss, R. D., Anton, R. F., Jr, George, T. P., Greenfield, S. F., Kosten, T. R., American Psychiatric Association, et al. (2007). Practice guideline for the treatment of patients with substance use disorders, 2nd ed. *American Journal on Psychiatry, 164*(4 Suppl.), 5–123.

Koesters, S. C., Rogers, P. D., & Rajasingham, C. R. (2002). MDMA ("ecstasy") and other "club drugs": The new epidemic. *Pediatric Clinics of North America, 49*(2), 415–433.

Lichtman, A. H., & Martin, B. R. (2005). Cannabinoid tolerance and dependence. *Handbook of Experimental Pharmacology, 168*, 691–717.

McArdle, P. A. (2006). Cannabis use by children and young people. *Archives of Disease in Childhood, 91*(8), 692–695.

Monitoring the Future Survey. 2005. Available from http://www.monitoringthefuture.org/.

Morris, B. J., Cochran, S. M., & Pratt, J. A. (2005). PCP: from pharmacology to modelling schizophrenia. *Current Opinion in Pharmacology, 5*(1), 101–106.

Nagy, J. (2006). Recent patents on pharmacotherapy for alcoholism. *Recent Patents on CNS Drug Discovery, 1*(2), 175–206.

National Institute on Drug Abuse. Infofacts: Ecstasy. Available from http://www.nida.nih.gov/.

National Institute on Drug Abuse. Infofacts: LSD. Available from http://www.nida.nih.gov/.

Neuspiel, D. R. (2007). Marijuana. *Pediatrics in Review, 28*(4), 156–157.

Nordstrom, B. R., & Levin, F. R. (2007). Treatment of cannabis use disorders: A review of the literature. *American Journal on Addictions, 16*(5), 331–342.

O'Brien, C. P. (2005). Benzodiazepine use, abuse, and dependence. *Journal of Clinical Psychiatry, 66*(Suppl. 2), 28–33.

Preti, A. (2007). New developments in the pharmacotherapy of cocaine abuse. *Addiction Biology, 12*(2), 133–151.

Rimsza, M. E., & Moses, K. S. (2005). Substance abuse on the college campus. *Pediatric Clinics of North America, 52*(1), 307–319.

Satel, S. (2006). Is caffeine addictive?: A review of the literature. *American Journal of Drug and Alcohol Abuse, 32*(4), 493–502.

Saunders, P. A., & Ho, I. K. (1990). Barbiturates and the GABAA receptor complex. *Progress in Drug Research, 34*, 261–286.

Skuza, G., & Wedzony, K. (2004). Behavioral pharmacology of sigma-ligands. *Pharmacopsychiatry, 37*(Suppl. 3), S183–S188.

Smith, D. E., & Landry, M. J. (1990). Benzodiazepine dependency discontinuation: Focus on the chemical dependency detoxification setting and benzodiazepine-polydrug abuse. *Journal of Psychiatric Research, 24*(Suppl. 2), 145–156.

Sofuoglu, M., & Kosten, T. R. (2006). Emerging pharmacological strategies in the fight against cocaine addiction. *Expert Opinion on Emerging Drugs, 11*(1), 91–98.

Stead, L. F., Perera, R., Bullen, C., Mant, D., & Lancaster T. (2008). Nicotine replacement therapy for smoking cessation. *Cochrane Database of Systematic Reviews, 2008*(1), CD000146.

Suh, J. J., Pettinati, H. M., Kampman, K. M., & O'Brien, C. P. (2006). The status of disulfiram: A half of a century later. *Journal of Clinical Psychopharmacology, 26*(3), 290–302.

Vadivelu, N., & Hines, R. L. (2007). Buprenorphine: A unique opioid with broad clinical applications. *Journal of Opioid Management, 3*(1), 49–58.

Vigezzi, P., Guglielmino, L., Marzorati, P., Silenzio, R., De Chiara, M., Corrado, F., et al. (2006). Multimodal drug addiction treatment: A field comparison of methadone and buprenorphine among heroin- and cocaine-dependent patients. *Journal of Substance Abuse Treatment, 31*(1), 3–7.

von Sydow, K., Lieb, R., Pfister, H., Höfler, M., Sonntag, H., & Wittchen, H. U. (2001). The natural course of cannabis use, abuse and dependence over four years: A longitudinal community study of adolescents and young adults. *Drug & Alcohol Dependence, 64*(3), 347–361.

NICHOLAS E. GOEDERS

DYNORPHIN.

Dynorphin is a neuropeptide transmitter; it is an opioid peptide, a member of the endorphin family of peptides. All neurotransmitters like Dynorphin have receptors. Its greatest affinity is for the Kappa opioid receptor. Dynorphin's role in drug abuse was originally anticipated based on its location in anatomical areas strongly associated with the mechanism of action of drugs of abuse. It is localized in the nucleus accumbens, amygdala, and ventral tegmental area.

Dynorphin induces feelings of dysphoria, or despair. This was first documented in animals, and later confirmed in humans. It is surprising because the best known opiate-like drugs are morphine and heroin, and they present great abuse liability since they illicit feelings of euphoria and absence of pain. However, there seem to be two opioid systems controlling behavior, one influencing feelings of reward (through endorphins) and one influencing feelings of aversion (through dynorphin). The physiological substrate underlying the effects of dynorphins is believed to be at the level of the mesolimbic dopamine neurons in the ventral tegmental area. Dynorphin tonically inhibits the firing of dopamine neurons, thus preventing its release in the striatum. Elevations of dopamine levels in the nucleus accumbens are believed to underlie the reinforcing properties of many psychostimulant-like drugs, as well as opiates.

Due to the adverse feeling associated with withdrawal from many drugs of abuse, the dynorphin system has been implicated in contributing to this state. Studies have found that there are long-term changes in dynorphin levels in brain areas associated with drug abuse, and that these changes also exist during withdrawal. Prenatal exposure to cocaine also affects the levels of dynorphin in the brain. These changes are present in both animal and human models of drug abuse. Since drugs modulate dynorphin systems, we can gain an understanding of how drugs work in the brain by studying the dynorphin system.

See also **Amygdala; Neurotransmitters; Nucleus Accumbens; Opiates/Opioids; Receptor, Drug; Ventral Tegmental Area.**

BIBLIOGRAPHY

Levine, B. A. (Ed.). (2007). *Neuropeptide research trends.* New York: Nova Science Publishers.

Lowinson, J. H. (2005). *Substance abuse: A comprehensive textbook.* Philadelphia, PA: Lippincott, Williams & Wilkins.

von Bohlen, O., & Halbach, R. D. (2006). *Neurotransmitters and neuromodulators: Handbook of receptors and biological effects.* Weinheim, Germany: Wiley-VCH.

EASTERN EUROPE. Eastern Europe is comprised of some of the countries of the former Soviet Union (Russian Federation, Ukraine, Belarus, Moldova, and the Baltic nations of Latvia, Lithuania, and Estonia) and its satellites (Poland, Romania, Bulgaria, Czech Republic, Slovakia, Hungary, Albania, and countries formed from the former Yugoslavia: Slovenia, Croatia, Serbia and Montenegro, Bosnia and Herzegovina, and Kosovo). The region is characterized by very high levels of alcohol use and, from the mid-1990s onward in the easternmost nations, by one of the highest rates of illicit injecting drug use in the world. Consequently, by the early twenty-first century, several Eastern European countries had the fastest-expanding HIV epidemics in the world, mostly among and from injecting drug users (also known as IDUs) to their sexual partners.

HISTORY OF SUBSTANCE USE
Alcohol has been used widely in Eastern Europe for several centuries. Large opium plantations existed on the Russian and Ukrainian steppes, and many Polish and Ukrainian villagers grew opium poppies near their homes as ingredients for homemade medicines to relieve pain and ease stomach ailments. The use of both cannabis and opium is believed to predate alcohol use by several millennia. The use of distilled alcohol (such as vodka) probably began in the sixteenth century, with tobacco use introduced in the early seventeenth century. Russia is also one of the leading tea-consuming nations, whereas Poland is the seventh largest consumer (in absolute terms) of coffee in the world.

Alcohol use rates in the easternmost countries of Eastern Europe are among the highest in the world. By 2007 Russia's average annual alcohol consumption had reached 15 liters per person, almost doubling the 2003 figure of 8.9 liters. For comparison, the 2003 statistics for selected other Eastern European nations were Czech Republic, 16.2 liters; Ukraine, 5.2; Belarus, 4.8; and Moldova, 10.2. In 2006, 12 billion liters of alcohol were sold in Russia, of which 75 percent was beer, 16 percent vodka and other hard liquor, 8 percent wine, and 1 percent cognac.

Although tobacco use has declined in many countries since the late twentieth century, it continues to rise in Eastern Europe. In 2004, 41.5 percent of Russians over the age of 15 smoked, compared to, for example, 21 percent of Canadians and 25 percent of Britons. Russia is the fourth largest market (in absolute terms) for tobacco in the world. The nation became an enormous market for transnational tobacco suppliers after a shortage of cigarettes in the early 1990s caused so-called tobacco riots, which led to a relaxation of import restrictions on tobacco products. A 2008 study showed that cigarette prices in Russia were low, making them widely accessible; tax on tobacco products was not keeping pace with inflation; Russia had no policies to restrict smoking in public places; Russian smokers did not have access to counseling or other support services to quit smoking; tobacco product advertising and promotion were not banned in the Russian mass media except for TV; and no functional national tobacco control agency existed in Russia to lead tobacco control efforts.

Despite the fact that imperial Russia bordered on and interacted with opiate- and hashish-using peoples, the abuse of these substances and cocaine was relatively rare. Russian medical literature of the nineteenth and early twentieth centuries barely addressed this topic, in contrast with the plethora of works fulminating against alcoholism and tobacco smoking. Three factors discouraged the abuse of narcotics in tsarist Russia. First, alcohol was the drug of choice. Second, although British and American physicians liberally prescribed opiates in the nineteenth century, Russian medical literature and textbooks for physicians, pharmacists, and paramedics consistently warned against the indiscriminate use of opiates and cocaine. In the late 1890s, shortly after heroin entered therapeutics, Russian physicians stressed that prolonged use could lead to addiction. Physicians also presented popular lectures on the evils of drug abuse. The third factor retarding drug abuse was the nature of Russian pharmacy. Russia lacked a large pharmaceutical industry and, furthermore, the Russian government closely controlled pharmaceutical practice.

The Soviet Union long denied the existence of drug users within its borders. Whereas Soviet medical literature candidly discussed narcotic abuse in the 1920s and early 1930s, from the late 1930s to the 1950s hard data on the number of abusers were scanty. But, by 1990 the number of registered drug addicts was admitted to be approximately 300,000, including 60,000 injecting drug users. These figures were assumed to be underestimates by five to ten times. Even so, during the 1990s the number of registered drug addicts grew 16-fold in the Russian Federation. By 2004 it was estimated that 2 percent of the adult population in the federation had tried opiates (with a 1999 study showing that 6% of 15- to 16-year-olds had tried heroin); 0.8 percent in Ukraine; 0.4 percent in Belarus; and 0.1 percent in Moldova.

Illicit drug use and drug injecting in the early twenty-first century has centered on a variety of opium products and a range of stimulants. Prior to the widespread availability of heroin in the region in the mid- to late 1990s, opium was consumed in liquid preparations known variously as hanka, chornye, or poppy straw. Considerable inter- and intra-country variation existed in the ways that these liquid opiates were prepared but all were most commonly used by injection. A group of injectors would generally meet at one drug user's apartment, combine the necessary ingredients (cook it), prepare and inject the drug, usually drawing several times from a common cup or vial.

The advent of widespread heroin use has reduced the utilization of communal equipment for drug preparation but needle and syringe sharing has continued, leading to massive HIV epidemics among injecting drug users in Russia and Ukraine; significant epidemics in Poland, Belarus, and the Baltic countries; and smaller epidemics in Moldova, Bulgaria, and Romania. In the countries formed from the former Yugoslavia, injecting drug use has played little role so far in HIV epidemics: In these nations, the most common mode of transmission is among men who have sex with men. Similarly, little transmission has occurred among or from drug users in Czech Republic, Slovakia, Hungary, or Albania. The *2006 Report on the Global AIDS Epidemic* released by the Joint United Nations Programme on HIV/AIDS (UNAIDS) reported that 220,000 people were newly infected with HIV in Eastern Europe and Central Asia in 2005, bringing to approximately 1.5 million the number of people living with HIV—representing a 20-fold increase in less than a decade. More than 50,000 adults and children died from the disease that year. Almost all the infections were confined to two countries: Russia and Ukraine.

In addition to opioids, each country in the region appears to have some level of psychostimulant use, including injection. In Russia, a homemade product known as ephedrone or *vint* was widely used in the 1990s, but in the first decade of the twenty-first century this appears to have been replaced mostly by amphetamine and Ecstasy use. In the Czech Republic, methamphetamine or pervitin is very popular. Poland is cited in the *World Drug Report 2007* issued by the United Nations Office on Drugs and Crime (UNODC) as one of the major sources of amphetamine production in Europe. Cocaine use in Eastern Europe is very low. As well as these classes of drugs, a range of other psychoactive drugs is used illicitly. In Moscow, for example, ketamine has been injected extensively by a subculture of street youth. In 2006 the Czech Republic was found to have the highest number of cannabis users in Europe. Czech per capita consumption of marijuana (22% of people aged 15–34 years) was about the same as that in the United States.

STATE POLICIES ON SUBSTANCE USE

Policies regulating drug and alcohol use vary widely across Eastern Europe, as do the methods available for treating drug and alcohol dependence. For licit drugs, a range of controls are in place with subtle variations from country to country. Although laws exist against under-age drinking in Russia, for example, vending machines selling cans of spirits (such as rum or gin) with mixers may be found at many Moscow Metro stations: As these are unsupervised, young people have easy access to alcohol. Alcohol use has been a major issue in Russia since at least the mid-1980s. By that time, the age at which people began to drink had fallen, increasing numbers of women and children were heavy drinkers, and in some cities the average consumption among working adults was a bottle of vodka each day. Newspapers reported that 3.5 percent of the workforce at one chemical plant were confirmed alcoholics, 2.2 percent showed early signs of addiction, and a further 18.8 percent were alcohol abusers, with only 1.4 percent abstainers. It was suggested that the loss of productivity associated with alcohol was the main reason for the Soviet Union's failure to achieve its 5-year plan in the early 1980s, with some estimates suggesting such alcohol-related loss of productivity as high as 20 percent.

The former Soviet Union was home to one of the greatest experiments in alcohol policy in the late twentieth century when the general secretary of the Communist Party, Mikhail Gorbachev, in 1985 introduced a series of measures to reduce alcohol production and sales. These included limiting the kinds of shops permitted to sell alcohol, closing many vodka distilleries and destroying vineyards in the wine-producing republics of Moldavia, Armenia, and Georgia, and banning the sale of alcohol in restaurants before two o'clock in the afternoon. (The policy lasted until 1988.) The results of this policy are still hotly debated, with some claiming a reduction in the number of cases of liver disease and other conditions several years

after the ban, and others pointing to the tens of thousands of Russians who died during the late 1980s from drinking homemade *samargon* (homemade vodka) or various other nonbeverage alcohols made from products such as aftershave lotion and shoe polish. At its height, the number of poisoning deaths was estimated at 40,000 annually and, even in 2006, 28,386 alcohol-linked deaths (mostly as a result of poisoning) were reported, representing 12 percent of all deaths in Russia.

In general, the use of illicit drugs is not criminalized in most nations of the region, although their supply, sale, manufacture, and trafficking are illegal. The possession of illicit drugs for personal use has been a topic of great debate in many Eastern European countries, and laws have changed both toward heavier penalties and criminal sanctions for those found to possess small quantities of drugs, and toward greater liberalization, amounting to de facto decriminalization of the possession of illicit drugs for personal use. In some cases, such as in Russia, Poland, and Bulgaria, both changes have occurred in the space of a few years.

Dependence treatment ranges from sophisticated, evidence-based treatment systems that are beginning to reach high levels of coverage in countries such as the Czech Republic and Slovenia, to very poor treatment systems in the easternmost nations, especially in the Russian Federation, Ukraine, Belarus, and Moldova. In these countries, most drug and alcohol treatment is based on narcological theories developed during the Soviet period. Analyses of narcological methods have shown them to be generally without a solid evidence base and to be implemented often in punitive, jail-like settings. Narcology relies heavily on detoxification as a stand-alone treatment despite international evidence that detoxification alone rarely assists in stopping drug or alcohol dependency.

Virtually all the nations of Eastern Europe allow (and in some cases provide at high coverage levels) opioid substitution treatment (OST) with either methadone or buprenorphine, or both. The exception is the Russian Federation, which has passed a law specifically banning any OST using methadone and as of early 2008 still had not allowed any buprenorphine programs to be implemented. Needle-exchange programs and other programs attempting to reach injecting drug users with HIV prevention education and materials are present in every country in Eastern Europe, although in most locations these activities are delivered at such low coverage levels that HIV epidemics continue to expand or pose the risk of rapid expansion.

See also **European Union; Foreign Policy and Drugs, United States; International Drug Supply Systems; Nordic Countries (Denmark, Finland, Iceland, Norway, and Sweden).**

BIBLIOGRAPHY

Bobrova, N., Rhose, T., Power, R., Alcorn, R., Neifeld, E., Krasiukov, N., et al. (2006). Barriers to accessing drug treatment in Russia: A qualitative study among injecting drug users in two cities. *Drug and Alcohol Dependence, 82*(Suppl.1), S57–S63.

Conroy, M. S. (1990). Abuse of drugs other than alcohol and tobacco in the Soviet Union. *Soviet Studies, 42*(3), 447–480.

Joint United Nations Programme on HIV/AIDS. (2007). *2006 Report on the global AIDS epidemic.* Available from http://www.unaids.org/.

Matic, S., Lazarus, J. V., & Donoghoe, M. C. (Eds.). (2006). *HIV/AIDS in Europe: Moving from death sentence to chronic disease management.* Copenhagen, Denmark: World Health Organization.

Pilkington, H. (2006). "For us it is normal": Exploring the "recreational" use of heroin in Russian youth cultural practice. *Journal of Communist Studies and Transition Politics, 22*(1), 24–53.

United Nations Office on Drugs and Crime. (2007). *World drug report 2007.* Vienna: UNODC.

White, S. (1996). *Russia goes dry. Alcohol, state and society.* Cambridge, UK: Cambridge University Press.

World Health Organization. (2008). *Russian Federation tobacco policy status.* Available from http://www.who.int/.

DAVE BURROWS

EATING DISORDERS. *See* **Anorexia Nervosa; Bulimia Nervosa.**

ECONOMIC COSTS OF ALCOHOL AND DRUG ABUSE. Alcohol and drug

abuse continue to be major health problems in the United States in the twenty-first century. As such, they cost the nation billions of dollars in health-care costs and reduced or lost productivity each year. Since the mid-1980s, researchers have regularly estimated the direct and indirect economic costs of alcohol and drug abuse in the United States. In 1985, alcohol abuse and dependence cost an estimated 70.3 billion dollars, and in 1988 the costs had risen to an estimated 85.8 billion dollars (Rice et al., 1991).

Other estimates on the various costs of substance abuse followed in the 1990s and first decade of the twenty-first century. In 1998, the National Institute on Drug Abuse (NIDA) and the National Institute on Alcohol Abuse and Alcoholism (NIAAA), which are parts of the National Institutes of Health (NIH), released a study on these costs based on 1992 survey data. In 2004 the Substance Abuse and Mental Health Services Administration (SAMHSA) released a report that estimated the cost for treatment of alcohol or drug abuse in outpatient facilities, and a 2008 report by the Johns Hopkins University School of Medicine examined the high rates and rising costs of alcohol and drug disorders in hospitalized patients. A 2004 study by the Office of National Drug Control Policy (ONDCP) estimated the costs of drug abuse between 1998 and 2002.

THE EXTENT OF THE PROBLEM IN 1992
The 1998 reports by NIAAA and NIDA found that the economic cost to society from alcohol and drug abuse was $246 billion in 1992. (Alcohol abuse and alcoholism cost an estimated $148 billion, while drug abuse and dependence cost an estimated $98 billion.) Although the data in the reports is slightly dated, the analytical methods used to assess the economic costs of alcohol abuse shaped later studies of drug abuse and defined the problem for the general public.

The 1992 estimates were 42 percent higher for alcohol than the 1985 estimate, over and above increases due to population growth and inflation. Between 1985 and 1992, inflation accounted for about 37.5 percent of this increase, and population growth accounted for 7.1 percent. Over 80 percent of the increase in estimated costs of alcohol abuse was attributed to changes in data and methodology employed in the new study. This suggests that the previous study significantly underestimated the costs of alcohol abuse.

In 1992, there were an estimated 107,400 alcohol-related deaths in the United States. Many of those who died were between 20 and 40 years of age—mainly because the major causes of death, such as motor vehicle crashes and other causes of traumatic death, are concentrated among this age group. However, alcohol is also involved in numerous premature deaths among the older population because of long-term, excessive alcohol consumption. Total costs attributed to alcohol-related motor vehicle crashes were estimated to be $24.7 billion. This included $11.1 billion from premature mortality and $13.6 billion from automobile and other property destruction.

In 1992 the total estimated spending for health-care services was $18.8 billion for alcohol problems and the medical consequences of alcohol consumption. Specialized services for the treatment of alcohol problems cost $5.6 billion. This included specialized detoxification and rehabilitation services as well as prevention, training, and research expenditures. Costs of treatment for health problems attributed to alcohol were estimated at $13.2 billion.

An estimated $67.7 billion in lost potential productivity was attributed to alcohol abuse in 1992. This accrued in the form of work not performed, including household tasks, and was measured in terms of lost earnings and household productivity. These costs were primarily borne by the alcohol abusers and by those with whom they lived. About $1 billion was for victims of fetal alcohol syndrome who had survived to adulthood and experienced mental impairment. This study did not estimate the burden of drug and alcohol problems on work sites or among employers.

The costs of crime attributed to alcohol abuse were estimated at $19.7 billion. These costs included reduced earnings due to incarceration, crime careers, and criminal victimization, as well as the costs of criminal justice and drug interdiction. Alcohol abuse is estimated to have contributed to 25 to 30 percent of violent crime.

The study estimated that 3.3 percent of social welfare beneficiaries in 1992 received benefits because of an administrative determination of drug- or alcohol-related impairment. While the 1996 federal welfare reform legislation has largely terminated alcohol or drug dependence as a primary cause for benefit eligibility, these impairments resulted in transfers of $10.4 billion in 1992, with administrative and other direct service expenses put at $683 million for those with alcohol problems.

A large amount of the economic burden of alcohol abuse falls on the part of the population that does not abuse alcohol. Governments bore costs of $57.2 billion (38.6 percent of the total) in 1992, compared with $15.1 billion for private insurance, $9 billion for victims, and $66.8 billion for alcohol abusers and members of their households. These costs are imposed on society in a variety of ways, including alcohol-related crimes and trauma (e.g., motor vehicle crashes); government services, such as criminal justice and highway safety; and various social insurance mechanisms, such as private and public health insurance, life insurance, tax payments, pensions, and social welfare insurance.

LATER STUDIES

The 2004 SAMHSA report found that in 2002 it cost an estimated $1,433 for each course of alcohol or drug treatment, while residential treatment cost $3,840 per admission. Outpatient methadone treatment was the most expensive, costing $7,415 per admission in 2002.

The 2008 report by researchers at Johns Hopkins found a high prevalence of hospital admissions for people who were abusing alcohol and drugs (Santora et al., 2008). The 43,000 patients admitted to Johns Hopkins between 1994 and 2002 who were abusing alcohol and drugs accounted for 13.7 percent of all hospital admissions during that time. Overall hospital costs for these patients, adjusted for inflation, increased 134 percent during the 12-year period. Medicaid and Medicare patients accounted for 70 percent of the patients and 70 percent of the costs. In 2002 the cost of caring for these patients was $28 million.

The 2004 study by the ONDCP estimated the economic costs of drug abuse in 2002 to be $180.0 billion. This amount represents both the use of resources to deal with health and crime consequences as well as the loss of potential productivity from disability, death, and withdrawal from the workforce. The study found the costs of drug abuse had increased an average of 5.3 percent a year from 1992 to 2002. This rate was slightly above the 5.1 percent annual growth in the U.S. gross domestic product during this period. Health-care costs accounted for $16 billion of the 2002 amount, while loss of productivity accounted for $128.6 billion. The greatest share of productivity loss was from criminal activities, which included the costs of incarcerating 660,000 offenders who committed crimes to support their drug use. Police protection, federal drug control efforts, and the operation of state and federal prisons were the other major cost components, totaling 36.4 billion in 2002.

The ONDCP study also confirmed that drug abuse is one of the most costly health problems in the United States. These costs are comparable to those for other health issues, including heart disease, cancer, diabetes, Alzheimer's disease, stroke, smoking, obesity, alcohol abuse, and mental illness. Alcohol and drug abuse are costly to the United States in terms of resources used for care and treatment of persons suffering from these disorders, lives lost prematurely, and reduced productivity. Data show clearly that the measurable economic costs of alcohol and drug abuse continue to be high.

See also **Accidents and Injuries from Alcohol; Accidents and Injuries from Drugs; Aging, Drugs, and Alcohol; Alcohol and AIDS; Cancer, Drugs, and Alcohol; Complications: Medical and Behavioral Toxicity Overview; Complications: Cardiovascular System (Alcohol and Cocaine); Complications: Cognition; Complications: Endocrine and Reproductive Systems; Complications: Immunologic; Complications: Liver (Clinical); Complications: Mental Disorders; Complications: Neurological; Complications: Nutritional; Complications: Route of Administration; Crime and Alcohol; Crime and Drugs; Driving, Alcohol, and Drugs; Drug Interactions and Alcohol; Productivity: Effects of Alcohol on; Social Costs of Alcohol and Drug Abuse.**

BIBLIOGRAPHY

American Psychiatric Association. (1987). *Diagnostic and statistical manual of mental disorders* (3rd ed., revised). Washington, DC: Author.

Harwood, H., Fountain, D., & Livermore, G. (1998). *The Economic Costs of Alcohol and Drug Abuse in the United States, 1992.* Bethesda, MD: National Institute on Drug Abuse & National Institute on Alcohol Abuse and Alcoholism. Available from http://www.nida.nih.gov/.

Office of National Drug Control Policy. (2004). *The economic costs of drug abuse in the United States, 1992–2002* (Publication No. 207303). Washington, DC: Executive Office of the President. Available from http://www.whitehousedrugpolicy.gov

Parker, D. A., & Harford, T. C. (1992). The epidemiology of alcohol consumption and dependence across occupations in the United States. *Alcohol Health & Research World, 16*(2), 97–105.

Rice, D. P., Kelman, S., & Miller, L. S. (1991). Estimates of economic costs of alcohol and drug abuse and mental illness, 1985 and 1988. *Public Health Reports, 106*(3), 280–292.

Rice, D. P., Kelman, S., & Miller, L. S. (1991). The economic cost of alcohol abuse. *Alcohol Health & Research World, 15*(4), 307–316.

Santora, P. B., & Hutton, H. E. (2008). Longitudinal trends in hospital admissions with co-occurring alcohol/drug diagnoses, 1994–2002. *Journal of Substance Abuse Treatment, 35*(1), 1–12.

Shultz, J. M., Rice, D. P., & Parker, D. L. (1990). Alcohol-related mortality and years of potential life lost—United States, 1987. *Morbidity and Mortality Weekly Report, 39*(11), 173–178.

Substance Abuse and Mental Health Services Administration, Office of Applied Studies. (2003). *The Alcohol and Drug Services Study (ADSS) Cost Study: Costs of substance abuse treatment in the specialty sector* (Analytic Series A-20, DHHS Publication SMA 03-3762). Rockville, MD: Author.

Williams, G. D., et al. (1987). Demographic trends, alcohol abuse and alcoholism, 1985–1995. *Alcohol Health & Research World, 11*(3), 80–83, 91.

DOROTHY P. RICE
REVISED BY FREDERICK K. GRITTNER (2009)

ED50. The ED50 is the median effective dose—the dose of a drug that is required to produce a specific effect (e.g., relief from headache) in 50 percent of a given population. The ED50 can be estimated from a dose-effect curve, where the dose of the drug is plotted against the percentage of a population in which the drug produces the specified effect. Therefore, if the ED50s for two drugs in producing a specified amount of relief from headache are 5 and 500 milligrams, respectively, then the first drug can be said to be 100 times more potent than the second for the treatment of headaches.

See also **LD50.**

BIBLIOGRAPHY

Hardman, J. G., et al. (Eds.). (1996). *The pharmacological basis of theraupeutics* (9th ed.). New York: McGraw-Hill Medical. (2005, 11th ed.)

Hollinger, M. A. (2003). *Introduction to pharmacology.* Boca Raton, FL: CRC Press.

NICK E. GOEDERS

EDUCATION AND PREVENTION.
See **Prevention, Education and.**

EMPLOYEE ASSISTANCE PROGRAMS (EAPS).
An Employee Assistance Program (EAP) consists of employer-sponsored services intended to aid employees with personal problems that may adversely affect their job performance. Initially developed to address alcohol-related problems, over the last fifteen years EAPs have emerged as a common response to the problems of alcohol and drug abuse in the workplace. In addition, they provide a variety of services to help employees and their families resolve health, emotional, marital, family, financial, or legal concerns.

While the exact mix of services provided depends on a number of variables, such as size and type of company, EAPs generally offer, at a minimum, confidential client counseling, problem assessment, and treatment referral. A comprehensive EAP offers

1. assessment and referral—EAPs conduct psychosocial assessments to guide decisions to refer clients to treatment and the choice among treatment alternatives

2. treatment follow-up—client follow-up and reintegration into the workplace is an essential EAP function

3. supervisor, management, and union representative training—training provides the information needed on how and when to use the program and how to best assist employees who use it

4. employee education—information on a broad range of problems and how to use the EAP.

The delivery of EAP services may take several forms, depending on such factors as the organization's size and structure. Large companies and organizations, unions, and employee groups often operate their own programs. These services are most often housed within the human resources or medical departments. Smaller organizations, or organizations with dispersed worksites may find it more advantageous to contract with an independent EAP provider located outside the company. A newer trend among small employers is the development of consortium EAP arrangements in which a number of small employers contract with an external provider to provide EAP services.

In the past 30 years, the number of EAPs has grown dramatically. A 2008 National Study of Employers found that the percentage of employers providing EAPs rose to 65 percent in 2008 from 56 percent in 1998. The Department of Labor's Bureau of Labor Statistics found that of those employers sampled the probability of an establishment offering EAP services increased as a function of establishment size, ranging from 79 percent of employers with over 250 employees, to 9 percent of employers with fewer than 50 employees.

Rapid growth in the number of EAP programs has led to heightened scrutiny concerning their cost effectiveness; in the current economic climate, EAP programs will experience increased pressure to conduct evaluation studies that provide empirical evidence of their efficacy. More research is needed to identify and improve the most essential program components and to aid in tailoring programs to fit specific needs.

Costs incurred in providing EAP services vary widely, but their presence has been clearly tied to overall savings in a number of areas. As of 2000, the Employee Assistance Program Association found that EAPs reduce lost time by 30 percent, reduce accident and sick pay by 60 percent, and reduce accidents by 70 percent.

For many companies, the approach taken to minimize the impact of drugs in the workplace incorporates a number of additional elements that complement EAPs and constitute a comprehensive strategy. These include a clearly stated formal policy prohibiting drug use, consequences for violating the policy, and alternative strategies to deter drug use.

The Employee Assistance Professionals Association may be consulted for further information: Suite 1001, 4601 North Fairfax Drive, Arlington, VA 22203, http://www.eapassn.org.

See also **Drug Testing Methods and Clinical Interpretations of Test Results; Industry and Workplace, Drug Use in; Military, Drug and Alcohol Abuse in the United States; Productivity: Effects of Alcohol on; Productivity: Effects of Drugs on.**

BIBLIOGRAPHY

Chan, K. K., Neighbors, C., & Marlatt, G. A. (2004). Treating addictive behaviors in the employee assistance program: Implications for brief interventions. *Addictive Behaviors, 29*, 9, 1883–1887.

Hayghe, H. V. (1991). Anti-drug programs in the workplace: Are they here to stay? *Monthly Labor Review, 114* 4, 26–29.

McClure, D. C. (2004). Employee assistance program strategies. In J. C. Thomas & M. Hersen (Eds.), *Psychopathology in the workplace: Recognition and adaptation*. London: Routledge.

STEVEN W. GUST

ENDORPHINS. Endorphins are a group of peptides with potent analgesic properties that occur naturally in the brain. The word *endorphin* is a contraction for the words *end*ogenous and *morphine*; it was coined by narcotics researchers in 1975 as the preferred term for a then hypothetical natural substance capable of action at receptors for opiates (such as heroin). The underlying hypothesis was that an endorphin neurotransmitter utilized the receptors at which morphine and related drugs exerted their actions. After extensive and intensely competitive research by many groups, three distinct types of such endogenous opioid peptides were found (*peptides* are segments of linked amino acids that can act as neurotransmitters). By 2008, additional peptides able to act at opioid receptors as well as to regulate pain sensitivity through nonopioid receptors had been identified.

Each type of opioid peptide gives rise to one or more opioid peptide prohormones, which are then modified by enzymes in tissues to convert the larger inactive peptides into smaller active ones. For example, the pro-opiomelanocortin prohormone is synthesized in the corticotropes in the anterior pituitary gland and separately in hypothalmic and medullary neurons. It is cleaved in those cells to β- endorphin, a 31 amino-acid peptide with the greatest intrinsic opioid activity. Each active natural opioid peptide contains the tetrapeptide tyrosine-glycineglycine-phenylalanine at its amino terminus. The fifth amino acid is either methionine (resulting in the so-called Met^5 enkephalin) or leucine (resulting in leu-enkephalin). Opioid peptides derived from plants—for example, caseimorphin— have also been described. The opioid peptides, of which the proenkephalin- and prodynorphin-derived peptides are most widespread, are found in specific neurons in the brain.

See also **Enkephalin; Opiates/Opioids.**

BIBLIOGRAPHY

Bear, M. F., Connors, B. W., & Paradiso, M. A. (2006). *Neuroscience: Exploring the brain*. Philadelphia, PA: Lippincott Williams & Wilkins.

Cooper, J. R., Bloom, F. E., & Roth, R. H. (1996). *The biochemical basis of neuropharmacology* (7th ed.). New York: Oxford University Press USA. (2002, 8th ed.)

FLOYD BLOOM

ENKEPHALIN. Enkephalin is either of two pentapeptides (containing five amino acids) with opiate and analgesic (painkilling) activity, occurring naturally in the brain, with a marked affinity for opiate receptors. Endorphin was initially the name for all opioid-like neurotransmitters in the brain; the research team of Hans Kosterlitz and John Hughes gave their own name, enkephalin (a variant of *en-cephal* ["of the brain"]), to the two opioid pentapeptides that they had purified from ox brains (ca. 1977). They confirmed their discovery by showing that the effects of synthetic peptides were the same in bioassays using opiate receptors and that both Met5enkephalin and Leu$_5$enkephalin were authentic endogenous opioid peptides.

See also **Opiates/Opioids.**

BIBLIOGRAPHY

Bear, M. F., Connors, B. W., & Paradiso, M. A. (2006). *Neuroscience: Exploring the brain.* Philadelphia, PA: Lippincott Williams & Wilkins.

Cooper, J. R., Bloom, F. E., & Roth, R. H. (1996). *The biochemical basis of neuropharmacology* (7th ed.). New York: Oxford University Press USA. (2002, 8th ed.)

FLOYD BLOOM

EPIDEMICS OF DRUG ABUSE IN THE UNITED STATES.

James Anthony defined an epidemic as

an unusual occurrence of an infection, disease, or other health hazard in a population. ... If the number of cases occurring in the population this month (or year) is notably greater than the number of cases that occurred in the population during each of the prior months (or years), then it is legitimate to talk of a growing epidemic. (2001, p. 487)

Epidemics of substance use may look very different depending on whether they are analyzed by substance type (tobacco, alcohol, cocaine, heroin, etc.), by geographic area, by demographic group, or by some criterion other than a national overview. A nationwide look at prevalence rates of marijuana or cocaine consumption may present a picture that does not reflect trends among, for example, inner city minority populations, or people of a specific age group, or residents of a particular city. The focus of this article is one of social history; it regards drug epidemics as large-scale cultural phenomena that reflect shifts in values or perspectives among significant portions of the population. Readers may wish to consult the entry on Epidemiology of Drug Abuse for a detailed look at how epidemiologists study national drug trends and some results from recent surveys of drug use and abuse.

A fundamental question in studying the social and cultural significance of substance-use epidemics over time is how to know what drives increases and decreases in overall consumption. Why is it that some types of drugs like heroin and cocaine appear to be repeatedly involved in successive epidemics? Social demographer K. Singh reasoned that, as the number of people aged 15 to 25 in the population declined, this by itself would change the balance of susceptibility to drug use (Anthony, 2001). Thus an epidemic in the use of a drug most attractive to youth would decline over time simply because their number in the population decreased. The underlying etiology may be that a susceptible age cohort (study group) is most likely to experiment with a substance from a prior epidemic that is perceived to be safe because memories of its effects disappear from society or are disregarded as antiquated. This group of new users then becomes the foundation population for a repeat epidemic that evolves over time until the age group learns from its own experience what previous generations had also learned, or simply outgrows the desire to use drugs (ages out). To be sure, this decline is not a specific event, and some portions of the population form the vanguard while others lag behind.

Lana Harrison, citing Eric Wish, pointed out that drug use patterns and trends among arrestees may be very different from those observed in the general population. Given the general picture of deviance among arrestees, it is possible to conclude that they use illegal drugs first as the substances become available, but realize the harms of drug use later than members of mainstream society and are more likely to resist pressures to abstain (Harrison, 1992). For these reasons, certain drugs may persist in more deviant groups even after they have been abandoned by the general population.

Significantly, the U.S. Census Bureau reported that the percentage of the population in the age group most susceptible to drug use, youths ages 15 to 25, hovered just under 20 percent from 1900 to 1910—the highest percentage of the twentieth century and coincident with high rates of alcohol and drug use. This age group rose from a low of about 13 percent to just over 19 percent between 1955 and 1975 and began another precipitous decline in 1980, again coinciding to some extent with falling levels of substance use. (Baby boomers were in their teens in the early 1960s, when marijuana became popular. They reached their 30s in the 1980s as drugs in general, and particularly cocaine, began to be seen as dangerous and undesirable.)

Although there were many attempts to estimate the number of addicts in the United States beginning in the 1920s, it was not until the early 1970s that the federal government supported systematic surveys to gauge the extent of the problem. The National Household Survey of Drug Abuse, now called the National Survey on Drug Abuse and Health (NSDAH), the Drug Abuse Warning Network (DAWN), the Monitoring the Future Survey, and Arrestee Drug Abuse Monitoring Program (ADAM) are discussed in separate entries in this work.

U.S. DRUG EPIDEMICS

What appear to be successive *waves* or cycles of substance use, followed by periods of reform have been studied by a number of scholars, particularly David F. Musto, David Courtwright, and Ruth Engs. Following is a chronological outline of these periods and a discussion of trends in acceptance and rejection of substances.

1865–1920—The First Epidemic. With the exception of the extremely high levels of alcohol use in colonial America and the early republic (Rorabaugh, 1979), the first epidemic of psychoactive substance abuse in the United States occurred in the second half of the nineteenth century and reached a peak in the first decade of the twentieth (when, as noted, the proportion of young people in the population was very high). Civil War veterans had become habituated to morphine through medical treatment, and large numbers of middle class women became addicted to opiate-based substances, either through doctors' prescriptions or self-medication with unregulated patent medicines.

The German pharmaceutical company Bayer introduced heroin in 1898 as a cough remedy, and it quickly became the drug of choice among young male slum dwellers and petty criminals. Opium dens in larger cities were frequented by prostitutes, pimps, and other marginal types as well as thrill-seeking socialites. Soft drinks and enhanced wines contained coca, and refined cocaine hydrochloride was available on the black market and in over-the-counter products such as inhalers for nasal congestion. David Courtwright reported that more than half the prostitutes in the Fort Worth, Texas, jail in 1900 were cocaine addicts.

Per capita ethanol consumption in the United States among people over the age of 14 ranged from a high of 2.6 gallons a year between 1906 and 1910 to 1.96 gallons just before National Prohibition was enacted in 1920. (By way of comparison, the years between 1935 and 1944 showed consumption well below two gallons, and below one gallon in 1934) (National Center for Health Statistics, 2006).

The excesses of the age inspired passionate reformist sentiments that found expression in temperance movements and drives for government regulation of food and medicine. These campaigns were instrumental in securing passage of federal legislation controlling commerce and consumption of psychoactive substances: the Pure Food and Drug Act of 1906, the Opium Exclusion Act of 1909, the Harrison Anti-Narcotics Act of 1914, and last but not least, the Nineteenth Amendment to the Constitution prohibiting "manufacture, sale, or transportation of intoxicating liquors," which became law in 1920.

1920–1960. Early in the twentieth century, about the same time that the International Opium Convention, the first international treaty on drug control, was signed at The Hague (January 23, 1912), the United States experienced an increase in tobacco smoking, with peak population levels of smokers occurring during World War II and the following two decades.

When one considers the social climate of the early twenty-first century, a time when tobacco smoking is not a socially approved drug-use practice, it may be difficult to imagine that, during World War II, Lucky Strikes and other cigarettes were passed out to soldiers as part of their daily food rations. This turned out to be an effective way to sustain the epidemic of tobacco smoking, but one cannot be sure whether the tobacco industry's intent was primarily to boost the morale of soldiers or to create and build market strength for tobacco cigarettes (Anthony, 2001)

From 1920 through the early 1960s, cocaine, heroin, and marijuana use in the United States was unusual outside of relatively small circles of entertainment stars, jazz musicians, and others who came into contact with illicit suppliers of drugs. The Marihuana Tax Act of 1937 succeeded in placating popular fears of the corrupting influence of alien minorities (mostly supposed to be Mexican) rather than responding to a documented increase in use. The Act served both to address a perceived threat and to demonstrate that H. J. Anslinger's Federal Bureau of Narcotics had the situation under control (Musto, 1987).

Alcohol use began a slow rise after repeal of Prohibition but did not reach new highs until 1970. In the early 1970s, when the federal government began supporting a series of national and state surveys of illicit drug use, cocaine use was found so rarely that it was difficult to get a reliable impression of the characteristics of the cocaine users—there were too few of them in the national survey samples. This was a period of low levels of drug use in all sectors of society and of enthusiasm for harsh penalties for drug trafficking and possession (the Boggs Act of 1951 and the Boggs-Daniels Act of 1956).

Retrospective data analyzed in the National Survey on Drug Abuse in 1977 indicated that lifetime experience with any illicit drug did not exceed 2 percent of the general population in the early 1960s. Marijuana use among young males and some ethnic minorities was estimated at approximately 5 percent. Then the spirit of the times changed. The reason may have been demographic, economic, political, or some combination of these forces, but the result was a period of extreme social stress in the United States.

1960–1980—The Second Epidemic. In the late 1960s and early 1970s, the middle class enjoyed unparalleled economic prosperity that permitted its sons and daughters long periods of intellectual and leisure activity. These young people, who as noted were becoming an ever-larger proportion of the population, adopted political positions and lifestyles at odds with the values of the preceding generation. In large numbers they took up the causes of civil rights, opposition to the war in Vietnam, and—what they saw as their right—use of mood-altering substances of various kinds. Thus, a process analogous to the large-scale violation of alcohol prohibition laws was set in motion: As a proscribed activity is adopted by some members of the middle class, the laws that apply to that behavior are increasingly questioned. The National Commission on Marijuana and Drug Abuse reported in 1972 that 83 percent of the adults surveyed and 65 percent of the youth would not incarcerate a youthful first offender; 54 percent

of the adults and 41 percent of the youth were opposed to imposing a police record on young offenders. By this time, drug policymaking reflected both the scientific and popular opinion that treatment should be the focus of drug policy, that severe penalties were counterproductive, and that abuse was a product of environment and could be controlled by manipulation of the external circumstances of the user. In spite of President Richard M. Nixon's declaration of "war on drugs" in 1971, his administration saw a large increase in budget allocations for treatment programs and the first large-scale implementation of methadone maintenance for heroin addicts. As part of this effort, the president established the Special Action Office for Drug Abuse Prevention (SAODAP) with Jerome Jaffe as its head.

In part, these policies were motivated by the return of Vietnam veterans, many of whom had become users of heroin and other opioid drugs during their overseas tours of duty. This surge in heroin use in the late 1960s and early 1970s was documented most readily by examining statistics on clients entering treatment for heroin dependence, including the lag of several years that separated users' initial injection of heroin to their first admission for treatment. Despite the war on drugs, another smaller increase in heroin use or dependence occurred during the mid-1970s, followed by apparent decreases in the occurrence of heroin dependence during the late 1970s and early 1980s. The early decrease appears to have coincided with the decrease in importation of heroin to the United States from supplier countries such as Turkey, and the mid-1970s increase with the emergence of Mexico and Southeast Asia as suppliers of illicit opiates.

The only drug-taking behavior that decreased during this period was tobacco smoking. The 1962 Surgeon Generals Report on Smoking and Health added new urgency to publicity campaigns about the health hazards of smoking. Per capita cigarette consumption did not decline significantly until the late 1970s, when that figure stood at under 4,000 cigarettes per year according to the American Lung Association (2004). After that, the number decreased steadily. While it is difficult to determine if social opprobrium was the primary factor in this trend, it is certainly true that smoking has become socially unacceptable among large segments of the population, and controlling legislation is popular in spite of protests from civil libertarians. It is ironic that a trend toward strict regulation of tobacco smoking began as efforts to decriminalize marijuana were gathering support.

Alcohol consumption also rose during this period to exceed levels registered at the beginning of the twentieth century. A high of 2.76 gallons per capita was recorded for 1980 and 1981. After that, consumption rates declined until 1998, when levels were reported at 2.14 gallons. Rates have increased somewhat since then (National Center for Health Statistics, 2006).

1980–1990. During the last years of the administration of President Jimmy Carter (1977–1981), parents of young teenagers complained that government leaders were promoting an attitude of accommodation to recreational drugs that was contributing to widespread use among their children. Carter endorsed decriminalization of marijuana in 1976, and his health adviser and drug czar was widely quoted as believing that cocaine was relatively benign. But rejection of these positions gradually took hold, at least among middle-class citizens. The period from 1978 to 1985 may be seen as a transition during which people in favor of moralistic and legalistic approaches to drug control struggled to gain political leverage, first over marijuana use among their own rebellious children, and later against the image of cocaine as the glamorous high of the media celebrity or hot-shot businessperson.

There may be a parallel between the story of cocaine and that of heroin. Heroin, the effects of which were initially hailed after it was first produced in 1898, later proved so devastating that by 1924 it was entirely rejected by the medical establishment, new manufacture was outlawed by Congress, and it became emblematic of degradation and marginalization. It never really emerged from this literal and figurative ghettoization. When it did appear among middle-class youth in the 1970s, it caused generalized consternation, and middle-class use, while an epidemic in the sense of an unusual and measurable increase, was relatively limited. In 1972 the National Household Survey on Drug Abuse reported that the rate of lifetime heroin use among young adults was 4.6 percent with current

use below measurable levels. Mainstream society had not forgotten that heroin was a dangerous and frightening drug—all the more so for its association with suspect urban subcultures and a mode of administration, intravenous injection, not likely to appeal to casual experimenters.

In the case of cocaine, it had been possible for middle-class drug users to forget or ignore the lessons that medical practitioners, social activists, and drug users themselves had learned between the late nineteenth century and the 1920s. Unlike heroin, cocaine had not remained a presence at the margins of middle-class experience and, when it emerged in the early 1970s, it seemed entirely new. Current (past month) use among young adults reached 9.3 percent in 1979. But as attitudes changed and experience grew, rates began a slow decline. Current use was down to 6.8 percent in 1982, 7.6 percent in 1985, and 4.5 percent in 1988. In the late 1980s, as middle-class cocaine use was already on the wane, crack, a new smokeable form of cocaine, appeared and quickly became a feature of life in urban areas populated by the minority poor, thereby effectively relegating cocaine to the list of "bad" drugs along with heroin.

While self-report surveys of the general population were showing declines in cocaine use, a new program, the Drug Use Forecasting program (DUF, now called ADAM) was showing a growing problem among arrestees. Urine tests obtained from samples of arrestees in booking facilities across the United States showed that 80 percent or more of arrestees, regardless of charge, tested positive for cocaine as well as other drugs. These findings alerted the nation to the extreme drug problems in offenders and led to new treatment and drug court programs to address this population. Even by the early twenty-first century, when levels of cocaine use declined markedly in the general population as the crack epidemic waned, a sizable minority of arrestees in the largest cities of the country still tested positive for cocaine and other illegal drugs.

A somewhat odd drug-taking fashion appeared between the mid-1980s and the early 1990s, mostly among adolescent males—smokeless tobacco (Nelson et al., 2006). This phenomenon has been traced to deliberate marketing strategies, including formulation of relatively low-cost, "unit dose" supplies of tobacco snuff that were flavored to increase palatability (Anthony, 2001).

The major drug surveys measure changing perceptions of the dangers of given substances among the selected responding populations, and increases in perception of risk are correlated to declines in use. Some specific events have been tied to increases in perceptions of risk, but other factors make the social environment more or less receptive to the lessons of these events. The drug-related deaths of Jimi Hendrix and Janis Joplin in the fall of 1970 had little impact on attitudes toward drug taking, while those of Don Rogers and Len Bias from the effects of cocaine in 1986 elicited a public response.

1991 to the Early Twenty-first Century. By the mid-1990s, multiple indications showed that the nation was in the end-stages of its second major drug epidemic. The peak years of the epidemic seem to have been in the early-to-mid-1980s. Past-month cocaine use in the general population over 12 years of age stayed below 1 percent throughout the decade of the 1990s, according to the National Household Survey on Drug Abuse (now called the National Survey on Drug Use and Health). That measure increased to one percent in 2003, decreased to 0.8 percent in 2004, and returned to one percent again in 2005 and 2006. The Monitoring the Future Survey reported past-month cocaine use among young adults aged 19 to 28 below two percent from 1992 through 2000, then a slight up-tick to 2.4 percent in 2003. Trends in annual prevalence in use of any illicit drug other than marijuana among all age groups reported in this survey show a peak in 1981 and relative stability after 1993, with some increases among young adults between the ages of 19 and 24. (People aged 21 to 22 reported an annual use rate of 22 percent in 2006—higher than the 13.5 percent recorded in 1993 but well below the 1981 level of 37 percent.)

With respect to smoking, the American Lung Association reports that adults consumed fewer than 2,000 cigarettes per capita in 2003. The percentage of American adults who were current smokers had declined to 22.5 percent in 2002, again according to the American Lung Association. The National Survey on Drug Use and Health puts the 2002 figure at 26 percent and 25 percent in

2006. The smokeless tobacco vogue, principally among adolescent males, had plummeted by nearly 50 percent by 2006 (Nelson et al., 2006).

As the use of cocaine and heroin declined in the general populations, other drugs took their place. Methamphetamine abuse has been reported in many states, especially in the west and southwestern parts of the United States. Spikes in use have been found from time to time in MDMA (Ecstasy) and marijuana by youths and in the misuse of prescription drugs. Stimulants are being shared by ADHD patients with their college peers. Increases in the use of prescription analgesics, including methadone, buprenorphine, and oxycodone, are showing up in surveys and in death statistics from medical examiners. The history of drug epidemics is consistent with the view that peoples' appetites for psychoactive drugs persist, while perceptions of risk and rates of use vary, and that the specific drugs of abuse change over time with each new generation.

See also **Anslinger, Harry Jacob, and U.S. Drug Policy; Arrestee Drug Abuse Monitoring (ADAM and ADAM II); Cocaine; Cola/Cola Drinks; Drug Abuse Warning Network (DAWN); Epidemiology of Drug Abuse; Harrison Narcotics Act of 1914; Heroin; International Control Policies; International Drug Supply Systems; Marijuana (Cannabis); MDMA; Methadone Maintenance Programs; Methamphetamine; Mexico; Monitoring the Future; Morphine; National Survey on Drug Use and Health (NSDUH); Opiates/Opioids; Oxycodone; Parent Movement, The; Prescription Drug Abuse; Prohibition of Alcohol; Psychoactive; Temperance Movement; Tobacco: Smokeless; U.S. Government Agencies: Special Action Office for Drug Abuse Prevention (SAODAP); Vietnam War: Drug Use in U.S. Military.**

BIBLIOGRAPHY

American Lung Association. (2004, November). *Trends in tobacco use.* Available from http://www.lungusa.org/.

Anthony, J. C. (1992). Epidemiological research on cocaine use in the U.S.A. In *Cocaine: Scientific and social dimensions.* Proceedings of the CIBA Foundation Symposium 166. Chichester, England: Wiley.

Anthony, J. C. (2001). Epidemics of drug abuse. *Encyclopedia of Drugs, Alcohol and Addictive Behaviors.* (2nd ed., pp. 487–494). Farmington Hills, MI: Macmillan Reference USA.

Bejerot, N. (1970). *Addiction and society.* Springfield, IL: Charles C. Thomas.

Courtwright, D. (2001). *Forces of habit: Drugs and the making of the modern world*. Cambridge, MA: Harvard University Press.

De Alarcon, R. (1969). The spread of heroin abuse in a community. *Bulletin on Narcotics, 21*, 17–22.

Ellinwood, E. H. (1974). The epidemiology of stimulant abuse. In E. Josephson & E. E. Carroll (Eds.), *Drug use: Epidemiological and sociological approaches*. Washington, DC: Halsted Press/Wiley.

Engs, R. C. (2000) *Clean living movements: American cycles of health reform*. Westport, CT: Praeger Publishers.

Harrison, L. D. (1992) Trends in illicit drug use in the United States; Conflicting results from national surveys. *International Journal of the Addictions, 27*(7), 817–847.

Helmer, J., & Vietorisz, T. (1974). *Drug use, the labor market, and class conflict*. Washington, DC: The Drug Abuse Council.

Hughes, P. H., & Crawford, G. A. (1974). Epidemiology of heroin addiction in the 1970s: New opportunities and responsibilities. In E. Josephson & E. E. Carroll (Eds.), *Drug use: Epidemiological and sociological approaches*. Washington, DC: Halsted Press/Wiley.

Hughes, P. H., & Jaffe, J. H. (1971). The heroin copping area: A location for epidemiologic study and intervention activity. *Archives of General Psychiatry, 24*, 394–400.

Johnston, L. D. (1991). Toward a theory of drug epidemics. In R. Donohew, H. Sypher, & W. Bukoski (Eds.), *Persuasive communication and drug abuse prevention*. Hillsdale, NJ: Erlbaum.

Musto, D. F. (1987). *The American disease: Origins of narcotic control*. (2nd ed.). New York: Oxford University Press.

Musto, D. F., & Korsmeyer, P. (2002). *The quest for drug control: Politics and federal policy in a period of increasing substance abuse, 1963–1981*. New Haven, CT: Yale University Press.

National Center for Health Statistics, Centers for Disease Control (2006). *Health, United States*. Available from http://www.cdc.gov/.

Nelson, D. E., Mowery, P., Tomar, S., Marcus, S., Giovino, G., & Zhao, L. (2006, May). Trends in smokeless tobacco use among adults and adolescents in the United States. *American Journal of Public Health, 96*(5), 897–905.

Rorabaugh, W. J. (1979). *The alcoholic republic: An American tradition*. New York: Oxford University Press.

Singh, K. (1995). Unpublished communication, presented and discussed in S. B. Sells (1977), Reflections on the epidemiology of heroin and narcotic addiction from the perspective of treatment data. In J. Rittenhouse (Ed.), *The epidemiology of heroin and other narcotics*. Washington, DC: U.S. Government Printing Office.

PAMELA KORSMEYER
ERIC WISH

EPIDEMIOLOGY OF ALCOHOL USE DISORDERS.

Epidemiology is the study of the distribution and determinants of health outcomes in a population. *Distribution* refers to the incidence and prevalence of health outcomes in the population as a whole or within subgroups of the population, as well as to trends over time in health outcomes. *Determinants* are factors that predict an increased risk for the onset or persistence of health outcomes. Unlike other branches of medicine, epidemiology focuses on factors affecting disease in a particular population or larger community. A "population of interest" may be a group defined by age, sex, or race and ethnicity, or it may be groups of patients in treatment facilities. A "community of interest" may comprise household residents in a particular geographic area.

Of concern here is the epidemiology of alcohol abuse and dependence (referred to together as "alcohol use disorders"). The definition of alcohol use disorders used throughout will refer to the *DSM-IV* definitions of the disorders. First, information on historical trends in alcohol consumption will be reviewed. As alcohol consumption is a necessary, but not sufficient, cause of alcohol abuse and dependence, the study of alcohol consumption can provide clues about trends in abuse and dependence in time periods for which diagnostic information is unavailable. Second, the design and results of major U.S. surveys in which the prevalence of alcohol abuse and dependence has been estimated will be analyzed. Third, the course of alcohol disorders will be examined by looking at onset, duration, recovery, and treatment rates. Finally, there will be an overview of major risk factors for alcohol abuse and dependence.

HISTORICAL TRENDS IN ALCOHOL CONSUMPTION

Long-term historical information on U.S. alcohol consumption is available through per capita alcohol consumption statistics derived from sales figures. These statistics do not reflect the prevalence of

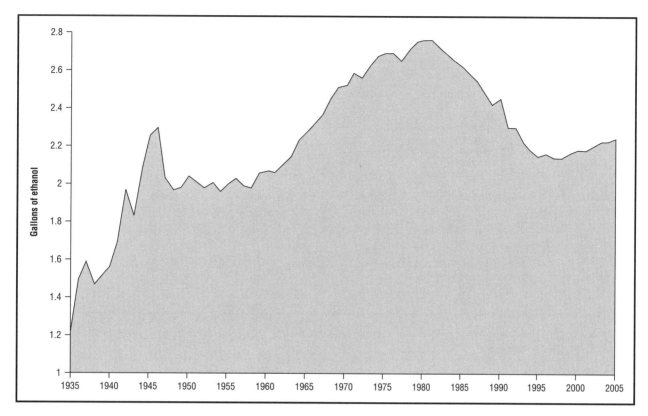

Figure 1. Total per capita ethanol consumption, United States, 1935–2005. (Source: Lakins et al., 2007.) ILLUSTRATION BY GGS INFORMATION SERVICES. GALE, CENGAGE LEARNING

alcohol use disorders, but the statistics do provide information from the 1700s to the present on alcohol consumption, a necessary condition for the development of alcohol dependence or abuse. However, these statistics only reflect alcohol sales, not the totality of alcohol consumption (especially during the period of Prohibition). Despite this limitation, studies of long-term trends in alcohol sales provide a historical picture of alcohol consumption in the United States, and this can give valuable clues regarding trends in alcohol abuse and dependence before specific diagnostic criteria were established.

These figures show drinking levels in the U.S. varied greatly over time (Lender & Martin, 1982). Per capita consumption levels ranged from extraordinarily high levels during the U.S. colonial period (from an estimated 5.8 gallons per year per capita in 1790 to 7.1 gallons in 1830) to very low levels before and during Prohibition, which began in 1919 (from an estimated 1.96 gallons in 1916 to 0.97 gallons in 1934). Levels were high during the colonial era because water supplies were unsafe, so

that even children drank alcohol. Figure 1 shows the estimated per capita alcohol consumption from the end of Prohibition in 1933 through 2005. From 1935 until 1982, per capita alcohol consumption increased steadily to a peak of nearly 2.8 gallons of ethanol per year in 1982 (Lakins et al., 2007). Since then, consumption has declined, leveling off at about 2.2 gallons of ethanol per year in 1993, and remaining at around that level until 2005, with a slight increase from 1999 to 2005. These data are generally consistent with liver cirrhosis mortality statistics, which show similar variations over time (Yoon et al., 2006).

Surveys are another source of alcohol consumption information. These surveys ask a representative sample of individuals to self-report on alcohol consumption. The advantage of surveys over alcohol sales data is that subgroup variations in alcohol consumption can be examined. The main disadvantages are that yearly information is often not available and individuals can underreport their alcohol consumption. Several national alcohol surveys have focused on direct questions about

Feature	ECA	NCS	NLAES	NCS-R	NESARC
Sponsoring institution	NIMH	NIMH	NIAAA	WHO	NIAAA
Years of data collection	1980–1984	1990–1992	1991–1992	2001–2003	2001–2002
Sample size	20,219	8,098	42,862	9,282	43,098
Response rate (approximate)	77.60%	82.60%	89.20%	70.90%	81.00%
Sample	5 U.S. communities	U.S. general population	U.S. general population	U.S. general population	U.S. general population
Sampling method	Probability, block sampling and oversampling in some sites	Probability	Probability, oversampling for minorities and young adults	Probability	Probability, oversampling for minorities and young adults
Individuals surveyed	Household + institutional residents	Household and college residents	Household residents	Household and college residents	Household and group quarters residents
Age range	18 and older	15–54	18 and older	18 and older	18 and older
Field work conducted by:	Independent academic researchers at the five sites	Survey Research Institute, University of Michigan	U.S. Bureau of the Census	Survey Research Institute, University of Michigan	U.S. Bureau of the Census
Follow-up component	1-year follow-up at all sites (N=10,167), ongoing 13-year follow-up at the Baltimore site	10-year follow-up (N=4,375)	None	None	1-year follow-up, N=34,653

Table 1. Design features of the five U.S. third-generation psychiatric epidemiological studies. ILLUSTRATION BY GGS INFORMATION SERVICES. GALE, CENGAGE LEARNING

consumption and nondiagnostic scales of alcohol-related problems. Conjoint analysis of several of these surveys showed that the lifetime and current prevalence of multiple alcohol-related problems increased in the U.S. general population from 1967 to 1984 (Hasin et al., 1990), but decreased from 1985 to 1995 (Greenfield et al., 2000; Hilton, 1987). The consistency of these findings lends credence to both sales-based and survey data.

PSYCHIATRIC EPIDEMIOLOGIC SURVEYS: AN OVERVIEW

Unlike alcohol consumption, which in itself is not a disorder, alcohol abuse and dependence are specific diagnoses defined by the *Diagnostic and Statistical Manual of Mental Disorders, Fourth Edition* (*DSM-IV*). The *DSM-IV* stipulates that individuals must exhibit a maladaptive pattern of alcohol consumption accompanied by specific criteria. Most available information on the prevalence of alcohol use disorders in the general U.S. population comes from large-scale psychiatric epidemiologic surveys conducted after the 1970s. Prior to the 1970s, large-scale epidemiologic studies did not address alcohol use disorders and generally used a very different methodology. In the mid- and late-1970s, diagnostic methods in psychiatry changed, allowing the use of specific diagnostic criteria for disorders including alcohol use disorders (Spitzer

et al., 1978). This advance in methodology led to five major large-scale psychiatric epidemiologic studies based on specific diagnostic criteria: the Epidemiologic Catchment Area Survey (ECA), the National Comorbidity Survey (NCS), the National Longitudinal Alcohol Epidemiological Survey (NLAES), the National Comorbidity Study Replication (NCS-R), and the National Epidemiologic Survey on Alcohol and Related Conditions (NESARC). Table 1 shows numerous features of each study.

PSYCHIATRIC EPIDEMIOLOGIC SURVEYS: DESCRIPTIONS OF EACH STUDY

In these surveys, large sample sizes and a wide geographic distribution of data collection has precluded the use of clinicians as interviewers. Therefore, structured diagnostic interviews were developed that could be administered by nonclinicians to collect data on symptoms and criteria of psychiatric disorders, including alcohol use disorders. Table 2 shows the diagnostic assessment procedures used in the five studies. Each interview form has distinctive structural features, and some, such as the NCS-R, appear to have influenced the rates of alcohol dependence obtained.

Epidemiologic Catchment Area Study (ECA).
The ECA, the earliest of the three major third-generation studies, was conducted between 1980

Feature	ECA	NCS	NLAES	NCS-R	NESARC
Diagnostic criteria used	DSM-III	DSM-III-R	DSM-IV	DSM-IV	DSM-IV
Diagnostic interview	Diagnostic Interview Schedule (DIS)	Composite International Diagnostic Interview - U. Michigan version (UM-CIDI)	Alcohol Use Disorders and Associated Disabilities Interview Schedule (AUDADIS)	Composite International Diagnostic Interview - WMH (WMH-CIDI)	Alcohol Use Disorders and Associated Disabilities Interview Schedule-IV (AUDADIS-IV)
Psychometric testing of interview	Comparison to other diagnostic procedures in varied settings indicated good reliability for alcohol diagnoses	None for this version of the CIDI	Test-retest reliability in three samples; kappas ranged from 0.70 to 0.84 for alcohol diagnoses	Clinical reinterviews with the Structured Clincial Interview for DSM-IV low sensitivity and excellent specificity for alcohol diagnoses	Test-retest reliability in two general population samples; kappas ranged from 0.70 to 0.74 for alcohol diagnoses
Time frame for "current" alcohol use disorder	Prior six months	Prior six months	Prior 12 months	Prior 12 months	Prior 12 months
Diagnostic coverage	Substance use, affective, anxiety, psychotic disorders	Substance use, affective, psychotic disorders	Substance and unipolar affective disorders	Substance, affective, anxiety, psychotic disorders	Substance use, affective, anxiety, personality disorders, psychotic screening
Notable interview features	Probe flowchart eliminates psychiatric symptoms if subject attributes them to alcohol/drugs	Screening questions all at start of interview, subject's commitment to disclosure requested then	Past alcohol disorders not diagnosed unless symptoms clustered together syndromally as specified in DSM-III-R and DSM-IV, alcohol abuse and dependence assessed hierarchically* and non-hierarchically	Screening questions all at start of interview, subject's commitment to disclosure requested then. In a departure from DSM-IV guidelines, alcohol dependence only assessed among individuals meeting criteria for alcohol abuse.	Past alcohol disorders not diagnosed unless symptoms clustered together syndromally as specified in DSM-III-R and DSM-IV, alcohol abuse and dependence assessed hierarchically* and non-hierarchically

*The DSM-IV specifies a hierarchical relationship between alcohol abuse and dependence. Individuals who meet lifetime criteria for alcohol dependence cannot be diagnosed with alcohol abuse. The NLAES interview collected information on alcohol abuse and dependence for all respondents regardless of alcohol dependence status so that diagnosis prevalence could be reported hierarchically or non-hierarchically.

Table 2. Assessment features of the five U.S. third-generation psychiatric epidemiologic studies. ILLUSTRATION BY GGS INFORMATION SERVICES. GALE, CENGAGE LEARNING

and 1984. One explicit purpose of this study was the assessment of psychiatric disorders according to the then-new *DSM-III* nomenclature. Unlike the remaining surveys discussed below, the ECA surveyed five communities, located in New Haven, Connecticut, Los Angeles, California, Baltimore, Maryland, St. Louis, Missouri, and Durham, North Carolina. Despite the sample's geographic distribution, weights were eventually derived to estimate national rates of alcohol use disorders (as well as other psychiatric disorders). The study's interview, the Diagnostic Interview Schedule (DIS), was developed specifically for the ECA.

The National Comorbidity Study (NCS). The NCS was designed to provide data on the comorbidity of alcohol and other psychiatric disorders based on a full national sample. With the publication of the revision of *DSM-III* in 1987, general population data using the more recent *DSM-III-R* diagnostic criteria were needed. The interview, the University of Michigan version of the Composite International Diagnostic Interview (UM-CIDI), was developed for this survey, with various features that differentiated it from other structured diagnostic interviews (see Table 2). Another difference between the NCS and the ECA interviews was the collection of risk factor data in the NCS to offer explanations for the etiology of disorders. Test-retest studies (which measure whether two independent evaluators produce the same results from a given respondent) for alcohol disorders and drug disorders in the CIDI indicated good reliability for these diagnoses (Wittchen, 1994).

The National Longitudinal Alcohol Epidemiologic Survey (NLAES). The NLAES, the first national survey with a primary focus on *DSM*-defined alcohol use disorders, was conducted in 1992. The survey aims were to provide accurate estimates of alcohol abuse and dependence, associated physical and mental disabilities, treatment utilization, information on risk factors for substance use disorders, and the economic impact of these disorders. This required a large sample and reliable diagnostic measures. As Table 1 demonstrates, the sample was very large, exceeding 40,000 people. The diagnostic interview developed for the NLAES was the Alcohol Use Disorders and Associated Disabilities Interview Schedule, or AUDADIS (see

Grant & Hasin, 1992). In the AUDADIS, alcohol dependence is not diagnosed unless symptoms cluster together chronologically. Although the NLAES was conducted prior to the publication of *DSM-IV*, the AUDADIS obtained the necessary information to make alcohol, drug, and psychiatric diagnoses according to *DSM-IV* criteria. The AUDADIS diagnoses were also subjected to test-retest reliability studies, and the results indicated good to excellent reliability for current and past alcohol disorders, and adequate to good reliability for drug disorder symptoms and diagnoses (Grant et al., 1995).

The National Epidemiologic Survey on Alcohol and Related Conditions (NESARC). From 2001 to 2002, the National Institute on Alcohol Abuse and Alcoholism (NIAAA) sponsored a survey whose sample design was similar to the NLAES, using a measurement instrument updated for *DSM-IV* (AUDADIS-IV). The NESARC included a national sample of over 43,000 respondents aged 18 and older, who were assessed for a wide range of psychiatric disorders, including alcohol disorders. Respondents were followed for three years and reassessed for psychiatric disorders from 2004 to 2005. Longitudinal studies are valuable in epidemiology because factors predicting the onset of disorder (as opposed to the prevalence of disorder) can be directly estimated without the potential for recall bias. Similar to the prior version of the AUDADIS, the updated version documented good to excellent test-retest reliability of alcohol diagnoses (Ruan et al., 2008).

National Comorbidity Study Replication (NCS-R). Part of a survey of 26 countries conducted by the World Mental Health (WMH) Survey Initiative, the NCS-R was conducted between 2001 and 2003. The NCS-R strived to study trends over time in psychiatric illness, and to update the prevalence of psychiatric disorders in accordance with the publication of the *DSM-IV.* Interview and study design features are similar enough to those of the NCS to make comparisons of the studies legitimate. An exception to this is the introduction of a new "skip feature" that eliminated all questions on alcohol and drug dependence among respondents that never met criteria for alcohol or drug abuse, respectively. A clinical

Disorder	Survey				
	ECA	NCS	NLAES	NCS-R	NESARC
Current*					
Any Alcohol Use Disorder	4.8	9.7	7.4	4.4*	8.5
Alcohol Abuse	1.9	2.5	3	3.1	4.7
Alcohol Dependence	2.8	7.2	4.4	1.3*	3.8
Lifetime					
Any Alcohol Use Disorder	13.5	23.5	18.2	18.6*	30.3
Alcohol Abuse	5.6	9.4	4.9	13.2	17.8
Alcohol Dependence	7.9	14.1	13.3	5.4*	12.5
*Dependence not assessed in those without abuse					

Table 3. Prevalence of current and lifetime alcohol disorders in five general population surveys. ILLUSTRATION BY GGS INFORMATION SERVICES. GALE, CENGAGE LEARNING

reappraisal study was conducted using a subset of the NCS-R respondents; with the results showing adequate sensitivity for alcohol abuse but low sensitivity for alcohol dependence (63.1% and 43.1%, respectively), and excellent specificity (98.1% and 99.9%, respectively) (Kessler & Merikangas, 2004). Low sensitivity for alcohol dependence was a marked departure from the normally excellent psychometric properties of alcohol dependence measured in other major surveys, and this difference was likely due to the aforementioned skip over alcohol and drug dependence questions.

PREVALENCE OF ALCOHOL USE DISORDERS: EVIDENCE FROM PSYCHIATRIC EPIDEMIOLOGIC SURVEYS

Prevalence refers to the proportion of the population with alcohol abuse OR dependence at a given moment or period in time. Prevalence estimates are used in describing the disease burden on a population. Table 1 details the prevalence of alcohol abuse and dependence in the five major epidemiologic surveys, which estimated both current and lifetime alcohol use disorders. While estimates differ due to variations in the measurement and definition of "current disorder" and the design of the surveys (see Tables 2 and 3), these studies, "taken together," provide a comprehensive assessment of the prevalence of alcohol abuse and dependence in the U.S. population.

The prevalence of current alcohol abuse ranges from 1.9 percent in the ECA to 4.7 percent in the NESARC. Current alcohol dependence ranges from 1.3 percent in the NCS-R to 7.2 percent in

the NCS. Overall, the prevalence of any current alcohol disorder ranges from approximately 4 percent to 10 percent. On a lifetime basis, estimates across surveys vary more widely. The lifetime prevalence of alcohol abuse ranges from 5.6 percent in the ECA to 17.8 percent in the NESARC, while alcohol dependence ranges from 5.4 percent in the NCS-R to 14.1 percent in the NCS. Together, these estimates indicate alcohol abuse and dependence are relatively common disorders compared to other psychiatric disorders and other chronic diseases in the population.

Because the NLAES and the NESARC used the same instrument in each survey, it is possible to examine trends over time (see Table 3). Overall, the prevalence of any current alcohol disorder increased from 7.4 percent to 8.5 percent, due mostly to an increase in the prevalence of alcohol abuse (3% to 4.7%). The prevalence of alcohol dependence decreased slightly during this period (4.4% to 3.8%). The prevalence of any lifetime alcohol disorder increased from 18.2 percent to 30.3 percent between 1991 and 1992, again due mostly to an increase in the prevalence of lifetime alcohol abuse (4.9% to 17.8%), for alcohol dependence decreased slightly (13.3% to 12.5%). Further discussion of these trends is provided by Grant and colleagues (2004).

LONGITUDINAL COURSE OF A DISORDER: ONSET, COURSE, AND RECOVERY

National surveys and longitudinal studies in both clinical and community samples have documented the course of alcohol disorders. Longitudinal studies have several advantages over cross-sectional studies in assessing the course of alcohol disorders, including minimal bias due to recall and selective mortality. However, longitudinal studies are often conducted among specialized samples, such as individuals in treatment. In general, longitudinal and cross-sectional studies concur regarding the course of alcohol use disorders.

Initiation of alcohol consumption often occurs during adolescence. Onset of alcohol abuse and dependence is most likely among individuals aged 18 to 29, although 15 percent of alcohol dependence cases begin before age 18 (Hingston et al., 2006). While alcohol abuse was once believed to be a prodromal form of alcohol dependence, evidence now suggests that over a third of those with alcohol dependence do not meet abuse criteria (Hasin et al., 2004). In addition, longitudinal studies suggest that many individuals with alcohol abuse do not develop alcohol dependence (Hasin et al., 1990; Schuckit et al., 2005). The duration of alcohol disorders is often, but not always, chronic, with an estimated mean of nearly four years for alcohol dependence (Hasin et al., 2007).

Often, alcohol abuse and dependence are not lifelong conditions. Indeed, a high rate of recovery has been documented in general population samples, even among individuals who have never sought treatment. Studies of the general population also show that a high proportion of recovered individuals return to moderate drinking as opposed to abstinence (Tucker, 2003; Watson & Sher, 1998). Data from the NESARC indicated that approximately 75 percent of individuals diagnosed with alcohol dependence at some point in the past did not have a current (i.e., past year) diagnosis, but that only about 20 percent of these individuals were abstinent from alcohol (Dawson et al., 2004). Thus, the transition to adulthood represents a key developmental phase in which alcohol disorders often remit, in a process termed "maturing out" (Bachman et al., 2002; Dawson et al., 2006). Major predictors of recovery include key lifestyle components, such as employment, marriage, and childbirth. Whether or not these factors have a causal influence on recovery or reflect common factors underlying the positive lifestyle components and the recovery remains unknown.

Despite substantial progress in the development of treatments for alcohol disorders, only about one-fifth of those individuals with an alcohol disorder seek treatment for the condition during their lifetime (Cohen et al., 2007). Further, the delay from onset of disorder to treatment is typically eight to ten years (Wang et al., 2005). Finally, in contrast to sharp increases in treatment utilization for disorders such as depression between 1990 and 2003, a corresponding increase in the proportion of individuals seeking treatment for an alcohol disorder did not occur during this period (Kessler et al., 2005).

DEMOGRAPHIC CHARACTERISTICS AND OTHER ESTABLISHED RISK FACTORS FOR ALCOHOL USE DISORDERS

The term *risk factor* refers to a characteristic of an individual or community that influences disease risk in a population. Risk factor epidemiology is an important method used to characterize factors that influence vulnerability to alcohol abuse and dependence, and to identify subpopulations for greater intervention and prevention efforts.

Demographic Risk Factors. Alcohol use disorders are not distributed randomly in the population. On the contrary, certain demographic groups exhibit a higher prevalence of alcohol use disorders than others. Gender is a well-documented risk factor, for example. In particular, men are more likely to have alcohol use disorders than women, although evidence suggests gender differences in the prevalence of disorder have decreased over time (Keyes, Grant, & Hasin, 2007). As noted above, age is strongly related to the development of alcohol use disorders, and alcohol disorders are often exhibited in young adulthood.

Socioeconomic status is inversely related to alcohol dependence, so that individuals in lower socioeconomic groups have a higher prevalence of disorder. Alcohol abuse, conversely, is more common among individuals with higher income and educational attainment (Van Oers et al., 1999). Finally, the prevalence of alcohol use disorders varies according to a person's self-described race or ethnic group. Of the largest such groups tracked in U.S. surveys, most surveys found that Native Americans and non-Hispanic whites have the highest prevalence of alcohol disorders, while individuals of Asian descent typically have the lowest prevalence (Huang et al., 2006).

Environmental factors. A particular substance must be available in the environment for individuals to be at risk for the development of disorders involving that substance. In Western societies, competing forces influence alcohol availability. Public health, moral or religious, "grassroots," and governmental organizations attempt to reduce availability and consumption by influencing public policy and laws, while the alcoholic beverage industry attempts to increase consumption through advertising and other means. Widespread social attitudes toward alcohol use, as well as political events, also influence availability and consumption, thereby influencing the risk of alcohol use disorders.

Other external environmental factors include home and family life. Poor parental monitoring and the modeling of heavy alcohol use contribute to the likelihood of adolescent alcohol initiation and binge drinking, although these factors may be mediators within the relationship between parental alcohol problems and adolescent alcohol use (Hawkins, Catalano, & Miller, 1992; Ellis, Zucker, & Fitzgerald, 1997; Repetti, Taylor, & Seeman, 2002). Peer influence and stressful life events are also strongly associated with adolescent alcohol abuse, while religiosity is a well-replicated protective factor (Kendler et al., 1997, Kendler et al., 2000; Walden et al., 2004; Dube et al., 2003).

Individual Risk Factors. Important risk factors for the development of alcohol disorders also exist within the individual, including positive alcohol expectancies and motivations for drinking. These beliefs and motivations can have roots in family and peer influences, but they are characteristics of the individual's internal environment. Individuals with certain personality traits, such as novelty or sensation seeking (Zuckerman & Kuhlman, 2000), may be more likely to experiment with heavy drinking, while co-occurring disorders associated with impulsivity and risk taking, such as conduct disorder and antisocial personality disorder, have been shown to predict the development of an alcohol disorder (Cloninger, Sigvardsson, & Bohman, 1988; Sher & Trull, 1994). Further, early onset of alcohol consumption is associated with a higher risk of alcohol disorder onset (Grant & Dawson, 1997; Grant et al., 2006), although evidence suggests that any early deviant behavior, including but not limited to alcohol consumption, is associated with later onset of an alcohol disorder (Kuperman et al., 2005; McGue & Iacono, 2005; King & Chassin, 2007). Thus, it is unclear whether early onset of drinking is a specific risk factor for alcohol disorders or a risk factor for a general category of externalizing behaviors.

Genetic factors are also important in the development of an alcohol disorder. Alcohol disorders are known to be familial (Cotton, 1979; Bierut et al., 1998), and twin studies of alcohol dependence show estimates of heritability (i.e., the proportion of risk attributable to genetics) of 50 percent to 60 percent (Klender et al., 2003; Heath, 1995; Rhee et al., 2003). The Collaborative Study on the Genetics of Alcoholism (COGA), a multisite family study of alcohol-dependent patients and their relatives, has contributed greatly to current knowledge of the genetic epidemiology of alcohol disorders, as have a series of case-control and family studies at Yale University and the University of Connecticut (Luo et al., 2006; Kaufman et al., 2007). In addition, linkage and association studies involving fine gene mapping have identified specific genes and alleles associated with alcohol dependence and related phenotypes through various mechanisms.

CONCLUSION

The field of epidemiology has facilitated estimates of the incidence and prevalence of alcohol use disorders and helped identify important risk factors for the onset and persistence of the disorders over time. Issues concerning major epidemiologic surveys include reliance on the self-reporting of problem behaviors and recall bias, which can affect lifetime estimates. Despite these limitations, however, epidemiologic studies present the most valid national picture of alcohol use disorders, their course, and factors associated with their occurrence. Thus, these findings play a vital role in advancing knowledge of alcohol use disorders in the general population.

See also **Alcohol: Chemistry and Pharmacology; Alcohol: History of Drinking; Alcoholism: Abstinence versus Controlled Drinking; Antisocial Personality Disorder; Diagnosis of Substance Use Disorders: Diagnostic Criteria; Diagnostic and Statistical Manual (DSM); Gender and Complications of Substance Abuse; Intimate Partner Violence and Alcohol/ Substance Use; Models of Alcoholism and Drug Abuse; Prohibition of Alcohol; Research: Developing Medications to Treat Substance Abuse and Dependence; Risk Factors for Substance Use, Abuse, and Dependence: An Overview; Treatment: An Overview of Alcohol Abuse/Dependence.**

BIBLIOGRAPHY

American Psychiatric Association. (1994). *Diagnostic and statistical manual of mental disorders* (4th rev. ed., *DSM-IV-R*), Washington, DC: Author.

Anton, R. F., O'Malley, S. S., Ciraulo, D. A., Cisler, R. A., Couper, D., Donovan, D. M., et al. (2006). Combined pharmacotherapies and behavioral interventions for alcohol dependence: The COMBINE study: A randomized controlled trial. *Journal of the American Medical Association, 295*(17), 2003–2017.

Bachman, J. G., O'Malley, P. M., Schulenberg, J. E., Johnston, L. D., Bryant, A. L., & Merline, A. C. (2002). *The decline of substance use in young adulthood: Changes in social activities, roles, and beliefs.* Mahwah, NJ: Lawrence Erlbaum.

Bierut, L. J., Dinwiddie, S. H., Begleiter, H., et al. (1998). Familial transmission of substance dependence: Alcohol, marijuana, cocaine, and habitual smoking—A report from the Collaborative Study on the Genetics of Alcoholism. *Archives of General Psychiatry, 55*(11), 982–988.

Cloninger, D. R., Sigvardsson, S., & Bohman, M. (1988). Childhood personality predicts alcohol abuse in young adults. *Alcoholism, Clinical and Experimental Research, 12*(4), 494–505.

Cohen, E., Feínn, R., Arias, A., & Kranzler, H. R. (2007). Alcohol treatment utilization: Findings from the National Epidemiologic Survey on Alcohol and Related Conditions. *Drug and Alcohol Dependence, 86*(2-3), 214–221.

Cooper, M. L. (1994). Motivations for alcohol use among adolescents: Development and validation of a four-factor model. *Psychological Assessment, 6*(2), 117–128.

Cooper, M. L., Frone, M. R., Russell, M., & Mudar, P. (1995). Drinking to regulate positive and negative emotions: A motivational model of alcohol use. *Journal of Personality and Social Psychology, 69*(5), 990–1005.

Cotton, N. S. (1979). The familial incidence of alcoholism: A review. *Journal of Studies on Alcohol, 40*(1), 89–116.

Dawson, D. A., Grant, B. F., Stinson, F. S., & Chou, P. S. (2006). Maturing out of alcohol dependence: The impact of transitional life events. *Journal of Studies on Alcohol, 67*(2), 195–203.

Dawson, D. A., Grant, B. F., Stinson, F. S., Chou, P. S., Huang, B., & Ruan, W. J. (2004). Recovery from *DSM-IV* alcohol dependence: United States, 2001-2002. *Addiction, 100*(3), 281–292.

Dube, S. R., Felitti, V. J., Dong, M., et al. (2003). Childhood abuse, neglect, and household dysfunction and the risk of illicit drug use: The adverse childhood experiences study. *Pediatrics, 111*(3), 564–572.

Ellis, D. A., Zucker, R. A., & Fitzgerald, H. E. (1997). The role of family influences in development and risk. *Alcohol Research & Health, 21*(3), 218–226.

Grant, B. F. (1997). Prevalence and correlates of alcohol use and *DSM-IV* alcohol dependence in the United States: Results of the National Longitudinal Alcohol Epidemiological Survey. *Journal of Studies on Alcohol, 58*(5), 464–473.

Grant, B. F., & Dawson, D. A. (1997). Age at onset of alcohol use and its associations with *DSM-IV* alcohol abuse and dependence: Results from the National Longitudinal Alcohol Epidemiologic Survey. *Journal of Substance Abuse, 9*, 103–110.

Grant, B. F., Dawson, D. A., & Hasin, D. S. (2001). *The alcohol use disorder and associated disabilities interview schedule—DSM-IV version (AUDADIS-IV).* Bethesda, MD: National Institute on Alcohol Abuse and Alcoholism.

Grant, B. F., Dawson, D. A., Stinson, F. S., Chou, S. P., Dufour, M. C., & Pickering, R. P. (2004). The 12-month prevalence and trends in *DSM-IV* alcohol abuse and dependence: United States, 1991–1991 and 2001–2002. *Drug and Alcohol Dependence, 74*(3), 223–234.

Grant, B., Harford, T., Dawson, D., Chou, P., & Pickering, R. (1995). The alcohol use disorder and associated disabilities interview schedule (AUDADIS): Reliability of alcohol and drug modules in a general population sample. *Drug and Alcohol Dependence, 39*(1), 37–44.

Grant, B., & Hasin, D. (1992). *The alcohol use disorders and associated disabilities interview schedule.* Rockville, MD: National Institution on Alcohol Abuse and Alcoholism.

Grant, B. F., Moore, T. C., Shepard, J., & Kaplan, K. (2003). *Source and accuracy statement for wave 1 of the 2001–2002 national epidemiologic survey on alcohol and related conditions.* Bethesda, MD: National Institute on Alcohol Abuse and Alcoholism. Available from http://www.niaaa.nih.gov/.

Grant, B., Stinson, F. S., Dawson, D. A., Chou, S. P., Ruan, W. J., & Pickering, R. P. (2004). Co-occurrence of 12-month alcohol and drug use disorders and personality disorders in the United States: Results from the National Epidemiologic Survey on Alcohol and Related Conditions. *Archives of General Psychiatry, 61*(4), 361–368.

Grant, J. D., Scherrer, J. F., Lynskey, M. T., Lyons, M. J., Eisen, S. A., Tsuang, M. T., et al. (2006). Adolescent alcohol use is a risk factor for adult alcohol and drug dependence: Evidence from a twin design. *Psychological Medicine, 36*(1), 109–118.

Greenfield, T. K., Midanik, L. T., & Rogers, J. D. (2000). A 10-year national trend study of alcohol consumption, 1984–1995: Is the period of declining drinking over? *American Journal of Public Health, 90*(1), 47–52.

Hasin, D. S., & Grant, B. F. (2004). The co-occurrence of *DSM-IV* alcohol abuse in *DSM-IV* alcohol dependence: Results of the National Epidemiologic Survey on Alcohol and Related Conditions on heterogeneity that differ by population subgroup. *Archives of General Psychiatry, 61*(9), 891–896.

Hasin, D., Grant, B., & Endicott, J. (1990). The natural history of alcohol abuse: Implications for definitions of alcohol use disorders. *American Journal of Psychiatry, 147*(11), 1537–1541.

Hasin, D., Grant, B., Harford, T., Hilton, M., & Endicott, J. (1990). Multiple alcohol-related problems in the U.S.: On the rise? *Journal of Studies on Alcohol, 51*(6), 485–493.

Hasin, D. S., Stinson, F. S., Ogburn, E., & Grant, B. F. (2007). Prevalence, correlates, disability, and comorbidity of *DSM-IV* alcohol abuse and dependence in the United States: Results from the National Epidemiologic Survey on Alcohol and Related Conditions. *Archives of General Psychiatry, 64*(7), 830–842.

Hawkins, J., Catalano, R. F., & Miller, J. Y. (1992). Risk and protective factors for alcohol and other drug problems in adolescence and early adulthood: Implications for substance abuse prevention. *Psychological Bulletin, 112*(1), 64–105.

Heath, A. C. (1995). Genetic influences on alcoholism risk: A review of adoption and twin studies. *Alcohol Health & Research World, 19*(3), 166–171.

Hilton, M. (1987). Drinking patterns and drinking problems in 1984: Results from a general population survey. *Alcoholism: Clinical and Experimental Research, 11*(2), 167–175.

Hingston, R. W., Hereen, T., & Winter, M. R. (2006). Age at drinking onset and alcohol dependence: age at onset, duration, and severity. *Archives of Pediatrics and Adolescent Medicine, 160,* 739–746.

Huang, B., Grant, B. F., Dawson, D. A., Stinson, F. S., Chou, S. P., Saha, T. D, et al. (2006). Race-ethnicity and the prevalence and co-occurrence of *Diagnostic and Statistical Manual of Mental Disorders, Fourth Edition,* alcohol and drug use disorders and Axis I and II disorders: United States, 2001 to 2002. *Comprehensive Psychiatry, 47*(4), 252–257.

Kaufman, J., Yang, B. Z., Douglas-Palumberi, H., Crouse-Artus, M., Lipschitz, D., Krystal, J.H., et al. (2007). Genetic and environmental predictors of early alcohol use. *Biological Psychology, 61*(11), 1228–1234.

Kendler, K. S., Bulik, C. M., Silberg, J., et al. (2000). Childhood sexual abuse and adult psychiatric and substance use disorders in women: An epidemiological and cotwin control analysis. *Archives of General Psychiatry, 57,* 953–959.

Kendler, K. S., Gardner, C. O., & Prescott, C. A. (1997). Religion, psychopathology, and substance use and abuse: A multimeasure, genetic-epidemiologic study. *The American Journal of Psychiatry, 154,* 322–329.

Kendler, K. S., Jacobson, K. C., Prescott, C. A., Neale, M. C. (2003). Specificity of genetic and environmental risk factors for use and abuse/dependence of cannabis, cocaine, hallucinogens, sedatives, stimulants, and opiates in male twins. *The American Journal of Psychiatry, 160,* 687–695.

Kessler, R. C., Berglund, P., Demler, O., Jin, R., Merikangas, K. R., & Walters, E. E. (2004). Lifetime prevalence and age-of-onset distributions of *DSM-IV* disorders in the National Comorbidity Survey Replication. *Archives of General Psychiatry, 62*(6), 593–602.

Kessler, R. C., Chiu, W. T., Demler, O., Merikangas, K. R., & Walters, E. E. (2005). Prevalence, severity, and comorbidity of 12-month *DSM-IV* disorders in the National Comorbidity Survey Replication. *Archives of General Psychiatry, 62*(6), 617–627.

Kessler, R. C., Demler, O., Frank, R. G., Olfson, M., Pincus, H. A., Walters, E. E, et al. (2005). Prevalence and treatment of mental disorders, 1990–2003. *New England Journal of Medicine, 352*(24), 2515–2523.

Kessler, R., McGonagle, K., Zhao, S., Nelson, C. B., Hughes, M., Eshleman, S., et al. (1994). Lifetime and 12-month prevalence of *DSM-III-R* psychiatric disorders in the United States: Results from the National Comorbidity Survey. *Archives of General Psychiatry, 51*(1), 8–19.

Kessler, R. C., & Merikangas, K. R. (2004). The National Comorbidity Survey Replication (NCS-R): Background and aims. *International Journal for Methods in Psychiatric Research, 13*(2), 60–68.

Kessler, R. C., & Ustum, T. B. (2004). The World Mental Health (WMH) Survey Initiative Version of the World Health Organization (WHO) Composite International Diagnostic Interview (CIDI). *International Journal for Methods in Psychiatric Research, 13,* 93–121.

Keyes, K. M., Grant, B. F., & Hasin, D. S. (2007). Evidence for a closing gender gap in alcohol use, abuse, and dependence in the United States population. *Drug Alcohol Dependence, 93*(1–2), 21–29.

King, K. M., & Chassin, L. A. (2007). Prospective study of the effects of age of initiation of alcohol and drug use on young adult substance dependence. *Journal of Studies on Alcohol and Drugs, 68*(2), 56–65.

Kuperman, S., Chan, G., Kramer, J. R., Bierut, L., Bucholz, K. K., Fox, L., et al. (2005). Relationship of age of first drink to child behavioral problems and family psychopathology. *Alcoholism, Clinical and Experimental Research, 29*(10), 1869–1876.

Lakins, N. E., LaVallee, R. A., Williams, G. D., & Yi, H. (2007). *Surveillance Report #82: Apparent Per Capita Alcohol Consumption: National, State, and Regional Trends, 1977–2005.* Rockville, MD: NIAAA, Division of Biometry and Epidemiology.

Lender, M., & Martin, J. (1982). *Drinking in America.* New York: The Free Press.

Li, T. K. (2000). Pharmacogenetics of responses to alcohol and genes that influence alcohol drinking. *Journal of Studies on Alcohol, 61*(1), 5–12.

Luo, X., Kranzler, H. R., Zuo, L., Lappalainen, J., Yang, B. Z., & Gelernter, J. (2006). ADH4 gene variation is associated with alcohol dependence and drug dependence in European Americans: Results from HWD tests and case-control association studies. *Neuropsychopharmacology, 31*(5), 1085–1095.

McGue, M., & Iacono, W. G. (2005). The association of early adolescent problem behavior with adult psychopathology. *American Journal of Psychiatry, 162,* 1118–1124.

Regier, D. A., Myers, J. K., Kramer, M., Robins, L. N., Blazer, D. G., Hough, R. L., et al. (1984). The NIMH Epidemiologic Catchment Area program. *Archives of General Psychiatry, 41*(10), 934–941.

Reich, T., Edenberg, H. J., Goate, A., Williams, J. T., Rice, J.P., Van Eerdewegh, P., et al. (1998). Genome-wide search for genes affecting the risk for alcohol dependence. *American Journal of Medical Genetics, 81*(3), 207–215.

Repetti, R. L., Taylor, S. E., Seeman, T. E. (2002). Risky families: Family social environments and the mental and physical health of offspring. *Psychological Bulletin, 128*(2), 330–366.

Rhee, S. H., Hewitt, J. K., Young, S. E., Corley, R. P., Crowley, T. J., Stallings, M. C. (2003). Genetic and environmental influences on substance initiation, use, and problem use in adolescents. *Archives of General Psychiatry,* 60,1256–1264.

Robins, L., Helzer, J., Croughan, J., & Ratcliff, K. (1981). National Institute of Mental Health Diagnostic Interview Schedule: Its history, characteristics, and validity. *Archives of General Psychiatry, 38*(4), 381–389.

Ruan, W. J., Goldstein, R. B., Chou, S. P., Smith, S. M., Saha, T. D., Pickering, R. P., et al. (2008). The Alcohol Use Disorder and Associated Disabilities Interview Schedule-IV (AUDADIS-IV): Reliability of new psychiatric diagnostic modules and risk factors in a general population sample. *Drug and Alcohol Dependence, 92*(1-3), 27–36.

Schuckit, M. A., Smith, T. L., Danko, G. P., Kramer, J., Godinez, J., Bucholz, K. K., et al. (2005). Prospective evaluation of the four *DSM-IV* criteria for alcohol abuse in a large population. *American Journal of Psychiatry, 162*(12), 350–360.

Sher, K. J., & Trull, T. J. (1994). Personality and disinhibitory psychopathology: Alcoholism and antisocial personality disorder. *Journal of Abnormal Psychology, 103*(1), 92–102.

Slutske, W. S., Cronk, N. J., Sher, K. J., et al. (2002). Genes, environment, and individual differences in alcohol expectancies among female adolescents and young adults. *Psychology of Addictive Behaviors: Journal of the Society of Psychologists in Addictive Behaviors, 16*(4), 308–317.

Spitzer, R., Endicott, J., & Robins, E. (1978). Research diagnostic criteria: Rationale and reliability. *Archives of General Psychiatry, 35*(6), 773–782.

Tucker, J. A. (2003). Natural resolution of alcohol-related problems. *Recent Developments in Alcoholism, 16,* 77–90.

Van Oers, J. A. M, Bongers, I. M. B, Van de Goor, L. A. M, & Garretsen, H. F. L. (1999). Alcohol consumption, alcohol-related problems, problem drinking, and socioeconomic status. *Alcohol and Alcoholism, 34*(1), 78–88.

Walden, B., McGue, M., Iacono, W., Burt, A., & Elkins, I. (2004). Identifying shared environmental contributions to early substance use: The respective roles of peers and parents. *Journal of Abnormal Psychology, 113*(3), 440–450.

Wang, P. S., Berglund, P., Olfson, M., Pincus, H. A., Wells, K. B., & Kessler, R. C. (2005). Failure and delay in initial treatment contact after first onset of mental disorders in the National Comorbidity Survey Replication. *Archives of General Psychiatry, 62*(6), 603–613.

Watson, A. L., & Sher, K. J. (1998). Resolution of alcohol problems without treatment: Methodological issues and future directions of natural recovery research. *Clinical Psychology: Science and Practice, 5,* 1–19.

Wittchen, H. U. (1994). Reliability and validity studies of the WHO-Composite International Diagnostic Interview (CIDI): A critical review. *Journal of Psychiatric Research, 28*(1), 57–84.

Yoon, Y. H., Yi, H. (2006). *Surveillance Report #75: Liver Cirrhosis Mortality in the United States, 1970–2003.* Rockville, MD: NIAAA, Division of Biometry and Epidemiology.

Zuckerman, M., & Kuhlman, D. (2000). Personality and risk-taking: Common biosocial factors. *Journal of Personality, 68*(6), 999–1029.

KATHERINE M. KEYES
DEBORAH S. HASIN

EPIDEMIOLOGY OF DRUG ABUSE.

Epidemiology can be thought of as the cornerstone of public health research. It is a branch of biomedical science that deals with measuring the occurrence and frequency of a disease in a population, as well as identifying the causes and mechanisms. Evidence gathered in epidemiologic investigations is used to inform future prevention efforts and management of the disease. Unlike general clinical practice, epidemiology focuses on populations at risk and their subgroups rather than individuals, although individual clinical experiences can be guided by epidemiology. The epidemiology of drug abuse is concerned with describing the distribution of drug use and its associated disorders. To do this, epidemiologists conduct surveys that seek information about all aspects of the population's drug experience and examine the intrapersonal and environmental factors that interact with each other and with genetic factors across development to identify patterns of exposure, initiation, maintenance, and desistance (i.e., cessation) of drug abuse. Furthermore, findings from epidemiologic studies can inform clinical practice, prevention programs, and other health and social services as avenues to improve public health.

There is, of course, good reason to wonder whether epidemiologic surveys of drug use and drug dependence have sufficient validity to be trusted. On the one hand, especially among young people, there may be a tendency to exaggerate drug taking, and to falsify survey responses in the direction of more drug taking than has really occurred. On the other hand, some people may be hesitant to disclose their histories of drug taking or drug problems; they might not agree to participate in the survey, or they might falsify their answers in the direction of less drug taking or fewer problems than have actually occurred.

Fortunately a body of methodologic research provides general assurance about the accuracy of estimates in drug abuse epidemiologic surveys. Accuracy of the survey results seems to be enhanced considerably when special care is taken to guarantee confidentiality of responses, to protect the privacy of the survey respondents, and to develop trust and rapport before asking survey questions about sensitive behavior, alcohol and drug problems, or illegal activities. In particular, except in poorly conducted surveys of very young respondents, there seems to be very little exaggeration of drug involvement, and older adolescents and adults rarely report drug use unless it actually has happened. Moreover, the accuracy of the estimates does not seem to be distorted greatly when the surveys concentrate on household residents and do not extend their samples to include homeless or imprisoned segments of the population. Although homeless people and prisoners often have significant and special needs for alcohol- and other drug-dependent treatment services that society cannot ignore without peril, the number of homeless and incarcerated persons is small relative to the considerably larger number of persons living in households.

It also is important to note the relatively large size of the survey estimates obtained in these epidemiologic surveys. For example, in 2007, as part of the annual Monitoring the Future (MTF) study, more than fifteen thousand high school seniors were asked to fill out confidential questionnaires about their use of such drugs as marijuana, cocaine, and nonmedical use of prescription drugs; about 47 percent reported having taken any illicit drug, 72 percent reported consuming alcoholic beverages, and 55 percent reported having consumed alcohol to the point of getting drunk. The same study also surveyed roughly thirty-four thousand tenth and eighth graders, and lifetime illicit drug use was reported by more than one-third and one-fifth, respectively, of these students. In 2006, nearly sixty-eight thousand American household residents aged twelve years and older participated in a U.S. government-sponsored National Survey on Drug Use and Health (NSDUH) and were asked to answer an interviewer's questions about the use of these drugs; illegal drug taking was reported by an estimated 28 percent of those twelve to seventeen years, 59 percent of those eighteen to twenty-five, and 46 percent of those twenty-six and older.

Furthermore, between 2001 and 2002 more than 43,000 Americans over the age of eighteen completed confidential interviews as part of the National Epidemiologic Survey on Alcohol and Related Conditions (NESARC). With the NESARC it is possible to estimate the proportion of drug users who have developed drug disorder syndromes, as defined in relation to *DSM-IV*, a set of diagnostic criteria for drug abuse or dependence that were developed by the American Psychiatric Association in 1994. Before the diagnoses of drug abuse or dependence are made, the survey must produce evidence that drug users experienced signs or symptoms of disorder such as unsuccessful efforts to cut down, recurrent social or interpersonal problems resulting from drug use, going through withdrawal, or taking drugs to avoid withdrawal symptoms. As such, 10 percent of the adults surveyed showed evidence of at some point having a drug use disorder (abuse or dependence).

While estimates across these surveys often tend to vary slightly, it must be noted that these surveys have methodological differences, including population structure under study, mode and location of administration, questionnaire wording, and response rates, among others (see Anthony & Helzer, Epidemiology of Alcohol Abuse and Dependence [2007] for a detailed description of methodologic features of recent national surveys of substance use and disorders). Despite the wide range of possible discrepancies, the trends in drug use reported by these surveys tend to be consistent over time, and unique characteristics of the individual surveys can be combined for an accurate picture of illicit drug abuse. Further, even if under-reporting were an issue, these survey-based estimates are already high enough to provoke social concern.

DRUG-SPECIFIC ESTIMATES
FOR THE U.S. POPULATION

It may be useful if, bearing in mind the potential limitations in the survey methods, one considers each broad drug class one by one, in order to convey the relative frequency of use of tobacco, alcohol, and other drugs in the United States, and to identify population subgroups within which drug use or drug dependence are most common. The estimates presented here are from the 2007 MTF, 2006 NSDUH, and 2001–2002 NESARC surveys. In view of recent attention to the caffeine-dependence syndrome and other health effects of drinking coffee, tea, "energy" drinks or consuming other caffeinated products, estimates concerning the use of caffeine and caffeine dependence might seem warranted. However there is not yet a stable base of epidemiologic data on caffeine use and caffeine dependence. These are among the topics that ought to be examined in future epidemiologic studies.

Tobacco Smoking. Monitoring the Future (MTF) estimates show that about 46 percent of high school seniors have smoked tobacco cigarettes at least once in their lifetime. An estimated 22 percent of high school seniors smoked tobacco cigarettes at least once during the month prior to the survey, and about 12 percent were daily tobacco smokers.

According to the NSDUH, which included household residents age twelve years and older, an estimated 66 percent smoked tobacco cigarettes at least once, for a total of about 162,991,000 smokers. An estimated 29.1 percent had smoked in the year prior to the survey, for a total of

71,676,000 recently active smokers; most of these had smoked in the month prior to the survey (25%; 61,565,000).

There are some important age- and sex-related variations in these NSDUH estimates. For example, 40 percent of young adults aged twenty-one to twenty-five reported current cigarette use, while 23 percent of adults age thirty-five or older were current smokers. While the rate of current cigarette smoking was similar for male and female youth aged twelve to seventeen, current use of any tobacco product among respondents aged twelve and older was reported by more males than females (36% vs. 23%, respectively). Among young adults eighteen to twenty-five, within the limits of survey error, there were differences between the sexes with an estimated 42 percent of males and 35 percent of females reporting smoking, and among those past age twenty-five, males were more likely than females to have been recent tobacco smokers (27.8% versus 21.8%).

Smokeless Tobacco Use. An estimated 15 percent of high school seniors had tried smokeless tobacco at least once, and about 6.6 percent had used it during the month prior to the survey (MTF estimates). NSDUH estimates indicate somewhat lower values for smokeless tobacco, except among males aged eighteen to twenty-five. For example, among twelve- to seventeen-year-olds, an estimated 7.1 percent had tried smokeless tobacco, and 2.4 percent had used it in the month prior to the survey. By comparison, about 20 percent of eighteen- to twenty-five-year-olds and individuals age twenty-six and older had tried smokeless tobacco. Males were much more likely to have tried smokeless tobacco (32.3% vs. 5.7% for females) and be recent users; 6.6 percent had used it during the month prior to the survey, while an additional 8.8 percent had used it at some time before the past month.

Alcohol Use. An estimated 72.2 percent of high school seniors have consumed alcohol at least once. About 66.4 percent had consumed alcoholic beverages in the year prior to the survey, and about 44.4 percent had done so during the month prior to the survey. Just over 3 percent had become daily drinkers (MTF estimates). An estimated 55.1 percent of high school seniors had been drunk at least once—about 46.1 percent during the year prior to the survey and almost 29 percent during the month prior to the survey. Nearly 30 percent had consumed five or more drinks in a row in the two weeks prior to the survey (an indicator of binge drinking), and just over 1 percent reported getting drunk daily (MTF estimates).

Among household residents aged twelve and older, an estimated 82.7 percent had consumed alcoholic beverages; this represents 203,368,000 individuals. During the month prior to the survey, an estimated 51 percent had consumed alcohol. As might be expected, the prevalence values for eighteen- to twenty-five-year-olds were somewhat higher than they were for the high school seniors, especially in relation to recent drinking: Almost 62 percent of the eighteen- to twenty-five-year-olds had consumed alcoholic beverages during the month prior to the survey. The values for twelve- to seventeen-year-olds were lower: About 40.4 percent in this age group had tried alcoholic beverages at least once, and about 16.6 percent had consumed alcohol during the month prior to the survey (NSDUH estimates).

An estimated 22.4 percent of respondents of all age groups from twelve years upward reported drinking at least once per week during the year prior to the survey. Corresponding estimates for respondents aged 12 to 17, 18 to 25, 26 to 34, and 35+ were 4.6, 24.5, 23.8, and 24.6 percent, respectively (NSDUH estimates).

Alcohol dependence was found to have affected 15 percent of those who had consumed alcoholic beverages: Of every six or seven persons who had tried alcohol, about one had become dependent on it. In relation to the total survey population that included drinkers as well as abstainers, an estimated 12.5 percent were found to qualify for the diagnosis of alcohol dependence, according to the *DSM-IV* criteria (NESARC estimates).

ILLICIT DRUG USE

When controlled substances such as marijuana, cocaine, and heroin, as well as inhalant drugs, were considered, it was found that an estimated 49 percent of respondents had used these drugs on at least one occasion, 37 percent during the year prior to the survey. About 23 percent had taken one or more of these drugs during the month prior to the survey (MTF estimates).

The NSDUH reported that an estimated 45.4 percent of the population aged twelve and older had engaged in illicit drug use at least once; this amounts to approximately 111,774,000 drug takers. The number of recently active drug takers was lower; past month users represented 8.3 percent of the population (NSDUH estimates).

According to the NESARC estimates, of every eight or nine persons who had tried marijuana, cocaine, hallucinogens, opioids, or other controlled substances and inhalant drugs, one had developed drug dependence (11.4%). In the total population of individuals (including both drug users and never users), 2.6 percent had fulfilled the criteria for drug dependence (NESARC estimates).

Cannabis Use. An estimated 42 percent of high school seniors had tried marijuana or hashish (*Cannabis*) on at least one occasion, and about 32 percent had smoked cannabis during the year prior to the survey. An estimated 19 percent had smoked cannabis during the month prior to the survey, and an estimated 5 percent reported daily cannabis use (MTF estimates).

Within the age range of twelve to seventeen, there are many individuals who have not yet started to use illicit drugs such as cannabis, as well as many others who never will start to use these drugs. As a result, one might expect a lower prevalence value in this age group as compared to the values for other age ranges. In fact, this is precisely what the national survey estimates indicate. Overall, an estimated 39.8 percent of respondents reported having tried cannabis, but among twelve- to seventeen-year-olds the estimate was only 17.3 percent, and among those aged twenty-six years and older it was 40.6 percent. Prevalence of cannabis use was most common among eighteen- to twenty-five-year-olds (52.4%). This also was true for recent cannabis use during the month prior to the survey: There was a prevalence of 6.0 percent for the population overall, 6.7 percent for twelve- to seventeen-year-olds, 16.3 percent for eighteen- to twenty-five-year-olds, and 4.2 percent for older adults (NSDUH estimates).

Among cannabis users, about 6.3 percent were found to have developed cannabis dependence. Also noteworthy, is that more than one-third of cannabis users also had a history of lifetime alcohol dependence. Among all respondents aged 18 and older (including both users and never users), 1.3 percent had become dependent on cannabis (NESARC estimates).

Inhalant Use. Inhalants had been used by an estimated 11 percent of high school seniors—about 4 percent within the year prior to the survey and just over 1 percent during the month prior to the survey. Unlike other illicit drugs assessed in this survey, inhalant use is more prevalent in the younger rather than older students; one in every six or seven eighth graders reported having used inhalants (MTF estimates).

The National Household Survey on Drug Abuse indicated that about 9.3 percent of its survey population had tried inhalants at least once; about 1 percent had done so during the year prior to the survey, and about 0.3 percent had used these drugs during the month prior to the survey. It was found, when considering age and sex, that the subgroup most likely to have used inhalant drugs during the month prior to the survey was that of females aged twelve to seventeen; in this group, 1.5 percent reported recently active inhalant use (NSDUH estimates).

An estimated 19 percent of the inhalant users have been found to qualify for the diagnosis of an inhalant disorder (abuse or dependence, although dependence was virtually nonexistent in the NESARC sample). Translated into an overall prevalence estimate for both users and nonusers, this amounts to about 0.3 percent of inhalant disorder in the total survey population (NESARC estimates).

Use of Psychedelic Drugs. Psychedelic drugs (hallucinogens) had been used by an estimated 8.4 percent of high school seniors. Around 5.4 percent of high school seniors had used them in the year prior to the survey, and about 1.7 percent had used them during the month prior to the survey. Some of the more commonly used types of hallucinogens are MDMA (methylenedioxymeth-amphetamine, or "Ecstasy"), lysergic acid diethyl-amide (LSD), and phencyclidine (PCP). Nearly 7 percent of twelfth graders reported use of MDMA, 3.4 percent used LSD, and PCP users were in the minority within this group of drug users—only 2.1

percent of the high school seniors had ever tried PCP (MTF estimates).

Among persons aged twelve years and older, around 14.3 percent of individuals had tried psy-chedelic drugs such as LSD, but for the most part these drug experiences were not recent: Only 0.4 percent reported taking psychedelic drugs during the month prior to the survey. Peak prevalence values for recent use of the psychedelic drugs were observed in the years of adolescence and early adulthood; only for eighteen- to twenty-five-year-olds did these values exceed a threshold of 1 percent (1.7%); otherwise, they were at the 0.7 percent level or lower (NSDUH estimates).

About 0.2 percent of adults aged eighteen and older surveyed in the NESARC had become dependent on psychedelic drugs, defined in rela-tion to the American Psychiatric Association criteria.

Cocaine Use. Among high school seniors, an esti-mated 7.8 percent had tried cocaine; within this group of cocaine users, almost one-half had tried crack-cocaine (3.2%). About 5.2 percent of high school seniors had used cocaine (including crack) during the year prior to the survey, and 2.0 percent had used it in the month prior to the survey (MTF estimates).

An estimated 14.3 percent of the NSDUH population reported having tried cocaine or crack smoking (or both) at least once. The correspond-ing value for twelve- to seventeen-year-olds was only 2.2 percent, and there was age-related varia-tion: 15.7 percent of the eighteen- to twenty-five-year-olds had taken cocaine (including crack) while the prevalence estimate for older adults was 15.8 percent. Translated into absolute numbers, an esti-mated thirty-five million Americans aged twelve and older had used cocaine (or crack). Recent use was substantially less common: Only 1.0 percent of the survey population reported having used these drugs during the month prior to the survey; this represented about 2.4 million recently active cocaine users in the United States.

The relatively low prevalence values for crack smoking among high school seniors was reflected in the NSDUH, which found that only 3.5 per-cent of its survey population had tried crack smok-ing; this amounted to more than 8.5 million individuals. The age groups with most crack-smoking experience were the twenty-six-year-olds and older, with a prevalence value of 3.9 percent. Prevalence of crack smoking during the month prior to the 2006 survey was 0.3 percent or lower for all age and sex groups under study (NSDUH estimates).

For every six individuals who had tried cocaine at least once, one had developed cocaine dependence. That is, among cocaine users, an estimated 16 percent had become sufficiently dependent upon cocaine to qualify for the American Psychiatric Association diagnosis. Nearly half of all cocaine users also had a diagnosis of alcohol dependence, and more than a quarter had some type of drug dependence diagnosis. In relation to all persons in the survey population, whether they had tried cocaine or not, an estimated 1 percent qualified for the diagnosis of cocaine dependence (NESARC estimates).

Use of Non-Cocaine Stimulants. The non-medical use of stimulants other than cocaine (such as amphetamines) was actually more prevalent than cocaine use among high school seniors. An estimated 11.4 percent of high school seniors had taken these stimulant drugs without any doctor's orders; 7.5 percent had done so in the year prior to the survey, and 3.7 percent had done so during the month prior to the survey. Ritalin, a stimulant used therapeutically for the management of Attention Deficit Hyperactivity Disorder (ADHD), had been used nonmedically by nearly 4 percent of seniors in the year prior to the survey. Among high school seniors, 3.4 percent had ever tried crystal methamphetamine ("ice"), 1.6 percent had done so in the year prior to the survey, and 0.6 percent had used during the prior month (MTF estimates).

Overall, the NSDUH population estimate for nonmedical use of these stimulant drugs was 8.2 percent, and the age group with the highest prevalence value was that made up of eighteen- to twenty-five-year-olds, at 10.7 percent. Within the survey population, recent use of the stimulant drugs was found to be 3.8 percent for the eighteen- to twenty-five-year-olds (NSDUH estimates).

Among adults surveyed in the NESARC, 4.7 percent reported any nonmedical use of amphetamines, and the corresponding rate of disorder

(abuse and/or dependence) was 2 percent (NESARC estimates).

Use of Anxiolytic, Sedative, and Hypnotic Drugs. About 9.3 to 9.5 percent of high school seniors had used tranquilizers (anxiolytic) or sedative-hypnotic (e.g., barbiturate) drugs without a doctor's orders. About 6.2 percent had done so during the year prior to the survey, and nearly 27 percent had done so during the month prior to the survey (MTF estimates, sedatives and tranquilizers reported separately).

About 8.7 percent of the NSDUH survey population reported nonmedical use of tranquilizers or anxiolytic drugs, while 3.6 percent reported nonmedical use of sedative-hypnotic drugs. For tranquilizers, this amounted to more than twenty-one million people using these drugs without a doctor's orders. For sedative-hypnotics, the total was 8.8 million nonmedical users. The estimated number of recently active users was less substantial; they represented 0.7 percent of the survey population for tranquilizers (1,766,000 nonmedical users) and 0.2 percent for the sedative-hypnotics (385,000 nonmedical users).

About 4 percent of adults surveyed in the NESARC had used sedatives nonmedically and around 0.3 percent had been diagnosed with dependence on sedatives. Similarly, 3.4 percent had used tranquilizers and 0.2 percent qualified for a diagnosis of dependence (NESARC estimates).

Use of Opioid Drugs. Any use of heroin was reported by 1.5 percent of high school seniors, with less than 1 percent using in the twelve months prior to the survey. Other opioid drugs often prescribed for the management of pain, such as oxycodone or hydrocodone, are being diverted to nonmedical use and an estimated 13 percent of twelfth graders report trying one of these drugs without a doctor's orders. In other words, more than one of every eight high school seniors have used these prescription opioids nonmedically (MTF estimates).

Similar to the twelfth grade estimates from MTF, 1.5 percent of the national household population aged twelve and older had used heroin at some time, and 0.2 percent or fewer had used within the year prior to the survey. Lifetime use peaks in early adulthood, where 2.4 percent of adults aged twenty-six to thirty-four had tried heroin. Nearly 14 percent of the sample surveyed have tried painkillers for nonmedical purposes, and about 5 percent had been using in the year prior to the survey (NSDUH estimates).

Nearly 5 percent of adults aged eighteen and older surveyed in the NESARC had used opioids nonmedically and 1.4 percent received a diagnosis of use disorder (abuse and/or dependence) (NESARC estimates).

TRENDS AND CURRENT ISSUES

One of the major benefits of these annual epidemiologic surveys is that they can paint a picture of historical, current, and emerging trends in relation to drugs of abuse. Trends tend to be complex and cycle based on the experience of a particular age cohort, as new drugs enter the scene and older drugs re-emerge among young people who have yet to experience the adverse consequences in their generation. For example, by the early 1990s, the second American epidemic of cocaine use had peaked, sustained for some time by crack smoking, and waned by the early 1990s when it became clear that crack smoking had not diffused broadly through the U.S. population. As illustrated by crack smoking, non-injecting heroin use, and crystal methamphetamine (ice), oftentimes the introduction of "new" drugs is merely a new formulation or mode of administration for drugs that have been around for generations.

Throughout this decade, abuse of prescription medications has emerged as one of the most prevalent categories of illicit drug use. Increased availability to consumers and perhaps a lower awareness of the risks of these drugs because they can be prescribed by doctors are just two of the factors that have brought abuse of these medications into the mainstream. More than one in five high school seniors had tried a prescription psychotherapeutic medication at least once without a doctor's orders, 15.4 percent in the year prior to the survey and nearly 8 percent in the month prior (MTF estimates). Similar estimates were reported by household residents aged twelve and older, suggesting that nearly fifty million people have used these medicines for nonmedical reasons (NSDUH estimates).

Despite this entry's unilateral focus on drug abuse there exists a high degree of comorbidity associated with drug use. Comorbidity refers to the occurrence of two or more substance or psychiatric disorders within a certain period of time, and there is a history of epidemiologic surveys such as the Epidemiologic Catchment Area (ECS) study, National Comorbidity Survey (NCS), and the NESARC that have shown mood, anxiety, and personality disorders to be related to drug use and disorders. These findings also have important implications for prevention and control of drug abuse, as it makes the course of these disorders more complex and often more chronic.

EPIDEMIOLOGY OF DRUG USE AND DRUG DEPENDENCE OUTSIDE THE UNITED STATES

Each year, the United States allocates more resources to epidemiologic surveys of drug use than does any other country in the world. For this reason, it has been possible to assemble a wealth of epidemiologic survey data on the prevalence of drug use and drug dependence within the United States. Other countries also have conducted surveys of this type and have produced valuable evidence about their experience with tobacco, alcohol, and other drugs. States, countries, and continents vary dramatically as to which drugs of abuse are more problematic than others, in terms of use as well as production and trafficking.

Of great concern globally is the transmission of HIV/AIDS through injection drug use; up to 10 percent of all HIV infections around the world could be attributable to injection drug use, and in some areas such as Eastern Europe or Central and Southeast Asia injection drug use might account for up to 80 percent of the cases of HIV. (See the bibliography for some references that can be consulted to gain more information about the results of these surveys.)

OTHER ASPECTS OF EPIDEMIOLOGY AS APPLIED TO DRUG USE AND DRUG DEPENDENCE

A broad range of research questions must be answered in order to gain a complete understanding of the epidemiology of drug use and drug dependence. The focus in this entry has been on quantity, or measuring the occurrence or frequency of drug abuse. Although many epidemiologists now devote their research careers to surveys that are needed to answer this kind of basic question, more stress ought to be placed on the other central aspects of epidemiology or aspects of public health that epidemiology can inform. These include the following:

Location, identifying where and within which population subgroups cases are more likely to arise. Location can incorporate geography, season, culture or society, or year in history in which drug involvement is examined. Interaction of geographical context, environmental, social, and economic factors and how they contribute to the etiology of drug abuse is one avenue that can inform this aspect of epidemiology.

Investigation of causes, determining what accounts for some people or populations, but not others, becoming affected. For example, family history has consistently been identified as a compelling risk factor for drug use and abuse, but does not guarantee that future generations will be affected. Advances in research of the interplay between genes and environment, such as studying the effects of the environment on gene expression (epigenetics), heritability, and gene-environment correlations and interactions, and how all these influences change throughout development, are helping scientists understand the causes of complex disorders like drug abuse and dependence.

Studies of linked sequences of causal conditions (i.e., mechanisms) as they relate to drug dependence explore the natural history and clinical course of drug use as it proceeds from exposure to initiation to disorder to remission.

Finally, *prevention and treatment* of drug abuse can improve the public's health and reduce the burden caused by drug disorders.

At its best, epidemiology contributes critically important evidence to each of these rubrics, and it works to ensure that new findings are translated rapidly into effective strategies for prevention. This is the future agenda for epidemiologic research on drug use and drug dependence.

See also **Amphetamine Epidemics, International; Diagnosis of Substance Use Disorders: Diagnostic Criteria; Diagnostic and Statistical Manual (DSM); Drug Abuse Warning Network (DAWN); Epidemics of Drug Abuse in the United States; Social Costs of Alcohol and Drug Abuse.**

BIBLIOGRAPHY

Anthony, J. C., & Helzer, J. E. (2002). Epidemiology of drug dependence. In M. Tsuang & M. Tohen (Eds.), *Textbook of psychiatric epidemiology* (pp. 479–562). New York: Wiley.

Compton, W. M., Thomas, Y. F., Conway, K. P., & Colliver, J. D. (2005). Developments in the epidemiology of drug use and drug use disorders. *American Journal of Psychiatry, 162,* 1494–1502.

Compton, W. M., Thomas, Y. F., Stinson, F. S., & Grant, B. F. (2007). Prevalence, correlates, disability, and comorbidity of *DSM-IV* drug abuse and dependence in the United States: Results from the national epidemiologic survey on alcohol and related conditions. *Archives of General Psychiatry, 64*(5), 566–576.

Heiman, G. A., Ogburn, E., Gorroochurn, P., Keyes, K. M., & Hasin, D. (2008). Evidence for a two-stage model of dependence using the NESARC and its implications for genetic association studies. *Drug and Alcohol Dependence, 92,* 258–266.

Huang, B., Dawson, D. A., Stinson, F. S., Hasin, D. S., Ruan, W. J., Saha, T. D., et al. (2006). Prevalence, correlates, and comorbidity of nonmedical prescription drug use and drug use disorders in the United States: Results of the National Epidemiologic Survey on Alcohol and Related Conditions. *Journal of Clinical Psychiatry, 67,* 1062–1073.

Johnston, L. D., O'Malley, P. M., Bachman, J. G., & Schulenberg, J. E. (2008). *Monitoring the Future national survey results on drug use 1975–2007 Vol. I: Secondary school students* (NIH Publication No. 08-6418A). Bethesda, MD: National Institute on Drug Abuse.

Petersen, R. C. (Ed.). (1978). *The international challenge of drug abuse.* National Institute on Drug Abuse Research Monograph. DHEW Publication No. ADM-78-654. Washington, DC: U.S. Government Printing Office.

Substance Abuse and Mental Health Services Administration. (2007). *Results from the 2006 National Survey on Drug Use and Health: National Findings* (Office of Applied Studies, NSDUH Series H-32, DHHS Publication No. SMA 07-4293). Rockville, MD.

United States Office on Drugs and Crime (UNODC). *2007 World Drug Report.* (United Nations Publication Sales No. E. 07.XI.5 ISBN 978-92-1-148222-5). Available from http://www.unodc.org/.

Winstanley, E. L., Gust, S. W., & Strathdee, S. A. (2006). Drug abuse and HIV/AIDS: International research lessons and imperatives. *Drug and Alcohol Dependence, 82,* S1–S5.

Wu, L-T., & Howard, M. O. (2007). Psychiatric disorders in inhalant users: Results from the National Epidemiologic Survey on Alcohol and Related Conditions. *Drug and Alcohol Dependence, 88,* 146–155.

MARSHA F. LOPEZ
WILSON M. COMPTON

ETHCHLORVYNOL. This is a complex alcohol that causes depression of the central nervous system (CNS). It is a sedative-hypnotic drug typically used on a short-term basis to treat insomnia and is prescribed and sold under the name Placidyl. Because of its depressant effects on the brain, it can impair the mental and/or physical abilities necessary to operate machinery, such as an automobile.

Continued use of ethchlorvynol can result in tolerance and physical dependence leading to abuse. Since the risk of abuse is not very great, it is included in Schedule IV of the Controlled Substances Act. Withdrawal signs, not unlike those seen after alcohol (ethanol) or barbiturates, occur upon termination of its use in addicts. Ethchlorvynol should never be combined with other CNS depressants, such as ethanol or barbiturates, because their depressant effects are additive. Because of their greater safety, the widespread use of benzodiazepines as sedative/hypnotics has largely supplanted the use of ethchlorvynol.

See also **Withdrawal.**

BIBLIOGRAPHY

Hanson, G. R., Venturelli, P. J., & Fleckenstein, A. E. (2005). CNS depressants: Sedative-hypnotics. In *Drugs and Society.* Sudbury, MA: Jones & Bartlett Publishers.

Hobbs, W. R., Rall, T. W., & Verdoorn, T. A. (1996). Hypnotics and sedatives: Ethanol. In J. G. Hardman, et al. (Eds.), *The pharmacological basis of therapeutics* (9th ed.). New York: McGraw-Hill Medical (2005, 11th ed.)

SCOTT E. LUKAS

ETHINAMATE. This is a short-acting sedative-hypnotic drug typically used to treat insomnia. It is prescribed and sold as Valmid. Structurally, it does not resemble the barbiturates, but it shares many effects with this class of drugs; the depressant effects of ethinamate are, however, generally milder than those of most barbiturates. Continued and inappropriate use of ethinamate can lead to tolerance and physical dependence, with withdrawal symptoms very similar to those of the barbiturates. Because of their greater safety, the widespread use of benzodiazepines as sedative/hypnotics has largely supplanted the use of ethinamate.

See also **Withdrawal.**

BIBLIOGRAPHY

Hanson, G. R., Venturelli, P. J., & Fleckenstein, A. E. (2005). CNS depressants: Sedative-hypnotics. In *Drugs and Society.* Sudbury, MA: Jones & Bartlett Publishers.

Hobbs, W. R., Rall, T. W., & Verdoorn, T. A. (1996). Hypnotics and sedatives: Ethanol. In J. G. Hardman, et al. (Eds.), *The pharmacological basis of therapeutics* (9th ed.). New York: McGraw-Hill Medical (2005, 11th ed.)

SCOTT E. LUKAS

ETHNICITY AND DRUGS. *See* **African Americans, Ethnic and Cultural Factors Relevant to Treatment for; Chinese Americans, Alcohol and Drug Use Among; Hispanic Americans, Alcohol and Drug Use Among; Jews and Alcohol; Racial Profiling.**

ETHNOPHARMACOLOGY. This branch of pharmacology studies the use and lore of drugs that have been discovered and developed by sociocultural (or ethnic) groups. It involves the direct observation and report of interactions between the societies and the drugs they have found in their natural environments and the customs that have evolved around such drugs, whether ceremonial, therapeutic, or other. These drugs, usually found in plants (hence similar study by ethnobotanists as well as ethnologists), are described—

as are their effects within the customs, beliefs, and histories of a traditional culture or a specific society.

Examples include descriptions of the use of coca leaves (*Erythroxylon coca*) by indigenous populations of Colombia and Peru, for increased strength and endurance in high altitudes; the ceremonial use of peyote (*Lophophora sp.*) by Native Americans of the Southwest and Mexico; and the use of kava (*Piper methysticum*) in ceremonial drinks by the indigenous populations of many South Pacific islands.

See also **Dover's Powder; Plants, Drugs From.**

BIBLIOGRAPHY

Efron, D. H., Ed. (1967). *Ethnopharmacological search for psychoactive drugs.* Public Health Service Publication No. 1645. Washington, D.C.: U.S. Department of Health, Education, and Welfare.

Etkin, N. L., & Elisabetsky, E. (2005). Seeking a transdisciplinary and culturally germane science: The future of ethnopharmacology. *Journal of Ethnopharmacology, 100,* 23–26.

Ratsch, C. (2005). *The encyclopedia of psychoactive plants: Ethnopharmacology and its applications.* Rochester, VT: Park Street Press.

NICK E. GOEDERS

EUROPEAN UNION. The European Union (EU) is a supranational organization created by a series of treaties. The twenty-seven member states pool their sovereignty to make joint decisions through shared institutions, such as the European Parliament, which is elected by EU citizens, and the Council of the European Union, which represents national governments. Representing the interests of the EU as a whole, the European Commission makes proposals for legislation and enforces the laws that have been adopted by the Council and Parliament. The European Court of Justice ensures that EU law is complied with, and that the various treaties are correctly interpreted and applied. The European Community began as the European Coal and Steel Community in 1952. This "community" was established to achieve the political goal of peace and the economic goal of a common market. During these early years, the European Community had only limited concern for occupational health, and it did not have the legal authority to engage in public health issues. Successive treaties have further unified the member states and expanded the competences to include a wide range of policy areas, including health policy.

The European Community started sponsoring public health education campaigns in the 1970s. However, the Community's first major public health initiative, the Europe Against Cancer Program (EACP), was not established by the Council until July 1986. The main components of this program were cancer prevention, information and public awareness, and training (Hervey, 2002). Within this mandate, the EACP developed legislative proposals for tobacco control, funded the Bureau for Action on Smoking Prevention (BASP), and encouraged the coordination of national cancer groups. In 1993, the Treaty of Maastricht expanded the authority of the community to establish the EU and included an article providing an explicit legal basis for health initiatives. However, Article 129 of the treaty still limited the EU to contributing "towards a high level of human health protection by encouraging cooperation between Member States, and, if necessary, lending support to their action."

In 1999, the Treaty of Amsterdam amended and renumbered the public health section of the Treaty of Maastricht, creating the current Article 152, which defines the role of the EU as complementing national policies, setting out procedures by which the EU institutions may act in the health field, and delineating the types of measures that may be enacted. Member states retain responsibility for the organization and delivery of health services and medical care. The EU Treaty is known as "primary legislation" because it gives the EU the authority to act. Secondary legislation consists mainly of regulations, directives, and recommendations adopted by the EU institutions. Although EU legislation sets minimum excise duties and product definitions for alcohol and tobacco, member states define their own tax structures. Thus, taxes and prices for alcohol and tobacco vary widely among member states.

To reduce the burden of disease and promote the health of the general population, the European Commission has developed a coordinated approach

1. A high level of human health protection shall be ensured in the definition and implementation of all Community policies and activities.
   Community action, which shall complement national policies, shall be directed towards improving public health, preventing human illness and diseases, and obviating sources of danger to human health. Such action shall cover the fight against the major health scourges, by promoting research into their causes, their transmission and their prevention, as well as health information and education.
   The Community shall complement the Member States' action in reducing drugs-related health damage, including information and prevention.

2. The Community shall encourage cooperation between the Member States in the areas referred to in this Article and, if necessary, lend support to their action. Member States shall, in liaison with the Commission, coordinate among themselves their policies and programmes in the areas referred to in paragraph 1. The Commission may, in close contact with the Member States, take any useful initiative to promote such coordination.

3. The Community and the Member States shall foster cooperation with third countries and the competent international organisations in the sphere of public health.

4. The Council, acting in accordance with the procedure referred to in Article 251 and after consulting the Economic and Social Committee and the Committee of the Regions, shall contribute to the achievement of the objectives referred to in this article through adopting:
   (a) measures setting high standards of quality and safety of organs and substances of human origin, blood and blood derivatives; these measures shall not prevent any Member State from maintaining or introducing more stringent protective measures;
   (b) by way of derogation from Article 37, measures in the veterinary and phytosanitary fields which have as their direct objective the protection of public health;
   (c) incentive measures designed to protect and improve human health, excluding any harmonisation of the laws and regulations of the Member States.
   The Council, acting by a qualified majority on a proposal from the Commission, may also adopt recommendations for the purposes set out in this article.

5. Community action in the field of public health shall fully respect the responsibilities of the Member States for the organisation and delivery of health services and medical care. In particular, measures referred to in paragraph 4(a) shall not affect national provisions on the donation or medical use of organs and blood.

Table 1. Treaty of the European Union, Public Health Article 152. ILLUSTRATION BY GGS INFORMATION SERVICES. GALE, CENGAGE LEARNING

to addressing major health determinants, including the harmful usage of illicit drugs, alcohol, and tobacco. The Health and Consumer Protection Directorate-General (DG) is primarily responsible for health policy within the Commission. EU health policy was first set out in the European Community health strategy put forward in May 2000. A new health strategy, outlined in the white paper "Together for Health: A Strategic Approach for the EU 2008–2013," was adopted on October 23, 2007. There are two main goals of this strategy. The first is to encourage and support the development of actions and networks for compiling, reporting, and exchanging information to evaluate and define policies, strategies, and programs, with the purpose of establishing effective health interventions. The second is to promote and stimulate member states' efforts to reduce negative health impacts through the regulation of harmful substances, information and education campaigns, and treatment programs.

TOBACCO

Following the EACP, EU tobacco policies have been criticized for the inconsistent objectives of reducing the negative health impacts of tobacco while simultaneously subsidizing tobacco farmers and protecting tobacco industry jobs. The EU is one of the largest cigarette manufacturing regions in the world, and there is an extensive export market. Subsidies for tobacco farmers were approximately one billion euros (US $1.5 billion) in 2005. These subsidies are being phased out, however, with a target date of 2010, and the Common Agricultural Policy (CAP) that manages the tobacco subsidy is encouraging sustainable economic development by rewarding the transition to healthful products and developing alternative sources of income and economic activity (European Commission, 2008). This shift toward public health policies taking precedent over agricultural interests stems from the fact that tobacco-related diseases are the single largest cause of death in Europe (ASPECT Consortium, 2004).

After the first wave of tobacco-control legislation, including taxation, directives on regulation, and an attempted ban on advertising, the tobacco industry implemented their own comprehensive lobbying strategy (Gilmore & Mckee, 2004). The industry's well-funded and multidimensional approach included the creation of the Confederation of European Community Cigarette Manufacturers, the funding of smokers' rights groups, and the support of research facilities. Tobacco industry documents later revealed close associations with both national government officials and EU staff. In particular, tobacco lobbyists encouraged and supported the German government's successful legal challenge overturning the EU's first Tobacco Advertising Directive in 2001. The German government complained that the official legal basis for the directive, the regulation of the single European market, did not support a total tobacco advertising

Public Health Agency	Created in January 2005 to manage all the phases of specific projects funded under the Program; to execute the budget for all operations necessary for the management of the Program; and to provide logistical, scientific and technical support for meetings and conferences. http://ec.europa.eu/phea/what_is_phea/what_is_phea_en.html
European Monitoring Centre for Drugs and Drug Addiction	Inaugurated in 1995, the EMCDDA is the hub of drug-related information in the European Union. It exists to provide the EU and its Member States with a factual overview of European drug problems and a common information framework to support the drugs debate. http://www.emcdda.europa.eu/
European Foundation for the Improvement of Living and Working Conditions EUROFOUND	Established in 1975, to collect information advice and expertise—on living and working conditions, industrial relations and managing change in Europe—for key actors in the field of EC social policy on the basis of comparative information research and analysis. http://www.eurofound.europa.eu/

Table 2. Selected health-related European Union agencies. ILLUSTRATION BY GGS INFORMATION SERVICES. GALE, CENGAGE LEARNING

ban. The European Court of Justice agreed, and found that the EU Treaty did not provide legal authority to justify the ban on public health grounds. The Commission quickly drafted a new directive, which was submitted to the Parliament and Council for approval. Negotiations were again strained, with Germany firmly supporting the tobacco industry's interests. Agreement on the new directive was not reached until November 2002, when the Parliament passed a watered-down draft. Thus, the Tobacco Advertising Directive (*Directive 2003/33/EC on the Approximation of the Laws, Regulations and Administrative Provisions of the Member States Relating to the Advertising and Sponsorship of Tobacco Products*) was ultimately adopted without the support of Germany and the United Kingdom. The Court rejected Germany's second legal challenge, ruling that the measures in the directive were appropriate for achieving the stated objectives.

The primary laws now regulating the tobacco market in the EU are the 2003 Tobacco Advertising Directive and the 2001 Tobacco Products Directive (*Directive 2001/37/EC on the Approximation of the Laws, Regulations and Administrative Provisions of the Member States Concerning the Manufacture, Presentation and Sale of Tobacco Products*). The Products Directive requires high-visibility, hard-hitting health warnings on all tobacco products sold in the EU, and misleading descriptors such as "light," "ultra light," and "mild," which give the impression that certain types of cigarette are less dangerous, are banned. The directive also regulates maximum levels of tar, nicotine, and carbon monoxide in cigarettes. The Advertising Directive bans all tobacco advertising

on the radio, the Internet, and in the print media in EU countries, and it prohibits tobacco sponsorship of cross-border events. The directive is limited, however, in that it does not cover advertising in cinemas, on billboards, or at strictly local sporting events. In April 2006 the European Commission sent formal notice of noncompliance to the Czech Republic, Italy, Hungary, and Spain for failure to enforce the Tobacco Advertising Directive. These states must bring their legislation into conformity with the directive or face infringement procedures (European Commission, 2006a). (For a detailed comparison of tobacco control legislation in thirty European countries, see the report written by Luk Joossens and Martin Raw in 2007.) As of 2007, all EU members have signed the Framework Convention on Tobacco Control (FCTC), and all but two have ratified the convention.

The EU has also sponsored significant anti-smoking media and education campaigns. From 2002 to 2004 the €18 million "Feel Free to Say No" antismoking campaign included television advertising geared toward adolescents. An evaluation of the campaign disclosed the need for more narrowly targeted strategies and greater focus on the independence of youth and the risks of addiction (Evalua, 2003). In 2005 the Commission launched a new campaign, "HELP—For a Life without Tobacco" with a budget of 72 million euros (US $113 million). This multimedia Europe-wide campaign includes Web-based advertising, more nationally tailored messaging, and information about the dangers of exposure to environmental smoke.

Policy trends in the EU have focused on encouraging member states to enact legislation expanding smoking bans in public places and requiring health labels to include color pictures. In an Annex to *Commission Decision 2003/641/ EC on the Use of Color Photographs or Other Illustrations as Health Warnings on Tobacco Packages*, in accordance with Article 5 of the Products Directive, the Commission adopted a library of forty-two selected source documents and technical specifications for printing combined pictorial and written warnings. Member states have also been encouraged to use combined warnings that include quitline phone numbers, Internet addresses, or other visual elements informing smokers about the support available to whose who want to stop smoking. However, a 2007 Commission report found that only Belgium, Romania, and the United Kingdom had plans to implement the combined pictorial warnings by autumn 2008 (European Commission, 2007e).

In 2007 the Commission published a green paper examining the health and economic burdens associated with passive smoking, public support for smoking bans, and the measures taken so far at national and EU level (European Commission, 2007b). The Commission had invited stakeholders to express their views on the scope of measures available to address the dangers of passive smoking and the most appropriate form of EU intervention. The responses verified that only a full smoking ban in all enclosed workplaces and public places could adequately protect the health of citizens and workers. However, mechanisms to achieve this goal must be addressed at both the member state and the EU level. The paper concluded that the EU should provide support in cases where national governments encounter political difficulties introducing comprehensive smoke-free legislation in the hospitality and leisure sector.

Cigarette smuggling into and across Europe has continued to be a problem since the creation of the Single European Market. On March 18, 2008, the European Anti-Fraud Office (OLAF) announced the arrest of twenty-six people in Poland and Germany, including the presumed main organizers of an international criminal gang responsible for smuggling millions of cigarettes into the EU from former Soviet Union countries and China. In addition to the arrests, the authorities in Poland seized nearly seven million cigarettes, a truck that was in the process of being loaded with contraband cigarettes, nearly three million euros in cash, and nine kilos of gold and jewelry (European Anti-Fraud Office, 2008).

ALCOHOL

The EU has the highest level of alcohol consumption in the world, with 11 liters of pure alcohol drunk per adult per year (Anderson & Baumberg, 2006). Alcohol has been produced and consumed in Europe for thousands of years, and it is deeply intertwined with many local cultural traditions. Prior to the major EU expansion in 1995, the European Commission defined alcohol as either an industrial or an agricultural product. Only distilled spirits were regulated as an alcoholic beverage, but the powerful Amsterdam Group, representing large international alcohol corporations, has effectively protected the industry's interests for many years (Kurzer, 1998).

The European Court of Justice has also played an active role in the harmonization of alcohol control regulations among member states. In two 2004 cases regarding the French ban on alcohol advertising on television (Cases C 262/02, *Commission v. France*, and C 429/02, *Bacardi France v. TF1, Groupe Jean-Claude Darmon and Girosport*), the Court held that the member states could justify legislation regulating the alcohol industry in order to protect public health and safety (Kurzer, 1998). In other cases, however, the court has ruled that the means used to regulate the alcohol market were not proportionate to attain the objective of protecting young persons from the harmful effects of alcohol. Under Swedish law, for example, private individuals must apply to the Swedish retail monopoly, called Systembolaget, to import any alcoholic beverages not available through the state-run stores. In Case C-170/04, *Klas Rosengren and Others v. Riksaklagaren* (2007), the court held that the prohibition was a quantitative restriction on the free movement of goods that could not be justified on public health grounds, since Sweden had failed to demonstrate that the process was necessary to prevent underage drinkers from gaining access to alcohol. Therefore the ECJ closely analyzes the restriction in each case to determine whether it is proportionate to the stated public interest goal, such as public health.

European Public Health Alliance http://www.epha.org	EPHA is an international non-profit association composed of not-for-profit organizations working on all aspects of public health. EPHA's mission is to promote and protect the health of all people living in Europe and to advocate for greater participation of citizens in health-related policy making at the European level.
European Network for Smoking Prevention http://www.ensp.org	ENSP's mission is to develop a strategy for coordinated action among organizations active in tobacco control in Europe by sharing information and experience and through coordinated activities and joint projects. ENSP aims to create greater coherence among smoking prevention activities and to promote comprehensive tobacco control policies at both national and European levels.
European Alliance on Drug Policy and Practice http://www.eadpp.eu	The mission of the EADPP is to create a channel for dialogue between the European Institutions and key stakeholders involved in prevention, treatment, care and (community) empowerment in the drug field; to influence the development of policy on reducing drug related harm; to encourage bottom up ideas and models of good practice from local or national level to European level; and to communicate European drug strategies and action plans back to national and local level.
EUROCARE European Alliance for Alcohol Policy http://eurocare.org	EUROCARE was formed in 1990 as an alliance of voluntary and non-governmental organizations representing a diversity of views and cultural attitudes and concerned with the impact of the European Union on alcohol policy in Member States. Member organizations are involved in the provision of information to the public; education and training of voluntary and professional community care workers; the provision of workplace and school based programs; counseling services, residential support and alcohol-free clubs for problem drinkers; and research and advocacy institutes.

Table 3. Relevant European non-governmental health organizations. ILLUSTRATION BY GGS INFORMATION SERVICES. GALE, CENGAGE LEARNING

The increased attention paid to alcohol-related harms encouraged a belated discussion of the public health aspects of underage and excessive alcohol consumption. In 2001 a Council Recommendation titled "Community Strategy to Reduce Alcohol Related Harm" recognized that alcohol was a key health determinant and invited the Commission to develop a comprehensive strategy to reduce the negative health impacts of alcohol. Accordingly, the Commission began public consultations and solicited reports to analyze the problem. One study estimated the economic cost of alcohol-attributable crime to be 33 billion euros in 2003. Alcohol is also responsible for about 195,000 deaths in the EU each year (Anderson & Baumberg, 2006). Based on these reports and public consultations the Commission published its 2006 Communication, the *EU Strategy to Support Member States in Reducing Alcohol-Related Harm*. The strategy focuses on five priority themes: (1) protect young people, children, and the unborn child; (2) reduce injuries and deaths from alcohol-related traffic accidents; (3) prevent alcohol-related harm among adults; (4) reduce the negative impact of alcohol in the workplace (such as absenteeism, drinking on the job, and health issues); and (5) develop, support, and maintain a common evidence base. The Commission defined its role as: (1) to inform, educate, and raise awareness about the major public health concerns regarding alcohol consumption, and to cooperate with member states in addressing these; (2) to initiate action at the EU level through public health programs; and (3) to support and help coordinate national actions by identifying and disseminating good practices across the EU.

In June 2007, the European Alcohol and Health Forum was established to facilitate the implementation of the 2006 Communication. Forum members include European umbrella organizations capable of playing an active role in reducing alcohol-related harm in the EU. These groups will engage in concrete and verifiable commitments to reach this goal. The forum meets twice a year and focuses on concrete actions to protect children and young people and prevent irresponsible commercial alcohol communication and sales. It has also created task forces to focus on youth-specific aspects of alcohol consumption and on alcohol marketing.

ILLICIT DRUGS

Due to the local nature of illicit drug use and related crime, there is a wide variation in national legislation, policies, and expenditures within the European Community. There are no directives specifically regulating drugs from a public health perspective, but the EU coordinates information gathering and dissemination, as well as the identification and sharing of best practices for drug treatment and control. In 2003 the Council of the European Union released its *Recommendation on the Prevention and Reduction of Health Related*

Tobacco	
Tobacco Products Directive 2001/37/EC	Directive on the approximation of the laws, regulations and administrative provisions of the Member States concerning the manufacture, presentation and sale of tobacco products
Tobacco Advertising Directive 2003/33/EC	Directive on the approximation of the laws, regulations and administrative provisions of the Member States relating to the advertising and sponsorship of tobacco products
Commission Decision 2003/641/ec	Commission Decision on the use of color photographs or other illustrations as health warnings on tobacco packages
Council Recommendation 2003/54/EC	Council Recommendation on the prevention of smoking and on initiatives to improve tobacco control
Council Decision 2004/513/EC	Council Decision concerning the conclusion of the WHO Framework Convention on tobacco control
Commission Green Paper January 2007	Towards a Europe free from tobacco smoke: policy options at EU level
Alcohol	
Council Recommendation 2001/458/EC	Council Recommendation on the drinking of alcohol by young people, in particular children and adolescents
Commission Communication COM(2006) 625	Commission Communication on an EU strategy to support Member States in reducing alcohol related harm
Drugs	
Council Recommendation 2003/488/EC	Council Recommendation on the prevention and reduction of health-related harm associated with drug dependence
Commission Green Paper COM(2006) 316	The Role of Civil Society in Drugs Policy in the EU

Table 4. Key European Union public health legislation. ILLUSTRATION BY GGS INFORMATION SERVICES. GALE, CENGAGE LEARNING

Harm Associated with Drug Dependence. This document focused on the need for member states to actively address drug-related health issues at the state and local level.

The European Monitoring Centre for Drugs and Drug Addiction (EMCDDA) compiles and reports data regarding the problem of illicit drugs in the EU, but it has no regulatory authority. EMCDDA helps to develop national monitoring systems based on common methodologies and standards, thus providing an evidence base for policymakers at the national and European levels. Generally, cannabis use seems to have leveled off in the first decade of the twenty-first century, while cocaine use is on an upward trend. Interventions in the 1990s were effective at controlling the spread of HIV among infected drug users in most of Europe, but HIV is still prevalent, especially in the Baltic states. Hepatitis C rates are high among injecting populations, and studies have shown that young injectors continue to acquire the disease relatively quickly, making early intervention crucial. The downward trend in drug-related deaths also seems to have leveled off, apparently because of an increase in overdoses by young users (EMCDDA, 2007).

The comparative information generated by the EMCDDA contributed to the development and implementation of the EU Drugs Strategy for 2005–2012, which was outlined in a 2004 Communication. The strategy is intended to reduce both the demand and supply of drugs, with a budget of 21,350,000 euros (US $33,551,000) (CEU, 2004). Due to the EU's limited competence to work in this field, the strategy focuses primarily on research, information dissemination, and evaluation. At the EU level, the Horizontal Working Party on Drugs, a coordinating committee within the Council, was established to monitor the implementation of the actions set out in the EU Action Plans on Drugs, and to coordinate other Council working groups dealing with drug-related issues. (Two action plans were announced, one covering the period 2005–2008, and the other covering 2009–2012.)

Demand-side strategies focus on the development and implementation of integrated and comprehensive knowledge-based demand reduction systems, including treatment, harm reduction, and rehabilitation and social integration. Supply-side strategies involve several branches of EU institutions. EU legislation provides a framework for the control of trade in the chemical precursors for drugs, both within the Community and in other countries. This legislation is enforced through the Commission's Environment Directorate-General (DG). With regard to money laundering, the Council set out a number of measures to prevent the laundering of drugs proceeds in the 2005 *Third Directive on Money Laundering*. The DG for Justice and Home Affairs, meanwhile, has encouraged cooperation between police, customs, and judicial authorities. Finally, in the area of external relations, the EU is taking international action through a combination of political initiatives, including the action plans, dialogue with various regions of the world, and assistance through development programs to third country sources of drug supply.

In June 2006 the Commission published its "Green Paper on the Role of Civil Society in Drugs Policy in the European Union." At the same time, The DG for Justice and Home Affairs organized the Civil Society Forum for Drugs, and it called for interested civil society organizations to formally express their interest in taking part in such a forum. The December 2007 meeting of the forum addressed current issues arising from the first EU Action Plan on Drugs, and a Progress Review was carried out by the Commission. The forum provides a channel for exchanging views, ideas, and information between the Commission and civil society organizations, and it provides for civil society input on the policy development and reflection process at the European level. The April 2007 *Commission Report on the Implementation of the 2003 Recommendation on the Prevention and Reduction of Health-Related Harm Associated with Drug Dependence* provides that the current status of implementation across EU will be used as a baseline for comparison with future studies. The Commission proposes that the action plan for 2009–2012 include a Council recommendation on reduction of drug-related harm in prisons, as well as a report on drug-treatment programs designed to encourage an exchange of good practice information.

CONCLUSION

EU institutions have become increasingly active in addressing public health risks and investing in programs to reduce the harm caused by tobacco,

Selected departments and initiatives	
DG Health and Consumer Protection, SANCO	Responsible for public health, consumer policy, food safety, animal health http://ec.europa.eu/dgs/health_consumer/index_en.htm
Commission's Public Health Strategy	Includes links to information, documents, and programs on the public health http://ec.europa.eu/health/index_en.htm
Health EU	Includes data and information on Public Health initiatives and programs at EU level http://ec.europa.eu/health-eu/health_in_the_eu/index_en.htm
DG Justice Freedom and Security	Illegal Drugs; Immigration policy and integration, protection of personal data concerning health http://ec.europa.eu/justice_home/web/policy/drugs/web_drugs_en.htm
DG Employment Social Affairs and Equal Opportunities	Safety and Health at work; coordination of Social security schemes including the EHIC card; access of people with disabilities to social health services; Europe Social Fund http://ec.europa.eu/employment_social/health_safety/index_en.htm
DG Agriculture and Rural Development	Nutritional aspects in promotional campaigns for EU agricultural products, information campaigns on smoking http://ec.europa.eu/agriculture/markets/tobacco/index_en.htm
Anti-Fraud Office OLAF	Illicit trade in tobacco products http://ec.europa.eu/anti_fraud/index_en.html

Table 5. European Commission, selected departments and agencies. ILLUSTRATION BY GGS INFORMATION SERVICES. GALE, CENGAGE LEARNING

alcohol, and illicit drugs. EU policies regulating these substances are a complex web of binding legislation and nonbinding recommendations. Member States are under increasing pressure, both politically and financially, to reduce the burden caused by unhealthy lifestyles that risk public health. Those responsible for designing and implementing EU policies in these fields include supranational, national, and local government organizations, as well as various nongovernmental organizations, such as the European Public Health Alliance, the European Network for Smoking Prevention, the European Alliance on Drug Policy and Practice, and EUROCARE (European Alliance for Alcohol Policy). The Commission's white paper "Together for Health: A Strategic Approach for the EU 2008–2013" identifies drugs, alcohol, and tobacco as key health determinants that must be addressed to realize the objective of fostering good health in an aging population. The strategy sets out implementation mechanisms for cooperation between partners, reinforcing health in all policies, and increasing understanding about health issues at the EU level.

The EU has frequently had difficulty balancing economic and social interests. As was mentioned above, for example, the EU simultaneously funds tobacco agricultural subsidies and antismoking campaigns, while large-scale alcohol production and distribution frustrates efforts to reduce harm from underage and excessive alcohol consumption. In addition, many of the funding streams and public health programs have not been adequately evaluated, either for efficiency or effectiveness. Indeed, the EU is still trying to define its role in addressing these issues, and it could take a more proactive role in promoting public health strategies to reduce the ill effects of drugs, alcohol, and tobacco.

See also **Britain; Eastern Europe; Foreign Policy and Drugs, United States; France; Germany; International Drug Supply Systems; Ireland, Republic of; Spain.**

BIBLIOGRAPHY

Anderson, P., & Baumberg, B. (2006). *Alcohol in Europe, a public health perspective: A report for the EU Commission.* Brussels: DG Health and Consumer Protection. Available from http://ec.europa.eu/health-eu/news_alcoholineurope_en.htm

ASPECT Consortium (Analysis of the Science and policy for European Control of Tobacco). (2004). *Tobacco or health in the European Union, past, present, and future.* Luxembourg: Office for Official Publications of the European Communities. Available from http://ec.europa.eu/.

Bitton, A., Neuman, M., & Glantz, S. (2002). Tobacco industry attempts to subvert European Union tobacco advertising legislation. *The Lancet, 359,* 1323–1330.

Cnossen, S. (2006). *Tobacco taxation in the European Union.* CESifo working paper no. 1718, May 2006. Maastricht: Center for Economic Studies and Ifo Institute for Economic Research (CESifo). Available from http://www.cesifo.de/.

Cnossen, S. (2007). Alcohol taxation and regulation in the European Union. *International Tax Public Finance, 14*(6), 699–732.

Council of the European Union. (2000). *Council Resolution: Action on health determinants 2000/C 218/03.* Brussels: Author.

Council of the European Union. (2001a). *Directive concerning the manufacture, presentation and sale of tobacco products.* Directive 2001/37/EC 2002 IP/02/1383. Brussels: Author.

Council of the European Union. (2001b). *Council Recommendation: Community strategy to reduce alcohol related harm.* 2001/458/EC. Brussels: Author.

Council of the European Union. (2003a). *Directive relating to the advertising and sponsorship of tobacco products.* Directive 2003/33/EC. Brussels: Author.

Council of the European Union. (2003b). *Council Recommendation on the prevention and reduction of health-related harm associated with drug dependence.* 2003/488/EC. Brussels: Author.

Council of the European Union. (2003c). *Commission Decision on the use of colour photographs or other illustrations as health warnings on tobacco packages.* 2003/641/EC. Brussels: Author.

Council of the European Union. (2004). *General Secretariat Communication to European Council on the EU drugs strategy (2005–2012).* 15074/04. Brussels: Author.

Council of the European Union. (2005). *Directive on the prevention of the use of the financial system for the purpose of money laundering and terrorist financing.* Directive 2005/60/EC. Brussels: Author.

European Anti-Fraud Office (OLAF). (2008). Press Release: International cigarette smuggling ring dismantled. OLAF/08/04, March 18, 2008. Brussels: Author. Available from http://ec.europa.eu/anti_fraud/.

European Commission. (2006a). Press Release: Tobacco advertising: European Commission takes action against four non-compliant Member States. IP/06/435. April 4. Brussels: Author.

European Commission (EC). (2006b). Commission Green Paper on the role of civil society in drugs policy in the European Union. COM (2006) 316 final. Brussels: Author.

European Commission (EC). (2006c). *Communication from the Commission: EU strategy to support member states in reducing alcohol related harm.* COM (2006) 625 final. Brussels: Author.

European Commission (EC). (2007a) *Report to the Council and the European Parliament on the implementation of the 2003 Council Recommendation on the prevention and reduction of health-related harm associated with drug dependence reports on the status of implementation across EU.* COM (2007) 199 final. Brussels: Author.

European Commission (EC). (2007b) Commission Green Paper: Towards a Europe free from tobacco smoke: policy options at EU level. COM (2007) 27 final. CEU. Brussels: Author.

European Commission (EC). (2007c) Commission Press Release: European Commission, businesses and NGO's create Forum to battle alcohol-related harm, June 7, 2007. Brussels: Author.

European Commission (EC). (2007d) Commission White Paper: Together for health: A strategic approach for the EU 2008–2013. COM (2007) 13 final. Brussels: Author.

European Commission (EC). (2007e) *Commission Report: Second report on the application of the tobacco products directive*. COM (2007) 754 final. CEU. Brussels: Author.

European Commission (EC). (2008) Commission Press Release: Commission proposes to continue financing community tobacco fund to pay for awareness raising on dangers of tobacco. Brussels: Author.

European Monitoring Centre for Drugs and Drug Addiction (EMCDDA). (2007). *Annual report 2007: The state of the drugs problem in Europe*. Lisbon: Author. Available from http://www.emcdda.europa.eu/.

Evalua. (2003). Evaluation process for the commission, tobacco prevention media campaign, "Feel Free To Say No," evaluation report, December 15, 2003. Available from http://ec.europa.eu/.

Gilmore, A., & McKee, M. (2004) Tobacco-control policy in the European Union. In E. A. Feldman & R. Bayer (Eds.), *Unfiltered: Conflicts over tobacco policy and public health* (pp. 219–370). Cambridge, MA: Harvard University Press.

Hervey, T. (2002). The legal basis of European Community public health policy. In R. Baeten, M. McKee, & E. Mossialos (Eds.), *The impact of EU law on health care systems* (pp. 23–56). Belgium: P.I.E. Peter Lang.

Holland, W., & Mossialos, E. (1999). *Public health policies in the European Union*. Aldershot, UK: Ashgate.

Joossens, Luk, & Raw, Martin. (2007) Progress in tobacco control in 30 European countries, 2005–2007. Paper presented at the 4th European Conference "Tobacco or Health" 2007, Basel, Switzerland, October 11–13, 2007.

Kurzer, P. Alcohol policy in Sweden and Finland: Challenges for the future. *Scandinavian Review*, Autumn 1998. Available from http://findarticles.com/p/articles/mi_qa3760/is_199810/ai_n8818952/pg_2.

ELIAS MOSSIALOS
JULIA LEAR

EXCLUSIONARY RULE. In legal proceedings, the exclusionary rule prohibits the use of any evidence obtained in contravention of the U.S. Constitution. The rule is frequently invoked when government authorities seize evidence in violation of the Fourth Amendment's prohibition against unlawful searches and seizures. Evidence may be illegally obtained when government officials do not have a warrant to search an individual's premises or the warrant is defective. Law enforcement officers may also lack sufficient probable cause to arrest a person. In addition, the courts may invoke the exclusionary rule when they find a violation of an individual's Fifth Amendment right against self-incrimination or a violation of a defendant's Sixth Amendment right to counsel. Courts often refer to evidence obtained in violation of the Fourth, Fifth, or Sixth Amendment as "tainted" or "the fruit of a poisonous tree."

The U.S. Supreme Court established the exclusionary rule in the early 1900s. It applies to all federal courts through the Fourth Amendment and to all state courts through the Due Process Clause of the Fourteenth Amendment. Before the rule was created, any evidence was admissible in a criminal trial if the judge found it relevant. It made no difference how the police had obtained it. In *Weeks v. United States*, 232 U.S. 383, 34 S.Ct. 341, 58 L.Ed. 652 (1914), the Supreme Court barred the use of evidence secured through a warrantless search of a defendant's house by federal agents. However, for almost fifty years the exclusionary rule only applied to federal courts.

The Supreme Court broadened the rule's coverage in *Mapp v. Ohio*, 367 U.S. 643, 81 S.Ct. 1684, 6 L.Ed.2d 1081 (1961). It held that the Due Process Clause of the Fourteenth Amendment requires states to exclude evidence obtained from an unconstitutional search or seizure. The Court has often cited an individual's right to privacy and the deterrence of unreasonable police conduct as the primary reasons for excluding evidence obtained from an unreasonable search and seizure.

A criminal defendant who claims an unreasonable search and seizure is usually allowed to make the claims in a suppression hearing that is conducted before the trial. At this hearing the judge must determine what evidence will be suppressed or excluded from trial.

A number of exceptions to the exclusionary rule have emerged to reduce the effects of the doctrine, such as a police officer's good-faith belief that an otherwise defective warrant is valid, evidence obtained in hot pursuit, or evidence seized in plain view of the law enforcement officer's sight and reach. There are other exceptions to the exclusionary rule. Evidence seized by private parties is not excluded from trial if the search was not at the direction of law enforcement officers. If a criminal defendant testifies in his or her own defense, illegally seized evidence may be used to discredit the defendant's testimony. Illegally seized evidence can also be used in grand jury proceedings and civil proceedings. However, a grand jury cannot use illegally seized evidence if it was obtained in violation of federal wiretapping statutes.

IMPORTANCE IN DRUG CASES AND ENFORCEMENT

The exclusionary rule prohibits the introduction of constitutionally tainted evidence. The effect of the doctrine has often been the exclusion of evidence that might be used to convict a suspected drug trafficker or abuser. Courts have excluded evidence of drug paraphernalia or supplies illegally seized, admissions obtained by coercion or without notifying the party of the right to remain silent, and evidence obtained in violation of a defendant's Sixth Amendment right to counsel, such as a lineup identification. The Supreme Court has determined that it is preferable to allow a drug trafficker to go free than to permit law enforcement officers to violate a citizen's constitutionally protected rights.

Two recent Supreme Court cases illustrate the polarities in Fourth Amendment exclusionary rule cases. In *Minnesota v. Carter*, 525 U.S. 83, 119 S.Ct. 469, 142 L.Ed.2d 373 (1998), the Court had to balance law enforcement and privacy interests in assessing the reasonableness of a drug search and seizure. The key issue was whether a police officer who looked in an apartment window through a gap in a closed window blind violated the privacy of the drug dealers in the apartment because they had an expectation of privacy that is protected by the Fourth Amendment. The Supreme Court held that the police officer did not violate the Fourth Amendment because the occupants of the apartment did not have an expectation of privacy. Therefore, the drugs that the police officer saw and later seized did not have to be excluded from evidence.

The outcome was much different in *Bond v. U.S.*, 529 U.S. 334, 120 S.Ct. 1462, 146 L.Ed.2d 365 (2000). In this case, the Court ruled that police cannot squeeze the luggage of bus passengers to try to find illegal drugs. The U.S. Border Patrol routinely squeezed carry-on luggage of bus passengers at a permanent Border Patrol checkpoint near the Texas-Mexico border. Border Patrol officers discovered a brick of methamphetamine after feeling the defendant's soft-sided bag. The Supreme Court noted that the Fourth Amendment provides that a person's effects are protected from unreasonable searches and seizures. A traveler's piece of luggage was clearly an effect protected by the amendment. It found that a "bus passenger clearly expects that his bag may be handled. He does not expect that other passengers or bus employees will, as a matter of course, feel the bag in an exploratory manner." Because the agent did manipulate the bag, he violated the Fourth Amendment. In addition, the Court ruled that the defendant's expectation of privacy was reasonable. It distinguished prior rulings that defeated exclusionary rule challenges because they were based on visual inspections, not tactile inspections.

The Supreme Court continued to relax the use of the exclusionary rule in *Hudson v. Michigan*, 547 U.S. 586, 126 S.Ct. 2159, 165 L.Ed.2d 56 (2006). The Court held that the exclusionary rule did not apply when police officers enter a home to execute a search warrant without following the knock-and-announce rule. This rule, which reaches back to medieval England, requires police to announce themselves and give the resident an opportunity to open the door. The Court reasoned that although the exclusionary rule serves to protect the interests of the Fourth Amendment, the purposes behind the knock-and-announce rule did not protect a person's interest in preventing the government from seizing evidence described in a warrant.

The Court also was concerned that there were considerable social costs in applying the exclusionary rule to knock-and-announce cases. Allowing dangerous criminals to go free was one cost; another was the prospect of many criminal defendants claiming a knock-and-announce violation in hopes of suppressing incriminating evidence. Another reason was that police officers would wait longer than the law required, leading to preventable attacks on officers and the destruction of evidence. Persons who have suffered a knock-and-announce violation could sue the police for damages under federal civil rights laws as a means of deterrence.

See also **Crime and Drugs; Drug Courts; Drug Laws, Prosecution of; Seizures of Drugs.**

BIBLIOGRAPHY

Cammack, M., & Garland, N. (2001). Advanced criminal procedure in a nutshell. St. Paul, MN: West Publishing Co.

Dash, S. (2004) The intruders: Unreasonable searches and seizures from King John to John Ashcroft. Rutgers, NJ: Rutgers University Press.

Long, C. (2006). Mapp v. Ohio: Guarding against unreasonable searches and seizures. Lawrence, KS: University Press of Kansas.

ROBERT T. ANGAROLA
ALAN MINSK
REVISED BY FREDERICK K. GRITTNER (2009)

EXPECTANCIES. The concept of *cognitive expectations* was introduced by psychologist Edward Tolman (1932), who later simplified the term to *expectancies* and defined them as cognitive "sets in the nervous system aroused by environmental stimuli" that influence subsequent behavior (1945, p. 165). Formalized by MacCorquodale and Meehl in 1953, and applied to human social behavior by Rotter in 1954, expectancies came to be understood as "stored information," that allows animals and humans to "act appropriately to impending events" (Bolles, 1972, p. 402). By "appropriately" Bolles meant in an "evolutionarily beneficial" manner.

The concept of *expectancy/anticipation/prediction* has emerged independently in increasingly diverse scientific venues (Goldman, 2002; Goldman et al., 2006), demonstrating that the brain may be well characterized as an "anticipatory machine" (Dennett, 1991) that includes "neural networks that match sensory input with learned expectations"; these processes "help explain how humans see, hear, learn, and recognize information" (Grossberg, 1995, p. 438). Venues in which expectancy

explanations have emerged include operant and classical conditioning, comparative judgment, models of memory, the neurobiology of animal and human reward and reinforcement, perception of motion, development of language, time perception, brain electrophysiology, music appreciation, visual orienting behavior in early infancy, and social functioning and the neurobiology of interpersonal trust, among others. At more basic levels, Kupfermann and colleagues (2000) refer to similar processes when they say, "homeostatic regulation is often *anticipatory*" (italics added; p. 1007). Adjustment of the homeostatic set point to anticipate repeated stressors has been called *allostasis*, a process implicated in alcohol and drug addiction.

In the clinical domain, expectancy has been related to mood dysfunction, fear, pain reduction, sexual dysfunction, asthma, drug abuse, alcohol abuse and dependence, smoking, placebo and nocebo (psychologically induced illness or even death) effects, psychotherapy, hypnosis, and medicinal effects of drugs, among others.

EXPECTANCY MEASUREMENT
Applied to substance use, expectancies have been most often characterized as individual cognitions, developed via past experience (direct or vicarious) of alcohol/drug use in one's environment, that anticipate affective, cognitive, and behavioral outcomes, thereby encouraging or discouraging alcohol/drug use. Because considerable variation (individual differences) in verbally reported expectancies has been found, the expectancy construct addresses why some substance users engage in drug use above and beyond beneficial outcomes (increased sociability, relaxation) to the point at which adverse outcomes (including death) are possible.

In the substance use arena, the development of expectancy measurement was preceded by *balanced placebo studies* of (primarily) alcohol effects, in which the influence of expectancies was inferred, rather than directly measured. In these studies, participants consumed a beverage that might or might not have contained alcohol but were independently told whether alcohol was present. This framework resulted in four groups: receiving alcohol and expecting alcohol, receiving alcohol and expecting placebo, receiving placebo and expecting alcohol, and receiving placebo and expecting placebo. Individuals who consumed placebo alcohol often displayed altered behaviors or mood, presumably as a result of expectancy activation. More recent neuroimaging research along the same lines has, in fact, shown that brain regions and neurotransmitters responsible for reward (e.g., dopamine) can be activated in response to substance cues, even in the absence of consumption.

These findings led to the use of psychometrically based instruments that explicitly capture the expectancies only inferred in the earlier balanced placebo designs. Too many instruments of this kind, tapping expectancies associated with a number of different substances, have been developed to list them all here. Examples include the Alcohol Expectancy Questionnaire (AEQ; Brown et al., 1980), the Cocaine and Marijuana Effect Expectancy Questionnaires (CEEQ; MEEQ; Schafer & Brown, 1991), Comprehensive Effects of Alcohol (CEOA; Fromme et al., 1993), the Smoking Consequences Questionnaire (SCQ; Brandon & Baker, 1991), and the Alcohol Expectancy Multi-Axial Assessment (A. E. Max; Goldman & Darkes, 2004). Within error-attenuated structural models, such instruments have accounted for as much as 50 percent of the variance in substance use, both concurrently and prospectively.

A further application of expectancy instruments is the development of models of alcohol expectancies as they are stored in hypothetical memory networks (Rather & Goldman, 1994.) As of 2008, these types of models had yet to be applied to other drug expectancies. These models suggest that more specific expectancies can be located in multidimensional space along dimensions of valence and arousal. Where a particular individual's expectancy profile falls within this space is reliably related to the individual's extent of alcohol use, such that heavier drinkers consistently endorse more positive and arousing effects of alcohol, and lighter drinkers and abstainers endorse more negative effects. Cross validation of these models has come from laboratory-derived cognitive techniques, such as free association.

Expectancies have also been probed in children, via scales such as the Alcohol Expectancy Questionnaire-Adolescent (AEQ-A; Christiansen et al., 1982), Marijuana and Stimulant Effect Expectancy Questionnaires for adolescents (Aarons et al.,

2001), and the Memory Model-based Expectancy Questionnaire (MMBEQ; Dunn & Goldman, 1996). These scales have shown expectancies to be present in children before drinking begins (demonstrating that they are not just a byproduct of consumption), and then to maintain a reciprocal relationship with drinking over time, with more positive expectancies leading to more drinking, and more drinking to increased expectancies (Smith et al., 1995). Initially, children endorse more negative expectancies of substance use, primarily before drinking or drug use begins. However, at some point during early adolescence but preceding the onset of substance use, children begin to develop more positive and arousing expectancies with substance use.

IMPLICIT EXPECTANCY MEASUREMENT

Expectancies have been measured using explicit verbal methods and have been addressed using implicit or indirect cognitive approaches such as the Stroop task, free associates, and expectancy priming. That expectancies can be implicit should come as no surprise given that expectancies were originally posited as explanatory devices in animal research, in which explicit verbal measurement of expectancies is obviously impossible. Although indices derived from these cognitive methods typically account for less variance in substance use behaviors than do explicit measures, they provide a window into the multiple pathways of expectancy operation.

For example, during a free associate task in which individuals were asked to quickly complete the sentence "Drinking alcohol makes me...," heavier drinkers first associated arousing effects of drinking (happy), while lighter drinkers first associated sedating effects (sick; Reich & Goldman, 2005a). Heavy drinkers also displayed increased interference during arousing and positive expectancy words on a modified Stroop task, during which they had to name the color of expectancy words after being primed with alcohol and neutral words (Kramer & Goldman, 2003). Lighter drinkers experienced interference during sedating and negative expectancy words. Essentially, heavier drinkers appeared to activate positive and arousing outcomes (and lighter drinkers to activate sedating and negative outcomes) following an alcohol prime. Heavier drinkers also associated alcohol-related meaning to ambiguous stimuli (e.g., "bar" or "pitcher"), and remembered positive, arousing expectancy words better if the first word on the list was alcohol-related (e.g., "beer" instead of "milk"; Stacy, 1997; Reich & Goldman, 2005b). These studies suggested that individualized implicit cognitive processes might mediate decisions people make about whether and how much to drink.

EXPECTANCIES AND ADDICTION

Expectancies have been related not only to the onset and maintenance of substance use, but also to the development of substance use disorders (SUDs). Drug addiction has been considered "an abnormal set of motivated behaviors" (Cardinal & Everitt, 2004, p. 156), and anticipation of reward plays a central role in motivating behavior. Individuals with the most problematic drug use typically have endorsed the greatest positive expectations of drug use. Expectancies also partially mediate the relationship between antecedents of risk (family history, gender, race, age, and personality variables) and the development of substance use disorders (Goldman et al., 1999).

Children of alcoholics with more positive alcohol expectancies experienced an earlier onset of regular drinking and were more likely to develop alcoholism themselves (Shen et al., 2001), especially if they were male (Ohannessian & Hesselbrock, 2004), impulsive (Finn et al., 2005), or had social anxiety disorder (Ham et al., 2002). Depressed individuals with a history of alcoholism were more likely to endorse more positive expectancies for drug use, rendering them more likely to fail in attempts to curb drug and alcohol use (Currie et al., 2001). These relationships have also been seen at the genetic level, such that alleles encoding enzymes that most efficiently break down alcohol in the body have been shown to contribute to the development of positive and arousing expectancies, which promote problematic drinking behavior (Hahn et al., 2006).

Expectancies also have significantly discriminated heavy drinkers who maintained very high levels of drinking from those who subsequently reduced drinking behavior over time (Greenbaum et al., 2005). In treatment studies, expectancies predicted post-treatment outcomes, such that those with less positive and less arousing expectancies were more likely to recover. Ultimately, expectancy

manipulation may have the potential to decrease drinking and encourage SUD recovery.

EXPECTANCY CHALLENGE

The aforementioned balanced placebo studies have shown that behaviors usually attributed to the neurochemical effects of alcohol were instead due to the activation, under appropriate cue conditions, of a drinker's expectancies about the presumed influences of alcohol. In addition, the development of questionnaires assessing alcohol expectancies has revealed that measured alcohol expectancies were directly related to drinking levels. It has thus become reasonable to suppose that disrupting, or challenging, a person's expectancies might decrease both motivation to drink and drinking behavior. Early tests of this supposition were carried out as experiments using limited participant pools. The challenge paradigm involved a group of individuals consuming either alcoholic beverages or placebo drinks in an experience that mimics a typical drinking situation (e.g., a party). Following this experience, participants were challenged to identify who amongst them actually received alcohol. If only two or three drinks had been consumed (maintaining low-to-moderate blood alcohol levels in those that actually consumed alcohol), participants were usually unsuccessful in correctly identifying the drinkers. Many positive and arousing effects of alcohol were then exposed to result from individual alcohol expectations, and not from the pharmacology of alcohol, and subsequent measured expectancies decreased and drinking over several weeks was diminished (Darkes & Goldman, 1993; 1998).

Subsequent alcohol expectancy challenge modifications have been tested, yielding varying results. Such modifications have included vicarious challenges via videotape (Keillor et al., 1999) and purely didactic (lacking the placebo manipulation) challenges (Corbin et al., 2001). The original protocols designed for use and demonstrated effective with college-aged males have also been modified for use with female drinkers (Dunn et al., 2000; Musher-Eizenman & Kulick, 2003), mixed gender groups (Wiers & Kummeling, 2004), for classroom presentation to elementary school children (Cruz & Dunn, 2003) and applied in combination with Brief Motivational Interviewing (BMI; Wood et al., 2007).

Results across this range of modifications have been mixed, with different effects reported across studies and populations, inconsistent changes in drinking (most notably in female attendees), and no apparent increase in the utility of the challenge when combined with brief motivational interviewing. These studies suggest that the experiential disconnection between alcohol consumption and alcohol-related behavior may play a role in reducing placebo effects of alcohol and could change substance use behavior.

Expectancies were originally identified as the mechanism by which organisms interact with their environment and behave in evolutionarily advantageous ways. It has become increasingly evident that the expectancy construct is vital to the understanding of behavioral phenomena across many disciplines, including addiction. The development of substance use expectancy measures (both explicit and implicit) have revealed that expectancies contribute to the onset and maintenance of substance use behavior and to some extent mediate the relationship between risk and SUDs. Furthermore, organized challenges (or disruptions) to more positive expectancies (via expectancy challenge paradigms) have reduced substance use behavior, with future potential for use as clinical interventions targeting problematic substance use behavior. The expectancy concept does not apply to one circumscribed domain. Consequently, to move forward in expectancy research, conscious efforts must be made to identify common expectancy pathways across multiple domains both in and outside the field of addiction and psychology.

See also **Coping and Drug Use; Models of Alcoholism and Drug Abuse; Prevention; Treatment; Women and Substance Abuse.**

BIBLIOGRAPHY

Aarons, G. A., Brown, S. A., Stice, E., & Coe, M. T. (2001). Psychometric evaluation of the Marijuana and Stimulant Effect Expectancy Questionnaires for adolescents. *Addictive Behaviors, 26,* 219–236.

Bolles, R. C. (1972). Reinforcement, expectancy, and learning. *Psychological Review, 79,* 394–409.

Brandon, T. H., & Baker, T. B. (1991). The smoking consequences questionnaire: The subjective utility of smoking in college students. *Psychological Assessment, 3,* 484–491.

Brown, S. A., Goldman, M. S., Inn, A., & Andersen, L. (1980). Expectations of reinforcement from alcohol: Their domain and relation to drinking patterns. *Journal of Consulting & Clinical Psychology, 48,* 419–426.

Cardinal, R. N., & Everitt, B. J. (2004). Neural and psychological mechanisms underlying appetitive learning: Links to drug addiction. *Current Opinion in Neurobiology, 14,* 156–162.

Christiansen, B. A., Goldman, M. S., & Inn, A. (1982). Development of alcohol-related expectancies in adolescents: Separating pharmacological from social learning influences. *Journal of Consulting & Clinical Psychology, 50,* 336–344.

Corbin, W. R., Mcnair, L. D., & Carter, J. A. (2001). Evaluation of a treatment-appropriate cognitive intervention for challenging alcohol outcome expectancies. *Addictive Behaviors, 26,* 475–488.

Cruz, I. Y., & Dunn, M. F. (2003). Lowering risk for early alcohol use by challenging alcohol expectancies in elementary school children. *Journal of Consulting & Clinical Psychology, 7,* 493–503.

Currie, S. R., Hodgins, D. C., El-Guebaly, N., & Campbell, W. (2001). Influence of depression and gender on smoking expectancies and temptations in alcoholics in early recovery. *Journal of Substance Abuse, 13,* 443–458.

Darkes, J., & Goldman, M. S. (1993). Expectancy challenge and drinking reduction: Experimental evidence for a mediational process. *Journal of Consulting & Clinical Psychology, 61,* 344–353.

Darkes, J., & Goldman, M. S. (1998). Expectancy challenge and drinking reduction: Process and structure in the alcohol expectancy network. *Experimental & Clinical Psychopharmacology, 6,* 64–76.

Del Boca, F. K., & Darkes, J. (2001) Is the glass half full or half empty? An evaluation of the status of expectancies as causal agents. *Addiction, 96,* 1670–1672.

Dennett, D. (1991). *Consciousness explained.* London: Penguin Books.

Dunn, M. E., & Goldman, M. S. (1996). Empirical modeling of an alcohol expectancy network in elementary children as a function of grade. *Experimental & Clinical Psychopharmacology, 4,* 209–217.

Dunn, M. E., Lau, H. C., & Cruz, I. Y. (2000). Changes in activation of alcohol expectancies in memory in relation to changes in alcohol use after participation in an expectancy challenge program. *Experimental & Clinical Psychopharmacology, 8,* 566–575.

Finn, P. R., Bobova, L., Wehner, E., Fargo, S., & Rickert, M. E. (2005). Alcohol expectancies, conduct disorder and early-onset alcoholism: Negative alcohol expectancies are associated with less drinking in non-impulsive versus impulsive subjects. *Addiction, 100,* 953–962.

Fromme, K., Stroot, E., & Kaplan, D. (1993). The Comprehensive Effects of Alcohol questionnaire: Development and psychometric evaluation of a new expectancy questionnaire. *Psychological Assessment, 5,* 19–26.

Goldman, M. S. (2002). Expectancy and risk for alcoholism: The unfortunate exploitation of a fundamental characteristic of neurobehavioral adaptation. *Alcoholism: Clinical & Experimental Research, 26,* 737–746.

Goldman, M. S., & Darkes, J. (2004). Alcohol expectancy multi-axial assessment (A. E. Max): A memory network-based approach. *Psychological Assessment, 16,* 4–15.

Goldman, M. S., Darkes, J., Reich, R. R., & Brandon, K. O. (2006). From DNA to conscious thought: The influence of anticipatory processes on human alcohol consumption. In M. R Munafo & I. P. Albery (Eds.), *Cognition and Addiction* (pp. 149–187). London: Oxford University Press.

Goldman, M. S., Del Boca, F. K., & Darkes, J. (1999). Alcohol expectancy theory: The application of cognitive neuroscience. In K. E. Leonard & H. T. Blane (Eds.), *Psychological theories of drinking and alcoholism.* New York: Guilford.

Greenbaum, P. E., Del Boca, F. K., Darkes, J., Wang, C., & Goldman, M. S. (2005). Variation in the drinking trajectories of freshman college students. *Journal of Consulting & Clinical Psychology, 73,* 229–238.

Grossberg, S. (1995). The attentive brain. *American Scientist, 83,* 438–449.

Hahn, C., Huang, S., Ko, H., Hsieh, C., Le, I., et al. (2006). Acetaldehyde involvement in positive and negative alcohol expectancies in Han Chinese persons with alcoholism. *Archives of General Psychiatry, 63,* 817–823.

Ham, L. S., Hope, D. A., White, C. S., & Rivers, P. C. (2002). Alcohol expectancies and drinking behavior in adults with social anxiety disorder and dysthymia. *Cognitive Therapy and Research, 26,* 275–288.

Jones, B. T., Corbin, W., & Fromme, K. (2001). A review of expectancy theory and alcohol consumption. *Addiction, 96,* 57–72.

Keillor, R. M., Perkins, W. B., & Horan, J. J. (1999). Effects of videotaped expectancy challenges on alcohol consumption of adjudicated students. *Journal of Cognitive Psychotherapy: An International Quarterly, 13,* 179–187.

Kramer, D. A., & Goldman, M. A. (2003). Using a modified Stroop task to implicitly discern the cognitive organization of alcohol expectancies. *Journal of Abnormal Psychology, 112,* 171–175.

Kupfermann, I., Kandel, E. R., & Iverson, S. (2000). Motivational and addictive states. In E. R. Kandel, J. H. Schwartz, and T. M. Jessell (Eds.), *Principles of neural science.* New York: McGraw-Hill.

Maccorquodale, K. M., & Meehl, P. E. (1953). Preliminary suggestions as to a formalization of expectancy theory. *Psychological Review, 60,* 55–63.

Musher-Eizenman, D. R., & Kulick, A. D. (2003). An alcohol expectancy-challenge prevention program for at-risk women. *Psychology of Addictive Behaviors, 17,* 163–166.

Ohannessian, C. M., & Hesselbrock, V. M. (2004). Do alcohol expectancies moderate the relationship between parental alcoholism and adult drinking behaviors? *Addictive Behaviors, 29,* 901–909.

Rather, B. C., & Goldman, M. S. (1994). Drinking-related differences in the memory organization of alcohol expectancies. *Experimental and Clinical Psychopharmacology, 2,* 167–183.

Reich, R. R., & Goldman, M. S. (2005a). Exploring the alcohol expectancy network: The utility of free associates. *Psychology of Addictive Behaviors, 19,* 317–325.

Reich, R. R., & Goldman, M. S. (2005b). Cue patterns and alcohol expectancies: How slight differences in stimuli can measurably change cognition. *Experimental & Clinical Psychopharmacology, 13,* 65–71.

Rotter, J. B. (1954). *Social learning and clinical psychology.* Englewood Cliffs, NJ: Prentice Hall.

Schafer, J., & Brown, S. A. (1991). Marijuana and cocaine effect expectancies and drug use patterns. *Journal of Consulting & Clinical Psychology, 59,* 558–565.

Shen, S., Locke-Wellman, J., & Hill, S. (2001). Adolescent alcohol expectancies in offspring from families at high risk for developing alcoholism. *Journal of Studies on Alcoholism, 62,* 763–772.

Smith, G. T., Goldman, M. S., Greenbaum, P. E., & Christiansen, B. A. (1995). Expectancy for social facilitation from drinking: The divergent paths of high-expectancy and low-expectancy adolescents. *Journal of Abnormal Psychology, 104,* 32–40.

Stacy, A. W. (1997). Memory activation and expectancy as prospective predictors of alcohol and marijuana use. *Journal of Abnormal Psychology, 106,* 61–73.

Tolman, E. C. (1932). *Purposive behavior in animals and men.* New York: Appleton-Century-Crofts.

Tolman, E. C. (1945). A stimulus-expectancy need-cathexis psychology. *Science, 101,* 160–166.

Wiers, R. W., & Kummeling, R. H. C. (2004). An experimental test of an alcohol expectancy challenge in mixed gender groups of young heavy drinkers. *Addictive Behaviors, 29,* 215–220.

Wood, M. D., Capone, C., LaForge, R., Erickson, D. J., & Brand, N. H. (2007). Brief motivational intervention and alcohol expectancy challenge with heavy drinking college students: A randomized factorial study. *Addictive Behaviors, 32,* 2509–2528.

ASHLEE C. CARTER
MARK S. GOLDMAN

FAMILIES AND DRUG USE. Despite increased primary school-based prevention efforts throughout the 1990s and the 2000s, alcohol and drug use among teens has remained stable, with a small percentage of teens (3.5%) developing alcohol dependence (Young et al., 2002). These individuals are at high risk of experiencing chronic substance-abuse-related problems into adulthood. Yet only about 16 percent of youth in need receive treatment for alcohol and drug problems, according to the Substance Abuse and Mental Health Services Administration (1996), and those that receive standard treatment in the community relapse at high rates within the year following treatment (Cornelius et al., 2003). Thus, more effective interventions for adolescent substance misuse are needed.

FAMILY FACTORS IN SUBSTANCE ABUSE

Substance abuse has multiple interacting precipitators, and family factors play a central role both in early substance use and its progression. A range of family risk factors correlate consistently with adolescent substance abuse, including poor family functioning, parent and sibling substance use, ineffective parental monitoring, family conflict, and low levels of family support. Family factors are also among the strongest protective influences against drug taking. Parents protect teens from early drug and alcohol initiation and abuse by setting clear standards against use and by setting limits. Family factors also exert an important mediational role in explaining other risk factors for drinking and drug use. While peers have a direct effect on teen substance abuse, parents mediate these influences by monitoring and maintaining close relationships with their adolescents. Family factors appear to operate both directly and indirectly to predict teen substance use, indicating the need for effective family-based interventions for alcohol and drug problems.

Several clinical trials have provided strong and consistent empirical support for the comparative efficacy of family-based interventions in reducing levels of adolescent drug use and increasing adaptive functioning (Waldron & Turner, 2008). Family-based interventions demonstrate considerable effectiveness in reducing teen drug use compared to individual therapy, adolescent group therapy, and family psychoeducational counseling. The superior posttreatment effects of family-oriented treatments have been retained for up to 12 months after termination (Liddle et al., 2002), and in one case for up to four years posttreatment (Henggeler et al., 2006). Furthermore, family-focused treatments improve family functioning, school performance, comorbid psychiatric symptomatology, and delinquency.

FAMILY-BASED INTERVENTION OUTCOMES

Progress has been made in developing treatments for adolescent alcohol abuse and outlining the critical factors and processes in alcohol recovery and relapse among youth. However, in the first year following standard community-based treatment, more than half of teens relapse (Maisto et al., 2001), and over time (from 1 to 8 years) alcohol use rises steadily in each consecutive year following treatment (Tapert et al., 2003). Few empirically developed models for adolescent alcohol abuse exist, and little is known about the intervention features that impact adolescent alcohol use following treatment. However, with new evidence about the multiple contributing factors to alcohol risk and protection, there is consensus that interventions for alcohol use disorders must simultaneously target the multiple factors and systems that create and maintain problems. Family-based approaches have potential in this regard, yet their promise with adolescent alcohol abusers has rarely been tested, and they certainly have yet to be fully realized.

There is some evidence that family-based interventions reduce alcohol use and related problems among teens. For instance, the Purdue Brief Family Therapy model significantly reduced adolescent alcohol use in fewer sessions than drug education and individual treatment as usual (Trepper et al., 1993), while behavioral family therapy was more effective than supportive counseling in reducing adolescent alcohol use up to nine months following treatment (Azrin et al., 1996).

FAMILY-BASED INTERVENTION FOR ADOLESCENT SUBSTANCE ABUSE

Efforts to intervene with youth at risk for substance use problems incorporate knowledge of both the developmental pathways to drug and alcohol use disorders and the multiple risk factors for these disorders. Family-based therapies target the major risk factors, established through longitudinal and cross-sectional studies, known to be the precursors to substance abuse in adolescence and young adulthood.

An example of one of the new generation of family-based therapies is multidimensional family therapy (MDFT). Other family-based treatments have also been developed that show evidence of positive outcomes, such as multisystemic therapy, functional family therapy, and brief strategic family therapy (see Austin, Macgowan, & Wagner, 2005; Vaughn & Howard, 2004; Waldron & Turner, 2008). The focus here is on MDFT in order to illustrate with some detail the main features of one of these models. The MDFT treatment system assesses and intervenes in four main areas: adolescent,

parent, family, and extrafamilial systems. With adolescents, therapists seeks to transform a substance-using lifestyle into a developmentally normative one with improved functioning across various domains (e.g., peers, identity, school, and family relationships). Goals for parents include increasing parental commitment and improving parent-teen communication and parenting practices such as monitoring. In family sessions, MDFT therapists promote supportive and effective communication among family members.

With adolescent alcohol problems, three areas deserve particular attention: alcohol expectancies, parental substance abuse, and family-based relapse prevention and aftercare services.

Alcohol Expectancies. The alcohol expectancies of an adolescent are a strong predictor of problem drinking (Colder et al., 1997). Alcohol expectancies include beliefs about the positive social and emotional effects of alcohol (e.g., appearing more comfortable to others and feeling more relaxed, respectively), as well as beliefs that alcohol is less harmful than it actually is. Adolescents' alcohol expectancies and attitudes connect to the norms families communicate about drinking. Children not only adopt their parents' drinking behaviors, they also adopt the coping strategies and motivations that are modeled by their parents (Ouellette et al., 1999). Thus, interventions to change adolescents' expectancies must also involve a shift in parents' messages and behaviors (Windle, 1996).

MDFT addresses the social cognitive aspects of substance use, the meaning and motivation for substance use, and the development of motivation for abstinence. Addressing expectancies, beliefs, and attitudes about alcohol is consistent with the MDFT therapist's work with teens to examine their motivations for using and to help them become aware of the health-compromising aspects of alcohol use. Individual sessions with the adolescent focus on highlighting discrepancies between stated personal goals or outcomes and current lifestyle choices, including beliefs about alcohol and its consequences. Continued use of substances is acknowledged to be incompatible with a nondrinking lifestyle and the benefits of positive changes, such as doing better in school and having less conflict at home. The pathways to achieve these changes also involve parents and other social systems. Therapists work with parents to examine their messages and norms about drinking, for example. Individual work with adolescents and parents provides a platform for families to talk together about drinking and help the adolescent develop more realistic beliefs about alcohol as well as new skills to avoid drinking.

Parental Alcoholism.

Parental alcoholism is one of the strongest and most consistent family risk factors for teen alcohol problems, and there is an increased risk even when the parent's alcoholism is in remission (DeLucia, Belz, & Chassin, 2001). Parental alcoholism increases young adolescents' risk of alcohol abuse through specific mechanisms that can be addressed in family interventions, such as family conflict and lack of cohesion, decreased monitoring, and alcohol expectancies (Chassin, Curran, Hussong, & Colder, 1996; Hussong, Curran, & Chassin, 1998; Sher, 1994).

Directly and systematically addressing parental alcoholism is part of core parent work in MDFT. MDFT targets the functioning of parents as individual adults, apart from their role as parents or caregivers. Because parenting practices are connected to the parent's functioning, parental substance abuse must be addressed. The therapist motivates the parent to take steps to change their own lives by resuscitating their love and commitment for the child, and therapists link parents' alcohol and substance use to their parenting, highlighting how alcohol use impairs their ability to be consistent, firm, and available to their child.

Family-based Relapse Prevention and Aftercare.

The most common precipitators of relapse following treatment are social pressures and negative affect. Protective factors against alcohol relapse include aftercare participation, better alcohol coping skills, and positive supports for recovery (Chung et al., 2004; Latimer et al., 2000). Family functioning has also been found to play a primary role in helping teens achieve and maintain abstinence (Hsieh et al., 1998). These findings underscore the importance of bolstering coping and relapse prevention skills during treatment and providing continued support and aftercare services following treatment.

In MDFT, primary family interventions are aimed at promoting new interactional patterns among family members. Because the family environment is an important context of adolescent functioning, one of the goals of MDFT is to create a new family environment in which the family becomes the therapeutic agent long after the MDFT therapist has completed work with the teen and the parents. Thus, MDFT family sessions use the technique of enactment to elicit and shape discussions of important topics, including alcohol use and ways to cope with drinking urges. These interventions provide opportunities for the therapist to take an active and directive stance toward the prompting of new responses and supportive behaviors from family members. Issues raised in individual sessions are brought into the family meetings, with the encouragement, support, and facilitation of the therapist.

A complementary component of work that helps to maintain the teen's recovery during and following treatment is in the extrafamilial realm. MDFT therapists aim to improve the parents' and adolescent's functioning relative to influential extrafamilial social systems, and also to promote the teen's involvement in prosocial activities. Added support during and following treatment is also facilitated by encouraging adolescents' participation in teen-focused Alcohol Anonymous (AA) meetings. Attendance at AA and other 12-step meetings has been shown to increase motivation for abstinence and predict better outcomes for youths in the three months following treatment (Kelly, Myers, & Brown, 2002). Multiple-systems oriented approaches such as MDFT have the advantage of addressing and providing coordinated comprehensive interventions with intrapersonal, social, familial, and extrafamilial relapse risk factors.

CONCLUSIONS

Experts recommend further development and application of family-based interventions that are comprehensive and multisystemic in scope (see Brannigan et al., 2004). A new wave of treatments based on the family therapy tradition have been created and developed in funded clinical research contexts, and these are increasingly available for dissemination in a wide variety of clinical settings. Variations of these approaches have been designed to more effectively target the needs of different clinical samples, such as adolescent girls, teens from different cultural groups, or those involved in juvenile-justice settings. The mechanisms by which these therapies achieve their effects have also been investigated (Diamond et al., 2000). This research has fed back into the treatment-development work of the models (Jackson-Gilfort et al., 2001) and helped improve the training and supervision of these science-supported therapies.

While it is known that families and drug use are linked, it is too simplistic and narrow a frame to think of family problems as causing drug use. Indeed, research does not support this notion of causation. It is more correct to say that family functioning is one of several factors that not only creates the conditions in which drug taking can begin, but also represents an important developmental arena that must be taken into account in drug treatment. Previous generations of theorizing and treatment development have either left families out of the recovery equation or blamed families unduly for being the cause of an individual's addiction. Numerous influential policy reports, practice guidelines, and research reviews now conclude that families must be included in the treatment of drug-using teens. Today's family-based therapies have a more enlightened clinical perspective, considerable empirical evidence, and a new family-friendly technology with which to engage and retain parents and teens, through nonblaming and nonpunitive means, in effective treatments.

See also **Adolescents and Drug Use; African Americans, Ethnic and Cultural Factors Relevant to Treatment for; Alcoholics Anonymous (AA); Codependence; Conduct Disorder and Drug Use; Risk Factors for Substance Use, Abuse, and Dependence: An Overview; Treatment, Behavioral Approaches to: Couples and Family Therapy; Treatment, Specialty Approaches to: Adolescents.**

BIBLIOGRAPHY

Austin, A. M., Macgowan, M. J., & Wagner, E. F. (2005). Effective family-based interventions for adolescents with substance use problems: A systematic review. *Research on Social Work Practice, 15*(2), 67–83.

Azrin, N. H., Acierno, R., Kogan, E. S., Donohue, B., Besalel, V. A., & McMahon, P. T. (1996). Follow-up results of supportive versus behavioral therapy for illicit drug use. *Behaviour Research and Therapy, 34*(1), 41–46.

Brannigan, R., Schackman, B. R., Falco, M., & Millman, R. B. (2004). The quality of highly regarded adolescent substance abuse treatment programs: Results of an in-depth national survey. *Archives of Pediatric Adolescent Medicine, 158*(9), 904–909.

Brown, S. A., Myers, M. G., Mott, M. A., & Vik, P. W. (1994). Correlates of success following treatment for adolescent substance abuse. *Applied & Preventive Psychology, 3*, 61–73.

Chassin, L., Curran, P. C., Hussong, A. M., & Colder, C. R. (1996). The relation of parent alcoholism to adolescent substance use: A longitudinal follow-up study. *Journal of Abnormal Psychology, 105*(1), 70–80.

Chung, T., Maisto, S. A., Cornelius, J. R., & Martin, C. S. (2004). Adolescents' alcohol and drug use trajectories in the year following treatment. *Journal of Studies on Alcohol, 65*(1), 105–114.

Colder, C. R., Chassin, L., Stice, E. M., & Curran, P. J. (1997). Alcohol expectancies as potential mediators of parent alcoholism effects on the development of heavy drinking. *Journal of Research on Adolescence, 7*(4), 349–374.

Cornelius, J. R., Maisto, S. A., Pollock, N. K., Martin, C. S., Salloum, I. M., Lynch, K. G., & Clark, D. B. (2003). Rapid relapse generally follows treatment for substance use disorders among adolescents. *Addictive Behaviors, 28*(2), 381–386.

DeLucia, C., Belz, A., & Chassin, L. (2001). Do adolescent symptomatology and family environment vary over time with fluctuations in paternal alcohol impairment? *Developmental Psychology, 37*(2), 207–216.

Diamond, G. M., Liddle, H. A., Hogue, A., & Dakof, G. A. (2000). Alliance building interventions with adolescents in family therapy: A process study. *Psychotherapy: Theory, Research, Practice, & Training, 36*(4), 355–368.

Ellis, D. A., Zucker, A., & Fitzgerald, H. E. (1997). The role of family influences in development and risk. *Alcohol Health & Research World, 21*(3), 218–226.

Henggeler, S. W., Borduin, C. M., Melton, G. B., Mann, B. J., Smith, L. A., & Hall, J. A. (1991). Effects of multisystemic therapy on drug use and abuse in serious juvenile offenders: A progress report from two outcome studies. *Family Dynamics of Addiction Quarterly, 1*, 40–51.

Henggeler, S. W., Halliday-Boykins, C. A., Cunningham, P. B., Randall, J., Shapiro, S. B., Chapman, J. E., et al. (2006). Juvenile drug court: Enhancing outcomes by integrating evidence-based treatments. *Journal of Consulting and Clinical Psychology, 74*(1), 42–54.

Hsieh, S., Hoffman, N. G., & Hollister, C. D. (1998). The relationship between pre-, during-, and post-treatment factors, and adolescent substance abuse behaviors. *Addictive Behaviors, 23*(4), 477–488.

Hussong, A. M., Curran, P. J., & Chassin, L. (1998). Pathways of risk for accelerated heavy alcohol use among adolescent children of alcoholic parents. *Journal of Abnormal Child Psychology, 26*(2), 453–466.

Jackson-Gilfort, A., Liddle, H. A., Tejeda, M. J., & Dakof, G. A. (2001). Facilitating engagement of African American male adolescents in family therapy: A cultural theme process study. *Journal of Black Psychology, 27*(3), 321–340.

Kelly, J. F., Myers, M. G., & Brown, S. A. (2002). Do adolescents affiliate with 12-step groups? A multivariate process model of effects. *Journal of Studies on Alcohol, 63,* 293–304.

Latimer, W. W., Newcomb, M., Winters, K. C., & Stinchfield, R. D. (2000). Adolescent substance abuse treatment outcome: The role of substance abuse problem severity, psychosocial and treatment factors. *Journal of Consulting and Clinical Psychology, 68*(4), 684–696.

Liddle, H. A. (2004). Family-based therapies for adolescent alcohol and drug abuse: Research contributions and future research needs. *Addiction, 99*(Suppl. 2), 76–92.

Liddle, H. A., Rowe, C. L., Dakof, G. A., & Lyke, J. (1998). Translating parenting research into clinical interventions for families of adolescents. *Clinical Child Psychology and Psychiatry, 3,* 419–443.

Liddle, H. A., & Dakof, G. A. (2002) A randomized controlled trial of intensive outpatient, family based therapy vs. residential drug treatment for co-morbid adolescent drug abusers. *Drug and Alcohol Dependence, 66,*(385), S2–S202.

Liddle, H. A., Rowe, C. L., Quille, T. J., Dakof, G. A., Mills, D. S., Sakran, E., & Biaggi, H. (2002). Transporting a research-based adolescent drug treatment into practice. *Journal of Substance Abuse Treatment, 22*(4), 231–243.

Liddle, H. A., Rowe, C. L., Henderson, C., Dakof, G. A., & Ungaro, R. A. (2004). Early intervention for adolescent substance abuse: Pretreatment to posttreatment outcomes of a randomized controlled trial comparing multidimensional family therapy and peer group treatment. *Journal of Psychoactive Drugs, 36*(1), 2–37.

Liddle, H. A., Rowe, C. L., Dakof, G. A., Henderson, C., & Greenbaum, P. (in press). Multidimensional Family Therapy for early adolescent substance abusers: Twelve-month outcomes of a randomized controlled trial. *Journal of Consulting and Clinical Psychology.*

Liddle, H. A., Dakof, G. A., Turner, R. M., Henderson, C. E., & Greenbaum, P. E. (in press). Treating adolescent drug abuse: A randomized trial comparing multidimensional family therapy and cognitive behavior therapy. *Addiction.*

Lowman, C. (2004). Developing effective evidence-based interventions for adolescents with alcohol use disorders. *Addiction, 99*(Suppl. 2), 1–4.

Maisto, S. A., Pollock, N. K., Lynch, K. G., Martin, C. S., & Ammerman, R. (2001). Course of functioning in adolescents 1 year after alcohol and other drug treatment. *Psychology of Addictive Behaviors, 15*(1), 68–76.

Ouellette, J. A., Gerrard, M., Gibbons, F. X., & Reis-Bergan, M. (1999). Parents, peers and prototypes: Antecedents of adolescent alcohol expectancies, alcohol consumption, and alcohol-related life problems in rural youth. *Psychology of Addictive Behaviors, 13*(3), 183–197.

Rowe, C. L. & Liddle, H. A. (2003). Substance abuse. *Journal of Marital and Family Therapy, 29,* 97–120.

Schmidt, S. E., Liddle, H. A., & Dakof, G. A. (1996). Changes in parenting practices and adolescent drug abuse during multidimensional family therapy. *Journal of Family Psychology, 10*(1), 12–27.

Sher, K. J. (1994). Individual-level risk factor. In: Zucker, R., Boyd, G., & Howard, J. (Eds.), *The development of alcohol problems: Exploring the biopsychosocial matrix of risk* (NIAAA Research Monograph No. 26, NIH Publication No. 94-34895). Rockville, MD: U.S. Department of Health and Human Services.

Sher, K. J., Walitzer, K. S., Wood, P. K., & Brent, E. E. (1991). Characteristics of children of alcoholics: Putative risk factors, substance use and abuse, and psychopathology. *Journal of Abnormal Psychology, 100*(4), 427–448.

Substance Abuse and Mental Health Services Administration (SAMHSA). (1996). *National household survey on drug abuse: Main findings.* Rockville, MD: Author.

Tapert, S. F., Cheung, E. H., Brown, G. G., Frank, L. R., Paulus, M. P., Schweinsburg, A. D., et al. (2003). Neural responses to alcohol stimuli in adolescents with alcohol use disorder. *Archives of General Psychiatry, 60*(7), 727–735.

Trepper, T. S., Piercy, F. P., Lewis, R. A., Volk, R. J., & Sprenkle, D. H. (1993). Family therapy for adolescent alcohol abuse. In O'Farrell, T. J. (Ed.), *Treating alcohol problems: Marital and family interventions* (pp. 261–278). New York: Guilford Press.

Vaughn, M. G., & Howard, M. O. (2004). Adolescent substance abuse treatment: A synthesis of controlled evaluations. *Research on Social Work Practice, 14*(5), 325–335.

Waldron, H. B. & Turner, C. W. (2008). Evidence-based psychological treatments for adolescent substance abuse. *Journal of Clinical Child and Adolescent Psychology, 37*(1), 238–261.

Windle, M. (1996). Effect of parental drinking on adolescents. *Alcohol Health & Research World, 20*(3), 181–184.

Young, S. E., Corley, R. P., Stallings, M. C., Rhee, S. H., Crowley, T. J., & Hewitt, J. K. (2002). Substance use, abuse and dependence in adolescence: Prevalence, symptom profiles and correlates. *Drug and Alcohol Dependence, 68*(3), 309–322.

HOWARD A. LIDDLE

FASHION INDUSTRY, INTERNATIONAL.

Although there is little to indicate that the fashion industry has a higher incidence of drug abuse than other, comparable branches of the entertainment industry, it developed a reputation for narcotic use in the last part of the twentieth century. This tendency reached a crescendo in 1996, when New York fashion photographer Davide Sorrenti died from a small dose of heroin. Sorrenti suffered from a rare blood disorder called Cooley's anemia or thalassemia, which explained his susceptibility to even small quantities of the drug; but because he was one of a group of photographers whose work had been dubbed *Heroin Chic* by the press, his death brought wide notoriety to the use and the alleged glorification of drugs in the fashion industry. Within the week, U.S. President Bill Clinton declared that "the glorification of heroin is not creative, it's destructive...It's not beautiful, it is ugly....This is not about art, it's about life and death" (*New York Times*, 1997, p. A22).

Clinton's speech resonated across the international fashion world and the industry responded almost immediately by promoting a new, healthier image. Nonetheless, when the model Kate Moss was secretly photographed taking cocaine at a party in September 2005, the British tabloids dubbed her "Cocaine Kate" (Stephen Moyes, *"Cocaine Kate,"* Daily Mirror, May 2005) and, a few months later, called her a "Cocaine Fiend" (Clodagh Hartley, "Kate on Coke at Mandela's," the *Sun*, March 2006). Clearly, the perceived association of fashion and drugs did not die out with the vogue for Heroin Chic at the end of the twentieth century.

VICTORIAN DRUG-USE IMAGERY

The association of drugs with fashion has roots that stretch well beyond the furor of the 1990s. One might begin with Elizabeth Siddal (1829–1862), model and muse of the mid-nineteenth-century Pre-Raphaelite Brotherhood of English painters (Yaeger, 2007). Siddal appeared in many of their paintings, perhaps most famously as the model for John Everett Millais's *Ophelia* (1851–1852). Siddal's depiction, especially in paintings by her eventual husband, Dante Gabriel Rosetti, shows her as young, strikingly beautiful, and somehow longing for things just beyond her grasp, beyond the frame's edge. Siddal's painted image figured youth, beauty, and tragically unfulfilled desire, associations that her 1862 death by laudanum overdose did nothing to diminish. Her demise resonated with the romanticized sense of drug use popularized in Thomas DeQuincey's *Confessions of an English Opium Eater* (1822). DeQuincey's memoir suggested that opium use (the opium and alcohol mixture called laudanum in DeQuincey's case) might offer an intellectual escape from the chains of Western reasoning, opening a path to a philosophical truth that was grander and more exotic than that which he found without the stimulus of drugs. Siddal's image conveyed a longing for a (usually medieval) world that was exotic and pure, one that could replace the industrial reality of mid-nineteenth-century England. Her painted image thus suggested youth, fragility, romantic longing for another, impossible world—all themes that would re-emerge in fashion photography of the late twentieth century.

DRUGS AND BODY IMAGE

Drugs and the fashion industry became closely linked as thinness became an important marker of female beauty. Its opposite, that is, obesity, is implicated in at least two of the seven deadly sins, sloth and gluttony, but any historical examination of western representations of beauty show that the interpretation of what counts as obese has been in constant flux. Obesity, however, is not only an aesthetic issue. It was increasingly treated as a medical condition throughout the twentieth century, according to Thomas C. Shevory (2000). Though the relationship between weight and health remained controversial in the early years of the twenty-first century, the negative health consequences of thinness, at least initially, received much less attention than did those of obesity. Being thin in the 1950s was commonly achieved with diet pills, which was particularly the case beginning in the 1950s, when physicians began to prescribe amphetamines, the first truly effective appetite suppressants, to patients whose goal was to reduce weight. As thinness became increasingly fashionable, those in the competitive world of fashion modeling soon realized the career-enhancing benefits of effective diet pills. Historian David Courtwright reports that the fashion model Jean Dawnay described her 1950s New York colleagues as living on Benzedrine, Dexedrine, and black coffee. She declared, "their incredible thinness staggered me" (Courtright, 2002, p. 109). Diet pills thus ensured that after the 1950s, fashion models, photographers, and those connected with them would be no strangers to drug use.

At the same time that diet pills were gaining a hold in the fashion industry, a visual discourse of narcotic addiction was being assembled in popular culture and also in law enforcement circles. The Federal Bureau of Narcotics (FBN), established in 1930, was headed by Harry J. Anslinger, who established harsh drug restrictions central to what Courtwright calls the "Classic Era" of anti-narcotic policy—a period when drug enforcement was simple, consistent, and rigid (2002, p. 3). The tone set within the FBN underlay the widespread production and dissemination of images intended to terrify the public—especially young people—in hopes of deterring them from using drugs. The images also played a large role in the popular culture of the mid-twentieth century. The demonization of drugs was also visible in films such as Louis Gasnier's 1936 *Ask Your Children* (more commonly known as *Reefer Madness*). Though part of a somewhat disreputable, exploitative genre, visions of "sex-crazed drug fiends" like those in Gasnier's film were the visual logic of the classic era of narcotic control (Newman, 1996, p. 509).

One consequence of the strong antidrug stance of the Anslinger years was the identification of drug use with inner-city vice districts and with a cultural underworld.

The most visible members of this urban, largely black population were the entertainers—especially jazz musicians—who worked in popular, big-city cabarets and nightclubs. For some people, the creativity of performers such as Charlie Parker and Billie Holiday became associated with their notorious drug use. The image of the drug addict as a deviant was conflated with this vibrant musical culture, and it acquired seductive appeal. Drug use seemed aligned with rejection of the conservative values and attitudes that the Harry Anslingers of the world hoped to promote. In other words, drug use seemed to signify a "hip" rebellion against an allegedly "square" mainstream culture.

Beat generation writers such as Jack Kerouac, Allen Ginsberg, and William S. Burroughs underscored precisely this alignment. Their texts, especially Kerouac's 1956 *On the Road*, idolized people whom the Beats imagined as being outside the dominant culture. From the Beats it is a very short way to the 1960s counterculture and its youth market. Kerouac, Ginsberg, Burroughs, and Neal Cassady all became influential figures within the 1960s counterculture. They brought drug use to the middle-class suburbs and college campuses of white America. Music, film, and fashion also began to glorify drug use as a fashionable rebelliousness. Edie Sedgwick, for instance, achieved celebrity through her connection with Andy Warhol's notoriously drug-associated studio Factory in the early sixties. As a model, she appeared in magazines such as *Vogue* (1965, 1966) and *Life* (1965). Sedgwick, who had been hospitalized with anorexia nervosa in 1962, appealed with her pronounced thinness.

Nonetheless, her modeling career never really took off, at least partly because "she was identified in the gossip columns with the drug scene" according to *Vogue* senior editor Gloria Schiff (Stein, 1982, p. 308). Other celebrity fashion icons such as Talitha Getty and Marianne Faithfull were similarly identified as drug users, but even the 1971 overdose deaths of Sedgwick and Getty did little to diminish their influence on the look of the era.

Drug use thus played a role in defining both the image and the personality of an array of glamorous, countercultural celebrities of the 1960s. The association persisted through the 1970s and 1980s. Partly it persisted because of the increasingly popular work of documentary photographers such as Larry Clark and Nan Goldin, who drew upon the older visual demonization of drugs and also the hip 1960s celebrity culture. Though none of this work glorifies drug use, its seductive images of hip, attractive, and apparently drugged young people contrast with the negative portraits propagated during the Anslinger years. Images depicting the squalor, physical demands, and loneliness of deviant addicts were here replaced by those of stylish, sophisticated people.

The marketing of this romanticized vision of intoxication, an obsession with thinness, a hip counterculture and tragic celebrity coalesced in the 1990s photographic phenomenon called Heroin Chic, which cemented the popular association of drugs and the fashion industry at the close of the twentieth century. The work of Clark and Goldin, and their evocation of a fashionable counterculture, was repeatedly cited as a major influence on a generation of young fashion photographers who sought what was understood to be a more authentic depiction of beauty than that embodied by the typically airbrushed, polished images presented in glossy fashion magazines (Kakutani, 1996, p. 16). The style chosen by photographers such as Corinne Day, Terry Richardson, Jürgen Teller, and Mario and Davide Sorrenti came to be known as Heroin Chic, a look that began to appear in British fashion and culture journals such as *The Face* and *I–D* during the early nineties, and also in U.S. publications such as San Francisco's *Detour*. It quickly spread across the international fashion scene. The style was connected to the popularity of Seattle's grunge music scene and what was then trumpeted as the *waif* look among fashion models. Heroin Chic images typically employ extremely thin models whose knotted hair, clammy skin and vacant, darkened eyes suggest a life of excess—a look associated with drug use but also with celebrity glamour. The bad publicity and notoriety that was drawn by Davide Sorrenti's death hastened the industry's move away from the fad but, as continuing controversy and negative attention show, the association of drugs with the fashion industry is a tenacious correlation.

See also **Anorexia; Bulimia Nervosa; Epidemics of Drug Abuse in the United States; Heroin; Media; Movies; Music; Sport, Drugs in International.**

BIBLIOGRAPHY

Arnold, R. (2001). *Fashion, desire and anxiety: Image and morality in the 20th century.* London: I. B. Taurus.

Clinton calls fashion ads' heroin chic deplorable. (1997, May 22). *New York Times,* Late Edition (East Coast), National Desk, p. A22.

Courtwright, D. T. (2002). *Forces of habit: Drugs and the making of the modern world.* Cambridge, MA: Harvard University Press.

Courtwright, D. T, Joseph, H., & Des Jarlais, D. (1989). *Addicts who survived: An oral history of narcotic use in America, 1923–1965.* Knoxville: University of Tennessee Press.

Hickman, T. A. (2002). Heroin chic: The visual culture of narcotic addiction. *Third Text: Critical Perspectives on Contemporary Art and Culture, 16*(2), 119–136.

Jonnes, J. (1996). *Hep–cats, narcs, and pipe dreams: A history of America's romance with illegal drugs.* New York: Scribner.

Kakutani, M. (1996, May 26). Culture zone: Slumming. *New York Times,* Late Edition, sec. 6, p. 16.

Newman, K. (1996). Exploitation and mainstream. In G. Nowell–Smith (Ed.), *The Oxford history of world cinema.* Oxford: Oxford University Press.

Shevory, T. (2000). *Body/politics: Studies in reproduction, production, and (re)construction.* Westport, CT: Praeger.

Spindler, A. M. (1996, May 7). The 90s version of the decadent look, *New York Times,* Late Edition, Final, p. B20.

Stein, J. (with George Plimpton). (1982). *Edie: An American biography.* New York: Alfred A. Knopf.

Sullum, J. (1997, May 23). Victims of everything. *New York Times,* Late Edition, p. A31.

Yaeger, L. (2007, March 27). High fashion: Styles come and go, but the glamour of drugs endures. *Village Voice.* Available from http://www.villagevoice.com/.

TIMOTHY A. HICKMAN

FERMENTATION. Fermentation is a natural metabolic process that produces energy by breaking down carbohydrates (such as sugars) in the absence of oxygen. It occurs in many microorganisms (such as yeasts), and the end product can be either ethyl alcohol (ethanol) or lactic acid; energy is typically given off in the form of heat. The chemical reaction of this process was first described in 1810 by the French chemist Joseph Louis Gay-Lussac. Fermentation is important to the production of many foods and beverages, the most popular of which are bread, butter, cheese, beer, and wine.

Fermented foods first occurred naturally, when stored or forgotten caches were found to be altered but edible. In ancient times, wheat and barley were domesticated, farmed, stored, and used to make breads and porridges—some of which fermented and formed brews. Since that time, the process of fermentation has been used worldwide. Industrial means provide huge quantities of fermented foods, as well as alcohol, which is obtained by distillation

Figure 1. Grapes. ILLUSTRATION BY GGS INFORMATION SERVICES. GALE, CENGAGE LEARNING

from fermented juices of fruits, grains, vegetables, and other plants.

See also **Beers and Brews.**

BIBLIOGRAPHY

Bamforth, C. W. (2005). *Food, fermentation and micro-organisms.* Malden, MA: Blackwell Publishing.

Briggs, D. E. (2004). *Brewing: Science and practice.* Cambridge, U.K.: Woodhead Publishing.

SCOTT E. LUKAS

FETAL ALCOHOL SYNDROME.

Fetal alcohol syndrome (FAS) is a constellation of behavioral, growth, and facial abnormalities resulting from prenatal alcohol exposure. Diagnosis is made by a specially trained physician and is based on the presence of three criteria: a pattern of distinct and specific facial abnormalities; growth deficiency; and central nervous system (CNS) damage, with or without confirmed maternal alcohol consumption. FAS is at one end of a spectrum, now termed "fetal alcohol spectrum disorders" (FASD). FASD is used as an umbrella term. If a child has some, but not all, of the criteria for FAS, they have one in a spectrum of disorders, covered by the terms ARBD, alcohol-related birth defects, and ARND, alcohol-related neurodevelopmental disorder. Use of the term FAE, fetal alcohol effects, is discouraged because of

non-specificity. FASD, short of full FAS, requires documentation of prenatal alcohol exposure.

HISTORY

The term *fetal alcohol syndrome* was first used in 1973 to describe the physical problems seen in the off-spring of alcoholic women. There have been admonitions against women drinking during pregnancy for literally thousands of years—at least as interpreted from biblical verses and in the writing of the ancient Greeks. The physical and social implications of women drinking during pregnancy first became highly noticeable during the gin epidemic of the 1750s. At that time, gin became a cheap and easily accessible beverage among low-income women. It was noted that there was a correlation between women who were consuming large amounts of gin and problems among their offspring.

A formal study was conducted in the 1890s by William Sullivan, a physician in England. He identified the offspring of 120 female "drunkards" in the Liverpool jail and compared them to the children of their non-drinking female relatives. From this study, Sullivan noted a perinatal mortality rate that was two and one-half times higher in the off-spring of the female alcoholics.

In 1968, Paul Lemoine published a study on the children of female alcoholics in a French medical journal. This article did not receive much attention until the landmark articles published in the *Lancet* by Jones, Smith, Ulleland, and Streissguth in 1973, in which the term *fetal alcohol syndrome* (FAS) was first used. Since 1973, about twenty thousand articles have been published detailing the effects of prenatal alcohol exposure from birth through middle age. In the early twenty-first century it has been commonly accepted that alcohol is a powerful teratogen (causative agent in fetal malformations) with lifelong consequences and that the severity of effects is associated with the amount and pattern of drinking. In particular, children who were exposed in utero to one or more drinks per day or to binge-like exposure (five or more drinks per occasion) tend to show adverse effects. These effects cannot be attributed to alcohol with certainty at lower levels of exposure, but there is strong evidence of differing susceptibility/vulnerability, so it is reasonable to advise women not to drink at all during pregnancy.

DISTRIBUTION

The prevalence of FAS ranges widely from community to community and is determined by the number of women consuming alcohol in any particular community. Every year in the United States, 500,000 women report drinking alcohol during pregnancy, with nearly one in five of those admitting to binge drinking. These statistics translate into a prevalence rate of nearly 13 percent for any consumption, and 6 percent for frequent and binge drinking. As of 2008, FAS was thought to be the leading cause of mental retardation in the United States, surpassing Down syndrome and spina bifida. It is estimated that approximately 1 to 4.8 of every 1,000 children born in the United States has FAS, with as many as 9.1 per 1000 (or nearly 1 in 100) born with FASD. However, few prevalence studies have been conducted as of 2008, and experts have different views as to the accuracy of the prevalence figures available. Additionally, prevalence rates vary widely by region and community, as well as by surveillance methodology. Some studies from the Centers for Disease Control and Prevention (CDC) suggest that drinking during pregnancy may be increasing despite public-health information designed to prevent FAS.

PHYSICAL EFFECTS

Drinking alcohol during pregnancy produces different effects, depending on the amount and when the alcohol is consumed. During the first trimester, there is a chance of major physical abnormalities (ARBDs) and CNS damage. During the first and second trimester, alcohol consumption leads to an increased rate of spontaneous abortion and CNS damage, as well as more subtle physical abnormalities. During the third trimester, alcohol consumption can lead to pre- and postnatal growth restriction and CNS damage.

Three major criteria must be met for a diagnosis of FAS. The common facial abnormalities include short palpebral (eye-slit) fissures; a long smooth philtrum (upper lip groove); and thin upper lip. Other common physical problems associated with prenatal alcohol use are cardiac (heart) malformations and defects; pectus excavatum (hollow at the lower part of the chest due to backward displacement of xiphoid cartilage); clinodactyly and camptodactyly (permanent curving or deflection of one or more fingers); fusion of the radius and ulna

at the elbow; scoliosis (lateral curvature of the spine); kidney malformations; and cleft lip and palate. Indeed, a large range of anatomic abnormalities in almost all body systems have been reported to be associated with prenatal alcohol exposure.

Growth deficiency in FAS is specifically noted in three parameters: height, weight, and head circumference. At birth, children with FAS and FASD tend to be small for gestational age with deficits in all three parameters, though deficiencies in all are not required for diagnosis. In addition, while some growth catch-up has been described, by puberty the vast majority of children with FAS/FASD still have growth retardation; they are generally short and thin. Significant changes in weight are noted as females enter puberty; although the growth deficiency remains in height and head circumference across the lifespan, females frequently gain weight and are plump. Males seem to remain comparatively short and slender until their late twenties or thirties.

CNS damage is frequently manifested in cognitive and memory deficits, sleep disturbances, developmental delays, hyperactivity/distractibility, a short attention span, an inability to understand cause and effect, lower levels of academic achievement, impulsivity, and difficulty in abstract thinking. The difficulties noted in infancy and early childhood are often precursors to later psychosocial deficits.

PSYCHOSOCIAL AND EDUCATIONAL ISSUES

Based mostly on caretaker experience and clinical observation (rather than clinical studies), the following describe the development patterns in FAS individuals.

Birth to Age Five Years. Diagnosis of FAS/FASD is possible at birth, but many physicians are either not trained to identify the characteristics or do not consider the possibility. Post-natal behavioral manifestations of FAS/FASD include the following: poor habituation, an exaggerated startle response, poor sleep/wake cycle, poor sucking response, and hyperactivity. Failure to thrive, alcohol withdrawal, and cardiac difficulties are medical concerns sometimes noted in those born with FAS. Also, developmental delays in walking, talking, and toilet training may be observed. Concerns such as hyperactivity, irritability, difficulty in following directions, and the inability to adapt to changes are commonly reported. The damage done to the brain by the prenatal alcohol exposure makes it problematic for children with FAS to learn in a timely and consistent fashion. The more abstract the task, the more apparent this learning gap becomes, particularly in adolescence and adulthood.

Recommended interventions before the age of five focus on the family as well as the child. Children with FAS/FASD are sometimes removed from the care of the biological mother owing to abuse, neglect, and/or maternal death. Newborns and infants with FAS/FASD often have trouble feeding; when this difficulty is coupled with a mother who may be deeply involved in substance abuse and not attentive to the needs of her infant, it can lead to medical crises. It may be necessary to provide the following services and interventions:

Health and medical monitoring

Safe, stable, structured residential placement with services provided to the mother, father, patient, and other family members, such as substance-abuse treatment and parenting training

Directions given to the caregivers in a simple, concrete fashion, one at a time; directions given to the child in similar fashion

Adaptation of the external environment to fit the child's ability to handle stimulation

Setting by caregivers of appropriate goals and expectations for the child

Respite care and ongoing support for caregivers

Ages Six to Eleven Years. Some of the problems noted earlier, primarily health issues, become less severe as others become more severe, with greater implications for negative social functioning. Hyperactivity, impulsivity, memory deficits, and inappropriate sexual behavior may emerge, as may difficulty predicting and/or understanding the consequences of behavior, difficulties in abstracting abilities, and poor comprehension of social rules and expectations. These are all common among children with FAS/FASD. Children with FAS/FASD may show decreasing ability to function in school as they get older. The abstracting deficits become more apparent when the child reaches the third and fourth grades and is expected to perform multiplication and division. Suggested interventions at this stage include the following:

Safe, stable, structured residential placement

Establishment of clear and reasonable expectations, goals, limits, and boundaries

Consistent structuring of leisure time and activities

Education of parents, caregivers, and the patient regarding age-appropriate sexual and social development

Appropriate educational placement that focuses on an activity-based curriculum, development of communication skills, development of appropriate behavior, and basic academic skills embedded with functional skills, in a structured environment, in which competing stimuli are avoided

Ages Twelve to Seventeen Years. Children with FAS/FASD have the same emotional needs as others do at this age, but adolescents with FAS/FASD may also exhibit cognitive deficits, impulsivity, faulty logic, low motivation, lying, stealing, depression, suicidal thoughts and attempts, and significant limitations in their adaptive behavior skills. Social deficits include financial/sexual exploitation and substance abuse. It is frequently difficult for people with FAS/FASD to articulate their feelings and needs, which typically occurs as these individuals reach their intellectual and academic ceiling.

Despite these problems and deficits, adolescents with FAS/FASD should be treated age appropriately within the limits of their developmental ability. The following are some interventions that may help them reach their social, emotional, and adaptive potential:

Changing the focus from academic to vocational and daily-living skills training

Structuring of leisure time and activities, such as involvement in organized sports and social activities

Educating patients, parents, and caregivers regarding sexual development and the need for birth control or protection against sexual exploitation and sexually transmitted diseases (STDs)

Planning for future vocational training and placements, financial needs, and residential placement

Increasing responsibility based on the patient's skills, abilities, and interests

Ages Eighteen through Adulthood. The problems, deficits, and difficulties seen prior to the age of eighteen are precursors to those seen in early adulthood and middle age. An additional problem experienced by people with FAS/FASD is the increased expectations placed on them by others. Not only can people with FAS often not meet these expectations but their impulsivity and poor judgment have more serious consequences than during their younger years. Issues such as poor comprehension of social rules and expectations, aggressive and unpredictable behavior, and depression coupled with impulsivity may lead to suicide attempts, antisocial behavior, hospitalization, and/or incarceration. Many can benefit from structured assisted living arrangements.

Other concerns noted in adults with FAS/FASD include social isolation and withdrawal, difficulties in finding and sustaining employment, poor financial management, problems accessing and paying for medical treatment or child care, and a need for help with social/sexual exploitation and unwanted pregnancy. The hyperactivity and distractibility seen in small children with FAS/FASD manifest in the adult's not being able to learn job skills or meet the requirements of many jobs. The following list contains suggested ways to help adults with FAS/FASD and their families deal with problematic issues in a productive fashion:

A guardianship for or assistance with finances
Residential placements or community housing to help ensure physical safety while allowing them to live as independently as possible
Support for medical care, along with birth control planning
Child-care and parenting classes, as needed
Education for others about FAS/FASD, including its limitations and skills, to foster acceptance
Long-term residential/vocational/psychosocial support for patient and/or caregivers

PREVENTION

The American College of Obstetricians and Gynecologists and the American Academy of Pediatrics recommend alcohol abstinence for both pregnant and pre-conception women because no safe threshold for consumption has been identified, and there is evidence of varying susceptibility/vulnerability to the effects of prenatal alcohol exposure. Prenatal practitioners are advised to question all women of reproductive age, and all pregnant women at their first prenatal visit about current and past alcohol use and to use a formal screen for risk-drinking, such as the T-ACE. Questioning again later in pregnancy is also recommended. For women identified as being at risk, intervention is indicated. For most pregnant women, a brief in-office intervention may be all that is needed to reduce the risk of an alcohol-exposed pregnancy. Brief interventions are evidence-based, low-cost, time-efficient, and effective self-help treatments involving counseling that can be delivered by health professionals who are not specialists in the treatment of alcohol use or dependence. Two randomized clinical trials and several other studies have shown that brief interventions, delivered as part of prenatal care, can significantly reduce rates of pregnancy drinking and consequent FAS/FASD neonates. However, for women with exceptionally high rates of consumption or who are diagnosed as alcoholics, more intensive intervention along with referral to specialized treatment programs is recommended.

FAS/FASD is a preventable birth defect; however, once it exists it has lifelong consequences. Special programs involving planning for the future vocational, educational, and residential needs of affected individuals should be implemented as early in childhood as possible. Education on the harmful effects of alcohol use and assistance for women prior to and during pregnancy is critical to help prevent or at least reduce this significant public health problem.

See also **Alcohol- and Drug-Exposed Infants; Alcohol: History of Drinking in the United States; Attention Deficit Hyperactivity Disorder; Fetus, Effects of Drugs on the; Pregnancy and Drug Dependence.**

BIBLIOGRAPHY

Abel, E. L., & Sokol, R. J. (1991). A revised conservative estimate of the incidence of fetal alcohol syndrome and its economic impact. *Alcoholism: Clinical and Experimental Research, 25,* 514–524.

Astley, S. J., & Clarren, S. K. (1995). A fetal alcohol syndrome screening tool. *Alcoholism: Clinical and Experimental Research, 19,* 1565–1571.

Bailey, B. N., Delaney-Black, V., Covington, C. Y., Ager J., Janisse, J., Hannigan, J. H., et al. (2004). Prenatal alcohol exposure to binge drinking and cognitive and behavioral outcomes at age 7 years. *American Journal of Obstetrics and Gynecology, 191,* 1037–1043.

Chang, G., McNamara, T. K., Orav, J., Koby, D., Lavigne, A., Ludman, B., et al. (2005). Brief intervention for prenatal alcohol use: A randomized trial. *Obstetrics and Gynecology, 105,* 991–998.

Chang, G., Wilkins-Haug, L., Berman, S., Goetz, M. A., Behr, H., & Hiley, A. (1998). Alcohol use and pregnancy: Improving identification. *Obstetrics and Gynecology, 91,* 892–898.

Coles, C. D., Brown, R. T., Smith, I. E., Platzman, K. A., Erickson, S., & Falek, A. (1991). Effects of prenatal alcohol exposure at school age: I. Physical and cognitive development. *Neurotoxicology and Teratology, 13,* 357–367.

Day, N. L., Leech, S. L., Richardson, G. A., Cornelius, M. D., Robles, N., & Larkby, C. (2002). Prenatal alcohol exposure predicts continued deficits in offspring size at 14 years of age. *Alcoholism: Clinical and Experimental Research, 26,* 1584–1591.

Dorris, M. (1989). *The broken cord.* New York: Harper & Row.

Jones, K. L., & Smith, D. W. (1973). Recognition of the fetal alcohol syndrome in early infancy. *Lancet, 2,* 999–1001.

Jones, K. L., Smith, D. W., Ulleland, C. N., & Streissguth, A. P. (1973). Pattern of malformation in offspring of chronic alcoholic mothers. *Lancet, 1,* 1267–1271.

Mattson, S. L., Riley, E. P., Gramling, L., Delis, D. C., & Jones, K. L. (1998). Neuropsychological comparison of alcohol-exposed children with or without physical features of fetal alcohol syndrome. *Neuropsychology, 12,* 146–153.

Olson, H. C., Burgess, D. M., & Streissguth, A. P. (1992). Fetal alcohol syndrome and fetal alcohol effects: A lifespan view with implications for early intervention. *Zero to Three, 13,* 24–29.

Sokol, R. J., Delaney-Black, V., & Nordstrom, B. (2003). Fetal alcohol spectrum disorder. *Journal of the American Medical Association, 290,* 2996–2999.

Sokol, R. J., Martier, S. S., & Ager, J. W. (1989). The T-ACE questions: Practical prenatal detection of risky drinking. *American Journal of Obstetrics and Gynecology, 160,* 853–868.

Streissguth, A. P. (1991). What every community should know about drinking during pregnancy and the life-long consequences for society. *Substance Abuse, 12,* 114–127.

Streissguth, A. P., Aase, J. M., Clarren, S. K., Randels, S. P., LaDue, R. A., & Smith, D. F. (1991). Fetal alcohol syndrome in adolescents and adults. *Journal of the American Medical Association, 265,* 1961–1967.

Streissguth, A. P., Barr, H. M., Kogan, J., & Bookstein, F. L. (1996). *Understanding the occurrence of secondary disabilities in clients with fetal alcohol syndrome and fetal alcohol effects.* Seattle: University of Washington Press.

Streissguth, A. P., Sampson, P. D., & Barr, H. M. (1989). Neurobehavioral dose-response effects of prenatal alcohol exposure in humans from infancy to adulthood. In D. E. Hutchings (Ed.), *Prenatal abuse of licit and illicit drugs* (pp. 145–158). New York: Annals of the New York Academy of Sciences.

ROBIN A. LADUE
REVISED BY BETH A. BAILEY (NORDSTROM) (2009)
ROBERT J. SOKOL (2009)

FETUS, EFFECTS OF DRUGS ON THE.

The pregnant substance-abusing or drug-dependent woman subjects her developing infant to a host of problems. When assessing the effects of drugs, whether illicit or appropriately administered (not abused) prescription drugs, on newborn infants (neonates) and young children, two factors must be considered: (a) the duration and concentration of the drug exposure on the developing fetus, and (b) any preexisting medical complications in the mother. These factors are interactive and together will influence, in varying ways, the eventual health, learning challenges, and potential capabilities of the child. Therefore, the long-term outcome of children exposed to drugs during fetal development should be assessed.

As cited by Dr. Nancy Young in her presentation on substance-exposed infants, the 2002 and 2003 Substance Abuse and Mental Health Administration (SAMHSA) Office of Applied Studies National Survey on Drug Use and Health (NSDUH) had a specific focus on substance use among pregnant women. It indicated that the reported incidence of pregnant women using any drug was highest in the first trimester, and decreased steadily thereafter: 7.7 percent of mothers affecting 315,161 infants in the first trimester, 3.2 percent of women affecting 130,976 infants in the second trimester, and 2.3 percent of women affecting 94,139 infants in the third trimester reported using any drugs whatsoever. Similar patterns were found for binge alcohol and alcohol use. For alcohol use the statistics were 19.6 percent of women affecting 802,228 infants in the first trimester, 6.1 percent of women affecting 249,673 infants in the second, and 4.7 percent of women affecting 192,371 infants in the third trimester of pregnancy. For binge drinking of alcohol the statistics were 10.9 percent of women affecting 446,137 infants in the first trimester of pregnancy, 1.4 percent of women affecting 57,302 infants in the second, and 0.7 percent of women affecting 28,651 infants in the third trimester (Young, 2006, p. 11). Roughly 4 million live births are recorded annually in the United States (Young, 2006, p. 16).

The 2006 NSDUH Report, which combined data collected during 2005 and 2006, indicated that among pregnant women between 15 and 44 years old, only four percent reported use of illicit drugs during the previous 30-day period; the rate among the non-pregnant, age-matched cohort was 10 percent (p. 25). In the same age group, 11.8 percent of pregnant women reported current use of alcohol, 2.9 percent reported binge drinking, and 0.7 percent indicated that they drank heavily. Among the non-pregnant group, the results for those categories were 53.0 percent, 23.6 percent, and 5.4 percent. Binge drinking of alcohol decreased from 10.9 percent to 4.6 percent during the first trimester, as reported in 2002–2003 (p. 34). The rates of tobacco use/cigarette smoking were also lower among pregnant than non-pregnant women between the ages of 18 and 25: 25.6 percent and 35.6 percent, respectively. Among those between the ages of 26 and 44, the rates of tobacco use were 10.3 percent for pregnant women and 29.1 percent for those who were not pregnant. In contrast, the rate for girls between the ages of 15 to 17 was higher in the pregnant than in the non-pregnant group: 23.1 percent and 17.1 percent, respectively (p. 44).

A pregnant drug-dependent woman puts her developing fetus at risk for a number of diseases, including hepatitis, human immunodeficiency virus (HIV), tuberculosis, and sexually transmitted diseases (STDs). A number of these diseases may be acquired through needle sharing. Mothers who are infected with these diseases are likely to deliver prematurely.

HEROIN AND METHADONE

In pregnant women who use heroin, the placenta typically shows microscopic evidence of oxygen deprivation. Infants are small for their gestational age, and all their organ systems are affected. In heroin-dependent women, a significant portion of the medical complications seen in their newborns is due to prematurity and low birth weight. Such complications include immature lungs, difficulties in breathing at birth, brain hemorrhage, low sugar and calcium levels, infections, and jaundice.

Women on methadone maintenance (an oral narcotic used for the treatment of heroin addiction) are more likely to give birth to normal- or almost normal-sized babies. Because they are in treatment, the complications in their infants are not as severe and generally reflect: (a) the amount of prenatal care the mother has received; (b) whether the mother has suffered any complications, including hypertension or infection; and, most importantly, (c) any multiple drug use that may have produced an unstable intrauterine environment for the fetus, perhaps complicated by withdrawal and/or overdose.

Multiple drug use may cause a series of withdrawals when the pregnant woman cannot obtain the drug she needs. This series of extreme physical conditions in the pregnant woman can severely affect the oxygen and nutrients that feed the developing fetus, causing various birth defects depending on when in each trimester the withdrawals occur. If the mother overdoses, a decreased oxygen supply to the fetus can cause aspiration pneumonia—if the mother survives the overdose to give birth.

Laboratory and animal studies have shown that opioids may have an inhibitory effect on enzymes that influence oxygen metabolism. They also alter the passage of oxygen and nutrients to the fetus by constricting the umbilical vessels and decreasing the amount of oxygen delivered to the developing fetal brain. Such metabolic side effects may cause a derangement in the acid/base balance (acidosis). In contrast, increased maturation of organ systems and certain enzymes have been seen in heroin-exposed infants, including maturation of the lungs, tissue-oxygen unloading, sweat glands, and liver enzymes. The stressful life of the pregnant woman probably contributes to this enhanced maturation in heroin-exposed infants.

The genetic risks to the offspring of addicts on heroin *and* methadone include an increase in the frequency of chromosome abnormalities; infants exposed predominantly to methadone *in utero* do not experience the same vulnerability to those abnormalities. The adverse environmental factors that may contribute to the abnormal findings in heroin-exposed infants may be less prominent in methadone mothers, as drug addiction is almost always compounded by poor maternal nutrition, extreme stress, infectious disease, and a lack of early and consistent prenatal care. However, in the absence of specific clinical abnormalities, it is impossible to isolate either methadone or heroin as agents linked to genetic damage. Given the obstetrical and medical complications, the lack of prenatal care, and the prematurity of the infants at delivery, it is not surprising that the death rate for addicted babies is higher than for infants born to non-addicts.

NEONATAL ABSTINENCE SYNDROME

The term neonatal abstinence syndrome (NAS) refers to the continuum of signs and symptoms evidenced by infants born to substance dependent mothers. Prenatally, NAS primarily describes the physiological, psychological, and cognitive impacts of substance use/abuse on the developing fetus. These impacts may be apparent at, or shortly after, birth or may not be detected until the child is older and develops learning, medical, or behavioral difficulties.

Whether born to heroin-addicted or methadone-dependent women, most infants seem physically and behaviorally normal at birth. The onset of their withdrawal may begin shortly after birth to two weeks of age, but most develop symptoms within seventy-two hours of birth. If the mother has been on heroin alone, 80 percent of the infants will develop clinical signs of withdrawal between four and twenty-four hours of age. If the mother has been on methadone alone, the baby's symptoms usually appear within forty-eight to seventy-two hours. The time of onset of withdrawal in individual infants depends on the type and amount of drug used by the mother, the timing of her last dose before delivery, the character of her labor, the type and amount of anesthesia and pain medication given during labor, and the maturity, nutrition, and presence or absence of systemic diseases in the infant.

Postnatal NAS includes the constellation of sequelae (secondary consequences) of maternal substance use, both developmental and medical. When first studied, the presence of NAS applied to the after-birth syndrome seen in infants born to heroin- or methadone-using mothers; over time it was broadened to include the aftereffects of cessation of virtually any chronic substance use—whether prescription medications used to control physiological or behavioral health disorders (such as seizures, depression, mood disorders, or other chronic medical or mental health conditions), as well as alcohol, tobacco, or illicit drugs used either recreationally or as a result of dependence. NAS is the most pronounced in infants born of women using opioids or narcotics.

Multiple, or polydrug, use increases the likelihood and severity of NAS. Infants born to mothers using stimulants, such as cocaine, methamphetamine, MDMA (Ecstasy), or medications used to treat ADHD (attention deficit hyperactivity disorder), often do not experience classic NAS, but show symptoms more closely associated with ongoing effects of the exposure to those substances. Drugs with a shorter half-life produce withdrawal effects more quickly after they are discontinued.

NAS typically involves multiple systems, with the greatest number of symptoms involving the central nervous and gastrointestinal systems. The type, number, and severity of symptoms will depend, to a large extent, on duration, amount, and frequency of drugs used as well as on the infant's own metabolism and physiological maturity. Opiates produce the most severe and obvious NAS effects and include premature birth, low birth weight for gestational age, and intrauterine growth retardation (IUGR). The effects of methadone use on the fetus are similar to those of heroin. It has a longer half-life, so acute NAS symptoms occur later, possibly even up to four weeks after birth.

Babies with NAS often exhibit signs and symptoms of central nervous system hyperirritability, gastrointestinal dysfunction, respiratory distress, and autonomic nervous system symptoms that include excessive yawning and sneezing, sweating, mottling, and fever. These infants frequently develop tremors that progress in severity. High-pitched crying, increased muscle tone, irritability, and exaggerated infant reflexes are common. Sucking of fists or thumbs is common, yet when fed, the infants have extreme difficulty in eating, and vomit frequently because of an uncoordinated and ineffectual sucking reflex. The infants may develop diarrhea and are therefore susceptible to dehydration and electrolyte imbalance. At birth the level of drug(s) in the blood begins to fall, and the newborn continues to metabolize and excrete the drug(s); withdrawal signs occur when critically low levels have been reached.

Studies indicate that more full-term infants require treatment for withdrawal than do preterm infants. Because withdrawal severity appears to correlate with gestational age, less mature infants show fewer symptoms. Decreased symptoms in preterm infants may be due to either (a) developmental immaturity of the preterm nervous systems, or (b) reduced total drug exposure because of shorter gestations.

The most severe withdrawal occurs in infants whose mothers have taken large amounts of drugs over a long period of time. Usually, the closer to delivery a mother takes heroin, the greater the delay in the onset of withdrawal and the more severe the baby's symptoms. The duration of symptoms may be anywhere from six days to eight weeks. The maturity of the infant's own metabolic and excretory mechanisms plays an important role. Although the infants are discharged from the hospital after drug therapy is stopped, some symptoms such as irritability, poor feeding, inability to sleep regularly, and sweating may persist for several months.

Drug-exposed infants show an uncoordinated and ineffectual sucking reflex as a major manifestation of withdrawal. Regurgitation, projectile vomiting, and loose stools may complicate the illness further. Dehydration, due to poor intake coupled with excessive losses from the gastrointestinal tract, may cause malnutrition, weight loss, subsequent electrolyte imbalance, shock, coma, and death. Untreated neonatal withdrawal carries a risk of death. The infant's respiratory system is also affected during withdrawal: Excessive secretions, nasal stuffiness, and rapid respirations are sometimes accompanied by difficulty breathing, blue fingertips and lips, and cessation of breathing. Severe respiratory distress occurs most often when the infant regurgitates, aspirates, and develops aspiration pneumonia.

PRENATAL OPIOID EXPOSURE

In addition to the heroin and methadone effects listed above, newborns exposed to opiates *in utero* are at increased risk for fetal distress or death or sudden infant death syndrome (SIDS). Thrombocytosis, an excessive production of platelets in the blood that can lead to blood clots, often occurs within the first few weeks of life and may last for several months.

PRENATAL STIMULANT EXPOSURE

Stimulants such as cocaine, amphetamines, and methamphetamine cross not only the blood–brain barrier of the mother, but the placental barrier as well. Stimulants have potent effects on the brain and cause prevention of reuptake or physiological alteration of several important neurotransmitters (substances that transmit nerve impulses), such as dopamine, epinephrine, norepinephrine, and serotonin. Infants exposed to stimulants often have an exaggerated startle reflex, a larger than normal Moro reflex (when exposed to a sudden noise, babies flex their legs and extend their arms abruptly), an excessive need to suck, and general jitteriness and irritability. There is ongoing research on the relationship between prenatal stimulant exposure and head circumference as well as on the long-term impact on the development of the brain.

Exposure is causally linked to smaller head circumference and therefore delayed brain development. Although most children do catch up in terms of overall head/brain growth over the first few years of life, there is a significantly increased rate of learning disabilities among children prenatally exposed to drugs, particularly in the areas of reading and math, as well as attention deficit disorders.

PRENATAL CAFFEINE AND TOBACCO EXPOSURE

Mothers who have excessive intake of caffeine (in any form) transmit a substance called methylxanthine to fetuses and breastfed infants. Tobacco use intensifies the effects of the drug on the fetus, because the blood vessels of the placenta increase their concentration in the developing infants' blood systems by up to 15 percent above that experienced by the mother. Tobacco use during pregnancy increases the likelihood of low birth weight and tobacco withdrawal in the neonate.

Exposure to either substance impairs the newborn's ability to habituate, to orient by sight or sound, to develop appropriate physiological mechanisms for autonomic regulation, and to be comforted. It can also cause a hyperreactive startle reflex, tachycardia, irritability, inefficient circulation, poor feeding, and tremors in the neonate—all indicators of nicotine toxicity in the body.

Behavioral studies have also been conducted with children exposed to prenatal smoking. Some research has shown that a child whose mother smoked during pregnancy is at increased risk of becoming a smoker. Because smoking activates neurotransmitters in the brain—including dopamine, which is involved in reinforcing the effects of addictive drugs—researchers have speculated that nicotine may have an effect on the developing dopamine system of the fetus and put the child at greater risk of addictive behavior in later life.

Prenatal exposure to cigarette smoking may affect a growing fetus in several ways. Carbon monoxide and high doses of nicotine obtained during inhalation of tobacco smoke can interfere with the oxygen supply to the fetus. Nicotine readily crosses the placenta, and it likely causes vasoconstriction of the umbilical arteries and impedes placental blood flow. Carbon monoxide can bind with hemoglobin to reduce the capacity of the blood to transport oxygen. These factors combined likely account for the developmental delays commonly seen in fetuses and infants of smoking mothers.

One of the most striking risks associated with prenatal smoking is that of Sudden Infant Death Syndrome (SIDS). A higher mortality rate exists for infants whose mothers have smoked compared to those who have not. Maternal smoking during pregnancy has also been cited as a major risk factor in almost every epidemiologic study of SIDS. The risk of sudden infant death syndrome is greater among infants exposed to both prenatal and postnatal smoking compared to those only exposed to postnatal smoking. The increase in SIDS risk also appears to be related to the *dose* of passive smoke to which the fetus or infant is exposed: The greater the exposure to smoke both before and after birth, the higher the risk of SIDS.

PRENATAL MARIJUANA EXPOSURE

To date, no research has shown the presence of a withdrawal syndrome in infants whose mothers used marijuana. However, prenatal exposure to marijuana may cause brain bleeds, jitteriness, sepsis

(severe infection), excessively low calcium, hypoglycemia, hypoxic encephalopathy (lack of sufficient oxygen to the developing brain causing brain damage, possibly resulting in mental retardation, developmental delays, or other neurophysiological deficits), and IUGR—particularly involving weight, length, and head circumference. The greater the mother's drug use during pregnancy, the more pronounced and severe the symptoms in the neonate. Nicotine toxicity effects, as mentioned above, may also be present. Although cognitive effects may last for several years, catch-up physiological growth typically occurs during the first year.

ANTIDEPRESSANT AND MOOD STABILIZER EXPOSURE

Pregnant women who use antidepressants (such as selective serotonin reuptake inhibitors, or SSRIs) or other mood stabilizers during their last trimester sometimes give birth to infants who express NAS. The signs and symptoms of NAS may include irritability, tremors, agitation, rapid and shallow breathing, stuffiness and nasal discharge, vomiting, and diarrhea. These effects are short in duration and generally only last for the first week or two of life.

T'S AND BLUES AND OXYCODONE EXPOSURE

T's and Blues are the street name for an intravenously injected drug cocktail comprised of a prescription painkiller called pentacozine (an opioid similar to morphine) and a nonprescription allergy medication. Babies born to women using this drug typically have reduced birth weight, may grow more slowly than their same-aged peers, and may experience withdrawal symptoms similar to infants with prenatal opioid exposure. The same is true for infants prenatally exposed to oxycodone.

PRENATAL CLUB DRUG EXPOSURE

Club drugs such as PCP (angel dust), ketamine (Special K), and lysergic acid (LSD), when used by pregnant women, may lead to NAS in the newborn. Prenatal exposure to these club drugs may result in learning and behavioral problems that endure.

PRENATAL MDMA (ECSTASY) EXPOSURE

There have been a small number of longitudinal human studies of the prenatal effects of MDMA to date. Thus far, the research suggests that use of MDMA during pregnancy may lead to permanent neurobiological changes; behavioral abnormalities such as hyperactivity; attention, focusing, and concentration deficits; and learning impairments.

PRENATAL INHALANT OR SOLVENT EXPOSURE

Women using inhalants (such as spray paint or gasoline fumes) or solvents (such as glues and resins) are at risk of kidney, liver, and brain damage; the mortality rate among this group of users is particularly high. Pregnant women who use them are at higher risk for miscarriage. Pregnancies that remain viable have increased incidence of premature birth, low birth weight, IUGR, and birth defects.

NAS ASSESSMENT AND MANAGEMENT

With proper management, the neonate's prognosis for recovery from the acute phase of withdrawal is good. When symptoms of withdrawal appear, simple nonspecific measures should be instituted, such as gentle, infrequent handling, maintaining calm and quiet surroundings, avoiding bright lights, swaddling, and feeding on demand. Careful attention to fluid-electrolyte balance and calorie support is essential, particularly in opioid-exposed infants undergoing withdrawal, because they display uncoordinated sucking and poor feeding, often develop vomiting and diarrhea, and have increased water loss due to rapid respirations and sweating.

Indications for specific treatment, dosage schedules, and duration of treatment have varied widely. As a general guide, if, in spite of nonspecific measures, babies have feeding difficulties, diarrhea, marked tremors, irritability even when undisturbed, or cry continuously; they should be given medication to relieve discomfort and prevent dehydration and other complications. Dosages must be carefully regulated to minimize symptoms without excessive sedation. Extremely low doses of drugs such as antiepileptic medications and mild opiates are effective in treating narcotic withdrawal symptoms in the infant.

NEUROBEHAVIOR IN NEWBORNS

Researchers using well-studied and clinically accepted neonatal assessment scales in evaluating drug-exposed infants noted that they were less able than non-drug-exposed infants to stay alert and less able to orient to auditory and visual stimuli; these effects were most pronounced at 48 hours of age. Drug-exposed infants were generally as capable of self-quieting and responding to soothing intervention as normal neonates, although they were substantially more irritable. These findings have important implications for caregivers' perceptions of infants, and thus may have long-term impact on the development of infant-caregiver interaction patterns.

On measures of social engagement, interactions between drug-dependent mothers and their infants have shown abnormalities. Abnormal interaction was explained by less positive maternal attachment as well as difficult infant behavior, which impedes social involvement. Many of these interactive abnormalities reverted to normal by four months of age, but the need for parenting training is obvious.

SUDDEN INFANT DEATH SYNDROME

Sudden infant death syndrome (SIDS) is defined as the sudden and unexpected death of an infant between one week and one year of age; the child's death remains unexplained after a complete autopsy examination, a full history, and a death-site investigation. Compared to an incidence of approximately 0.55 per 1,000 live births in the general population, narcotic-exposed infants appear to have an increased risk of SIDS. Other high-risk factors for SIDS, such as low socioeconomic status, low birth weight, young maternal age, membership in a racial minority group, and maternal smoking, were all overrepresented in studies of drug-using groups. In a large-scale study, New York City SIDS rates were calculated in 1.2 million births from 1979 to 1989. Maternal opiate use, after controlling for high-risk variables, increased the risk of SIDS by three to four times that of the general population.

LONG-TERM OUTCOMES FOR CHILDREN

Although a drug-exposed newborn may seem free of physical, behavioral, or neurological deficits at the time of birth, the effects of pharmacological agents (used or abused) may not become apparent for many months or years. Although heroin abuse during pregnancy has been recognized for more than fifty years and methadone treatment has been employed for more than thirty years, longitudinal follow-up of opioid-exposed infants is still fragmentary. The difficulties encountered in long-term follow-up of this population include an inability to fully document the mother's drug intake, difficulty separating the drug effects from high-risk obstetric variables, problems in maintaining a cohesive group of infants for study, and the need to separate drug effects from those of parenting and the home environment.

The easiest part of caring for the neonate is actually over when drug therapy has been discontinued and the infant is physically well. The most difficult parts then begin—the care involved in discharge planning and assuring optimal growth and development throughout infancy and childhood. Because there is no standard for the disposition of these infants, some may be released to their mothers, some to relatives, and others placed in the custody of a state agency. Other infants may be voluntarily released by their mothers to private agencies for temporary or permanent placement.

In the United States pressure to separate infants from their addicted mothers has been growing. This solution may not be practical in cities where social services and courts are already understaffed and overworked. There is a nationwide shortage of appropriately trained, licensed, and available foster parents qualified to care for high-risk infants. Pediatricians typically believe that the mother-infant association should not be dissolved except in extreme situations. In addition to intensive drug rehabilitation and medical treatment, these women need extensive educational and job training to become productive citizens and loving mothers who will positively socialize their children. Supportive therapies, such as outpatient care or residential treatment, may help eliminate some of the medical and social problems experienced by drug-dependent women and their children.

Most of the children evaluated for long-term development have been exposed to methadone. Evaluations have occurred at various intervals: at 6, 12, 18, and 24 months; then at 3, 4, and 5 years of age. Testing procedures utilized include the Gesell Developmental Schedule, the Bayley Scales of Infant Development, the McCarthy Scales of Infant Abilities, the Stanford-Binet, and the Wechsler Preschool and Primary Scale of Intelligence. Infants exposed to drugs prenatally have shown overall developmental scores in the normal range but a tendency to decrease in scores at about two years of age, which suggests that environment may confound long-term infant outcome. Low socioeconomic groups suffer from this factor particularly because of poor language stimulation and development.

The developmental scores in these early years, although useful in identifying areas of strength and weakness, are not valid predictors of subsequent intellectual achievement. Many studies have proposed multiple-factor models to assess infant outcome following intrauterine drug exposure. One such postnatal influence involves maternal-infant interaction. Drug-exposed infants are often irritable, have decreased rhythmic movements, and may display increased muscle tensing when handled. Mothers may interpret such behaviors as rejection, leading to inappropriate maternal caretaking and possible neglect of the infant. Studies of mother-infant interactions indicate that (a) infants born to narcotic-addicted women show deficient social responsiveness after birth; (b) this deficient mother-infant interaction persists until the infants' treatment for withdrawal is completed; and (c) maternal drug dosages may affect that interaction.

Available data suggest that at five years of age, children born to women maintained on methadone, in contrast to heroin-exposed babies, generally appear to function within the normal developmental range. In addition, no significant differences in language and perceptual skills were observed between them and a matched control group consisting of children of mothers not involved with drugs. Difficulty in following large cohorts (study groups) of drug-exposed infants has led to the study of very limited samples.

Positive and reinforcing environmental influences can significantly improve drug-exposed infant development. Women who show a caring concern for their infants are most likely to pursue follow-up pediatric care and cooperate in neurobehavioral follow-up studies. Lacking a large database, there is a significant need for comprehensive studies assessing the development of large populations of drug-exposed infants.

See also **Alcohol- and Drug-Exposed Infants; Attention Deficit Hyperactivity Disorder; Complications: Route of Administration; Fetal Alcohol Syndrome; Pregnancy and Drug Dependence.**

BIBLIOGRAPHY

Berghella, V., Lim, P. J., Hill, M. K., Cherpes, J., Chennat, J., & Kaltenbach, K. (2003). Maternal methadone dose and neonatal withdrawal. *American Journal of Obstetrics and Gynecology* 189(2): 312–317.

Breshears, E. M., Yeh, S., & Young, N. K. (2004). *Understanding substance abuse and facilitating recovery: A guide for child welfare workers.* U.S. Department of Health and Human Services. Rockville, MD: Substance Abuse and Mental Health Services Administration.

Carroll, J. L., & Siska, E. S. (1998). SIDS: Counseling parents to reduce the risk. (Sudden infant death syndrome). *American Family Physician, 57,* 1566.

Council on Cardiovascular Disease in the Young, American Heart Association. (1994). Active and passive tobacco exposure: A serious pediatric health problem. A statement from the Committee on Atherosclerosis and Hypertension in Children. Dallas, TX: Author.

Finnegan, L. P., & Kandall, S. R. (1992). Maternal and neonatal effects of drug dependence in pregnancy. In J. Lowinson, P. Ruiz, R. B. Millman, & J. G. Langrod (Eds.), *Comprehensive textbook of substance abuse.* (2nd ed.). Baltimore: Williams & Wilkins.

Griesler, P. C., Kandel, D. B., & Davies, M. (1998). Maternal smoking in pregnancy, child behavior problems, and adolescent smoking. *Journal of Research on Adolescence, 8,* 159–185.

Hadeed, A. J., & Siegel, S. R. (1989). Maternal cocaine use during pregnancy: Effect on the newborn infant. *Pediatrics, 84,* 205.

Hamilton, B. E., Martin, J. A., & Sutton, P. D. (2003) Births: Preliminary data for 2002. *National Vital Statistics Reports, 51*(11). Hyattsville, MD: National Center for Health Statistics.

Hughes, A., Sathe, N., & Spagnola, K. (2008). *State estimates of substance use from the 2005–2006 National Surveys on Drug Use and Health.* (DHHS Publication No. SMA 08-4311, NSDUH Series H-33). Rockville, MD: Substance Abuse and Mental Health Services Administration, Office of Applied Studies.

Kaltenbach, K., & Finnegan, L. P. (1988). The influence of the neonatal abstinence syndrome on mother-infant interaction. In E. J. Anthony & C. Chiland (Eds.), *The child in his family: Perilous development.* New York: Wiley-Interscience.

MacDorman, M. F., Cnattingius, S., Hoffman, H. J., Kramer, M. S., & Haglund, B. (1997). Sudden infant death syndrome and smoking in the United States and Sweden. *American Journal of Epidemiology, 146,* 249–257.

Makin, J., Fried, P. A., amp; Watkinson, B. (1991). A comparison of active and passive smoking during pregnancy: Long-term effects. *Neurotoxicology & Teratology, 13,* 5–12.

Mathias, Robert. (1998). Prenatal exposure to drugs of abuse may affect later behavior and learning. National Institute on Drug Abuse: *NIDA Notes, 13*(4). Available from http://www.nida.nih. gov/.

National Institute on Drug Abuse. *NIDA research report— Nicotine addiction.* (NIH Publication No. 98–4342). Rockville, MD: National Clearinghouse on Alcohol and Drug Information. Available from http://www.quit smoking.com/.

Office of Applied Studies. (2003). *Results from the 2002 national survey on drug use and health: National findings.* (DHHS Publication No. SMA 03-3836, NHSDA Series H-22). Rockville, MD: Substance Abuse and Mental Health Services Administration, Office of Applied Studies.

Office of Applied Studies. (2007). *Results from the 2006 National Survey on Drug Use and Health: National findings.* (DHHS Publication No. SMA 07-4293, NHSDA Series H-32). Rockville, MD: Substance Abuse and Mental Health Services Administration, Office of Applied Studies.

Schoendorf, K. C., & Kiely, J. L. (1992). Relationship of sudden infant death syndrome to maternal smoking during and after pregnancy. *Pediatrics, 90,* 905–908.

Young, N. K. (2006, June 20). Presentation. Substance-exposed infants: Policy and practice.

Zuckerman, B., Frank, D. A, Hingson, R., Amaro, H., Levenson, S. M., & Kayne, H. (1989). Effects of maternal marijuana and cocaine use on fetal growth. *New England Journal of Medicine, 320,* 762.

LORETTA P. FINNEGAN
MICHAEL P. FINNEGAN
GEORGE A. KANUCK
REVISED BY PATRICIA OHLENROTH (2001)
PAMELA V. MICHAELS (2009)

FINLAND. *See* **Nordic Countries (Denmark, Finland, Iceland, Norway, and Sweden).**

FLY AGARIC. A poisonous mushroom of Eurasia (*Amanita muscaria*), having typically a bright red cap with white dots. A preparation, consisting primarily of the dried mushroom, is ingested by the people of Siberia as a hallucinogen. Intoxication by ingestion of several mushrooms moistened with milk or fruit juice leads to a progression of symptoms—beginning with tremors, continuing through a period of visual hallucination that may be interpreted as having religious significance, and finally ending in deep sleep. A similar preparation may be identified with the deified intoxicant *soma* of the ancient Hindus. In some cultures, the urine of intoxicated individuals is ingested by others to induce intoxication, since the active components of the preparation pass unmetabolized through the body.

The active components found in fly agaric are ibotenic acid and several of its metabolites. The predominant metabolite is muscimol, which has agonist properties at a subset of receptors recognizing the neurotransmitter GABA. Ibotenic acid itself has agonist properties at certain excitatory amino acid receptors and has been shown to be neurotoxic.

See also **Plants, Drugs From.**

BIBLIOGRAPHY

Houghton, P. J., & Bisset, N. G. (1985). Drugs of ethno-origin. In D. C. Howell (Ed.), *Drugs in central nervous system disorders.* New York: Marcel Dekker.

Lewis, W. H. (2005). *Medical botany: Plants affecting human health.* Hoboken, NJ: John Wiley & Sons.

Spinella, M. (2005). *Concise handbook of psychoactive herbs.* New York: Haworth Press.

ROBERT ZACZEK

FOREIGN POLICY AND DRUGS, UNITED STATES.

Drug control is a relative newcomer to the list of global issues that are now an integral part of U.S. foreign policy. Although arms control and human rights were already important international issues in the 1970s, drug control lagged behind. In 1971 and 1972 some members of Congress tried to impose foreign-aid restrictions on Turkey to stop the entry of its heroin, but the U.S. government did not want to risk hurting relations with an important defense ally over heroin, which was not then considered a mainstream drug. The government instead found a compromise through diplomatic efforts, which led to the Turkish government severely limiting the cultivation of opium poppies (from which heroin is made) and changing the way

in which poppies were processed into legitimate medicinal opium. Parallel diplomatic negotiations with Mexico resulted in cooperation on marijuana eradication efforts. On the international front, the U.S. government pressed hard for the ratification of the 1971 United Nations (UN) Convention on Psychotropic Drugs and created the UN Fund for Drug Abuse Control (UNFDAC), the predecessor of today's UN Drug Control Program (UNDCP). During the rest of the decade, however, drug control gradually declined as a key U.S. foreign policy objective.

Drug control only gained full diplomatic legitimacy in the 1980s when cocaine use became widespread among entertainers, athletes, and stockbrokers. U.S. relations with the government of Panama and its leader, General Manuel Noriega, soured when it became clear that Noriega had cooperated with the Medellin drug cartel. A U.S. federal grand jury in Miami indicted Noriega on drug-trafficking charges in 1988, alleging that he had facilitated money laundering by the cartel and permitted the cartel to operate cocaine-processing facilities in Panama. In 1989 the United States invaded Panama and brought Noriega to Florida for a trial. In 1992 he was convicted on the drug-trafficking charges and sentenced to 40 years in prison.

Despite targeted efforts on prominent officials such as Noriega, the government's inability to stop the drug epidemic at home prompted Congress to address the role of foreign governments in drug trafficking. In 1986, in the first of a series of comprehensive international antidrug laws (the Anti-Drug Abuse Act of 1986), Congress placed the burden of halting drug flows on the governments of the drug-producing countries. Using a traditional carrot-and-stick approach, the law required the major drug-producing and transit countries to cooperate fully with the United States in drug matters in order to receive American foreign aid. Half of all assistance was withheld every year until the office of the president certified that the country concerned had met the criteria for receiving aid. Subsequent laws have expanded this requirement, obliging the major drug-producing and transit countries to also comply with the 1988 UN Convention against Illicit Traffic in Narcotics Drugs and Psychotropic Substances. Countries that do not comply not only lose U.S. assistance but also incur U.S. opposition to loans from the World Bank and other international financial institutions. For many countries in the developing world, losing access to these loans is an even greater hardship than losing U.S. assistance. Although the certification process has raised tensions with some foreign governments, it has become an accepted part of U.S. foreign policy. However, critics note that the United States has recertified countries such as Mexico and Colombia, despite the political corruption in these nations that has seriously undercut narcotics enforcement efforts.

In earning its diplomatic legitimacy, drug control has had to overcome the same obstacles encountered by other global issues, such as human rights or nuclear nonproliferation. The U.S. foreign policy establishment has favored strategic issues affecting vital U.S. national security or trade interests over law enforcement or scientific endeavor. It has been reluctant to allow multilateral "functional" questions to affect traditional bilateral negotiations. However, after the terrorist attacks on September 11, 2001, the State Department placed greater emphasis on drug control. It maintains that counternarcotics programs complement the war on terrorism, both directly and indirectly, by promoting the modernization of and supporting operations by foreign criminal justice systems and law enforcement agencies charged with the counterterrorism mission.

Congress has consistently worked to keep drug control high on the list of U.S. foreign policy issues. By denying virtually all forms of aid—excluding humanitarian and drug-control assistance—to countries that refuse to cooperate, Congress has devised an effective form of leverage over drug countries. Because the law also allows the president to waive sanctions when clearly stated national interests are at stake, Congress has made it difficult for foreign policy agencies to evade their drug-control responsibilities.

RESPONSIBLE AGENCIES

The U.S. Department of State is responsible for formulating international drug policy. Its Bureau for International Narcotics and Law Enforcement Affairs oversees the annual certification process and prepares an annual report. Since 1989 formal coordination authority has rested with the White House Office of National Drug Control Policy (ONDCP) and the National Security Council. Drug-control programs, however, involve a broad spectrum of government agencies, including the Central Intelligence Agency, the Department of Defense, the Department of Homeland Security (which now includes the U.S. Customs Service and the Coast Guard), the Department of Treasury, the Justice Department, the Drug Enforcement Administration, and the Department of Health and Human Services. A small percentage of the U.S. drug-control budget is spent on international programs. The bulk of the money goes to domestic law enforcement, drug treatment, and public education.

THE REALITIES OF DRUG CONTROL

As presidential administrations have discovered, an effective drug policy is easier to design than to carry out. The drug issue is a typical chicken-and-egg problem. Does supply drive demand or vice versa? Drug-consuming countries traditionally blame the suppliers for drug epidemics, whereas drug-producing countries allege that without foreign demand, local farmers would not grow the drug crop at all. Planners must therefore strike the right balance between reducing drug supply and demand. In theory, eliminating drug cultivation in the source countries is the most economical solution, because it keeps drugs from entering the system and acquiring any value as a finished product. Few source-country governments—all of which are in developing nations—will, however, deprive farmers of a livelihood without substantial compensation from abroad. And the price they seek is usually more than the U.S. government is prepared to pay.

THE NATURE OF THE THREAT

The illegal drug trade in the early twenty-first century is one of the most lucrative, and therefore powerful, criminal enterprises in history. Drugs generate profits on a scale without historical precedent—especially given their abundance and low production costs. Such financial resources, which are well beyond those of most national budgets, give drug traffickers the means to buy sophisticated arms, aircraft, and electronic and technical equipment available to few countries. More importantly, illegal drug revenues allow trafficking organizations to buy themselves protection at almost every level of government in the drug-producing and drug-transit countries, where drug-related corruption remains the single largest obstacle to effective control programs.

Efforts to control the quantity of drugs have had mixed results. Opium production, which declined in the years 2001 to 2006, rebounded in 2007. Opium poppy cultivation in Southeast Asia increased by 22 percent in 2007, mainly driven by a 29 percent increase in opium cultivation in Myanmar (the former Burma) and increased cultivation in Afghanistan. In South America, coca production has been reduced, yet it is enough to satisfy world demand twice over. This surplus is so large that the drug trade easily absorbs losses inflicted by drug-control authorities and still makes enormous profits.

Traffickers have the option of expanding the cultivation of drug crops into new areas. For example, although coca plants are currently confined to Latin America, coca once flourished in Indonesia and could do so again if market conditions were right. Opium poppy cultivation is spreading into nontraditional areas, including South America. South American cocaine-trafficking organizations have diversified into opium poppy cultivation. Without active government antidrug programs, production will grow until the new expanding market is saturated.

The popularity of methamphetamine grew dramatically in the United States beginning in the late 1990s. Local meth labs were the original source of most meth consumed in the United States, but state and federal laws have severely restricted the availability of the chemicals needed to produce it. Consequently the illegal production of meth in Mexico and its importation to the United States have become a major problem. By 2008 the majority of meth consumed in America came from Mexico.

EARLY-TWENTY-FIRST-CENTURY POLICY

The U.S. government's first priority is to stop the flow of cocaine, which still poses an immediate threat to potential drug users. Because of rising heroin use promoted by the new, cheaper Latin American producers, the United States must also focus on opium-producing countries. The U.S.

goal is to limit the cultivation of drug crops to the amount necessary for international medical applications. Because all the cocaine that enters the United States comes from coca plantations in Peru, Bolivia, and Colombia, the U.S. government maintains active drug-control programs in these three countries. During the 1990s the United States also assisted Bolivia and Peru in their efforts to reduce coca cultivation. Although these efforts dramatically reduced production, drug traffickers increased coca production in Colombia. This resulted in increased political corruption and political destabilization. In 2000 the United States approved $1.3 billion in emergency assistance for Colombia; the aid package contained money for police and military training, administration of justice programs, and economic development programs. The United States has also increased its military assistance to Latin America to help fight narcotics trafficking. Although Colombia leads the world in coca cultivation and is the source of 90 percent of the cocaine entering the United States, by 2008 it had made some progress in combating cultivation. In 2007, with U.S. assistance, Colombia eliminated a record-breaking 153,000 hectares of coca through aerial eradication and another 66,000 through manual eradication.

Opium control is more difficult than coca suppression, because most of the world's opium poppy grows in countries where the United States has minimal diplomatic influence (Myanmar, Laos, and Iran). The U.S. military presence in Afghanistan since 2001 has not led to the destruction of the opium trade. In 2007 that nation produced 90 percent of the world's opium poppy. As the former leaders of the Taliban government have regained control of the southern provinces, they have used increased opium production to fund the insurgency.

AN INTERNATIONAL APPROACH

Because bilateral programs seldom provide solutions to global problems, the United States has been an active proponent of collective action under the 1988 UN Convention. This latest agreement covers not only the traditional aspects of drug production and trafficking but also requires signatories to control drug-processing chemicals and outlaw drug-money laundering. The money-laundering provisions are critical innovations, as they target the enormous international cash flows that sustain the drug trade. As astronomical as drug profits may be, drug money is useless unless it can enter the international banking system. The major industrialized countries are therefore pressing for uniform laws and regulations to exclude drug money in all key financial centers. If honestly implemented, strict money-laundering controls, along with better use of existing programs to suppress drug supply and decrease consumption, offer the hope of reducing the drug trade from an international threat to a manageable concern. However, efforts by the European Union (EU) to create a uniform set of procedures to combat this problem have been flawed. A 2006 review by an EU committee found that procedures for identifying and reporting suspicious transactions differed between countries. Some members took too long to report suspicious deals, ruling out action.

See also **Bolivia; Coca/Cocaine, International; Colombia; Crop Control Policies; Drug Interdiction; Drug Laws: Financial Analysis in Enforcement; Golden Triangle as Drug Source; International Drug Supply Systems; Opium: U.S. Overview; Peru; Terrorism and Drugs; U.S. Government Agencies.**

BIBLIOGRAPHY

Ehrenfeld, R. (1990). *Narco-terrorism*. New York: Basic Books.

MacDonald, B., & Zagaris, B. (Eds.). (1992). *International handbook on drug control*. Westport, CT: Greenwood.

Simmons, L. R. S., & Said, A. A. (Eds.). (1974). *Drugs, politics, and diplomacy: The international connection*. Beverly Hills, CA: Sage.

Taylor, A. H. (1969). *American diplomacy and narcotics traffic, 1909–1939*. Durham, NC: Duke University Press.

U.S. Congress. Senate Committee on the Judiciary. (1975). *Poppy politics*. Hearings before the Subcommittee to Investigate Juvenile Delinquency. Washington, DC: U.S. Government Printing Office.

U.S. Department of State. (March 2008). *International narcotics control strategy report*. Washington, DC: U.S. Government Printing Office.

White House Office of National Drug Control Policy. (2008). *National drug control strategy: 2008 annual report*. Washington, DC: Author.

W. KENNETH THOMPSON
REVISED BY FREDERICK K. GRITTNER (2009)

FRANCE. France is a western European country with a population of about 60 million. It belongs to the European Union and uses the Euro; however, many of the available statistics through the 1990s are in francs. It is the leading world consumer and exporter of alcoholic beverages. Drinking wine with meals has deep cultural roots in France. Tobacco was long a monopoly of the state, and its use is still widespread. There has long been a small traffic of illicit drugs. In the last third of the twentieth century, an increase was observed in the use of illicit drugs, chiefly cannabis, among youths. The French government has developed several programs, mainly since the 1990s, to protect the public's health from the harm caused by these substances.

GEOGRAPHY

France is at the Western end of Europe. It produces its own alcoholic beverages and tobacco products, along with some imports. Its cannabis comes mainly from Morocco, usually by way of Spain. Cocaine and crack come from the new world, often by way of the French Antilles. Opium is produced chiefly in Afghanistan; heroin is produced in Turkey and other countries and travels through Germany and various European countries to reach France.

HISTORY

Alcoholic Beverages. Wine has been used in the diet since antiquity, and spirits were used medically since the late middle ages. In the nineteenth century the consumption of wine nearly quadrupled (from 33 to 120 liters per capita between 1830 and 1900), and use of beer and spirits markedly increased in all classes of society. Inebriety became more prominent. Temperance movements emerged after 1870 (Societé Française de Tempérance, 1872; Union Française Antialcoolique, 1894; Ligue Nationale Antialcoolique and Fédération Ouvrière Antialcoolique, both early in the 1900s). Members of the movement took a moral stance. Calls for governmental control over alcohol increased during World War I, and absinthe drinks were made illegal in 1915. After World War I the temperance movement collapsed (Brennan, 1989). Use of alcoholic beverages gradually increased until concern about alcohol-related health problems emerged in the 1950s. During his brief tenure as prime minister, Pierre Mendès-France initiated several proposals and decrees to reduce alcohol production and consumption, but he encountered great resistance from the wine industry as well as the public (Ugland, 2003). However, attention to alcohol-related harm had increased. A governmental High Committee for Study and Information about Alcoholism was formed in 1954. Government intervention to decrease alcohol use, especially among youths, intensified in the 1990s.

Tobacco. Tobacco was introduced in France early in the sixteenth century. Jean Nicot popularized it for medical purposes in the 1560s. In the next century it became fashionable to use it as snuff or for pipe smoking. The first commercial cigarettes were produced in 1843 by the Manufacture Française des Tabacs, a state run outfit that started the French government monopoly on tobacco. The French monopoly was later know as SEIT (Service d'Exploitation Industrielle des Tabacs), and its profits were used from 1926 on to reduce the public debt. In 1935 it became SEITA by adding a monopoly on matches (*allumettes*). In 1959 it became a public establishment to manage the state monopoly. In 1984 the State became the only investor in SEITA. In 1995 SEITA was privatized, and in 1999 it fused with Tabacalera, a Spanish tobacco monopoly to become Altadis. Altadis is now the sixth-largest producer of cigarettes in the world and the first of cigars (Tabagisme.net).

World War I markedly increased the use of tobacco by soldiers who kept the habit after discharge. Prevalence of smoking steadily increased during the first three-quarters of the twentieth century. Knowledge of the causal role of tobacco in lung cancer, in other cancers, and in heart disease spread in the 1970s. Laws to control tobacco advertising and smoking in public places were passed in 1976 and 1991.

Illicit Psychoactive Substances. Cannabis, opium derivatives, and cocaine have been used in France for several centuries for both medicinal and recreational use. LSD, hallucinogenic mushrooms, ecstasy, and amphetamines were introduced after the middle of the twentieth century. The twentieth century saw an increase in nonmedical use of psychoactive pharmaceuticals. Initially, these drugs were used by a relatively small number of people looking for new sensations and by socially marginalized people. In the 1960s youths began to experiment with, and eventually use, many of these drugs. In subsequent years cannabis became very widely used by teenagers and young adults. Use of pharmaceutical drugs has increased steadily, especially among girls. The government responded with a punitive law in 1970, followed in the 1990s by risk reduction measures. In the past two decades a large set of governmental structures has been organized to integrate the various actors in the fight against drugs.

THE FIGHT AGAINST DRUGS

No single agency or ministry is charged with coordinating the various aspects of the fight against drugs in France at the national level; rather, control is divided among several ministries. State control of drug use includes the Ministry of Justice and the law courts. The Ministry of the Interior is in charge of the police in localities with more than 100,000 residents, whereas the Ministry of Defense oversees the *gendarmerie* (police) in rural areas and small towns. Assistance to drug users has been primarily a function of the Ministry of Health; however, social services have become increasingly involved. Several other agencies are also involved, such as customs in the Ministry of Treasury or the newly-created Ministry of Research. In order to create some coherence among these various activities, the French government has established two bodies: Mission Interministerielle de Lutte contre la Drogue et la Toxicomanie (MILDT), and the Observatoire Français des Drogues et des Toxomanies (OFDT).

The MILDT was founded in 1982 as a task force and elevated in 1996 to its present title and rank, reporting directly to the prime minister. It prepares government plans for the fight against drugs and monitors the implementation of these plans. It coordinates the policies of 17 ministries and supports the work of several other state and private partners, including local governments, specialized institutions, professional bodies, and associations. It also finances public interest groups. Its budget comes from the various ministries. (MILDT, 2004)

The OFDT is one of the public interest groups financed by MILDT. It is charged with the collection, analysis, synthesis, and distribution of data concerning alcohol, tobacco, cannabis, and other psychoactive drugs in France. Their statistics are secondary analyses based on primary data from various public or private surveys. Statistics are available at OFDT for number of sales, level of consumption, associated morbidity and mortality, and methods of repression of prohibited use and of traffic. (OFDT, 2006)

CURRENT SUBSTANCE USE

National surveys (ESCAPAD in 2003 and 2005 and Barometer Santé 2005) provided the following quantitative information on the adult population aged 12 to 75. Adults who had used psychoactive substances at least once in their lifetime numbered 42.5 million for alcohol, 34.8 million for tobacco, 15.1 million for psychotropic medications, 12.4 million for cannabis, 1.1 million for cocaine, 0.9 million for ecstasy, and 0.36 million for heroin. Adults who used the substance daily numbered, in millions, 6.4 for alcohol, 11.8 for tobacco, and 0.55 for cannabis (OFDT, 2006).

In 2005 a study of 17-year-olds showed the following percentage of monthly usage in the study population: 82 percent of boys and 75 percent of girls for alcohol, 41.5 and 40.9 for tobacco, 33.5 and 22.5 for cannabis, 3.7 and 11.8 for psychotropic medications, 1.7 and 1.0 for ecstasy, 1.2 and 0.7 for cocaine, 1.0 and 0.5 for amphetamines, 0.54 and 0.3 for LSD, 0.3 and 0.2 for heroin, and 0.32 and 0.1 for crack (OFDT, 2006).

Alcohol. There has been a steady decrease in alcohol sales since the 1950s. Sales expressed in liters of pure alcohol per resident decreased from 15.7 in 1970 to 11.7 in 1998 (OFDT, 2002). Daily use of alcohol decreased from 23 percent of adults in 1995 to 15 percent in 2005 (Beck, 2006). Daily use in 1998 was greater in men (31.3%) than in women (12.5%). Daily use of alcohol increased with age from 10 percent at age 30 to 32 percent at age 40, 41 percent at age 50, and 60 percent at age 60 and above. Problematic drinking (risky drinking or dependence) was found in 8.3 percent of adults in 1995 and 8.9 percent in 1999. The rate of problematic drinking in men increased with age from 9.3 percent at age 20 to 19.4 percent at age 50 and then decreased, although it is not known to what extent this is an aging effect or a group effect (OFDT, 2002). The percentage of risky drinking

(i.e. excessive drinking without dependence) declined from 30 percent of drinkers at age 20 to 10 percent at age 60, but the percentage of dependent drinkers rose from 2.5 percent at age 20 to 10 percent of drinkers at age 60 (Beck, 2006). First use of alcohol begins on average at 13 years of age. By age 16, 84 percent of boys and 83 percent of girls had experimented with alcohol.

Tobacco. Sales of cigarettes have decreased steadily from about 100 billion units in 1990 to about 55 billion in 2004 and remained stable until 2006 (OFDT, 2006). The value of these sales increased from 6.4 billion euros in 1991 to 13.4 billion in 2007 despite the decrease in volume of sales; this was due to a marked increase in the price of cigarettes. Among adults, 30 percent of men and 23 percent of women smoked daily in 2005 (Beck, 2006). Use of tobacco decreased steadily among adult men from 60 percent in 1970 to about 40 percent in 2004, whereas in women, it moved from 28 percent in 1970 to about 35 percent in 1980 and back to 28 percent in 2004 (Beck, 2006). In 2005, 34 percent of boys and 43 percent of girls aged 17 reported daily use of tobacco, and one-third of them already showed evidence of tobacco addiction.

Cannabis. Cannabis use increased markedly among youths. The percentage of 17-year-old boys who experimented with cannabis rose from 24.7 percent in 1993 to 52.3 percent in 2003 and remained stationary until 2005, whereas that of 17-year-old girls rose from 17.2 percent in 1993 to 47.2 percent in 2003. Regular use of cannabis (more than 10 days a month) remained close to 15 percent among 17-year-old boys and 5 to 6 percent in 17-year-old girls from 2000 to 2005. Cannabis is used chiefly by the younger generations. Its yearly prevalence decreases steadily to 8 percent of men and 3 percent of women by age 40 and lower still later (Beck, 2006).

Other Drugs. Experimentation with cocaine, amphetamine, and heroin by percentage of the population ages 28 to 44 was 1.3, 1.0, and less than 0.1, respectively in 1992; it rose to 3.5, 3.0, and 1.8, respectively in 2005. Yearly use in 2005 for ages 18 to 25 was 1.5 for cocaine, 1.4 for Ecstasy, 0.8 for hallucinogenic mushrooms, 0.5

for solvents, 0.4 for LSD, 0.4 for heroin, and 0.3 for amphetamines (Beck, 2006). In 2005 psychotropic medications were used during the past year by 24 percent of women and 14 percent of men. Lowest use was among the 18 to 25 age group, with 15 percent of women and 9 percent of the men using them during the previous year. Frequency of use increased with age until ages 45 to 54 and remained steady thereafter (Beck, 2006).

POLYCONSUMPTION

The levels of polyconsumption are: (a) polyexperimentation; (b) repeated polyconsumption; (c) polyconsumption at the same occasion; and (d) polydependency. Among the general adult population 18 to 44 years of age, people who used cannabis had an average polyexperimentation of 1.4 drugs. For those who used heroin, the average polyexperimentation was 4.7 drugs; for the rest it varied between 3.8 and 4.2. With regard to repeated polyconsumption, only alcohol, tobacco, and cannabis had enough subjects to get reliable data. In the population ages 18 to 44, 9.6 percent used alcohol and tobacco; 3.4 percent used tobacco and cannabis; 1.7 percent used alcohol, tobacco, and cannabis; and 0.4 percent used alcohol and cannabis. (OFDT, 2002). Among adolescents aged 17 in 2000, those who used cannabis experimented with 1.4 other drugs (not including alcohol and tobacco), those using psychotropic medications experimented with 1.7 percent other drugs, and those who used heroin, LSD, amphetamines, or cocaine experimented with more than five drugs. A relatively small number of adolescents used two or more drugs at the same occasion for one of the following purposes: to maximize the effects, to correct the effects of one drug with another to obtain the optimal combination, to master the negative effects following the first drug, or because there was not enough of one type of drug (OFDT, 2002).

GOVERNMENTAL POLICY

French government policies are based on laws that are implemented by specific ministries or agencies. Ministries use *décrets* that entail an obligation (analogous to regulations in the U.S.) and *ciculaires* that are advisory (analogous to guidelines in the U.S., but somewhat stronger). The actual effect of the law depends not only upon the strength of the provisions in the law but also on the manner in which it is implemented through *décrets* and *circulaires*, and through the penalties for violations. The interval of time between enactment of a law and implementation is also an important variable.

ALCOHOL LEGISLATION

The objects of policies are to limit harmful effects, to decrease the total use of alcohol in the population, and to delay the age when youth start drinking. Gradual approaches are used because use of alcohol is ingrained in the culture and because of the importance of the alcohol industry to the economy and its political power.

Efforts to decrease car accidents when the drivers are under the influence of alcohol led to the first definition of legal alcohol levels of 0.4 grams per liter of exhaled air and 0.8 grams per liter of blood in the law of July 8, 1970. Subsequent laws increased the penalties for driving under the influence and lowered the legal blood limit to 0.5 grams per liter in 1990.

The Barzarch law of July 10, 1987, targeted advertising and other means of publicizing alcohol products. It prohibited television advertising and alcohol companies' sponsorship of sports events. It was ineffective as the industry found ways of getting around the law. A stronger law was passed on January 10, 1991. It is named the loi Evin, after the minister of health Claude Evin. It prohibits direct or indirect advertising or sponsorship of public events, with specified exceptions. It also mandates statements about health dangers of alcohol on product labels. It sets relatively high fines on infractions of these rules, up to 100,000 euros. It has encountered opposition both within France and in Europe, but the government has been steady in implementing it over a number of years.

TOBACCO

The production and sale of tobacco was for a long time a state monopoly that provided an important source of revenue. It was privatized in 1995, but it remains an important source of tax funds. Tobacco, an addictive substance, is an ingrained habit among much of the French public. The Veil law of July 9, 1976, allowed publicity only in the press, forbid sponsorship of sports events, required a message about health risks on the package, and forbade smoking in public places when it posed a health hazard for others. The law was ineffective, and both advertising and sponsorship expenses increased in the following decade.

The Evin law of January 10, 1991 (Logifrance, 1991) took up the challenge. It prohibited advertising and other publicity except for certain specified sites and increased the fine for violations; it prohibited smoking in public places; it maintained messages about health risks on product labels and set significant fines (e.g. 5,000 francs for the smoker); and it removed tobacco from the national price index, thus facilitating a rise in the cost of cigarettes. However, it was implemented very gradually; for instance, restaurants were allowed to have a smoking section until December 31, 2007, and only in 2008, 17 years after passage of the law, did restaurants become totally smoke free.

ILLICIT DRUGS PHASE 1: LAW OF 1970
The problem of illicit drug use became pressing in France in the 1960s when an increasing number of French youths started to use these substances. The government's response was initially repressive. The law of December 31, 1970, set the use of heroin and other drugs, such as cocaine and cannabis, as an infraction punishable by jail time. However, an arrestee may escape a jail sentence through treatment with a psychiatrist with the goal of becoming drug free. At that time French professionals and policy makers saw the problem of drug addiction as an individual's own problem, a deviation for which that person needed treatment. This contrasts with the social approach to the problem that developed at the same time in the Netherlands There, the addict was conceptualized as a marginalized person, living in a state of social misery, and management allowed the use of morphine or other opium derivatives, along with helping to reintegrate the individual into society (Van Solinge, 1996).

French opposition to this approach was slow in developing. There was a small effort to develop methadone substitution programs on an experimental basis, sponsored by Institut National de la Santé et de la Recherche Médicale (INSERM) that led to two programs for 20 people each in 1973. They were not followed up by other programs, however, as the opinion of politicians as well as professionals was strongly against substitution for nearly two decades, so psychiatry maintained a monopoly on treatment (Augé-Caumon et al., 2002).

However, a more important opposition developed in the 1980s, stimulated in part by the HIV/AIDS epidemic among drug users. In the 1980s, 30 percent of heroin addicts tested sero-positive for HIV and 60 percent for hepatitis B or C. Associations that included consumers and professionals organized to "limit the damage or reduce harm" (Van Solinge, 1996). Individuals engaged in auto-substitution therapy with opium derivatives available without prescription, including derivatives of codeine (Augé-Caumon, 2002). Several primary care physicians led by Jean Carpentier treated heroin addicts with morphine sulfate (Van Solinge, 1996) and with buprenorphine that had been developed by Schering-Plough. (Augé-Caumon, 2002).

PHASE 2: *DÉCRET* AND *CIRCULAIRES*
The new phase did not start with a new law, but rather with the *décret* of June 29, 1992, which established the Centres Spécialisés de Soins aux Toxicomanes (CSST), with a mission not only for psychiatric care, but also for social and educative functions to help patients during the period of withdrawal and give social support in the familial environment. There was no mention of methadone substitution in that *décret*. However, within a year the minister of health issued two *circulaires* (1993 and 1994) that set the CSSTs as methadone-substitution sites in large cities of France, with strict standards for eligibility to the treatment (including duration of heroin dependency of at least five years), for control of utilization and storing of methadone, and for services offered (Augé-Caumon, 2002). The number of patients rose from 53 in 1993 to more than 1000 in 1995 (Van Selinge, 1996). A third *circulaire* in 1995 deleted the requirement for a five-year previous period of dependency. Finally, a fourth *circulaire* in 1995 set up the present system of substitution treatment. Methadone could be initiated only in specialized centers, but the treatment could be continued by the patient's physician. High-dose buprenorphine was also approved for substitution, and it could be prescribed by primary care physicians. By 2001, 12,000 persons were treated with methadone, and 80,000 persons were treated with buprenorphine (Augé-Caumont, 2002).

PHASE 3: MONITORING AND EVALUATION
By 2007, Centres d'Évaluation et d'Information sur la Pharmacodépendance (CEIP) had been

organized in 11 large cities (Bordeaux, Caen, Grenoble, Lille, Lyon, Marseille, Montpellier, Nancy, Nantes, Paris, and Toulouse). Their functions are (a) to develop statistics on pharmacodependence or abuse of drugs and evaluate the addicting potential of new illicit drugs or pharmaceuticals; (b) to inform professionals, the public, and policy makers about the risks of pharmacodependence and drug abuse by responding to queries or through bulletins or meetings; and (c) to do research, including animal experimentation and human surveys, to study toxicity and addictive potential of new drugs or substances.

The CEIPS utilize several tools to fulfill their functions:

- The OPPIDUM (Observatoire des Produits Psychotropes Illicites ou Détournés de leur Utilisation Médicamenteuse) does yearly surveys of patients in substitution therapy or with a diagnosis of pharmacodependence in health facilities. In 2006, it followed 3,867 patients and 7,737 prescriptions.

- OSIAP (Ordonnances Suspectes Indications d'Abus Possible) is a network of sentinel pharmacists attached to each CEIP. In 2006 it identified 314 prescriptions involving 514 medications.

- SINTES (Système d'Identification National des Toxicants et des Substances) is a social and health partnership to identify new substances or changes in degree of toxicity of substances, based on studies conducted in relation to social events or "rave parties."

- Enquête ASOS (Analgésiques, Stupéfiants, et Ordonnaces Sécuritées) is a survey of 800 pharmacies for utilization of analgesic, sedative, or other restricted drugs.

- Enquête Soumission Chimique investigates reported cases of people who were given drugs without being aware of it at parties or other occasions, usually to perform sexual or other acts on them (chemical submission).

- DRAMES (Décès en Rellation avec l'Abus de Médications et de Substances) reports on postmortem studies by toxicology laboratories on drug addicts suspected of dying from overdoses. It conducted studies on 177 postmortems in 2006.

Coordination and Information Transfer. Each of the above studies is administered by one CEIP (for instance, OPPIDUM is administered by a CEIP in Marseille) that integrates the results to present a national evaluation. The material collected by the CEIP is presented to and evaluated by the Commission Nationale des Stupéfiants et des Psychotropes (CNSP) which, in turn, transmits its findings and advice to the Agence Française de Sécurité Sanitaire des Produits de Santé (AFSSPS). The AFSSPS has a broader mission over all health products and drugs (somewhat similar to the Food Drug Administration of the United States). It also exchanges information with a parallel system of data on drugs, the Observatoire Francais des Drogues et des Toxicomanes (OFDT).

The ministry of health requests and receives information and advice from the CNSP and the AFSSPS. The AFSSPS communicates with the European Medication Agency (EMEA) and the European Observatory of Drugs and Toxic substances (EODT) and the WHO (World Health Organization) Expert Committee on Pharmacodependence.

The CEIPs also serve as a source of local information for health facilities and health professionals. In turn, they receive spontaneous notifications of drug abuse from physicians, pharmacists, and other health professionals and often perform studies based on such local notifications.

CONCLUSION

The French government's initial punitive approach to illicit drugs use (imprisonment or injunction to psychiatric treatment) in the 1970s has evolved since the 1990s into a more comprehensive and socially-oriented approach. The development of methadone therapy, although late in comparison to other countries, has proceeded rapidly and is now well established, along with a pharmaceutical alternative administered by primary care physicians. The comprehensive approach developed by the CEIP may pave the way for a more socially-oriented approach to illicit drug use, as opposed to a punitive one. However, except for the success of replacement therapy, the fight against illicit drugs has not yet progressed to the point of decreasing use of these drugs in the population. This is in contrast to the success of the steady gradual methods that have led to the decreased prevalence of alcohol use in the adult population and the decreased use of tobacco by men and, following an earlier increase, by women.

The main problem with alcohol and tobacco as well as illicit drugs concerns the adolescent generation. Education about tobacco in schools from the earliest to the final grade levels is a promising approach that might also work for alcohol. Cannabis represents a special problem because a vast majority of adolescents as well as a significant part of the adult population do not consider it a dangerous drug, and it is now well implanted. France may have to consider a legalization of cannabis complemented by strong regulation and extensive education and surveillance of youth for psychosocial complications of its use. In addition, the problem of the marginalized population, major drug users, must be addressed in dealing not only with drugs, but by the related problems of low income, high levels of unemployment or underemployment, and lack of integration into society.

See also **Alcohol; Amphetamine; Cannabis Sativa; Cocaine; Crack; European Union; Foreign Policy and Drugs, United States; Germany; Hallucinogens; Heroin; International Control Policies; International Drug Supply Systems; Italy; Lysergic Acid Diethylamide (LSD) and Psychedelics; Methadone Maintenance Programs; Netherlands; Opiates/Opioids; Opium: International Overview; Polydrug Abuse; Psychoactive; Rave; Spain; Substance Abuse and AIDS; Tobacco: Dependence; Treatment, Pharmacological Approaches to: Buprenorphine; Treatment, Pharmacological Approaches to: Methadone; World Health Organization Expert Committee on Drug Dependence.**

BIBLIOGRAPHY

Agence Française de Sécurité Sanitaire des Produits de Santé (AFSSPS) (2007). *Centres d'Évaluation et d'Information sur la Pharmacodépendence (CEIP). Rapport d'activité 2006.* Paris: Bilan Scientifique.

Augé-Caumont, M.-J., Blocj-Lainé, J.-F., Lowenstein, W., & Morel, A. (2002). L'accès à la methadone en France: Bilan et recommendations. Rapport réalisé à la demande de Bernard Kouchner, Ministre Délégué de la Santé. Ministère délégué à la Santé, Paris. Available from http://www.ladocumentationfrancaise.fr/.

Beck, F., Legleye, S., Spilka, S., Briffault, X., Gautier, A., Lamboy, B., et al. (2006). Les niveaux d'usage des drogues en France en 2005. Observatoire Français des Drogues et des Toxicomanies. (Tendances numero 48, Mai 2006). Available from http://www.ofdt.fr.

Brennan, T. (1989). Toward the cultural history of alcohol in France. *Journal of Social History 23*(1),71–92.

Choquet, M., Beck, F., Hassler, C., Splika, S., Morin, D., & Legley, S. (2004). Les substances psychiactives chez les collégiens et les lycéens: Consummation en 2003 et evolution depuis 10 and Paris, Observatoire français des drogues et des toxicomanies. (Tendances numero 35, Mars 2004). Available from http://www.ofdt.fr.

Guichard, A., Lert, F., Calderon, C., Gaige, H., Maguet, O., Soletti, J., et al. (2003). Illicit drug use and injections practices among drug users on methadone and buprénorpine maintenance treatment in France. *Addiction 98*(11), 1585–1597.

Logifrance. (1991). Loi no. 91–32 du 10 Janvier 1991 relative à la lutte contre le tabagisme et l'alcoolisme. Available from http://www.logifrance.gouv.fr/.

Lopez, D. (2002). Use of illicit drugs and social exclusion: State of knowledge in France. (Trends No. 24, October 2002). Available from http://www.drogues.gouv.fr/.

Mildt. (2004). Plan Gouvernemental de Lutte contre Les Drogues Illicites, Le Tabac et L'Alcool, 2004–2008. Paris: Mission Interministerielle de Lutte Contre La Drogue et La Toxicomanie. Available from http://www.drogues.gouv.fr/.

Observatoire Français des Drogues et des Toxicomanies (OFTD). (2002). Drugs and drug addictions—indicators and trends: Alcohol. Available from http://www.ofdt.fr/.

Observatoire Français des Drogues et des Toxicomanies (OFTD) (2006). Recherche thematique. Available from http://www.ofdt.fr.

Tabagisme.net. Available from http://www.tabagisme.net/.

Ugland, T. (2003). A case of strange bedfellows: An institutional perspective on French-Swedish cooperation and alcohol control. *Scandinavian Political Studies, 26*(3),269–286.

Van Solinge, T.B. (1996) L'héroine, la cocaine, et le crack en France: Trafic, usage, et politique. Amsterdam: CEDRO Centium voer Drugssonderzoek: Universiteit van Amsterdam.

RENÉ JAHIEL

FREEBASING. The illicit practice of smoking cocaine is generally referred to as freebasing. The hydrochloride form of cocaine (powder) is highly soluble in water and, therefore, is efficiently absorbed by the mucous membranes when taken intranasally (snorted) or via blood when injected intravenously (shot up). This form of cocaine is, however, destroyed when it is heated to the temperatures required for smoking it. Therefore, the cocaine alkaloid, called *crack* or *freebase*, is the form that is smoked. Although not always differentiated, freebase actually refers to cocaine in the base state with all the adulterants removed (Inciardi, 1991). Cocaine hydrochloride is combined with an alkaline substance, such as sodium hydroxide or ammonia, to remove the hydrochloride. The *free* cocaine *base* is then dissolved in ether, and pure cocaine-base crystals are formed. It has been estimated that approximately 560 milligrams of cocaine freebase can be extracted from one gram of street cocaine hydrochloride (Siegel, 1982). Cocaine freebase has a melting point of 208°F (98°C) and is volatile at temperatures above 194°F (90°C), therefore providing an active drug for smoking. Crack, in contrast, although also in the base state and used for smoking (or freebasing), does not have the adulterants of the street cocaine removed. Cocaine base is soluble in alcohol, acetone, oils, and ether—but is almost insoluble in water.

Cocaine freebase is usually smoked in a water pipe containing fine mesh screens, which trap the heated cocaine as it melts. A temperature of 200°F (93°C) is the most efficient. Although the amount of cocaine absorbed by the smoker varies—depending on the kind of pipe used, the temperature of the heat source, and the inhalation pattern of the user—under optimal conditions approximately 30 to 35 percent of the cocaine placed on the mesh screen is absorbed by the smoker.

COMPARISON OF COCAINE AND METHAMPHETAMINE SMOKING

Vapor inhalation of the (+) isomer of methamphetamine hydrochloride, colloquially known as *ice* has several differences when compared to vapor inhalation of cocaine freebase. Although both methamphetamine and cocaine freebase have their origin as a salt, cocaine hydrochloride must be pretreated with an alkaline substance to remove the hydrochloride, thus creating the freebase of cocaine that can be heated and inhaled as vapor. In contrast, methamphetamine hydrochloride can be heated and inhaled without adulterating the original compound.

When heated, cocaine freebase has a melting temperature of 208°F while methamphetamine hydrochloride melts at 268°F. Once the appropriate melting temperature is met for each substance, vapors will form and can be inhaled. Significant

amounts of cocaine freebase vapor are lost through pyrolysis (chemical change caused by heat) and little condensation appears on the water pipe, suggesting decreased amounts of inhaled vapor. Methamphetamine hydrochloride, however, condenses as a crystalline solid on the cooler areas of the glass pipe. It is thought that this same phenomenon occurs in the mouth and throat of the user, leading to rapid methamphetamine absorption through the lungs as well as delayed absorption through the oral mucosa.

These differences in drug absorption have been demonstrated by comparisons of plasma levels of cocaine and methamphetamine after smoking the individual substances. Plasma levels of cocaine peak and decline rapidly, with a half-life of approximately forty-five to sixty minutes. Methamphetamine plasma levels also rise rapidly, but the half-life is approximately eight to twelve hours. The delayed absorption of methamphetamine from the oral mucosa is thought to play a role in the extended half-life. Differences in the metabolism of cocaine and methamphetamine also contribute to the disparity in plasma half-life. Cocaine is quickly degraded to inactive metabolites by plasma esterases (enzymes) and cleared from the bloodstream. Methamphetamine is eliminated by enzymes with limited plasma distribution and limited activity and, unlike cocaine, is converted to active metabolites that prolong the action of the drug. These active metabolites can accumulate, and repeated smoking of methamphetamine and its active metabolites can lead to dangerous levels of methamphetamine in the plasma.

In summary, differences between cocaine freebase vapor inhalation and methamphetamine hydrochloride inhalation include method of preparing the substance, melting temperature, metabolism, and length of plasma half-life. These differences can have important clinical implications. For example, methamphetamine can cause paranoid symptoms that last considerably longer than those ordinarily seen after cocaine smoking. Distinguishing between drug-induced paranoia and other causes of paranoia thus requires a different length of drug-free observation depending on which drug was inhaled. Understanding the differences between cocaine freebase inhalation and methamphetamine inhalation, particularly the difference in duration of action of the two drugs, can be important in the evaluation and management of patients with stimulant abuse.

Although in use since the mid-1970s, freebasing cocaine became popular in the United States in the early 1980s. The popularity of this route of administration was responsible for the rise in U.S. cocaine use during the mid-1980s. When cocaine is smoked, it is rapidly absorbed and reaches the brain within a few seconds. Thus, users get a substantial immediate rush and an almost instant "high," comparable to that after intravenous cocaine. This is in contrast to intranasal use of cocaine, which engenders a high with a much slower onset. Free-basing is thus a convenient way of taking cocaine, with the possibility of repeated and substantial doses. Since the likelihood of abuse is related to the rapidity with which a drug reaches the brain, smoking cocaine makes it more likely that use will lead to abuse than does snorting the drug. Despite losses of more than half of the cocaine when it is smoked, sufficient cocaine rapidly reaches the brain, providing an intense drug effect—which users repeat, often to toxicity. The danger of free-basing, in addition to the inherent danger of cocaine use, lies in what some users perceive to be the greater social acceptability of a route of administration that requires minimal paraphernalia and can achieve toxic levels of cocaine with relative ease.

See also **Amphetamine Epidemics, International; Coca Paste; Complications: Cardiovascular System (Alcohol and Cocaine); Methamphetamine; Pharmacokinetics: General.**

BIBLIOGRAPHY

Brownlow, H. A., & Pappachan, J. (2002). Pathophysiology of cocaine abuse. *European Journal of Anesthesiology, 19*, 395–414.

Chu, A. K. (1990). Ice: A new dosage form of an old drug. *Science, 249*, 631–634.

Cook, C. E. (1991). Pyrolytic characteristics, pharmacokinetics, and bioavailability of smoked heroin, cocaine, phencyclidine, and methamphetamine. In M. A. Miller & N. J. Kozel (Eds.), *Methamphetamine abuse: Epidemiologic issues and implications* (pp. 6–23). NIDA Research Monograph no. 115. Rockville, MD: National Institute on Drug Abuse.

Inciardi, J. A. (1991). Crack-cocaine in Miami. In S. Schober & C. Schade (Eds.), *The epidemiology of cocaine use and abuse*. NIDA Research Monograph no. 110. Rockville, MD: National Institute on Drug Abuse.

Karch, S. B. (2005). *A brief history of cocaine*, 2nd ed. Boca Raton, FL: CRC Press.

Lowinson, J. H. (2005). *Substance abuse: A comprehensive textbook*. Philadelphia, PA: Lippincott Williams & Wilkins.

Perez-Reyes, M., et al. (1982). Freebase cocaine smoking. *Clinical Pharmacology and Therapeutics, 32*, 459–465.

Siegel, R. (1982). Cocaine smoking. *Journal of Psychoactive Drugs, 14*, 271–359.

MARIAN W. FISCHMAN
REVISED BY GRACE O'LEARY (2001)
ROGER WEISS (2009)

FREUD AND COCAINE. Sigmund Freud (1856–1939), Austrian neurologist and founder of psychoanalysis, became interested in cocaine in 1884. The following year (1885) he published "Contribution to the Knowledge of the Effect of Cocaine." At the time he was in his late twenties and was a medical house officer at the Vienna hospital, Allgemeine Krankenhaus. He was able both to gain access to the literature about cocaine and, at some expense, to the substance itself (which was not illegal at that time). In a letter to his fiancée Martha Bernays, Freud referred to the role cocaine played in the discovery of his medical vocation. Freud indicated that he wanted to medically cure patients from their suffering, and he hoped he had found a panacea in the form of cocaine. (There had been articles in the U.S. medical literature describing cocaine used in the treatment of various ills and for drug dependencies as a panacea.)

Freud noticed the ability of cocaine to fend off fatigue and enhance mood. He was particularly taken by suggestions that cocaine might be an adjunct to, or even a cure for, alcohol or opioid dependencies. His interest was heightened because one of his teachers and close friends, Ernst von Fleischl-Marxow, had become an opiate addict. Using cocaine, Freud treated him with almost disastrous results. At the time, there was no opprobrium attached to the use of cocaine and relatively little concern about any adverse effects.

Freud performed a number of cocaine experiments on himself and reported the results in the aforementioned experimental paper, "Contribution to Knowledge of the Effects of Cocaine." These were reasonable studies that provided useful data about the physiological and psychological effects of cocaine. Freud mentioned that individuals react differently to the drug. Biographies of Freud, such as Ernest

Freud had hoped to use cocaine to medically treat patients suffering from mood disorders or fatigue. THE LIBRARY OF CONGRESS.

Jones's *The Life and Work of Sigmund Freud*, have tended to disparage his experimental paper and other works on cocaine. Although his work was done on himself and was limited in its scope, it has been confirmed in modern replications. Freud was initially skeptical about the possible addictive properties of cocaine in normal individuals, but later, in the face of evidence and criticism, he was less vehement on the subject. He became, in later life, very sensitive to criticism of his earlier views on cocaine.

From 1884 to 1887 Freud wrote four papers concerning cocaine, including a definitive review in 1884. In the last of his cocaine papers, "Craving for and Fear of Cocaine" (1887), Freud wrote that cocaine affected people in different ways; it had become an unpredictable object, and it was not possible to know who would have a general reaction to it. Regarding addiction, Freud's so-called cocaine episode demonstrates two related and crucial aspects

of his thought on the subject: First, the ultimate cause of addiction is not situated in the drug but in the individual predisposition of the user; and second, drugs have effects that are particular because they are dependent on the constitution of the user. He obviously felt comfortable in both taking cocaine and writing about it in his letters. He mentions and discusses his use of and dreams about cocaine in the *Interpretation of Dreams* (1889). The true extent and duration of his self-experiments is not known, since access to his correspondence has been severely restricted.

Freud is sometimes credited with the discovery of local anesthesia because of his proposal in his cocaine review paper that the substance could be used for this purpose. He also claims suggesting the idea to both Koenigstein and Carl Koller prior to their experiments in ophthalmology, which led to the initial papers on local or topical anesthesia. There is a semantic problem in understanding these claims. Almost all investigators of cocaine had noticed the numbing properties of the drug when placed on the tongue. The idea that this property had a practical use in ophthalmological surgery does belong to Carl Koller, a friend and colleague of Freud, who did the proper experiments and published them promptly. The controversy about the discovery between Koller and Koenigstein with Freud's mediation is well covered in the article by Hortense Koller Becker, "Carl Koller and Cocaine," in *Psychoanalytic Quarterly* (1963).

Extreme viewpoints that attribute Freud's behavior and writings to the influence of the toxic effects of cocaine are unsubstantiated by evidence. Clearly, he used cocaine as a psychotropic agent on himself, and this experience led to his faith in its relative safety. Despite these facts, there is no real support for a viewpoint that he was an addict or that his thought was markedly affected by his drug usage. The combined notoriety of both Freud and cocaine has led to speculative exaggerations that make better newspaper headlines than history.

See also **Cocaine; Psychoanalysis.**

BIBLIOGRAPHY

Becker, H. K. (1963). Carl Koller and cocaine. *Psychoanalytic Quarterly, 32,* 309–343.

Byck, R. (1974). *Cocaine papers: Sigmund Freud.* (Edited, with an introduction by R. Byck). New York: Stonehill.

Jones, E. (1953–1957). *The life and work of Sigmund Freud.* 3 vols. New York: Basic Books. (See Vol. 1, chap. 4, "The Cocaine Episode [1884–1887].").

Karamel, R. (2003). Freud's "Cocaine Papers" (1884–1887): A commentary. *Canadian Journal of Psychoanalysis, 11,* 161–169.

Loose, R. (2002). *The subject of addiction: Psychoanalysis and the administration of enjoyment.* London: Karnac. (See Chap. 1.)

Malcolm, J. (1984). *In the Freud archives.* London: Jonathan Cape.

ROBERT BYCK
REVISED BY R. LOOSE (2009)

FUNDING AND SERVICE DELIVERY OF TREATMENT.

There is no single best method or setting for the treatment of substance abuse disorders. Treatment is offered in specialty units of general and psychiatric hospitals, residential facilities, halfway houses, outpatient clinics, mental health centers, jails and prisons, general medical practitioners' offices (e.g., family physician, pediatrician), collaborative-care settings, and the offices of private practitioners. (Collaborative care involves settings in which case management and a multidisciplinary consultation between the case manager, the primary care provider, and a consulting psychiatrist are central to the care of the individual; this type of setting is particularly effective for the treatment of depression.) Since the 1970s, there has been significant progress in the movement to unify the treatment of substance abuse and mental health disorders under the banner of "behavioral health service delivery." There has also been a recognition that substance abuse and mental health disorders occur together in many individuals, who are said to be suffering from "co-occurring disorders." In the United States during the 1970s and 1980s, persons with disorders of drug abuse or dependency were commonly treated in programs completely separate from those programs serving persons with alcohol abuse or dependency. By the late 1980s and early 1990s, however, the two treatment systems were merged in most areas across the country.

TREATMENT COSTS

The cost of substance abuse treatment and substance dependence treatment vary greatly depending on the setting. During the first decade of the twenty-first century, the annual national cost estimate for nonhospital residential substance abuse treatment in a specialty setting (the most expensive form of service delivery for this population) was around $62 per patient per day, with an overall annual cost of $2.3 billion. For outpatient nonmethadone treatment in a specialty treatment setting, the cost per patient per day was about $10, with an annual cost estimate of $2.7 billion. For methadone maintenance in specialty settings, the cost was just over $9 per day per patient, with an annual cost of $0.6 billion. In total, the cost of substance abuse treatment in a specialty setting was about $5.5 billion per year, with nonhospital residential admissions costing about $2.2 billion, outpatient methadone clinic services costing around $800,000, and outpatient nonmethadone treatment costing $2.5 billion. Roughly 100,000 people were served in around 50 nonhospital residential specialty settings, 152,000 were served in 44 outpatient methadone clinics, and 807,000 were served in 222 nonmethadone outpatient specialty settings.

Within the outpatient settings, the average cost per visit was significantly lower for methadone clinic visits ($14.50, with a reported range of $7.82 to $58.81) than for nonmethadone outpatient facilities (about $22, with a reported range of $4.43 to $204.13). On average, the cost for an inpatient nonhospital residential admission was about $3,000, with a range of $308 to $18,482. The cost per admission for outpatient methadone treatment was around $6,000, with a range of $2,109 to $32,630, and the cost of nonmethadone outpatient treatment was just over $1,100, with a range of $188 to $12,650. The total cost for all treatment types was $5.5 billion, or $1,900 per admission, with around 3 million people receiving services. Inpatient programs, although they are the most costly, are generally of the shortest duration, averaging around 30 days. Outpatient programs vary in duration from a few months to several years or more.

At the beginning of the twenty-first century, behavioral health treatments in the United States (substance abuse and mental health services combined) cost $104 billion, putting them among the top fifteen health-care areas in terms of expenditures. Eighteen billion dollars, or 18 percent of the total, was spent on substance abuse treatment. These figures do not take into account the significant percentage of substance abuse and behavioral health services provided in general medical settings by health care professionals who are not behavioral health specialists, nor do they consider the cost of medications used in the treatment of behavioral disorders.

PRIVATE HEALTH INSURANCE

The availability of private health-insurance coverage for substance abuse treatment began to grow exponentially in the 1980s. By the first decade of the twenty-first century, more than 98 percent of health insurance plans had explicit coverage for behavioral health services. Individuals with private insurance have a greater range of treatment providers to choose from than those who are indigent and have only government-funded programs at their disposal. Programs that mainly rely on insurance reimbursement, however, tend to be more expensive than those that receive the bulk of their support from government sources. Private insurance pays about 20 percent of the overall costs for behavioral health treatment annually.

U.S. GOVERNMENT FINANCING

In the general health care system (medical and behavioral health combined) in the United States, about 70 percent of the cost of services is borne by the individual, an insurance company, or some other private third-party payer. For substance abuse or mental health care, in contrast, the government (public health services) supplies nearly 70 percent of the funds for treatment.

States often finance treatment by reimbursing providers through public-welfare programs, local public health facilities, or through grants and contracts. Some states transfer funds to county and local governments, which, in turn, purchase services from providers. Another financing mechanism is Medicaid, a combined state and federal program that pays medical bills for low-income persons. Under Medicaid, states can pay for substance abuse care in inpatient general hospitals, clinics, outpatient hospital and rehabilitation services, and group homes with sixteen or fewer beds.

Medicare is a federal program that pays the health-care costs of persons 65 years of age or older and those who are disabled. For individuals with substance abuse disorders, this program primarily covers inpatient hospital treatment of alcohol or drug abuse, as well as some medically necessary services in outpatient settings. The primary federal mechanism for paying for alcohol and drug treatment is the Substance Abuse Prevention and Treatment (SAPT) Block Grant, administered by the Department of Health and Human Services. Funds from the block grant are distributed to the states (and territories) using a formula that takes the characteristics of each state's population into account. In fiscal year 2009, Congress appropriated approximately $1.7 billion for the SAPT Block Grant, per the 2009 Health and Human Service Budget Appropriations request. The federal government also makes grants to individual treatment providers to support innovative treatment approaches, improve the quality of treatment, or ensure services are available for underserved or special populations.

See also **U.S. Government Agencies.**

BIBLIOGRAPHY

Braden, B. R., Cowan, C. A., Lazenby, H. C., Donham, C. S., Long, A. M., Martin, A. B., et al. (1998). National health expenditures, 1997. *Health Care Financing Review, 20*(1), 83–126.

Coffey, R. M., Mark, T., King, E., Harwood, H., McKusick, D., Genuardi, J., et al. (2000). *National estimates of expenditures for mental health and substance abuse treatment, 1997.* SAMHSA Publication No. SMA-00–3499. Rockville, MD: Center for Substance Abuse Treatment and Center for Mental Health Services, Substance Abuse and Mental Health Services Administration.

Department of Health and Human Services. (2007). Fiscal Year 2008 Substance Abuse and Mental Health Services Administration. *Justification of estimates for appropriations committees.* Available from http://www.samhsa.gov/.

Department of Health and Human Services. (2008). Fiscal Year 2009 Substance Abuse and Mental Health Services Administration. *Justification of estimates for appropriations committees.* Available from http://www.samhsa.gov/.

French, M. T., Dunlap, L. J., Zarkin, G. A., McGeary, K. A., & McLellan, A. T. (1997). A structured instrument for estimating the economic cost of drug abuse treatment: The drug abuse treatment cost analysis program (DATCAP). *Journal of Substance Abuse Treatment, 14*(5), 445–455.

Mark, T. L., Coffey, R. M., King, E., Harwood, H., McKusick, D., Genuardi, J., et al. (2000). Spending on mental health and substance abuse treatment, 1987–1997. *Health Affairs, 19*(4), 108–120.

Mark, T. L., Coffey, R. M., Vandivort-Warren, R., Harwood, H. J., King, E. C., & the MHSA Spending Estimates Team (2005). U.S. spending for mental health and substance abuse treatment, 1991–2001. *Health Affairs, W5,* 133–142.

President's New Freedom Commission on Mental Health. (2003). *Achieving the promise: Transforming mental health care in America, final report.* DHHS Publication No. SMA-03-3832. Rockville, MD: Department of Health and Human Services.

Ringel, J. S., & Strum, R. (2001). National estimates of mental health utilization and expenditures for children in 1998. *The Journal of Behavioral Health Services & Research 28*(3), 319–333.

Ringel, J. S., & Strum, R. (2001). Financial burden and out-of-pocket expenditures for mental health across different socioeconomic groups: Results from healthcare for communities. *Journal of Mental Health Policy and Economics, 4*(3), 141–150.

Substance Abuse and Mental Health Services Administration, Office of Applied Studies (2001). *2000 National household survey on drug abuse.* Rockville, MD: Author.

Substance Abuse and Mental Health Services Administration, Office of Applied Studies. (2003). *The ADSS cost study: Costs of substance abuse treatment in the specialty sector.* DHHS Publication No. SMA 03-3762, Analytic Series A-20. Rockville, MD: Author.

Substance Abuse and Mental Health Services Administration, Office of Applied Studies. (2004). *Results from the 2003 national survey on drug use and health: national findings.* NSDUH Series H-25, DHHS Publication No SMA 04-3964. Rockville, MD: Author.

Substance Abuse and Mental Health Services Administration, Office of Applied Studies. (2005). *Overview of findings from the 2004 national survey of drug use and health.* DHHS Publication No. SMA 05-4061. Rockville, MD: Author.

Thorpe, K. E., Florence, C. S., & Joski, P. (2004). Which medical conditions account for the rise in healthcare spending? *Health Affairs, W4,* 437–444. Available from http://content.healthaffairs.org/.

U.S. Department of Health and Human Services. (1999). *Mental health: A report of the surgeon general—executive summary.* Rockville, MD: Author. Available from http://www.surgeongeneral.gov/.

SALVATORE DI MENZA
REVISED BY PAMELA V. MICHAELS (2009)

GAMBLING. The formal group of impulse control disorders (ICDs) in the *Diagnostic and Statistical Manual Fourth Edition Text Revision* (*DSM-IV-TR*) is termed *ICDs Not Elsewhere Classified* and includes pathological gambling (PG), intermittent explosive disorder, kleptomania, pyromania, trichotillomania, and ICDs not otherwise specified. The ICDs are described as a heterogeneous cluster of disorders linked by a "failure to resist," impulses to engage in harmful, disturbing or distressing behaviors (p. 663). PG is the ICD that, as of 2008, has been most widely studied. PG and other ICDs have been conceptualized both as *obsessive-compulsive spectrum disorders* and *behavioral addictions*. Consistent with the latter formulation, ICDs are considered to have a core set of clinical features, including the following: (1) compulsive and repetitive performance of the problematic behavior despite adverse consequences; (2) loss of control over the behavior; (3) an appetitive urge or *craving* state before starting the behavior; and (4) a pleasurable quality associated with its performance. As an example, individuals with PG "often increase the frequency of their bets or the amount of money gambled in order to achieve the desired level of excitement," suggestive of tolerance (Dell'Osso et al., 2005, p. 2).

With emphasis on its impulsive characteristics, PG can be thought of as an obsessive-compulsive spectrum disorder, in which affected individuals experience an intense unpleasantness resulting in an attendant neurophysiological compensation, which promotes an intense drive to perform a specific behavior. The model for PG as a non-substance related addiction is supported by the frequent co-occurrence of PG and substance use disorders (SUDs), whereas there is less consistent evidence of comorbidity between PG and OCD. Because depression and suicidality, as well as impaired judgment (suggestive of bipolar disorder) are seen at a rate greater than chance among individuals with PG, it has been proposed that PG is an affective spectrum disorder (Dell'Osso et al., 2005, p. 2).

CHARACTERIZATION, CLINICAL COURSE, AND PREVALENCE

PG is characterized by persistent and recurrent maladaptive patterns of gambling behavior and is associated with impaired functioning, reduced quality of life, and a high frequency of bankruptcy, divorce, and incarceration. PG usually begins in adolescence or early adulthood, with males tending to start at an earlier age. Although prospective studies are largely lacking, PG appears to follow a similar trajectory as substance dependence, with high prevalence rates among adolescents and young adults and lower rates in older adults, along with periods of abstinence and relapse. Other phenomenological similarities exist between PG and SUDs, such as a *telescoping* pattern in women that signifies a foreshortened timeframe between age at onset of the behavior and the development of a problem relative to the course seen in men.

Treatment interventions are common to PG and SUDs. For example, the opioid antagonist naltrexone, a drug that is approved by the U.S. Food and Drug Administration for the treatment of alcohol dependence and opiate dependence, has also been found in placebo-controlled trials to be helpful in the treatment of PG. In alcohol dependence, naltrexone appears particularly linked to reduced alcohol cravings and heavy drinking. Analogously, naltrexone appears particularly helpful for individuals with strong gambling urges. Other approaches (e.g., behavioral therapies such as motivational enhancement and cognitive behavioral therapy) that have been found to be effective in the treatment of SUDs also appear helpful in PG. Twelve-step programs initially developed to deal with alcohol and other SUDs (e.g., Alcoholics Anonymous) have been widely used for PG (e.g., Gambler's Anonymous).

In comparison to other psychiatric disorders, the pathophysiology of PG is poorly understood. Until shortly before 2008, PG had been excluded from many major psychiatric epidemiological surveys, such as the National Comorbidity Survey. PG and other ICDs have historically been excluded from widely used structured clinical instruments used to diagnose psychiatric disorders. This latter point is important because the under-diagnosis and treatment of PG and other ICDs are suggested by some studies indicating high frequencies of these disorders co-occurring with other psychiatric disorders. One study found that over 30 percent of 204 hospitalized psychiatric inpatients had a current ICD, compared to less than 2 percent who were diagnosed with such a disorder at the time of their initial hospital admission. Improved identification and treatment of ICDs could be facilitated by brief screening instruments because the lack of efficient screening mechanisms may put these patients at risk for worse treatment outcomes.

DEFINING ADDICTION

The concept of addiction has changed over time. One view is that addictions result from one's genetic predisposition and access to the specific reward stimulus that signals a cue for the addictive behavior (for example, an individual with PG having free access to casinos). A key component of addiction is diminished *behavioral control*, which leads to behaviors *in the service of the addiction*; behaviors that are performed despite anticipated, longer term adverse consequences. This diminished

behavioral control does not always occur in individuals who develop tolerance to a particular drug. An example involves the development of physiological (physical) tolerance while taking a prescribed medication (for example, a beta-blocker used in the treatment of heart disease). Chronic administration may lead to tolerance, physical dependence, and withdrawal upon immediate cessation of the drug. However, use of the drug is generally not associated with addiction (i.e., drug-seeking behavior and drug use that interferes with major areas of life functioning).

TOWARD A MODEL OF ADDICTION, IMPULSIVITY, AND PATHOLOGICAL GAMBLING

The core clinical features of addiction overlap with a definition proposed for impulsivity that emphasizes "a predisposition toward rapid, unplanned reactions to internal or external stimuli with diminished regard to the negative consequence of these reactions to the impulsive individual or others" (Moeller et al., 2001, p. 1784). PG has been described as a *behavioral addiction* or an *addiction without the drug* because of shared similar features with substance dependence. A strong connection between addiction and the impulsive behavior seen in PG is highlighted in the proposed Reward Deficiency Syndrome model, which suggests that diminished dopamine (DA) function in brain reward pathways places vulnerable individuals at risk for addictive, impulsive, and compulsive behaviors. Similar models postulating the relevance of DA reward pathways in individuals vulnerable to drug addiction, excessive eating, and PG are suggested by the "impaired response inhibition and salience attribution" model of addiction (Goldstein & Volkow, 2002, p. 1643) and the addiction development model put forth by Koob and Le Moal (2001). Each of these models incorporates environmental and genetic factors as factors in the development of addictions.

Brain network models of addiction have been proposed to explain both PG and SUDs. These models have focused on neural circuits underlying motivated behaviors and how they may become dysregulated in addictive processes. A fundamental aspect of an evolving addiction is the progressive development of repetitive, habitual behaviors, which rely upon progressive activation of specialized brain structures; for example, increased usage of upper (dorsal) portions of a subcortical brain structure known as the striatum (consisting of the caudate nucleus and the putamen), as opposed to other, lower (ventral) parts of striatal brain networks. The encoding of such behavior may begin early with the acute rewarding effects of a drug or a stimulating experience and may involve dopamine release and alterations in cellular signaling. Later, changes in brain cellular protein, receptor sub-unit, and enzyme synthesis, may be seen later in the addiction process. Thus, behavior becomes more habitual over time or the associated learned cues become potent in the absence of reward. It is hypothesized that a drug cue or related stimulus leads to heightened motivation for drug-seeking, and this results in craving and addictive behaviors.

NEUROBIOLOGY

The dopamine system influences rewarding and reinforcing behaviors and has been implicated in addictions. Alterations in dopaminergic pathways have been proposed to underlie reward seeking and pleasure in PG and SUDs. Acute ingestion of drugs of abuse increases DA transmission in the basal ganglia, an important biological process for behavioral reinforcement and learned associations encoding addictive behaviors.

Other monoamine systems have been implicated in the pathophysiology of PG and SUDs. Serotonin (5-HT) has been implicated in the initiation and cessation of the problematic behavior and norepinephrine (NE) has been associated with arousal and excitement. These findings are central to hypotheses that underlie the use of medications in the treatment of PG, which are based on the neurobiology of PG and other impulse control disorders. Thus, effective pharmacological treatments can provide insight into the pathophysiology of PG, and vice versa.

ANIMAL MODELS OF IMPULSIVITY AND NEURONAL ACTIVATION

Animal models of impulsivity, specifically those designed to assess levels of motor activity, lack of impulse control, and impulsive decision making have been developed. Some of these models involve choice preference paradigms that include the simultaneous assessment of real-time neurophysiological and neurochemical measures. This experimental approach has been used as a means of mapping impulsive behavior (e.g., deficits in impulse regulation under stress) onto specific brain circuitry. It has been suggested that upper and lower cortical brain regions represent distinct areas of impulsive behavior which carry unique brain chemicals transmitting signals that are separately regulated. In particular, discrete areas of frontal cortex have been divided into functionally "dissociable areas," whose distinctive brain chemistries could reflect the divergence of serotonin and dopamine signal modulation implicated in impulsive choice (Winstanley et al., 2006, p. 112).

GENETIC CONSIDERATIONS

Data from twin studies suggest that a substantial degree of the risk for PG is heritable. Shah and colleagues determined that the prevalence of PG in the Vietnam Era Twin Registry was 1.4 percent. Of twins reporting gambling at least twenty-five times in a year in their lifetime, 29 percent (7.6% of the total cohort) also reported at least one symptom of PG. Subsequent investigations of the same sample indicate that genetic and environmental factors contribute to PG, and that overlap exists in the genetic and environmental contributions between PG and alcohol dependence and PG and adult antisocial behaviors. In addition, the majority of the co-occurrence between PG and major depression appears to be determined by common genetic factors. Thus, environmental and intrinsic genetic factors contribute to vulnerability to both PG and substance abuse. An increased prevalence of these disorders is seen within families and across generations and is determined by the genetic variance in risk for substance addiction (estimated to be approximately 60%) and in the liability for symptomatology in PG (estimated to be between 35% to 54%).

Regarding particular molecular genetic mechanisms, specific variants of serotonergic and dopaminergic genes have been implicated in preliminary studies of PG. The genes implicated include those coding for monamine oxidase A (MAO-A), the serotonin transporter, and the D1, D2, and D4 dopamine receptors. Some differences in allelic variation related to PG appear influenced by sex status, raising the possibility that genetic contributions to PG among males and females are different.

It should be noted that findings from genetic association studies should be viewed cautiously, particularly since many have methodological limitations (e.g., lack of definitive diagnoses and stratification by racial/ethnic identity). The extent to which these preliminary findings are substantiated in PG and generalize to other ICDs requires further research. More comprehensive diagnostic evaluations, larger population samples, and genome-wide investigation should provide important data that will help delineate more precisely the genetic underpinnings of PG, other ICDs, and SUDs.

PG shares core features with SUDs, including tolerance, withdrawal, repeated attempts to cut back or stop, and impairment in major areas of life functioning. Further research is needed to understand the molecular and biochemical factors underlying the unique and overlapping behavioral features seen in PG and SUDs. An improved understanding of the neurobiology of these disorders will facilitate clinical advances in their identification, prevention, and treatment.

See also **Addiction: Concepts and Definitions; Addictive Personality and Psychological Tests; Gambling Addiction: Assessment; Gambling Addiction: Epidemiology.**

BIBLIOGRAPHY

American Psychiatric Association, Committee on Nomenclature and Statistics. (2000). *Diagnostic and Statistical Manual of Mental Disorders* (4th ed.). Washington, DC: American Psychiatric Association.

Brewer, J. A., & Potenza, M. N. (2008). The neurobiology and genetics of impulse control disorders: Relationships to drug addictions. *Biochemical Pharmacology, 75*(1), 63–75.

Chambers, R. A., & Potenza, M. N. (2003). Neurodevelopment, impulsivity and adolescent gambling. *Journal of Gambling Studies, 19*(1), 53–84.

Dell'Osso, B., Allen A., & Hollander, E. (2005). Comorbidity issues in the pharmacological treatment of pathological gambling: A critical review. *Clinical Practice and Epidemiology in Mental Health, 1*, 1–9.

Goldstein, R. Z., & Volkow, N. D. (2002). Drug addiction and its underlying neurobiological basis: Neuroimaging evidence for the involvement of the frontal cortex. *American Journal of Psychiatry, 159*(10), 1642–52.

Koob, G. F., & Le Moal, M. (2001). Drug addiction, dysregulation of reward, and allostasis. *Neuropsychopharmacology, 24*(2), 97–129.

Kreek, M. J., Nielsen, D. A., Butelman, E. R., & LaForge, K. S. (2005). Genetic influences on impulsivity, risk taking, stress responsivity, and vulnerability to drug abuse and addiction. *Nature Neuroscience, 8*(11), 1450–1457.

Moeller, F. G., Barratt, E. S., Dougherty, D. M., Schmitz, J. M., & Swann, A. C. (2001). Psychiatric aspects of impulsivity. *American Journal of Psychiatry, 158*(11), 1783–93.

Petry, N. M. (2006). Should the scope of addictive behaviors be broadened to include pathological gambling? *Addiction, 101*(Suppl. 1), 152–160.

Potenza, M. N. (2006). Should addictive disorders include non-substance-related conditions? *Addiction, 101*(Suppl. 1), 142–151.

Shah, K., Eisen, S., Xian, H., & Potenza, M. N. (2005). Genetic studies of pathological gambling: A review of methodology and analyses of data from the Vietnam era twin registry. *Journal of Gambling Studies, 21*(2), 179–203.

Winstanley, C., Theobald, D., Dalley, J., Cardinal, R., & Robbins, T. (2006). Double dissociation between serotonergic and dopaminergic modulation of medial prefrontal and orbitofrontal cortex during a test of impulsive choice. *Cerebral Cortex, 16*(1), 106–114.

WENDOL A. WILLIAMS
MARC N. POTENZA

GAMBLING ADDICTION: ASSESSMENT.

Although pathological gambling (PG) is associated with adverse functioning and is approximately as prevalent as schizophrenia and bipolar disorder, there is some indication that both clinicians and researchers fail to screen for, diagnose, and properly assess the disorder. This entry describes instruments available as of 2008 for the assessment of PG, and provides information on each instrument's psychometric properties. More detailed information on the gambling screening and assessment instruments can be found in chapter 14 and the appendix section of the book *Pathological Gambling: A Clinical Guide to Treatment* (Grant & Potenza, 2004).

SCREENING AND DIAGNOSTIC INSTRUMENTS: SELF-REPORT MEASURES

South Oaks Gambling Screen (SOGS). The South Oaks Gambling Screen (SOGS) is a twenty-item, self-report screening instrument for PG. The time frame of the SOGS is based on lifetime gambling activity and does not differentiate pathological gamblers in remission from those actively gambling problematically. The SOGS is scored by summing selected items, with a score of ≥5 indicating probable pathological gambling.

The SOGS has demonstrated excellent internal consistency (alpha=0.97) and one-month test-retest reliability (r=0.71). Validity was examined by correlating the SOGS with counselors' independent assessments (r=0.86), family member assessment (r=0.60), and *DSM-III-R* PG diagnosis (r=0.94). The SOGS was compared to a *DSM-III-R* diagnosis of PG and demonstrated satisfactory overall diagnostic accuracy among Gamblers Anonymous members (98.1 percent), university students (95.3 percent), and hospital employees (99.3 percent).

The SOGS has also demonstrated satisfactory internal consistency and validity for a one-year time frame. Satisfactory internal consistency was demonstrated in general (alpha=0.69) and treatment (alpha=0.86) samples. Satisfactory validity was also observed for the SOGS, as shown by correlation with *DSM-IV* criteria (r=0.77 and r=0.83, in general and treatment samples, respectively).

The SOGS has been further modified to assess the last three months of a person's gambling behavior, for which it demonstrated good internal consistency (alpha=0.83). The three-month version of the SOGS also showed good convergent validity (r=0.79) when correlated with the National Opinion Research Center *DSM-IV* Screen for Gambling Problems (NODS).

The SOGS has shown poorer classification accuracy in the general population. The SOGS overestimated the number of pathological gamblers in the general population compared to *DSM-IV* criteria (sensitivity rate=0.67). It also showed a high false positive rate, such that one-half of the cases identified as probable pathological gamblers by the SOGS did not meet *DSM-IV* criteria for PG.

Gamblers Anonymous Twenty Questions (GA-20). The Gamblers Anonymous twenty questions (GA-20) is a self-report measure for identifying problem gamblers. A score of ≥7 indicates that the

respondent is a problem gambler. The GA-20 correlates highly with gambling frequency. The GA-20 has also demonstrated high internal consistency (alpha=0.94) and excellent validity (correlation with the SOGS; r=0.94).

Massachusetts Gambling Screen (MAGS). The Massachusetts Gambling Screen (MAGS) is a fourteen-item (only seven of which are scored), self-report screen for problem gambling among adolescents and adults. The MAGS measures past-year behaviors. The MAGS classifies respondents into non-problem, in-transition, or pathological gamblers using a weighted scoring derived from a discriminant function analysis. The seven-item MAGS scale has demonstrated good internal consistency (alpha=0.84) and validity (r=0.83) as correlated with the total *DSM-IV* score.

DSM-IV-MR (MR=Multiple Response). The *DSM-IV-MR* is a ten-item self-report questionnaire based on the 10 *DSM-IV* diagnostic criteria for PG. Most items have four response options: (1) never, (2) once or twice, (3) sometimes, and (4) often. Each item is allocated one point, and scores range from 0 to 10. A score of 3 or 4, including at least one point from criteria 8, 9, or 10, indicates that the respondent is a problem gambler, and an individual receiving a score of 5 or greater is classified as a severe problem gambler. The *DSM-IV-MR* has demonstrated satisfactory internal consistency (alpha=0.79) but lacks validity data.

Lie/Bet Questionnaire. The Lie/Bet Questionnaire is a two-item screen for PG that can be used in a self-report format: (1) "Have you ever had to lie to people important to you about how much you gambled?" and (2) "Have you ever felt the need to bet more and more money?" The Lie/Bet Questionnaire has a sensitivity of 0.99 to 1.00, specificity of 0.85 to 0.91, positive predictive power of 0.78 to 0.92, and negative predictive power of 0.99 to 1.00 in comparing Gamblers Anonymous members and non-problem gambling controls.

Early Intervention Gambling Health Test (EIGHT). The Early Intervention Gambling Health Test (EIGHT) is an eight-item, self-report screening instrument designed for use by general practitioners. A score of ≥4 indicates possible PG. The EIGHT correlates highly with the SOGS (r=0.83) and shows high sensitivity (0.91), but low specificity (0.50) and positive predictive value (0.59) using a *DSM-IV* diagnosis as a criterion measure.

SCREENING AND DIAGNOSTIC INSTRUMENTS: CLINICIAN-ADMINISTERED MEASURES

Structured Clinical Interview for Pathological Gambling (SCI-PG).

The Structured Clinical Interview for Pathological Gambling (SCI-PG) is a clinician-administered, *DSM-IV*-based diagnostic interview that is compatible with the Structured Clinical Interview for *DSM-IV* (SCID). The SCI-PG assesses both the ten inclusion criteria and the exclusionary criterion of PG: "not better accounted for by a Manic Episode." The SCI-PG has demonstrated excellent reliability (r=0.97), validity (correlation with the SOGS; r=078) and classification accuracy (sensitivity=0.88, specificity=1.00, positive predictive value=1.00, and negative predictive value=0.67).

Diagnostic Interview for Gambling Schedule (DIGS).

The Diagnostic Interview for Gambling Schedule (DIGS) is a structured clinician-administered interview that includes twenty diagnostic symptom items (lifetime and past-year), gambling treatment history, age of onset of gambling, and family and social functioning. The *DSM-IV* diagnostic criteria items have demonstrated good internal consistency (alpha=0.92), and the total diagnostic score has shown moderate correlations with measures of gambling severity (r=0.31–0.50).

National Opinion Research Center DSM-IV Screen for Gambling Problems (NODS).

The NODS is a seventeen-question clinician-administered interview based on the *DSM-IV* diagnostic criteria. The NODS includes both a lifetime and a past-year time frame, and the past-year items are asked only if the subject endorses the corresponding lifetime items. An individual with a score of zero is considered a low-risk gambler; one with a score of one or two is an at-risk gambler; while scores of three or four identify a problem gambler; and scores of ≥5 identify a pathological gambler. In initial studies, the NODS has demonstrated test-retest coefficients of r=0.99 and r=0.98 for lifetime and past year, respectively.

Gambling Assessment Module (GAM).

The GAM is a structured diagnostic gambling interview that examines eleven different types of gambling activities. The GAM can be administered by a clinician, as well as in a self-report or computerized format. The GAM has demonstrated good test-retest reliability (kappa=0.51–0.79) and poor-to-good validity on specific diagnostic criteria when compared to clinician ratings (kappa=0.0–0.7).

Gambling Behavior Interview (GBI).

The Gambling Behavior Interview (GBI) is a 106-item structured interview of problem gambling behaviors used to measure *DSM-IV* diagnostic criteria for PG. The GBI has a twelve-month time frame and consists of eight content domains: (1) gambling attitudes (4 items), (2) frequency of different types of gambling (15 items), (3) time and money spent gambling (4 items), (4) gambling frequency at different venues (7 items), (5) South Oaks Gambling Screen (25 items), (6) *DSM-IV* diagnostic criteria (10 items), (7) research diagnostic items (32 items), and (8) demographics (9 items).

The ten diagnostic criteria have demonstrated high factor loadings, ranging from 0.60 to 0.87. Convergent validity ranged from r=0.32 to r=0.90 and a standard *DSM-IV* cut score of five yielded respectable overall diagnostic accuracy (0.91), with good sensitivity (0.83) and a low false negative rate (0.13).

MEASURES OF GAMBLING SEVERITY AND TREATMENT RESPONSE: SELF-REPORT MEASURES

Gambling Symptom Assessment Scale (G-SAS).

The G-SAS is a twelve-item, self-rated scale assessing gambling urges, thoughts, and behaviors during the previous seven days. Each item is rated zero to four with a possible total score of forty-eight. Higher scores reflect greater severity of PG symptoms. The G-SAS has demonstrated good one-week test-retest reliability (r=0.56–0.70) and high internal consistency (alpha=0.86–0.89). In terms of validity, G-SAS scores showed excellent correlation with the PG-YBOCS in terms of change during treatment (r=0.81).

MEASURES OF GAMBLING SEVERITY AND TREATMENT RESPONSE: CLINICIAN-ADMINISTERED MEASURES

Pathological Gambling Modification: Yale-Brown Obsessive Compulsive Scale (PG-YBOCS). The PG-YBOCS is a ten-item, clinician-administered scale that rates gambling symptoms within the last seven days, on a severity scale from zero to four for each item (total scores range from zero to forty with higher scores reflecting greater illness severity). The first five items of the PG-YBOCS are the gambling urge/thought subscale (time occupied with urges/thoughts; interference and distress due to urges/thoughts; resistance against and control over urges/thoughts), and items six through ten are the gambling behavior subscale (time spent gambling and amount of gambling; interference and distress due to gambling; ability to resist and control gambling behavior).

The PG-YBOCS has demonstrated excellent inter-rater reliability (ICC=0.97), internal consistency for the total score (alpha=0.97), as well as for the urge/thought (alpha=0.94) and behavior (alpha=0.93) subscales, and excellent validity with the SOGS (r=0.89). Good sensitivity to change was shown by comparison to the Clinical Global Impression scale score (r=-0.69).

Canadian Problem Gambling Index (CPGI). The CPGI is a thirty-one-item measure with nine items scored as a measure of gambling severity. The CPGI problem gambling total score is the sum of the nine items (scored from zero "never" to three "almost always"). The interpretation of the total score ranges from zero (non-gambling) to a score of ≥8 (problem gambling). The CPGI has demonstrated good internal consistency (alpha=0.84) and four-week test-retest reliability (r=0.78). The CPGI scores correlate highly with those derived from the SOGS (r=0.83) and *DSM-IV* (r=0.83).

Gambling Treatment Outcome Monitoring System (GAMTOMS). The GAMTOMS is a multidimensional assessment system that includes the following instruments: (a) gambling treatment admission questionnaire, (b) primary discharge questionnaire, (c) client follow-up questionnaire, (d) staff discharge form, (e) significant other intake questionnaire, and (f) significant other follow-up questionnaire. Internal consistency for the scales

has ranged from alpha=0.59 to 0.79. Validity of the gambling frequency section was modest based on correlation with the TLFB for the past four weeks (r=0.55).

Clinical Global Impressions: Pathological Gambling (CGI). The Clinical Global Impressions (CGI) is a clinician-administered instrument consisting of two reliable and valid seven-item Likert scales used to assess severity and change in clinical symptoms. The improvement scale ranges from one = "very much improved" to seven = "very much worse," whereas the CGI severity scale ranges from one = "not ill at all" to seven = "among the most extremely ill." The CGI has been used to assess PG severity and to measure "global gambling improvement" in psychopharmacological studies. CGI scores have been highly correlated with PG-YBOCS (r=0.89) and G-SAS (r=0.78–0.81) scores.

Addiction Severity Index (ASI). The Addiction Severity Index (ASI) was modified for PG to include six gambling items that are scored to create a composite score, the Gambling Severity Index (ASI-G). The ASI-G has demonstrated satisfactory reliability (alpha=0.73–0.90) and validity (r=0.57–0.75 with the SOGS).

TimeLine Follow-Back (TLFB). The TimeLine Follow-Back (TLFB) assesses the number of days and amount of money spent gambling over a six-month period. The TLFB has shown adequate three-week test-retest reliability (r=0.42–0.98) for both days and dollars gambled. Agreement with collaterals was fair to good with intra-class correlations of 0.46 to 0.65 for both days and dollars gambled. The TLFB has been adapted to assess gambling over a four-week period. The TLFB showed modest correlations with other measures of gambling frequency (r=0.24–0.53).

Multiple instruments have been developed in response to a need to detect and measure problem gambling. No single instrument is best suited for all purposes. Instead a variety of instruments are available, each with both advantages and disadvantages. In choosing an instrument to use, clinicians should consider the sample to be studied, the purpose of the assessment, the length of the battery, and the psychometric properties of the instrument.

The existing instruments all require additional psychometric evaluation, particularly with regard to specific populations. Information generated from these studies enables clinicians and researchers to make more informed decisions as to how, within specific settings and for specific purposes, to best identify, assess, and monitor individuals with gambling problems.

See also **Gambling Addiction: Epidemiology; Gambling as an Addiction.**

BIBLIOGRAPHY

American Psychiatric Association. (2000). *Diagnostic and statistical manual of mental disorders* (4th ed.). Washington, DC: Author.

Cunningham-Williams, R. M., Ostmann, E. L., Spitznagel, E. L., & Books, S. J. (2007). Racial/ethnic variation in the reliability of *DSM-IV* pathological gambling disorder. *Journal of Nervous and Mental Disease, 195,* 551–559.

Grant, J. E., & Potenza, M. N. (Eds.). (2004). *Pathological gambling: A clinical guide to treatment.* Washington, DC: American Psychiatric Press.

Stinchfield, R., Govoni, R., & Frisch, G. R. (2005). *DSM-IV* diagnostic criteria for pathological gambling: Reliability, validity, and classification accuracy. *American Journal of Addiction, 14,* 73–82.

Wulfert, E., Hartley, J., Lee, M., Wang, N., Franco, C., & Sodano, R. (2005). Gambling screens: Does shortening the time frame affect their psychometric properties? *Journal of Gambling Studies, 21*(4), 521–536.

JON E. GRANT
MARC N. POTENZA

GAMBLING ADDICTION: EPIDEMIOLOGY.

Gambling is a common activity in almost all societies around the world. Evidence of gambling has been found in early civilizations and throughout history. Gambling may be defined as risking something of value on the outcome of an event when the probability of winning or losing is determined by chance (Korn & Shaffer, 1999). Although the vast majority of individuals who gamble never experience any adverse consequences from the behavior, it is estimated that approximately 5 percent of adults in the United States (as many as ten million people) have serious problems related to gambling. An additional 1 percent (around two million people) of the population meet criteria for pathological gambling diagnosis. For this reason, pathological gambling is gaining increasing attention from patients, clinicians, and policy makers. It is considered to be an impulse control disorder characterized by persistent and recurrent maladaptive gambling behavior resulting in damage to vocational, employment, family, and social interests. It is also associated with financial losses and legal problems, along with medical and psychiatric comorbidity (American Psychiatric Association 2000). In 1980, the American Psychiatric Association officially included pathologic gambling in the *Diagnostic and Statistical Manual of Mental Disorders,* third edition (*DSM-III*), and it remains in the fourth edition (*DSM-IV*).

There is considerable debate about the appropriate conceptualization of pathological gambling and its place in psychiatric nosology. There are two dominant models of pathological gambling: a non-pharmacologic addiction and an obsessive-compulsive spectrum disorder. The data available from different areas seem to converge, showing that pathological gambling has characteristics that are similar to those of a substance use disorder, and less closely resemble those of obsessive-compulsive disorder, although those conceptualizations are not mutually exclusive. Pathological gambling and substance use disorders share many features: an intense desire to satisfy the need, loss of control over the behavior, periods of abstinence and tolerance, recurrent thoughts about the behavior, and continued engagement in the behavior despite negative consequences. One important difference is that substance use is generally ego-syntonic (i.e., the individual does not experience his/her condition as problematic), while obsessions and compulsions are most often ego-dystonic (i.e., the individual experiences subjective distress from his/her condition).

RAPID GROWTH OF LEGALIZED GAMBLING

Historically, gambling in the United States was not considered a major recreational pastime until the largest continuous expansion ever of legalized gambling that began during the last quarter of the twentieth century. Gross gambling revenues have increased dramatically. Data suggest that the total expended on gambling, including that occurring in casinos, through lotteries, and in other settings (after accounting for winnings), was about $91 billion in 2006, up 7.7 percent from 2005, and representing 0.7 percent of the U.S. gross domestic product (GDP). That compares with $45.1 billion expended in 1995, which represented 0.6 percent of U.S. GDP. In the 1990s, there were major increases in the availability of some forms of gambling (casino and lottery) and it was initiated in new locations (riverboats and Native American reservations), including many that were immediately accessible (convenience stores). By the end of the twentieth century, gambling in the public mind had shifted from being associated with immorality, personal deviance, and crime to become a major and socially acceptable form of entertainment. As of 2008, lottery and casino gambling are the most prominent forms of legal gambling in the United States, and there is no indication that the trend is slowing.

The factors contributing to an increase in legalized gambling include the perceived need by governments for lottery revenue to avoid raising taxes and to stimulate economic growth in distressed areas. Also contributing are the efforts of gambling entrepreneurs in the private sector and the simultaneous development of new forms of gambling technology, principally electronic gaming devices.

The private gaming industry and state governments trumpet gambling as exciting entertainment that also brings the benefits of more jobs and lower taxes. However, gambling is not solely a societal plus. When gambling is legalized and made more accessible, the number of people who engage in it increases and a certain percentage of those new gamblers develop a gambling problem. Adverse effects of pathological gambling, such as co-occurring substance use disorders and increased rates of bankruptcy, divorce, and crime have been found to be severe in clinical samples of pathological gamblers. Assessment on a large scale of these social costs has only just begun (Lesieur 1998).

PREVALENCE OF PROBLEM GAMBLING

The first national study of gambling and problem gambling in 1974 indicated that 0.8 percent of the sample had at some time in their lifetime been probable pathological gamblers, with another 2.33 percent being potential pathological gamblers (University of Michigan Survey Research Center, 1976). The second federally supported national study was conducted by the National Gambling Impact Study Commission (NGISC) in 1999. It found that 1.2 percent (2.5 million) of the adult population were considered to be probable pathological gamblers in their lifetime and 1.5 percent (three million) were lifetime problem gamblers (National Research Council, 1999). In another major national survey, the National Epidemiologic Survey on Alcohol and Related Conditions (NESARC), conducted during the period 2001–2002, the prevalence of pathological gambling was 0.42 percent among the adult general population (Petry et al., 2005) with an additional 5 percent of adults being considered problem gamblers (Blanco et al., 2006).

SUBGROUPS AT RISK

An important consideration in the epidemiology of gambling is how pathological gambling affects various groups. Evidence suggests that men, youth, unmarried people, people with low income, and ethnic minorities are at increased risk of pathological gambling. The reasons for the overrepresentation in these groups are an active area of research that could help to elucidate the etiology of pathological gambling.

Gender. Prevalence rates of pathological gambling are higher in men than in women. The reasons for gender difference in prevalence rates are unknown, but are likely to be multifactorial. First, men appear to engage in regular gambling behavior more often than women. It is possible that increased exposure to gambling opportunities may partially account for prevalence differences. Social norms may oppose gambling (or higher levels of gambling) more strongly in women than men, exerting a protective effect in certain otherwise vulnerable individuals. Studies have shown different motivations to gamble in men and women, with men possibly more driven by underlying impulsivity and economic incentives, and women more motivated by emotional reasons. There are also differences in the types of gambling activities and venues among men and women with pathological gambling. Specifically, men are significantly more likely to engage in forms of gambling such as sports betting or stock trading that can be done over the phone or electronically and are therefore easily available regardless of the individual's location. In contrast, women are more likely to engage in the types of gambling that are more often associated with escape, rather than action or strategies (Blanco et al., 2006).

Age. Gambling rates are higher among adolescents and in young adults and tend to decrease with age. However, due to the cross-sectional nature of the available data it is unknown whether differences in prevalence across age groups are due to period effects. Of concern is that there has been a substantial increase in adolescent gambling rates in the past two decades. It is estimated that 50 percent to 90 percent of adolescents gamble in a given year, despite legal restrictions on underage gambling, and 3 percent to 8 percent of adolescents are pathological gamblers.

Also of concern is that young pathological gamblers are underrepresented in treatment. Pathological gambling in adolescents has been associated with poor school or college performance, delinquency or illegal behaviors, higher rates of tobacco and alcohol use and drug abuse, risky behaviors such as having multiple sexual partners, disruption of familial relationships, low self-esteem, depressive symptoms, and suicidal ideation and attempts.

Ethnic Minorities. Several studies in the United States and other countries have suggested that some ethno-racial minorities may be at increased risk for disordered gambling. In the case of Native Americans, the establishment of casino gambling on several reservations through the 1988 Federal Indian Gaming Regulatory Act may have increased exposure to gambling activities in this population, leading to an increased risk for disordered gambling among vulnerable individuals. Increased risk for problem and pathological gambling in certain ethno-racial groups is partially due to the highest prevalence of risk factors in those groups. For example, Native Americans have been consistently found to have a higher prevalence of psychiatric disorders, specifically alcohol and drug use disorders, than any other ethno-racial group, a factor strongly associated with problem and pathological gambling. Cultural factors also appear to influence the prevalence of problem and pathological gambling in ethnic minorities. For example, gambling is part of the tradition, history, and lifestyle of some Asian cultures. In other cultures, acceptance of

magical thinking and the existence of fate may allow such beliefs to be extended to gambling. Difficulties related to post-immigration adjustment, such as unemployment, language barriers, and social isolation, which can affect many members of ethno-racial minorities, have been also associated with problem and pathological gambling among Asians.

Socioeconomic Factors. Lower socio-economic status is consistently associated with increased pathological gambling rates. One hypothesis concerning the basis for this relationship is that individuals with less education are less able to understand the probabilities associated with gambling, but little empirical evidence is yet available to support this. Other researchers have suggested that this relationship could be explained by the poorer economic conditions experienced by some people, resulting in a strong motivation to engage in gambling behaviors in order to increase income.

Marital Status. Pathological gamblers are more likely to be divorced or separated. It has been suggested that separation and divorce are a result, rather than a cause for the development of pathological gambling. Others have suggested that pathological gamblers may be less likely to get or stay married because of an inability to maintain stable relationships.

PREDISPOSING FACTORS

Personality traits such as high impulsivity and extraversion have been associated with problem gambling. Problem gambling often occurs jointly with substance abuse, mood disorders, and personality disorders. In certain cases, gambling may serve to provide escape from depression or anxiety. Offspring of pathological gamblers are at increased risk of pathological gambling, because they are exposed to parental approval of gambling, though genetic factors also play a role. Earlier onset of gambling behavior seems to be directly related to a greater likelihood of progression to pathological gambling.

Community-level Factors. The prevalence of gambling problems is affected by many factors, including the number of legal and accessible gambling opportunities, as well as illegal ones. Prevalence rates may also be affected by the increasing availability of forms of electronic gaming (slots, video poker, video lottery terminals). This form of gambling involves an interaction between person and machine, which provides the opportunity for more frequent play and reinforcement than other forms of gambling. Because of the short time between the bet and the outcome, this form of gambling is likely to become more addictive. In addition, electronic gaming is often available twenty-four hours a day, which further increases its addictive potential.

Higher prevalence rates for problem gambling may also result when there is an increased societal acceptance of financial risk-taking. Although many forms of financial risk-taking, such as investing in stocks and other financial markets, are socially acceptable, they can also become arenas for problem and pathological gambling. In 1997 the U.S. Securities and Exchange Commission acknowledged for the first time that problem gambling occurs in the financial markets, distributing a pamphlet on investor problem gambling (Connecticut Council on Problem Gambling, 1997). The presence of the Internet has also increased the accessibility of gambling opportunities. As a result, the number of gambling sites available and the number of online gamblers have been increasing rapidly, as indicated by the sharp increase in Internet gambling revenues, from $445.4 million in 1997 (Barry, 1998) to $5.9 billion in 2005, according to Christiansen Capital Advisors (CCA 2007). As a response to this, in 2006, Sen. John Kyl (R-Ariz.) and Senate Majority Leader Bill Frist (R-Tenn.) secured the passage of the first federal legislation restricting the rapidly increasing online gambling industry when they attached the Unlawful Internet Gambling Enforcement Act (UIGEA) to federal legislation crafted to increase the security of U.S. ports.

TREATMENT INTERVENTIONS

Despite increasing awareness of the disorder, most pathological gamblers do not seek treatment. If they do, they may first seek treatment for a comorbid disorder rather than for the pathological gambling itself. Pathological gambling remains largely undiagnosed and untreated, even among high-risk populations such as youth and substance abusers.

The treatment of pathological gambling is complicated by high rates of comorbidity with mood, substance use, and personality disorders (Petry et al., 2005) and high rates of treatment dropout. Treatment compliance is of great concern when it comes to pathological gambling as it is for other addictions. Promising evidence suggests that pathological gambling can be treated successfully with pharmacotherapy and psychotherapy.

Pharmacotherapy. Although several medications have been examined as potential treatments for pathological gambling, there are no medications approved by the Food and Drug Administration for its treatment. Selective serotonin reuptake inhibitors (SSRIs) have shown mixed results. Some reports have shown beneficial effects of fluvoxamine (Hollander et al., 2000) especially in young men (Blanco et al., 2002). A single-site, double-blind, randomized clinical trial of paroxetine showed that gambling behavior decreased after sixteen weeks of treatment, but in a later study it failed to show efficacy compared with placebo. A study of sertraline (Saiz-Ruiz et al., 2005) further supports the finding that antidepressant medication may be beneficial only for some pathological gamblers. In studies in which participants had few or no signs of comorbid anxiety or depression, treatment with SSRIs were effective in reducing gambling behaviors.

Other researchers have tested the use of opioid antagonists in the treatment of pathological gambling, with promising results. A study using naltrexone in pathological gamblers showed high rates of response (Kim, 2001). This medication was more effective in gamblers with more severe urges to gamble. Also, in a clinical trial, nalmefene was superior compared with placebo in reducing gambling urges and behavior (Grant et al., 2006), although the study had very high dropout rates. Overall, although several medications have shown promise, further research is needed into this area.

Psychotherapy. Although a vast number of theoretical approaches to treat pathological gamblers exist, limitations on patients' follow-up and the inappropriate use of treatment outcomes makes it difficult to evaluate the efficacy of these approaches. However, several controlled studies on the efficacy of cognitive-behavioral therapy for patients with pathological gambling have yielded promising results (Sylvain et al., 1997; Echeburua et al., 1996; Petry, 2005). According to a cognitive-behavioral model, stimuli that become associated with gambling can over time develop into triggers for gambling. Once a trigger is encountered, it leads to an involuntary response of heightened autonomic arousal that is accompanied by gambling-related cognitions (e.g., "This is my lucky day") and urges to gamble. Whether or not a person gambles is mediated by coping skills. Treatment involves interventions that aim to enhance coping skills such as stimulus control and response prevention, problem-solving skills, assertiveness training, erroneous cognition modification, relaxation training, and relapse prevention (Petry, 2005).

Step-based Program. The most common step-based program for problem gamblers over the world is Gamblers Anonymous. This program uses a twelve-step program adapted from Alcoholics Anonymous and offers peer support for its attendants. This program is recommended as a complement to professional treatment, but seems to have very limited effect when used as the only intervention (Petry et al., 2006).

GROWTH OF COUNCILS ON PROBLEM GAMBLING

To meet the challenges of problem gambling, which increased with the growth of gambling in the last quarter of the twentieth century, councils on problem gambling have been created in the United States and Canada. As spiritual advisor to Gamblers Anonymous, Monsignor Joseph Dunne, along with recovering compulsive gamblers and family members, founded the National Council on Problem Gambling (NCPG) in 1972. The first state affiliate of the NCPG was Connecticut in 1980, and by 2000 there were thirty-four state affiliate councils. The NCPG was the first professional organization to educate the public about compulsive gambling as a serious public health problem and to advocate for treatment services. Other major priorities of the NCPG and its affiliates include sponsoring helplines, conducting prevention programs, training human services personnel, conducting surveys on problem gambling, and collaborating with a variety of relevant organizations, including the public and private gaming industry.

RECOMMENDATIONS OF THE NATIONAL GAMBLING IMPACT STUDY COMMISSION (NGISC)

The 1999 examination by the NGISC was the most extensive and systematic study of gambling in the United States. The study made seventy-four recommendations for changes in policies and practices for the public, private, and Native American sectors of the gambling industry, including state regulators and the federal government. As of 2008, most of these recommendations have not been implemented, which suggests that this is an important area for future advocacy.

Some of the major recommendations include:

A pause in the processing of all new gambling premises licenses applications to allow for adequate assessment of the gambling establishments already in place

A rollback of all convenience gambling in communities and a halt to authorization of all new convenience gambling

A restriction of the minimum legal gambling age to twenty-one

A ban on betting on collegiate and amateur athletics

A ban on all aggressive gambling advertisements and the creation of responsible gambling advertisement guidelines

Prohibition of Internet gambling not already authorized

A ban on ATM and credit card machines within or near the immediate gambling area

Gambling establishment policies to ensure the safety of children and prevent underage gambling

School programs from the elementary through college level should include warning of the dangers of gambling

See also **Gambling as an Addiction.**

BIBLIOGRAPHY

American Gaming Association. (1998). *Responsible gaming resource guide.* Washington, DC: Author.

American Psychiatric Association. (2000). *Diagnostic and statistical manual of mental disorders* (4th ed.). Washington, DC: Author.

Barry, G. (1998). Seven billion gambling market predicted. *Interactive Gambling News.* Available from http://igaming.com.

Blanco, C., Hasin, D. S., Petry, N., Stinson, F. S., & Grant, B. F. (2006). Sex differences in subclinical and *DSM-IV* pathological gambling: Results from the National Epidemiologic Survey on Alcohol and Related Conditions. *Psychological Medicine, 36,* 943–953.

Blanco, C., Petkova, E., Ibanez, A., & Saiz-Ruiz, J. (2002). A pilot placebo-controlled study of fluvoxamine for pathological gambling. *Annals of Clinical Psychiatry, 14,* 9–15.

Christiansen Capital Advisors LLC. (2007). Available from http://www.cca-i.com/.

Connecticut Council on Problem Gambling. (1997). *Investing and gambling problems.* Guilford, CT: Author.

Echeburua, E., Baez, C., & Fernandez-Montalvo, J. (1996). Comparative effectiveness of three therapeutic modalities in the psychological treatment of pathological gambling: Long-term outcome. *Behavioral and Cognitive Psychotherapy, 24,* 51–72.

Grant, J., Kim, S. W., & Cunningham-Williams, R. (2006). A multicenter investigation of fixed-dose nalmefene in the treatment of pathological gambling. *American Journal of Psychiatry, 163,* 303–312.

Hollander E., Decaria, C. M., Finkell, J. N., Begaz, T., Wong, C. M., Cartwright, C. (2000). A randomized double-blind fluvoxamine/placebo crossover trial in pathological gambling. *Biological Psychiatry, 47,* 813–817.

Kim, S. (2001). Double-blind naltrexone and placebo comparison study in the treatment of pathological gambling. *Biological Psychiatry, 49,* 914–921.

Korn, D., & Shaffer, H. (1999). Gambling and the health of the public: Adopting a public health perspective. *Journal of Gambling Studies, 15,* 289–365.

Lesieur, H. (1998). Costs and treatment of pathological gambling. In *The Annals of the American Academy of Political and Social Science, 556,* 153–171.

National Gambling Impact Study Commission. (1999). *National Gambling Impact Study Commission report.* Washington, DC: Author.

National Research Council. (1999). *Pathological gambling: A critical review.* Washington, DC: National Academy Press.

Petry, N. (2005). *Pathological gambling: Etiology, comorbidity, and treatment.* Washington DC: American Psychological Association.

Petry, N., Ammerman, J. B., Doersch, A., Gay, H., Kadden, R., Molina C., et al. (2006). Cognitive-Behavioral Therapy for Pathological Gamblers. *Journal of Consulting and Clinical Psychology, 74,* 555–567.

Petry, N., Stinson, F. S., & Grant, B. F. (2005). Comorbidity of *DSM–IV* pathological gambling and other psychiatric disorders: Results from the National Epidemiologic Survey on Alcohol and Related Conditions. *Journal of Clinical Psychiatry, 66,* 564–574.

Saiz-Ruiz, J., Blanco, C., Ibanez, A., Masramon, X., Gomez, M. M., Madrigal, M., et al. (2005). Sertraline treatment of pathological gambling. *Journal of Clinical Psychiatry, 66,* 28–33.

Sylvain, C., Ladoceur, R., & Boisvert, J. M. (1997). Cognitive and behavioral treatment of pathological gambling: A controlled study. *Journal of Consulting and Clinical Psychology, 65,* 727–32.

University of Michigan Survey Research Center. (1976). *Report for Commission on the review of the national policy toward gambling.* Ann Arbor, MI: Author.

ANALUCIA ALEGRIA
MAYUMI OKUDA
CARLOS BLANCO

GAMMA-AMINOBUTYRIC ACID (GABA).

Gamma-aminobutyric acid (GABA) is an amino acid neurotransmitter that is derived from glutamate by a single-step decarboxylation (a chemical reaction in which a carboxyl group [-COOH] is split off as carbon dioxide). GABA is the most abundant (in micromolar concentrations/mg of protein) inhibitory neurotransmitter, and it is found throughout the animal kingdom. Its role as a neurotransmitter was first defined for the inhibitory nerve in lobster muscle, where GABA accounted for the total inhibitory potency of nerve extracts. A central inhibitory neurotransmitter role for GABA was securely established only when selective antagonists (such as bicuculline) discriminated GABA receptors and pathways from those involving glycine, a related inhibitory amino acid neurotransmitter.

GABA actions, and receptors for GABA, have been linked to central nervous system sedatives such as alcohol and benzodiazepines. Recently, the GABA system has been targeted for the treatment of substance abuse. Vigabatrin is an irreversible inhibitor of GABA-transaminase, an enzyme that breaks down GABA, thereby increasing intracellular GABA concentrations. The drug effectively inhibits increases in brain dopamine concentrations induced by cocaine, amphetamine or methamphetamine, alcohol, nicotine, phencyclidine, heroin, or morphine. Further, increased GABA tone blocks behaviors associated with drugs of abuse, including drug self-administration, conditioned place preference, and the reinstatement of both of these phenomena. Clinical trials using the anticonvulsant vigabatrin in cocaine-dependent subjects have yielded promising results. In addition, studies have demonstrated that targeting the GABA system may also be an effective strategy for treating binge-eating disorder.

See also **Dopamine; Glutamate; Neurotransmitters.**

BIBLIOGRAPHY

Cooper, J. R., Bloom, F. E., & Roth, R. H. (2003). *The biochemical basis of neuropharmacology* (8th ed.). New York: Oxford University Press.

FLOYD BLOOM
REVISED BY STEPHEN L. DEWEY (2009)

GANGS AND DRUGS. The gang is an American phenomenon. Reports of groups of youth involved in criminal activities called "gangs" emerged over 200 years ago in the United States (Fagan, 2001). Since then, the gang has held a particular fascination in the United States, and young people in gangs are the contemporary image of the rogue, the bad guy, the criminal "other" (cf. Jefferson, 1993; Sanders, 2005). In the twenty-first century, gangs remain an important criminal justice concern, as they are responsible for a disproportionate amount of crime. For instance, in large cities such as Los Angeles and Chicago, half of the total number of homicides has been considered "gang related" (Egley & Ritz, 2006). As of 2004, statistics indicate that approximately three-quarters of a million gang members were active in the United States (Egley & Ritz, 2006). These numbers are based largely on police records, and more gang youth may exist due to their hidden nature (Valdez & Kaplan, 1999).

While ganging has traditionally been a male phenomenon, research indicates the number of female gang members has risen significantly in recent years (Miller, 2001a; Miller, 2001b). Esbensen and Lynsky (2001, p. 98), for instance, reported in their findings that "there are more girls in gangs than is commonly assumed" whereby 38 percent of all gang members in their 8th grade sample were females. Young women in gangs are no longer considered strictly to be sexual auxiliaries of male gangs, but are rather autonomous groups who engage in crime and violence at levels paralleling their male

counterparts (Miller, 2001b; Moore & Hagedorn, 2001; however, see Wang, 2000).

Defining what exactly constitutes a gang has been an important focus of gang research, and the definition has changed over the years (Brotherton & Barrios, 2004; Klein, 1971, 2006; Miller, 1958; Sanders, 1994; Spergel, 1964, 1995; Yablonsky, 1962). One contemporary definition is offered by Klein, who classifies a gang as "any durable, street-oriented youth group whose own identity includes involvement in illegal activities" (Klein, 2006). This definition is similar to the one utilized by law enforcement in some states such as California (see California Penal Code 186.22 [f]). Gangs can be further broken down by type based on their structure and activities. The Klein/Maxson gang typology indicates characteristics of five different gang types (Klein & Maxson, 2006):

1. The traditional gang: Such gangs are well-established (over 20 years old) and regenerate themselves through the recruitment of younger members. They often have cliques separated by age, location of neighborhood or gang status, with a wide age-range of members (e.g., 10–30 years old). Such gangs are very large, numbering in the hundreds, and they strongly identify with a particular neighborhood or "turf."

2. The neo-traditional gang: Similar to the traditional gang, but somewhat smaller (e.g., 50–100 members, though it can reach a couple of hundred) with a shorter length of existence (e.g., 10 years or less).

3. The compressed gang: Unlike the above gangs, the compressed gang is small (50 members or less), has no subgroups, and a narrow age range (i.e., 10 or fewer years between younger and older members). These gangs have been around less than 10 years and may be territorial.

4. The collective gang: Unlike the compressed gang, the collective gang has a wider age range (i.e., 10 or more years between younger and older members), a larger size (around 100 or more members), and has been in existence longer (i.e., 10–15 years). No subgroups exist in this gang. The collective gang may be territorial.

5. The specialty gang: Whereas the previous gangs engage in a wide variety of offenses, those in the specialty gang engage in particular offenses (e.g.,

drug selling) for which they become known. Issues of territoriality are related to these offenses. Such gangs are usually small, with 50 members or less, and likely have been around less than 10 years.

Another gang type could be added to this typology: the multinational gang. One gang in particular, Mara Salvatrucha 13—commonly known as MS-13—may be considered a multinational gang. Little academic research on MS-13 has emerged, and most of what is known about the gang is drawn from media reports or intelligence assessments (Darnton, 2005; Del Barco, 2005; Federal Bureau of Investigation, 2008; National Drug Intelligence Center, 2002). Based on these data, it can be gathered that MS-13 consists of Latinos from Honduras, Guatemala, and, in particular, El Salvador. MS-13 cliques can be found throughout several nations including the United States, Canada, and some European countries. Moreover, MS-13 has reportedly been involved in crimes typical of organized syndicates, such as weapons and drug smuggling, but also human trafficking, which is an offense unique to this type of gang.

Debates continue on whether gang characteristics are clearly outlined or vague, antisocial or constructive, or responsible for a large portion of crime and violence or a fraction of it (see Brotherton & Barrios, 2004; Egley & Major, 2004; Katz, 2000; Katz & Jackson-Jacobs, 2004; Klein, 1971, 2006; Miller, 2001a; Sanders, 1994; Spergel, 1995, cf. Sanders & Lankenau, 2006). Outlining what exactly constitutes a gang and the different types of gangs is relevant for a discussion on drug use and sales, because most gangs *do not* sell drugs and some gang members have very hostile attitudes toward the use of certain drugs.

GANG YOUTH AND SUBSTANCE USE

According to national sentinel data, such as Monitoring the Future, the National Survey on Drug Use and Health, and the Youth Risk Behavior Survey, cannabis and alcohol are the most commonly reported substances used by young people in the United States (Eaton et al., 2006; Johnston et al., 2008; Substance Abuse and Mental Health Services Administration, 2007). Correspondingly, the use of these drugs is the most commonly reported among gang youth (Fagan, 2001).

Studies specifically on gangs have indicated that at least 90 percent of their samples have ever used alcohol, and between 80 percent and 90 percent have ever used cannabis (e.g., Hagedorn, 1998; Mata et al., 2002). Much of gang life consists of "hanging around"—a relatively consistent finding among gang researchers over time (Klein, 1995; Sanders, 1994; Short & Strodbeck, 1965; Vigil, 1988). During such times, the use of alcohol and cannabis is a prominent activity. Hunt and Joe-Laidler (2001) discuss various symbolic roles of alcohol in the lives of gang members related to issues of displaying masculinity, maintaining a "cool" image, facilitating violence, gang initiation, and ritualistic mourning (e.g., pouring alcohol on the ground in remembrance of deceased peers; see also Moore, 1991; Valdez et al., 2006; Vigil, 1988). Similar to much research on gang males, Joe-Laidler and Hunt (1997) also reported that among both African American and Latino gang females, "hanging out" and "partying" were major activities, where drinking alcohol and smoking cannabis featured prominently (see also Harris, 1988).

Gang members also use a variety of other drugs. Phencyclidine (PCP) and crack cocaine have been found among Latino gang youth in East Los Angeles (Moore, 1991; Vigil, 1988; see also Joe-Laidler and Hunt, 1997). Valdez et al. (2006), in their study of gang members, found approximately 90 percent of their sample had ever used cocaine, 57 percent had ever injected heroin, 35 percent had ever used inhalants, and 29 percent had ever used amphetamines. Robinson (2001) noted that up to 50 percent of gang members reported ever using crystal methamphetamine, a drug commonly associated with Caucasians and outlaw motorcycle groups. Brotherton (1996) also reported on a wide variety of substance use among gang females in San Francisco including crack, PCP, and LSD (i.e., acid). Hagedorn and Devitt (1999) reported that daily cocaine use was prevalent among the Latina gang members, with two-thirds indicating such behavior, while only around a quarter (27.8%) of the African American gang females used cocaine daily. However, about twice as many African American gang females than Latina gang members in Hagedorn and Devitt's study reported going to school "while high" (presumably on cannabis) on a daily basis.

Some gang researchers have indicated that gang members have harsh views of some hard drugs. Vigil (1988), for instance, reported that Latino gang members had very critical attitudes towards heroin use, and similar sentiments were expressed by Latino gang members in South Texas (Valdez & Sifaneck, 2004). Likewise, Chin (1996) found that while Chinese gang members used alcohol, few were regular users of cannabis and very small percentages used "hard" drugs such as cocaine or heroin.

Emerging topics of concern related to substance use, such as non-medical prescription drug use and polydrug use (i.e., the simultaneous or sequential use of two or more substances), have received peripheral attention in the research literature on gang youth. Sanders et al. (2007) found that many gang youth reported lifetime rates of using prescription drugs, particularly opiates (e.g., Vicodin) and benzodiazepines (e.g., Valium; see also Valdez et al., 2006). Moreover, many of the gang youth in the Sanders et al. study reported polydrug use, particularly the use of alcohol alongside cannabis, but also alcohol, cannabis, and one other drug, especially crystal methamphetamine, powder cocaine or crack cocaine (cf. Bennett & Holloway, 2005). Cannabis joints containing crack cocaine were also reported by Sanders et al. (cf. Bourgois, 1995). Valdez et al. (2006) reported that 44 percent of their sample had ever used a mixture of heroin and cocaine (i.e., "speedballs").

Gang members clearly use a variety of substances. Comparative research often indicates that gang youth use *more* drugs and alcohol in comparison to their non-gang peers. Evidence from several longitudinal studies on youth development in North America (Denver, Rochester, Seattle, Pittsburgh, and Montreal) all indicate that gang youth, compared to non-gang youth, not only have higher rates of crime and violence perpetration, but also drug and alcohol use (see, e.g., Thornberry et al., 2003).

In Seattle, Hill and colleagues (2001) found that gang youth were more likely to binge drink alcohol and use marijuana in comparison to non-gang youth. Over half of the gang youth in the Hill et al. study had used marijuana, though only about a quarter of non-gang youth had done so. In Rochester, Thornberry et al. (1993) found that gang youth reported drug use that was four to five times higher in comparison to the non-gang youth in

the sample. In Montreal, Gatti et al. (2005) found that rates of drug use for gang youth were three to four times higher when compared to non-gang youth. In a similar vein, Bjerregaard and Smith (1993), utilizing the Rochester data set, found that gang females were more likely to report alcohol and marijuana use in comparison to the non-gang females. Moreover, gang females have been found to report higher involvement in drug sales and drug use than the non-gang males (Esbensen & Winfree, 1998).

Even studies on other groups of high risk youth, such as homeless youth, find that former and current gang involvement is related to increased substance use. For instance, in a study among homeless youth in Midwestern states, Yoder et al. (2003) found that those who also identified as gang members or as gang "involved" reported higher overall rates of substance use compared to the homeless youth with no such identification. Similar findings were reported in a study by Harper and colleagues (2008) in Chicago, who found that homeless youth with gang ties were more likely to use substances (Harper et al., 2008). Further still, Harper et al. developed a "level of gang involvement scale," and found a significant positive relationship between level of gang involvement and lifetime use of alcohol and cannabis. This finding corroborates Klein's earlier work on differences he found between "core" and "fringe" gang members, with the former more likely to report greater substance use (see Klein & Maxson, 2006). Together, the comparative studies indicate the significant effect of both gang participation itself and the *intensity* of gang participation on increased levels of reported substance use (see also Walker-Barnes & Mason, 2004; Zhang et al., 1999).

Gang youth are an important criminal justice concern due to the elevated rates of crime and violence committed by gang members. Gang youth may also be considered a public health concern, as their elevated rates of substance use suggest they are at an increased likelihood of suffering from the many related negative health outcomes such as cognitive impairment, overdose, addiction, exposure to hepatitis C and HIV, and even death (Sanders & Lankenau, 2006).

GANG YOUTH AND DRUG SELLING
Media representations and law enforcement proclamations closely link drug selling with gang membership

(Curtis, 2003). It has been argued, however, that most gangs have been poorly organized to sustain a system of drug distribution (Decker, 2001; Esbensen et al., 2002; Klein, 1995; Spergel, 1995). Curtis (2003, p. 42) found that, between 1990 and 2000, drug distribution among gang youth was "inconsequential" to the overall drug market in New York City. Certain members within gangs may sell drugs but drug distribution is often reported as not being central to the gang's overall purpose (see Decker & Van Winkle, 1996). Such findings stand in sharp contrast to what is generally perceived about gang members and drug selling.

Of all the gang types discussed earlier, the "specialty" gang may be organized explicitly around drug selling. Several studies have emerged that have examined gangs that may be considered specialty gangs, particularly those involved in corporation-style crack cocaine distribution, whereby members view such distribution as "employment" or "enterprise" (Hagedorn, 1988; Padilla, 1992; Taylor, 1989; see also Decker, 2001). Drug selling in such cases is a business akin to those within the service industry such as fast food restaurants (Anderson, 1990; Ruggiero & South, 1995; Sanders, 2005). Even the language of drug selling in such instances mirrors fast food language, where users are talked about as "customers" and selling drugs to them is discussed as "serving" (Padilla, 1992; Ruggiero & South, 1995; Sanders, 2005; Williams, 1989).

Moore and Hagedorn (2001) reported that selling drugs is among the most common offenses committed by female gang members. Miller and Decker (2001) indicate that approximately two-thirds (63%) of the gang females had sold marijuana and/or crack cocaine, and that approximately a quarter (22%) had sold other drugs. Joe-Laidler and Hunt (1997) found that, among African American gang females, selling crack was a primary source of income, and that among Latina gang members, over one-third sold drugs, primarily cannabis and cocaine. Hagedorn and Devitt (1999) found that among African American females, those who sold drugs on their own were equal in proportion to those who sold drugs as part of "the guy's operation" (each at 8.3% of the sample). In contrast, very few (1.9%) of the Latina gang members sold drugs on their own but more than two-fifths (42.3%) sold drugs alongside the gang males.

Taylor (1993) notes that African American female gang members were directly involved in crack cocaine distribution.

The phrase "don't get high on your own supply" is a colloquialism cautioning individuals tempted to use the drugs they sell (Sanders, 2005). While selling crack cocaine may be sanctioned among fellow gang members, using the drug may not be. Taylor (1989) and Fagan (1996), in writing about gangs who sell crack, have mentioned harsh consequences for gang members found to use the drug (Bourgois, 1995; Jacobs, 1999; Sanders, 2005). In other words, selling crack was not viewed as problematic among gang youth, but using the drug was a completely different story.

Valdez and Sifaneck (2004) offer a valuable portrait of the relationship between drug users and drug sellers within Mexican American gangs in South Texas. Similar to other researchers (e.g., Klein, 1995), Valdez and Sifaneck identified two different gang types: the street gang and the drug gang. In the street gang, the authors identify two types of drug sellers: the homeboy and the hustler. The homeboy is a drug user/seller who sells a small amount of drugs in order to cover the costs of personal use and perhaps generate a small income. The hustler, in contrast, sells drugs strictly for personal profit (see also Decker, 2001). While the drug profits the hustler, the earnings do not support the street gang; the hustler benefits from the protection the gang offers as part of membership. The drug gang also has two types of drug sellers: the slanger and the baller. The slanger, like the homeboy, is a drug user/seller, who sells small portions of drugs to offset the costs associated with personal use and earn a small profit. The baller, in contrast, controls drug distribution business in a gang that is organized around such an endeavor, whereby profits from this business benefit the entire gang. Ballers may also be users but are less ubiquitous and rarely seen.

Most youth in gangs, like most young offenders, do not specialize in one type of offense, but engage in a variety of offenses (Decker, 2001; Klein, 1995). And while gang members may sell drugs, and their gang may offer some sort of direct or indirect support for drug distribution, most gangs do not focus on selling drugs and are not organized to do so.

BIBLIOGRAPHY

Anderson, E. (1990). *Streetwise: Race, class, and change in an urban community.* Chicago: Chicago University Press.

Bennett, T., & Holloway, K. (2005). The association between multiple drug misuse and crime. *International Journal of Offender Therapy and Comparative Criminology, 49*(1), 63–81.

Bjerregaard, B., & Smith, C. (1993). Gender differences in gang participation, delinquency, and substance use. *Journal of Quantitative Criminology* 9:329–355.

Bourgois, P. (1995). *In search of respect: Selling crack in El Barrio.* Cambridge, UK: Cambridge University Press.

Brotherton, D. (1996). "Smartness," "Toughness," and "Autonomy": Drug use in the context of gang female delinquency. *Journal of Drug Issues, 26,* 261–277.

Brotherton, D. C., & Barrios, L. (2004). *The almighty Latin king and queen nation: Street politics and the transformation of a New York City gang.* New York: Columbia University Press.

Chin, K. (1996). *Chinatown gangs: Extortion, enterprise, and ethnicity.* Oxford: Oxford University Press.

Curtis, R. (2003). The negligible role of gangs in drug distribution in New York City in the 1990s. In L. Kontos, D. Brotherton, & L. Barrios (Eds.), *Gangs and society: Alternative perspectives* (pp. 41–61). New York: Columbia University Press.

Darnton, K. (2005). The fight against MS-13: Dan Rather on difficult fight against dangerous gang. Available from http://www.cbsnews.com/.

Decker, S. (2001). The impact of organizational features on gang activities and relationships. In M. Klein, H. J. Kerner, C. L. Maxson, & E. G. M. Weitekamp (Eds.), *The Eurogang paradox: Street gangs and youth groups in the U.S. and Europe.* Dordrecht: Kluwer Academic Publishers.

Decker, S., & Van Winkle, B. (1996). *Life in the gang: Family, friends and violence.* Cambridge, UK: Cambridge University Press.

Del Barco, M. (2005). The international research of the Mara Salvatrucha. Available from http://www.npr.org/.

Eaton, D. K, Kann, L., Kinchen, S., Ross, J., Hawkins, J., Harris, W. A., et al. (2006). Youth risk behavior surveillance–United States, 2005. *Morbidity and Mortality Weekly Report 55*(SS05). Atlanta: Centers for Disease Control and Prevention.

Egley, A., Jr., & Major, A. K. (2004). Highlights of the 2002 National Youth Gang Survey. *OJJDP Fact Sheet* March 2004-01. Washington, DC: U.S. Department of Justice, Office of Juvenile Justice and Delinquency Prevention.

Egley, A., Jr., & Ritz, C. (2006). Highlights of the National Youth Gang Survey. *OJJDP Fact Sheet* April 2006-01.

Washington, DC: U.S. Department of Justice, Office of Juvenile Justice and Delinquency Prevention.

Esbensen, F. A., & Lynskey, D. P. (2001). Youth gang members in a school survey. In M. Klein, H. J. Kerner, C. L. Maxson, & E. G. M. Weitekamp (Eds.), *The Eurogang paradox: Street gangs and youth groups in the U.S. and Europe* (pp. 93–114). Dordrecht, Germany: Kluwer Academic Publishers.

Esbensen, F. A., & Winfree, L. T., Jr. (1998). Race and gender differences between gang and non-gang youth: Results from a multisite survey. *Justice Quarterly, 15*(3), 505–526.

Esbensen, F., Peterson, D., Freng, A., & Taylor, T. J. (2002). Initiation of drug use, drug sales, and violent offending among a sample of gang and non-gang youth. In R. Huff (Ed.), *Gangs in America* (3rd ed.) (pp. 37–50).

Fagan, J. (1996). Gangs, drugs, and neighborhood change. In C. R. Huff (Ed.), *Gangs in America* (2nd ed.). Thousand Oaks, CA: Sage Publications.

Fagan, J. (2001). Gangs and drugs. In R. Carson DeWitt (Ed.), *Encyclopedia of drugs, alcohol and addictive behavior* (2nd ed.). New York: Macmillan.

Federal Bureau of Investigation. (2008). *The MS-13 threat: A national assessment.* Headline Archives. Available from http://www.fbi.gov/.

Gatti, U., Tremblay, R. E., Vitaro, F., & McDuff, P. (2005). Youth gangs, delinquency and drug use: A test of the selection, facilitation, and enhancement hypotheses. *Journal of Child Psychology and Psychiatry, 46*(11), 1178–1190.

Hagedorn, J. (1988). *People and folks: Gangs, crime and the underclass in a rust-belt city.* Chicago: Lake View Press.

Hagedorn, J. M. (1998). Cocaine, kicks, and strain: Patterns of substance use in Milwaukee gangs. *Contemporary Drug Problems, 25,* 113–145.

Hagedorn, J. M., & Devitt, M. L. (1999). Fighting female: The social construction of female gangs. In M. Chesney-Lind & J. M. Hagedorn (Eds.), *Female Gangs in America: Essays on Girls, Gangs and Gender* (pp. 256–276).

Hall, G. P, Thornberry, T. P., & Lizotte, A. J. (2006). The gang facilitation effect and neighborhood risk: Do gangs have a stronger influence on delinquency in disadvantaged areas? In J. F. Short Jr. & L. A. Hughes (Eds.), *Studying Youth Gangs.* Lanham, MD: Altamira Press.

Harper, G. W., Davidson, J., & Hosek, S. G. (2008). Influence of gang membership on negative affect, substance use, and antisocial behavior among homeless African American male youth. Available from http://jmh.sagepub.com/.

Harris, M. G. (1988). *Cholas: Latino girls and gangs.* New York: AMS Press.

Hill, K. G., Lui, C., & Hawkins, J. D. (2001). *Early Precursors of Gang Membership: A study of Seattle youth.* Bulletin. Youth Gang Series. Washington, DC: U.S. Department of Justice, Office of Juvenile Justice and Delinquency Prevention.

Hunt, G. P., & Joe-Laidler, K. (2001). Alcohol and violence in the lives of gang members. *Alcohol Research and Health, 25,* 66–71.

Jacobs, B. A. (1999). Crack to heroin?: Drug markets and transition. *British Journal of Criminology, 39,* 555–574.

Jefferson, T. (1993). The racism of criminalisation: Police and the reproduction of the criminal other. In L. Gelsthorpe (Ed.), *Minority ethnic groups in the criminal justice system* (Cropwood Conference Series No. 21). University of Cambridge, Institute of Criminology.

Johnston, L. D., O'Malley, P. M., Bachman, J., & Schulenberg, J. E. (2008). *Monitoring the future national results on adolescent drug use: Overview key findings, 2007* (NIH Publication No. 08-6418). Bethesda, MD: National Institute on Drug Abuse.

Katz, J. (2000). The gang myth. In S. Karstedt & K. D. Bussmann (Eds.), *Social dynamics of crime and control: New theories for a world in transition* (pp. 171–187). Portland, OR: Hart.

Katz, J., & Jackson-Jacobs, C. (2004). The Criminologists' Gang. In C. Sumner (Ed.), *The Blackwell companion to criminology* (pp. 91–124). Malden, MA: Blackwell.

Klein, M. (1971). *Street gangs and street workers.* Englewood Cliff, NJ: Prentice Hall.

Klein, M. (1995). *The American street gang: Its nature, prevalence and control.* New York: Oxford University Press.

Klein, M. (2006). The value of comparisons in street gang research. In J. F. Short & L. A. Hughes (Eds.), *Studying youth gangs* (pp. 129–144). Thousand Oaks, CA: Altamira Press.

Klein, M. W., & Maxson, C. L. (2006). *Street gang patterns and policies.* New York: Oxford University Press.

Mata, A., Valdez, A., Alvarado, J., Capeda, A., Cervantes, R., & Kaplan, C. D. (2002) Drug related violence among Mexican American youth in Laredo, Texas: Preliminary findings. *Free Inquiry in Creative Sociology, 30,* 25–39.

Miller, W. B. (1958). Lower class culture as generating a milieu of gang delinquency. *Journal of Social Issues, 14,* 5–19.

Miller, J. (2001a). *One of the guys: Girls, gangs, and gender.* New York: Oxford University Press.

Miller, J. (2001b). Young women's involvement in gangs in the United States: An overview. In M. Klein, H. J. Kerner, C. L. Maxson & E. G. M. Weitekamp (Eds.), *The Eurogang paradox: Street gangs and youth groups in the US and Europe* (pp. 115–134). Amsterdam: Kluwer Academic Publishers.

Miller, J., & Decker, S. H. (2001) Young women and gang violence: Gender, street offending, and violent victimization in gangs. *Justice Quarterly, 18*(1), 115–140.

Miller, W. B. (1958). Lower class culture as generating a milieu of gang delinquency. *Journal of Social Issues, 14,* 5–19.

Moore, J. (1991). *Going down to the barrio: Homeboys and homegirls in change.* Philadelphia: Temple University Press.

Moore, J. W., & Hagedorn, J. M. (2001). Female gangs: A focus on research. *Juvenile Justice Bulletin, Youth Gang Series.* Washington, DC: U.S. Department of Justice, Office of Juvenile Justice and Delinquency Prevention.

National Drug Intelligence Center. (2002). *Virginia drug threat assessment.* Available from http://www.usdoj.gov/.

Padilla, F. (1992). *The gang as an American enterprise.* New Brunswick, NJ: Rutgers University Press.

Robinson, C. (2001). Methamphetamine use and sales among gang members: The cross-over effect. *Journal of Gang Research, 9*(1), 39–52.

Ruggiero, V., & South, N. (1995.) *Eurodrugs: Drug use, markets, and trafficking in Europe.* London: UCL Press.

Sanders, B. (2005). *Youth crime and youth culture in the inner city.* London: Routledge.

Sanders, B., & Lankenau, S. (2006). A public health model for studying youth gangs. In J. Short & L. Hughes (Eds.), *Studying Youth Gangs* (pp. 117–128). Latham, MD: Altamira Press.

Sanders, B., Lankenau, S., & Jackson-Bloom, J. (2007). Illicit substance use among gang-identified youth in Los Angeles. Poster presented at the 2007 Annual Meeting of the College on Problems of Drug Dependence. Quebec City, Quebec.

Sanders, W. B. (1994). *Gangbangs and drive-bys: Grounded culture and juvenile gang violence.* New York: Aldine de Gruyter.

Short, J. F., Jr., & Strodbeck, F. L. (1965). *Group process and gang delinquency.* Chicago: University of Chicago Press.

Spergel, I. (1964). *Racketville, Slumtown, Haulberg.* Chicago: University of Chicago Press.

Spergel, I. (1995). *The youth gang problem: A community approach.* Oxford: Oxford University Press.

Substance Abuse and Mental Health Services Administration. (2007). *Results from the 2006 National Survey on Drug Use and Health: National findings* (Office of Applied Studies, NSDUH Series H-32, DHHS Publication No. SMA 07-4293). Rockville, MD.

Taylor, C. S. (1989). *Dangerous society*. East Lansing: Michigan State University Press.

Taylor, C. S. (1993). Female gangs: A historical perspective. In C. S. Taylor (Ed.), *Girls, gangs, women and drugs*. East Lansing: Michigan State University Press.

Thornberry, T. P., Krohn, M. D., Lizotte, A. J., & Chard-Wierschem, D. (1993). The role of juvenile gangs in facilitating delinquent behavior. *Journal of Research in Crime & Delinquency, 30*, 55–87.

Thornberry, T. P., Krohn, M. D., Lizotte, A. J., Smith, C. A., & Tobin, K. (2003). *Gangs and delinquency in developmental perspective*. Cambridge, UK: Cambridge University Press.

U.S. Department of Justice, Office of Justice Programs, Office of Juvenile Justice and Delinquency Prevention. (2006). *Highlights of the 2004 National Youth Gang Survey*. Washington, DC: Egley, A., Jr., Ruiz, C. E.

U.S. Department of Justice, Office of Justice Programs, Office of Juvenile Justice and Delinquency Prevention. (2001). Early precursors of gang membership: A study of Seattle youth. *Juvenile Justice Bulletin*. Washington, DC: Hill, K. G., Lui, C., Hawkins, J. D.

U.S. Department of Justice, Office of Justice Programs, Office of Juvenile Justice and Delinquency Prevention. (2001). *Female gangs: A focus on research*. Washington, DC: Moore, J., Hagedorn, J.

Valdez, A., & Kaplan, C. D. (1999). Reducing selection bias in the use of focus groups to investigate hidden populations: The case of Mexican-American gang members from South Texas. *Drugs and Society, 14*(1), 209–224.

Valdez, A., Kaplan, C. D., & Cepeda, A. (2006). The drugs-violence nexus among Mexican-American gang members. *Journal of Psychoactive Drugs, 38*(2), 109–121.

Valdez, A., & Sifaneck, S. J. (2004). "Getting high and getting by": Dimensions of drug selling behaviors among American Mexican gang members in South Texas. *Journal of Research in Crime & Delinquency, 41*(1), 82–105.

Vigil, J. D. (1988). *Barrio gangs: street life and identity in Southern California*. Austin: University of Texas Press.

Walker-Barnes, C. J., & Mason, C. A. (2004). Delinquency and substance use among gang-involved youth: The moderating role of parenting practices. *American Journal of Community Psychology, 34*, 235–250.

Wang, J. A. (2000). Female gang affiliation: Knowledge and perceptions of at-risk girls. *International Journal of Offender Therapy & Comparative Criminology, 44*, 618–632.

Williams, T. (1989). *The cocaine kids*. Reading, MA: Addison-Wesley.

Yablonsky, L. (1962). *The violent gang*. New York: Macmillan.

Yoder, K. A., Whitbeck, L. B., & Hoyt, D. R. (2003). Gang involvement and membership among homeless and runaway youth. *Youth & Society, 34*(4), 441–467.

Zhang, L., Welte, J. A., & Wieczorek, W. F. (1999). Youth gangs, drug use and delinquency. *Journal of Criminal Justice, 27*(2), 101–109.

BILL SANDERS

GANJA. Ganja is a Hindi word (derived from Sanskritic) for the hemp plant, *Cannabis sativa* (marijuana); the term *ganja* entered English in the late seventeenth century. Ganja is a selected and potent preparation of marijuana used for smoking.

The hemp plant was introduced into the British West Indies by indentured laborers from India who arrived in Jamaica in 1845. Considered to be a "holy" plant, ganja is often used in religious ceremonies in both countries. The Indian Hemp Drug Commission traced the origin of ganja use to India.

Although usually smoked, *Cannabis* may also be mixed with foods or drinks; it is considered a remedy for many ailments in herbal medicine. A medical-anthropological study of ganja users in Jamaica was conducted in 1972; the results revealed little evidence of a deleterious effect among users, as compared with nonusers. These conclusions were criticized, however, by investigators who claim that the tests of maturation and mental capacity that were used were not sensitive enough to detect decrements in higher level mental skills or motivation.

See also **Bhang; Plants, Drugs From.**

BIBLIOGRAPHY

Booth, M. (2005). *Cannabis: A history*. New York: MacMillan.

Roffman, R. A., & Stephens, R. S. (2006). *Cannabis dependence: Its nature, consequences and treatment*. Cambridge, U.K.: Cambridge University Press.

Rubin, V. & Comitas, L. (1975). *Ganja in Jamaica: A medical anthropological study of chronic marihuana use*. The Hague: New Babylon Studies in the Social Sciences.

LEO E. HOLLISTER

GENDER AND COMPLICATIONS OF SUBSTANCE ABUSE.

Despite a lower overall level of alcohol and drug consumption and rates of substance use disorder, women suffer more negative physical and psychiatric consequences from substance use than men. In this entry, the evidence for gender differences in the complications of substance abuse will be reviewed in three overall areas: (1) alcohol, (2) nicotine, and (3) illicit drugs.

ALCOHOL

Gender differences in the consequences of alcohol use and abuse are extensively researched and well documented in both human populations and animal models. Women exhibit higher blood alcohol levels than men at the same level of consumption, due to smaller average body size (Lieber, 1997), body water content (Lieber, 1997), and lower gastric alcohol dehydrogenase (an enzyme that is involved in the oxidation of alcohol through the liver) activity among younger adults. Further, alcohol-dependent women exhibit higher rates of physical illness compared to alcohol dependent men including overall mortality (Klatsky, Armstrong, & Friedman, 1992), cirrhosis of the liver (Deal & Gavaler, 1994), heart attacks (Hanna, Chou, & Grant, 1997), and brain damage (Schweinsburg et al., 2003; Hommer et al., 2001). Heavy alcohol use is also a risk factor for breast cancer (Key et al., 2006). Alcohol disorders often co-occur with other psychiatric disorders such as depression and anxiety disorders. Studies suggest that women are more likely to exhibit anxiety disorders when presenting for alcohol treatment (Brady et al., 1993), but larger population-based studies have found little evidence for gender differences in rates of coexisting diseases among alcoholics (Regier et al., 1990; Kessler et al., 1996).

The consequences of heavy alcohol use during pregnancy are also well documented. In addition to Fetal Alcohol Syndrome in the offspring, even moderate use of alcohol during pregnancy is associated with adverse outcomes in the offspring. These include low birth weight and premature birth (Sokol, Delaney-Black, & Nordstrom, 2003) as well as impairments throughout childhood, including slow growth as measured up to age six and learning disorders as measured up to age 10 (Jacobson & Jacobson, 2000). Moderate alcohol use is also associated with increased risk of miscarriage and stillbirth (Kesmodel et al., 2002). Although the amount of alcohol that adversely affects the fetus is still debated, most women are advised to abstain from alcohol throughout pregnancy (Coles et al., 2000).

NICOTINE

Gender differences in the adverse effects of nicotine, particularly via cigarette use, have been consistently observed. Although it is generally believed that the acute effects of nicotine are similar in men and women, women are less likely than men to experience positive effects from nicotine. Instead, women respond to smoke stimuli, secondary social reinforcement, and other sensory aspects of the smoking experience. Clinical evidence suggests that women experience more severe nicotine withdrawal syndromes, which may contribute to a lower abstinence rate compared to men (Leventhal et al., 2007). Further, women experience greater depressive and anxiety symptoms when they stop smoking (Borelli et al., 2001) and are subject to effects involving the menstrual cycle in which stimulation and withdrawal from nicotine is stronger in the menstrual phase that immediately precedes menstruation (Mello, Mendelson, & Palmieri, 1987; Craig, Parrott, & Coomber, 1992). Despite fewer reinforcing effects of nicotine, nicotine-dependent women may be at higher risk for smoking-related diseases such as lung cancer (Zang & Wynder, 1996) as well as heart attacks than men (Prescott et al., 1998). Women also suffer reproductively from nicotine dependence, as smoking during pregnancy has been known for decades to have adverse effects on the fetus (Wilcox, 1993).

Studies show that women in smoking cessation treatment have lower rates of abstinence than men whether the treatment includes counseling, nicotine replacement therapy vs. placebo (Cepeda-Benito, Reynoso, & Erath, 2004), or a medication such as buprorion vs. placebo (Sharf & Shiffman, 2004). Some researchers hypothesize that women may have more difficulty quitting smoking due to a more severe withdrawal syndrome, greater psychiatric symptoms, or social factors, such as fear of weight gain (Borelli et al., 2001; Etter, Prokhorov, & Perneger, 2002). The development of smoking prevention and cessation treatments targeted toward women remains a vitally important research topic, especially as evidence indicates that adolescent girls are smoking at a higher rate than boys (Johnston et al., 2007).

ILLICIT DRUGS

Gender differences in the consequences of illicit drug use are less studied, although extensive work has been done on sex differences in cocaine and stimulant addiction in animal models. These models indicate that sex differences occur at many stages of the cocaine addiction process, including more rapid acquisition of cocaine and opiates among females, more bingeing and craving during the maintenance phase, and greater risk for relapse (Becker & Hu, 2008; Lynch, Roth, & Carroll, 2002; Lynch, 2006). Further, female rats have an exaggerated behavior response as well as higher stress levels (as measured by corticosterone release) after both acute and chronic cocaine administration (Festa et al., 2003; Hu & Becker, 2003; Hu, Robinson, & Becker, 2006). These animal studies indicate a biological basis for addiction through a combination of factors including sex differences in neurotransmission and pharmacokinetics (i.e., how the body handles the drug) (Lynch, Roth, & Carroll, 2002; Becker, 1999; Carroll et al., 2004). Additionally, extensive literature shows the effect of hormones such as estrogen and progesterone in modulating the brain activity important during cocaine use and affecting toxicity of cocaine differently in males and females (Becker & Hu, 2008). Evidence from animal models also indicates that chronic cocaine administration can lead to menstrual cycle disruptions and amenorrhea (loss of menses) in females (Mello et al., 1997). The translation of this research to human populations remains an important yet complex task for addiction researchers.

Serious social consequences also adversely affect female drug users. Among illicit drug users, women experience a higher risk of physical and sexual assault (Silverman et al., 2001), although men experience more legal problems associated with drug use than women (Su et al., 1997). Infections with the hepatitis C virus and HIV are also serious health consequences of drug use, and more than half of AIDS cases in women in the United States are related to injection drug use either through personal use or sex with an injection drug user, compared with 31 percent of cases among men (Schneider et al., 2006). Interestingly, in contrast to other substances in which women have greater health risks following prolonged use, men may be at greater risk for ischemic stroke from chronic cocaine abuse, although there is some evidence to refute this (Petitti et al., 1998).

In conclusion, the harmful long-term effects of alcohol, nicotine, and illicit drugs are different between men and women. Typically, women exhibit more harmful effects of substance use disorders, including increased disease and death. More research into the consequences of illicit drug use in human populations is necessary, but animal models show robust sex differences in every phase of drug self-administration, suggesting that biological factors may affect the consequences of drug use. Regardless, research indicates the necessity of prevention and treatment efforts specifically addressing the needs of substance-using women.

See also **Fetal Alcohol Syndrome; Pregnancy and Drug Dependence; Women and Substance Abuse.**

BIBLIOGRAPHY

Becker, J. B. (1999). Gender differences in dopaminergic function in striatum and nucleus accumbens. *Pharmacology, Biochemistry, and Behavior, 64*, 803–812.

Becker, J. B., & Hu, M. (2008). Sex differences in drug abuse. *Frontiers in Neuroendocrinology, 29*, 36–47.

Borelli, B., Spring, B., Niaura, R., Hitsman, B., & Papandonatos, G. (2001). Influences of gender and weight gain on short-term relapse to smoking in a cessation trial. *Journal of Consulting and Clinical Psychology, 69*, 511–515.

Brady, K. T., Grice, D. E., Dustan, L., & Randall, C. (1993). Gender differences in substance use disorders. *American Journal of Psychiatry, 150*, 1707–1711.

Carroll, M. E., Lynch, W. J., Roth, M. E., Morgan, A. D., & Costrove, K. P. (2004). Gender and hormones influence drug abuse. *Trends in Pharmacological Sciences, 25*, 273–279.

Cepeda-Benito, A., Reynoso, J. T., & Erath, S. (2004). Meta-analysis of the efficacy of nicotine replacement therapy for smoking cessation: Differences between men and women. *Journal of Consulting and Clinical Psychology, 72*, 712–722.

Coles, C. D., Kable, J. A., Drews-Botsch, C., & Falek, A. (2000). Early identification of risk for effects of prenatal alcohol exposure. *Journal of Studies on Alcohol, 61*, 607–616.

Conway, K. P., Compton, W., Stinson, F. S., & Grant, B. F. (2006). Lifetime comorbidity of *DSM-IV* mood and anxiety disorders and specific drug use disorders: Results from the National Epidemiologic Survey on Alcohol and Related Conditions. *Journal of Clinical Psychiatry, 67,* 247–257.

Craig, D., Parrott, A., & Coomber, J. (1992). Smoking cessation in women: Effects of the menstrual cycle. *International Journal of the Addictions, 27,* 697–706.

Deal, S. T., & Gavaler, J. S. (1994). Are women more susceptible than men to alcohol-induced cirrhosis? *Alcohol Health and Research World, 18,* 189–191.

Etter, J. F., Prokhorov, A. V., & Perneger, T. V. (2002). Gender differences in the psychological determinants of cigarette smoking. *Addiction, 97,* 733–743.

Festa, E. D., Jenab, S., Chin, J., Gazi, F. M., Wu, H. B. K., Russo, S. J., et al. (2003). Frequency of cocaine administration affects behavioral and endocrine responses in male and female Fischer rats. *Cellular and Molecular Biology, 49,* 1275–1280.

Hanna, E. Z., Chou, S. P., & Grant, B. F. (1997). The relationship between drinking and heart disease morbidity in the United States: Results from the National Health Interview Survey. *Alcoholism, Clinical and Experimental Research, 21,* 111–118.

Hommer, D. W., Momenan, R., Kaiser, E., & Rawlings, R. R. (2001). Evidence for a gender-related effect of alcoholism on brain volumes. *American Journal of Psychiatry, 158,* 198–204.

Hu, M., & Becker, J. B. (2003). Effects of sex and estrogen on behavioral sensitization to cocaine in rats. *Journal of Neuroscience, 23,* 693-699.

Hu, M., Crombag, H. S., Robinson, T. E., & Becker, J. B. (2006). Biological basis of sex differences in the propensity to self-administer cocaine. *Neuropsychopharmacology, 29,* 81–85.

Jacobson, S. W., & Jacobson, J. L. (2000). Teratogenic insult and neurobehavioral function in infancy and childhood. In C. A. Nelson (Ed.), *The Minnesota symposia on child psychology* (Vol. 31). The effects of early adversity on neurobehavioral development (pp. 61–112). Mahwah, NJ: Lawrence Erlbaum.

Johnston, L. D., O'Malley, P. M., Bachman, J. G., & Schulenberg, J. E. (2007). Monitoring the Future national survey results on drug use, 1975–2006: Volume I, Secondary school students (NIH Publication No. 07-6205). Bethesda, MD: National Institute on Drug Abuse.

Kesmodel, U., Wisbor, K., Olsen, S. F., Henriksen, T. B., & Secher, N. J. (2002) Moderate alcohol intake during pregnancy and the risk of stillbirth and death in the first year of life. *American Journal of Epidemiology, 155*(4), 305–312.

Kessler, R. C., Nelson, M. B., McGonagle, K. A., & Edlund, M. J. (1996). The epidemiology of co-occurring addictive and mental disorders: Implications for prevention and service utilization. *American Journal of Orthopsychiatry, 66*(1), 17–31.

Key, J., Hodgson, S., Omar, R. Z., Jensen, T. K., Thompson, S. G., Boobis, A. R., et al. (2006). Meta-analysis of studies of alcohol and breast cancer with consideration of the methodological issues. *Cancer Causes Control, 17*(6), 759–770.

Klatsky, A. L., Armstrong, M. A., & Friedman, G. D. (1992). Alcohol and mortality. *Annals of Internal Medicine, 117,* 646–654.

Leventhal, A. M., Waters, A. J., Boyd, S., & Moolchan, E. T. (2007). Gender differences in acute tobacco withdrawal: Effects on subjective, cognitive, and physiological measures. *Experimental and Clinical Psychopharmacology, 15*(1), 21–36.

Lieber, C. S. (1997). Gender differences in alcohol metabolism and susceptibility. In R. W. Wilsnack & S. C. Wilsnack (Eds.), *Gender and alcohol: Individual and social perspectives* (pp. 77–89). Piscataway, NJ: Rutgers Center for Alcohol Studies.

Lynch, W. J. (2006). Sex differences in vulnerability to drug self-administration. *Experimental and Clinical Psychopharmacology, 14*(1), 34–41.

Lynch, W. J., Roth, M. E., & Carroll, M. E. (2002). Six differences in drug abuse: Preclinical and clinical studies. *Psychopharmacology, 164,* 121–137.

Mello, N. K., Mendelson, J. H., Kelly, M., Diaz-Migoyo, N., & Sholar, J. W. (1997). The effects of chronic cocaine self-administration on the menstrual cycle in rhesus monkeys. *The Journal of Pharmacology and Experimental Therapeutics, 281,* 70–83.

Mello, N. K., Mendelson, J. H., & Palmieri, S. L. (1987). Cigarette smoking by women: Interactions with alcohol use. *Psychopharmacology, 93,* 8–15.

Petitti, D. B., Sidney, S., Quesenberry, C., & Bernstein, A. (1998). Stroke and cocaine or amphetamine use. *Epidemiology, 9*(6), 587–588.

Prescott, E., Hippe, M., Schnohr, P., Hein, H. O., & Vestbo, J. (1998). Smoking and risk of myocardial infarction in women and men: Longitudinal population study. *British Medical Journal, 316,* 1043–1047.

Regier, D. A., Farmer, M. E., Rae, D. S., Locke, B. Z., Keith, S. J., Judd, L. L., et al. (1990). Comorbidity of mental disorders with alcohol and other drug abuse: Results from the epidemiologic catchment area (ECA) study. *Journal of the American Medical Association, 264*(19), 2511–2518.

Schneider, E., Glynn, M. K., Kajese, T., McKenna, M. T., Division of HIV/AIDS Prevention, National Center for HIV/AIDS, Viral Hepatitis, STD and TB

Prevention (proposed), CDC. (2006). Epidemiology of HIV/AIDS—United States, 1981–2005. *Morbidity and Mortality Weekly Report, 55*(21), 589–592

Schweinsburg, B. C., Alhassoon, O. M., Taylor, M. J., Gonzalez, R., Videen, J. S., Brown, G. G., et al. (2003). Effects of alcoholism and gender on brain metabolism. *American Journal of Psychiatry, 160,* 1180–1183.

Sharf, D., & Shiffman, S. (2004). Are there gender differences in smoking cessation, with and without bupropion? Pooled- and meta-analyses of clinical trials of Bupropion SR. *Addiction, 99,* 1462–1469.

Silverman, J. G., Raj, A., Mucci, L. A., & Hathaway, J. E. (2001). Dating violence against adolescent girls and associated substance use, unhealthy weight control, sexual risk behavior, pregnancy, and suicidality. *Journal of the American Medical Association, 286,* 572–579.

Sokol, R. J., Delaney-Black, V., & Nordstrom, B. (2003). Fetal alcohol spectrum disorder. *Journal of the American Medical Association, 290*(22), 2996–2999.

Su, S. S., Larison, C., Ghadialy, R., Johnson, R. A., & Rohde, F. (1997). *Substance use among women in the United States.* Rockville, MD: Substance Abuse and Mental Health Services Administration; SAMHSA Analytic Series A-3.

Wilcox, A. J. (1993). Birthweight and perinatal mortality: The effect of maternal smoking. *American Journal of Epidemiology, 137,* 1098–1104.

Zang, E. A., & Wynder, E. L. (1996). Differences in lung cancer risk between men and women: Examination of the evidence. *Journal of the National Cancer Institute, 88,* 183–192.

KATHERINE M. KEYES
DEBORAH S. HASIN

GENE.

A gene is a unit of heredity that confers some trait or function on the organism. Most genes are thought to be essential to development and normal functioning. Genes are often a primary determinant of interpersonal differences; for example, they determine whether you have blue or brown eyes. A disrupted or mutated gene can cause serious, even fatal problems. Genes are composed of DNA and found in the chromosomes in the nucleus of a cell. At present, we are on the verge of identifying all the human genes due to the efforts of the genome projects.

See also **Chromosome.**

BIBLIOGRAPHY

Cummings, M. (2008). *Human heredity: Principles and issues.* Belmont, CA: Brooks Cole.

Maldonado, R., Ed. (2002). *Molecular biology of drug addiction.* Totowa, NJ: Humana Press.

MICHAEL J. KUHAR

GENE REGULATION: DRUGS.

A gene, made of DNA, is transcribed to produce a messenger RNA (mRNA), which is then translated to produce a protein product. *Gene regulation* refers to alterations in the production of mRNA from a gene.

All cells of an organism contain the same genes, but not every gene is turned on (producing its mRNA) at all times. During development, different cell types and organs are generated by the selective expression of genes. Likewise, during adulthood, altered expression of genes within mature neurons mediates their ability to adapt to the environment. Such gene regulation is thought to play a crucial role in mediating positive adaptations (e.g., learning, therapeutic response to an antidepressant medication, or psychotherapy), as well as maladaptations associated with disease states (e.g., pathological responses to drugs of abuse or stress).

Gene regulation in neurons is governed by highly complex processes. DNA exists in the neuron's nucleus within chromatin, where the DNA is wrapped around complexes of histone proteins; these DNA-histone units are called nucleosomes. Genes present within tightly packed nucleosomes are inactive because they are inaccessible to the enzymatic machinery required for mRNA transcription. In contrast, genes become active when the nucleosomes become less tightly packed. This occurs when specialized proteins, called transcription factors, bind to specific sequences of DNA present within the regulatory (promoter) regions of genes. Transcription factors recruit enzymes to the genes which modify the nearby histones (e.g., by acetylation), which causes further loosening of the nucleosomes. Genes are then inactivated when other enzymes remove the acetyl groups from the histones, allowing restoration of more tightly packed nucleosomes. Transcription factors can cause the opposite effects when they bind to other responsive genes and inhibit gene function by reducing histone acetylation and tightening nucleosomes.

This highly simplified summary of gene regulation provides a context within which individuals can begin to appreciate how a drug of abuse alters gene regulation in the brain. After a drug is taken, it enters the brain where it interacts with its initial protein target (e.g., the dopamine transporter for cocaine or mu opioid receptor for opiates); binding to the target alters the activity of endogenous neurotransmitter systems (dopamine or opioids), which alters the activity of postreceptor signaling proteins. These proteins signal to the neuron's nucleus where they alter the activity and levels of particular transcription factors. The transcription factors then bind to the promoters of certain genes, which increases or decreases the rate at which the genes produce their mRNAs, which ultimately changes the levels of protein products in the neurons. In this manner, drugs of abuse change the biochemical composition of individual neurons in the brain and cause profound changes in brain function that underlie key aspects of drug addiction.

An example of this process is the transcription factor, ΔFosB. Administration of virtually any type of drug of abuse causes the induction of a small amount of ΔFosB in important brain reward regions. Unlike most proteins, ΔFosB is highly stable, which means that repeated administration of the drug leads to the gradual accumulation of ΔFosB. As ΔFosB accumulates within the neurons, it binds to an increasing number of gene promoters where it can either increase or decrease transcription of those genes' mRNAs. Increasing evidence indicates that such ΔFosB-mediated gene regulation creates a state of heightened reward, which promotes further drug use. This research raises the interesting possibility that medications that block ΔFosB may be useful in the treatment of addiction. To determine if this is, in fact, true will require much further research. Nevertheless, studies of gene regulation offer novel insight into the molecular basis of addictive states and the hope that such knowledge will be mined one day to develop more effective treatments and possibly even cures for drug addiction.

See also **Neurotransmitters.**

ERIC J. NESTLER

GENOME PROJECT. The Human Genome Project started in 1990 with the goal of sequencing the entire human genome and the genomes of five model organisms: bacterium (*Escherichia coli*), yeast (*Saccharomyces cerevisiae*), nematode (*Caenorhabditis elegans*), fruit fly (*Drosophila melanogaster*), and mouse (*Mus musculus*). The human genome is the complete set of deoxyribonucleic acid (DNA, the genetic material) in a typical human cell; it is approximately three billion nucleotides, contained in 22 pairs of autosomal chromosomes, two sex chromosomes (X and Y), and the mitochondrion. The human genome contains all of the genetic information needed for the development of a human from a single cell. The human genome is diploid, meaning there are two copies of each chromosome, which are nearly, but not completely, the same. The original target for the Human Genome Project was to get a reference sequence that would represent a haploid copy (equivalent to one copy of each chromosome).

The Human Genome Project, by generating the genome sequence and knowledge of genetic variations and stimulating development of technologies that allow one to measure the variations present in an individual, has greatly stimulated research to find which genes contain variations that can affect the risk for contracting complex diseases such as alcoholism and other addictions, diabetes, and various cancers. Continuing work on annotating the genome (i.e., determining which sequences encode genes or other functional elements) and understanding the functions of many sequences is necessary; it will further aid in finding and understanding how genetic variations affect these diseases.

The Human Genome Project was an international effort that drove advances in DNA sequencing technology and the computational tools to analyze the vast amounts of data generated. Projects to explore how the genetic information might have an impact on individuals and society were also part of the effort. The initial goals of creating genetic and physical maps of the genome were completed early in the process and contributed to the ability to map genes whose variations affect the risk for diseases. The public genome project adopted a strategy based on mapping the genome, creating a "tiling path" of overlapping large clones (a set of clones, primarily bacterial artificial chromosomes, which overlap and extend from one end of each chromosome to the other), and then sequencing those large clones by fragmenting them and cloning them in smaller pieces; the final challenge was to assemble the data based upon the physical map. The public genome project put sequence data into the public domain as they were generated and made the data available to all through the Internet, along with tools to allow analyses. This allowed scientists to use the data in real time and accelerated progress in many areas of genetic research. A competing private project by Celera Genomics developed a "whole genome shotgun approach" that involved fragmenting the genome into pieces of different sizes, sequencing both ends of the cloned fragments, and assembling the data computationally based in part on the known distance between paired reads. The competition stimulated an earlier than expected completion of the project. The human genome was declared completed in April 2003, the 50th anniversary of the determination of the structure of DNA by James Watson and Francis Crick.

Researchers now have the sequence of nearly all of the three billion base pairs that make the haploid human genome, although some repetitive regions are missing due to technical issues. The reference human genome sequences—both from the public project and from Celera—are mosaics, each derived from several individuals. Since then, new techniques and strategies have allowed sequencing of the diploid genome of some individuals, which has revealed additional sequences and some structural variations. A new target is to develop technology that permits the sequencing of individual genomes at low cost.

Understanding the genome and annotating the sequence is a major project that will take many more years. The data have already provided surprises, such as finding that there are fewer than 25,000 human genes (although there are disagreements about how to recognize and count genes). More recent studies, enabled by the genome sequence, have shown that alternative splicing (whereby different forms of messenger ribonucleic acid [mRNA] are produced from the same DNA template, leading to different protein products) is far more widespread than initially thought and generates a much greater number of proteins from this small number of genes. The fact that a small number of genes can lead to the great

complexity that characterizes the human species suggests that gene regulation at both transcriptional and post-transcriptional levels plays a crucial role in the development and maintenance of an organism.

Many new genes have been identified from the genome sequence, and families of genes have been recognized. There is much work remaining, including discovering the function of the vast majority of the DNA, which does not code for proteins. Comparative genomics, in which genome sequences from other organisms are determined, is an important tool in this effort. Comparing these genomes to each other and to the human genome is contributing greatly to the task of recognizing new genes and understanding the function of the sequences.

Evolutionary conservation is one way to recognize functionally important sequences. The original design for the genome project included sequencing genomes of the five model organisms listed above as tests of the methods, to assist research on these widely studied organisms, and for comparative analyses. Comparative genomics has been greatly enhanced by the tremendous drop in the cost of sequencing that resulted from the genome project, and many additional genomes have been sequenced. As of April 2008, 464 eukaryotic genome sequencing projects were completed or underway. Information on these can be found online at the National Center for Biotechnology Information: National Institutes of Health Web site.

Another extension of the Human Genome Project has been the search for genetic variability among humans. An international effort called the HapMap project has discovered millions of positions in the genome that differ from one individual to another. Genomes of many individuals are now being sequenced in whole or in part in the "1000 Genomes Project" to discover more genetic variations, including variations in the number of copies of some regions. These data are important for projects designed to find genetic variations that are related to the risk for diseases.

Complex diseases, including alcohol and drug dependence, result from the interplay of genetic variation and the environment. No two individuals, except identical twins, have exactly the same genome sequence. In fact, there are more than six million differences between a pair of randomly chosen individuals. While many of these variations have no functional significance, some affect the sequence of proteins or the regulation of their expression. The reference sequences, catalogs of variations, and technologies to measure these variations that resulted from the Human Genome Project have tremendously aided the search for the variations that affect disease.

See also **Risk Factors for Substance Use, Abuse, and Dependence: Genetic Factors.**

BIBLIOGRAPHY

Collins, F. S., Patrinos, A., Jordan, E., Chakravarti, A., Gesteland, R., Walters, L., & the members of the U. S. Department of Energy (DOE) and the National Institutes of Health (NIH) planning groups. (1998). New goals for the U.S. human genome project: 1998–2003. *Science, 282,* 682–689.

International HapMap Project. (2008, April 14). Available from http://www.hapmap.org.

International Human Genome Sequencing Consortium. (2004). Finishing the euchromatic sequence of the human genome. *Nature, 431,* 931–945.

National Center for Biotechnology Information: National Institutes of Health. (2008, April 14). *Genome project.* Available from http://www.ncbi.nlm.nih.gov/.

National Human Genome Research Institute: National Institutes of Health. (2008, April 7). *All about the human genome project (HGP).* Available from http://www.genome.gov/.

Venter, J. C., Adams, M. D., Myers, E. W., Li, P. W., Mural, R. J., Sutton, G. G., et. al. (2001, February 16). The sequence of the human genome. *Science, 291,* 1304–1351.

HOWARD J. EDENBERG

GERMANY. In the geographic area that became Germany, tobacco entered society first and foremost as an addition to the pharmacopoeia in the sixteenth century. Its recreational use was frowned upon and restricted through legislation, and many German states issued edicts against smoking throughout the eighteenth century. Despite this, smoking (mostly pipe smoking) spread, paralleling a rise in drinking. Prior to the nineteenth century, the most popular alcoholic beverage was beer. Distilled spirits were the preserve of wealthier sections of society or used for festive occasions. After the Napoleonic wars, however, disastrous harvests limited the grain available for beer production. The potato provided a substitute and, with depressed agricultural conditions, there was a surplus of potatoes that could be converted to spirits. Between 1806 and 1831, the consumption of spirits tripled, becoming widespread among the laboring poor. There was a close connection between inadequate nutrition and drinking, as spirits provided a source of calorific energy. There was also a popular perception that alcohol had medicinal properties.

Between 1855 and 1873, per capita consumption of spirits increased nearly 50 percent, while that of beer doubled. This increase was a result of rising real incomes during the Industrial Revolution. Alcohol was one of the few consumer goods available to the lower classes at the time. The consumption of tobacco also rose, particularly as cigars became popular. By 1878 there were just under 4,000 cigar manufacturers in Germany. These were small-scale, family-owned businesses, and production was labor intensive. The main types of tobacco consumed were heavier Oriental tobaccos; consumers were male; and cigars were everyday, as opposed to luxury, items.

The turn of the twentieth century saw the cigarette grow in popularity as a result of mechanized production. This growth threatened to overtake cigar consumption, and the German government sought to protect the labor-intensive cigar industry through differential taxation. In 1906, cigarettes became subject to a revenue seal (meaning that an additional duty had to be paid), following the imposition of a similar revenue seal on *sekt* (sparkling wine) in 1902. Taxation underwent various changes during the First World War and the Great Depression of the 1930s, but cigars remained more favorably taxed than cigarettes. Thus, cigar consumption maintained parity with cigarette consumption until after the Second World War. In 1938, 36.8 percent of tobacco was made into cigars, 34.9 percent into cigarettes, and 28.3 percent into other tobacco articles.

HOSTILITY TO SMOKING AND DRINKING
Beginning in the 1820s, increased alcohol consumption among the laboring poor gave rise to middle-class fears about drunkenness. The temperance movement began in America but spread across Britain and through the Protestant states of northern Germany as part of a wave of religious revival, which fitted within *Bürgertum* (bourgeoisie) ideals of self-help through personal discipline. The first German temperance

association was formed in 1830 in Hamburg. An estimated 600,000 adult men took the pledge by 1846, and more than 1,250 organizations were founded. The 1848 revolutions saw a decline in the popularity of temperance, however, as other social causes became more dominant. Further, poor harvests in 1846 and 1847 limited supply and made alcohol more expensive.

The temperance movement reemerged in the 1880s, following concerns about the pervasive nature of drinking in working-class life. There were also sporadic publications against smoking. In 1910 the *Bund Deutscher Tabakgegner* (Alliance of German Anti-Tobacconists) was established through an amalgamation of earlier German-language antismoking organizations. Critics saw youth smoking and drinking as a particular threat, for young people were not seen to be developed enough to tolerate nicotine, while drinking was seen as a sign of waywardness. Antismoking movements were overshadowed by anti-alcohol movements, but both merged with ideologies of racial and social hygiene. Proponents of hereditary theories correlated alcohol with degenerative diseases, criminality, and prostitution. Such beliefs led to calls for the compulsory sterilization of alcoholics.

In 1934, the main German agency against alcoholism, the *Deutsche Reichstelle gegen den Alkoholismus*, became part of government efforts to fight addiction, and in 1939 the *Reichstelle gegen die Alkohol und Tabakgefahren* (Reich Agency against the Dangers of Alcohol and Tobacco) was formed by the National Socialist regime. Here, the aims of the anti-alcohol and the antismoking movements coalesced with Nazi ideology, and the *Reichstelle gegen die Alkohol und Tabakgefahren* issued propaganda against smoking and drinking. In addition, many states passed legislation prohibiting youth smoking. The government funded smoking research, building on the first studies linking smoking with lung cancer in the late 1930s. Measures against alcoholics were more sinister, with the creation of a register of alcoholics, compulsory sterilization under the 1933 Sterilization Law, and some alcoholics being sent to concentration camps. By the early 1940s the regime had shied away from antismoking measures because of tobacco shortages and the hostility that the restrictive measures aroused. Anti-alcohol campaigns also had little success, and consumption rose throughout the period.

CHANGES IN ADDICTIONS AFTER THE SECOND WORLD WAR

After the Second World War, the tobacco market underwent a drastic change due to shortages of German and Oriental tobacco and the availability of American cigarettes through the black market. Within five years, West German tastes had changed toward lighter Virginian cigarettes, which assumed prominence in the market. From the 1950s onward, per capita consumption, particularly of cigarettes, grew annually. For health reasons, filter cigarettes were particularly popular, and by 1956 around half the smoking population had switched to a filtered brand. Through the 1950s, around 10 percent of population income was spent on alcohol and tobacco, with the larger proportion of this money being spent on alcohol.

The West German government followed a relatively liberal line on smoking and drinking, believing it was up to adults to make decisions about their own consumption. The government therefore focused its attention on young people. In the 1950s, with increased disposable income and more freedom, the proportion of young people smoking increased to over half of the young men and 15 percent of the young women in the nation. This increase was seen by youth protection agencies as a psychological reaction to the trauma of the immediate postwar period and the breakdown of the traditional family, for many men were either killed or took several years to return from POW camps. The *Deutsche Gesundheitsmuseum* issued two booklets on the dangers of smoking in the 1960s, as well as a film, *Der Tod gibt eine Party* (Death gives a Party), which aimed to shock.

Drinking was also seen as a problem. With the inception of the *Bundeszentrale für Gesundheitliche Aufklärung* (BZgA, the Federal Agency for Health Education) in 1967, more funding became available for health education, and campaigns against smoking and drinking intensified. Television advertising of cigarettes was stopped in 1970 on a voluntary basis by the tobacco companies, although the subject of press and poster advertising remained hotly debated until 2006, when Germany finally adopted an EU resolution prohibiting tobacco advertising. For much of the second half of the twentieth century, the German government maintained a close relationship with the tobacco industry, which was generally held to have stalled progress in promoting antismoking policies. The early twenty-first century has seen tax increases and moves toward restricting smoking in public places.

DRUGS

In contrast to the use of alcohol and tobacco, drug use in West Germany began to assume its current dimensions only in the early 1970s, when the "drug wave" occurred. This "wave" came in the wake of an increase in the use of cannabis, speed and heroin during the mid- to late 1960s. Previously, drug use had been most apparent in those with a therapeutic addiction to morphine, and in the cocaine use that was part of Weimar nightlife. The postwar expansion of drug use in West Germany emerged from two social trends: (1) the growth of the nation's youth as a distinct cultural category due to increasing financial independence, and (2) increased mass consumption, particularly of so-called *Genußmittel* (luxury goods), such as alcohol and tobacco.

The drug scene in West Germany emerged later than in other Western countries, but it was shaped by the same forces: rock and roll, unprecedented disposable income, and a context of international cultural exchange. The development of a drug "scene" varied from city to city and from region to region. Throughout the nation, "beat clubs" dominated as places where young people could congregate away from adults and listen to music from the United Kingdom and the United States, as well as from Germany. In Hamburg, the key area was along the Reeperbahn; in Berlin it was the Kurfürstendamm; in Munich, the Nikolaiplatz. A contributing factor was the disaffection some young people felt with postwar affluence and capitalism. These were the so-called *Gammler*, or "drop outs," who drifted from city to city, or country to country, seeking new experiences, smoking hashish, and using LSD. West Germans traveled in search of an alternative lifestyle and immigrants entered West Germany in search of a better standard of living, and this increased travel and tourism opened up drug routes from the Far East.

By the early 1970s, amid a climate of public fear about drug use, the authorities rushed through amendments to *Betäubungsmittelgesetz*, the main law dealing with drug trafficking and use. These amendments increased the sentences for the trafficking and posession of drugs to three years, and for major offenses the penalty increased to ten years; in 1983 the maximum penalties were increased to four years and fifteen years, respectively. The medical profession supported punitive measures against drug use, as did the police and youth protection agencies. Nonetheless, a rapid growth in drug use occurred throughout the 1970s and 1980s. By 1989 it was estimated that around 100,000 people were regular drug users. The main problem had become heroin, however, rather than cannabis and LSD. In addition, the space occupied by the drug scene expanded. In 1987, for example, Frankfurt's downtown drug scene covered a square mile and involved over 5,000 people dealing and using drugs.

In the late 1960s and 1970s, drug use, like smoking and drinking, was seen primarily as a youth protection issue. As well as penalizing drug use, the government, through the BZgA, funded and ran health education programs. The goal of such campaigns was to raise awareness of drug misuse, but the drug problem was clearly set in the context of wider patterns of deviant behavior and seen to be a failure of upbringing. Campaigns not only targeted young people, but also those with a responsibility for their education and upbringing. Adults were addressed in their capacity as drug consumers (of alcohol, tobacco, and over-the-counter pharmaceuticals), and the consequences of their own drug use was brought to their attention. Thus, problematic drug use was conceived and addressed in broad terms by targeting addiction in general, rather than one drug in particular. Young people were also targeted through popular culture. The youth magazine *Bravo* carried educational articles on drug use, commenting in a January 4, 1971, article titled "Tödliche Träume" ("Deadly Dreams") that "ever more young people are sucked into the drug wave," and warning, through teenage examples, of the dangers of hash and LSD. The magazine also set up advice centers in major cities.

The focus of intervention changed in the 1980s with the appearance of HIV infection among intravenous drug users. HIV/AIDS threatened the general public, as well as the users, and (as in other countries) this forced a paradigmatic shift in health policy. The threat of HIV led to a policy of harm reduction, with less emphasis on punitive legislation.

Needle-exchange programs began in the mid-1980s, providing and delivering clean needles to users, and "injecting rooms," also known as "health rooms," were established to provide a clean and safe environment for drug injection. These were initially clandestine operations, but they were legalized in 1999. Further, by the 1990s, methadone substitution programs had been put in place to combat the dangers from black market and potentially adulterated drug use. Such substitution programs initially faced political opposition, but by 1995 over 1,000 drug users in Frankfurt were participating in a methadone program, and these programs expanded in urban centers. From 1984 onward, the number of drug-related deaths declined, though they began to rise again in 2007. The use of drugs such as methamphetamine and cocaine also increased, and by 2008 around 200,000 people were using opiates, cocaine, amphetamines, and hallucinogenics.

By 2008, the focus of concern about addiction had shifted back to alcohol. The annual drugs report (*Drogen und Sucht Bericht*, 2008, published by the Bundesministerium für Gesundheit) noted a decrease in the number of young people using cannabis and tobacco, but it also reported an alarming rise in alcohol consumption, binge drinking, and the number of hospital admissions from alcohol poisoning, particularly among young people. Around 600,000 people, mostly young people, were found to be regular cannabis users, but fewer were taking up the substance. Smoking also declined among young people, from 28 percent to 18 percent between 2000 and 2007. In 2008 the German government was preparing a national campaign against alcohol consumption, with a particular focus on the nation's youth.

See also **Alcohol: History of Drinking in the United States; Alcohol: History of Drinking (International); Club Drugs; European Union; Foreign Policy and Drugs; Injecting Drug Users and HIV; International Drug Supply Systems; Temperance Movement; Tobacco: An International Overview.**

BIBLIOGRAPHY

Drogen und sucht bericht. (2008). Bundesministerium für Gesundheit. Bonn, Germany: Publisher.

Fischer, B. (1995). Drugs, communities, and "harm reduction" in Germany: The new relevance of "public health" principles in local responses. *Journal of Public Health Policy, 16*(4), 389–411.

Hengartner, T. and Merki, C. (Eds.). (1996). *Tabakfragen: Rauchen aus kulturwissenschaftlicher sicht.* Zürich: Chronos.

Proctor, R. N. (1999). *The Nazi war on cancer.* Princeton, NJ: Princeton University Press.

Roberts, J. S. (1984). *Drink, temperance, and the working class in nineteenth-century Germany.* Boston: Allen & Unwin.

Scheerer, S. (1978). The new Dutch and German drug laws: Social and political conditions for criminalization and de-criminalization. *Law and Society Review, 12*, 585–606.

Spode, H. (1993). *Die macht der trunkenheit: Kultur- und sozialgeschichte des alkohols in Deutschland.* Opladen: Leske & Budrich.

Stephens, R. (2003). Drugs, consumption, and internationalization in Hamburg, 1960–1968. In D. F. Crew (Ed.), *Consuming Germany in the cold war*, 179–207. Oxford: Berg.

ROSEMARY ELLIOT

GINSENG. Ginseng is the most revered and well-known plant of Chinese herbal medicine; it is sold over the counter in Asian apothecaries and groceries worldwide. This plant of the family Araliaceae grows on both sides of the Pacific, with *Panax schinseng* the Asian form and *Panax quinquefolius* the North American form. It is a perennial herb with five-foliate leaves, and its fleshy aromatic root is valued as a tonic and a medicine.

Figure 1. Ginseng. ILLUSTRATION BY GGS INFORMATION SERVICES. GALE, CENGAGE LEARNING

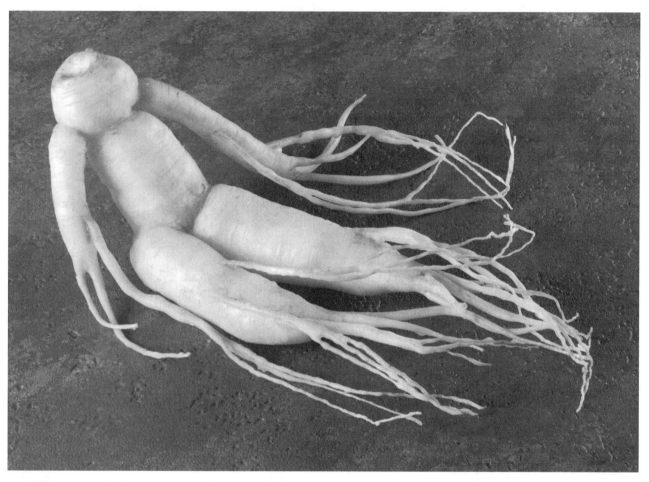

Ginseng root. FOODFOLIO/ALAMY.

The root has been used by Native Americans, Siberians, Chinese, and other Asians for millennia. Usually it is taken as a tea—once a day as a general preventative tonic, more frequently for therapeutic purposes. Since the North American form is considered the most potent, it is now grown in Asia along with the local variety. American ginseng is also exported to Asia, then sometimes reimported into the United States as a Chinese or Korean herbal. Both the wild and cultivated forms are used. Roots older than five years are needed for good effect, and the older and larger the root (seven to fifteen years is prized), the more the ginseng costs. Dried roots are heated and sliced thinly to make tea, but pieces may be kept in the mouth, sucked, and eaten. The many ginseng products now sold (sodas, candies, etc.) have no real tonic or therapeutic value.

Ginseng has a bittersweet aromatic flavor, contains alkaloids, and is said to be good for mental arousal and general well-being. It has not been established in Western medicine and pharmacology, although it contains properties that might be isolated and used pharmacologically.

See also **Plants, Drugs From.**

BIBLIOGRAPHY

Lewis, W. H. (2005). *Medical botany: Plants affecting human health.* Hoboken, NJ: John Wiley & Sons.

Taylor, D. (2006). *Ginseng, the divine root: The curious history of the plant that captivated the world.* Chapel Hill, NC: Algonquin Books.

MICHAEL J. KUHAR

GLUTAMATE. Glutamate (GLU) is a dicarboxylic aliphatic amino acid, the chemical symbol for which is COOH-CH$_2$-CH$_2$[NH$_2$]-COOH. It is abundant in all cells of the body. In many neurons (nerve cells) glutamate is packaged into synaptic vesicles and serves as an excitatory neurotransmitter in the brain. Once released as a transmitter, glutamate binds to both ionotropic (containing an ion channel) and metabotropic (signaling through intracellular second messengers) receptors and is removed or sequestered by a high-affinity uptake system that transports glutamate into both neurons and glia. As the primary excitatory neurotransmitter in the brain, glutamate, along with other neurotransmitter systems, regulates most behaviors, including emotional and cognitive perceptions. Accordingly, a role for glutamate has been proposed in a variety of pathologic conditions, ranging from schizophrenia and addiction to Alzheimer's and Parkinson's diseases. Consequently, developing drugs that regulate glutamate neurotransmission has become a high priority. Drug development is focusing on agonists and antagonists at glutamate receptors. In addition to neuronal receptors, it is now clear that release and elimination of glutamate by glial cells (non-neuronal cells that serve a variety of brain functions) represents a critical homeostatic function in regulating glutamate neurotransmission. These mechanisms are also emerging as targets for medications to treat brain-related disorders.

See also **Dopamine.**

BIBLIOGRAPHY

Parsons, C. G., Danysz, W., & Zieglgansberger, W. (2005). Excitatory amino acid neurotransmission. *Handbook of Experimental Pharmacology, 169,* 249–303.

PETER W. KALIVAS

GLUTETHIMIDE. Glutethimide was introduced into clinical medicine in 1954. It was prescribed to treat insomnia and sold as Doriden. It was first acclaimed as a safer "nonbarbiturate" hypnotic—implying that it was free of the problems of abuse, addiction, and withdrawal that were, by then, recognized drawbacks of the older barbiturate sedative-hypnotics. Within ten years, however, it was recognized that, in most respects, its actions are like those of the barbiturates and it shares the same disadvantages.

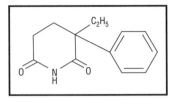

Figure 1. Chemical structure of glutethimide. ILLUSTRATION BY GGS INFORMATION SERVICES. GALE, CENGAGE LEARNING

Glutethimide is structurally related to the barbiturate drugs and, like the short–acting barbiturates, it depresses or slows the central nervous system. Side effects from its proper use are relatively minor, but a rash is often seen. Like barbiturates, it can produce intoxication and euphoria; tolerance and dependence can result with daily use. Glutethimide is metabolized somewhat differently than barbiturates, and overdose is often far more difficult to treat than barbiturate overdose; fatalities are not uncommon. As a consequence of this and its abuse potential, glutethimide is included in Schedule III of the Controlled Substances Act. Since the introduction of the benzodiazepines to treat short–term insomnia, the use of glutethimide has decreased considerably.

See also **Barbiturates; Sedatives: Adverse Consequences of Chronic Use.**

BIBLIOGRAPHY

Hanson, G. R., Venturelli, P. J., & Fleckenstein, A. E. (2005). CNS depressants: Sedative-hypnotics. In *Drugs and Society.* Sudbury, MA: Jones & Bartlett Publishers.

Harvey, S. C. (1975). Hypnotics and sedatives: Miscellaneous agents. In L. S. Goodman & A. Gilman (Eds.), *The pharmacological basis of therapeutics* (5th ed.). New York: Macmillan. (Brunton, L., et al. [2005]. 11th ed. New York: McGraw-Hill Medical.)

SCOTT E. LUKAS

GOLDEN TRIANGLE AS DRUG SOURCE. Opium, the sap of the opium poppy (*Papaver somniferum* Linnaeus), is a bitter, brownish, and sticky substance. This alkaloid-rich and addictive narcotic drug has been known to humanity since time immemorial. Between the early 1950s and the early 1990s—that is, before Afghanistan's opium production surpassed that of Burma—most of the world's illicit opium originated in the so-called Golden Triangle, the name given to the area of Mainland Southeast Asia known for its large illicit opium production. (The Union of Burma was renamed "Myanmar" on June 25, 1989, by the military dictatorship then known by the acronym SLORC [State Law and Order Restoration Council]. This name change was recognized by the United Nations and a number of countries, including France, but not by others, such as the United Kingdom and the United States.)

The Golden Triangle is located in the highlands of the fan-shaped relief of the Indochinese peninsula, where the international borders of Burma, Laos, and Thailand intersect. Opium poppy cultivation has taken place in the border regions shared by the three countries since the mid-nineteenth century, and it developed considerably beginning in the 1950s. However, this production receded markedly in the 1990s, and it is now confined to the Kachin and Shan States of northern and northeastern Burma, along the borders of China, Laos, and Thailand.

ABOUT THE GOLDEN TRIANGLE

The Golden Triangle is not only an isolated mountainous and heavily forested area overlapping the contiguous and outlying border areas of three countries, it is also populated by many extremely diverse ethnic groups, many of them tribal and semi-nomadic slash-and-burn agriculturalists. In fact, the international borders of Burma, Laos, and Thailand also cut across two zones that are intricately woven together: the Tai linguistic zone, composed of Shan, Thai, and Lao peoples, over which is superimposed a more complex zone of numerous other ethnic groups that are dispersed throughout the three-border area and in neighboring China.

The term *Golden Triangle* was coined by the Assistant Secretary of State Marshall Green of the United States during a press conference on July 12, 1971. Referring to a polygon whose angles could be found in Burma, Laos, and Thailand, where opium production was indeed concentrated, Green implicitly acknowledged (and probably rightly so) the absence of large-scale commercial opium production in China. Once the world's main opium producing country, China drastically reduced poppy cultivation and opium trade after the Communist victory in 1949. Green's exclusion of China from the so-called Golden Triangle was all the more necessary because it was made three days prior to the announcement by President Richard Nixon of his official visit to the People's Republic of China in February 1972. This was the first visit of a U.S. president to Communist China.

In addition to being a politically grounded geographic reference, the term *Golden Triangle* also refers to one of the region's most important economic features: opium production. Mainland Southeast Asia became a major source of opium over the course of the second half of the twentieth century. According to the Swedish journalist and veteran Burma-watcher Bertil Lintner, the first traders in the three-border region—especially those of the Thai-Burmese border towns of Mae Sai (northernmost Thailand) and Tachilek (Shan State, eastern Burma)—reportedly exchanged the precious substance for 99 percent pure gold ingots. Such reports inspired the name, Golden Triangle.

TRENDS IN POPPY CULTIVATION AND OPIUM PRODUCTION

Opium production in Mainland Southeast Asia has always been concentrated in the three-border region, where rugged hills and mountains, heavy monsoon rains, and a lack of transportation infrastructure have long protected rebel armies and illicit crops from the writ of central governments and national and international antidrug agencies. Yet after decades of expansion of poppy cultivation in the three countries, opium production has progressively receded—it almost completely disappeared from Thailand in the 1990s, and it seriously decreased in Laos during the early 2000s. Poppy cultivation has diminished, concentrating in northern and northeastern Burma, where it had originated in the mid-nineteenth century. Although Burmese opium production has also considerably decreased since 1998, it has nevertheless proven to be extremely geographically and historically resilient.

Burma's turbulent political history since its independence from Britain in 1948 can clearly be held responsible for Asia's longest illicit opium production. The opium economy and the war economy have clearly nurtured one another in a country that has suffered an internal war for over sixty years (the Karen National Union [KNU] has fought Burma's central government since the country's independence). Indeed, as an extremely valuable economic resource, opium has often enabled warring factions to fund their respective war efforts. Opium production has also weighed upon strategic negotiations, offering both state and nonstate actors opportunities to gain political leverage or create ad hoc strategic alliances. For instance, the Burmese government has continually integrated opium into its negotiation strategy so as to affect power struggles, something that some antigovernment forces have directly or indirectly benefited from.

Yet Burma's opium production progressively decreased between the mid-1990s and the mid-2000s, dropping from a record of 1,791 tons in 1993 to only 315 tons in 2006, according to the United Nations Office on Drugs and Crime. But production surged to 460 tons in 2007, mostly as an economic consequence of hasty and uncompensated opium bans. In fact, opium production in Burma abated not as a result of central government policies but as a consequence of bans issued by the leaders of three of the private armies controlling the country's largest opium-producing areas: Shan State's Special Region 4 (Mong La) in 1997, Special Region 1 (Kokang) in 2003, and Special Region 2 (Wa) in 2005. Yet opium is still produced in Burma, the world's second largest illicit opium producing country after Afghanistan (in 2007, Afghanistan produced 8,200 tons, 18 times more than Burma). In the mid-2000s, Burmese opium is still mostly produced in southern Shan State, where poppy acreage has increased in 2005, 2006, and 2007, when 65 percent of Burma's poppies were cultivated in South Shan State and 25 percent were cultivated in East Shan State. Parts of Kachin State and Kayah State also produce opium in significant quantities. In 2007, after years of decline, the overall Burmese opium production increased by 46 percent, due to higher yields than in 2006 and a 29 percent increase in opium poppy cultivation.

METHAMPHETAMINE PRODUCTION
While opium production ebbed in Burma from the mid-1990s on, methamphetamine production quickly developed, especially in Shan State. Methamphetamine is a synthetic drug that is classified as an amphetamine-type stimulant (ATS). It is known as *yaa baa* ("madness drug") in Thailand, where consumption developed considerably after the mid-1990s and especially in the early 2000s. During this period, between 500 and 800 million *yaa baa* pills were reportedly produced on a yearly basis in Burma. These pills were then trafficked to consuming countries such as Thailand and China.

In November 2000, the head of the Thai National Security Council identified drug trafficking as the major threat to Thailand's national security. Various Thai officials blamed the situation on neighboring Burma and denounced Rangoon's "narcotic aggression" against Thailand. *Yaa baa* seizures doubled between 1996 and 1997 (to 1.5 tons), between 1997 and 1998 (to 2.8 tons), and again in 1999 (to 4.5 tons). During the same period, heroin seizures declined by almost 30 percent, with only 511 kilograms confiscated in 1998. This increase in *yaa baa* trafficking coincided with an increase in violence along the Thai-Burma border, where numerous incidents of varying intensity led to major crises between the two countries.

Upon taking office in February 2001, Thailand's prime minister, Thaksin Shinawatra, vowed to prevent and suppress both drug trafficking and drug consumption in the kingdom. On February 1, 2003, he launched a nationwide "war on drugs" aimed at making the country drug-free within three months. His government crackdown resulted in the seizure of 40 million *yaa baa* pills; the arbitrary arrest of 92,500 drug addicts, 43,000 dealers, and 750 drug producers and importers; and the unexplained killing of more than 2,500 persons. Although the Thai government claimed that the operation had been a "victory beyond expectation," Thaksin called for a second "war" in October 2004. Of course, in 2008, methamphetamine trafficking and consumption had not disappeared from Thailand. In fact, the trend was in the opposite direction, as the 2008 launch of a new "war on drugs" indicates.

DRUG TRAFFICKING ROUTES OF MAINLAND SOUTHEAST ASIA
Since the emergence of the Golden Triangle, opiate trafficking has followed the main caravan axes of Southeast Asia and southern China. Indeed, Chinese opium was already being exported to Southeast Asia at the end of the nineteenth century, when Chinese production was double the amount of

imports forced onto the Chinese Empire by the British. The Haw (Chinese Muslims), the Hmong, and the other tribal populations who migrated from China to Southeast Asia played an important role in spreading opium production in the Indochinese peninsula, and they had a positive impact on the emergence of the Golden Triangle by perpetuating a few trafficking and contraband routes. The caravan tracks of the Haw, which crisscrossed Siam (modern-day Thailand) very early, played a large role in turning Thailand into a privileged hub of heroin trafficking after World War II.

Thailand remained the main heroin trafficking route in Southeast Asia until the early 1990s. However, a number of factors have contributed to the reorientation of drug trafficking routes within Southeast Asia, and to the development of new routes to other parts of the continent. The Thai crackdown on heroin trafficking that took place after the 1984 nationwide opium eradication campaign considerably reduced the use of its well-developed road system by smugglers and traffickers from the Thai-Burma border. Subsequent patrols of the northern and northwestern Thailand borders by the Thai Third Army and the Border Patrol Police also disrupted the routes across the Thai-Burma border used by opium and heroin traffickers. While China is now certainly the main transshipment destination for heroin from Burma, it is not the only one, as northeast India also draws some of the traffic.

In the late 1990s, the diversification of drug trafficking routes increased, as did the diversification of illicit drug production. The explosion of methamphetamine production in Burma has led to a resurgence in use of the Thai route, for Thailand is by far the first consumer market of *yaa baa* in the region. *Yaa baa* traffickers differ from others in that they are more numerous and carry small quantities of pills across the Thai-Burma border. They form what Thai authorities have referred to as an "ant army," crisscrossing the border along countless hill paths and using small tribal villages as staging posts. The strong crackdown led by the Thai army and police in the early 2000s in the northernmost part of the country has recently diverted the flux of methamphetamine, pushing traffickers to use new itineraries.

The roads of Laos are frequently used for transporting illicit drugs bound for Thailand, even though drug trafficking aboard speedboats along the Mekong River—which demarcates the international border between the two countries—is the first choice. Further south along the Thai border and lower on the Mekong, Cambodia is also increasingly used as a staging point for trafficking methamphetamine into Thailand. Vietnam has similarly been turned into a drug trafficking route, either from or to China; overseas trafficking is frequently organized from Vietnamese seaports. While most (80%) of the drugs entering Thailand still allegedly come across the northern part of the Thai-Burma border, the constant strengthening of Thai antidrug actions has clearly fostered a wide diversification of drug trafficking routes, as well as a diminution of the quantity of drugs being transported at any one time.

See also **Crop Control Policies; Foreign Policy and Drugs, United States; International Drug Supply Systems.**

BIBLIOGRAPHY

Booth, M. (1998). *Opium: A History.* New York: St. Martin's Press.

Chouvy, P.-A. (2002). *Les territoires de l'opium: Conflits et trafics du Triangle d'Or et du Croissant d'Or.* Geneva: Olizane.

Chouvy, P.-A., and Meissonnier, J. (2004) *Yaa Baa: Production, Traffic, and Consumption of Methamphetamine in Mainland Southeast Asia.* Singapore: Singapore University Press.

Lintner, B. (1994). *Burma in Revolt: Opium and Insurgency since 1948.* Boulder, CO: Westview Press.

McCoy, A. W. (2003). *The politics of heroin: CIA complicity in the global drug trade—Afghanistan, Southeast Asia, Central America, Colombia* (3rd ed.). New York: Lawrence Hill Books.

Renard, R. D. (1996). *The Burmese connection: Illegal drugs and the making of the Golden Triangle.* Studies on the Impact of the Illegal Drug Trade, Vol. 6. Boulder, CO: Lynne Rienner.

United Nations Office on Drugs and Crime. (2007). *World drug report 2007.* Vienna: UNODC.

PIERRE-ARNAUD CHOUVY

HAIR ANALYSIS AS A TEST FOR DRUG USE.

Because every drug taken becomes a permanent part of the user's hair, laboratory analysis of hair can reveal the presence of a variety of drugs including opiates, cocaine, amphetamines, phencyclidine, marijuana, nicotine, and barbiturates. Hair analysis is widely used and accepted by courts, law enforcement bureaus, and government agencies. It is used for a variety of purposes including employment screening, determination of maternal or fetal drug exposure, and validating self-reports of drug use (Kintz, 1996; Harrison & Hughes, 1997).

Unlike urinalysis, which can only detect comparatively recent drug ingestion (e.g., depending on the drug, between days and weeks), hair analysis can reveal the ingestion of drugs during the past ninety days or even longer. Because head hair grows at a relatively constant rate of one-half inch (1 cm) (1 inch = 2.54 cm) per month, segmental analysis of hair strands could localize the period of drug exposure to within as little as one particular week. Although various hair treatments such as tinting and perming may affect test readings, detectable traces are indelible in the hair (Kintz, 1996).

DRUGS IN HAIR

Hair is nonliving tissue composed primarily of a sulfur-rich protein called keratin. Hair grows from the follicle (a saclike organ in the skin) at a rate of 0.3 to 0.4 millimeters (0.011 to 0.012 inches) per day in cycles of active growth followed by a resting phase.

For an adult, approximately 85 percent of scalp hair is in the growing stage at any time. Two sets of glands are associated with the follicle: the sebaceous glands, which excrete sebum (a waxy substance), and the apocrine glands, which excrete an oil that coats the hair. Hair color is determined by genetic programming for varying amounts of melanin, a pigment that is synthesized in hair cells called melanocytes.

Although the exact mechanism by which drugs and drug metabolites are incorporated into hair is still unknown, they enter into hair by multiple processes. Drugs and drug metabolites may be deposited from the capillaries, which supply blood to the follicles, or they may be excreted in the sebum, oil, or sweat that coats the hair shafts. Drugs can also be deposited on the hair by environmental exposure (such as marijuana smoke or cocaine powder in the air) (Kintz, 2008).

When hair is analyzed for drug use a sample is taken from either the head or another part of the body. It's washed to remove dirt and any external drug deposits (the wash medium is also tested) then stripped of melanin. The actual analysis is performed by radioimmunoassay, which detects not only traces of drugs but their metabolites, breakdown products that appear only when the body has metabolized the drug. All positive samples are confirmed by gas chromatography/mass spectrometry (GC/MS). This second test has a cutoff level to eliminate specimens containing drug levels that could come from environmental exposure such as inhaling second-hand marijuana smoke or eating food that contains poppy seeds (Kintz, 1996).

SIGNIFICANCE OF HAIR DRUG TESTING

Once a drug is embedded in hair it appears to be stable indefinitely although its concentration diminishes somewhat over time. Cocaine metabolite, for example, has been detected in hair from a pre-Columbian mummy more than 500 years old. This is an obvious advantage over other methods of drug testing such as urinalysis, which can detect drugs ingested only within the past few days or weeks. Depending on the length of the hair, analysis can determine that drug use has occurred from months to years. Hair is also easily collected and stored. If more testing is required another sample may be easily obtained. One disadvantage of hair analysis is that it will not reveal drug use during the three to five days before testing since hair does not grow quickly enough to show this. Urine testing can thus be used to complement the results of hair analysis. Hair analysis is also more expensive than urinalysis and the results take longer to be determined.

CONTROVERSY

Hair drug testing techniques have been greatly improved over time. However, quantitative detection of some drugs and their metabolites—particularly THC, the major active component of cannabis—is still considered difficult (Uhl & Sachs, 2004).

Some groups have raised concerns that hair testing may be biased against minority populations such as African Americans. Multiple cross-comparison studies between self-report and hair testing on cocaine demonstrate discrepancies to be correlated with hair color (Ledgerwood et al., 2008). A number of in vitro experiments show that hair samples from different gender and racial groups incorporate differing amounts of drugs under identical conditions (Kidwell et al., 2000). Hair testing labs claim that their processes, which remove melanin from samples, eliminate any chance of distinction or discrimination by race or ethnic group. Combining urinalysis and hair testing may be needed to assess a more complete profile of the individual's past and present drug use for forensic and occupational applications.

See also **Industry and Workplace, Drug Use in; Military, Drug and Alcohol Abuse in the United States.**

BIBLIOGRAPHY

Harrison, L., & Hughes, A. (1997). The validity of self-reported drug use: Improving the accuracy of survey estimates. *NIDA Research Monograph, 167* (NIH Publication No. 97–4147).

Kidwell, D. A., Lee, E. H., & DeLauder, S. F. (2000). Evidence for bias in hair testing and procedures to correct bias. *Forensic Science International, 107,* 39–61.

Kintz, P. (Ed.). (1996). *Drug testing in hair.* Boca Raton, FL: CRC Press.

Kintz, P. (2008). Drug testing in hair. In A. J. Jenkins (Ed.) *Forensic science and medicine: Drug testing in alternate biological specimens,* (pp. 67–81). Totowa, NJ: Humana Press.

Ledgerwood, L. M., Goldberger, B. A., Risk, N. K., Lewis, C. E., & Price, R. K. (2008). Comparison between self-report and hair analysis of illicit drug use in a community sample of middle-age men. *Addictive Behaviors.* Available from http://www.science-direct.com.

Uhl, M., & Sachs, H. (2004). Cannabinoids in hair: Strategy to prove marijuana/hashish consumption. *Forensic Science International, 145,* 143–147.

EDWARD J. CONE
REVISED BY AMY LOERCH STRUMOLO (2001)
RUMI KATO PRICE (2009)
BRUCE A. GOLDBERGER (2009)

HALLUCINATION. The word *hallucinate* is derived from the Greek *halyein,* meaning "to wander in mind." Hallucinations are perceptions that occur in the absence of a corresponding external sensory stimulus. They are experienced by the person who has them as immediate, involuntary, vivid, and real. They may involve any sensory system, and hence there are several types of hallucinations: auditory, visual, tactile (e.g., sensations on the skin), olfactory (smell), and gustatory (tastes). Visual hallucinations range from simple (e.g., flashes of light) to elaborate visions. Auditory hallucinations can be noises, a voice, or several voices carrying on a conversation. In command hallucinations, the voices often order the person to do things that at times involve acts of violence.

Hallucinations have been a hallmark of mental illness throughout history. They are an important clinical feature of several psychiatric conditions in which psychosis can occur, such as schizophrenia, manic-depressive illness, major depression, and dissociative states. Withdrawal from alcohol can cause visual as well as other sensory hallucinations. In alcoholic hallucinosis, a person dependent on alcohol develops mainly auditory hallucinations that can persist after the person has stopped drinking. Hallucinations may be induced by illicit drugs, such as cocaine, amphetamines, and LSD. These hallucinations are usually visual, but they can also be auditory or tactile, as in the sensation of insects crawling up the skin (an example of a haptic hallucination). Occasionally, after repeated ingestion of drugs, some people experience "flashbacks"—that is, spontaneous visual hallucinations during a drug-free state, often months or years later.

The cause of hallucinations is not known, but it is likely to be multifactorial through a combination of physiological, biological, and psychological variables. Numerous hypotheses have been proposed. According to a perceptual release theory, hallucinations develop from the combined presence of intense states of psychological arousal and decreased sensory input from the environment (e.g., sensory deprivation) or a reduced ability to attend to the sensory input (e.g., in delirium). This leads to the emergence of earlier images and sensations that are interpeted as originating in the environment. Other researchers suggest that abnormalities in brain cell excitability or in the information processing system of the central nervous system cause hallucinations. Biochemical theories implicate brain neurotransmitters such as dopamine. Drugs that block brain dopamine activity (antipsychotics) alleviate hallucinations, whereas drugs that stimulate dopamine release induce hallucinations.

Hallucinations can occur in people who are not mentally ill. In acute bereavement, some people report seeing or hearing the deceased. Sensory, sleep, food, and water deprivation can produce hallucinations, as can the transition from sleep to wakefulness and vice versa (called hypnopompic and hypnogogic hallucinations, respectively). These hallucinations can occur as side effects of prescribed medications, such as drugs that treat cardiac conditions, or in various medical disorders (e.g., migraines, Parkinson's disease, infections). They have been described in persons with hearing loss and blindness; in these instances, it has been hypothesized that they may be due to chronic sensory deprivation.

The treatment of hallucinations is part of the treatment of the entire psychotic syndrome. Antipsychotic medications (e.g., haloperidol, chlorpromazine) are effective in reducing and often eliminating hallucinations. When the hallucinations are part of a medical disorder, it is necessary to correct the underlying condition, or remove the causative agent, in addition to prescribing antipsychotic medication.

See also **Complications: Mental Disorders; Delirium Tremens (DTs); Hallucinogenic Plants; Hallucinogens.**

BIBLIOGRAPHY

Aleman, A., & Laroi, F. (2008). *Hallucinations: The science of idiosyncratic perception*. Washington, D.C.: American Psychological Association.

Asaad, G., & Shapiro, B. (1986). Hallucinations: Theoretical and clinical overview. *American Journal of Psychiatry, 143*, 9, 1088–1097.

Burton, N. L. (2006). *Psychiatry*. Malden, MA: Blackwell Publishing.

Yager, J. (1989). Clinical manifestations of psychiatric disorders. In H. I. Kaplan & B. J. Saddock (Eds.), *Comprehensive textbook of psychiatry* (5th ed.). (Vol. 1). Baltimore: Williams & Wilkins. (2004, 8th ed.)

MYROSLAVA ROMACH
KAREN PARKER

HALLUCINOGENIC PLANTS.

Literally hundreds of hallucinogenic substances are found in many species of plants. For example, a variety of mushrooms contain indole-type hallucinogens, the most publicized being the Mexican or "magic" mushroom, *Psilocybe mexicana*, which contains both the hallucinogenic compounds psilocybin and psilocin, as do some of the other *Psilocybe* and *Conocybe* species. The peyote cactus (*Lophophra williamsii* or *Anhalonium lewinii*), which is found in the southwestern United States and northern Mexico, contains mescaline. The seeds of the morning glory, *Ipomoea*, contain hallucinogenic lysergic acid derivatives, particularly lysergic acid amide. Many of these plants and plant by-products were and are used during religious ceremonies by Native Americans and other ethnic groups.

Some plant substances may contain prodrugs, that is to say, compounds that are chemically altered in the body to produce psychoactive substances. For example, nutmeg contains elemicin and myristicin, whose structures have some similarities to the hallucinogen mescaline as well as the psychostimulant amphetamine. It has been hypothesized that elemicin and myristicin might be metabolized in the body to form amphetamine-and/or mescaline-like compounds, but this has not been proven. The fact that hallucinogenic substances are found in nature does not mean that they are safer or purer than compounds that have been synthesized in the laboratory. Some common edible mushrooms that can be purchased in any supermarket may be sprinkled with LSD or other hallucinogens to be misrepresented as magic mushrooms. In addition, serious problems—even death—may occur when species of hallucinogenic plants are misidentified and people mistakenly ingest highly toxic plants, such as poisonous mushrooms.

See also **Ayahuasca; Ibogaine; Jimsonweed; Plants, Drugs From.**

BIBLIOGRAPHY

Efron, D. H., Holmstedt, B., & Kline, N. S., Eds. (1979). *Ethnopharmacologic search for psychoactive drugs.* New York: Raven Press.

Lewis, W. H. (2005). Hallucinogens. In *Medical botany: Plants affecting human health.* Hoboken, NJ: John Wiley & Sons.

Siegel, R. K. (1989). *Intoxication.* New York: Dutton.

Spinella, M. (2005). *Concise handbook of psychoactive herbs.* New York: Haworth Press.

Weil, A. (1972). *The natural mind: An investigation of drugs and the higher consciousness.* Boston: Houghton Mifflin. (1998, rev. ed.)

DANIEL X. FREEDMAN
R. N. PECHNICK

Figure 1. Belladonna. ILLUSTRATION BY GGS INFORMATION SERVICES. GALE, CENGAGE LEARNING

HALLUCINOGENS. Hallucinations are audio, visual, and temporal distortions. Hearing or seeing things that do not really exist or feeling that time has slowed down, sped up, or ceased altogether are typical hallucinations. *Seeing* sounds, *hearing* colors, and perceiving that still objects are moving are other examples of hallucinations. Out-of-body experiences also may be considered hallucinations. Of course, these things actually do not happen, but are the result of chemical reactions that alter the way the brain perceives information from the senses. These reactions may occur naturally when an individual goes through periods of illness, pain, hunger, or fatigue. Hallucinations may be produced also through ingesting particular substances.

Seeing pink elephants after drinking alcohol (though perhaps more appropriately associated with alcohol withdrawal) is an enduring image within U.S. culture. Inhaling large doses of marijuana or hashish may make users feel as if they were viewing the world through dream-like spectacles. Binge-use—whereby individuals consistently use drugs over several days without rest—of stimulants, such as cocaine (powder and crack) and crystal methamphetamine, has been associated with paranoia and delusions. Alcohol, heroin, and opiate withdrawal have also been linked with delirium. Even drinking excess cough syrup may cause the user to see, hear, or feel things that do not actually exist. While all of these substances may produce hallucinations, none is classified as a hallucinogen.

A review of the literature and Web sites indicates that hundreds of drugs, legal and illicit, natural and synthetic, are hallucinogens (Shulgin & Shulgin, 1991, 1997). An exhaustive review of these hallucinogens is beyond the scope of this entry. Rather, the focus here is on some well- and lesser-known hallucinogens that are consumed for recreational purposes—that is, for pleasure. These can be broken down into three rough categories: tryptamines, phenethylamines, and dissociative anesthetics.

TRYPTAMINES: LSD, PSILOCYBIN, AND DMT

Perhaps the most popular hallucinogens are LSD (lysergic acid diethylamide, commonly referred to as *acid*) and psilocybin *magic* mushrooms. These drugs fall under the category *tryptamine*. Recreational use of LSD and psilocybin was introduced widely into popular culture during the 1960s and 1970s, with LSD associated particularly with hippie counterculture (Yablonsky, 1968). Both drugs enjoyed a renaissance during the late 1980s and through the 1990s with the advent of underground rave culture (Sanders, 2006). Rave culture was commercialized across the United States in the 1990s and into the new millennium. Raves are dance parties where electronic dance music is played, often together with laser light shows, projected images, and artificial fog. During this same time period, rates of LSD and psilocybin use rose, particularly among young people (Hunt, 1997). The rise in popularity of raving and clubbing within popular culture and the reported increases in LSD and psilocybin among youth most likely influenced one another. The effects of LSD and psilocybin complement the rave/club atmosphere with its loud, bass heavy music, flashing lasers, disco lights, and colorful outfits worn by the clubbers (Sanders, 2006). To an extent, these drugs fit with this culture.

Another less well-known tryptamine, with a history of recreational use, is N, N-dimethyltryptamine, or DMT. DMT is one of the active ingredients in ayahuasca, a plant and bark mixture that has been used for sacramental purposes among people in South America for thousands of years and relatively recently among Westerners seeking novel psychedelic experiences (McKenna, 2004; Rushkoff, 1994). Hallucinations resulting from ingesting ayahuasca may be many hours long. In contrast, the hallucinations from using DMT by itself may be much shorter—perhaps 10 to 20 minutes depending on the dosage. The recreational use of DMT, whether organic or synthesized, dates back to at least the 1960s, when it was referred to

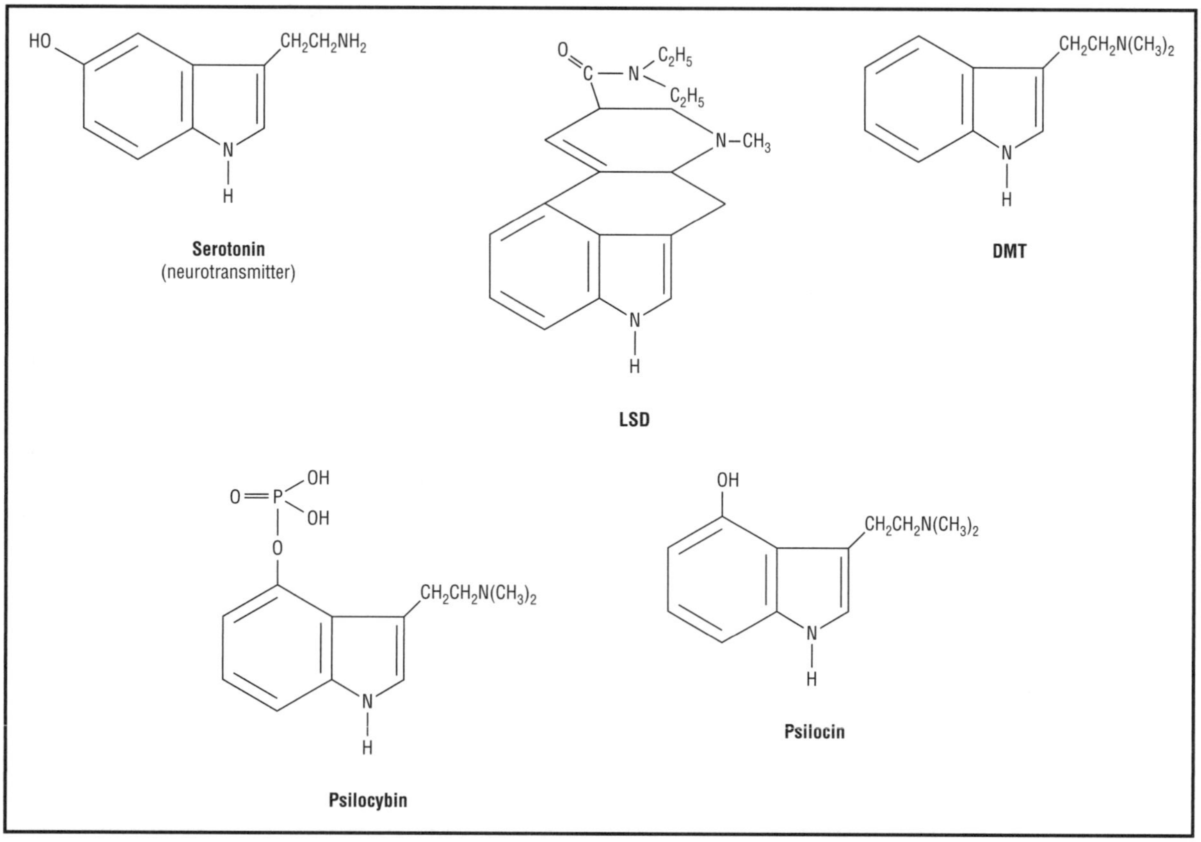

Figure 2. Indole-type hallucinogens. ILLUSTRATION BY GGS INFORMATION SERVICES. GALE, CENGAGE LEARNING

as "the businessman's lunch" because an individual could use the drug, feel its effects, and then return to a relatively normal state within a short time period, such as a lunch break (Halpern, 2004).

Other hallucinogens within the tryptamine family include alpha-methyltryptamine (AMT), diisopropyltryptamine, (DIPT), and their 5-methoxy (i.e., 5-MEO) counterparts (e.g., 5-MEO-AMT and 5-MEO-DIPT). Other tryptamines include N,N-dipropyltryptamine (DPT), N-isopropyl-N-methyltryptamine (MIPT), 4-hydroxy-N,N-diisopropyltryptamine (4-HO-DIPT), and many more (Shulgin & Shulgin, 1997). Similar to DMT, these drugs are dose-sensitive and are measured in milligrams, because tiny amounts may cause very powerful hallucinations lasting anywhere from 15 minutes to 24 hours or more. Very few accounts of these drugs have emerged within the research literature, though DMT and 5-MEO-DIPT, also known as *Foxy*, have been reported within rave and club culture (Sanders, 2006; cf. Measham, 2004).

PHENETHYLAMINES: MESCALINE, MDMA AND 2C-B

Other hallucinogens fall under the category *phenethylamine*. One relatively well-known hallucinogenic phenethylamine is mescaline. Mescaline occurs naturally in several types of cacti, but is most associated with peyote. Mescaline has a long history of recreational use, and reports of human use for sacramental purposes can be traced back millennia. Scientists in 2005 reported on the discovery of prehistoric peyote use in humans, dating to around 3700 BCE (El-Seedi et al., 2005).

MDMA is a stimulant-hallucinogenic phenethylamine. Commonly expressed feelings after using MDMA are empathy and euphoria; the street name of the drug is *ecstasy*. Ecstasy has been considered the club drug par excellence because of its tight association with rave and club culture (Shapiro, 1999; Sanders, 2006). Similar to LSD and psilocybin, the effects of ecstasy reportedly work well with rave culture environments. Moreover, prior to the emergence of raving in popular culture, ecstasy was relatively unheard of, so the rise of ecstasy use among youth has somewhat paralleled the rise of rave and club culture.

Other phenethylamines include hallucinogens within the *2C* series, such 2C-B (4-bromo-2, 5-dimethoxyphenethylamine), 2C-E (2,5-dimethoxy-4-ethyl-phenethylamine), and 2C-T-7 (2,5-dimethoxy-4-(n)-propylthiophenethylamine). Additional hallucinogenic phenethylamines are DOI (2,5-dimethoxy-4-iodoamphetamine) and DOB (2,5-dimethoxy-4-bromoamphetamine). Analyses of people's use of these drugs within the research literature are limited (Carmo et al., 2005). However, 2C-B, also

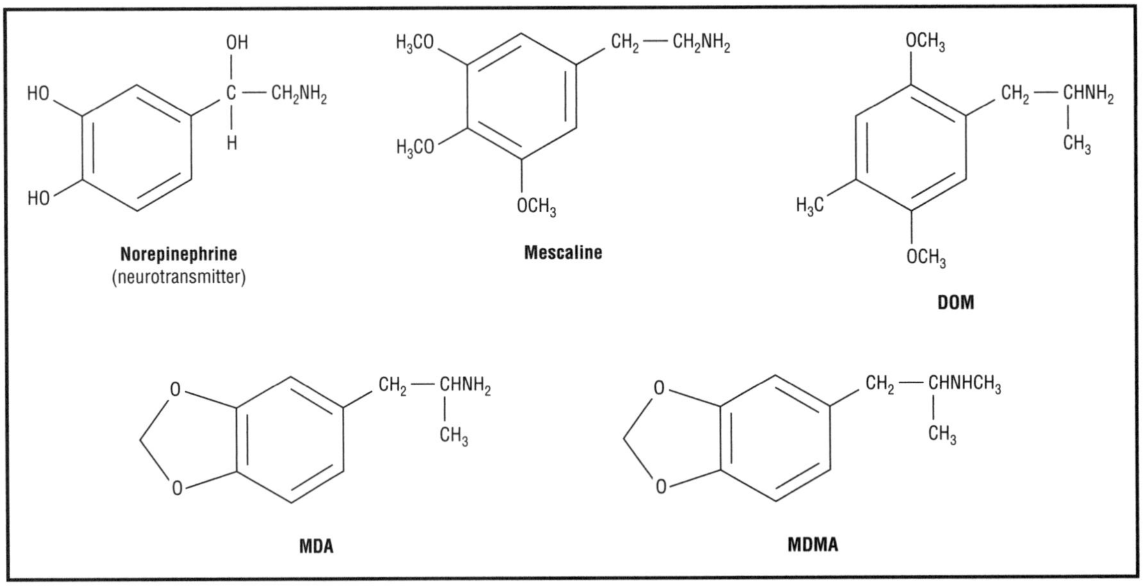

Figure 3. Substituted phenethylamines. ILLUSTRATION BY GGS INFORMATION SERVICES. GALE, CENGAGE LEARNING

known as *Nexus*, has been reported in rave and club culture (Sanders, 2006; Sanders et al., 2008), and qualitative experiences from users can be found on Internet Web sites (www.lycaeum.org; www.erowid.org). Reported dosages of these drugs are measured in milligrams, with the effects lasting up to several hours.

DISSOCIATIVE ANESTHETICS: PHENCYCLIDINE AND KETAMINE

Phencyclidine (PCP) and ketamine are chemically analogous substances that are considered dissociative anesthetics. Both were first designed for use as general anesthetics, and both can make users feel disconnected or detached from their bodies or their minds, which may include out-of-body experiences. Both PCP and ketamine use in humans was discontinued after adult patients described horrific nightmares and visions while sedated (Lankenau, 2006; Wish, 1986). Ketamine is used widely in veterinary practices, hence the street names of *cat* or *horse* tranquilizer in reference to the drug (Lankenau & Sanders, 2007).

PCP may come in liquid form, whereby users smoke cigarettes, *joints* or *blunts*, pre-soaked with PCP. PCP can also be used as a dry powder, suggesting a variety of other administrations (e.g., sniffing, injecting). PCP use has been linked with violence (Wish, 1986). Some academic findings, though, suggest the relationship between PCP use and violence may be overstated (Brecher et al., 1988; Hoaken & Stewart, 2003).

Ketamine has been considered a *club drug*, because of its association with rave and club culture, where it is often used with other drugs (Lankenau & Clatts, 2005). Using enough ketamine may produce what is referred to as the *K-hole*, distorted feelings of space and time and colorful visions (Lankenau, 2006). Ketamine may be administered intramuscularly—within a muscle—a relatively unique administration for any recreationally used substance.

LAWS AND POTENTIAL THERAPEUTIC VALUES

Certain hallucinogens are legal and may be purchased over the counter from particular shops in the United States as well as from businesses selling them on the Internet. One such drug is Salvia divinorum, a plant within the mint family. The psychoactive ingredient of the plant is called *salvinorin A* and is commonly sold under the name *Salvia* in extracts of various strengths.

In a report on the use of uncommon tryptamines and phenethylamines, youth purchased a variety of these drugs legally over the Internet where they were sold as "research chemicals" (Sanders et al., 2008; cf. Halpern & Pope, 2001; Kikura-Hanajiri et al., 2005; McCandless, 2004). Moreover, a variety of plants and fungi that naturally grow in the United States and that are legal to possess contain illegal substances that can be extracted (Halpern, 2004; McKenna, 2004).

Some tryptamines and phenethylamines have been illegal for many years, though other chemically analogous substances that produce roughly similar effects are not, for instance, tryptamine DMT. DMT is a Schedule I drug in the United States—the same legal status as heroin or crack cocaine—and is illegal to use. However, its chemical cousin, 5-MEO-DMT, is legal to use. Likewise, the phenethylamine 2C-B has been a Schedule I drug since 1994, but a related drug, 2C-I, may still be used legally. Under the Analogue Statute of the Controlled Substance Act, though, the trafficking of any substances chemically analogous to scheduled tryptamines and phenethylamines is illegal. In other words, while it remains legal to use 5-MEO-DMT, 2C-I and a host of other similar drugs, selling them is illegal.

Alexander Shulgin synthesized hundreds of tryptamines and phenethylamines (Shulgin & Shulgin, 1991, 1997). Dr. Shulgin predicted that by the year 2060, over a thousand similar hallucinogens would be discovered (Biello, 2008). A reason to highlight these potential findings is the therapeutic qualities of some hallucinogens.

The Multidisciplinary Association for Psychedelic Studies (MAPS) has been conducting research for many years into the use of certain hallucinogens among humans in the search for cures for many mental and physical health conditions. A visit to their Web site indicates a variety of lines of inquiry. For instance, researchers have been involved in studies examining the utility of MDMA, or ecstasy, to treat patients suffering from post-traumatic stress disorder; the drug could also be used to relieve anxiety and pain in end-stage cancer patients

(Check, 2004; Sessa, 2005). Researchers are also examining the use of psilocybin and LSD to alleviate cluster headaches (Sewell et al., 2006). Other researchers have examined the use of psilocybin to achieve spiritual significance and personal meaning (Griffiths et al., 2006). Ketamine has been used to treat chronic pain associated with Reflex Sympathetic Dystrophy (see Harbut & Correll, 2002).

An additional utility of some hallucinogens is their potential for treatment of drug and alcohol addiction. Ibogaine—a very powerful hallucinogen—is one such drug. Ibogaine is illegal in the United States, though legal in many other countries, and dozens of clinics worldwide have used ibogaine in the treatment of addiction (Vastag, 2005). Ketamine, as well, has been used effectively in the treatment of heroin addiction (Krupitsky et al., 2002). Many findings on the medicinal qualities of hallucinogens have emerged in the early 2000s, and the potential therapeutic utility of those, which are yet unexplored, is promising.

SUMMARY

Hallucinogens include a variety of psychoactive substances that produce audio, visual, and temporal distortions commonly referred to as hallucinations. Hundreds of substances have hallucinogenic properties, though common and relatively unique hallucinogens discussed here can be broken down into three general categories: tryptamines (LSD, psilocybin, DMT), phenethylamines (mescaline, MDMA, 2C-B) and dissociative anesthetics (phencyclidine (PCP), ketamine). Hallucinogens were once popular within hippie culture in the 1960s and 1970s, and enjoyed a renaissance within rave/club culture from the 1990s into the new millennium. Many hallucinogens are illegal to use or possess, though others are not. Some hallucinogens also have medicinal qualities that have been proven to be effective remedies for a variety of ailments affecting physical and mental health.

See also **Ayahuasca; Complications: Mental Disorders; Hallucinogenic Plants; Ibogaine; Plants, Drugs From.**

BIBLIOGRAPHY

Biello, D. (2008, March 20). Self-experimenters: Psychedelic chemist explores the surreality of inner space, one drug at a time. *Scientific American.* Available from http://www.sciam.com/.

Brecher, M., Wang, B. W., Wong, H., & Morgan, J. P. (1988). Phencyclidine and violence: Clinical and legal issues. *Journal of Clinical Psychopharmacology, 8,* 397–401.

Carmo, H., Hengstler, J. G., de Boer, D., Ringel, M., Remiao, F., Carvalho, F., et al. (2005). Metabolic pathways of 4-bromo-2,5-dimethoxyphenethylamine (2C-B): Analysis of phase I metabolism with hepatocytes of six species including human. *Toxicology, 206*(1), 75–89.

Check, E. (2004). The ups and downs of ecstasy. *Nature, 429,* 126–128.

El-Seedi, H. R., De Smet, P. A. G. M., Beck, O., Possnert, G., & Bruhn, J. G. (2005). Prehistoric peyote use: Alkaloid analysis and radiocarbon dating of archaeological specimens of *Lophophora* from Texas. *Journal of Ethnopharmacology, 101* (1–3), 238–242.

Erowid. (May 22, 2008). *Documenting the complex relationship between humans & psychoactives.* Available from http://www.erowid.org.

Griffiths, R. R., Richards, W. A., McCann, U., & Jesse, R. (2006). Psilocybin can occasion mystical-type experiences having substantial and sustained personal meaning and spiritual significance. *Psychopharmacology.* Available from http://www.hopkinsme dicine.org/.

Halpern, J. H. (2004). Hallucinogens and dissociative agents naturally growing in the United States. *Pharmacology Therapeutics, 102*(2), 131–138.

Halpern, J. H., & Pope, Jr., H.G. (2001). Hallucinogens on the Internet: A vast new source of underground drug information. *American Journal of Psychiatry, 158*(3), 481–483.

Harbut, R. E., & Correll, G. E. (2002). Successful treatment of a nine-year case of complex regional pain syndrome type-I (reflex sympathetic dystrophy) with intravenous ketamine-infusion therapy in a warfarin-anticoagulated adult female patient. *Pain Medicine, 3,* 147–155.

Hoaken, P. N. S., & Stewart, S. H. (2003). Drugs of abuse and the elicitation of human aggressive behavior. *Addictive Behaviors, 28,* 1533–1554.

Hunt, D. (1997, October). *Rise of hallucinogen use.* (Research Brief). National Institute of Justice: U. S. Department of Justice. Washington DC: Office of Justice Programs.

Kikura-Hanajiri, R., Hayashi, M., Saisho, K., & Goda, Y. (2005, October 15). Simultaneous determination of nineteen hallucinogenic tryptamines/beta-calbolines and phenethylamines using gas chromatography-mass spectrometry and liquid chromatography-electrospray ionisation-mass spectrometry. *Journal of chromatography. B, Analytical technologies in the biomedical and life sciences, 825*(1), 29–37.

Krupitsky, E., Burakov, A., & Romanova, T. (2002). Ketamine psychotherapy for heroin addiction. *Journal of Substance Abuse Treatment, 23,* 273–283.

Lankenau, S.E., (2006). On ketamine: In and out of the K hole. In B. Sanders (Ed.) *Drugs, Clubs and Young People: Sociological and Public Health Perspective.* Aldershot, UK: Ashgate.

Lankenau, S. E., & Clatts, M. C. (2005). Patterns of poly-drug use among ketamine injectors in New York City. *Substance Use & Misuse, 40,* 1381–1398.

Lankenau, S. E., & Sanders, B. (2007). Patterns of ketamine use by young injection drug users. *Journal of Psychoactive Drugs, 39*(1), 21–30.

McCandless, D. (2004, February 16). Goodbye ecstasy, hello 5-Meo-DMT: New designer drugs are just a click away. *The Guardian.* Available from http://www.guardian.co.uk/.

McKenna, D. J. (2004). Clinical investigations of the therapeutic potential of ayahuasca: Rationale and regulatory challenges. *Pharmacology and Therapeutics, 102*(2), 111–129.

Measham, F. (2004). Play space: Historical and socio-cultural reflections on drugs, licensed leisure locations, commercialization, and control. *International Journal of Drug Policy, 15,* 337–345.

Multidisciplinary Association for Psychedelic Studies. (2008, April 20). Available from http://www.maps.org.

Rushkoff, D. (1994). *Cyberia: Life in the trenches of hyperspace.* Manchester, UK: Clinamen Press.

Sanders, B. (2006). Young people, clubs and drugs. In Sanders, B. (Ed.), *Drugs, Clubs and Young People: Sociological and Public Health Perspectives.* Aldershot, UK: Ashgate.

Sanders, B., Lankenau, S. E., Jackson Bloom, J., & Hathazi, D. (2008). "Research chemicals": Tryptamine and Phenethylamine use amongst high-risk youth. *Substance Use and Misuse, 43*(3), 389–402.

Sessa, B. (2005). Can psychedelics have a role in psychiatry once again? *British Journal of Psychiatry, 186,* 457–458.

Sewell, R. A., Halpern, J. H., & Pope, Jr., H. G. (2006). Response of cluster headache to psilocybin and LSD. *Neurology, 66*(12), 1920–1922.

Shapiro, H. (1999). Dances with drugs: Pop music, drugs and youth culture. In N. South (Ed.), *Drugs: Cultures, controls and everyday life* (pp. 17–35). Sage, London.

Shulgin, A., & Shulgin, A. (1991). *PiHKAL (Phenethylamines I have known and loved).* Berkeley: Transform Press.

Shulgin, A., & Shulgin, A. (1997). *TiHKAL (Tryptamines I have known and loved): The continuation.* Berkeley: Transform Press.

Vastag, B. (2005). Addiction research: Ibogaine therapy: A "vast, uncontrolled experiment." *Science, 308* (5720), 345–346.

The Lycaeum. Available from http://www.lycaeum.org.

Wish, E. D. (1986). PCP and crime: Just another illicit drug? In D. H. Clouet (Ed.), *Phencyclidine: An update.* Bethesda, MD: National Institute of Drug Abuse.

Yablonsky, L. (1968). *The Hippie Trip.* New York: Pegasus.

BILL SANDERS

HARM REDUCTION.

Between the mid-1980s and the early 2000s, harm reduction emerged as a third alternative to the stark choice between legalization and a strict law enforcement oriented prohibition. It is not the only such alternative. Among others, Reuter (1992) suggests pragmatic and compassionate prohibition as an "owlish" alternative to prohibition hawks and legalizing doves. Nevertheless, harm reduction is arguably the most prominent alternative, particularly in the developed world outside the United States.

DIFFERENT DEFINITIONS OF HARM REDUCTION

The term *harm reduction* is highly controversial, particularly in the United States, in part because it is variously defined by different people. For example, MacCoun (1998) distinguishes between micro- and macro-harm reduction by using the following simple equation: The total drug-related harm equals the amount of drug use multiplied by the average harm per unit of drug use.

The goal to reduce total drug-related harm, what MacCoun terms "macro- harm reduction," is not particularly controversial, but there are broadly speaking two schools of thought concerning how best to achieve this end. One school, which might be termed *use reduction*, argues that the surest way to reduce drug-related harm is to reduce drug use.

The second school advocates reducing total harm by making drugs less harmful, that is, by reducing the average harm per unit of drug use. In MacCoun's terms, this is "micro- harm reduction," or what is more commonly called simply *harm reduction*. This school of thought questions aggressive efforts to reduce drug use because they can increase the average harm per unit of drug use so much that total harm goes up, even if drug use is reduced. For example, restricting syringes might have a modest effect on injection drug use yet greatly increase the frequency of needle sharing and, hence, transmission of blood-borne diseases, including HIV/AIDS and Hepatitis C.

Just as some harm reduction advocates fear that suppressing drug use might increase harm per unit of drug use, some use reduction advocates fear that reducing drug harmfulness might increase the amount of drug use. This second effect could occur because of *risk compensation*: Reducing the costs of an activity can increase the likelihood and frequency of participation, whether the costs reduced are direct dollar costs (economists such as Grossman [2004] have shown convincingly that drug use goes up when drug prices go down) or non-dollar costs such as health risks. This second effect could also occur if government funding of harm reduction programs was misunderstood as tacitly condoning drug use.

PROBLEMS WITH EVALUATING PROGRAMS AND POLICIES

In principle, programs or policies targeted at either term on the right hand side of the equation above (amount of drug use or average harm per use) have potential to either reduce or increase total drug-related harm. So the merits of a program or policy are hard to establish deductively. But in theory one could simply measure or estimate whether a program or policy had a greater effect in the intended direction on the targeted term or a greater unintended adverse effect on the other term in the equation. In practice, data and other limitations interfere, so researchers can make only rough estimates of the magnitude of intended effects and sometimes almost no reliable quantitative estimates of unintended side-effects.

Opiate Substitution Therapies. Perhaps the strongest evidence in support of such programs and policies come from opiate substitution therapies (OST). When people who are dependent on heroin receive treatment that includes an opiate agonist, substantial improvements in health, social, and criminal justice outcomes often follow. Some opiate agonists, such as the methadone, are not particularly controversial among use reduction advocates. Indeed, methadone maintenance was traditionally seen as a form of drug treatment, not a harm reduction program.

Three factors complicated this view. The first was the advent of HIV/AIDS in the 1980s. Whereas historically it was common to try to gradually reduce the methadone dose over time to get a patient drug-free, high relapse rates and the great risk that relapsing injectors would become HIV-infected encouraged a shift toward viewing indefinite maintenance on methadone as a successful outcome. Second, there has been a more general conceptualization of drug dependence as a chronic relapsing condition that should be managed indefinitely, akin to asthma, not as something to be *cured* by emphasizing abstinence. Third, evidence has accumulated from Switzerland and elsewhere that medically supervised legal heroin prescription produces improved outcomes not altogether different than those offered by methadone maintenance. Some claim that recruitment and retention into such heroin maintenance programs can exceed that achieved with methadone maintenance.

As of 2008, in countries where use reduction policy dominates, methadone maintenance is generally accepted as a legitimate form of drug treatment, whereas heroin maintenance is dismissed as an irresponsible form of harm reduction. Among those advocating harm reduction there is generally more openness toward heroin maintenance, although implementation is still not widespread.

Syringe Exchange Programs. Among harm reduction programs, the second largest body of evidence concerns syringe exchange programs (SEP). The conventional wisdom among scholars who study drug policy is that SEP is effective at reducing the spread of HIV without increasing rates of injection drug use among existing users. SEP are not as effective at controlling the spread of Hepatitis C (which is more virulent), but these programs can have the important side benefit of bringing injection drug users into regular contact with service providers who can offer treatment referrals and other support services.

Supervised Injection Facilities. The third largest body of literature concerns supervised injection facilities (SIFs). The most common form of acute drug-related mortality is heroin overdose. Heroin overdose is readily treatable if detected early enough, so harm reduction advocates suggest allowing heroin users to inject in a supervised facility where there is a staff member who can contact emergency medical personnel promptly if there is a problem.

DRUG TESTING, EDUCATION, AND LOCAL CODES

Another type of harm reduction is offering free testing of drugs. Particularly for some so-called club drugs such as ecstasy, adverse reactions are often caused by an adulterant (e.g., amphetamine), not by the drug that the user intended to consume. Informal drug testing services provided by the user community itself were not uncommon in the U.S. in the 1970s, but more formal versions have emerged in Australia and several European countries over the last ten years (MacCoun, 2007).

Education about responsible or safe drug use is another form of harm reduction. A classic example concerns drug use at all night dance parties, or raves, where drug-related dehydration and hyperthermia are important and sometimes fatal risks, but ones that can easily be countered by drinking plenty of water and taking breaks.

Those same risks can be countered not only via user education but also via municipal code enforcement. Some night clubs eliminate cold water taps in bathrooms to encourage patrons to buy alcoholic drinks, but that practice can be banned, with the ban enforced in the same way that fire codes and other public health codes are enforced by threatening to close the establishment or revoke its liquor license.

U.S. VERSUS INTERNATIONAL VIEWS ON HARM REDUCTION

There are many drug-related harms, and harm reduction efforts as of 2008 have primarily focused on only a subset, notably (1) transmission of blood-borne diseases via injection drug use, (2) heroin overdose, and (3) harms associated with club drugs. Perhaps not coincidentally, those harms account for a substantial share of all drug-related harms in Australia and many European countries, which are seen as leaders in harm reduction. However, in the United States, roughly three-fourths of drug-related harms are associated with

cocaine (including crack) and methamphetamine and are often connected to drug-related crime and drug markets, not directly to drug use per se.

Perhaps harm reduction is viewed more skeptically in the United States because it less relevant to most of the U.S. drug problem, or perhaps harm reduction is less relevant for the bulk of U.S. drug problems because international leaders of the harm reduction movement have focused on inventing ways of dealing with the issues that are of greatest concern in those countries.

If the United States were to adopt a harm reduction philosophy that focused on drug-related crime and market violence, the resulting policies might look very different than those typically associated with the harm reduction movement. In particular, currently police often play a passive role in harm reduction. For example, they may not arrest injection drug users for possessing a syringe, and as a result, those users are less likely to need to borrow a syringe when they next inject themselves. However, if the harm reduction objective is reducing drug market–related violence, police may need to play a more active role. Indeed, interventions such as Boston's Operation Ceasefire that dramatically reduced drug-related homicide among youthful drug sellers (Braga et al., 2001) can be seen as successful harm reduction interventions. These programs greatly reduce drug-related homicides without specifically trying to reduce drug use. However, they are rarely conceptualized or discussed as such because the term "harm reduction" is so controversial in the United States.

Some of the controversy regarding harm reduction may derive unfortunately from its association for some people with legalization. While certainly many people who support legalization also support harm reduction, it may not be true that most people who support harm reduction also support legalization. Then, too, some controversy may derive from a generalized belief that drug use is bad. Harm reduction replaces such an inclusive and simplistic position with one that is more nuanced (e.g., drug use may be bad, but HIV/AIDS is worse, so we will focus on the latter) in the hopes of achieving certain pragmatic outcomes.

Graduated enforcement of prohibitions with particular attention to activities that are seen as most harmful has been accepted in some societies for certain vices: Prostitution in the early 2000s and gambling in former times might be examples in the United States. Whether harm reduction is good policy toward drugs in a particular jurisdiction depends on the values and preferences of local voters and on program effectiveness. The public needs to examine how much a harm reduction approach may reduce harmfulness and what if any adverse consequences exist for drug use. Neither is easily measured. People may continue to debate harm reduction proposals, but one can hope that the debate will be based on reasoned rather than false arguments.

See also Drug Testing Methods and Clinical Interpretations of Test Results; Legal Regulation of Drugs and Alcohol; Legalization vs. Prohibition of Drugs: Historical Perspective; Legalization vs. Prohibition of Drugs: Policy Analysis; Methadone Maintenance Programs; Needle and Syringe Exchanges and HIV/AIDS.

BIBLIOGRAPHY

Braga, A. A., Kennedy, D. M., Waring, E. J., & Piehl, A. M. (2001). Problem-oriented policing, deterrence, and youth violence: An evaluation of Boston's Operation Ceasefire. Journal of Research in Crime and Delinquency 38(3), 195–225.

Grossman, M. (2004). Individual behaviors and substance abuse: The role of price (NBER Working Paper No. 10948). Cambridge, MA: National Bureau of Economic Research.

MacCoun, R. J. (1998). Toward a psychology of harm reduction. American Psychologist, 53(11), 1199–1208.

MacCoun, R. J. (2007). Testing drugs versus testing users: Private risk management in the shadow of the criminal law. DePaul Law Review, 56, 507–538. Available from http://repositories.cdlib.org/.

Reuter, P. (1992). Hawks ascendant: The punitive trend of American drug policy. Daedalus, 121(3), 15–52.

JONATHAN P. CAULKINS

HARRISON NARCOTICS ACT OF 1914.

The first international drug-control initiative, the 1909 Shanghai Opium Commission, brought the international community together in an effort to curb the illicit traffic and consumption of the narcotic drug opium. The Commission met at conferences at the Hague, Netherlands in 1911 and 1913 and encouraged participants to enact national legislation that would address the narcotics problem in their own countries. During this period the U.S. Congress became aware of the public opinion favoring prohibition of all moral evils, especially alcohol and drugs. New York Representative Francis B. Harrison was motivated by both the Shanghai Commission directive to curb narcotics and by the reformists in the Progressive movement in the United States who wanted to eradicate drug use. He proposed two measures: (1) prohibit the importation and nonmedical use of opium and (2) regulate the production of opium in the United States.

Congress enacted the Harrison Narcotics Act in December 1914 with minimal debate because of the general public opinion about drugs.

PROVISIONS OF THE HARRISON NARCOTICS ACT

Congress regulated narcotic drugs by imposing licensing requirements on manufacturers, distributors, sellers, importers, producers, compounders, and dispensers. The Harrison Act required that these parties register with the director of the Internal Revenue Service within the Treasury Department and that they pay a gradually increasing occupational tax. Congress wanted to monitor the flow of opium and coca leaves so that government authorities would have records of any transaction involving these drugs. The drugs were allowed only for limited medical and scientific purposes. Those individuals found in violation of the act faced a maximum penalty of five years in jail, a $2,000 fine, or both.

TREASURY DEPARTMENT REGULATIONS

The Harrison Act was intended to generate revenue by imposing taxes on parties involved in the trade, sale, and distribution of drugs. As a result, Congress entrusted the Treasury Department with enforcement responsibility, in particular the Internal Revenue Service and subsequently the Narcotics Unit of the Bureau of Prohibition. The Treasury Department attempted to limit narcotics to medical and scientific use and prevent their illegal diversion by physicians and druggists. The Harrison Act required pharmacists to review prescriptions to determine if they were a suspicious or coerced prescription (i.e., unusually large quantity).

Sales and transfers of narcotics could only be made through official order forms obtained from the director of the IRS. District offices of the IRS maintained these records for two years. The act permitted a few notable exceptions to filing these forms. For example, qualified practitioners (physicians, dentists, and veterinarians) could prescribe or dispense narcotics to patients without completing the order forms but were required to maintain records of all the substances distributed. Druggists could also fill lawful prescriptions without completing the forms.

The Treasury Department interpreted the Harrison Act to mean prohibiting drug addicts from obtaining narcotics. Addicts were prohibited from registering and could receive narcotics only through a licensed physician, dentist, or veterinarian. The department regulations also prohibited physicians from maintaining a patient-addict on narcotics, a practice frequently used to help addicts avoid severe withdrawal pain while they were weaned from narcotic dependence. The department interpreted possession of narcotics as prima facie evidence of a Harrison Act violation, and the burden of proof shifted to the suspect, who had to document that the narcotics were obtained legally.

The Treasury Department enforced the Act primarily through warnings. However, the department charged physicians and druggists with conspiracy when authorities arrested an individual who possessed narcotics without a prescription made in good faith, and a connection could be made that proved that the physician or the druggist provided the narcotics.

THE HARRISON ACT AND U.S. DRUG POLICY
According to the Harrison Act, physicians could prescribe opiates in the course of professional practice. The police and judiciary, however, interpreted the law broadly in ways that resulted in the arrest, the prosecution, and imprisonment of some physicians under the new law. Health professionals therefore chose not to work with substance users, providing a stark choice for their patients to either stop their drug use or buy from the thriving illicit market. An unintended effect of the law shifted heroin and cocaine consumption into the illicit market. Until 1914 heroin, cocaine, and opium could be purchased at a pharmacy; after 1914 they could only be bought from the illicit market.

In 1918 a government committee attempted to determine the impact of the Harrison Act. The committee estimated that opium and other narcotic drugs (including cocaine, which Congress had erroneously labeled as a narcotic in 1914) had over a million adherents. The committee concluded that the reasons for the growth in narcotic use were due to lax implementation, and thus it called for more rigorous application. A growth in organized crime made drug smuggling profitable. Another unintended consequence was the virtual eradication of opium smuggling because of its bulk but a rise in heroin smuggling because it was a concentrated form of opiate and therefore less bulky.

In 1924 Congress attempted to further tighten restrictions by banning heroin for medicinal use. It also prohibited doctors from working with addicts. Pharmaceutical morphine supplies, which were unadulterated, began to rapidly dwindle and were replaced by a thriving illicit trade in adulterated heroin.

Many critics of the Harrison Act argue that the legislation created more problems than it solved. In particular, they charge that the measure failed to eradicate the narcotics problem, primarily because it failed to prohibit the sale and distribution of marijuana. In addition detractors argue that the act did not resolve the issue of whether drug addicts should be treated as criminals or as patients requiring medical treatment. They also contend that the courts hampered the Treasury Department's enforcement authority. Specifically, courts prohibited the department from seizing narcotics, interpreting the Act as a means to collect revenue, rather than as a penal measure. After the Harrison Act was passed, illicit use of narcotics increased initially as a result of these omissions or ambiguities.

Despite these criticisms, the Harrison Act is significant because it led to a national focus on the dangers of narcotics and drug abuse. Most important is that the Act served as the impetus for further legislation, such as the 1970 Controlled Substances Act, in the attempt to combat the illegal sale, distribution, and consumption of narcotics and other abusable substances in the United States, while ensuring their availability for medical purposes.

See also **Controlled Substances Act of 1970; Legal Regulation of Drugs and Alcohol; Prohibition of Alcohol.**

BIBLIOGRAPHY

Anslinger, H. J., & Tompkins, W. F. (1953). *The traffic in narcotics*. New York: Funk & Wagnalls.

McWilliams, J. C. (1990). The history of drug control policies in the United States. In J. A. Inciardi (Ed.), *Handbook of drug control in the United States*. New York: Greenwood Press.

Musto, D. F. (1973). *The American disease: Origins of narcotic control*. New Haven: Yale University Press.

ROBERT T. ANGAROLA
ALAN MINSK
REVISED BY DEAN WHITTINGTON (2009)

HASHISH. Hashish is the Arabic word for a particular form of Cannabis sativa; it came into English at the end of the sixteenth century. Hashish is the resin derived principally from the flowers, bracts, and young leaves of the female hemp plant. The resin contains cannabinoids—the one of major interest being tetrahydrocannabinol (THC). The THC content will vary depending upon the composition of the hashish, but often it is about 4 percent or more. Usually the resinous portion is sticky enough to allow the material to be compressed into a wafer or brick. Some preparations contain only the resin and are known as hashish oil. Similar preparations of the resinous material and flowering tops of the plant have been given a variety of names in different regions—*charas* in India, *esvar* in Turkey, *anascha* in areas of the former USSR, *kif* in Morocco and parts of the Middle East.

One of the ways in which hashish is prepared is to boil *Cannabis* leaves in water to which butter has been added. THC, being extremely fat-soluble, binds with the butter, which can then be used for making various confections, cookies, and sweets; these are eaten to obtain the effects of the drug. Although hashish is often taken by mouth, it can also be smoked, just as marijuana is.

Hashish was introduced to the West in the middle of the nineteenth century by a French psychiatrist, Moreau de Tours, who experimented with the drug as a means of understanding the phenomenon of mental illnesses. He not only experimented on himself but on a coterie of friends of considerable literary talent. These included Théophile Gautier, Alexander Dumas, and Charles Baudelaire. This group named themselves "Le Club des Haschischins" or "The Club of Hashish-Eaters." The lurid descriptions of the drug effects by these talented writers no doubt helped popularize the drug. Most of their accounts dwelt on beautiful hallucinations and a sense of omnipotence. Doses must have been large, since the effects described are more characteristic of hallucinogenic drugs than effects experienced by present-day users (smokers) of marijuana.

Hashish was introduced into England at about the same time, by an Irish physician, William Brooke O'Shaughnessy, who had spent some time in India, where he had become familiar with it. The material was soon hailed as a wonder drug, being used for all sorts of complaints: pain, muscle spasms, convulsions, migraine headaches, and inflamed tonsils. As most of the preparations were weak and the doses used were small, any beneficial effects might be attributable to a placebo effect.

A preparation, Tilden's Extract of Cannabis Indica, became a popular remedy in the United States in the 1850s. An amateur pharmacologist, Fitz Hugh Ludlow, used this preparation for self-experiments in which he was able to explore its hallucinogenic properties. He may have become somewhat dependent on hashish but finally gave it up. His descriptions of the effects of the drug were similar to what had previously been experienced by Asian users: euphoria and uncontrollable laughter; altered perceptions of space, time, vision, and hearing; synesthesias and depersonalization.

Hashish is currently the most potent of all *Cannabis* preparations: A lot of drug effect is packed into a small parcel. Regulation of the dose is difficult because of its variable potency, and labels for street drugs are notoriously unreliable, however. What may be sold as hashish may often be closer to ordinary marijuana in potency.

See also **Amotivational Syndrome; Creativity and Drugs; Epidemics of Drug Abuse in the United States; Plants, Drugs From.**

BIBLIOGRAPHY

Booth, M. (2005). *Cannabis: A history*. New York: Macmillan.

ElSohly, M. A., Ed. (2006). *Marijuana and the cannabinoids*. Totowa, NJ: Humana Press.

Moreau, J. J. (1973). Hashish. In H. Peters & G. G. Nahas (Eds.). *Hashish and mental illness.* New York: Raven Press.

Nahas, G. G. (1973). *Marihuana—deceptive weed.* New York: Raven Press.

LEO E. HOLLISTER

HEMP. In the narrow sense, hemp refers to a fiber derived from certain strains of *Cannabis sativa*, a bushy herb that originated in Asia. In the broader sense, it also denotes the other use of the plant, as a source of marijuana. Although *Cannabis sativa* is generally considered to be a single species, two genetic strains show considerable differences. One is used for fiber production and has been so used for centuries to make rope, floor coverings, and cloth. Hemp plants have been grown for this purpose as commercial crops in Asia and even in colonial America; during World War II, they were grown in the midwestern United States when the Asian supply was unavailable.

The other strain of the hemp plant produces a poor fiber but has a relatively high drug content; it is used for its psychoactive effect. Near the end of the nineteenth century, the Indian Hemp Drug Commission (1895) produced one of the first major assessments of *cannabis* as a drug, finding it not a major health hazard. Consequently, it remains in legal use in India for both medicinal and social purposes, where it is called bhang.

Figure 1. Hemp plant. ILLUSTRATION BY GGS INFORMATION SERVICES. GALE, CENGAGE LEARNING

See also **Plants, Drugs From.**

BIBLIOGRAPHY

Booth, M. (2005). *Cannabis: A history.* New York: MacMillan.

Ebadi, M. S. (2006). *Pharmacodynamic basis of herbal medicine.* Boca Raton, FL: CRC Press.

LEO E. HOLLISTER

HEPATITIS C INFECTION. In the 1970s it became clear that infection with hepatitis A or B could not explain a large proportion of cases of both acute and chronic hepatitis, and another virus was suspected. This non-A, non-B hepatitis virus was identified in 1989 and designated the hepatitis C virus (HCV). HCV belongs to the flaviviridae family that is distantly related to hepatitis G virus but not to any other known hepatitis viruses. HCV is an RNA virus with a single strand molecule of about 9,500 nucleotides. The enzyme responsible for viral replication lacks the ability to correct copying errors, resulting in the large viral diversity that is characteristic of HCV. This heterogeneity is extremely important because it affects immune response, diagnosis, and response to treatment. Closely related viral strains are called quasispecies and are about 95 percent similar in their RNA sequence. More distantly related strains share only about 80 percent or less of their genetic sequence and are called *genotypes.* Over time HCV virus evolved into six distinct genotypes. The world distribution of these genotypes is approximately as follows: Genotype 1 is most common (60 to 70% of isolates) in the United States and Europe; genotypes 2 and 3 are less common in these areas, while genotypes 4, 5, and 6 are rare. Genotype 2 is present worldwide, and genotype 3 is most common in India, the Far East, and Australia; genotype 4 is most common in Africa and the Middle East; genotype 5 is most common in South Africa; and genotype 6 is most common in Hong Kong, Vietnam, and Australia. The clinical significance of viral genotypes is in their response to interferon-based therapy. The sustained virologic response to therapy by pegylated interferon plus ribavarin ranges from about 40 to 50 percent with genotype 1 (including

1a and 1b) to as high as 70 to 80 percent with genotypes 2 and 3 (Lauer & Walker, 2001).

EPIDEMIOLOGY

It is estimated that there are about 20,000 new acute cases of HCV infection per year in the United States, a decline from 230,000 cases per year in the 1980s. Most of these cases appear to be related to drug use. Transfusion associated acute HCV infection has been reduced almost to zero in the past 20 years. Chronic HCV infection is the most common chronic liver disease and the majority of liver transplants in the United States are performed for this condition. Additionally, about 8,000 to 13,000 people die each year as a consequence of chronic HCV infection. Approximately 1.6 percent of people in the United States are positive for HCV antibody, or 4.1 million people who are positive for antibody, translating to about 1.3 percent or 3.2 million persons that test positive for HCV virus in their blood. Most cases of acute hepatitis C have no symptoms and only 25 percent are clinically detected. Severe acute hepatitis C cases are rare (Alter & Mast, 1994).

TRANSMISSION AND RISK ODDS

The majority of HCV-infected patients in the United States acquired the disease through intravenous drug use or blood transfusion. However, as of 2008, transfusion-related infection is rare since testing of blood-derived products began in 1990. About 40 percent of patients lack identifiable risk factors for HCV infection but high-risk behavior at some point in their lives often can be detected on careful questioning. About 60 percent of newly acquired infection is attributable to drug use. A variety of behaviors and exposures have been shown to substantially increase the risk of infection with HCV. Intravenous drug use confers an odds ratio of infection of about 50, meaning that individuals who use drugs intravenously have 50 times the risk of HCV infection as individuals who do not inject drugs. Shared needles or other paraphernalia remain the most common route of acute HCV infection in the United States. HCV is also associated with intranasal cocaine use, most likely due to blood on shared snorting devices. Before routine screening of blood-derived products began, blood transfusion carried an odds ratio of about 11. The estimated risk as of 2008 is less than one in a million per unit transfused. Sexual activity with an intravenous drug user results in an odds ratio of about 6. A jail stay of more than three days confers an odds ratio of about 3. Religious scarification (i.e., creating ritual scars on the skin) carries an odds ratio of about 3. Injury by a bloody object or piercing one's ears or other body parts increases the odds ratio to about 2. A history of an immunoglobulin injection carries an odds ratio of 1.6. Other important risk factors include being a healthcare worker, transmission in the context of receiving health care (e.g., while in the hospital), organ transplantation and perinatal transmission (where the risk is about 5% higher if a baby's mother is co-infected with HIV). Sexual contacts with either heterosexual or homosexual partners appear to increase risk for HCV transmission only slightly. The estimated risk is about 0.1 percent a year. However, the risk is higher if partners are co-infected with HIV. Routine household contacts are at no increased risk of transmission. Tattooing, body piercing, and commercial barbering may also transmit HCV on rare occasions (Alter & Mast, 1994).

CLINICAL PRESENTATION AND PROGNOSIS

Acute infection with HCV most often produces no symptoms and rarely results in liver failure. It is responsible for about 20 percent of acute cases of hepatitis in the United States. Less that 25 percent of patients develop jaundice. Other symptoms are non-specific and include malaise, nausea, and right upper abdominal pain. About 80 to 100 percent of acute cases develop chronic presence of the virus in their blood and 60 to 80 percent have abnormal liver enzymes tests. Approximately 15 percent of patients may spontaneously clear the virus early after acute infection, but this is unlikely to occur after the virus has persisted for more than 6 months. Patients with chronic infection often show no symptoms or have non-specific complaints such as fatigue (most frequent), nausea, anorexia, sore muscles or joints, and weight loss. These symptoms often alter the individual's quality of life and may improve after successful treatment of the HCV infection. There is no correlation between symptoms, laboratory abnormalities, or liver biopsy histology, but patients with cirrhosis are more likely to be symptomatic. Interestingly, HCV infection is also associated with cognitive impairment independent of the severity of liver disease.

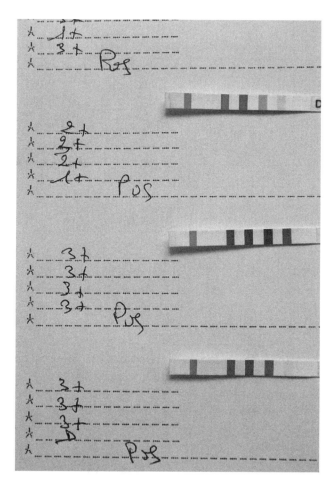

Hepatitis C virus screening with Western-Blot, or immunoblot assay. Test Serum is incubated on nitrocellulose strips, on which four recombinant viral proteins are blotted. Color changes indicate that antibodies are adhering to the proteins. An immunoblot is considered positive if two or more proteins react and is considered indeterminate if only one positive band is detected. GARO/PHOTO RESEARCHERS, INC.

The natural history of HCV infection is difficult to define both because of the long course and the fact that the disease is not progressive in all patients. Both host and viral factors are responsible for the variability in progression. Factors that appear to hasten disease progression include positive HIV status, alcohol and marijuana use, infection after the age of 40 to 55, obesity, diabetes, and liver steatosis (also known as fatty liver). Some studies suggest that after 10 to 20 years the rate of cirrhosis in patients with chronic HCV infection may be as high as 50 percent, though much lower rates of cirrhosis have also been reported. Survival is probably not affected by HCV infection, but overall mortality increases once cirrhosis develops.

The risk of liver decompensation in the setting of cirrhosis is about 3 to 4 percent annually. The most common sign of decompensation is accumulation of ascites (fluid in the abdomen). Once decompensation occurs the likelihood of survival at 5 years is 50 percent. The risk of hepatocellular carcinoma (a cancer of the liver) is about 1 percent per year once cirrhosis develops, so that screening for this complication is recommended every 6 months. (Alter & Mast, 1994).

DIAGNOSIS

The presence of viral RNA in the blood is detectable within days after acute exposure. Serum liver test markers (aminotransferases) become elevated in 6 to 12 weeks after exposure, and an HCV antibody test may become positive as soon as 8 weeks after exposure. Patients with known exposure should also undergo testing.

TREATMENT

The goal of treatment of chronic HCV infection is to achieve viral eradication that improves clinical outcomes. Several small studies suggest that treatment of acute HCV infection may result in rates of sustained virologic response rates in excess of 80 percent, but the optimal regimen and timing of therapy remain to be determined. The majority of treatment trials for acute HCV infection used interferon treatment alone. Successful eradication was predicted by achieving a sustained virologic response, that is, no detectable virus 6 months after treatment is completed. Abstaining from alcohol and maintaining a healthy weight are also part of the management of chronic HCV infection. The treatment of chronic HCV infection as of 2008 consists of combination therapy with pegylated interferon injection administered weekly and daily ribavirin tablets. For reasons discussed below, some patients with chronic HCV infection are not candidates for treatment; others do not agree to be treated, so that less than 20 percent of patients ultimately receive treatment. Further, not all individuals in whom treatment is begun successfully complete a full course (i.e., 48 weeks) of treatment. Sustained virologic response depends on many factors and typically ranges from 40 percent to 80 percent depending on the viral genotype and the patient's pretreatment characteristics. Typical patients for whom therapy is widely accepted are older than 18 years of age and have an abnormal alanineaminotransferase (a liver enzyme) level and a liver biopsy showing significant fibrosis with compensated liver disease. Although the decision to undergo treatment has to be individualized, persons with uncontrolled major depression, autoimmune hepatitis, untreated hyperthyroidism, or who are recipients of a renal, heart, or lung transplant should not be treated. This is also true for those who are pregnant or unwilling to practice adequate contraception (Seef & Hoofnagle, 2002; Hoofnagle & Seef, 2006).

See also **Complications; Injecting Drug Users and HIV.**

BIBLIOGRAPHY

Alter, M. J., & Mast, E. E. (1994). The epidemiology of viral hepatitis in the United States. *Gastroenterology Clinics of North America, 23*, 437–455.

Hoofnagle, J. H., & Seef, L. B. (2006). Peginterferon and ribavirin for chronic hepatitis C. *New England Journal of Medicine, 355*(23), 2444–2451.

Lauer, G. M., & Walker, B. D. (2001). Hepatitis C virus infection. *New England Journal of Medicine, 345*(1), 41–52.

Seef, L. B., & Hoofnagle, J. H. (2002). National institutes of health consensus development conference: Management of hepatitis C: 2002. *Hepatology* (Suppl. 1), S1.

PETR PROTIVA

HEROIN. Morphine was first identified as the pain-relieving active ingredient in opium in 1806. But morphine was not free of the habit-forming and toxic effects of opium. By the late nineteenth century, the idea of modifying molecules to change their pharmacological actions was well established. It seemed quite reasonable to use this approach to develop new chemical entities that might be free of the problems seen with morphine. In Germany, in 1898, H. Dresser introduced such a new drug—3,6-diacetylmorphine—into medical use; it was named there by the Bayer Company, which produced and marketed it, named it heroin (presumably from *heroisch*, meaning "heroical"), because it was more potent than morphine.

Although heroin is structurally very similar to morphine, it was hoped that it would relieve pain

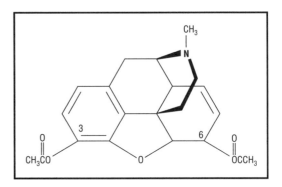

Figure 1. Chemical structure of heroin. ILLUSTRATION BY GGS INFORMATION SERVICES. GALE, CENGAGE LEARNING

without the tendency to produce addiction. Turn-of-the-century medical writings and advertisements, both in Europe and the United States, claimed that heroin was effective for treating pain and cough. Many suggested that it was less toxic than morphine and was nonaddictive. A few even suggested that heroin could be a nonaddicting cure for the morphine habit. Clearly, this was not the case, and within a year or two of its introduction, most of the medical community knew so. By the 1920s, heroin had become the most widely abused of the opiates.

PHARMACOLOGY
Heroin is a white powder that is readily soluble in water. The introduction of just two esters onto the morphine molecule changes the physical properties of the substance such that there is a significant increase in solubility, permitting solutions with increased drug concentrations. A more subtle advantage of heroin is its greater potency compared to morphine. The volume of drug injected may be particularly important when high doses are used. Thus, 1 gram of heroin will produce the effects of 2 to 3 grams of morphine; by converting morphine to heroin, producers increase both the potency and the value of the drug.

Following injection, heroin is very potent, with the ability to cross the blood-brain barrier and enter the brain. This barrier results from a unique arrangement of cells around blood vessels within the brain, which limits the free movement of compounds. Many factors contribute to the barrier—in general, the less polar a drug, the more rapidly it enters the brain. Heroin, however, has a very short half-life in the blood (amount of time that half the drug remains). It is rapidly degraded by esterases, the enzymes that break ester bonds. The acetyl group at the 3-position of the molecule is far more sensitive to these enzymes than the acetyl group at the 6-position. Indeed, the 3-acetyl group is attacked almost immediately after injection and, within several minutes, virtually all the heroin is converted to a metabolite, 6-acetylmorphine. The remaining acetyl group at the 6-position is also lost, but at a slower rate. Loss of both acetyl groups generates morphine. It is believed that a combination of 6-acetylmorphine and morphine is responsible for the actions of heroin.

MEDICINAL USE

The pharmacology of heroin is virtually identical to that of morphine. This probably reflects its rapid conversion to 6-acetylmorphine and morphine. Detailed studies comparing the actions of heroin and morphine in cancer patients with severe pain have shown very little difference between the two agents, other than simple potency. Heroin may have a slightly more rapid onset of action than morphine and it is certainly two to three times as potent (presumably due to its greater facility in crossing the blood-brain barrier). This difference in potency is lost with oral administration. The pain relief (analgesia) from both agents is comparable when the doses are adjusted appropriately. At equally effective analgesic doses, even the euphoria seen with heroin is virtually identical to that of morphine. From the clinical point of view, there is little difference between one drug and the other. Both are effective analgesics and can be used beneficially in the treatment of severe pain. Heroin is more soluble, which makes it somewhat easier to give large doses by injection, with smaller volumes needed. Many of the similar semisynthetic agents, such as hydromorphone, however, are many times more potent than heroin and offer even greater advantages.

One widespread use of heroin in the United Kingdom was in the early formulations of Brompton's Cocktail, a mixture of drugs designed to relieve severe pain in terminal cancer patients. The heroin employed in the original formula is now typically replaced with morphine without any loss in effectiveness. For many years, some groups have maintained that heroin is more effective in the relief of cancer pain than morphine is. Careful clinical studies show that this is not true, but the most important issue is using an appropriate dose. Thus, heroin offers no major advantage over morphine from the medical perspective.

STREET HEROIN

Since heroin has no approved medical indications in the United States, it is only available and used illicitly. The marked variability of its purity and the use of a wide variety of other substances and drugs to "cut" street heroin poses a major problem. This inability to know what is included in each drug sale makes the street drug more than doubly dangerous. Typically, heroin is administered intravenously, which provides a rapid "rush," a euphoria, which is thought to be the important component of heroin's addictive properties. It can be injected under the skin (subcutaneously, SC) or deep into the muscle (intramuscularly, IM). Multiple intravenous injections leave marks, called tracks, in a much-used injection site, which often indicate that a person is abusing drugs; but heroin can also be heated and the vapors inhaled through a straw (called "chasing the dragon"). It can also be smoked in a cigarette. While the heat tends to destroy some of the drug, if the preparation is pure enough, a sufficient amount can be inhaled to produce the typical opiate effect.

Heroin use is associated with tolerance and dependence. Chronic use of the drug leads to a decreased sensitivity toward its euphoric and analgesic actions, as well as to dependence. Like morphine, the duration of action of heroin is approximately 4 to 6 hours. Thus, addicts must take the drug several times a day to prevent the appearance of withdrawal signs. Many believe that the need to continue taking the drug to avoid withdrawal enhances its addictive potential.

Patients taking opiates medicinally can be taken off them gradually, without problems. Lowering the opiate dose by 20 to 25 percent daily for two or three days will prevent severe withdrawal discomfort and still permit rapid taper off the drug. Abrupt withdrawal of all of the drug is very different—and leads to a well-defined abstinence syndrome that is very similar for both heroin and morphine. It includes eye tearing, yawning, and sweating after about eight to twelve hours past the last dose. As time goes on, people develop restlessness, dilated pupils, irritability, diarrhea, abdominal cramps, and periodic waves of gooseflesh. The term *cold turkey* is now used to describe abrupt withdrawal with the associated gooseflesh. The heroin withdrawal syndrome peaks between two and three days after stopping the drug, and symptoms usually disappear within seven to ten days, although some low-level symptoms may persist for many weeks. Babies of mothers dependent on opiates are born dependent, and special care must be taken to help them withdraw during their first weeks. Medically, although miserable, heroin withdrawal is seldom life threatening—unlike withdrawal from alcohol, which can sometimes be fatal.

OVERDOSE

Overdosing is a common problem among heroin addicts. The reason is not always clear, but wide variation in the purity of the street drug can make it difficult for the addict to judge a dose. Some impurities used to cut the drug may be toxic themselves. With overdose, a person becomes stuporous and difficult to arouse. Pupils are typically small and the skin may be cold and clammy. Seizures may occur, particularly in children or babies. Breathing becomes slow, and cyanosis—seen as a darkening of the lips to a bluish color—may develop, indicating inadequate levels of oxygen in the blood. With respiratory depression, blood pressure may then fall. These last two signs are serious, since most people who die from overdose, die from respiratory failure. Complicating the problem is the fact that many addicts may have taken other drugs, used alcohol, and so on. Some of them may have been taken on purpose, and some may have been a part of the street drug.

Naloxone can readily reverse some opiate problems, since it is a potent opiate antagonist. This drug binds to opiate receptors and can reverse morphine and heroin actions. The appropriate dose may be a problem, however, since naloxone can also precipitate a severe abstinence syndrome in a dependent person.

See also **Addiction: Concepts and Definitions; International Drug Supply Systems; Methadone Maintenance Programs; Opioid Complications and Withdrawal; Treatment: A History of Treatment in the United States.**

BIBLIOGRAPHY

Egendorf, L. K. (2007). *Heroin*. San Diego, CA: ReferencePoint Press.

Jaffe, J. H. (1990). Drug addiction and drug abuse. In A. G. Gilman et al. (Eds.), *Goodman and Gilman's the pharmacological basis of therapeutics* (8th ed.). New York: Pergamon. (2005, 11th ed. New York: McGraw-Hill Medical.)

Jaffe, J. H., & Martin, W. R. (1990). Opioid analgesics and antagonists. In A. G. Gilman et al. (Eds.), *Goodman and Gilman's the pharmacological basis of therapeutics* (8th ed.). New York: Pergamon. (2005, 11th ed. New York: McGraw-Hill Medical.)

Mold, A. (2008). *Heroin: The treatment of addiction in twentieth-century Britain*. DeKalb, IL: Northern Illinois University Press.

Musto, D. F. (2002). *One hundred years of heroin*. Westport, CT: Auburn House.

GAVRIL W. PASTERNAK

HIGH SCHOOL SENIOR SURVEY.
See **Monitoring the Future.**

HISPANIC AMERICANS, ALCOHOL AND DRUG USE AMONG.
Hispanic Americans are a large, growing, diverse group. More precisely, revised U.S. Census Bureau figures released in May 2006 put the total at 44.3 million—of these, 64 percent are Mexican in origin, 9 percent Puerto Rican in origin, and 3 percent Cuban in origin. Yet another 24 percent are classified by the U.S. Bureau of the Census as "other Hispanic," 55 percent of which are from the various Central and South American countries. The rapid growth of the Latino population within the United States also is noteworthy: This population grew by 57.9 percent between 1990 and 2000. A high birth rate and continuous new immigration fuel this growth. The terms *Hispanic* and *Latino* are used interchangeably. Hispanic is commonly used in official statistics, and Latino is more widely used within the population itself.

On average, Hispanics are younger than other minorities and other American population groups. When youthfulness is combined with poverty or discriminatory practices, the result sometimes is a disproportionate degree of conflict with law enforcement, especially in connection with drug abuse and drug dealing. The media coverage of these conflicts may lead to prejudicial beliefs about Latinos and drug use.

Most Hispanic Americans live in urban areas of the United States. Lacking other options, they are steadily crowding into the poorest sections of New York, Los Angeles, Chicago, and other large cities. In 1999, 22.6 percent of Latinos in the United States lived in poverty compared with 24.9 percent of black families and 12.4 percent of all other Americans. Poor education, difficulty with the English language, and urban concentration can compound this impoverishment—as it has for the other immigrant minorities in the United States—thereby contributing to the complexity of modern urban problems that they must face daily.

All segments of this highly diverse group are changing rapidly. From 1999 to 2003, Mexican immigration accounted for one-third of the overall flow of more than 1 million immigrants to the United States per year, and these numbers are rising. The foreign-born population is expected to grow, until by 2050, it is estimated that nearly 25 percent of the U.S. population will be of Hispanic origin. Many of the newcomers crowd into old *barrios* (neighborhoods), and this reduces the quality of life for older residents. Great pressure is therefore exerted on local educational services, health resources, job sources, and job-training services—a pressure that is compounded by problems of acculturation.

Many Mexican-American communities predate the Mexican-American War of the 1840s, but other Latino communities have become established in significant numbers only since World War II. Puerto Ricans, for example, settled mostly in the large cities of the Rust Belt (or Manufacturing Belt formed by parts of the Northeast, Mid-Atlantic, and Upper Midwest states) in the late 1940s and early 1950s, forming a particularly large concentration in New York City. Like Mexican Americans (Chicanos), they have been sharply affected by shifts in the American economy that relegate poorly educated workers to lower paid service jobs. Central and South Americans are found in diverse locations, with concentrations in New York, Houston, and Los Angeles, where they tend to work at the bottom of the labor market. Cubans, who are concentrated

primarily in Miami, have been helped both by a vigorous enclave economy (with Cubans owning many of the enterprises and hiring fellow Cubans) and by Miami's emergence as a center for Latin American trade.

HISPANICS AND ILLICIT DRUGS

Latinos often are typecast as drug users. Such stereotypes persist partly because there is little research information. National statistics about Hispanics mask important variations within the population, not only in ethnicity but also in class and culture. Drug problems of the community are treated principally as criminal phenomena, and indeed, in many states a disproportionate number of Latinos are imprisoned for drug-related offenses. The context for drug use is little studied.

What then is really known about drug use by Hispanics? Specifically, the 2007 National Survey on Drug Use and Health (NSDUH) report showed that Hispanics are generally less likely to use any illicit drug than either blacks or whites. The same survey reported illicit drug use among Hispanics at 6.9 percent (Substance Abuse and Mental Health Services Administration, 2007). Hispanics are most likely to use cocaine, and next most likely (after blacks) to use crack cocaine.

While heroin has posed problems for Latinos, particularly in New York and the Southwest, the prevalence rates for this drug are low. The general population had 136,000 current heroin users in 2005, a figure that rose to 338,000 in 2006 (SAMHSA). Heroin use has been studied in several southwestern communities, in particular in the context of peer group and family in Los Angeles barrios.

The aggregate figures also conceal significant subgroup and geographic differences. Puerto Ricans are especially likely to use cocaine, for example, and Cubans are notably less likely to use any drug. (However, clinical data indicate that Cuban drug use is actually higher than survey data show.) Studies of persons arrested for crimes, for example, show that more than two-thirds of Hispanic arrestees in Chicago, New York, Philadelphia, and San Diego were using drugs, but proportions were far lower in most other cities (U.S. Department of Justice, 1991). More than two-thirds of local jail inmates (68%) were dependent on or abusing drugs or alcohol, according to a 2002 survey of men and women held in local jails. While 78 percent of white inmates and 64 percent of black inmates were reportedly dependent on or abusing drugs and alcohol, only 59 percent of Hispanic inmates were dependent on or abusing drugs or alcohol (U.S. Department of Justice, 2002).

Differences in drug use by males and females are sharper for Hispanics than for other ethnic or cultural groups. Mexican American and Puerto Rican boys and girls are socialized very differently to alcohol and drug use—that is, there is more parental and community disapproval for girls and more permissiveness for boys. Research also shows that most female heroin addicts usually begin to use the drug with a male friend, spouse, or common-law partner, thus suggesting that the use depends on a relationship. Hispanic women appear to be greatly influenced by traditional ideas about the role of women, even under the pressures of urbanization, acculturation, and poverty (Moore, 1990).

As to adolescents, the most susceptible group, there is little information about how adolescent Hispanic groups differ from other adolescent groups in drug use. National surveys of high school seniors discover only small differences, but the surveys omit dropouts, who are often the adolescents most at risk, and Hispanic adolescents have very high dropout rates. Most studies confirm that the same risk factors that are important for other youth are important for Hispanics: above all, a disruptive family environment, availability of drugs, peer influences, and patterns of unconventional behavior (such as low school achievement, rebelliousness, and early sexual activity). These influences (plus the degree of acculturation and individual judgments of the adolescent) seem to be related, in a general way, with beginning drug use and a steady use of drugs (Booth, Castro, & Anglin, 1990).

One recent study indicated that acculturated Hispanics show patterns of substance abuse that are similar to non-Hispanic whites. "The study showed that 6.4 percent of whites reported using illicit drugs in the previous month, compared to 7.2 percent of acculturated Hispanics. However, less than 1 percent of non–acculturated, Spanish-speaking Hispanics reported use in the same time period" (Medical News Today, 2007). The authors of the study explained that, in states such as California, large Hispanic enclaves have a protective effect on new arrivals that mitigates drug experimentation.

A special factor that affects Latinos is the overriding importance in the culture of the family. This influence has both positive and negative effects. The extended family among Puerto Ricans in New York may limit drug use by protecting and controlling youngsters in both single and two-parent households (Fitzpatrick, 1990). In Cuban families, by contrast, illicit drug use may occur when the family structure is severely disrupted, often by the trauma of refugee migration, and researchers argue that the very cohesiveness of the Cuban family may be associated with parental overprotectiveness and adolescent rebellion, sometimes accompanied by drug use as a symptom (Rio et al., 1990).

Research suggests that Hispanic clients achieve only mixed success in treatment, but that finding needs qualification, due to the limitations of available treatment programs. Because of poverty and residence in blighted areas, a disproportionate number of Latino heroin users, for example, are enrolled in programs that simply administer blocking drugs (e.g., methadone) with virtually no other treatment. Urban drug treatment programs generally face chronic shortages of money and personnel. When drug abusers gain access to broader treatment, failure can often be blamed upon the absence of culturally sensitive therapies (Rio et al., 1990). Fitzpatrick (1990) has suggested that Puerto Ricans in New York City show an "extraordinary" ability to cope with a community saturated with drugs and that efforts should be made to build on this ability.

HISPANICS AND ALCOHOL

Among Hispanic and many other groups, alcohol use has been easier to study than the use of illicit drugs; many of its patterns are similar to and may shed light on drug use. As they do with drugs, Hispanics use less alcohol over their lifetimes than do Anglos (i.e., non-Hispanic white U.S. inhabitants in general, not just those of English ancestry), and their usage is only very slightly more than that of blacks. Again as with drugs, sharp gender differences occur in alcohol use, which are especially noteworthy among immigrants. Among Mexican Americans, the gap between male and female drinking narrows but never disappears in succeeding generations, and much recent research focuses on this acculturation effect, so critical in a large new immigrant population (Canino, 1994). Among younger women, the narrowing gap seems to reflect both acculturation and upward social mobility. Even within one city, Mexican-American drinking habits vary greatly by class (Trotter, 1985). However, Gilbert found that Mexican Americans in California also identify family, financial, and job problems as factors in abusive drinking; they tend to recognize alcoholism not as a medical problem but as a failure of will (Gilbert, 1985). Certainly there is no one set of beliefs, behaviors, or norms associated with Latinos and drinking. Lifestyle diversity within Latino subgroups suggests the need for a corresponding diversity of treatment approaches. The failure of such standard treatments as Alcoholics Anonymous among Hispanics in certain areas should be noted.

Finally, as noted before regarding drugs, there are important differences in drinking behavior between subgroups of Hispanics. Pentecostal church groups have had notable success in influencing the drinking behavior of some Puerto Ricans, although some clinicians have expressed the view that Puerto Ricans are reluctant to use treatment services. Cuban drinking patterns are generally moderate: Cultural values of self-control forbid discernible drunkenness for both men and women. Increasing acculturation gradually increases alcohol usage but reduces reliance on minor tranquilizers by Cuban women. Of the little information available on the subject, all stresses the importance of individual ethnic experience.

See also **Alcoholics Anonymous (AA); Cocaine; Coping and Drug Use; Crack; Crime and Drugs; Criminal Justice System, Treatment in the; Dropouts and Substance Use; Families and Drug Use; Heroin; Marijuana (Cannabis); Methadone Maintenance Programs; Mexico; National Survey on Drug Use and Health (NSDUH); Opiates/Opioids; Prisons and Jails, Drug Treatment in; Risk Factors for Substance Use, Abuse, and Dependence: Gender; Risk Factors for Substance Use, Abuse, and Dependence: Race/Ethnicity; U.S. Government Agencies: Substance Abuse and Mental Health Services Administration (SAMHSA).**

BIBLIOGRAPHY

Booth, M. W., Castro, F. G., & Anglin, M. D. (1990). What do we know about Hispanic substance abuse? A review of the literature. In R. Glick & J. Moore (Eds.), *Drugs in Hispanic communities.* New Brunswick, NJ: Rutgers University Press.

Canino, G. (1994). Alcohol use and misuse among Hispanic women. *International Journal of the Addictions, 29,* 1083–1100.

Fitzpatrick, J. P. (1990). Drugs and Puerto Ricans in New York City. In R. Glick & J. Moore (Eds.), *Drugs in Hispanic communities.* New Brunswick, NJ: Rutgers University Press.

Gilbert, M. J. (1985). Mexican Americans in California: Intercultural variation in attitudes and behavior related to alcohol. In L. A. Bennett & G. M. Ames (Eds.), *The American experience with alcohol.* New York: Plenum.

Glick, R. (1990). Survival, income, and status: Drug dealing in the Chicago Puerto Rican community. In R. Glick & J. Moore (Eds.), *Drugs in Hispanic communities* (pp. 77–101). New Brunswick, NJ: Rutgers University Press.

Gonzalez, D. H., & Page, J. B. (1981, January–March). Cuban women, sex role conflicts and the use of prescription drugs. *Journal of Psychoactive Drugs, 13*(1), 47–51.

Medical News Today. (2007, August 14). Drug use by Hispanics rises in US culture. Available from http://www.medicalnewstoday.com/.

Moore, J. (1990). Mexican American women addicts. In R. Glick & J. Moore (Eds.), *Drugs in Hispanic communities.* New Brunswick, NJ: Rutgers University Press.

Rio, A., Santisteban, D., & Szapocznik, J. (1990). Treatment approaches for Hispanic drug-abusing adolescents. In R. Glick & J. Moore (Eds.), *Drugs in Hispanic communities.* New Brunswick, NJ: Rutgers University Press.

Substance Abuse and Mental Health Services Administration. (2007). *Results from the 2006 National Survey on Drug Use and Health: National Findings* (Office of Applied Studies, NSDUH Series h–32, DHHS Publication No. SMA 07–4293). Rockville, MD: U.S. Government Printing Office.

Trotter, R. (1985). Mexican-American experience with alcohol: South Texas examples. In L. A. Bennett & G. M. Ames (Eds.), *The American experience with alcohol.* New York: Plenum.

U.S. Department of Justice. (1991). *Drug use forecasting. Drugs and crime (1990 Annual Report).* Washington. DC: National Institute of Justice.

U.S. Department of Justice. (2002). *Substance dependence, abuse, and treatment of jail inmates.* Washington. DC: National Institute of Justice. Available from http://www.ojp.usdoj.gov/.

JOAN MOORE
REVISED BY PUBLISHER (2009)

HIV (HUMAN IMMUNODEFICIENCY VIRUS). *See* Alcohol and AIDS; Injecting Drug Users and HIV; Needle and Syringe Exchanges and HIV/AIDS; Prisons and Jails: Drug Use and HIV/AIDS in; Substance Abuse and AIDS.

HIV RISK ASSESSMENT BATTERY (RAB).

The Risk Assessment Battery (RAB) is a self-administered questionnaire designed for use with substance-using populations. It was developed to provide a rapid (less than 15 minutes) and confidential, non interview method of assessing both needle use practices and sexual activity associated with HIV transmission.

The forty-five questions of the RAB are simply worded and use discrete response categories. Respondents are asked to "check off" the answer that best describes their behavior. There are no open-ended questions, minimizing the need for writing skills. A brief set of instructions is included on the first page of the RAB. However, as with all self-administered questionnaires, it is particularly important to provide the respondent with a proper introduction and explanation of the form, its purpose, and how it is to be completed. A staff member should be available during administration of the test to screen for reading difficulties, answer questions as they arise, and ensure that the form is being filled out properly. Given the very sensitive nature of the information collected, it is also important that individuals administering the RAB address the issue of confidentiality. Although the more private approach of the self-administered questionnaire should reinforce the confidential nature of the assessment, it is very important that respondents understand the confidentiality of their responses will be protected.

There are two global sections within the RAB: 1) drug and alcohol use during the past 30 days, and 2) needle use and sexual behavior during the previous 6 months. Questions have been constructed to provide maximum coverage and sensitivity to potential risk behaviors within these categories. Since self-reports may be expected to provide underestimates of behaviors that are socially unaccepted, items have been assembled that assess a wider range of behaviors associated with HIV infection. Thus, questions ask not only about the behaviors directly responsible for viral transmission such as needle sharing and unprotected sexual activity, but also those associated with such activities (e.g., needle acquisition, shooting gallery attendance, exchange of money or drugs for sex). The inclusion of these items is intended to identify individuals at increased risk of HIV exposure even if transmission behaviors are not directly reported. However, endorsement of these "peripheral behaviors" does not prove that transmission behaviors have actually occurred. For example, an individual who indicates that he or she has visited a shooting gallery on numerous occasions during the assessment interval may not have shared a needle or had unprotected sex even though these behaviors are common in shooting galleries. Instead, these peripheral behaviors may be more readily reported by some respondents despite their reluctance to report primary transmission events such as sharing a syringe or unprotected sexual activity.

Scoring. Sixteen items from the RAB are used in the computation of three scores: a drug-risk score, a sex-risk score, and a total score. These scores are calculated by adding responses to selected items. For individual questions, the values range from zero to a maximum of 4. Higher values for items reflect greater frequency of occurrence for the behavior. The eight-item drug-risk score has a range of 0 to 22. The range of the sex-risk score, comprised of nine items, is 0 to 18. This simple scoring system was designed to capture frequency of engaging in each of the reported risk behaviors. Scores for the various items are not differentially weighted. This scoring strategy serves to guard against underestimates of risk resulting from the tendency to underreport participation in behaviors known to be most likely to transmit the AIDS virus.

As a self-administered questionnaire, the RAB offers an efficient tool for screening individuals who may be at risk for HIV infection. The RAB provides a measure of HIV-risk behaviors, which is broken down into subscales for drug risk and sex risk and combined to yield a measure of total risk. A number of studies conducted by the authors and others suggest that when properly administered, the RAB responses are equivalent to those collected via a personal interview. Test-retest reliability has also been found to be relatively high. Most importantly, the RAB has demonstrated discriminant validity in differentiating between respondents engaging in different drug-use patterns and predictive validity in identifying seroconverters on the basis of higher-risk scores.

As the AIDS epidemic enters its third decade, it has become increasingly important to have valid, reliable, and cost-effective tools to monitor behaviors associated with the transmission of HIV. It is no longer sufficient to direct prevention resources toward populations at risk in a "shotgun" approach to risk reduction. Such a strategy is costly and inefficient since many individuals within risk groups have instituted safer behaviors. Targeting risk-reduction interventions to specific segments of the population at risk and evaluating their efficacy are necessary components in a well-planned approach to HIV prevention. Measures of risk behavior, such as the RAB, are needed to target and evaluate interventions in a more precise manner.

See also **Alcohol and AIDS; Substance Abuse and AIDS.**

BIBLIOGRAPHY

Krupitsky, E. M., et al. (2005). Alcohol use and HIV risk behaviors among HIV-infected hospitalized patients in St. Petersburg, Russia. *Drug and Alcohol Dependence, 72,* 2, 251–256.

Metzger, D., et al. (1992). The impact of HIV testing on risk for AIDS behaviors. In L. Harris (Eds.), *Problems of drug dependence.* NIDA research monograph 119, Washington, D.C.: National Institute on Drug Abuse. 297–298.

Metzger, D., et al. (1993). Human immunodeficiency virus seroconversion among in- and out-of-treatment intravenous drug users: An 18-month prospective follow-up. *Journal of Acquired Immune Deficiency Syndromes, 6,* 1049–1056.

DAVID S. METZGER
HELEN A. NAVALINE
GEORGE E. WOODY

HOMELESSNESS, HISTORY OF ASSOCIATION WITH ALCOHOL AND DRUGS.

As Robert Frost observed in *The Death of the Hired Man,* "home is the place where, when you have to go there, they have to take you in." Not everyone has that privilege, however. The history of homelessness is the history of the social contexts that create both the necessity of refuge and the specific forms it takes. While data about individuals are clues to the larger processes of displacement, they do not explain them. Debates about whether a third or a half of today's sheltered population suffers with current substance abuse often miss this point. Simply put, substance abuse is a significant, but not pervasive, problem among homeless people. It is concentrated among (but not unique to) single men and those who spend unusually long stretches of time in shelters or who "make the loop" among shelters and other institutions reserved for the ill, the wayward, and the dispossessed. This is hardly surprising. While substance abuse usually came before prolonged homelessness, so did a lifetime of poverty, family disruption, and modest educational achievement and vocational development. This constitutes the bundle of liabilities associated with homelessness. But whereas previous generations of impoverished substance abusers scuffled their way through a variety of makeshift economic and housing arrangements that would have disqualified them as homeless by the twenty-first-century definition, the liabilities of that generation play out in a world grown unforgiving at its economic margins and highly dependent on congregate shelters to contain and measure the fallout.

HISTORY

The word *homeless* has a long and complex use. In its most literal meaning of houseless, it has been employed since the mid-1800s to describe those who sleep outdoors or in various makeshifts or who reside in temporary accommodations such as police-station lodgings of earlier generations or emergency shelters of the present day. Another early meaning of the word is not belonging to a place or with the people who live there. This usage was handed down from the largely rural and small-town society of the nineteenth century, in which the coincidence of family and place provided the basis for community and social order, nurturing traditions of mutual aid and the control of troublesome behavior. To be homeless was to be *unattached,* outside this web of support and control; it was to be without critical resources and, equally important, beyond constructive restraint. Many of the young men and women who moved from farm to city, or those who emigrated from abroad during the nineteenth and early twentieth centuries, were unattached in this respect. Organizations like the YWCA, the YMCA, and various ethnic mutual-aid societies were invented both to help and superintend them by creating surrogate social ties.

By the 1840s many Americans linked homelessness with habitual drunkenness. In the popular view, habitual drunkards, usually men, drank up their wages and impoverished their families; they lost their jobs and their houses and drove off their wives and children by cruel treatment. They became outcasts and drifters, and their wives entered poorhouses while their children became inmates of orphanages. By the 1890s the same logic served to explain the downward, isolated spiral of opiate and cocaine *fiends* (as they were called) and the unhappy circumstances of their families.

Until the early years of the Great Depression (which began in 1929), habitual drunkenness, in particular, often was cited as a principal cause of homelessness. Even so, after the financial collapse of 1893 and an ensuing five-year depression of unprecedented severity, most thoughtful observers did not believe heavy drinking or habitual drug use caused homelessness in any *direct* manner. Although scholarly studies during the first decades of the 1900s were crude by today's technical standards, their explanations of homelessness were not simple-minded. In fact, they foreshadowed twenty-first-century explanations.

Perhaps most important, pre-Depression students of homelessness noted that the ranks of the dispossessed grew and diminished in close relation to economic conditions. They understood that the profound depressions that haunted the economy long before 1929 caused large numbers of people to lose their grip on security. They noted as well that certain occupations were especially affected by seasonal fluctuations in the demand for labor and by technological change. For example, by the 1920s, agricultural workers, cigar makers, printers, and others had high rates of *structural* unemployment. That is, their jobs had been lost permanently to changes in methods of production and distribution.

These scholars also understood the importance of decisions that employers made about hiring and firing. Workers without families to support and those regarded as the least productive were let go first when the economy soured. Usually these were single young women assumed able to return to their natal families, married women presumed to be working for *pin money* (people who today are known as secondary wage earners), older men, and in particular, single men known to drink heavily. Minority racial and ethnic status also marked people for layoff. Conversely, in times of high demand for labor, employers relaxed their standards for hiring and job performance. In boom times all but the most seriously disabled or the most erratic and disruptive heavy drinkers and drug users could find some kind of work. The ranks of the homeless thus thinned considerably.

Pre-Depression observers also emphasized the impact of working conditions, disability, and the absence of income supports on the creation of homelessness. In an era of dangerous work and widespread chronic disease (especially tuberculosis), large numbers of men, in particular, became substantially disabled, often at a young age. In an era before significant public disability benefits or much in the way of welfare or effective medical treatment, they rapidly became abjectly poor, reduced to begging, eating in soup kitchens, and bedding down in mission shelters or the cheapest, most verminous lodging houses (*flophouses*, as they came to be called).

Some of these men were heavy drinkers, and some were habitual drug users, but these problems often developed in the context of poverty and rootlessness. The miseries and long stretches of boredom endemic to poverty were understood to promote frequent intoxication—even during the Prohibition years (1920–1933), when illicit alcohol could be had by arrangement, as could illicit drugs. Certain *hobo* occupations that demanded rootlessness and brought together large groups of men without families were regarded as corrupting and debilitating. Railroad gangers, cowboys, farm workers, lumberjacks, and sailors, among others, pursued risky occupations and lived in ways that provided both motive and opportunity for dissipation. During the Depression it was widely feared that tens of thousands of homeless young people in the United States would be maimed hopping freights and would learn bad habits on the road that would transform them into lifelong tramps.

Finally, related to their understanding of homelessness as an unwholesome and demoralizing experience, early observers paid a great deal of attention to the milieu of homelessness—the urban areas where homeless people congregated and the constellation of institutions with which they were involved. Commonly called *hobohemias* before the Depression and *skid rows* thereafter, such areas were characterized by a particular way of life and a peculiar set of economic and social resources. They were honeycombed with cheap restaurants, residential hotels and lodging houses, private and eventually public welfare agencies, and formal and informal labor exchanges that offered casual (day) work. Skid row (and the segregated satellites that developed in minority communities) was also a world dominated by single men. Saloons (later bars) and sex workers saturated the area. Some were the sites of a vigorous drug trade.

By the 1940s, winnowed by wartime labor demand, skid row was both repository and refuge, mainly for impoverished single men disabled by age, injury, and/or chronic illness. They survived on private charity, meager public welfare allowances, modest pensions, and undemanding work. However, skid-row denizens were not homeless, and from the 1940s through the 1970s, they were more often described as *unattached* or *disaffiliated*. They were homeless in the broader, social sense. Further, and contrary to the enduring stereotype, the residents of skid row were not usually heavy drinkers or habitual drug users. Although perhaps one-third could be so described and while public intoxication was common and visible, heavy drinking or drug taking was, as today, the exception and not the rule.

With the sustained prosperity of the period between 1941 and 1973 and the simultaneous elaboration of the American welfare state, many observers believed that skid row would wither away. The older men would die off or—helped by federal Old Age Security and later by Medicare/Medicaid, state and federal disability benefits, and subsidized housing—would move to better neighborhoods. Or they would remain on a skid row that would be uplifted and transformed by urban renewal projects and effective rehabilitation programs for heavy drinkers and drug users.

In a limited sense, these optimists were correct. The expansion of the welfare state dramatically improved the economic circumstances of the elderly, who are rare among the early twenty-first-century homeless. Aided by federal funds, some cities bulldozed their skid-row areas, thus causing their bricks and mortar, at least, to disappear. But homelessness did not disappear; instead, it underwent an astonishing and tragic transformation. If literal houselessness is used as the definition and measure of the problem, only the Depression produced the prodigious dispossession that characterizes the early twenty-first century.

As opposed to the domiciled isolation of skid row, something like the houseless poverty of the early twenty-first century was first reported in news magazines and the occasional scholarly publication as early as 1973. But it was not until the early 1980s that a new generation of younger homeless people achieved widespread notice. At first, most observers were struck by the apparently very high rates of mental illness, heavy drinking, and drug use among these new homeless people. Explanations of the problem pointed toward nationwide changes in policies that governed commitment to and retention in mental hospitals and incarceration for public drunkenness and minor drug offenses. During the 1960s and 1970s many states deinstitutionalized both people with mental illness as well as alcoholics and addicts. State hospital patients were discharged in wholesale fashion, and new laws made initial involuntary commitments difficult; they also severely limited the duration of involuntary treatment. Many states also decriminalized public drunkenness, referring inebriates to places where they could sober up rather than housing them in jail for thirty days to six months. Similarly, many minor drug offenders were diverted from jails. During the early 1980s many observers, notably those within the Reagan administration, characterized the resurgence of homelessness as a problem related to mental disorder, excessive drinking, habitual drug use, and the new policies that kept people with such problems from their customary lodgings in state hospitals and county jails. Homelessness was described mainly as a problem in the rehabilitation and control of troubled and troublesome people who were not only houseless but barred from their traditional institutional shelters and estranged from family and friends who might take them in.

EARLY TWENTY-FIRST CENTURY VIEWS

Although not discounting this view entirely, most scholars now find it simplistic and unsupported by the evidence. Although some popular treatments of the subject continue to claim that perhaps 85 percent of homeless people are substance abusers and/or mentally ill, such huge figures are drawn from old studies that were seriously flawed by two related methodological problems. The first requires little explanation: These studies relied for their estimates on *lifetime* rather than *current* measures of problems. In any group not in treatment or recently discharged, a lifetime measure (a determination of whether a person has ever had a severe mental illness or substance-use disorder) will always produce much higher prevalence rates than a measure of current disorder (customarily defined as present within the previous six months or one year).

The second problem is a matter of how homeless respondents were sampled for these studies and concerns the distinction epidemiologists make between *point prevalence* and *period prevalence*. Point prevalence refers to counts conducted at a single moment in time (a snapshot), whereas period prevalence refers to counts taken over time (a motion picture). Longitudinal (period) counts of homeless people will produce much higher numbers than cross-sectional (point-in-time) enumerations, for many more people are homeless during a year than on a given night. People with problems of substance abuse and mental illness move out of homelessness more slowly, so they will be overrepresented in snapshot studies because they are more likely to be counted. Longitudinal studies during the 1990s demonstrated conclusively that a fairly small group of people with very high rates of disorder (usually single men under forty years old) account for a very large percentage of shelter nights in most cities. Since most studies of homeless populations conducted in the 1980s sampled from shelters on a cross-sectional basis, their estimates of substance abuse and mental illness were correspondingly inflated.

With these caveats in mind, it is probably fair to say that among all homeless adults during the previous year, something like half had a substance-use disorder or a major mental illness, alone or in combination. These rates are substantially higher among single men and significantly lower among adults who are homeless in family groups, most often single women.

Even so, prevalence estimates do not explain the causal relationship between homelessness and substance abuse and mental illness. Clearly, most people with such problems never become homeless. To explain why some do, current scholarship has returned—often unwittingly—to themes first sounded a century ago: the relationship of homelessness to changes in the economy and the nature and supply of housing, to the availability (or coverage) and sufficiency of income supports and medical care, and to the tolerance and support capacity of kin. Heavy drinking, habitual drug use, and mental illness are considered in this larger context. Such problems are understood to be among many risk factors that make it more likely that some people will become homeless repeatedly or remain so for a long time. Moreover, scholars are concerned with how such experience wears people down, introduces or rekindles bad habits or poor health, and makes exits from homelessness less likely or short-lived.

Briefly and simply, early twenty-first-century scholarship suggests the following relationship between homelessness and heavy drinking and habitual drug use. The problem of poverty has worsened considerably since the mid-1970s. Changes in the economy have added high-skill, well-paid technical jobs and low-skill, poorly paid service positions, but these changes have simultaneously produced job losses among semiskilled but highly paid workers, primarily in manufacturing. This process of deindustrialization—the historic passage from a manufacturing to a service economy—has been especially hard on those younger members of the huge baby-boom group (boomers are those born between 1946 and 1964), especially Hispanics and African Americans, who have entered a glutted labor market without the advantage of prolonged higher education or advanced technical training.

At the same time, the 1980s brought startling inflation in rental housing costs and a steep decline in the inflation-adjusted value of federal and state welfare benefits and unemployment insurance. In consequence poor people had an increasingly difficult time forming independent households, and poor families became increasingly hard put to support dependent adult members. Simultaneously, America's most rudimentary housing, the old hotels and lodging houses of skid row and similar areas, was decimated by urban renewal.

Ironically, the unprecedented, sustained economic growth of the 1990s aggravated the problem of homelessness. As the decade wore on, shelter counts rose all over the country. In some part, this was because the general prosperity of the 1990s had little effect in the lowest reaches of the income distribution from which most homeless people come. Cutbacks in federal, state, and local welfare eligibility compounded the problem. Further, rapid economic expansion had a significant inflationary effect on rents. Indeed, for the poorest 20 percent of American households, rents increased faster than incomes between 1995 and 1997. Moreover, the number of units renting for $300 per month (in inflation-adjusted dollars) decreased by 13 percent from 1996 to 1998, resulting in the loss of almost one million such units nationwide. At the same time, the number of households assisted by subsidies from the Department of Housing and Urban Development dropped by 65,000 between 1994 and 1998. In sum, the crisis in affordable housing became worse during the great boom (U.S. Department of Housing and Urban Development, 1999). For a variety of reasons, the supply of affordable housing continued to erode during the first decade of the twenty-first century, whereas the need for it spiked. In 2008 about 8 million low-income households paid more than 50 percent of their income in rent, a figure that increased by a third since 2000 (Locke, Khadduri, & O'Hara, 2007).

CHRONIC HOMELESSNESS AND SUPPORTIVE HOUSING

The most significant change in anti-homelessness policy since the 1990s has been federal emphasis on attending to chronic homelessness. With access to federal resources at stake, states have brought their priorities into line. By government definition, a *chronically homeless* person is someone "with a disabling condition" and a substantial and recent history of continuous or episodic homelessness (Caton, Wilkins, & Anderson, 2007). Roughly 20 percent of the homeless (sheltered) adult population meets these criteria, or about 200,000 people. The *lifetime* prevalence of substance use disorder among the members of this group appears to be very high (Caton, Wilkins, & Anderson, 2007).

The chronic homelessness initiative, as it is known, is controversial for a number of reasons but none more important than its tacit reframing of homelessness as a problem of disability rather than income distribution relative to housing costs. By focusing resources on chronic homelessness, the policy addresses the material basis of homelessness in a limited way by combining federal disability benefits with housing subsidies. Given the inadequacy of unskilled wages to housing costs and the poor coverage and low benefits of American income maintenance programs, it is a stopgap approach dictated by political considerations.

Programs implemented under the initiative rely heavily on *supportive housing*. This combines rehousing efforts with medical and social services. The myriad approaches to supportive housing make generalizations difficult, especially in terms of their effectiveness. The most important distinction among models concerns the role of independent housing. In the most traditional approach—the so-called *staircase* or *continuum of care* model— independent living is preceded by a lengthy period of transitional housing in which homeless people live in supervised, congregate arrangements while they get therapeutic and social support and become *housing ready*. In a more recently developed approach, usually called *housing first*, homeless people are placed immediately in their own residences (often with the service agency as the leaseholder) and get services in their homes or by visiting a program. While there is some evidence that the *housing first* approach is highly effective with people with mental illness (compared to *community-based treatment as usual*), there is far less evidence of its effectiveness with substance abusers or those with multiple problems. Understanding and evaluating these approaches to combining housing with treatment is the most important research problem of the current era. Even so, neither approach can succeed outside experimental conditions in the absence of available, affordable housing.

CONCLUSION

Poor people have been badly squeezed since the early 1970s. As a consequence, perhaps three percent of all American adults, about 5.5 million people, experienced at least one spell of homelessness between the beginning of 1985 and the end of 1990 (Burt, 1996). Some, however, experience frequent and prolonged episodes of homelessness, and it is among these people that rates of heavy drinking and habitual drug use are very high. It is not simply the case, however, that drinking and taking drugs has caused their homelessness. The problems often associated with such habits may have played an important role in job loss, familial estrangement, or displacement from housing, but this is not a new phenomenon.

Now, though, the absorptive mechanisms of earlier generations have gone awry. Deinstitutionalization has been a factor in this breakdown, mainly because community care never has been equal to the unprecedented need. Nonetheless, more important factors in the creation of widespread houseless poverty among heavy drinkers and habitual drug users have been the disappearance of casual labor, the erosion of public benefits and the capacities of kinship, and the virtual destruction of the tough but viable refuge of skid-row housing. In 1970 impoverished heavy drinkers and habitual drug users could almost always find some port in the storm, often by moving from one decrepit hotel to another, frequently pooling resources to rent a room by the week. Since the 1980s they can no longer do this. Thus they have become a large and highly visible proportion of those who inhabit our public places and persist in our shelters month after month.

See also **Alcohol- and Drug-Free Housing; Alcohol: History of Drinking in the United States; Treatment: A History of Treatment in the United States.**

BIBLIOGRAPHY

Blumberg, L. U., Shipley, T. F., Jr., & Barsky, S. F. (1978). *Liquor and poverty: Skid row as a human condition.* New Brunswick, NJ: Rutgers Center of Alcohol Studies.

Burt, M.R. (1996). Homelessness: Definitions and counts. In J. Baumohl (Ed.), *Homelessness in America* (pp. 15–23). Phoenix, AZ: Oryx Press.

Caton, C. L. M., Wilkins, C., & Anderson, J. (2007). People who experience long-term homelessness: Characteristics and interventions. In *Toward understanding homelessness: The 2007 National Symposium on Homelessness Research.* Retrieved May 27, 2008, from http://aspe.hhs.gov/.

Hopper, K. (2003). *Reckoning with homelessness.* Ithaca, NY: Cornell University Press.

Kusmer, K. (2002). *Down and out, on the road: The homeless in American history.* New York: Oxford University Press.

Locke, G., Khadduri, J., & O'Hara, A. (2007). Housing models. In *Toward understanding homelessness: The 2007 National Symposium on Homelessness Research.* Retrieved May 27, 2008, from http://aspe.hhs.gov/.

U.S. Department of Housing and Urban Development. (1999). *Waiting in vain: An update on America's housing crisis.* Washington, DC: U.S. Government Printing Office.

Jim J. Baumohl

HOOKAH. A hookah—also known as a water-pipe, hubble bubble, nargile, argileh, shisha, boory, and goza—is a long-necked device used to smoke tobacco. Hookahs may vary in size, shape, and composition, but they all have four main parts: (1) the head, where the tobacco is placed and indirectly heated, (2) a pipe that connects the bowl to the base and dips into the water in the base, (3) the base, which is partially filled with water, and (4) one or more flexible connecting hoses and mouthpieces from which the smoke is inhaled. To use a hookah, charcoal is placed on perforated foil or another type of screen on top of the tobacco-filled head. The charcoal is then lit, and as the user inhales through the mouthpiece, the tobacco smoke passes through the water in the base of the pipe and passes through the hose to the user.

While the exact origin of hookah smoking is unclear, the use of hookahs to smoke opium, hashish, and tobacco is centuries old. Hookah tobacco smoking in the Middle East declined for most of the twentieth century, but it experienced a resurgence in the 1990s. This resurgence occurred at the same time as the introduction of maassel (also spelled mu'essel or mu'assel, and sometimes referred to as shisha in the U.S.), a tobacco sweetened with honey or molasses that is available in a variety of flavors, including apple, banana, strawberry, chocolate, mint, coffee, rose, and vanilla. Hookah use began to spread globally in the late 20th and early twenty-first centuries. In 2007 the American Lung Association described waterpipes as the "first new tobacco trend of the twenty-first century."

Hookahs are generally used in a group setting, either in a private residence or in a public place. In Middle Eastern and Indian countries, hookahs are widely used in coffee houses, restaurants, and hookah cafes by individuals from many age groups and social classes. In Europe and the United States, hookah lounges (also called hookah bars or cafes) are growing in popularity, especially in cities and near colleges and universities. In 2006 an estimated two-thirds of U.S. states had hookah lounges, with California, Illinois, New York, Texas, and Virginia having the greatest number. U.S. hookah users are primarily young adults between the ages of 18 and 25, and hookahs are particularly popular among college students. Studies published in 2008 estimated that between 15 and 20 percent of college freshmen have smoked tobacco in a hookah in the past month (Eissenberg, et al., 2008; Grekin & Ayna, 2008).

The increasing popularity of hookah use among young adults in the U.S. can be linked to several factors. Unlike cigarette smoking, hookah smoking is an intermittent, uniquely social activity. Hookah lounges provided an opportunity for socialization similar to that of bars and clubs, but hookah lounges have the added appeal of sometimes being open later hours (until 4:00 a.m. in some instances) and sometimes being open to those who are under 21. (Most hookah lounges require customers be of legal adult age, but some establishments that sell herbal maassel may have a lower minimum age.)

Hookah smoking is relatively inexpensive, which also increases its appeal. Waterpipes and maassel are widely available for purchase on the Internet and in certain retail establishments, such as hookah lounges and Middle Eastern markets. In 2008, online prices for packaged maassel range from $7 to $20 for 250 grams, (enough to fill approximately 20 to 30 hookah heads). Maassel is also sold in single-serve packages, called "shots," for less than $1 each. The cost for the use of a hookah and a bowl of maassel at hookah bars ranges from $5 to $20.

The increasing popularity of hookah smoking in the U.S. can also be attributed to the belief, held by the majority of hookah smokers, that hookah smoking is less harmful than cigarette smoking. The fact that hookah smoke is smoother and less irritating than cigarette smoke may help to perpetuate this belief. Unfortunately, this smoothness, combined with the pleasurable smell and taste of the sweetened, flavored tobacco, may actually encourage a hookah smoker to smoke for a longer period of time and to inhale more deeply. The

World Health Organization (2005) estimates that hookah users may inhale as much smoke during one hookah session as a cigarette smoker would inhale consuming one hundred or more cigarettes.

A common misperception is that the water in a hookah filters out the dangerous ingredients of the tobacco smoke. While there is minimal research on the subject, it appears that the water in a hookah may filter out only a small amount of the carbon monoxide, nicotine, tar, and heavy metals found in hookah smoke. For example, Shafagoj, Mohammed, and Hadidi (2002) found that less than five percent of nicotine is filtered out into the water. This nominal reduction of nicotine may be offset by a tendency for the hookah smoker to inhale more deeply or more often to get the desired amount of nicotine. It is estimated that a person who smokes a hookah daily absorbs as much nicotine as someone who smokes ten cigarettes per day, while an occasional hookah smoker (someone who smokes once during a four-day period) absorbs as much nicotine as smoking two cigarettes per day (Neergaard et al., 2007).

This nicotine exposure means that hookah smoking has potentially the same risks of dependence as any other way of using tobacco. However, the risks may be slightly decreased because of the intermittent, recreational nature of hookah use. The limited research on hookah dependence suggests that a transition from social to individual patterns of use, sharing less frequently, or a modification of behavior to accommodate hookah use may be signs of possible dependence. A multidimensional approach to both assessment and treatment of hookah smoking may be necessary to take into account the unique intermittent and social nature of this practice.

Several studies have found that tobacco smoked through a hookah produces more tar than tobacco smoked in a cigarette. However, tobacco smoked through a hookah is heated, not burned, and thus reaches much lower temperatures than in a cigarette. The temperature at which tar is produced may be related to how hazardous and carcinogenic it is. More research is needed to determine the amount and nature of tar produced from hookah smoking, including how this varies by type of tobacco, hookah size and composition, and smoking patterns.

The levels of carbon monoxide (CO) produced and absorbed by hookah smoking may be as high or higher than that of cigarettes. A significant amount of this CO is produced by the combustion of charcoal used to heat the hookah tobacco. CO levels can vary greatly, depending on hookah size (CO levels are higher with smaller hookahs), the type of hose used (CO levels are higher with a plastic hose), the type of charcoal, and the type of tobacco. Hookah smoke also has higher levels of toxic heavy metals—such as arsenic, nickel, and lead—than cigarette smoke. It is unclear whether these metals come from the tobacco, the charcoal, the foil often used as a screen, or the metal coating of the hookah bowl. Another health hazard unique to hookah smoking is the spread of infectious diseases. Sharing a waterpipe can spread tuberculosis and viruses such as herpes and hepatitis. The use of disposable mouthpieces can help reduce this risk.

Many factors make it difficult to assess the specific health consequences directly attributable to hookah smoking, including a lack of studies, differing study methodologies (e.g., smoking machines versus human subjects), the simultaneous use of other tobacco products, and the distinct method of smoking involved in using a hookah (e.g., frequency of puffing, depth of inhalation, length of smoking session). In general, however, the available research indicates that hookah smoking carries many of the same risks as cigarette smoking, including exposure to nicotine and tar, and that it may have some unique risks, such as an increased exposure to carbon monoxide, heavy metals, and infectious diseases.

See also **Tobacco: A History of Tobacco; Tobacco: An International Overview.**

BIBLIOGRAPHY

American Lung Association. (2007). An emerging deadly trend: Waterpipe tobacco use. (Tobacco Policy Trend Alert.) http://www.lungusa2.org/.

Asotra, K. (2006). Hooked on hookah? *Burning Issues: Tobacco-Related Disease Research Program Newsletter.* http://www.trdrp.org/.

Chaouachi, K. (2006). A critique of the WHO TobReg's "Advisory Note" report entitled: "Waterpipe tobacco smoking: Health effects, research needs, and recommended actions by regulators." *Journal of Negative Results in BioMedicine,* 5(17). http://www.jnrbm.com/.

Chaouachi, K. (2007). The medical consequences of narghile (hookah, shisha) use in the world. *Revue d'Epidemiologie et de Sante Publique, 55*(3), 165–170.

Eissenberg, T., Ward, K. D., Smith-Simone, S., & Maziak, W. (2008). Waterpipe tobacco smoking on a U.S. college campus: Prevalence and correlates. *Journal of Adolescent Health, 42*(5), 526–529.

El-Nachef, W. N., & Hammond, S. K. (2008). Exhaled carbon monoxide with waterpipe use in U.S. students. *Journal of the American Medical Association, 299*(1), 36–38.

Grekin, E. R., & Ayna, D. (2008). Argileh use among college students in the United States: An emerging trend. *Journal of Studies of Alcohol and Drugs, 69*(3), 472–475.

Knishkowy, B., & Amitai, Y. (2005). Water-pipe (narghile) smoking: An emerging health risk behavior. *Pediatrics, 116*(1), e113–e119.

Maziak, W., Ward, K. D., Afifi Soweid, R. A., & Eissenberg, T. (2004). Standardizing questionnaire items for the assessment of waterpipe tobacco use in epidemiological studies. *Public Health, 119*(5), 400–404.

Maziak, W., Ward, K. D., Afifi Soweid, R. A., & Eissenberg, T. (2004). Tobacco smoking using a waterpipe: A re-emerging strain in a global epidemic. *Tobacco Control, 13*(4), 327–333.

Maziak, W., Eissenberg, T., & Ward, K. D. (2005). Patterns of waterpipe use and dependence: Implications for intervention development. *Pharmacology, Biochemistry and Behavior, 80*(1), 173–179.

Maziak, W., Ward, K. D., & Eissenberg, T. (2007). Interventions for waterpipe smoking cessation. *Cochrane Database of Systematic Reviews 2007* (Issue 4, Art. No. CD005549).

Neergaard, J., Singh, P., Job, J., & Montgomery, S. (2007). Waterpipe smoking and nicotine exposure: A review of the current evidence. *Nicotine & Tobacco Research, 9*(10), 987–994.

Sajid, K. M., Akhter, M., & Malik, G.Q. (1993). Carbon monoxide fractions in cigarette and hookah (hubble bubble) smoke. *Journal of the Pakistan Medical Association, 43*(9), 179–182.

Salameh, P., Waked, M., & Aoun, Z. (2008). Waterpipe smoking: Construction and validation of the Lebanon Waterpipe Dependence Scale (LWDS-11). *Nicotine & Tobacco Research, 10*(1), 149–158.

Saleh, R., & Shihadeh, A. (2008). Elevated toxicant yields with narghile waterpipes smoked using a plastic hose. *Food and Chemical Toxicology, 46*(5), 1461–1466.

Shafagoj, Y., Mohammed, F., & Hadidi, K. (2002). Hubble-bubble (water pipe) smoking: Levels of nicotine and cotinine in plasma, saliva, and urine. *International Journal of Clinical Pharmacology, Therapy, and Toxicology, 40*(6), 249–255.

Smith-Simone, S., Maziak, W., Ward, K. D., & Eissenberg, T. (2008). Waterpipe tobacco smoking: Knowledge, attitudes, beliefs, and behavior in two U.S. samples. *Nicotine & Tobacco Research, 10*(2), 393–398.

Ward, K. D., Eissenberg, T., Gray, J. N., Srinivas, V., Wilson, N., & Maziak, W. (2008). Characteristics of U.S. waterpipe users: A preliminary report. *Nicotine & Tobacco Research, 9*(12), 1339–1346.

WHO Study Group on Tobacco Product Regulation. (2005). *Waterpipe tobacco smoking: Health effects, research needs and recommended actions by regulators* (TobReg Advisory Note). Geneva: World Health Organization.

WANDA HAUSER

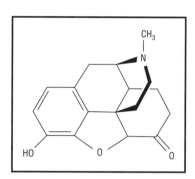

Figure 1. Chemical structure of hydromorphone. ILLUSTRATION BY GGS INFORMATION SERVICES. GALE, CENGAGE LEARNING

HYDROMORPHONE. Hydromorphone is a semisynthetic opioid analgesic (painkiller) derived from thebaine, an alkaloid of the opium poppy (*Papaver somniferum*). It is one of the most widely used and effective analgesics for moderate to severe pain and is often referred to as Dilaudid, one of the brand names under which it is sold. Its potency is almost eightfold greater than is morphine's. Structurally, it is quite similar to morphine but most like dihydromorphine, differing only in the replacement of the hydroxyl (–0H) group at the 6-position with a ketone (=0). Thus, it is not surprising that hydromorphone has many of the same side effects—including sedation, constipation, and depression of breathing. Chronic use will produce tolerance and physical dependence, much like morphine. This drug is reported to have high abuse potential, perhaps due, in part, to its very high potency.

See also **Alkaloids; Analgesic; Morphine; Opiates/ Opioids; Papaver Somniferum; Tolerance and Physical Dependence.**

BIBLIOGRAPHY

Davis, M., Glare, P., & Hardy, J. R. (Eds.). (2005). *Opioids in cancer pain.* New York: Oxford University Press USA.

Jaffe, J. H., & Martin, W. R. (1990). Opioid analgesics and antagonists. In A. G. Gilman et al. (Eds.), *Goodman and Gilman's the pharmacological basis of therapeutics,* 8th ed. New York: Pergamon. (2005, 11th ed. New York: McGraw-Hill Medical.)

Kenakin, T. (2003). *A pharmacology primer: theory, application and methods.* New York: Academic Press.

GAVRIL W. PASTERNAK

IATROGENIC ADDICTION. Addiction can occur as a side effect of some medical care, and physicians need to understand iatrogenic addiction to weigh the risks and benefits associated with the use of medications such as opioids, benzodiazepines, and stimulants. Not only is the use of these addictive medications a concern, but their underuse is as well, because withholding them from patients out of the fear of causing addiction can result in needless suffering. Physicians are also often reticent to prescribe addictive drugs out of fear of retribution from law enforcement and licensing boards.

DEFINING ADDICTION

There has been confusion surrounding the terminology used to discuss addiction. To help promote uniformity, experts from the American Society of Addiction Medicine, the American Pain Society, and the American Academy of Pain Medicine formed a consensus panel in 2001 to define tolerance, physical dependence, and addiction. According to this panel, *tolerance* can be defined as a state of adaptation in which exposure to a drug induces changes that result in a diminution of one or more of the drug's effects over time. *Physical dependence* is defined as a state of adaptation that is manifested by a drug class-specific withdrawal syndrome that can be produced by abrupt cessation, rapid dose reduction, decreasing blood levels of the drug, or administration of an antagonist. It should be noted that tolerance and physical dependence are secondary physical manifestations that can be

expected to occur in virtually all patients treated with opioids and benzodiazepines.

In contrast, *addiction* is a primary neurobiological disorder with genetic, psychosocial, and environmental underpinnings. It manifests as behavior, such as impaired control over drug use, compulsive use, continued use despite harm, and craving. It is also characterized by denial, prompting the phrase often heard in addiction treatment settings: "addiction is the only disease that tells you that you don't have it." However, what appears to be addiction is not always addiction. The term *pseudoaddiction* is used to describe behavior that can occur when symptoms such as pain are inadequately controlled. In an attempt to attain relief due to inadequate dosing or increasing symptoms, a patient may repeatedly request more medications or take higher doses than prescribed. What appears to be noncompliance and a loss of control is instead an effort by a suffering patient to bring his symptoms under control. Thus, inadequate dosing in an attempt to avoid addiction can result in behaviors that resemble addiction.

DRUG CONTROL MEASURES

To understand the reticence of many physicians to prescribe addictive medications, it is helpful to review the history of drug control legislation in the United States. In the nineteenth century, few laws in the U.S. governed addictive medications. Opioids and cocaine were ingredients in many patent medications, and physicians freely prescribed them for many medical conditions. Dependence became a major problem, and—as reported in the October 17, 1903 issue of the Journal of the American Medical Association—physicians were thought to be largely responsible:

> Unfortunately, a large number of cases are reported as directly due to careless prescribing by physicians. Physicians must be guarded and careful in the use of such remedies and must discourage in every possible way the use of proprietary remedies containing them; we must work with all our might for national and local legislation restricting the use of the habit-producing drugs and for the suppression of drug habits. (Drug Habits, 2003)

This perception led to legislation such as the 1906 Pure Food and Drug Act, which required that products containing substances such as opioids and cocaine indicate this on the label. In 1914, the Harrison Narcotics Act was introduced. Though a seemingly reasonable piece of legislation designed to control the nonmedical use of narcotics through taxation and record keeping, the Harrison Act evolved into a drug enforcement instrument that led to the arrest and prosecution of tens of thousands of American physicians over the next 50 years.

The transition of the Harrison Act from a taxation- and documentation-regulatory Act to a drug trafficking control Act can be traced to three Supreme Court cases between 1916 and 1919. In the first, *United States v. Jin Fuey Moy*, 241 U.S. 394 (1916), Dr. Jin Fuey Moy was tried for prescribing 1/16 of an ounce of morphine to a patient who was dependent on opioids. The rationale for prescribing opioids was to prevent the patient from experiencing withdrawal and reduce cravings. This was a common medical treatment strategy at the time, and indeed it is still utilized in methadone and buprenorphine maintenance programs. The Supreme Court decided that the scope of the Harrison Act was limited to taxation and documentation and could not be used for federal control over the practice of medicine. Furthermore, it was the court's decision that the use of the act to suppress the trafficking of opium and other drugs was unconstitutional. As a result of the Court's decision, the Harrison Act could not be used to justify prosecuting physicians such as Dr. Moy.

However, over the next three years, sentiment grew increasingly hostile toward those with an addiction (often referred to as "dope fiends"), as well as the doctors who prescribed opioid medications for them. In 1919, two cases were brought before the Supreme Court to challenge the Harrison Act. In *United States v. Doremus*, 249 U.S. 86 (1919) and *Webb v. United States*, 249 U.S. 96 (1919), the Harrison Act was reinterpreted as having "the moral purpose of discouraging the use of drugs except as a medicine." This wording opened the door to the prosecution of doctors, because addicts were no longer considered patients, and thus satisfying their need for opioids could not be considered medical care. The Supreme Court thus agreed with a lower court's statement that "to call such an order for the use of morphine a physician's prescription would be so plain a perversion of meaning that no discussion of the subject is required." Thus the constitutionality of the use of the Harrison Act to enforce legal penalties on physicians who prescribed addictive medications to addicts was established. Over the next 14 years more than 77,000 violations, mostly by physicians, were prosecuted (Hohenstein, 2001). The Harrison Act was eventually repealed in 1970. The Controlled Substances Act was introduced that year, giving rise to the U.S. Drug Enforcement Administration (DEA) in 1973. In the late 1990s, stories of iatrogenic OxyContin addiction and the well-publicized arrest of overprescribing doctors continued to perpetuate unease over prescribing opioids for the management of chronic pain.

CAUSES OF ADDICTION

Exactly how great a role an exposure to drugs has in causing addiction is a source of continued controversy. The etiology of addiction is thought to be multifactorial. For instance, research into heredity suggests that there is often a strong genetic component. Studies of families in which many members are alcoholic have confirmed that addictions, especially alcohol dependence, run in families. However, genetic analysis has not shed light on which genes, or how many genes, are involved, and the relative contribution of genes versus environment is still actively debated, but it is clear that genes are important. They may determine, for example, how much dopamine is released after a person ingests a standard drink (Yoder, 2005). Also important is early, teenage, binge drinking. Studies in the early 2000s showed that addictions tend to be diseases with a clear pediatric onset, and adolescent drinking is a major culprit (Bonomo, 2004). There is also evidence suggesting that psychological trauma and chronic stress can be contributory (Brady, 2005).

However, the question of whether opioids, stimulants, and other so-called "addictive" medications can themselves cause iatrogenic addiction is still being debated. Certainly these drugs can trigger a relapse in those already diagnosed with addiction, and they can possibly trigger addiction in those who are predisposed to it. Less clear is whether they can cause iatrogenic addiction in those without risk factors. An oft-quoted study from the 1980s estimated addiction to be as low as 5 percent in nonmalignant chronic-pain patients (Portenoy, 1986). However, a more recent meta-analysis looking at only the most valid studies found a prevalence of lifetime substance use disorders among this population ranging from 36 percent to 56 percent, and current substance use disorders were found to be as high as 43 percent (Martell, 2007). Whatever figure is believed or accepted, the true incidence of addiction in opioid-treated patients with chronic pain is unknown.

THE EFFECTS OF ADDICTION

There is evidence that chronic exposure to addictive drugs can have long-lasting effects on the brain. For example, drugs such as opioids and stimulants can alter dendritic density and branching. Furthermore, long-term use may reorganize brain circuits, moving the focus away from circuits associated with "reward" to those related to "habit" in the more dorsal parts of the striatum. This may explain why people with the disease of addiction keep using drugs, despite the loss of the ability to experience pleasure from drugs (Koob, 2003). A 2004 study suggests the possibility that chronic exposure to trace opioids may result in neuroplastic changes in the brain that may predispose to addiction (Gold, 2004). This study points out that while only 5.6 percent of licensed physicians in Florida are anesthesiologists, nearly 25 percent of those with substance abuse or dependence are anesthesiologists. The authors show that fentanyl, a powerful opioid, and anesthetics such as propofol are exhaled in measurable amounts by patients under general anesthesia. Further, in the operating room, direct exposure is common through inhalation, spilling, and "cracking off" the glass top of the vial containing the anesthesia drug. An intriguing hypothesis proposed by Gold is that long-term exposure to these opioids may sensitize or change the brain, resulting in vulnerability to addiction and relapse.

Also intriguing is the possible damaging effect of commonly used sedatives and stimulants on the developing brain. Ikonomidou et al. (2001) have shown that many commonly used anesthetic agents that are NMDA receptor antagonists or $GABA_A$ agonists may induce apoptotic neuronal cell death if administered to patients under the age of four, possibly resulting in later behavioral disturbances. Other studies, though controversial, on the use of stimulants in children being treated for attention deficit hyperactivity disorder (ADHD) have suggested that stimulants may reduce the incidence of the development of later addiction in this population (Beiderman, 2008).

PREVENTION

Given the uncertainty and controversy over the relationship between "addictive" but potentially helpful medications and iatrogenic addiction, the correct approach remains elusive, and always subject to change as our knowledge increases. However, some recommendations and observations can be made. Intensive screening for addiction and risks factors is warranted in patients being considered for potentially addictive medications such as opioids, benzodiazepines, and stimulants. Questions regarding any personal or family history of addiction, tobacco use, and social history can be very enlightening. This can also be problematic, however, since addiction carries stigma, and patients may not be forthright about their personal or family histories. Collateral information may be very helpful, especially since denial and minimization are hallmarks of addiction.

Physicians who treat pain, anxiety, and ADHD should have a low threshold for consulting an addiction medicine specialist to help evaluate and care for these often challenging patients. ASAM is working on the development of a core curriculum to address the overlap between pain management and addiction medicine. Innovative multidisciplinary clinics and rehabilitation facilities are needed that address both pain and addiction. Patients with the disease of addiction may also suffer from a chronic pain condition. These conditions can be successfully comanaged with appropriate medication choices and vigilant monitoring for compliance and recovery.

Finally, medications can be chosen to minimize their addictive potential. Since reinforcement is related to the rapidity of drug increase, medications that are time released, or have long half-lives may be less addictive than quick-release short-acting medications. For this reason, although breakthrough short-acting pain medications are sometimes helpful, they should be used sparingly. Nonreinforcing adjuncts are helpful, and urine monitoring for medications that should be present (as well those that should not) is suggested. If stimulants for ADHD or benzodiazepines for anxiety are warranted, long-acting medications may be preferred.

More research is clearly needed into the potential for iatrogenic addiction as a result of occupational exposure. Operating rooms should be well ventilated, scavenger systems operational, and gloves worn. Finally, addiction should be viewed as a life-threatening disease rather than a moral shortcoming. Those who suffer from it deserve to be treated with compassion and dignity.

See also **Addiction: Concepts and Definitions; Harrison Narcotics Act of 1914; Physicians and Medical Workers, Substance Abuse among.**

BIBLIOGRAPHY

American Society of Addiction Medicine. (2001). Development of a core curriculum in pain medicine and addiction medicine. (ASAM Public Policy Statement). Chevy Chase, MD: Author. Available from http://www.asam.org/.

Biederman, J., Monuteaux, M.C., Spencer, T., Wilens, T. E. Macpherson, H. A., & Faraone, S. V. (2008). Stimulant therapy and risk for subsequent substance use disorders in male adults with ADHS: A naturalistic controlled 10-year follow-up study. *American Journal of Psychiatry*, 165(5), 597–604.

Bonomo, Y., Bowes, G., Coffey, C., Carlin, J. B. & Patton, G. C. (2004). Teenage drinking and the onset of alcohol dependence: A cohort study over seven years. *Addiction*, 99(12), 1520–1528.

Brady, K. T., & Sinha, R. (2005). Co-occurring mental and substance use disorders: The neurobiological effect of chronic stress. *American Journal of Psychiatry*, 162(8), 1483–1493.

Courtwright, D. T. (2004). The controlled substances act: How a "big tent" reform became a punitive law. *Drug and Alcohol Dependence*, 76(1), 9–15.

Drug habits. (1903). *Journal of the American Medical Association*, 41, 968–969.

Flugsrud-Breckenridge, M. R., Gervitz, C., Paul, D., & Gould, H. J. (2007). Medications of abuse in pain management. *Current Opinions in Anesthesiology*, 20(4), 319–324.

Gold, M. S., Byars, J. A., & Frost-Pineda, K. (2004). Occupational exposure and addiction for physicians: Case studies and theoretical implications. *Psychiatric Clinics of North America*, 27(4), 745–753.

Gold, M. S., Melker, R. J., Pomm, R., Frost-Pineda, K., Morey, T., & Dennis, D. M. (2004). Anesthesiologists are exposed to fentanyl in the operating room: Addiction may be due to sensitization. *International Journal of Neuropsychopharmacology*, 7(S1), P01–P023.

Hohenstein, K. (2001). Just what the doctor ordered: The Harrison Anti-Narcotic Act, the Supreme Court, and the federal regulation of medical practice, 1915–1919. *Journal of Supreme Court History*, 26(3), 231–256.

Ikonomidou, C., Bittigau, P., Koch, C., Genz, K., Hoerster, F., Felderhoff-Mueser, U., et al. (2001). Neurotransmitters and apoptosis in the developing brain. *Biochemical Pharmacology*, 62(4), 401–405.

Kalivas, P.W., & Volkow, N. (2007). The neural basis of addiction: A pathology of motivation and choice. *American Journal of Psychiatry*, 162, 1403–1413.

Koob, G. F. (2003). Neuroadaptive mechanisms of addiction: Studies on the extended amygdala. *European Neuropsychopharmacology*, 13 (6), 442–452.

Koob, G. F., & Le Moal, M. (2005). Plasticity of reward neurocircuitry and the "dark side" of addiction. *Nature Neuroscience*, 8(11), 1442–1444.

Martell, B. A., O'Connor, P. G., Kerns, R. D., Becker, W. C., Morales, K. H., Kosten, T. R., et al. (2007). Systemic review: Opioid treatment for chronic back pain: Prevalence, efficacy, and association with addiction. *Annals of Internal Medicine*, 146(2), 114–127.

Morse, R. M., & Flavin, D. K. (1992). Definition of alcoholism. *Journal of the American Medical Association*, 268(8), 1012–1014.

Porrino, L. J., Lyons, D., Smith, H. R., Daunais, J. B., & Nader, M. A. (2004). Cocaine self-administration produces a progressive involvement of limbic, association, and sensorimotor striatal domains. *Journal of Neuroscience*, 24(14), 3554–3562.

Portenoy, R. K., & Foley, K. M. (1986). Chronic use of opioid analgesia in nonmalignant pain: Report of 38 cases. *Pain*, 25(2), 171–186.

Savage, S. R., Joranson, D. E., Covington, E. C., Schnoll, S. H., Heit, H. A., & Gilson, A. M. (2003). Definitions related to the medical use of opioids: Evolution towards universal agreement. *Journal of Pain Symptom Management*, 26(1), 665–667.

Singer, M. (2001). Toward a bio-cultural and political integration of alcohol, tobacco and drug studies in the coming century. *Social Science & Medicine*, *53*(2), 199–213.

Volkow, N. (2006). Prescription stimulants: Retaining the benefits while mitigating the risk of abuse. *Child and Adolescent Psychopharmacology News*, *11*(3), 1–4.

Yoder, K. K., Constantinescu, C. C., Kareken, D. A., Normandin, M, D., Cheng, T.-E., O'Connor, S. J., et al. (2007). Heterogeneous effects of alcohol on dopamine release in the striatum: A PET study. *Alcoholism: Clinical and Experimental Research*, *31*(6) 965–973.

MARK S. GOLD
JOHN A. BAILEY

IBOGAINE. The roots of the shrub *Tabernanthe iboga* first aroused pharmacological interest in 1864 when a French naval surgeon brought some back from Gabon, West Africa. The root was eaten by various Gabonese tribes as part of initiation ceremonies of puberty and was said to produce intoxication, visions, and a reduced need for sleep.

An active alkaloid, ibogaine ($C_{20}H_{26}N_2O$), was isolated in 1901 from the roots, bark, and leaves of *Tabernanthe iboga*. In the early 1900s, some medical researchers in France recommended ibogaine for use in treating neurasthenia and asthenia (syndromes that would probably be diagnosed in the twenty-first century as depression or fatigue syndrome). Although the drug was part of a proprietary medication marketed in Europe in the late 1930s and throughout the 1940s, ibogaine attracted little medical or scientific attention until the emergence of interest in indole alkaloids that accompanied the use of reserpine in the 1950s. During the 1960s, when there was considerable research on the use of lysergic acid diethylamide (LSD) and other psychedelic agents (hallucinogens) in psychotherapy, ibogaine was also studied, since it appeared to produce mental effects similar in some ways to other hallucinogens. At about the time of these studies, 1967–1968, the World Health Organization and the U.S. Food and Drug Administration (FDA) classified ibogaine as a hallucinogen, along with LSD, mescaline, and psilocybin.

In 1962, Howard Lotsof, who was at the time addicted to heroin, ingested ibogaine in search of a different drug experience. Lotsof came out of a long psychedelic experience, during which he had not taken any heroin, and found that he had no withdrawal symptoms and did not crave drugs. At the time, he noticed that ibogaine had a similar effect on several other heroin addicts. He subsequently remained drug free, completed law school, eventually obtained a patent on the use of ibogaine for the treatment of addiction (brand name Endabuse), and became active in seeking funding to urther develop the drug and to obtain FDA approval for its medical use in treatment of addiction.

As a Schedule I drug under the Controlled Substances Act, ibogaine is considered to be highly subject to abuse and without any approved medical use. To be approved by the FDA, an agent must be shown to be safe and effective. The only reports of the efficacy of ibogaine have been anecdotal ones from individuals in Europe who were addicted to heroin, cocaine, and tobacco. Those who take ibogaine are generally highly motivated since the drug is expensive, costing up to several thousand dollars. While many reported a decrease in drug craving after taking ibogaine, relapse to drug use within a few months was also observed.

As a result of pressure from activists, the U.S. government funded animal studies of ibogaine's actions on opioid and cocaine withdrawal, opioid and cocaine self-administration, and neurotoxicity. Studies in animals have not been entirely consistent. High doses of ibogaine reduced some manifestations of opioid withdrawal in monkeys. Studies in opioid-dependent rodents have shown that ibogaine decreases withdrawal, but other studies have not. Some rodent studies have shown a decrease in drug self-administration. Studies of ibogaine toxicity have also produced mixed results. Some studies in monkeys produced no obvious nervous system toxicity, but a study in rats produced damage to neurons in the cerebellum, the part of the brain known best for its role in control and coordination of movement. Other research studies indicate that ibogaine is not similar to opioids such as morphine and heroin nor to hallucinogens such as LSD in terms of actions at drug receptors.

Despite these inconclusive research findings, the National Institute on Drug Abuse (NIDA) has sponsored studies to evaluate the pharmacology and toxicology of ibogaine. The FDA has not approved ibogaine for treatment of addiction and NIDA discourages human trials. At least twelve deaths have been attributed to the use of ibogaine in the treatment of heroin addiction.

See also **Ayahuasca; Hallucinogenic Plants; Hallucinogens; Treatment, Pharmacological Approaches to: An Overview.**

BIBLIOGRAPHY

Blakeslee, S. (1993). A bizarre drug tested in the hope of helping drug addicts. *New York Times*, October 27, p. C11.

Deecher, D. C., et al. (1992). Mechanisms of action of ibogaine and harmaline congeners based on radioligand binding studies. *Brain Research, 571,* 242–247.

Goutarel, R., Gollnhofer, R., & Sillans, R. (1993). Pharmacodynamics and therapeutic applications of iboga and ibogaine. Translated by William Gladstone. *Psychedelic Monographs and Essays, 6,* 71–111.

Jetter, A. (1994). The psychedelic cure. *New York Times Magazine*, April 10.

Karel, R. (1993). FDA approves trials of hallucinogen for treating cocaine, heroin addiction. *Psychiatric News*, September 17, p. 7.

Lewis, W. H. (2005). Hallucinogens. In *Medical botany: Plants affecting human health*. Hoboken, NJ: John Wiley & Sons.

Qiu, J. (2005). Herbal Remedy. *Nature Reviews Neuroscience, 6,* 3, 167.

Rumsey, S. (1992). Addiction and obsession. *New York Newsday*, Thursday, November 19, p.1.

Schultes, R. E. (1967). The place of ethnobotany in the ethnopharmacologic search for psychotomimetic drugs. In D. H. Efron, B. Holmstedt, & N. S. Kline (Eds.), *Ethnopharmacologic search for psychoactive drugs*. Public Health Service Publication no. 1645. Washington, D.C.: U.S. Government Printing Office.

JEROME H. JAFFE

IMAGING TECHNIQUES: VISUALIZING THE LIVING BRAIN.

The term *brain imaging* is most broadly used to encompass all non-invasive methods that depict internal features of the brain. Those most typically associated with imaging of the brain for studies of substance abuse and dependence are single photon emission tomography (SPECT), positron emission tomography (PET), magnetic resonance imaging (MRI), and magnetic resonance spectroscopy (MRS). Each of these four major categories of techniques possesses strengths and weaknesses and they are increasingly becoming complementary tools for investigating the brain. As a group, they have the capacity to measure the concentrations of neurochemicals and rates of metabolic pathways, quantify specific proteins such as subtypes of neurotransmitter receptors or transporters, assess blood flow, observe changes in the brain caused by alterations in brain function, and map connections among brain regions. They are increasingly being used to address the little-studied issues of gender differences (Cosgrove, et al., 2007). This entry describes the technological basis of the imaging techniques and with each, briefly describes examples that highlight particular strengths of the methods with regard to their ability to study substance use, abuse, and dependence.

SINGLE PHOTON EMISSION TOMOGRAPHY (SPECT)

This technique might be considered an x ray from the inside, so a description of the principle of x ray is useful for understanding SPECT. An x ray is created by shining a beam of x rays at an object. A photographic plate or digital detector is placed behind the object (a hand, for example). The tissue absorbs some of the x rays and reduces the film exposure behind the hand. Bone absorbs more x rays than soft tissue, so where there are bones, the film is less exposed. Upon development, the outline of the hand is visible with bones readily apparent inside.

SPECT imaging, by contrast, makes use of injectable radioisotopes placed in chemicals that are associated with particular features of interest in the brain, such as blood flow or benzodiazepine receptors. The radio-labeled compound is injected, travels through the blood stream to the brain, where it is taken up and trapped, ideally in proportion to the quantity of the protein target or physical effect that is being studied. The radioisotope atoms that are part of the injected chemical emit x rays, which are measured with an array of detectors around the head. When the measurements are analyzed to form images, one can determine the distribution of the isotope through the brain. The sensitivity of this technique is high enough to make the measurements of chemoreceptor binding in the brain. In new SPECT cameras, the resolutions, defined as the full-width of the signal at half the maximum amplitude from a small sample, are 6 to 8 millimeters, which means that areas of the brain that small and in some cases a little smaller can be visualized.

Isotopes commonly used with SPECT include iodine-123 and technecium-99m. A laborious and creative task for radiochemistry is the design of compounds that bind to brain targets at low concentrations, allow labeling with radioisotopes, and can enter the brain in sufficient quantities to allow their detection at doses that are safe for humans. Once promising chemicals are identified, additional work is carried out to measure whether the chemical's binding is specific enough to be useful and whether it yields sufficient sensitivity to support brain studies at safe concentrations.

SPECT is in use to study the effects on the brain of many drugs, including nicotine. For example, smokers have more nicotinic acetylcholine receptors than do nonsmokers (Staley et al., 2006). Among alcoholics, those in early abstinence show elevated benzodiazepine receptor numbers compared to nondependent healthy subjects, with nonsmokers showing greater elevations than smokers (Staley, 2005).

POSITRON EMISSION TOMOGRAPHY (PET)
Conceptually related to SPECT, the radioisotopes used with this technique do not themselves emit the x rays for detection by the scanner. Instead, they emit positrons, which are the positively charged equivalent of an electron. The positron travels randomly for up to a few millimeters until it encounters an electron, at which point the positron and electron annihilate one another and from the site of the collision, two x rays are emitted in almost exactly opposite directions. The PET camera has detectors around the head. A count is registered when two x rays are detected simultaneously 180 degrees apart. Background radiation is a source of noise in PET and SPECT imaging, and the requirement that detection be simultaneous at opposite detectors decreases the likelihood of random counts and increases the spatial resolution of the detection, with machines available as of 2008 with resolution of 4 to 5 millimeters.

PET is most commonly used to measure the uptake of the sugar glucose. Under most circumstances, glucose provides the primary fuel for brain energy metabolism. The analog of glucose, deoxyglucose, is taken into cells and almost entirely trapped by the first step of glucose metabolism, so by injecting radio-labeled deoxyglucose and mapping the radioactivity in the brain, one can measure how quickly various regions of the brain are using glucose, as developed in pioneering work by Louis Sokoloff and colleagues in 1977 and adapted and validated for use in humans in 1979 by Michael Phelps and coworkers with the positron emitter fluorine-18 in fluoro-deoxyglucose (FDG). FDG-PET is as of 2008 used widely to investigate cerebral metabolic changes that occur in substance abuse and other psychiatric disorders. Other isotopes that have found use are carbon-11 and oxygen-15.

Carbon-11 and oxygen-15 can be useful because those elements are common in many biological compounds. For example, instead of the glucose analogue FDG, it is possible to use glucose labeled with carbon-11, which is chemically identical to naturally occurring glucose in the body. Oxygen-18 can be used to create labeled water and image its uptake into the brain tissue as a measure of blood flow. A technical difficulty with some isotopes, including carbon-11 and oxygen-15, is their short radiological half-life, 20 minutes and 122 seconds, respectively. Facilities that use such short-lived isotopes must have a cyclotron on site to generate the isotopes immediately before each measurement.

These and other radioisotopes can be used to create ligands used to study dopamine release, dopamine receptor binding, serotonin receptor binding, and many other systems that are of interest for substance abuse. One example of PET applied to improve the understanding of addiction and craving was of dopamine receptor binding in cocaine-addicted patients (Wong et al., 2006). The results showed that the more each individual craved cocaine, the more dopamine that individual had bound to dopamine receptors. The authors concluded that there was likely to be more dopamine release in response to cues in strongly craving subjects than in those who craved cocaine less. Amphetamine, cocaine, and many other drugs of abuse share some effects on dopamine neurotransmission, and this piece of information about cocaine was anticipated to have relevance to craving for alcohol, nicotine, and other drugs.

MAGNETIC RESONANCE IMAGING (MRI)
As a technology that is ubiquitous in the industrialized world and is spreading through the developing

world, MRI has gained widespread utility for clinical evaluations of numerous disorders. MRI is also used widely as a research tool. Because it uses no ionizing radiation, it is often a method of choice for studying children and for following people sequentially over time to track the course of disease development or therapeutic effects.

MRI uses magnetic fields that are tens of thousands of times stronger than the earth's field. Certain atomic nuclei, including hydrogen, have a property called *spin*. When nuclei with spin are put into such a strong magnetic field, a very small minority, much less than one tenth of 1 percent, become aligned with the magnetic field. This small minority provides the sensitivity of the technique. Because the minority is so small, MRI is a relatively insensitive method, on a per-atom basis, but because hydrogen is so abundant in the body, MRI is able to provide measurements of less than one cubic millimeter. If energy is applied to the head in very brief bursts, typically microseconds or milliseconds in length, the nuclei change their distribution. As they gradually return to their slightly biased orientation in the magnetic field, they emit energy, and this energy is detected and used to make images. The frequency of the energy transmitted to the head and received from the head depends on the magnetic field strength and generally lies in the FM radio band. For this reason, MRI suites are generally shielded against outside radio signals, which appear as noise in MRI. A typical hospital MRI machine uses a 1.5 Tesla magnet that operates at 60 MHz, or increasingly, a 3 Tesla magnet that requires 120 MHz, and the frequency of operation depends directly on the magnetic field strength. Stronger magnets are in use for human research projects, as of 2008 as high as 9.4 Tesla. The rate of return to the orientation in the magnetic field is governed by the physical property called *T1*, and the rate at which their radiofrequency signal dies away is under the control of the property called *T2*. T1 and T2 are called *relaxation times*, and their respective values in the brain are typically measured in seconds (for T1) and tens to hundreds of milliseconds (for T2).

A magnet and radiofrequency transmission and reception are sufficient to measure a signal, but not to make images, which requires mapping the locations where the signals originate. MRI machines are equipped with what are called *gradient coils* that are used to induce magnetic field *gradients*. When electric currents pass through the gradient coils, they create linear ramps to the field of the large magnet. Because the frequency of reception at a given location depends on the magnetic field strength at that place in the brain, it is possible in the presence of gradients to determine where in the brain a signal arose, by determining the precise frequency of the signals. The gradient coils are also responsible for most of the loud noises that emanate from MRI machines. Gradient coils make MRI feasible for clinical work and human research, and for their dramatic breakthroughs Paul Lauterbur of SUNY Stonybrook and Peter Mansfield of Nottingham, England, shared the 2003 Nobel Prize for Physiology or Medicine.

Although MRI uses no ionizing radiation, there are risks to its use that must be considered carefully. The primary risk is that of metallic objects being pulled toward the magnet. Such an object could be an iron-containing tool that flies toward the scanner, injuring anyone in its path, or it could be an implanted metal object such as an aneurysm clip. Also at risk are electronic implants that may malfunction in the magnetic field, such as a pacemaker. As magnetic field strengths rise, it has become more important than ever to verify the MRI-safety of implanted medical devices. Some devices are said to be MRI safe, but they may only have been approved for use at magnetic field strengths of 1.5 Tesla, and not above. Some have been approved for use at 3 Tesla, but each device should be checked for safety at any magnetic field.

MRI can be subdivided into structural, functional, perfusion, diffusion, and under development as of 2008, molecular imaging, and magnetic resonance spectroscopy. Each is unique in its application and is discussed below as a separate imaging modality. What is common about each is its goal to create contrast to distinguish particular features of interest.

Structural MRI. This most common form of MRI provides anatomic information about the brain. The images generally resemble what would be seen in an anatomy text, but acquisition parameters and methods can be tailored to emphasize particular aspects, such as vasculature (blood vessels) or fluid-filled lesions (such as areas of dead tissue), for examples. Image contrast often uses the T1 and T2 relaxation times to differentiate tissue, with what are called T1- or T2-weighted images. Images can be obtained under conditions that black out tissues with long T1 values, such as fluid, so that the ventricles (fluid-filled structures in the brain) and sulci (fissures in the surface of the brain) appear black in an image, and the rest of the brain is light. Images can also be measured in ways that emphasize tissues with long T2 values, such as fluid that fills small strokes in the white matter. Contrast agents as of 2008 function primarily by shortening the T1 relaxation time in their vicinity and may be introduced to delineate where the blood-brain barrier has been compromised by acquiring images with scanning procedures that show brighter features where T1 is reduced by the contrast agent.

In research projects, structural images are sometimes used to rule out neurologic contraindications for study participants, but many studies use structural MRI as the primary goal, obtaining measurements of volumes and shapes of brain regions in disorders of the brain. For example, it is possible to measure the thickness of the layer of gray matter that covers the brain, or the size of the fluid-filled ventricles inside the brain, the total volume of white matter in the brain, or the size of particular regions like the frontal lobes or the hippocampus.

MRI image intensity varies according to the type of tissue present (cerebral spinal fluid, white matter, gray matter, or abnormalities such as strokes). The MRI contrast can also depend on factors such as proximity to the ears, the sinuses, the mouth, or deposits of iron in the brain. Any factor that disrupts the magnetic field in the brain has the potential to distort the signal and reduce the image intensity near the object. A bobby pin lodged firmly in a subject's hair might not move in the magnetic field but would eliminate the signal from large regions of the brain. Likewise, deposits of iron in the cerebellum can darken the image at the site of the deposits. Boundaries between air and tissue, as occurs in the sinuses or the ear canals, also can lead to image darkening. These factors must be considered when analyzing structural MRI.

Structural MRI has been used to observe changes in the brain in a variety of disorders. MRI showed reduced volumes of the frontal cortex in recently abstaining cocaine addicts (Fein et al., 2002) and smaller hippocampus and amygdala in marijuana smokers (Yucel et al., 2008). Heavy drinkers have reductions in brain volume that recover significantly after the patients stop drinking, although the recovery is less in tobacco smokers (Gazdzinski, 2008). Indeed, knowledge of that recovery often gives hope to alcohol-dependent patients seeking treatment, providing them with tangible evidence that sobriety will quickly change something so measurable as the sizes of structures in their brains. These are only three examples in the early 2000s of the numerous applications of structural MRI to research on substance abuse.

Functional MRI (fMRI). A common MRI research tool for studies of substance abuse and dependence is fMRI. Most fMRI depends on blood oxygen level-dependent (BOLD) contrast and depends on the magnetic susceptibility caused by deoxygenated hemoglobin (Ogawa et al., 1990; Kwong et al., 1992). Deoxygenated hemoglobin distorts the magnetic field locally and thereby reduces the image signal intensity in its vicinity, whereas oxygenated hemoglobin does not. When blood oxygen levels drop, the MRI signal intensity nearby decreases, and when blood oxygen increases, the MRI signal rises. One might expect, then, that if brain function increases in a particular region of the brain, the brain energy requirements will rise, oxygen levels will be reduced in the nearby capillary bed, and the MRI signal would drop. Paradoxically, however, the MRI signal increases when brain activity increases, and this occurs because blood flow rises rapidly and compensates with oxygen beyond the tissue's immediate needs. Therefore, MRI can be acquired under different conditions, often taking measurements in tens of milliseconds. The images acquired during different activities can be compared, and areas in which intensity changes are observed are designated as having been affected by the change in functional state. Using the principles of the changes in image intensity, brain activity can be evaluated with respect to functional tasks, pharmacologic influences, and changes caused by disease states.

When evaluating an fMRI study, some factors must be considered. One factor is the baseline state, because fMRI necessarily compares two conditions.

For example, if a higher BOLD response is observed in the dorsolateral prefrontal cortex during a functional challenge in a cocaine addict relative to a healthy comparison subject, it could be that the patient required more functional activity to achieve the same task, or it could be that the patient had a lower baseline activity than the control subject but used the same amount of energy to perform the task. Another important factor to consider is that although the contrast is called BOLD, the signal change results not only from the blood oxygenation, but also from the blood volume and the rate of blood flow in the vicinity of the activation. Blood flow or volume can themselves change the BOLD response either independently or interactively with function. Pharmacologic agents (medications) or disease states may therefore alter fMRI findings by themselves. An fMRI is sensitive to brain function but must be interpreted carefully since it is also sensitive to misleading interpretation.

Although structural MRI generally provides information about long-term conditions and changes, fMRI may also be used to assess acute effects. One such example is a study of methadone treatment for heroin addiction that showed significant brain functional responses to heroin-related cues and that methadone reduced those responses (Langleben et al., 2008). The finding is consistent with a vulnerability to relapse that is greatest shortly before the daily dose of methadone. A different strategy to evaluate substance abuse is to use a compound that mimics particular aspects of a substance, like using ketamine to simulate some glutamatergic effects of alcohol, in which case fMRI studies of ketamine (Honey et al., 2005) may provide insights into alcoholism (Krystal et al., 2003; Petrakis et al., 2004).

Perfusion MRI. As a research tool, perfusion MRI can be achieved by various means. Prevalent as of 2008 is a non-invasive approach that uses radiofrequency to effect changes in blood water signal selectively in the neck and then acquire images in the brain. Cerebral perfusion can be assessed by the appearance of the altered blood signal arriving in image slices. Perfusion MRI has been combined with pharmacologic challenges to create *pharmacological MRI* (phMRI), and it has been combined with functional challenges for purposes similar to what is done with fMRI: for example, to determine

how brain perfusion changes before and after a drug is administered.

Perfusion MRI has been used to investigate a variety of substances. One study of cocaine abusers took the novel step of using both SPECT imaging of blood flow and perfusion MRI. Both methods showed significant reductions of blood flow in several deep brain regions and in frontal white matter (Ernst et al., 2000). This study illustrates the benefits of combining imaging techniques and highlights the impact on white matter in psychiatric diseases in general and substance abuse and dependence in particular.

Diffusion MRI. As was illustrated in the discussions of deoxygenated hemoglobin and the presence of magnetic objects, one of the factors that reduces the signal in MRI is magnetic field disruption in some part of the image. Imagine, then, that on a microscopic scale, some water molecules wander randomly from one location to another, where the magnetic field is slightly different. The signal from that water molecule will be lower. Typically, the magnetic field does not vary so strongly on a microscopic scale, but gradient coils can be used to apply a deliberate disruption of the field. The stronger the magnetic field gradient applied, the greater is the sensitivity of the method to the movement of the water molecules, so water that is able to move more freely has its signal reduced. It is possible to apply gradients in different orientations to assess the directionality of the water diffusion. Under those circumstances, one can evaluate the loss of structure in the tissue (diffusion anisotropy) and carry out fiber tracking to evaluate connections among brain regions.

Numerous applications of diffusion MRI have been used, many with diffusion anisotropy rather than the more computationally demanding fiber tracking. Among them is a study of children exposed prenatally to cocaine, which showed that poorer cognitive functioning was directly related to greater fractional anisotropy in frontal white matter (Duckworth Warner et al., 2006). White matter in the normal brain is highly structured, with fibers running from one part of the brain to another. Anisotropy in this case represents a breakdown of that organization in the white matter, perhaps by loss of fibers or by less uniform orientation of fibers in the white matter. This example was selected because it demonstrates the use of MRI in children and because it targets themes that are repeated in investigations of drugs of abuse: damage to white matter and loss of white matter organization.

Molecular Imaging. An area of MRI with enormous potential is the use of contrast agents that target particular chemical receptors or reactions and change image intensity once at the target. Approaches to molecular imaging as of 2008 include the tagging of iron to chemicals that bind to targets of interest in the brain, analogous to the radio-labeling strategies of SPECT and PET: where the iron goes, the signal amplitude is reduced in the images, so MRI darkening represents the presence of the tagged chemicals. Another approach is to use genetic engineering to introduce a protein that can convert an inactive contrast agent to an active one, so that the contrast agents will be effective in cells that express the new gene. Such a gene can be introduced linked to a section of DNA of interest, so that cells that are affected by the contrast are known to carry the section of DNA. A new approach as of 2008 is imaging of transcription of messenger RNA from DNA, which is the first step toward protein synthesis (Liu et al., 2007): This technology allows the mapping of mRNA non-destructively in animals and holds potential for helping researchers understand the processes of drug addiction, treatment, and recovery at the level of generation of RNA from DNA for particular proteins.

MAGNETIC RESONANCE SPECTROSCOPY (MRS)

Magnetic resonance has the ability to measure multiple distinct neurochemicals at the same time. To be detected, chemicals typically must have concentrations of at least a few hundred micromolar, with most scanners limited to 0.5 millimolar or more, but even so, the approach can yield measurements of important chemical entities. The primary chemicals detected by MRS are N-acetylaspartate (NAA), creatine combined with phosphocreatine (Crtotal), a combination of choline, phosphorylcholine, and glycerophosphorylcholine (Cho), myoinositol, and glutamate, glutamine, and gamma-amino butyric acid (GABA). The latter three are usually detected as a combined set of chemicals called *Glx*. With specialized techniques, it is possible to measure GABA, glutamate, and glutamine separately from one another, but the

approaches as of 2008 still require some specialized implementation. NAA is found in neurons, and its purpose as of 2008 is not established, although it is known to decrease when neuronal health is compromised, often recovering with clinical improvement. Crtotal is a crucial element in energy metabolism, but because creatine is not resolved from the energy-rich form, phosphocreatine, Crtotal provides little information about energy states. Choline is generally believed to reflect membrane breakdown and or synthesis. Glutamate, glutamine, and GABA are closely interrelated through energy metabolism and neurotransmitter release and uptake, although their total levels have not yet been related to rates of neurotransmitter release.

An example of the utility of MRS in studying children was an evaluation of effects of cocaine exposure during gestation. Although structural MRI showed no abnormalities, creatine levels were 13 percent higher in the children exposed to cocaine (Smith et al., 2001). MRS can also be used to investigate acute effects of drugs, such as acute changes in brain GABA induced by the nicotine after smoking and drinking.

The neurochemicals discussed are all detected by monitoring the hydrogen signature of the brain, but phosphorus metabolism can also be assessed with MRS, allowing the detection of high-energy phosphates such as ATP in the brain, as well as phosphomonoesters and diesters. A newer and novel technology is carbon MRS, which detects the nonradioactive isotope carbon-13 that occurs naturally as 1 percent of all carbon. Because the natural carbon signal is so low, it is possible to inject glucose, acetate, or other compounds labeled with the material and using MRS observe the gradual increase of glucose products in the brain, including glutamate, glutamine, and GABA. The more rapid is the labeling, the faster the rate of synthesis. The kinetic information (reflecting changes in concentration over time) obtainable with carbon-13 MRS holds promise for understanding the effects of substances of abuse on amino acid neurotransmission and energy metabolism, but such applications are as of 2008 in their infancy.

Technology development continues for all of the methods of imaging described in this entry. For PET and SPECT, new chemicals are continuously under development and testing is being done to target particular proteins more effectively at lower doses, or with better time resolution, or with greater specificity. PET and SPECT are constantly pushing for higher spatial resolution (to provide clear images of smaller brain areas), as are MRI techniques. For MRI, improvements in sensitivity occur as magnetic field strengths rise and as the technology for coil designs, transmission, and reception improves. Great excitement has arisen in the early 2000s in the MR community over hyperpolarized carbon-13. Although it has not been shown as of 2008 to be useful for metabolic studies of the brain, its success in studies of other organs and in cancer leave the possibility open for new solutions to allow its effective application to studies of the brain in general and substance abuse in particular.

See also **Brain Structures and Drugs; Reward Pathways and Drugs.**

BIBLIOGRAPHY

Cosgrove, K. P., Mazure, C. M., & Staley, J. K. (2007). Evolving knowledge of sex differences in brain structure, function, and chemistry. *Biological Psychiatry, 62*(8), 847–855.

Duckworth Warner, T., Behnke, M., Davis Eyler, F., Padgett, K., Leonard, C., Hou, W., et al. (2006). Diffusion tensor imaging of frontal white matter and executive functioning in cocaine-exposed children. *Pediatrics, 118,* 2014–2024.

Ernst, T., Chang, L., Oropilla, G., Gustavson, A., & Speck, O. (2000). Cerebral perfusion abnormalities in abstinent cocaine abusers: A perfusion MRI and SPECT study. *Psychiatry Research: Neuroimaging, 99,* 63–74.

Fein, G., Di Sclafani, V., & Meyerhoff, D. J. (2002). Prefrontal cortical volume reduction associated with frontal cortex function deficit in 6-week abstinent crack-cocaine dependent men. *Drug & Alcohol Dependence, 68*(1), 87–3.

Gazdzinski, S., Durazzo, T. C., Yeh, P.-H., Hardin, D., Banys, P., & Meyerhoff, D. J. (2008). Chronic cigarette smoking modulates injury and short-term recovery of the medial temporal lobe in alcoholics. *Psychiatry Research, 162*(2), 133–145.

Honey, G. D., Honey, R. A., O'Loughlin, C., Sharar, S. R., Kumaran, D., Suckling, J., et al. (2005). Ketamine disrupts frontal and hippocampal contribution to encoding and retrieval of episodic memory: An fMRI study. *Cerebral Cortex, 15,* 749–759.

Krystal, J. H., Petrakis, I. L., Krupitsky, E., Schutz, C., Trevisan, L., & D'Souza, D. C. (2003). NMDA receptor antagonism and the ethanol intoxication signal:

From alcoholism risk to pharmacotherapy. *Annals of the New York Academy of Sciences, 1003,* 176–184.

Kwong, K. K., Belliveau, J. W., Chesler, D. A., Goldberg, I. E., Weisskoff, R. M., Poncelet, B. P., et al. (1992). Dynamic magnetic resonance imaging of human brain activity during primary sensory stimulation. *Proceedings of the National Academy of Science USA, 89,* 5675–5679.

Langleben, D. D., Ruparel, K., Elman, I., Busch-Winokur, S., Pratiwadi, R., Loughead, J., et al. (2008). Acute effect of methadone maintenance dose on brain FMRI response to heroin-related cues. *American Journal of Psychiatry, 165*(3), 390–394.

Liu, C. H., Kim, Y. R., Ren, J. Q., Eichler, F., Rosen, B. R., & Liu, P.K. (2007). Imaging cerebral gene transcripts in live animals. *Journal of Neuroscience, 27,* 713–722.

Ogawa, S., Lee, T. M., Nayak, A. S., & Glynn, P. (1990). Oxygenation-sensitive contrast in magnetic resonance image of rodent brain at high magnetic fields. *Magnetic Resonance in Medicine, 14,* 68–78.

Petrakis, I. L., Limoncelli, D., Gueorguieva, R., Jatlow, P., Boutros, N. N., Trevisan, L., et al. (2004). Altered NMDA glutamate receptor antagonist response in individuals with a family vulnerability to alcoholism. *American Journal of Psychiatry, 161*(10), 1776–1782.

Phelps, M. E., Huang, S. C., Hoffman, E. J., Selin, C., Sokoloff, L., & Kuhl, D. E. (1979). Tomographic measurement of local cerebral glucose metabolic rate in humans with (F-18)2-fluoro-2-deoxy-D-glucose: Validation of method. *Annuals of Neurology, 6,* 371–388.

Smith, L. M., Chang, L., Yonekura, M. L., Gilbride, K., Kuo, J., Poland, R. E., et al. (2001). Brain proton magnetic resonance spectroscopy and imaging in children exposed to cocaine in utero. *Pediatrics, 107*(2), 227–231.

Sokoloff, L., Reivich, M., Kennedy, C., Des Rosiers, M. H., Patlak, C. S., Pettigrew, K. S., et al. (1977). The [14C]-deoxyglucose method for the measurement of local cerebral glucose utilization: Theory, procedure, and normal values in the conscious and anesthetized albino rat. *Journal of Neurochemistry, 28,* 879–916.

Staley, J. K., Gottschalk, C., Petrakis, I. L., Gueorguieva, R., O'Malley, S., Baldwin, R., et al. (2005). Cortical gamma-aminobutyric acid type A-benzodiazepine receptors in recovery from alcohol dependence: Relationship to features of alcohol dependence and cigarette smoking. *Archives of General Psychiatry, 62*(8), 877–888.

Staley, J. K., Krishnan-Sarin, S., Cosgrove, K. P., Krantzler, E., Frohlich, E., Perry, E., et al. (2006). Human tobacco smokers in early abstinence have higher levels of beta2* nicotinic acetylcholine receptors than nonsmokers. *Journal of Neuroscience, 26*(34), 8707–8714.

Wong, D. F., Kuwabara, H., Schretlen, D. J., Bonson, K. R., Zhou, Y., Nandi, A., et al. (2006). Increased occupancy of dopamine receptors in human striatum during cue-elicited cocaine craving. *Neuropsychopharmacology, 31*(12), 2716–2727. [Erratum appears in *Neuropsychopharmacology, 32*(1), 256.]

Yucel, M., Solowij, N., Respondek, C., Whittle, S., Fornito, A., Pantelis, C., et al. (2008). Regional brain abnormalities associated with long-term heavy cannabis use. *Archives of General Psychiatry, 65*(6), 694–701.

GRAEME F. MASON

IMMUNOASSAY.

Immunology is a laboratory science that studies the body's immunity to disease. The basic mechanism of immunity is the binding of drugs or other chemical compounds to antibodies (large proteins produced by the body's immune system). An assay is a general term for an analytical laboratory procedure designed to detect the presence of and/or the quantity of a drug in a biological fluid such as urine or serum (the fluid component of the blood obtained after removal of the blood cells and fibrin clot). An immunoassay, therefore, is an analytical procedure which has as its basis the principles of immunology—specifically the binding of drugs to antibodies.

Several different types of immunoassay are routinely performed in the laboratory. Although they differ in the types of reagents and instrumentation used, they are all based on the same scientific principle (the binding of drugs to antibodies). The three types of immunoassay that are commonly used for drug testing are the radioimmunoassay (RIA), enzyme multiplied immunoassay (EMIT), and fluorescence polarization immunoassay (FPIA).

It may facilitate the reader's understanding of immunoassay to envision the reactions that occur in the body following a vaccination (e.g., polio). The vaccine contains a weak or a killed solution of (polio) virus. When the vaccine is injected into the body, the immune system recognizes the presence of a foreigner (the polio virus), and it generates antibodies to that virus. These antibodies circulate in the blood, and they constitute the body's protection; if at some later date a live (polio) virus invades the body, the antibodies recognize it by its unique size and shape (similar to the fit of a lock and key); they spontaneously bind to the virus, leading to its inactivation and removal from the body.

This binding of antibodies to drugs forms the basis for immunoassay. In the development of an immunoassay, the first step is to inject an animal (host) with the drug that we ultimately wish to analyze. The host immune system, recognizing the drug as a "foreigner," generates antibodies to this drug, and these antibodies can then be harvested from the serum of the animal. In the test-tube environment of the laboratory (*in vitro*), these antibodies can be recombined with the appropriate drug. Just as it did inside the body (*in vivo*), the antibody will recognize the drug based on the lock-and-key fit and will spontaneously bind to it.

The second step in the development of an immunoassay is to synthesize a "labeled" drug. This involves the chemical addition of a "marker" to the drug. This marker can be small, such as an atom of radioactive iodine, or it can be large, such as an enzyme, which is a fairly large protein. Irrespective of its size, this marker is added in such a way that it does not interfere with the lock-and-key recognition between the antibody and the drug.

Commercially available immunoassay kits contain the antibody (which the company has prepared as described above) and the labeled drug (which has been chemically synthesized) necessary to perform the assay. In the laboratory, a fixed amount of antibody and a fixed amount of labeled drug are placed into a reaction vessel (test tube). If these were the only two ingredients, all the binding sites on the antibody would react with (bind to) the labeled drug. A third ingredient added to the assay is, however, the unlabeled drug (i.e., the urine, saliva, or serum specimen containing the drug that is being measured). Because the label on the labeled drug is placed in a position that does not interfere with binding to the antibody (i.e., it is "hidden"), the antibody cannot distinguish between the labeled and unlabeled drug.

Immunoassays are always designed so that there are fewer antibody-binding sites present in the reaction mixture than there are molecules of (labeled plus unlabeled) drug. Because the labeled and unlabeled drug appear the same to the antibody, they will compete equally for the limited number of available binding sites on the antibody. By measuring the amount of labeled drug bound to the antibody, the analyst can calculate the amount of unlabeled drug in the biological specimen.

All immunoassays work in the same basic fashion. They differ in the types of labels that are added to the labeled drug and in the analytical methods by which the amount of binding of labeled drug to the antibody is measured.

RADIOIMMUNOASSAY

Radioimmunoassay (known as RIA) was the earliest of the immunoassay techniques. It was developed during the 1950s by a pair of research immunologists in New York City, Dr. Solomon A. Berson and Dr. Rosalyn S. Yalow. Their initial RIA was designed to detect very low blood levels of insulin and they published their findings in 1959. Their development of this technique was considered of such importance to science that Dr. Yalow was awarded a Nobel prize in 1977 for their work (since Dr. Berson died in 1972 and Nobels are not awarded posthumously, Berson's contribution was remembered in Yalow's acceptance speech).

In RIA, the marker is an isotope of a radioactive element, hence the name *radio*immunoassay. In most RIAs performed in the laboratory today, the radioactive isotope used as the marker is iodine 125, although tritium (hydrogen 2), carbon 14, and cobalt 57 are used in some assays. RIAs can be used in two different fashions to give information about the drug in a sample: (1) they can be used qualitatively—to determine whether a drug is present or absent (e.g., in urine drug testing); (2) they can be used quantitatively—to determine how much of a drug is present (e.g., to measure serum levels of drugs such as digoxin, a heart medication, or theophylline, an asthma medication).

RIA is an extremely powerful tool. One of its main advantages is the sensitivity that can be achieved. Drug levels in serum and urine that are as low as 10 to 100 parts per billion are routinely measured. Two of the most sensitive of the radioimmunoassays are the urine LSD assay and the serum digoxin assay, both of which can detect less than one part per billion. RIA is also an extremely versatile tool. It is used to measure a wide range of drugs of abuse in blood, serum, saliva, and urine, as well as therapeutic (physician administered) drugs in blood or serum. It is also used as a diagnostic tool to detect and quantify numerous naturally occurring chemicals in human serum and urine. Another characteristic that makes RIA such a

powerful tool is the specificity of the assay. The antibodies are highly specific for the drugs analyzed and they rarely make a mistake in recognizing the lock-and-key fit between antibody and drug.

One of the major limitations of the radioimmunoassay is that it generates radioactive waste. To avoid spreading the radioactive compounds and contaminating the environment, the laboratory must conform to very strict regulations, including very elaborate procedures for waste disposal—and undergo frequent inspections. Because of a short half-life for some isotopes, another limitation is that the reagents with a radioactive label have a short shelf life. For instance, the majority are RIAs labeled with iodine 125; they have a shelf life of only approximately sixty days.

Some very sophisticated automated equipment is available for performing RIA or, if need be, the assays can be performed manually. All RIAs require the use of an instrument called a gamma counter, which measures the amount of gamma radiation given off by the radioactive drug bound to the antibody. In 2008, gamma counters could be purchased for several thousand dollars. The reagents are moderately expensive (costing from less than fifty cents per test to two to three dollars per test, depending on the specific assay and the volume of reagents purchased).

ENZYME MULTIPLIED IMMUNOASSAY

The enzyme multiplied immunoassay technique, also known as EMIT^{TM}, is a variation of the general immunoassay technique, in which the marker used to prepare the labeled drug is an enzyme, rather than a radioactive isotope. EMIT is a two-stage assay. As in the other immunoassays, the sample, which contains some amount of the drug being measured, is combined with the antibody plus a fixed amount of the enzyme-labeled drug. In the first reaction, the labeled and the unlabeled drug compete for the available binding sites on the antibody (standard immunoassay reaction). A secondary reaction is then performed, which involves only the enzyme portion of the labeled drug. The results of this secondary reaction are used to calculate the amount of enzyme-labeled drug that is bound to the antibody and thus how much (unlabeled) drug there was in the original urine or serum specimen.

As with other forms of immunoassay, the EMIT can be used either qualitatively or quantitatively. In urine specimens, it is used to detect the presence of drugs, such as THC (marijuana), cocaine, PCP, opiates (heroin), amphetamines, and barbiturates. In serum specimens, EMIT is used to determine the amount present of drugs used for therapeutic (medical) purposes. Such drugs include acetaminophen (Tylenol), salicylate (aspirin), theophylline (widely used to treat asthma), several drugs used to treat epilepsy, and several drugs used to treat heart abnormalities.

Advantages that the EMIT technology has over the RIA are (1) that no radioactivity is involved, so the waste is more readily disposable; (2) the reagents are relatively stable, which may be particularly attractive to a small laboratory, which runs only a few specimens. The EMIT reagents are also less costly than the RIA reagents. The basic instrumentation requires less capital outlay than does the RIA, however the expense grows as more sophisticated automation is acquired.

Some limitations of the EMIT technique are (1) that it is somewhat less sensitive than the RIA (in particular, the LSD assay requires detection of such minute levels of the drug in urine that it can only be done by RIA); (2) also, EMIT is less specific than RIA and is subject to some interferences that do not affect the RIA—for example, the EMIT assay for amphetamines in urine gives a positive response with several other drugs that are similar in structure to amphetamines.

FLUORESCENCE POLARIZATION IMMUNOASSAY

Fluorescence polarization immunoassay (known as FPIA) is a technique that was developed by Abbott laboratories and marketed under the trade name TD$_X$. As the name FPIA implies, the marker for the labeled drug is a molecule of a naturally fluorescent compound called fluorescein. The amount of labeled drug that binds to the antibody is measured by a sophisticated instrument called a spectrofluorometer. As with the other immunoassays, this measurement is used to calculate the amount of labeled drug bound to the antibody and thus the amount of drug in the original urine or serum specimen.

The instrumentation necessary to perform the FPIA is only made by Abbott. It is expensive to purchase (upwards of $50,000) but can be leased

from the manufacturer. The reagents are more expensive than EMIT reagents, being roughly comparable in cost to RIA reagents. They come in a liquid form and have a more limited shelf life than those for EMIT, but they tend to be more stable than RIA reagents.

The attractiveness of FPIA is in the speed and ease of operation of the instrument. The reagents come in a kit that is bar coded and is placed right into the instrument. All the operator has to do is fill the sample cups with serum or urine, place the reagent pack inside the instrument, and push a button marked "run." The instrument reads the bar code, enters the necessary programs into its memory, performs the assay, and prints out the results. For the routine hospital lab or small drug-testing lab, it is as fast or faster than EMIT or RIA and a lot easier; however, the instrument can only run twenty specimens at a time. For the large drug-testing laboratory, more rapid results can be achieved with the automated instrumentation available for the EMIT or RIA techniques.

FPIA is nearly as sensitive as RIA; digoxin can be run by FPIA, although LSD is still not available. The specificity of FPIA is also comparable to that of RIA.

See also **Drug Testing Methods and Clinical Interpretations of Test Results; Hair Analysis as a Test for Drug Use.**

BIBLIOGRAPHY

Blake, C. C. F. (1975). Antibody structure and antigen binding. *Nature, 253,* 158.

Chard, T. (1990). *Laboratory techniques in biochemistry and molecular biology: An introduction to radioimmunoassay and related techniques* (4th ed.). Amsterdam: Elsevier.

Ekins, R. (1989). A shadow over immunoassay. *Nature, 340,* 599.

Howanitz, J. H., & Howanitz, P. J. (1979). Radioimmunoassay and related techniques. In J. B. Henry (Ed.), *Clinical diagnosis and management by laboratory methods* (16th ed.). Philadelphia: W. B. Saunders. (2006, 21st ed.)

Nakamura, R. M., Tucker, E. S., III, & Carlson, I. H. (1991). Immunoassays in the clinical laboratory. In J. B. Henry (Ed.), *Clinical diagnosis and management by laboratory methods* (18th ed.). Philadelphia: W. B. Saunders. (2006, 21st ed.)

Pier, G. B., Lyczak, J. B., & Wetzler, L. M. (Eds.). (2004). *Immunology, infection, and immunity.* Washington, DC: ASM Press.

Stewart, M. J. (1985). Immunoassays. In A. C. Moffat (Ed.), *Clark's isolation and identification of drugs.* London: Pharmaceutical Press.

Tietz, N. W. (1982). Radioimmunoassay. In *Fundamentals of clinical chemistry.* Philadelphia: W. B. Saunders.

van Emon, J. M. (2006). *Immunoassay and other bioanalytical techniques.* Boca Raton, FL: CRC Press.

Wild, D. (2005). *The immunoassay handbook* (3rd ed.). Philadelphia: Elsevier Science.

JEFFREY A. GERE

IMPULSIVITY AND ADDICTION.

Impulsivity is a construct that has relevance to a broad range of psychiatric disorders and behaviors, including attention deficit hyperactivity disorder, bipolar disorder, substance use disorders, cluster B personality disorders (e.g., antisocial and borderline personality disorders), formal impulse control disorders (e.g., pathological gambling and kleptomania), and suicidal and other self-injurious behaviors. *Impulsivity* is defined as a predisposition toward rapid, unplanned reactions to internal or external stimuli with diminished regard to the negative consequences of these reactions to the impulsive individuals or others.

Impulsivity is a complex construct composed of multiple elements. Domains of impulsivity (e.g., those related to risk/reward decision-making, response disinhibition, and attention) have been identified in factor analyses. Measures of impulsivity often show little to modest correlations across these domains or are sometimes inversely related to one another. For example, rapid response has been shown to correlate inversely with disadvantageous decision-making in cocaine dependent subjects when they perform on some measures such as the Iowa Gambling Task. Behavioral and self-report measures of similar constructs within each domain of impulsivity also do not uniformly show expected correlations. For example, consider delay discounting, the process by which individuals temporally discount the value of rewards. More impulsive individuals tend to show greater preferences for small, immediate rewards as compared to larger delayed ones. The steepness of discounting of rewards can thus be considered a measure of impulsivity. However, individuals can report preferences for specific smaller immediate rewards as opposed to larger delayed rewards, though their responses may not correlate with real-life measures of preferred immediate versus delayed reward.

For example, self-report and behavioral measures of delay discounting were collected in adolescent smokers. The self-report measures asked about hypothetical reward preferences; for example, "Would you prefer US $54 today or US $55 in 117 days?" The behavioral task involved individuals sitting in front of a computer monitor and selecting immediate rewards (for example, 15 cents) or larger ones (for example, 30 cents) delayed for a period of time (for example, 30 seconds), with subsequent amounts adjusted according to the immediately preceding selection (for example, if the larger, delayed amount was selected, the immediate amount would increase). Self-report and real-life measures were not correlated with one another, and the real-life measures were associated with successful smoking cessation, whereas the hypothetical measures were not. These findings might parallel others in real-life settings, for example, with dieting behaviors, in which one might report placing a higher value on a delayed reward (better physical fitness) over a smaller immediate reward (dessert) but behave differently in the setting of being served a dessert.

Impulsivity has particular relevance to drug addiction and multiple stages of the process by which addiction develops. Animal and human studies indicate that impulsivity can predispose to experimentation with drugs and thus may be particularly relevant to initiation of drug use. Impulsivity has also been associated with relapse to substance use by addicted individuals. Measures of impulsivity and related constructs have also been associated with severity of and treatment outcome for psychiatric disorders. For example, measures of impulsiveness have been repeatedly found to be elevated in groups of individuals with pathological gambling, and decreases in gambling symptomatology have correlated with decreases in measures of impulsiveness. Brain imaging studies as of 2008 were beginning to identify specific aspects of brain circuitry that influence specific aspects of impulsivity and related constructs in mentally healthy and psychiatric populations, including those with addictions. Such approaches, particularly when integrated into treatment studies, were expected to inform the development of improved prevention and treatment strategies.

See also **Risk Factors for Substance Use, Abuse, and Dependence: Sensation Seeking and Impulsivity.**

BIBLIOGRAPHY

Brewer, J. A., & Potenza, M. N. (2008). The neurobiology and genetics of impulse control disorders: Relationships to drug addictions. *Biochemical Pharmacology, 75*, 63–75.

Dalley, J. W., Fryer, T. D., Brichard, L., Robinson, E. S. J., Theobald, D. E. H., Laane, K., et al. (2007). Nucleus accumbens d2/3 receptors predict trait impulsivity and cocaine reinforcement. *Science, 315*, 1267–1270.

Kreek, M. J., Nielsen, D., Butelman, E., & LaForge, K. (2005). Genetic influences on impulsivity, risk taking, stress responsivity, and vulnerability to drug abuse and addiction. *Nature Neuroscience, 8*(11), 1450–1457.

Krishnan-Sarin, S., Reynolds, B., Duhig, A. M., Smith, A., Liss, T., McFetridge, A., et al. (2007). Behavioral impulsivity predicts treatment outcome in a smoking cessation program for adolescent smokers. *Drug and Alcohol Dependence, 88*, 79–82.

Moeller, F., Barratt, E., Dougherty, D., Schmitz, J., & Swann, A. (2001). Psychiatric aspects of impulsivity. *American Journal of Psychiatry, 158*(11), 1783–1793.

Potenza, M. N. (2007). To do or not to do? The complexities of addiction, motivation, self-control and impulsivity. *American Journal of Psychiatry, 164*, 4–6.

Reynolds, B., Ortengren, A., Richards, J. B., & de Wit, H. (2006). Dimensions of impulsive behavior: Personality and behavioral measures. *Personality and Individual Differences, 40*, 305–315.

Reynolds, B., Penfold, R. B., & Patak, M. (2008). Dimensions of impulsive behavior in adolescents: laboratory behavioral assessments. *Experimental and Clinical Psychopharmacology, 16*(2) 124–131.

MARC N. POTENZA

INDIA AND PAKISTAN. Intoxicants of various kinds have been used in the Indian subcontinent for millennia. Opium entered India through Arab medicine, cannabis was traditionally consumed in religious and social festivals, and alcohol was consumed despite the prohibitionist ethos of many of the subcontinent's religious traditions. The local trade in intoxicants was well established before the advent of European colonizers, but Portuguese and, later, British officials created sophisticated economic and financial networks rapidly increasing its scope.

Of the intoxicants consumed on the subcontinent, opium and its derivatives have received the most attention due to the continuing controversy over the Indo-Chinese opium trade and the region's contemporary role in trafficking narcotics. The impact of opium in the domestic market only began to be analyzed in the early twenty-first century, at least in the detail previously reserved for its export (Richards, 2002). Research into the consumption of other intoxicants, both licit and illicit, has also increased, so that a more balanced understanding of their long-term impact is emerging from under opium's shadow.

The Indian trade evolved into a complex business operation involving millions of people, from cultivators of the poppies to local merchant intermediaries, government factory workers, and laborers on to the docks of Calcutta and Bombay. Profits, naturally, remained skewed to the higher echelons, and they were more evenly distributed in the western districts of India. Nevertheless, opium remained an important element of the local economy as well as a major source of revenue for the East India Company (EIC), the British Government of India, and the western princely states.

EARLY USE OF OPIUM
Opium had been used as a medicine in India since its introduction by Arab traders. The eating of opium as a daily general tonic was widespread; however, unlike farther east in Asia, in India it was consumed in the form of tablets and liquors, and recreational opium smoking was viewed with distaste. Demand for Indian opium in China was rooted in its mellow taste. Indian opium had a lower morphia content of 3 to 6 percent compared to the domestic Chinese product and the 12 percent of Turkish opium, and its mellowness was much desired by smokers, in particular the mild Patna opium. As a result, the trade in Indian opium expanded rapidly (Winther, 2003).

At first, opium smoking in China was a form of medication against fevers, dysentery, and that nineteenth-century scourge, cholera. As the price was reduced throughout the century, usage expanded from the medical market to the country's poorer classes. With the leaching of opium from medicinal use, the number of addicts increased, creating a near constant demand for Indian opium throughout the century. However, the trade was shrouded in controversy.

THE OPIUM TRADE

While the opium trade expanded—along with global trading in other intoxicants of the new consumer age, such as coffee—the commercialization of a narcotic ensured that the trade was couched in double standards. The East India Company board of directors insisted that company ships could not be involved in the trade after the Chinese Government placed embargoes on opium imports. However, the EIC ensured that there were ample supplies of good-quality opium from Patna for auction at Calcutta for the British and American merchants who smuggled the product into China. The company monopolized the production from field to factory to port, and it knew the final destination of the trade, but the profits available for the constantly cash-strapped EIC, which was tasked with acting as the de facto colonial government of India, were too high to resist.

Initially, the EIC did not gain from the Malwa opium trade in the West, which was in the hands of officials of the princely states and merchant and banking intermediaries. The desire to force the trade through Bombay and dent the independence of the princely states was part of the motive behind the British annexation of Oudh. Opium, therefore, was a key element in the expansion of the British Empire, both within and outside of the Indian subcontinent. When the Crown finally took control of the government of India in 1857, the profits of the opium trade were once again too attractive to forgo, despite an increasing clamor against the immorality of the commerce.

CANNABIS

Cannabis use was also rooted in medical systems in India, but was regarded as controversial by the colonists. Although William O'Shaughnessy (1809–1889), the editor of the *Bengal Pharmacopoeia* (1844), advocated cannabis as a powerful remedy in cases of rabies, tetanus, cholera and convulsive disorders, many early travelers commented upon its intoxicating effects and regarded its use as predominantly recreational and social rather than

medicinal. The government's 1871–1872 report on cannabis linked its habitual consumption to an increased risk of insanity. Cannabis became a key element in the prohibitionist platforms, including that of the Society for the Suppression of the Opium Trade (SSOT). William Sproston Caine (1842–1903), a temperance reformer and member of the British Parliament, declared it to be "the most horrible intoxicant the world has ever produced," and the Indian government was demonized in prohibitionist circles for deriving substantial revenue from an intoxicant. While the opium trade was regarded as the public sin of the Indian authorities, their condoning of cannabis consumption was the private sin.

Cannabis aroused economic fears about the weakening of the India labor force, as well as social fears of the creation of a criminal class driven insane through the overconsumption of *ganja*. The resulting seven-volume Indian Hemp Drugs Commission Report of 1894 simply fuelled the controversy further. This commission, also known as the Young Commission, sat for over two years and heard 1,193 witnesses from throughout the subcontinent with widely diverging views. The report likened cannabis consumption in India to that of alcohol in Britain, arguing that as long as the latter was tolerated, the former must be as well. Indeed, the Majority Report decreed that the banning of *bhang* (cannabis liquor) was unjustified because it was far less potent than alcohol. While accepting that smoking *ganja* and *charas* (hashish), if consumed habitually and in sufficient amounts, was an activity potentially more addictive than drinking alcohol, the prohibition of these substances was rejected. Not only would it be regarded as an attack on the cultural and religious practices of the population, a ban would be counterproductive and simply lead to a search for other illicit, and possibly more potent, intoxicants. It would also raise the cost of policing.

THE POLITICS OF OPIUM

The controversy over governmental attitudes toward intoxicants increased with the publication of the Report of the Royal Commission on Opium in the following year. The Majority Report declared that opium was fundamental to government revenue in India and, through the Home Charges, to the British Government as well. Further, the use and trading of opium could not be banned because citizens of both

India and Britain would not accept the new taxes required to replace revenue lost from opium. The report also expressed skepticism that the Indian opium habit was necessarily harmful, deeming anti-opium propaganda exaggerated and unduly alarmist. So convincing were the arguments condemning a ban, that the former prohibitionist Arthur Pease was drummed out of the SSOT for signing the Majority Report. Temperance campaigners were horrified by both the cannabis and opium reports, declaring that the commissioners had been unduly influenced by financial over moral considerations.

With the rise of the use of Indian indentured servants and Indian seamen throughout the British Empire and beyond, local consumption patterns were exported around the globe. This helped to increase fears of narcotic criminality and degeneration. At the turn of the twentieth century, Indians would often appear in contemporary accounts of Chinese opium dens being used by missionaries, anti-narcotics campaigners, and politicians alike to condemn the "opium habit."

The Indian narcotics reports came in for excoriating criticism in a later report by the missionary Bishop Charles Brent in the Philippines, which formed the basis of American attempts to introduce international drug controls. By then, however, the government of India had accepted that the opium trade was prejudicial to its prestige, and it had already reached agreement with the Chinese government to end the opium trade between their nations over the next decade if the latter controlled its domestic production. Only five years later, the Indo-Chinese trade was ended, at a cost of approximately US $8 million to India. At the Hague Opium Convention of 1911–1912, the government of India agreed to end the opium trade to those countries, including the Philippines, in which an embargo on imports was already in place. However, if the West wanted any further concessions, India demanded that pharmaceutical-manufacturing countries be treated in the same way as producing countries, with the manufacture of morphine and heroin strictly limited to the amount required for medicinal needs. Such demands, naturally, were unpopular with these countries, which argued that their products were used strictly for medicinal purposes.

India's request for limitations on cocaine did not meet with any greater success. Such limitations would have impinged further upon the export trade of Western nations, and the government of India was accused of attempting to divert attention away from its role in the opium trade. However, both central and provincial authorities in India were concerned about the rising level of cocaine consumption. Cocaine was considered an intoxicant foreign to India, but it seemed to be taking a speedy hold of addicts in the major drug trafficking centers such as Bombay, Calcutta, and Rangoon. Indian authorities were among the first to try to control the supply of cocaine, with Bengal (1900), Bombay (1903), and Madras (1905) all introducing legislation attempting to restrict its sale to pharmacists and physicians. However, officials felt that, as an imported narcotic, the trade in cocaine would not be stemmed without international cooperation. India, then, had a genuine interest in controlling the cocaine trade—an ironic position given its role in the opium trade. Despite the rhetoric of the temperance movements, it appeared at the Hague that the Government of India was among those attempting real control of the trade in intoxicants.

With narcotics control built into the principles of the League of Nations, the controversy continued after 1918. Under pressure from the Home Office, the Viceroy of India announced in February 1926 that all remaining nonmedicinal exports of opium would be prohibited within a decade. As suspected by those involved, this simply resulted in the substitution of Turkish for Indian opium, rather than diminishing the availability of opium on the black market. Even worse was the fact that the substitutes were of a higher and more addictive quality than the Indian product had been. As such, the attempts to reduce India's role in the opium trade offered a template for many of the problems of international narcotics control since then.

Historically, opium was a major component of the South Asian colonial economy. It bolstered government revenues, brought bullion into the country, and provided India with a trade surplus with its Asian neighbors. It also provided the financial wherewithal underpinning the expansion of the British Empire in the region. Opium, ironically, which had nourished empire, also helped to undermine its foundations. Not only did it form part of the nationalist argument against the colonial rulers, it also divided them. The debates over opium were a fundamental element in the gradual split between the British government in Whitehall and the British Government of India. However, the story of opium did not end with the end of empire.

MODERN PRODUCTION

In another of history's ironies, in the modern world India remains the largest producer of raw opium for the licit medicinal market. Not only does world consumption of morphine-based medications such as codeine continue to rise, Indian opium is also an excellent raw material for the new generation of thebaine-based opiates such as oxycodone (thebaine is an opiate alkaloid and a minor constituent of opium). India was designated one of only seven countries permitted to produce export grade opium for pharmaceuticals under the 1948 Paris Protocol, which, after much negotiation, formed the basis of the 1961 Single Convention on Narcotic Drugs. Pakistan, however, was only permitted to produce opium for domestic consumption and its government refused to sign the protocols. Apart from again upsetting the fragile regional political balance, there are serious concerns about the trade's control and the quantities of opium produced. Opium leaches from the licit into the illicit narcotics market because traffickers can pay significantly more than government buyers. At the same time, thebaine-based pharmaceutical products are being abused by drug addicts because of their stimulatory effects, re-creating the historical pattern of medicinal-to-illicit drug use.

In the modern narcotics trade, India and Pakistan continue to be geographically vulnerable. Whereas northeastern India increasingly serves as an outlet for the illicit opium and amphetamine products of the Golden Triangle (e.g., Southeast Asia), Pakistan has become the primary conduit for the narcotics smuggled out of the Golden Crescent (the drug-producing regions of Afghanistan, Iran, and Pakistan). Seventy percent of Afghanistan's poppies are grown in the provinces bordering Pakistan. This fact, combined with the civil strife and political corruption within Pakistan itself, has created the perfect conditions for the expansion of opium and heroin production in the region. The U.S. Central Intelligence Agency (CIA) has been charged with repeating its mistakes of the Vietnam era, with covert American operations in Afghanistan and Pakistan

providing local warlords the wherewithal to link the region into the complex web of international narcotics criminals.

In South Asia, American geopolitics has once again come into conflict with the local governments and peoples through the U.S. desire to destroy narcotics traffic at its source. Just as America once attempted to reduce the subcontinent's role in the nineteenth century Chinese opium trade, its actions in the late twentieth century bolstered the narcotics trade of South Asia. Illicit raw opium production in Pakistan, which had been decreasing until the 1990s due to a relatively effective alternative development program, once again increased, and the region has also become the base for the manufacture of heroin from Afghan opium. It is assumed that the illicit laboratories are based in Pakistan because of easier access to supplies of acetic anhydride and other precursor chemicals required for the manufacture of heroin.

India has repeated this pattern. Political instability in its states that border Burma (Myanmar) has created the perfect condition for narcotics trafficking. International financial contributions to reduce the production and trafficking of opium in the subcontinent have increasingly come under the umbrella of the "war on drugs," and therefore fewer resources are focused on the alternative development of new cash crops. Instead, these resources are part of a frontline battle against local suppliers, including aid for helicopters and equipment for the Pakistan Anti-Narcotics Force. The battle is not going well. In 2005 the Pakistan authorities seized 24 metric tons of heroin and morphine products, which amounted to 27 percent of annual global seizures (United Nations, 2008).

The narcotics trade has resulted in several long-term consequences for the region. Authorities in both countries are concerned that the increased role in international distribution networks for illicit drugs has massively increased domestic consumption. Patterns of consumption have also changed from traditional forms to the more highly addictive practices of opium smoking and heroin injection, further increasing the number of addicts, which, in turn, has been linked to the high incidence of HIV/AIDS in South Asia. Attempts over the years by Indian and Pakistani anti-narcotics forces to coordinate their operations have been hampered by the geopolitics of the Kashmir situation. Both countries also face the environmental fallout of cultivation, including land erosion and deforestation.

OTHER DRUGS

While government interest has been focused upon the opium and heroin trade, policies against other intoxicants have received a lower priority. There is evidence that suggests that cannabis consumption remains high, buoyed by relatively low prices and ease of production. The evidence also suggests that, as in the West, there has been increased abuse of amphetamines, benzodiazepines, and other synthetic intoxicants—an increase made easy by the proximity of India and Pakistan to Thailand. The control of the abuse of benzodiazepine and other pharmaceutical products is made more difficult by the fact that they are licit medicinal drugs.

Of course, not all the intoxicant problems of the subcontinent stem from consumption of illicit narcotics. The countries also have problems with licit intoxicants such as alcohol and nicotine. The 1950 constitution of the newly independent India enshrined the temperance ethos of Gandhi. The consumption of liquor, as well as tea and coffee, was regarded by many nationalists as an unwelcome infiltration of Western habits that altered long-established local patterns of consumption. It was also felt that this contributed to the cultural as well as political hegemony of the colonizers. However, most provinces ignored prohibition in practice, deriving some 20 percent of their taxable income from alcoholic beverages. This was a continuation of earlier ambivalent attitudes toward alcohol in the colonial period. While distilled beverages had long been part of social custom in the subcontinent, there were strong prohibitionist ethics within its major religions. Unlike government attitudes to opium and cannabis use, the *abkari* (excise) policies of the British colonial state toward alcohol had a strongly prohibitive stance, no doubt reflecting metropolitan attitudes toward alcohol consumption by the working classes as detrimental to their efficiency and morality, as well as raising the specter of racial degeneracy.

In South Asia, colonial officials viewed the unregulated distilling of alcohol as a potential source of social unrest and criminality, and they sought to restrict brewing to licensed premises only. Imported alcoholic beverages, including medicinal products, were also heavily taxed. However, *abkari* became a significant element in provincial state income, and increasing numbers of licenses were granted—alongside an increasingly sophisticated and expensive police operation against unlicensed liquor distilling. This unlicensed production has continued into the twenty-first century, with regular reports of fatalities and injuries caused by adulterated "country" liquor in both India and Pakistan.

TOBACCO

By the late nineteenth century, India was the largest producer of tobacco in Asia, and its output of 340 million pounds was four-fifths that of the American harvest. However, the bulk of India tobacco at this time was retained for the domestic market, augmented by significant imports of British manufactured cigarettes (Goodman, 1993). The smoking of cigarettes and *bidis* (roll-ups) in India has had a significant long-term impact upon its population. According to the World Health Organization, 12 percent of the world's smokers are to be found in India, and it remains one of the few countries in which cigarette consumption continues to grow. This has resulted in high levels of mortality and morbidity from smoking-related cancers and cardiac and respiratory disease. For instance, India has the world's highest incidence of oral cancers, and its high tuberculosis rates have also been associated with smoking.

As the price of cigarettes has tumbled in the region, the consumption levels soared. A 2008 report on smoking in India suggests that the problem is serious, with one in five children in India using some form of tobacco regularly. The report estimates that 20 percent of deaths in men aged 30 to 69 result from a smoking-related illness, and it predicts that smoking will result in around 1 million deaths annually (Jha et al., 2008).

India has banned smoking in public places, but with India having been a major exporter of cigarettes since the 1970s, it remains to be seen if there will be a more sustained campaign against smoking. Tobacco is also grown in the North-West Frontier Province of Pakistan, and there are fears that exploitation by the large cigarette manufacturers pushes cultivators into poppy production. Cigarette smuggling from throughout Asia into Pakistan is also a major problem, and the health problems linked to smoking are increasing, just as they are in India.

In South Asia, as is the case elsewhere in the world, the distinction between illicit intoxicants and the licit products of tobacco and alcohol will require a major change in public perception of the dangers of smoking and drinking before any long-term change in habits is possible. Intoxicants, both licit and illicit, continue to play a major role in the lives of the peoples of India and Pakistan, and it remains to be seen how effective the recent internationally backed public health and anti-narcotics policies of the two nations will prove to be.

See also **Afghanistan; Alcohol: History of Drinking (International); China; Coca/Cocaine, International; Foreign Policy and Drugs, United States; Golden Triangle as Drug Source; Hashish; International Control Policies; International Drug Supply Systems; Marijuana (Cannabis); Middle East; Opiates/Opioids; Opium: International Overview; Oxycodone; Religion and Drug Use; Substance Abuse and AIDS; Tobacco: An International Overview.**

BIBLIOGRAPHY

Berridge, V., and Edwards, G. (1981). *Opium and the people: Opiate use in nineteenth-century England.* New York: St. Martin's Press

Booth, M. (2003). *Cannabis: A history.* London: Bantam Books.

Emdad-ul Haq, M. (2000). *Drugs in South Asia: From the opium trade to the present day.* London: Palgrave.

Ghosal, S. (2003). *The politics of drugs and India's Northeast.* New Delhi: Anamika Publishers & Distributors.

Goodman, J. (1993). *Tobacco in History: The cultures of dependence.* London: Routledge.

Jha, P., Jacob, B., Gajalakshmi, V., Gupta, P. C., Dhingra, N., Kumar, R., et al. (2008). A nationally representative case-control study of smoking and death in India. *New England Journal of Medicine, 358*(11), 1137–1147.

McCoy, A. W. (2003). *The politics of heroin: CIA complicity in the global drug trade.* Rev. ed. Chicago: Lawrence Hill.

Mills, J. H. (2003). *Cannabis Britannica: Empire, trade and prohibition, 1800–1928.* Oxford: Oxford University Press.

Mills, J. H., & Barton, P. (Eds.). (2007). *Drugs and empires: Essays in modern imperialism and intoxication, c. 1500 to c. 1930.* London: Palgrave.

Ramana, M. (2002). *Western medicine and public health in colonial Bombay, 1845–1895.* New Delhi: Orient Longman.

Richards, J. F. (2002). The opium industry in British India. *Indian Economic and Social History Review, 39* (2–3), 149–180.

Trocki, C. A. (1999). *Opium, empire, and the global political economy: A study of the Asian opium trade, 1750–1950.* London: Routledge.

United Nations Office on Drugs and Crime. (2008). *Illicit drug trends in Pakistan.* Islamabad: U.N. Country Office, Pakistan. Available from http://www.unodc.org/unodc/.

Winther, P. (2003). *Anglo-European science and the rhetoric of Empire: Malaria, opium, and British rule in India, 1756–1895.* Lanham, MD: Lexington Books.

PATRICIA BARTON

INDUSTRY AND WORKPLACE, DRUG USE IN.

The drugs that have the most impact on the U.S. workforce are marijuana and cocaine, although heroin and illicit prescription-drug use also pose a significant risk. Besides impacting productivity, these drugs affect workplace safety because they may reduce an individual's reaction time, impair judgment and memory, promote aggression, and further a worker's delusions of performance capability. Their use also impacts workplace morale because of attendance and co-worker relationship problems.

In 2004 and 2005, over 8 percent of full-time U.S. workers aged 18 to 64 regularly used illicit drugs. Workers in food service and accommodations, construction, entertainment and recreation, and mining had the highest rates, which exceeded 13 percent in these industries. Rates among part-time employees are also significantly higher, and men regularly use illicit drugs more often than women, although this gap narrowed between 1997 and 2007, according to the National Survey on Drug Use and Health.

SUBSTANCE USE BY EMPLOYMENT STATUS AND WORKER CHARACTERISTICS

Drug use among workers impacts the workplace in a variety of ways:

- Drug use lowers productivity. The George Washington University Medical Center reported in 2002 that problems related to alcohol and drug abuse cost American businesses over $134 billion

Industry categories	Percent
Accommodations and Food Services	16.9
Construction	13.7
Arts, Entertainment, and Recreation	11.6
Information	11.3
Mangement of Companies and Enterprises, Administrative, Support, Waste Management, and Remediation Services	10.9
Retail Trade	9.4
Other Services (Except Public Administration)	8.8
Wholesale Trade	8.5
Professional, Scientific, and Technical Services	8.0
Real Estate, Rental, and Leasing	7.5
Mining	7.3
Finance and Insurance	6.8
Manufacturing	6.5
Transportation and Warehousing	6.2
Agriculture, Forestry, Fishing and Hunting	6.2
Health Care and Social Assistance	6.1
Public Administration	4.1
Educational Services	4.0
Utilities	3.8

Table 1. Past month illicit drug use among full-time workers aged 18 to 64, by industry categories: 2002–2004 combined. (Source: Substance Abuse and Mental Health Services Administration, 2002, 2003, and 2004 National Survey on Drug Use and Health.) ILLUSTRATION BY GGS INFORMATION SERVICES. GALE, CENGAGE LEARNING

in lost productivity annually, and that work performance drops significantly among those using drugs.

- Drug use causes accidents and injuries. According to the 1999 National Household Survey on Drug Abuse, employees who use drugs are over three times more likely to be involved in a workplace accident.

- Absenteeism and turnover are increased. A 1991 report by the National Association of Treatment Providers found that employees who regularly use drugs are absent from work more and change employers with greater frequency.

- Drug use increases an employer's medical costs. The National Institute on Drug Abuse reports that employees who use drugs cost their employers about twice as much in medical claims as employees who do not use drugs.

- Workers' compensation costs are increased. Nearly half of all workers' compensation claims are related to substance abuse, according to the National Council on Compensation Insurance (DWI Resource Center, 2008).

- Drug use promotes workplace theft and violence. James Reaves (1994) found that 80

percent of drug abusers steal from their workplaces to support their drug use, and a 1994 study by the Society of Human Resource Management found that substance abuse is the third leading cause of workplace violence.

EMPLOYER RESPONSE

Employers have implemented workplace drug-testing programs in an attempt to reduce these consequences. As a preventive measure in the workplace, drug testing had its beginnings in the Department of Defense, which initially used it to address the high addiction rates of soldiers returning from Vietnam in the 1970s. In 1981, after an aircraft accident on the USS *Nimitz* revealed drug use among the ship's crew, the Department of Defense launched an aggressive drug-testing program that included random testing.

Drug testing in the civilian workplace began in earnest in the late 1980s. It was driven at first by the nuclear power industry, which was concerned about the quality of construction of new plants and the safe operation of all nuclear plants. In 1988, the Nuclear Regulatory Commission (NRC) mandated random drug testing for all employees and contractors who had unescorted access within their licensed nuclear facilities.

In 1989 the United States Department of Transportation (DOT) mandated comprehensive drug-testing programs for all safety-sensitive personnel involved in the aviation, highway, railroad, mass transit, pipeline, and maritime industries, including robust random-testing programs. As of 2008, over 12 million workers were covered under these DOT programs. Many other civilian employers have implemented drug-testing programs, though most are limited to pre-employment and "for cause" testing.

In 1988, Congress passed the Drug-Free Workplace Act, which requires all federal grant recipients and federal contractors whose contracts exceed $25,000 to certify that they will provide a drug-free workplace, including awareness programs for employees and training for supervisors. However, there are no drug-testing requirements for employees. Today's drug-testing programs, whether mandated by the government or not, follow a time- and court-tested approach to ensure that an employer's obligation to maintain the health and safety of its workplace is

Employment status	Illicit drug use		Heavy alcohol use	
	Percent	Number in thousands	Percent	Number in thousands
Total	9.2	16,363	8.4	15,017
Full-Time	8.2	9,413	8.8	10,113
Part-Time	11.9	2,903	8.6	2,094
Unemployed	18.6	1,405	13.6	1,026
Other*	8.3	2,642	5.6	1,783

Table 2. Substance use by employment status and worker characteristics. Past month illicit drug use and heavy alcohol use among persons aged 18 to 64, by Employment Status: 2002–2004 combined. (Source: National Survey on Drug Use and Health, The NSDUH Report, U.S. Department of Health and Human Services, July 23, 2007.) ILLUSTRATION BY GGS INFORMATION SERVICES. GALE, CENGAGE LEARNING

unhindered and that the rights of the individual are safeguarded.

Best practice drug-testing programs include the following elements:

- A written policy, distributed to all employees, that establishes the employer rules regarding drug use, possession, and sale while at work, as well as the penalties for violating these rules.

- A drug-testing program that includes pre-employment testing for all applicants; random, for cause, and post-accident testing for employees; and return-to-work and follow-up testing for those employees who have tested positive, completed employer-designated counseling or rehabilitation, and returned to work after the successful completion of either effort.

- A helping program that employees and their families can use if they voluntarily seek help for drug use or other related family problems. These services are mainly provided by employee assistance programs (EAPs) funded by the employer, but they may also include referral to community based counseling and treatment programs.

DRUG-TESTING METHODOLOGY

When people use drugs, including tobacco, the drugs are found in all parts of the body. The drugs (and their breakdown products, called metabolites) are excreted in the urine, laid down in growing hair, and found in sweat and oral fluids (saliva). The most common drug test is a urine test. Hair tests are also widely used, and sweat patches and oral swabs are increasingly used to detect drug use. The chemical tests used for each type of sample are

the same, beginning with an immunoassay screening test and going on to a more sophisticated confirming test when necessary.

Urine testing is used exclusively in all federally mandated drug-testing programs (e.g., NRC, DOT). Most other workplace drug-testing programs also use urine testing. The period of time in which a drug remains in the body and can be successfully found by a drug test is called the "window of detection." Drugs are usually found in urine for one to three days after the most recent drug use. Marijuana can be detected for longer periods for people who smoke every day for weeks at a time, but urine tests are usually negative after a day or two for people who smoke marijuana only occasionally.

Hair testing is used by employers who want a wider window of detection. The collection of the specimen is much less invasive than urine, and it is much easier to collect. A standard hair sample is one and a half inches long. Since hair grows about one half inch a month, this length of hair has information about drug use over the prior 90 days.

Sweat and oral-fluid testing are less common in employer-directed workplace programs, although the technology continues to develop. Ease of use is a major factor for using oral fluids or sweat. These methodologies also negate the requirements for time-consuming and costly urine collection procedures. Sweat patches are often used to monitor drug abstinence over time. Sweat is tested by applying a patch to the skin, and drug use is detected over the period the patch is worn, usually from one to three weeks. Oral fluids are tested by taking a swab from a person's mouth. They generally detect drug use within the last day or two after

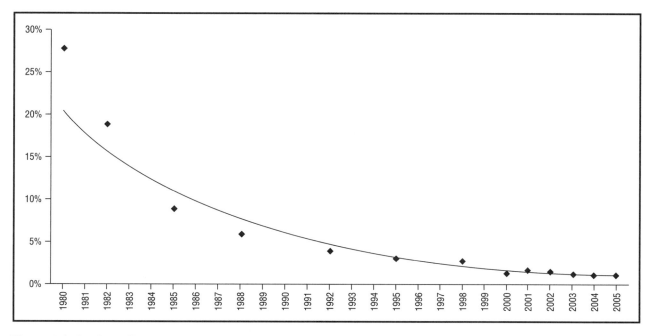

Figure 1. Active duty military drug positive rate, 1980–2005. (Source: Status of Drug Use in the Department of Defense Personnel, Fiscal Year 2005, Drug Testing Statistical Report, Office of the Deputy Assistant Secretary of Defense for Counternarcotics.) ILLUSTRATION BY GGS INFORMATION SERVICES. GALE, CENGAGE LEARNING

the most recent drug use. Oral-fluid testing is often used in criminal justice and drug treatment programs, as well as the workplace.

THE TESTING PROCESS

The drug-testing programs themselves have three important elements: a controlled specimen-collection process, testing at a certified drug-testing laboratory, and a review of all tests by a medical review officer before the result is sent to the employer.

Collection efforts are designed to ensure that a collected specimen is not diluted, adulterated, or otherwise tampered with, while at the same time respecting the privacy and sensibilities of the donor. Well-developed specimen collection protocols are used by trained collectors, regardless of the methodology. The specimen protocols used for federally mandated drug-testing programs are outlined in the *Urine Specimen Collection Handbook for Federal Agency Workplace Drug Testing Programs* (2004), which is available online.

Analysis of the specimen is performed by certified laboratories. All drug tests performed under federally mandated programs must be tested at a laboratory certified by the National Laboratory Certification Program (NLCP), a program established

and directed by the Department of Health and Human Services (DHHS). Laboratories will report out all test results only to a medical review officer. Drug tests that are conducted by employers but not mandated by the federal government will usually be analyzed at these certified laboratories, but they may be analyzed at laboratories certified by other credentialing agencies, such as the College of American Pathologists (CAP).

A medical review officer (MRO) is a physician who has been trained in the field of addictions. (According to the DHHS Medical Review Officer Manual for Federal Agency Workplace Drug Testing Programs, medical review officers must have the following background and credentials: knowledge about and clinical experience in controlled substance abuse disorders; detailed knowledge of alternative medical explanations for laboratory positive drug test results; knowledge about issues relating to adulterated and substituted specimens; and knowledge about possible medical causes for specimens reported as having an invalid result.) The MRO's primary duty is to determine whether there is a legitimate medical explanation for a laboratory positive test. If a laboratory test is positive, the MRO will contact the donor to discuss the results.

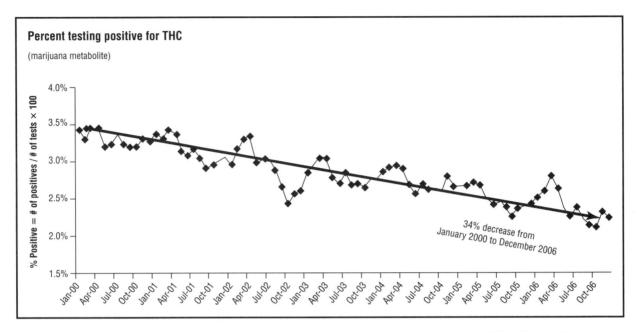

Figure 2. National workforce positives are down. (Source: Quest Diagnostics, through December 2006. Office of National Drug Control Policy, National Drug Control Strategey, 2008 Annual Report.) ILLUSTRATION BY GGS INFORMATION SERVICES. GALE, CENGAGE LEARNING

In the discussion with the donor, the MRO will determine if the donor was using a properly prescribed drug that could have caused the laboratory positive result. If the MRO can verify the prescription with a pharmacist, physician, or dentist, the MRO will report the test as negative. If there is no verification, then the MRO will report the test as positive. Test results are sent to the employer by the MRO. The employer will usually receive an MRO report that says that the test was negative, positive, or invalid for a specific reason.

HELPING PROGRAMS

Comprehensive drug-free workplace programs usually include a helping component, which is designed to provide information, counseling, and other services for employees (and often for their families) who are having problems with drugs. Employee assistance programs (EAPs) are the most prevalent employer helping program. EAPs are intended to help employees deal with personal problems that might adversely impact their work performance, health, and well-being. They often include short-term counseling and referral services. Department of Transportation programs for the U.S. transportation industry also require that employees who have tested positive, in order to return to work, meet with a substance abuse

professional, who will provide the employer with an assessment and a counseling or treatment regimen that must be completed before the employee can return to a safety sensitive job.

Other employees may provide information to employees regarding available community counseling and treatment programs, as well as other programs that are available. These programs may or may not be covered by the employee's health insurance. Twelve-step programs are often a viable option. Enrollment in employee assistance programs has risen steadily. In 1993, there were 27.2 million individuals enrolled in EAP programs, and by 2002 there were 80.2 million, representing a 194 percent increase since 1993 (Open Minds, 2002).

THE IMPACT OF DRUG TESTING

The results, where reported, are notable. For example, before the military began drug testing in 1981, its surveys indicated that over 25 percent of active duty military were regularly using illegal drugs. However, in a 2005 Department of Defense survey, the last one comparable with the 1980 data, that number was only 3.4 percent. Within DOT programs, the Federal Railroad Administration reports that the occupational injury rate among railroad workers was halved in the ten years following the implementation of random drug testing in January 1990. Finally, a prominent index of national workplace drug testing has reported that the positive rate in the overall U.S. workforce decreased from 18.1 percent in 1987 to 4.1 percent in 2006 and that the positive rate for marijuana, the most widely used illegal drug, decreased by over one-third between 2000 and 2006 (Quest Diagnostics, 2007).

As reported by the White House Office of National Drug Policy, "[l]arger workforces were far more likely to have incorporated a comprehensive drug-free workplace program which has resulted in approximately 50 percent lower positive drug test rates, and 75 percent fewer self-reports of current drug use among workers compared to smaller worksites."

CONCLUSION

Substance use in the workplace negatively affects U.S. industry through lost productivity, workplace accidents and injuries, employee absenteeism, low morale, and increased illness. The loss to U.S. companies due to employees' alcohol and drug use and related problems is estimated at billions of dollars per year. Research shows that the rate of substance use varies by occupation and industry. Employers have responded by establishing drug-free workplace programs that include comprehensive drug-testing programs. Credible drug testing requires protocols that insure the rights of the individual while protecting the employers' rights to provide a safe and healthful workplace. Workplace-based employee assistance programs (EAPs) and community programs can be valuable resources for obtaining help for substance-using workers.

See also **Accidents and Injuries from Drugs; Drug Metabolism; Hair Analysis as a Test for Drug Use; Prevention.**

BIBLIOGRAPHY

DuPont, R. L., & Bucher, R. H. (2005). *Family guide to drug testing.* Self-published.

DWI Resource Center. (2008). *What does employee alcohol and drug use cost your business?* Albuquerque, NM: Author. Available from http://www.dwiresourcecenter.org/.

George Washington University Medical Center (GWUMC). (2002). *Alcohol problems cost American business.* Washington, DC: GWUMC, Ensuring Solutions to Alcohol Problems. Available from http://www.ensuringsolutions.org/.

National Association of Treatment Providers. (1991). *Treatment is the answer: A white paper on the cost-effectiveness of alcoholism and drug dependency treatment.* Laguna Hills, CA: Author.

National Institute on Drug Abuse. *NIDA InfoFacts: Workplace trends.* Available from http://www.drugabuse.gov/.

Open Minds. (2002). *Managed behavioral health & employee assistance program enrollment reaches 227 million in 2002.* Press release, October 30, 2002. Available from http://www.openminds.com/.

Quest Diagnostics. (2007). Drug Testing Index®, 2007. Madison, NJ: Author. Available from http://www.questdiagnostics.com/.

Reaves, J. J. (1994). Drug crimes in the workplace: A survey of drug use and its effects on crimes in the workplace, and a small study of workplace drug abusers under rehabilitative care. *Security Journal, 5*(1), 32.

Society for Human Resources Management. (1994). SHRM survey reveals extent of workplace violence. *EAP Digest, 14*(3), 25.

U.S. Department of Defense. (2006). *2005 Department of Defense survey of health related behaviors among active duty military personnel.* Triangle Park, NC: RTI International. Available from http://www.ha.osd.mil/.

U.S. Department of Health and Human Services, Substance Abuse and Mental Health Services Administration (SAMSHA). (2000). *1999 National Household Survey on Drug Abuse.* Rockville, MD: Author. Available from http://ncadi.samhsa.gov/.

U.S. Department of Health and Human Services, Substance Abuse and Mental Health Services Administration (SAMSHA). (2007). *National survey on drug use and health: Worker substance use, by industry category. Washington, DC: SAMHSA, Office of Applied Studies.* Available from http://oas.samhsa.gov/.

U.S. Department of Health and Human Services, Substance Abuse and Mental Health Services Administration (SAMSHA). *Urine specimen collection handbook for federal agency workplace drug testing programs.* Available from http://www.workplace.samhsa.gov/.

White House Office of National Drug Control Policy. *Drug-Free Workplace.* Washington, DC: Author. Available from http://www.whitehousedrugpolicy.gov/.

RICHARD H. BUCHER

INFANTS EXPOSED TO ALCOHOL AND DRUGS. *See* **Alcohol and Drug Exposed Infants.**

INHALANTS. Inhalants are volatile solvents or anesthetics that are subject to abuse by inhalation. Most are central nervous system (CNS)

depressants, but some are convulsants. As a class they are characterized by high vapor pressure and significant solubility in fat at room temperature. Vapors and gases have been inhaled since ancient times for religious or other purposes, as at the oracle at Delphi in Greece. Experimentation with inhalants did not occur to any significant extent, however, until after the discovery of nitrous oxide and the search for volatile anesthetics commenced in earnest.

Arguably the most toxic and least studied among abused substances, inhalants can produce a wide range of injuries, depending on the chemical constituents of the products inhaled. Many are very complex mixtures formulated for a specific purpose or are used because they are the least expensive alternative, or both. Thus, their purity and safety are in no way comparable with those achieved by pharmaceutical companies manufacturing medications for human consumption.

METHOD OF USE AND EFFECT MECHANISM

Inhalants are typically abused by achieving a high airborne concentration of a substance and deliberately inhaling it. With solvents, doing so typically involves putting the solvent in a closed container or saturating a piece of cloth and inhaling through it. Compressed gases are sometimes released into balloons and inhaled; directly releasing these substances into the mouth may freeze the larynx, causing laryngospasm and death by asphyxiation. Once the chemical is inhaled, its uptake and duration of action are determined by its solubility in blood and brain and by the respiratory rate and cardiac output.

The mechanism of action of this class of agents is less well understood than those of other drugs and medications. As CNS depressants, they have been thought to exert their actions by dissolving in membranes and altering their function in a nonspecific way; the potency of these compounds is frequently related to their solubility in membranes. Many consider this relationship to better predict the access of the agent to the site of action and to be unrelated to the mechanism by which the solvents exert their effects. Solvents impair conduction in isolated nerves and affect nerves with smaller diameters first, which suggests that parts of the nervous system such as the cortex would be

Teenager huffing inhalant from plastic bag. © James Marshall/ Corbis.

affected before systems consisting of large fibers. There is significant interest in the GABA receptor complex as the site of action of many of these compounds. Some findings indicate that the rewarding effects of inhalant abuse are mediated through the same brain neurotransmitter systems and anatomical areas as have been implicated in other forms of substance abuse.

TYPES OF INHALANTS

Alkanes. Alkanes are hydrocarbons of the general formula C_nH_{2n+2}. The potency of this family of straight-chain chemicals increases with the number of carbons. The smaller molecules (methane, ethane, butane, propane) are gases at room temperature; their deliberate inhalation can produce cardiac arrhythmias and sudden death. Pentane, hexane, and longer alkanes are liquids that become progressively less volatile. Hexane can produce a devastating neurotoxicity. Alkanes are paraffins; cycloparaffins are rings without alternating double bonds; and alkylcycloparaffins have a short substituent on the ring. Alkylcycloparaffins such as methylcyclopentane and methylcyclohexane (hexahydrotoluene) are convulsants.

Amyl Nitrite. Amyl nitrite is a volatile, oily liquid with a sweet, banana-like odor. It is sold by prescription in glass ampules for the treatment of angina pectoris, chest pain caused by the narrowing of vessels supplying the heart, resulting in inadequate blood flow. When the glass ampules are broken, they pop; hence, they are sometimes called *poppers.* Amyl nitrite relaxes the vessels of the heart by relaxing the muscles of the veins as well as all other smooth muscles in the body. When the veins throughout the body dilate, blood pressure falls. Because a minimum blood pressure is required to maintain blood supply to vital organs such as the brain, a reflex protects the brain by increasing heart rate and blood flow. This produces a *rush* as the heart pounds, and there is a throbbing sensation in the head. Users also experience a warm flush as the blood accumulates near the skin because of the dilation of veins. Vision also may redden as the retinal vessels dilate. The user may faint if the heart cannot maintain blood flow to the brain. If fainting occurs, the user falls to the floor, and blood flows to the brain, restoring consciousness. Use in a situation in which it is impossible to become horizontal may result in brain damage.

The duration of action of the drug is very brief, and as the effect wears off, the user may experience headache, nausea, vomiting, and a chill. The drop in body temperature occurs because of the loss of heat when the veins dilate and the skin flushes. Use of the drug for prolonged periods, or swallowing the liquid, may produce fatal methemoglobinemia, a blood condition in which the blood is brown and cannot carry oxygen to the brain. The drug produces a thick, crusty brown rash if it is spilled on the skin and is irritating to the lungs. It is flammable and explosive. Volatile nitrites are converted to nitrosamines in the body, and most nitrosamines are potent cancer-causing chemicals. Volatile nitrites impair the function of the immune system. There is an association of the use of volatile nitrites with Kaposi's sarcoma, an AIDS-related skin cancer, but this may be a surrogate variable for other hazards associated with the frequency of high risk sexual behaviors. The physiology of sexual intercourse involves smooth muscle; the nitrites relax those muscles as well and so will affect sexual function.

The prescription requirement for amyl nitrite was eliminated in 1960, and its use became popular; in 1964 prescription requirements were reestablished. So-called designer nitrites, such as butyl and isobutyl nitrites, were then bottled and sold as room deodorizers with such names as RUSH and Locker Room, and Aroma of Men (so named because it smelled like a locker room). Since these products were not controlled substances or sold as medicines, they were once legal products but were subsequently removed from the market, only to return when the formulation of the products was changed to escape regulation, as cyclohexylnitrite was not captured by the legislation.

Anesthetics. Anesthetics are used in medicine to permit surgical procedures without pain or consciousness. They are of two types: local and general. A local anesthetic is usually injected near nerves to prevent pain in a limited area, such as a procaine injection to anesthetize a tooth. General anesthetics are administered to the whole body and depress the CNS to such an extent that major surgery can be performed without killing the patient from the shock resulting from procedures that otherwise would be unendurable. General anesthetics were developed in the mid-nineteenth century by doctors experimenting, usually on themselves, with the organic solvents available at the time. These experiments were sometimes done by groups of people who inhaled the vapors and described the effects or passed out. Later, careful experimental work identified volatile chemicals that are used to save lives by permitting surgery that would otherwise be impossible to perform and that have relatively low toxicity and are relatively safe to use in medical contexts.

Some anesthetics can be given by injection. Short-acting anesthetics are used for brief procedures in medicine and dentistry when inhalation anesthesia is inappropriate or difficult or for starting anesthesia before longer-acting agents are given to the patient. Drugs that have been used for this purpose include barbiturates such as sodium methohexital and sodium thiopental, and benzodiazepines such as midazolam. Fentanyl and related opioid compounds are used for a longer duration of action. A dissociative anesthetic, ketamine, is used for treating burn patients and small children. These agents affect the brain in a more selective way than other anesthetics, so that there is more muscle tone and better circulation in the head and neck. A related veterinary drug, phencyclidine (PCP), has a longer duration of action; when given to humans, however, it has produced terrifying hallucinations upon recovery. It is subject to abuse.

Volatile Anesthetics. Volatile anesthetics induce unconsciousness and loss of reflexes. This CNS depression can be induced by a wide variety of different chemicals; agents used in clinical medicine are selected for reasons that include low toxicity, ease of maintaining and adjusting a given depth of anesthesia, and freedom from adverse effects upon recovery. Many compounds were examined in the search for modern anesthetic agents.

The depth of anesthesia depends on how much of the medication is present in the CNS. This, in turn, depends on how much is in the air that is inhaled, to what extent the anesthetic divides between air and blood, and between blood and brain. An agent that is highly insoluble in blood, such as nitrous oxide, achieves a plateau, or saturation, concentration rapidly. More soluble agents take a longer time to plateau and to be exhaled as well, so recovery from them takes longer. Nitrous oxide and cyclopropane have the same solubility in blood and take the same amount of time to come to a steady concentration in blood; cyclopropane is more soluble in brain and fat, however, so it takes a much lower concentration to achieve the same effect. (Cyclopropane is explosive and, therefore, is no longer used in the operating room.) The way an anesthetic functions in a given individual depends on a number of variables, including the amount of fat in the individual's body, the volume of air inspired per minute, the amount of blood pumped through the lungs per minute, and various pre-existing medical conditions.

Aromatic Hydrocarbon Solvents. Aromatic hydrocarbon solvents have a structure that includes a benzene ring. The simplest form is benzene, a six-membered ring with double bonds and six hydrogen atoms. All other aromatic hydrocarbons have alkyl substituents around the ring; for example,

toluene has one methyl group and xylene has two methyl groups.

Benzene. Benzene is a volatile aromatic hydrocarbon. Its presence in consumer products and in the workplace has been reduced because it causes a form of leukemia. Its chemical formula is C_6H_6; it is a six-membered ring with alternating double bonds and a hydrogen on each carbon. The ring opens when metabolized, causing the formation of reactive and toxic chemicals. Benzine, a name applied to automotive fuel in Europe, is a solvent mixture and should be distinguished from benzene.

Black Jack. Black Jack is the trade name for several inhalant products that contain either volatile nitrites or ethyl chloride.

Chlorinated Hydrocarbons. These substances comprise a large class of industrial chemicals. Those that are highly volatile are sometimes subject to abuse. Chlorinated hydrocarbons undergo significant metabolism in the body, and these changes in chemical structure usually result in an increase in the solvent's toxicity. Because many of these metabolic products are reactive chemicals, they can produce injuries to the kidneys, the liver, and the blood-forming organs. Chlorinated hydrocarbon inhalation is also associated with lethal disorders of heart rhythm, that is, ventricular arrhythmias.

Chlorofluorocarbon Propellants. Halogenated hydrocarbons are relatively non-reactive chemicals with high vapor pressure that have been used to blow products out of containers through a tiny hole. Their widespread use in the early 1960s was followed by an epidemic of aerosol sniffing that led to cardiac arrhythmias and death among young people. The halogens—chlorine, fluorine, and bromine—have been used to make various chemicals for purposes ranging from propellants and refrigerants to fire extinguishers. Their use has been severely limited since the recognition that their release into the atmosphere depletes the upper layers of ozone, exposing the Earth to excessive amounts of ultraviolet radiation. Freon is a brand name for a family of commercial products.

Chloroform. Chloroform ($CHCl_3$) was one of the earliest solvents put to use as an anesthetic agent, and it was widely abused in the nineteenth century.

It has been replaced with agents that are much less toxic. Its use in cough and cold medications is obsolete.

Ethyl Chloride. Ethyl chloride is a local anesthetic, CNS depressant, and refrigerant that has been subject to abuse by inhalation. Ethyl chloride has a high vapor pressure; spraying it directly into the mouth may freeze the tissues of the throat and cause fatal laryngospasm (contraction of the muscles of the throat and larynx), and the shutoff of the flow of air to the lungs. Ethyl chloride has been sold in canisters and spray cans (e.g., Black Jack). A related chemical, methyl chloride, has similar effects and was used in refrigerators until it was recognized as highly poisonous in closed spaces.

Ethyl Ether. A volatile anesthetic agent subject to abuse by inhalation, ethyl ether was used as an inhalation anesthetic for many years. It has been supplanted by other agents with fewer recovery side effects, such as headache, nausea, and vomiting. It is explosive. Ethyl ether was drunk during the Whiskey Rebellion of the eighteenth century, when heavy taxes were imposed on whiskey. Consumed by this route, ether *tanned* (hardened dramatically) the soft palate. When swallowed, profound intoxication follows, but recovery is faster than from alcohol. Alcohol is metabolized at a fixed number of grams per hour, except under extreme conditions; ethyl ether is eliminated by exhalation.

Freon. Freon is a brand name applied to a class of aerosol propellants commonly used as refrigerants. The availability of Freon has been limited since the 1990s due to increased recognition that chlorofluorocarbons and hydrochlorofluorocarbons negatively impact the Earth's ozone. Deliberate inhalation has been associated with sudden death from cardiac rhythm disturbances.

Gasoline. Gasoline, a fuel that powers internal combustion engines, is a complex petroleum product subject to abuse by inhalation. The toxicity produced from gasoline exposure depends on the constituents of the mixture and the route of administration. Oral ingestion of gasoline is usually followed by vomiting; subsequent aspiration of gasoline liquid into the lungs is followed by a frequently fatal chemical pneumonia. Deliberate inhalation of leaded gasoline fumes can lead to brain injury related to absorption of tetraethyl lead, a very toxic chemical.

Glue. Glues are made by dissolving a sticky or adhesive material in a solvent. When the solvent evaporates, the adhesive material remains attached to the surfaces to which it is applied, sticking them together. Glues are complex mixtures formulated for specific purposes. They are not designed for human consumption. When inhaled, they may produce severe injury or death. Most of the solvents used in glues are flammable, and fires have resulted from their inappropriate use. The solvent mixtures in glues and glue thinners are designed to dissolve the solid glue material and to evaporate evenly at a rate appropriate for the product. Solvents of relatively low industrial purity are used in these products; they are usually complex mixtures whose formulation changes with market price. Their toxicity can be great when concentrated and inhaled. Some manufacturers label their products or add irritants in an attempt to prevent youths from deliberately inhaling these products.

Hexane. Hexane is a volatile solvent that contains six carbons in a straight chain (i.e., an alkane) and has the chemical formula C_6H_{14}. It can cause severe damage to the peripheral nervous system, producing destruction of long myelinated nerves (distal axonopathy). This condition results in an inability to walk, loss of muscle mass in all limbs, and sometimes loss of bowel and bladder control. This injury occurs because hexane is metabolized to a gamma diketone. Another solvent subject to abuse that undergoes the same change in the body is methylbutylketone.

Nitrous Oxide. Nitrous oxide is a volatile analgesic and anesthetic agent. It was discovered at the beginning of the nineteenth century by Sir Humphry Davy, who was looking for gases and vapors that might have some therapeutic use. It is also used to increase the power output of engines, especially in race cars. Nitrous oxide quickly produces an inebriation that many found pleasurable, and it rapidly became the subject of much experimentation and merrymaking, which is why it is sometimes referred to as *laughing gas*. Nitrous oxide parties became very fashionable but could not long be limited to the upper classes. Popular demonstrations were conducted, and at one such demonstration Horace Wells noticed that a participant had injured his leg, yet seemed oblivious to the pain. Although Davy had noted that nitrous oxide deadened the pain of his toothaches, it was Wells who underwent the first tooth extraction using nitrous oxide for pain relief. The first use of nitrous oxide for clinically significant pain relief was its use in childbirth by the physician Stanislav Klikovich (1853–1910). Nitrous oxide inhalation is about as effective as 30 mg of morphine for pain relief.

Nitrous oxide is not very soluble in either blood or brain tissue, and consequently it has a short duration of action and requires very high levels to produce effects, on the order of 15 to 30 percent by volume. Because the use of gases at this high a concentration might result in asphyxiation, special equipment is used to guard against this possibility in medical settings. Because it displaces oxygen, nitrous oxide can kill those who inhale it for pleasure in closed rooms or automobiles.

Nitrous oxide was long thought to be a relatively innocuous anesthetic, almost as safe as inert gases. Research has demonstrated, however, that its inhalation irreversibly inactivates methionine synthetase, and this enzyme inhibition produces a vitamin deficiency that can injure the peripheral nervous system. This was first observed in dentists and others with access to nitrous oxide who inhaled it habitually. This nervous system injury is associated with numbness and clumsiness of the hands and with Lhermitte's sign, a lightning-like shooting sensation that occurs when the patient bends the neck.

Nitrous oxide is used in dentistry because it has both analgesic and anxiety-relieving properties. It is used as a carrier gas and inducing agent in major surgery, facilitating induction of anesthesia maintained by other agents. Given that it is not very soluble in blood, oxygen must be provided to patients at the end of the surgery because the nitrous oxide can displace oxygen as it rushes out of the patient's body (diffusion hypoxia).

Perchloroethylene. This chlorinated hydrocarbon solvent, which was used in the dry-cleaning industry, is also known as PERC (see Chlorinated Hydrocarbons, above).

Toluene. Toluene (methyl benzene, toluol) is an aromatic hydrocarbon solvent widely used in industrial processes, fuels, and consumer products. It is among the least irritating of the aromatic hydrocarbon solvents. When inhaled, it can produce CNS depression, like alcohol and other solvents. Its pharmacologic effects resemble those of other CNS depressant drugs, displaying actions like those of medications used for the treatment of epilepsy or for the clinical management of anxiety.

Toluene is removed from the body by exhalation and by metabolism. It is metabolized to methylhippuric acid and is excreted by the kidneys. Overexposure to toluene can produce distal tubular acidosis of the kidney, an injury attributable to excess acidity that is reversible upon termination of exposure. Toluene has been demonstrated to produce loss of high-frequency hearing in laboratory animals following repeated high exposure, such as occurs during solvent abuse. Toluene also has been implicated in severe injuries to the nervous system in a large number of patients who deliberately inhaled toluene-containing solvents. These injuries are characterized by injury and loss of brain tissue. Patients display flattened emotional responses, impaired cognitive abilities, and a wide, shuffling gait associated with injury to the cerebellum. As of 2008, animal studies had not conclusively demonstrated that toluene alone is responsible for this severe brain injury syndrome; nonetheless, solvent abusers who inhale toluene-containing mixtures run a very high risk of irreversible brain injury.

1,1,1 Trichloroethane (TCE). This chlorinated hydrocarbon solvent has a high vapor pressure. It is useful in products that need to dry quickly, such as liquid paper products once commonly used to cover errors. The deliberate inhalation of these products has been associated with sudden death from ventricular arrhythmias (see Chlorinated Hydrocarbons, above).

Trichloroethylene. A chlorinated hydrocarbon solvent used as a degreaser and dry-cleaning agent, trichloroethylene is subject to abuse by inhalation. When alcohol is consumed after exposure to trichloroethylene, profound blushing of the face occurs, the so-called degreaser's flush. One of the metabolites of trichloroethylene is chloral hydrate, an anesthetic agent used in a Mickey Finn, a spiked drink used criminally to anesthetize robbery victims.

Whippets. Whippets are small canisters of nitrous oxide used at soda fountains to make whipped cream. They have been incorporated into various products, such as balloon inflators, carburetor pipes, and other drug paraphernalia (see Nitrous Oxide, above).

See also **Inhalants: Extent of Use and Complications; Monitoring the Future.**

RONALD W. WOOD
REVISED BY BRIAN E. PERRON (2009)
MATTHEW O. HOWARD (2009)

INHALANTS: EXTENT OF USE AND COMPLICATIONS.

Inhalant abuse first became prevalent in the United States in the 1850s and is in the early twenty-first century endemic among adolescents. One of the most common forms of substance abuse, it is aptly referred to as the *silent epidemic*. Inhalants are also one of the most understudied types of substances. Commonly abused inhalants include acetone, butanone, n-hexane, and toluene, although varied mixtures of chemicals are found in many abused products. Intoxication presents as a general syndrome marked by slurred speech, ataxia, stupor or coma, and other signs similar to alcohol intoxication. Inhalant abusers may inhale vapors from a rag soaked with a substance placed over the mouth or nose, a bag into which a substance has been placed, or directly from a container. Intoxication is rapid in onset and short-lived, although some users repeatedly administer inhalants to maintain a preferred level of intoxication.

The *Diagnostic and Statistical Manual of Mental Disorders* (*DSM-IV*) distinguishes inhalant use disorders (i.e., disorders caused by the inhalation of aliphatic, aromatic, and halogenated hydrocarbons, as well as esters, ketones, and glycols) from disorders related to the abuse of anesthetic gases (e.g., nitrous oxide) or short-acting vasodilators such as amyl or butyl nitrite. Unlike other substance use disorders, withdrawal symptoms are not a criterion used for defining inhalant dependence in *DSM-IV*.

PREVALENCE AND CORRELATES OF INHALANT USE

Results from the 2006 Monitoring the Future (MTF) survey indicated that approximately 16.1 percent of eighth graders reported lifetime inhalant use. This rate of use was slightly higher than the comparable rate of marijuana use (15.7%) and substantially higher than the lifetime prevalence of cocaine use (3.4%) among this age group. Results from the National Survey on Drug Use and Health (NSDUH, 2002–2004) showed that an average of 598,000 youth twelve to seventeen years of age reported initiating inhalant use in the year prior to being surveyed. The NSDUH data also revealed that trends in past year inhalant use among this age group remained stable for males between 2002 and 2005. However, the prevalence of use increased from 4.1 percent to 4.9 percent for girls over this period.

Recreational inhalant use progresses to serious involvement with inhalants for many youth. For example, findings from the National Comorbidity Survey indicated that nearly 8.0 percent of youth fifteen to twenty-four years of age who tried inhalants eventually met *DSM-III-R* criteria for inhalant dependence. Inhalant use is found at epidemic levels in juvenile justice populations, with some estimates as high as approximately 40.0 percent (Howard et al., 2007). While inhalant use appears to be less prevalent among adults, it is important to note that it is problematic among disenfranchised adult populations, such as Native Americans who live on reservations, convicts, and other persons of low socio-economic status.

Asthma inhalers are typically not considered to be a substance of abuse. However, one study involving adolescents in the juvenile justice system found that approximately one-third of the sample had used an asthma inhaler without a prescription. Among youth with an inhaler prescription, approximately 27 percent reported using the inhaler more than prescribed (Perron & Howard, 2008). Coupled with other cases of inhaler misuse and abuse/dependence that are reported in the medical literature, it is likely that misuse and abuse of asthma inhalers is a greater problem than previously considered to be.

CONSEQUENCES OF INHALANT USE

Medical Consequences. Recreational inhalant use results in chemical exposures at levels dramatically higher than those typical of toxic occupational exposures. Inhalant intoxication can lead to emergencies, including sudden sniffing death and serious accidents. Recurrent inhalant intoxication is associated with conditions, including Parkinsonism and other brain, liver, and kidney disorders. Neurological findings in inhalant abusers include cerebral atrophy, thinning of the corpus callosum, and lesions of the white matter. Brain imaging studies (e.g., fMRI and SPECT) indicate that regional decrements in cerebral blood flow can be observed after one year of inhalant abuse, whereas white matter changes may take years to develop (Okada et al., 2000). Such studies have found inhalant abusers to exhibit hypoperfusion foci and nonhomogeneous uptake of radiopharmaceuticals (Kucuk et al., 2000).

Legal and Social Consequences. Use of inhalants is associated with a wide range of adverse legal and social consequences. Inhalant users have higher rates of aggressive behavior, criminal offending, school problems, conduct disorder, substance abuse, and involvement in high-risk behaviors (including unprotected casual sex and IV-drug use) than other drug users/nonusers. Inhalant users in juvenile justice settings are more likely to commit a crime while intoxicated, sell drugs, or steal to acquire money with which to buy drugs than their inhalant-nonusing peers. Research on juvenile offenders has also revealed a wide variety of deleterious consequences attributable to inhalant use, including fistfights, property crime, and failure to meet social and vocational obligations.

Cognitive Consequences. Studies of occupationally exposed workers form the basis of much of what is known about cognitive deficits in inhalant-exposed persons (Hoek et al., 2000). Inhalant-related cognitive problems are slow to resolve in many patients, and even a single occupational exposure leading to inhalant intoxication can produce long-term memory problems and processing speed impairments (Stolley, 1996). This finding is ominous given that inhalant abuse is often characterized by repeated exposures to neurotoxins at levels that greatly exceed those of occupational exposures. The most common deficits found in this line of research include learning problems, auditory and visual abnormalities, memory and attentional deficits, and errors in recall and judgment. Cognitive impairment may be the most disabling consequence of inhalant abuse and the earliest sign of neurological damage.

Psychiatric Dysfunction. Inhalant users display high rates of multiple-drug use and conduct disorder as youth and substance dependence and antisocial personality disorder in adulthood. Inhalant users tend to exhibit an earlier onset of behavior problems and greater diversity in antisocial conduct than non-inhalant abusers. Prior reports have identified higher rates of mood disorders, particularly major depression, in inhalant exposed workers than controls. For example, journeyman painters were significantly more likely than controls (41.0% vs. 16.0%) to meet lifetime *DSM-IV* criteria for major depression, and eleven of twelve painters who met criteria for a mood disorder experienced their first episode of mood disorder after they had commenced their painting careers (Condray et al., 2000). Various studies also show an association of inhalant use with suicidal ideation, suicide attempts, paranoia, psychosis, impulse control disorders, and anxiety disorders among antisocial youth and other adolescent populations.

An important gap in the research is on the temporal ordering of psychiatric dysfunction and inhalant use. Specifically, it is unknown whether inhalants are used to alleviate psychiatric dysfunction (i.e., self-medication hypothesis) or if inhalants cause or exacerbate psychiatric dysfunction (i.e., super-sensitivity hypothesis). Most likely, there are heterogenous causal mechanisms within the population of inhalant abusers. A reciprocal relationship is probably at play.

TREATMENT AND PREVENTION

Research on treatment and prevention of inhalant use and abuse remained undeveloped in the first decade of the twenty-first century. As of 2008, no clinical trial of inhalant treatment had ever been funded by the National Institute of Drug Abuse, and no freestanding treatment facilities specializing in inhalant treatment existed in the United States. Moreover, inhalants are very rarely screened for in the United States, even within the substance abuse treatment service delivery system. Significant efforts are needed to effectively and efficiently identify persons who use inhalants. The identification of characteristic patterns of early cognitive dysfunction in inhalant users would contribute to future efforts to prevent inhalant-related brain damage. Psychiatric and substance abuse treatment providers should have knowledge about inhalants, including risk factors for, and consequences of, inhalant abuse. Despite the absence of empirically supported treatments for inhalant use disorders, this knowledge can be beneficial in structuring treatment modalities to meet individual needs.

The most successful treatment approaches would likely focus on issues of psychosocial functioning. Attention would be directed toward social influences related to use, including identifying and avoiding risky situations, developing skills to manage peer influence, building social networks that do not include inhalant users, and creating opportunities for meaningful social engagement.

Prior research involving youth in the juvenile justice system indicate that adolescents used inhalants due to curiosity about their effects, feelings of boredom, ease of access, and enjoyment (Perron, Vaughn, & Howard, 2007). These reasons suggest that social marketing campaigns that heighten awareness of adverse consequences are needed to dispel myths that recreational inhalant use is an innocuous activity. Although current research shows that adolescents involved in the juvenile justice system are at elevated risk of inhalant use, further epidemiological research is needed in order to more effectively target social marketing campaigns. Other prevention efforts can occur with the manufacturing of substances that are commonly abused, such as changing formulas to reduce toxicity and adding irritants.

See also **Complications.**

BIBLIOGRAPHY

Condray, R., Morrow, L. A., Steinhauer, S. R., Hodgson, M., & Kelley, M. (2000). Mood and behavioral symptoms in individuals with chronic solvent exposure. *Psychiatry Research, 97,* 191–206.

Hoek, J. A. F., Verberk, M. M., & Hageman, G. (2000). Criteria for solvent-induced chronic toxic encephalopathy: A systematic review. *International Archives of Occupational and Environmental Health, 73,* 362–368.

Howard, M. O., Balster, R. L., Cottler, L. B., Wu, L. T., & Vaughn, M. G. (2007). Inhalant use among incarcerated adolescents in the United States: Prevalence, characteristics, and correlates of use. *Drug & Alcohol Dependence, 91,* 129–133.

Kucuk, N. O., Kilic, E. O., Aysev, A., Gencoglu, E. A., Aras, G., Soylu, A., et al. (2000). Brain SPECT findings in long-term inhalant abuse. *Nuclear Medicine Communications, 21,* 769–773.

Okada, S., Yamanouchi, N., Kodama, K., Uchida, Y., Hirai, S., Sakamoto, T., et al. (2000). Regional cerebral blood flow abnormalities in chronic solvent abusers. *Psychiatry and Clinical Neurosciences, 53,* 351–356.

Perron, B. E., & Howard, M. O. (2008). Endemic asthma inhaler abuse among antisocial adolescents. *Drug and Alcohol Dependence.*

Perron, B. E., Vaughn, M. G., & Howard, M. O. (2007). Reasons for using inhalants: Evidence for discrete classes in a sample of incarcerated adolescents. *Journal of Substance Abuse Treatment.*

Stolley, B. T. (1996). Long-term cognitive sequelae of solvent intoxication. *Neurotoxicology and Tetratology, 18,* 471–476.

BRIAN E. PERRON
MATTHEW O. HOWARD

INJECTING DRUG USERS AND HIV. One of the major risk behaviors for infection by the human immunodeficiency virus (HIV) is the multi-person use (sharing) of needles and syringes for injecting drugs; the other risk behavior is unprotected sexual intercourse with an HIV-infected partner. The National Institute on Drug Abuse (NIDA) estimated that there were between 1.1 and 1.3 million injecting drug users (IDUs) in the United States in the late 1980s (Centers for Disease Control, 1987). The number of injecting drug users has probably declined somewhat since then because fewer people are injecting, people are transitioning to non-injecting drug use, and more people are dying due to AIDS and other causes.

BACKGROUND

In 2006, 22 percent of the estimated 433,000 people in the United States living with the HIV infection reported injecting drug use as their primary risk, and an additional 3 percent reported both male-with-male sexual behavior and injecting drug use as risk. Injecting drug use has been declining as a route of HIV transmission in the United States (Santibanez et al., 2006) and in Western Europe (European Monitoring Centre for Drugs and Drug Addiction [EMCDDA], 2007) but has been increasing dramatically in Eastern Europe and Asia. Approximately one-third of new cases of HIV infection outside of sub-Saharan Africa are related to injecting drug use (UNAIDS, 2007).

Historically the most commonly injected drug has been heroin; however, the increased availability of cocaine has resulted in an increased use by IDUs since the late 1980s. Injecting cocaine has elevated the risk of spreading HIV because the shorter duration of a cocaine high leads to more frequent injecting (Gottlieb & Hutman, 1990), and the possibility that cocaine injectors may confuse whose syringe is whose in a session with multiple injections by each person.

The prevalence of HIV and AIDS among injectors varies widely from region to region in the United States. The highest rates of IDU and HIV are found along the East Coast and West Coast, in the Southwest, Florida, Puerto Rico, and in major metropolitan areas. The prevalence of HIV infection is also related to the social context of needle sharing. In areas where injectors go to *shooting galleries*—where anyone using a previously used needle may not know who else used the needle—there are generally high rates of HIV infection. Conversely, in areas where the IDUs share syringes within small social networks, transmission is likely to be much lower

While IDUs with HIV infection are predominantly Hispanic and African American men in their late 20s to mid-40s, variations and exceptions are noted and reflect dynamics in individual metropolitan areas. Historically, HIV prevalence among IDUs has been highest in the mid-Atlantic states (New York, New Jersey, Pennsylvania).

REDUCING RISK-TAKING BEHAVIOR

Drug-abuse treatment and prevention can be effective in controlling the spread of AIDS among IDUs and for reducing the risk of exposure to the HIV virus. The goal of treatment is to eliminate injecting drug use as a risk factor in the spread of HIV. The goal of prevention is to reduce and eliminate harmful behaviors, such as sharing needles, that place the IDU at risk for either becoming infected or infecting others with HIV. Prevention does not necessarily focus on changing drug-seeking and needle-using behavior. Four areas are considered to be of prime importance:

1. Increase the number of drug abusers in treatment;
2. Enhance the effect of treatment;
3. Develop outreach and counseling strategies;

4. Develop prevention strategies for reducing the risk-taking behavior among IDUs

Drug Treatment. Several organizations and groups have suggested that drug-abuse treatment is important in helping to decrease and prevent the spread of AIDS. These organizations include the World Health Organization (WHO); the American Medical Association (AMA); the National Academy of Sciences, Institute of Medicine; and the Presidential Commission on the HIV Epidemic.

Drug-abuse treatment can play an important role in preventing HIV transmission. Treatment reduces the number of people engaging in risky behavior. In addition to reducing the number of active drug addicts, treatment can also reduce the number of people recruiting new drug addicts (Brown, 1991). Barriers to treatment now exist for IDUs with HIV. The most serious barrier to drug-abuse treatment is the lack of treatment availability and programs.

Drug-abuse treatment incorporates several modalities, which include drug-free outpatient services, methadone maintenance programs, and therapeutic communities (Leukefeld, 1988), as well as a number of programs that do not fit into these categories. Ideally, HIV and drug treatment should be integrated to increase social support systems, which should increase adherence to medication schedules and resistance to drugs (Stein et al., 2000).

Outreach and Counseling. One way to increase the number of IDUs in treatment is to increase the number of outreach and counseling programs. The National AIDS Drug Abuse Research Demonstration Program is an example of outreach and counseling (National Institute on Drug Abuse, 1988). This demonstration program, initiated in 1987, provided an opportunity to assess the characteristics and risk-taking behaviors of injecting drug abusers not in treatment. Additional purposes included focusing on sexual partners of IDUs at high risk for AIDS, determining and monitoring HIV seroprevalence (rate that a given population tests positive) across cities, and evaluating prevention strategies. The overall goal was to reduce the spread of HIV infection by reducing and eliminating drug-use practices and certain high-risk sexual practices. Counseling and outreach approaches were applied, tested, and evaluated at each community site. Projects were targeted on three levels: (a) high-risk individuals, (b) family and social networks of IDUs, and (c) the larger community. Although intervention components varied across sites, the focus and objectives were similar (McCoy et al., 1990; Leukefeld, 1988). These projects provided information about protective behaviors, and IDUs were encouraged to enroll in drug-abuse treatment programs. Trained indigenous outreach workers distributed and discussed materials through informal groups or through one-on-one interactions. Sixty-three communities were involved in this demonstration project (McCoy & Khoury, 1990; Leukefeld, 1988).

Strategies for community outreach differ between the IDU, their sex partners, and commercial sex workers. Reaching the IDU means that outreach workers go to places where IDUs hang out and buy their drugs, as well as visit jails, prisons, and courts, drug-treatment centers, and the health-care system. Although there is inherent danger in many of these settings, recovering drug users—savvy men and women of the same backgrounds as IDUs—have achieved success in contacting IDUs in these settings (Serrano, 1990; Brown, 1990).

Many male IDUs hang out on the street or can be found in places where other IDUs hang out. However, female sex partners of IDUs are often employed and frequently stay close to home with children. (Margolis, 1991). While women may purchase drugs for their partners, they do not generally hang out at those locations. Thus, targeting female partners of IDUs requires different strategies than those used for contacting the IDU.

The YES project of San Francisco is an example of a program that targeted female sex partners of IDUs. It began by supporting high-risk women in meeting their basic needs by helping them get general assistance, food, clothing, and health care. A second strategy was to rent a hotel room, called A Room of Her Own in which education and counseling was provided to the female partner of the IDU. Another project (serving Bridgeport, Connecticut; San Juan, Puerto Rico; and Juarez, Mexico) contacted the female sex partners of male IDUs. It examined an approach that attracted women to a safe setting established by the program—a clothing boutique where women could pick up new clothes and then stay to view an AIDS information video. Another strategy of this project was to have outreach staff available in the afternoons and evenings, hours when these women were available (Moini, 1991). There was also a project in Long Beach, California, where a drop-in center was established for youth and women (Yankovich, Archuleta, & Simental, 1991).

Commercial sex workers are another high-risk group and require strategies appropriate to their environment. Contacting commercial sex workers can be difficult because their pimps can severely restrict contact with social-service workers. In one study, contact was made when the pimp was not around and through the Salvation Army mobile canteen that served coffee to the sex workers in the late night and early morning hours (Moini, 1991). Another study reported that sex workers are aware of AIDS, know how it is transmitted, and are aware that their drug use and unsafe sexual behavior are putting them at risk (Shedlin, 1990). However, barriers to behavioral changes in commercial sex workers include low self-esteem and low levels of education, along with poverty, addiction, hopelessness, lack of knowledge, and lack of support services.

Prevention Strategies. Prevention is of central importance in controlling the spread of HIV among IDUs. Reducing syringe sharing among people who continue to inject drugs is the most important aspect of preventing HIV transmission among drug users. Preventing infection is a self-preservation issue, while preventing the spread of HIV is an altruistic issue (Moini, 1991). Reports have indicated that among IDUs there is greater resistance to changing sexual behaviors (using condoms) than drug-use behaviors (sharing needles) (Sorenson, 1990). Thus, it is important to target not only IDUs but also their sex partners and commercial sex workers who engage in unsafe sex practices. These people may also be exchanging drugs for sex and may be IDUs themselves (Centers for Disease Control, 1990a). There are three prevention strategies available:

1. Education
2. Needle-exchange programs
3. Community-based interventions

Education. In addition to the community-outreach programs, Jean Schensul and Margaret Week (1991) indicate that three overarching prevention-education strategies have been developed

1. Prevention education for HIV-antibody-negative individuals;

2. AIDS pre- and posttest counseling;

3. Prevention and support for HIV-antibody-positive individuals

AIDS prevention education involves delivery of information related to the spread of HIV, risk behaviors, and preventing the spread of the virus. Educational activities target the general public, school-aged populations, and populations at risk, like IDUs. The U.S. Centers for Disease Control (CDC) National Public Information Campaign produced numerous educational materials for the radio, television, and print media. Education targeting individuals at risk for HIV infection has included counseling, testing, teaching of behavioral responses to risky behaviors, and providing support for low- or no-risk behaviors (Roper, 1991).

Prevention education for IDUs includes several informational components. Of primary importance to active-drug users are issues related to needle sharing as a risk behavior for HIV transmission. Safe-sex issues and knowledge of HIV transmission through unsafe sex are important to IDUs, the sex partners of IDUs, and commercial sex workers.

Pre- and posttest AIDS counseling is another strategy for HIV prevention. In the early 1980s, at the beginning of the AIDS epidemic, testing was controversial because of the fear of discrimination, the concern about the accuracy of tests, the usefulness of the results, and the psychological distress associated with a positive result. However, because there is more effective treatment for symptomatic AIDS and early treatment for HIV-infected individuals, the resistance is diminishing.

Generally, individuals seek HIV testing for one of two reasons: (a) an agency or person (like a plasma center, a penal institution, or a medical professional) requests it, or (b) the individual seeks to be tested because of identified high-risk behaviors (Roggenburg et al., 1991). When an individual is tested for HIV, it can represent a crisis in the life of that individual. Receiving the results can be difficult due to the anxiety surrounding the situation, even if the results are negative. Pre- and posttest counseling are necessary to assess the psychological well-being of the individual being tested.

A very important approach for preventing HIV infection is providing legal access to sterile injection equipment for IDUs (Committee on the Prevention of HIV Infection among Injecting Drug Users in High Risk Countries, 2006). Access is provided through sales in pharmacies, needle exchange programs, or both. In needle exchange programs, a clean needle and sometimes injection equipment (works) are exchanged for used ones. Large-scale syringe exchange programs have been associated with both preventing HIV epidemics among IDUs (Des Jarlais et al., 1995) and reducing high seroprevalence epidemics (Des Jarlais et al., 2005). Syringe exchange started in the United States in the late 1980s, and there are now approximately 180 needle exchange programs in the United States (McKnight et al., 2007) and a number of states (Connecticut, New York, Minnesota) have changed their laws to permit pharmacies to sell sterile needles and syringes to drug users. While it is difficult to draw strict causal relationships, the number of HIV infections among injecting drug users in the United States has been declining substantially (McKnight et al., 2007) since the expansion of syringe exchange in the country.

FUTURE DIRECTIONS FOR PREVENTION AND TREATMENT

Preventing the spread of AIDS for IDUs and their sex partners requires a multidisciplinary, multiple-strategy approach. Community-intervention strategies have proven to be partially effective in reducing IDU risk behaviors. Much remains to be accomplished, however, particularly in low- and middle-income countries (Committee on the Prevention of HIV Infection among Injecting Drug Users in High Risk Countries, 2006). Targeting HIV-prevention approaches and interventions will receive additional emphasis as the epidemic progresses. Research needs to continue to examine methods to reduce HIV in IDUs, to reinforce IDU behavior changes, to increase the effectiveness of drug-abuse treatment, and to provide antiretroviral treatment with psychosocial support and other support systems for HIV-infected IDUs.

See also **Cocaine; Eastern Europe; Harm Reduction; Heroin; Hispanic Americans, Alcohol and Drug Use Among; HIV Risk Assessment Battery (RAB); National Survey on Drug Use and Health (NSDUH); Needle and Syringe Exchanges and HIV/AIDS; Prevention, Education and; Prisons and Jails, Drug Use and HIV/AIDS in; Risk Factors for Substance Use, Abuse, and Dependence: An Overview; Substance Abuse and AIDS; U.S. Government: Agencies Supporting Substance Abuse Prevention and Treatment.**

BIBLIOGRAPHY

Battjes, R. J., Leukefeld, C. G., Pickens, R. W., Haverkos, H. W. (1988). The Acquired Immunodeficiency Syndrome and intravenous drug abuse. *Bulletin on Narcotics, 40* (1), 21–34.

Brown, L. S. (1990). Black intravenous drug users: Prospects for intervening in the transmission of human immunodeficiency virus infection. In C. G. Leukefeld, R. J. Battjes, & Z. Amsel (Eds.), *AIDS and intravenous drug use: Future directions for community based prevention research.* National Institute on Drug Abuse Research Monograph 93. Washington, DC: U.S. Department of Health and Human Services.

Brown, L. S. (1991). The impact of AIDS on drug abuse treatment. In R. W. Pickens, C. G. Leukefeld, & C. R. Schuster (Eds.), *Improving drug abuse treatment.* National Institute on Drug Abuse Research Monograph 106. Washington, DC: U.S. Department of Health and Human Services.

Centers for Disease Control. (1987). *A review of current knowledge and plans for expansion of HIV surveillance activities: A report to the Domestic Policy Council.* Washington, DC: U.S. Government Printing Office.

Centers for Disease Control. (1990a). AIDS in women— United States. *Morbidity and Mortality Weekly Report, 39*(47), 845–846.

Centers for Disease Control. (1990b). *National HIV seroprevalence surveys: Summary of results,* 2nd ed. Washington, DC: U.S. Department of Health and Human Services.

Centers for Disease Control. (1991). Mortality attributable to HIV infection/AIDS—United States, 1981–1990. *Morbidity and Mortality Weekly Report, 40,* 42–44.

Centers for Disease Control. (1992). The second 100,000 cases of acquired immunodeficiency syndrome— United States, June 1981–December 1991. *Morbidity and Mortality Weekly Report, 41,* 28–29.

Centers for Disease Control. (1999). Drug-Associated HIV Transmission Continues in the United States. *HIV Prevention Saves Lives.*

Centers for Disease Control. (2007). *HIV/AIDS surveillance report,* 17, 1-54.

Chaisson, R. E., Baccheti, P., Osmond, D., Brodie, B., Sande, M. A., Moss, A. R. (1989). Cocaine use and HIV infection in intravenous drug users in San Francisco. *Journal of the American Medical Association, 261,* 561–565.

Childress, A. R., et al. (1991). Are there minimum conditions necessary for methadone maintenance to reduce intravenous drug use and AIDS risk behaviors? In R. W. Pickens, C. G. Leukefeld, & C. R. Schuster (Eds.), *Improving Drug Abuse Treatment.* National Institute on Drug Abuse Research Monograph 106. Washington, DC: U.S. Department of Health and Human Services.

Committee on the Prevention of HIV Infection among Injecting Drug Users in High Risk Countries. (2006). *Preventing HIV infection among injecting drug users in high risk countries: An assessment of the evidence.* Washington, Institute of Medicine.

Des Jarlais, D. C., Friedman, S. R., Sotheran, J. L., Stoneburner, R. (1988). The sharing of drug injection equipment and the AIDS epidemic in New York City: The first decade. In R. J. Battjes & R. W. Pickens (Eds.), *Needle sharing among intravenous drug abusers: National and international perspectives.* National Institute on Drug Abuse Research Monograph 80. Washington, DC: U.S. Department of Health and Human Services.

Des Jarlais, D. C., et al. (1995). Maintaining low HIV seroprevalence in populations of injecting drug users. *Journal of the American Medical Association 274*(15), 1226-1231.

Des Jarlais, D. C., et al. (1999). Audio-computer interviewing to measure risk behavior for HIV among injecting drug users: A quasi-randomised trial. *The Lancet, 353,* 1657.

Des Jarlais, D.C., et al. (2005). HIV incidence among injection drug users in New York City, 1990 to 2002: Use of serologic test algorithm to assess expansion of HIV prevention services. *American Journal of Public Health, 95*(8), 1439–1444.

European Monitoring Centre for Drugs and Drug Addiction (EMCDDA). (2007). *Annual report on the state of the drug problem in Europe.* EMCDDA, Lisbon, Portugal.

Gottlieb, M. S., & Hutman, S. (1990). The case for methadone. AIDS Patient Care 4, 15–18.

Henderson, C. W. (2000a). Infectious outbreaks among drug users studied. *AIDS Weekly* (January).

Henderson, C. W. (2000b). Unsafe injection practices have serious, large-scale consequences. *World Disease Weekly* (April).

Henderson, C. W. (2000c). Various types of drug use affect HIV risks. *AIDS Weekly* (April).

Lange, W. R., et al. (1988). Geographic distribution of human immunodeficiency virus markers in parenteral drug abusers. *American Journal of Public Health, 78,* 443–446.

Leukefeld, C. G. (1988). HIV and intravenous drug use. *Health and Social Work*, 247–250.

Leukefeld, C. G., Battjes, R. J., & Amsel, Z. (1990). Community prevention efforts to reduce the spread of AIDS associated with intravenous drug abuse. *AIDS Education and Prevention*, 2(3), 235–243.

Leukefeld, C. G., Battjes, R. J., & Pickens, R. W. (1991). AIDS prevention: Criminal justice involvement of intravenous drug abusers entering methadone treatment. *Journal of Drug Issues, 21*(4), 673–683.

Margolis, E. (1991). Evaluating outreach in San Francisco. In *Community-based AIDS prevention: Studies of intravenous drug users and their sexual partners*. Rockville, MD: National Institute on Drug Abuse.

McCoy, C. B., & Khoury, E. (1990). Drug use and the risk of AIDS. *American Behavioral Scientist, 33*(4), 419–431.

McCoy, C. B., Chitwood, D. D., Khoury, E. L., & Miles, C. E. (1990). The implementation of an experimental research design in the evaluation of an intervention to prevent AIDS among IV drug users. *Journal of Drug Issues, 20*(2), 215–222.

McKnight, C., et al. (2007). Syringe exchange programs—United States, 2005. *Morbidity and Mortality Weekly Report, 56*(44) 1164–1167.

Moini, S. (1991). AIDS and female partners of HIV drug users: Selected outreach strategies, accomplishments, and preliminary data from one project. In *Community-based AIDS prevention: Studies of intravenous drug users and their sexual partners*. Rockville, MD: National Institute on Drug Abuse.

National Institute on Drug Abuse. (1988). *Community research branch AIDS research demonstration project research plan*. Bethesda, MD: Author.

Primm, B. (1990). Needle exchange programs do not involve the problem of HIV transmission. *AIDS Patient Care, 4*(August), 18–20.

Roggenburg, L., et al. (1991). The relation between HIV-antibody testing and HIV risk behaviors among intravenous drug users. In *Community-based AIDS prevention: Studies of intravenous drug users and their sexual partners*. Rockville, MD: National Institute on Drug Abuse.

Roper, W. L. (1991). Current approaches to prevention of HIV infections. *Public Health Reports, 106*, 111–115.

Santibanez, S. S., Garfein, R. S., Swartzendruber, A., Purcell, D. W., Paxton, L. A., & Greenberg, A. E. (2006). Update and overview of practical epidemiologic aspects of HIV/AIDS among injection drug users in the United States. *Journal of Urban Health, 83*(1), 86–100.

Schensul, J. J., & Week, M. (1991). Ethnographic evaluation of AIDS-prevention programs. In *Community-based AIDS prevention: Studies of intravenous drug users and their sexual partners*. Rockville, MD: National Institute on Drug Abuse.

Serrano, Y. (1990). The Puerto Rican intravenous drug user. In C. G. Leukefeld, R. J. Battjes, & Z. Amsel (Eds.), *AIDS and intravenous drug use: Future directions for community based prevention research*. National Institute on Drug Abuse Research Monograph 93. Washington, DC: U.S. Department of Health and Human Services.

Shedlin, M. G. (1990). An ethnographic approach to understanding HIV high-risk behaviors: Prostitution and drug abuse. *NIDA Research Monograph, 93*, 139–149.

Sorenson, J. L. (1990). Preventing AIDS: Prospects for change in white male intravenous drug users. In C. G. Leukefeld, R. J. Battjes, & Z. Amsel (Eds.), *AIDS and intravenous drug use: Future directions for community based prevention research*. National Institute on Drug Abuse Research Monograph 93. Washington, DC: U.S. Department of Health and Human Services.

Stein, M. D., Rich, J. D., Maksad, J., Chen, M. H., Hu, P., Sobota, M., & Clarke, J. (2000). Adherence to antiretroviral therapy among HIV-infected methadone patients: Effect of ongoing illicit drug use. *American Journal of Drug and Alcohol Abuse, 26*, 195.

UNAIDS. (2007). AIDS epidemic update: December 2006. *Joint United Nations Programme on HIV/AIDS*, Geneva, Switzerland: Author.

Yankovich, D., Archuleta, E., & Simental, S. (1991). A mobile outreach program to intravenous drug users and female sexual partners in Long Beach, California. In *Community-based AIDS prevention: Studies of intravenous drug users and their sexual partners*. Rockville, MD: National Institute on Drug Abuse.

FAYE E. REILLY
CARL G. LEUKEFELD
REVISED BY DON C. DES JARLAIS (2009)

INJURIES FROM ALCOHOL AND DRUGS. *See* Accidents and Injuries from Alcohol; Accidents and Injuries from Drugs.

INTERNATIONAL CLASSIFICATION OF DISEASES (ICD). International Classification of Diseases (ICD) is the official classification system of the World Health Organization (WHO), which is mandated to issue periodic revisions. As a general system for the classification of diseases, injuries, causes of death, and

related health problems, the ICD is used throughout the world as a frame of reference for statistical reporting of morbidity and mortality, clinical practice, and education. The ICD is a system of categories to which specific disease entities can be assigned consistently in different parts of the world. As of 2008, it has become the international standard of diagnostic classification for epidemiological and many health management purposes, including analysis of the general health situation of population groups and the monitoring of disease prevalence and incidence. It is used extensively to classify psychiatric disorders, including alcohol and drug dependence, and related health problems recorded on many types of health records, including death certificates and hospital reports.

Recognizing the growing importance of alcohol and drug misuse, the ninth revision of ICD published in 1975 (*ICD-9*) for the first time introduced the terms *dependence* and *abuse* into the international nomenclature. *Drug dependence* was defined as "a state, psychic and sometimes also physical, resulting from taking a drug, and characterized by behavioural and other responses that always include a compulsion to take the drug on a continuous or periodic basis in order to experience its psychic effects, and sometimes to avoid the discomfort of its absence" (WHO, 1977, 1978, p. 42). *Alcohol dependence* was defined in a similar way. The category Non-Dependent Abuse of Drugs was designed for cases in which a person "has come under medical care because of the maladaptive effect of a drug on which he is not dependent and that he has taken on his own initiative to the detriment of his health or social functioning" (WHO, 1978, pp. 43–44).

In 1994, the tenth revision of ICD was introduced. *ICD-10* replaced *ICD-9* as the official classification system for international use (WHO, 1992b). Chapter V, which describes mental and behavioral conditions (WHO, 2007), includes a section for the classification of disorders based on ten kinds of psychoactive substances: alcohol, sedative-hypnotics, cannabis (marijuana), cocaine, other stimulants, opioids, hallucinogens, tobacco, volatile solvents, and multiple drugs. The major disorders associated with these substances are acute intoxication, harmful use, dependence syndrome, withdrawal state, amnesic syndrome, and psychotic disorders (WHO, 2007). The identification of the substance used may be made on the basis of an interview with the patient, laboratory analysis of blood or urine specimens, or other evidence (such as clinical signs and symptoms or reports from third parties).

Acute intoxication is a transient condition following the ingestion of alcohol or other psychoactive substances. It results in disturbances in consciousness, cognition, perception, mood, or behavior. According to *ICD-10*, psychoactive substances are capable of producing different types of effect at different dose levels. For example, alcohol may have stimulant effects at low doses, lead to agitation and aggression with increasing dose levels, and produce clear sedation at very high levels. The term *pathological intoxication* in *ICD-10* refers to the sudden onset of violent behavior that is not typical of the individual when sober. This sudden onset occurs very soon after amounts of alcohol are drunk that would not produce intoxication in most people.

A central feature of the *ICD-10* approach to substance-use disorders is the concept of a dependence syndrome, which is distinguished from disabilities caused by harmful substance use (Edwards, Arif, & Hodgson, 1981). The *dependence syndrome* is defined as "a cluster of behavioral, cognitive, and physiological phenomena that develop after repeated substance use and that typically include a strong desire to take the drug, difficulties in controlling its use, persisting in its use despite harmful consequences, a higher priority given to drug use than to other activities and obligations, increased tolerances, and sometimes a physical withdrawal state" (WHO, 2007). A central characteristic of the dependence syndrome is the strong and persistent desire to take psychoactive drugs, alcohol, or tobacco. Another feature is the rapid reappearance of the syndrome soon after alcohol or drug use is resumed after a period of abstinence. A definite diagnosis of dependence is made only if three or more of the following have been experienced during the previous year: (1) a strong desire or sense of compulsion to take the substance; (2) difficulties in controlling substance-taking behavior in terms of its onset, termination, or levels of use; (3) a physiological withdrawal state; (4) evidence of tolerance; (5) progressive neglect of alternative pleasures or interests because of substance use; and (6) persisting with substance use despite clear evidence of overtly harmful consequences.

Harmful use, a new term introduced in *ICD-10* is a pattern of using one or more psychoactive substances that causes damage to health. The damage may be of two sorts: (1) physical (physiological), such as fatty liver, injuries associated with alcohol intoxication, or hepatitis from a contaminated needle used to inject drugs; or (2) mental (psychological), such as depression related to heavy drinking or drug use. Adverse social consequences often accompany substance use, but they are not in themselves sufficient to result in a diagnosis of harmful use.

A *withdrawal state* is a group of symptoms occurring on cessation or reduction of substance use after repeated and usually prolonged high-dose use of that substance. Onset and course of the withdrawal state are related to the type of substance and the dose being used immediately before abstinence. The withdrawal state may be complicated by convulsions.

Amnestic disorder refers to chronic impairment of recent memory induced by alcohol or other psychoactive substances. Disturbances of time sense and ordering of events are usually evident, as are difficulties in learning new material.

Psychotic disorder in the context of psychoactive substance use is a cluster of psychotic symptoms characterized by vivid hallucinations (typically auditory, but often in more than one sensory modality), misidentifications, delusions, ideas of reference (often of a paranoid or persecutory nature), psychomotor disturbances (excitement of stupor), and an abnormal affect, which may range from intense fear to ecstasy. The disorder typically resolves at least partially within one month and fully within six months.

Chapter 5 of *ICD-10* is available in several different versions. The *Clinical Descriptions and Diagnostic Guidelines* is intended for general clinical, educational, and service use (WHO, 2007). *Diagnostic Criteria for Research* is designed for use in scientific investigations and epidemiological studies. A shorter and simpler version of the classification is available for use by primary healthcare workers.

See also **Addiction: Concepts and Definitions; Alcoholism: Origin of the Term; Diagnostic and Statistical Manual (DSM); Models of Alcoholism and Drug Abuse.**

BIBLIOGRAPHY

Edwards, G., Arif, A., & Hodgson, R. (1981). Nomenclature and classification of drug- and alcohol-related problems: A WHO memorandum. *Bulletin of the World Health Organization, 59*, 225–242.

World Health Organization. (1977). *Manual of the international statistical classification of diseases, injuries, and causes of death* (Vol. 1). Geneva: Author.

World Health Organization. (1978). *Mental disorders: Glossary and guide to their classification in accordance with the ninth revision of the international classification of diseases.* Geneva: Author.

World Health Organization. (1992a). *The ICD-10 classification of mental and behavioural disorders: Clinical descriptions and diagnostic guidelines.* Geneva: Author.

World Health Organization. (1992b). *International classification of diseases and related health problems* (10th ed., rev.). Geneva: Author.

World Health Organization. (1993). *The ICD-10 classification of mental and behavioural disorders: Diagnostic criteria for research.* Geneva: Author.

World Health Organization. (2007). *The* ICD-10 *classification of mental and behavioral disorders: Mental and behavioral disorders due to substance use.* Geneva: Author.

THOMAS BABOR

INTERNATIONAL CONTROL POLICIES.

The international control of drugs, such as opium, coca, cannabis, alcohol, and tobacco, started at the end of the nineteenth century. Before these drugs came under international control, their global exchange had been ruled by free trade. In fact, many of the states shaping the international control system in the twentieth century had profited from the drug trade in the centuries before. The most evident example was the flourishing trade in opium between China and the British colony of India in the nineteenth century, which provided the British Empire with crucial revenues.

The shift from free drug trade to control was the result of economic and political changes. Industrialization and growing world trade were the bases for the expanding global use and production of substances such as alcohol, tobacco, and opium. In response to this expansion, social reformers gathered political momentum against the, in their eyes, immoral drug trade at the end of the nineteenth century. In particular, Christian missionaries were among the first to pressure the British and U.S. governments to limit their involvement in the alcohol and opium trade. Bishop Charles Henry Brent, who had gained firsthand experience of opium smoking and trade in the U.S. colony of the Philippines, zealously advocated the international prohibition of dangerous drugs (McAllister, 2000).

Moral crusaders inspired by Brent also found support for their cause in new medical research, which highlighted the health risks of drug use. Although opium and alcohol-based remedies had been indispensable to the medical chest for centuries, at the end of the nineteenth century medical research started to portray opium, alcohol, and manufactured drugs, such as heroin and cocaine, as great risks to people's health. Growing medical consensus on the dangers of drugs aided the campaigns of social reformers (Courtwright, 2001).

Against this background the first international meetings were held to discuss the regulation of the trade in opium, particularly in China. The 1909 Shanghai Opium Commission was the first such meeting, having been initiated by the U.S. and Chinese governments and presided over by Bishop Brent himself. The aim of the conference was to prohibit nonmedical opium use and to stop state-sanctioned opium exports.

In contrast to Brent's moral position, the U.S. government favored opium trade restrictions because they offered the United States strategic advantages. By supporting drug control, the U.S. government gained inroads into the opium-dominated Chinese market and improved U.S.-Chinese relations by supporting a policy in China's interest. The United States also claimed the moral high ground without having to compromise its economic interests in Asia. In contrast, major drug producing and manufacturing countries strongly opposed U.S. policy, as it threatened their favorable position in the opium market. As a result of these divergent political interests, the Shanghai Commission and the subsequent Hague Opium Conference (1911–1912) had few tangible effects on the international control of the drug trade.

DRUG CONTROL AFTER WORLD WAR I
The major step toward an international control system for opium, coca, and cannabis only occurred after World War I had reshuffled global power relations. The strongest opponents and potential losers of international drug control, such as drug-manufacturing Germany and drug-producing Turkey, were forced into the system at the peace conferences following the war. In addition, the newly founded League of Nations, the predecessor of the United Nations (UN), provided a permanent institutional basis for the negotiation and coordination of international drug control.

The two most important treaties negotiated under the League were the 1925 International Opium Convention and the 1931 Convention for Limiting the Manufacture and Regulating the Distribution of Narcotic Drugs. The 1925 Convention obliged members to report national opium exports and imports to the League-based Permanent Central Opium Board. The board also oversaw restrictions on the trade in coca and cannabis. The 1931 Convention concentrated on manufactured drugs and established a system by which governments estimated the quantity of drugs they required for medical and scientific use. This convention also introduced a drug-scheduling system that classified drugs according to the danger(s) they posed to health. The predecessor of the World Health Organization (WHO) was involved in this scheduling mechanism. In general, these two conventions established a reporting, estimating, and scheduling system that remained the basis for all later drug treaties (McAllister, 2000).

This early international control system under the League was effective at reducing the legal world trade in opium, coca, and cannabis products. It was the first time in history that a prosperous global trade was shrunk by international cooperation (Courtwright, 2001). However, after World War II the illegal smuggling of drugs soon caught up with the declining legal trade. In response, new treaties were drafted to close loopholes and to devise stricter controls on the illegal side of the drug trade. Compared to the legal trade, international cooperation would remain unsuccessful at stopping the rise of illegal drug trafficking throughout the twentieth century.

POST–WORLD WAR II
After World War II the UN and its specialized bodies inherited the drug-control mandate of the

League. UN bodies such as the International Narcotics Control Board (INCB) and the WHO replaced their forerunners. Traditional focal points for international control, such as China and Turkey, were replaced by new countries, such as Afghanistan and Colombia. But as in the first half of the twentieth century, the preferences of powerful Western governments continued to dominate the formulation and implementation of international control policies. Western preference for a supply stop of opium, coca, and cannabis from producer countries has remained the guiding principle of UN drug control. The U.S. government also continued to use its diplomatic and economic powers to force this preference onto producer states.

The treaties negotiated under UN auspices reflect these political preferences. The treaties extended the scope of international drug control, in particular in the field of illegal trade, and consolidated the ideas introduced in the first three decades of the twentieth century. The 1961 Single Convention on Narcotic Drugs was the culmination of the international drug-control effort started at the beginning of the century. The treaty had the dual goals of ensuring adequate medical and scientific supply of opium, coca, and cannabis products, as well as limiting all other cultivation, manufacture, trade, and use by strengthening the established reporting, estimating, and scheduling system. The treaty has remained the principal and most universally accepted agreement on drug control.

Through its aims and mechanisms, the 1961 Convention prioritizes a clear set of ideas on drug control, which is worth highlighting. The foremost method prescribed to intervene in the drug market is through supply-dominated measures, such as export and import controls. The convention mentions drug demand measures but does not institutionalize a single binding mechanism in this field. The main focus of the treaty is to minimize drug production, manufacture, smuggling, and distribution rather than use.

Besides supply control, the treaty prioritizes the control of opium, coca, cannabis, and their derivates over other drugs. In fact, during negotiations on the 1961 Convention drugs such as synthetic amphetamines were intentionally excluded because Western pharmaceutical companies opposed their control. These substances appeared in subsequent,

less stringent treaties. Drugs more socially accepted in Western states, such as alcohol and tobacco, were not even discussed during the course of drafting the 1961 Convention and other treaties. Therefore, the 1961 Convention and international legal framework prioritize the control of opium, coca, and cannabis products over other drugs (McAllister, 2000).

It is important to note that the 1961 Convention and related international agreements do not establish the total prohibition of heroin, cocaine, and cannabis use, although this is often claimed in official statements. The international control system regulates as well as prohibits drug use and trade. It regulates the medical and scientific use of controlled substances and prohibits any other use. The line between regulated medical and prohibited nonmedical use is open to states' own interpretation. For instance, it allowed the government of the United Kingdom to legalize the medical prescription of heroin to addicts, although this practice was illegal in other countries. This and similar interpretative spaces in the international framework offer governments a certain level of discretion when implementing the international treaties.

In general, even though this interpretative discretion leaves some space for national decisions on drug control, the 1961 Convention and other drug-control treaties are clear in their preference for the supply control of opium, coca, and cannabis. They purport these preferences not only through the supply-control-dominated language used in treaties but also through obligatory mechanisms, which are confined to the drug-supply side. In this sense, the treaties clearly reflect the powerful interests of the main drug consumer states in Europe and North America, which have attempted to shift the burden of control to producer states. In addition, interpretative discretion is often unfeasible for poorer states, which are more vulnerable to pro-prohibitionist pressures from the U.S. administration. For instance, Turkey was bullied into the international control system with the threats of U.S. economic sanctions in the 1950s and 1960s.

UNITED NATIONS TREATIES AFTER 1961
The treaties that followed the 1961 Convention confirmed its dominant ideas. The 1972 Protocol Amending the Single Convention on Narcotic Drugs

continued to focus on minimizing illegal supplies of opium, coca, and cannabis products and the 1971 Convention on Psychotropic Substances extended the 1961 approach to a greater variety of drugs.

The second major UN drug-control convention besides the Single Convention was negotiated in 1988. The UN Convention against Illicit Traffic in Narcotic Drugs and Psychotropic Substances was a direct outcome of U.S. President Ronald Reagan's domestic and international war on drugs from the mid-1980s onward and the realization among other UN member states that the existing conventions were lagging behind the growing global trade in illegal drugs.

The 1988 Convention reaffirmed the dominant drug-control system of earlier treaties and strengthened the importance of criminal justice—that is, policing, prosecution, and imprisonment—as the major method of drug control. Its main goal was to increase police and legal cooperation in the field of supply control. As in the treaties before, discussion of such issues as demand control and health were absent from the treaty and international debates at the time. This fact prompted observers at the time to state that until the 1980s, "the history of national and international narcotics control can be written without reference to addicts or addiction" (Stein, 1985, p. 5).

Together, the 1961 and 1988 treaties are the principal pillars supporting the international drug-control system. Drug-control agreements made after 1988 have had less impact on the legal control framework. However, these post-1988 agreements are important as this period witnessed a shift toward a more balanced international drug control approach. In particular, drug-demand reduction became more central in debates about international drug control throughout the 1990s.

DEMAND REDUCTION AS AN INTERNATIONAL PRIORITY

The main international agreements that represent this shift were made in 1987 and 1998. The principal product of the 1987 International Conference on Drug Abuse and Illicit Traffic was the Comprehensive Multidisciplinary Outline of Future Activities in Drug Abuse Control (CMO), which consisted of four equally important parts: drug-supply control, illicit drug traffic, illicit drug demand, and drug user treatment. For the first time, the CMO elevated drug-demand control to the same level of importance as supply control. The CMO especially served the interests of poor drug-producing states, which had advocated an equal international focus on the different aspects of drug control. In particular, Latin American states had opposed the overemphasis on the supply control of cocaine and the international neglect of U.S. drug demand.

Latin American states were also crucial in pushing for the revision of the international drug-control system at a major drug-control meeting in 1998, the UN General Assembly Special Session on the World Drug Problem (UNGASS). The meeting reaffirmed the CMO's aims and sought to establish a more equal relationship not only between supply and demand efforts but also between rich and poor states and their respective responsibilities in solving the world drug problem. In addition, states participating in UNGASS agreed to commit to attaining a "significant and measurable" reduction of drug demand (Donnelly, 1989; Jelsma, 2003).

RECENT DEBATE

Coinciding with UNGASS in the 1990s were broader international policy debates over drug legalization and harm reduction. These debates were part of a backlash against the ineffectiveness of the international control system, which had led to no significant reduction in illegal drug consumption, production, and trade. On one hand, proponents of a personal-freedom-centered approach, such as U.S. economist Milton Friedman, proposed drug legalization as an alternative to the internationally dominant approach. Legalization was meant to be a return to unregulated drug trade. The legalized trade in drugs would lead to the disappearance of criminal drug industries, which had developed as a result of drug control. In this view, legalization would also make the ineffective and expensive drug enforcement bureaucracy redundant. Legalization proponents saw control as the major problem that needed to be abolished.

On the other hand, harm reduction approaches grew out of medical concerns over the spread of HIV/AIDS through injecting drug use. In response to these concerns, harm reduction proposed a focus on the reduction of major drug-related harms rather than a reduction of drug use per se. Among the many practices advocated by harm reduction, needle-exchange programs aiming to prevent the spread of HIV/AIDS through shared syringes as well as a more balanced emphasis on demand and supply control were common (Courtwright, 2001). In general, harm reduction emphasized the underlying reason behind drug control, that is, the protection of individuals' and societies' health, which had been sidelined by international drug control.

In international political circles, legalization remained of marginal importance, unless it was used by conservatives to discredit policy reformers. Harm reduction was practiced in several European countries and therefore had some impact on the sidelines of international conferences and on the practical work of the UN. But harm reduction also never made its way into international policy documents because it was strongly opposed by the UN's major donor, the United States.

Overall, if seen from a legal perspective, these policy debates as well as UNGASS had limited effects on the international drug-control system and its supply-control bias. It did not introduce any new binding mechanisms and institutional responsibilities. Even rhetorically, supply control still dominates the international drug-control system. At UN drug-control meetings, the language of "drug war" and "drug scourge" continues to be used by a majority of state representatives. This language affirms the dominance of supply control, criminal justice, and policing and has little in common with demand reduction, prevention, and medical patient treatment (Room, 1999).

However, a slight shift has occurred, if just on the rhetorical and not on a legal level. Drug-demand control was not considered worth debating until the 1990s and only then became significant enough to be reflected in international policy statements, such as the CMO and at UNGASS. Harm reduction has also been discussed in UN studies on alternative drug control, such as the 1997 World Drug Report (Jelsma, 2003). This shift has not reached, and might never reach, a level where supply control and demand control are equally important in the international legal framework. Nonetheless, there was an important shift away from pure supply control to the prescription of a more balanced approach in the 1990s.

NEW CONTROLS ON TOBACCO AND ALCOHOL

Finally, although few international policy reforms have evolved in the field of opium, coca, and cannabis control during the last few decades, in large part due to U.S. opposition, the control of alcohol and tobacco has seen new initiatives since the late 1990s. International measures to control tobacco gained new impetus after 1999, when the WHO began preparing a Framework Convention on Tobacco Control. That convention was adopted in 2003 and proposes restrictive sales measures, labeling requirements, protection from exposure to tobacco smoke, as well as measures against the smuggling of cigarettes. The treaty is most stringent in the field of advertising, although none of its provisions amount to the type of obligations existent in the field of opium, coca, and cannabis control. As the convention is primarily a framework for future legal developments, it remains to be seen how far international tobacco control will emulate the control of illegal drugs.

Nonetheless, international tobacco controls go much further than control measures for the world's most widespread legal drug, alcohol. International alcohol control has its historical precedents in alcohol prohibition in the Islamic world, as well as in treaties on liquor trade restrictions in colonial Africa. About a century after these unsuccessful colonial treaties, the WHO initiated the negotiation of a global strategy to control alcohol internationally. This strategy will be presented to the World Health Assembly and adopted in 2010. It will be of a lower legal status than the tobacco convention and will not be legally binding.

Compared to tobacco, alcohol is much less regulated, and compared to opium, coca, and cannabis, alcohol and tobacco are traded almost freely on the international level. The reasons why alcohol and tobacco are not as strictly controlled is that large industries are behind the production and distribution of these drugs and their use is socially integrated in most modern countries. Companies such as Philip Morris International or SABMiller are not only powerful political actors by themselves; they also bring large tax incomes to governments. Hence, it is understandable that drugs produced by such big economic players are not as tightly regulated as opium and coca. In addition, in contrast to opium and coca that are traditionally produced in Asia and

South America, global alcohol and tobacco production is concentrated in rich Western states, which have more bargaining power at international negotiation tables.

Only in the field of the global tobacco trade is it possible to see more controls in the near future. Not only is demand for this drug slowly decreasing in richer countries but also recent international agreements have directly attacked powerful economic interests. It is possible that the flourishing tobacco trade will face the same fate as the trade in opium, coca, and cannabis products confronted at the beginning of the twentieth century. However, if the international tobacco-control system will also prioritize the supply side of the trade and ignore health issues, the danger exists that it will lead to another failed international initiative, which merely strengthens the illegal trade in drugs.

See also **Afghanistan; China; Colombia; Crop Control Policies; Foreign Policy and Drugs, United States; Harm Reduction; International Drug Supply Systems; Opium: International Overview; Terrorism and Drugs.**

BIBLIOGRAPHY

Courtwright, D. (2001). *Forces of habit: Drugs and the making of the modern world.* Cambridge, MA: Harvard University Press.

Donnelly, J. (1989). The United Nations and the global drug control regime. In W. Walker (Ed.), *Drug control policy in the Americas* (pp. 282–304). Albuquerque: University of New Mexico Press.

Jelsma, M. (2003). Drugs in the UN system: The unwritten history of the 1998 United Nations General Assembly Special Session on Drugs. *International Journal of Drug Policy, 14*(2), 181–195.

McAllister, W. (2000). *Drug diplomacy in the twentieth century: An international history.* London: Routledge.

Room, R. (1999). The rhetoric of international drug control. *Substance Use & Misuse, 34*(12), 1689–1707.

Stein, S. (1985). *International diplomacy, state administrators, and narcotics control: The origins of a social problem.* Brookfield, VT: Gower for London School of Economics.

GERNOT KLANTSCHNIG

INTERNATIONAL DRUG SUPPLY SYSTEMS. While drug use and drug abuse have been a part of human cultures for thousands

of years, the international drug control system to prohibit the trade in drugs such as opium and cocaine only began in the early 1900s. The first instrument of international law to deal with psychoactive drugs was the Hague Opium Convention of 1912. It required each signatory to enact domestic legislation controlling opium and cocaine so they could be restricted to medical use, thus beginning a process that evolved into the multilateral drug control system of the early twenty-first century. From these origins, a still-continuing process broadened and deepened the scope of control over drugs, from opium and cocaine to cannabis, LSD, amphetamines, Ecstasy, methamphetamines, and many other psychotropic substances.

The century since the Hague Opium Convention saw a number of illicit drug epidemics sweep across the world. The World Drug Report (2006) argued that there was evidence that the multilateral system had reduced and contained the drug problem at a global level because world opium production stood at 30,000 metric tons in 1907/1908 (before the convening of the Shanghai Opium Convention), and opium production had fallen to 5,000 tons in 2005, even though the world population had expanded from 2 billion to 6 billion. The problem with this comparison is that opium had widespread medical use in 1907; it was the basis for countless soothing syrups and popular panaceas in Europe and North America: Unless the percentage consumed for nonmedical use at that time is known, the comparison between production levels in 1907 with those in 2005 is pointless. As well, a fair inventory of the market for illicit substances in 2005 would need to include 45,000 tons of cannabis, 910 tons of cocaine, and 450 tons of amphetamine-like stimulants, as well as the 5,000 tons of opium. The nonmedical use of opium may have fallen over the century, but the use of cannabis and other drugs has increased enormously (UN Office on Drugs and Crime, 2006).

After the arms trade (with which it shares an unusual symbiosis), the illicit drug trade is the largest trade in the world, worth an estimated 1 to 2 trillion U.S. dollars. Ninety percent of this trade is based on three plants, the opium poppy (the source of heroin), the coca bush (the source of cocaine), and the cannabis plant. Cannabis is the largest of the illicit crops, and because of hydroponics techniques, cannabis can now be grown almost anywhere. The cultivation of the coca shrub remains limited to western and northern areas of South America, whereas Afghanistan, southeast Asia, Mexico, and Colombia account for most of the world's illicit opium production. Although the U.S. drug market remains the largest global market and the United States is the destination for much of the global drug trade, Europe has emerged as a significant rival. The drug routes that begin in Afghanistan, southeast Asia, and Colombia snake their way across the globe to these two great markets where most of the tens of thousands of tons of cannabis and the hundreds of tons of heroin, cocaine, and amphetamine-like substances are consumed.

Heroin production declined in southeast Asia between 1995 and 2008, and one of the significant developments in the global illicit drug trade has been a move away from heroin production to methamphetamine production by southeast Asian criminal organizations to fuel the growing global methamphetamine market. Other major developments that shaped the global drug trade at the start of the twenty-first century were the rise of Afghanistan to a dominant position in the global heroin trade and the preponderance of hydroponics cannabis in the cannabis market.

OPIUM

The opium poppy (*Papaver somniferum*) is the source of heroin. It is grown in three principal geographic regions: southeast Asia, southwest Asia, and Latin America. After 1971, when modern international drug control efforts began, a number of major shifts occurred in the opium-producing capabilities of various countries. For example, in the early 1970s, after the so-called French Connection was broken (Turkish opium was processed into heroin in France), Mexico and southeast Asia replaced Turkey as the major source of U.S. heroin; Pakistan then supplanted Mexico after 1979, when the Soviet Union occupied Afghanistan, and the resistance movements there increased opium cultivation to generate income and finance the war.

In 1991, the southeast Asian Golden Triangle countries of Myanmar (Burma until 1989), Laos, and Thailand cultivated approximately 81 percent of the world's total opium, which would yield 250 metric tons of heroin. The Golden Crescent countries of Afghanistan, Iran, and Pakistan cultivated approximately 11 percent, and the Latin American countries of Mexico, Guatemala, and Colombia produced approximately 8 percent.

Figure 1, Global opium production (1990–2005) from the 2006 World Drug Report, shows

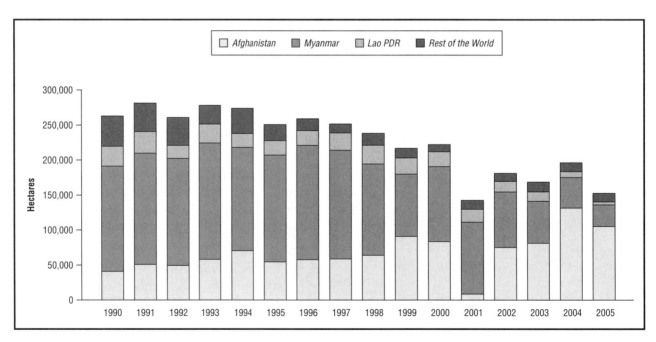

Figure 1. Global opium production (1990–2005). Illustration by GGS Information Services. Gale, Cengage Learning

the gradual decline in southeast Asian heroin production between 1990 and 2005. This decline was due to environmental factors (a drought in Myanmar between 1997 and 1999) and also a preference for methamphetamine in the southeast Asian market. A spectacular decline in opium production occurred in Afghanistan between 1999 and 2001 from an estimated 89,172 hectares in 2000 to an estimated 7,606 hectares in 2001, a reduction of 91 percent. Afghanistan produced an estimated 79 percent of the world's illicit opium in 1999, but this dropped to 70 percent in 2000, following a decree issued by the Taliban authorities in September 1999, requiring all opium-growers to reduce output by one-third. A second decree, issued in July 2000, required farmers to completely stop opium cultivation. As a consequence, 2001 saw the lowest level of global opium production in the period. Perhaps not coincidentally, Australia experienced a spectacular heroin shortage in 2001. While opium and morphine seizures fell in Europe and Asia in 2001, the year of the opium poppy cultivation ban in Afghanistan, heroin seizures fell in 2002 (mainly reflecting a delay of about a year in the production of opium in Afghanistan and the arrival of heroin in western European markets). Opiate seizures grew strongly again in subsequent years.

Between 2002 and 2004, the proportion of opiate seizures along the Afghanistan-Europe trafficking route increased from 78 percent to 85 percent, reflecting rising levels of opium production in Afghanistan and rising levels of opiate trafficking from Afghanistan. The volume of opiate seizures along the other two main routes showed a downward trend (from 7% to 4% in the Americas and from 15% to 11% for the southeast Asia/Oceania route). Global opiate seizures in 2004 were 21 percent higher than in 2000. Over the 1994–2004 period opiate seizures grew, on average, by 8 percent per year. Europe's opiate seizure rose by 49 percent in 2004 and reached almost 29 metric tons (in heroin equivalents), the highest such figure ever recorded. While most of the opiates for the Commonwealth of Independent States (CIS) countries and some of the opiates for the Nordic countries were trafficked via central Asia, most of the opiates for western Europe were trafficked from Afghanistan to Turkey and then along various branches of the Balkan route. More than 90 percent of opiates in Europe originated in post-Taliban Afghanistan (after 2001).

While environmental and political factors had a detrimental effect on heroin production in southeast Asia, other changes in the Asian drug trade in the 1990s also contributed to the decrease in heroin production in the region. In China and Thailand, which are the major markets for producers in the Golden Triangle, heroin was displaced as drug of choice in the 1990s by *yaa-baa*, an amphetamine-type stimulant.

Yaa-baa was originally known in Thailand as *yaa-ma* (literally, horse medicine), but in 1996 Thai health minister Sanoh Thienthong substituted the name *yaa-baa* (madness drug) in order to disenchant the public with a product whose consumption levels had already reached alarming proportions. Not surprisingly, as *yaa-baa* the drug became even more popular. The thriving trade in *yaa-baa* stimulated methamphetamine production in Burma and Thailand and attracted players from heroin production. According to a 2004 study by Chouvy and Meissonnier, methamphetamine production was easier, more flexible, and cheaper than heroin production, and it did not need vast areas devoted to its production. Thus, methamphetamine manufacture was more attractive to many big players in the heroin market, and Chouvy and Meissonnier suggest that the very public retirement of Khun Sa and his United Wa State Army from the heroin industry in 1996 masked a move into methamphetamine production (Chouvy & Meissonnier, 2004).

CANNABIS

An estimated 4 percent of the world's adult population consumes cannabis each year, more than all the other illicit drugs combined. In some countries, more than half of the young people polled had tried it. However, when it comes to the mechanics of the market, the world's biggest illicit drug is the least understood. The advent of indoor cannabis cultivation techniques (hydroponics) in the last decades of the twentieth century revolutionized the cannabis market to the extent that cannabis can be grown virtually anywhere, and there are no countries where it can be definitively said that cannabis is not cultivated. Moreover, because cannabis is both easy to grow and highly productive, yielding a large quantity of ready-to-use drug per plant, many users can, and do, produce their own supply. Unlike other drug crops, illicit crop monitoring techniques, such as satellite surveillance, are of little use in assessing cannabis cultivation, which is taking place in private homes and small plots in communities spread across the globe. As a consequence, this critical sector of the cannabis trade is almost invisible. Few governments can confidently give an estimate of the scale of cultivation in their own countries, and even in the United States, a country with both resources and a strong infrastructure for cannabis control, official estimates of the extent of domestic cultivation vary considerably.

However, the evidence of cannabis seizures show that, in terms of both volume and geographic spread, cannabis remains the most widely trafficked illicit drug in the world, accounting for the majority of all illicit drug seizures. Globally, herbal cannabis (marijuana) seizures surpassed the 6,000 metric ton mark in 2004, and an additional 1,470 metric tons of cannabis resin (hashish) were seized. Cannabis seizures were reported from 176 countries and territories (90% of the UN list), and the UN estimated global cannabis production was 45,000 metric tons. Cannabis was almost ubiquitous, trafficked in nearly every country in the world, and the upward trend in cannabis seizures, which began in the early 1990s, continued in 2004. Most herbal cannabis seizures were reported from Mexico, followed by the United States, South Africa, Nigeria, and Morocco, whereas most seizures of cannabis resin were made by Spain, followed by Pakistan, France, Morocco, and Iran. While cannabis resin (hashish) retained its traditional popularity in Eurasia and north Africa, herbal cannabis dominated in the markets of the Western hemisphere and grew in popularity in Europe and Africa.

Most of the global total of cannabis herb was seized in North America, notably Mexico and the United States. With seizures of 2,164 metric tons in 2004, Mexico accounted for 35 percent of global seizures, followed by the United States, where 1,118 metric tons of cannabis herb were seized in 2004. North America dominates the world cannabis market, and, as a consequence of hydroponics technology, the cannabis markets in North America have become largely self-sufficient.

According to the United States Office of National Drug Control Policy estimates (which are about 30% lower than UN estimates), 10,100 metric tons of cannabis herb were produced in Mexico in 2005. This estimate made Mexico the largest cannabis herb producer in the world. In the United States, about 4,455 metric tons of cannabis herb were produced in fiscal year 2004–2005, while an estimated 800 metric tons of cannabis herb were produced in Canada.

In the late 1980s and early 1990s, herbal cannabis was chiefly grown in tropical and subtropical climates. For example, in 1990 South America accounted for 46 percent of global herbal cannabis seizures, but this share fell to 7 percent in 2004. However, hydroponics technology enabled Canada, and its western province British Columbia in particular, to become a major producer and supplier to the U.S. market. The hydroponics revolution, which transformed cannabis production so that cannabis can be grown indoors almost anywhere, radically transformed the U.S. cannabis trade, allowing cannabis to be grown in countries closer to the U.S. market and disadvantaging traditional suppliers in South America and the Caribbean.

Despite this change, Colombia continued to be the major cannabis producer in South America with an estimated production of 2,000 metric tons, though its role as a supplier of the U.S. market declined as a consequence of the hydroponics revolution. Colombia's decline was accelerated by the extensive crop eradication programs conducted by the United States and the government of Colombia beginning in the 1980s. Paraguay emerged as the second-largest producer in South America, with much Paraguayan cannabis destined for the Brazilian market.

African cannabis production increased significantly between 1990 and 2004: African seizures were 16 percent of global herbal cannabis seizures in 1990; 20 percent in 2002; and 31 percent in 2004. The major producing countries of cannabis herb in Africa, according to UN estimates, were Morocco (3,700 metric tons), South Africa (2,200 metric tons), and Nigeria (2,000 metric tons). Morocco was also the world's largest producer of cannabis resin, producing an estimated 40 percent of global production. The area under cannabis cultivation in Morocco decreased significantly by 40 percent from 120,500 hectares to 72,500 hectares in 2004, largely due to a severe drought. Eradication campaigns in the provinces of Larache, Tanouate, and Chefchaouen, targeting over 15,000 hectares of cannabis in total, further decreased Morocco's total production figure for cannabis.

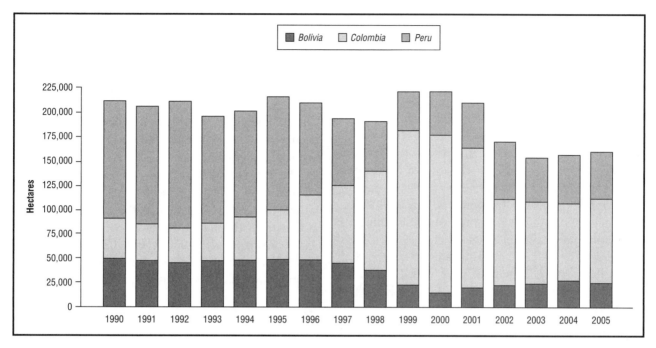

Figure 2. Global Coca Bush Cultivation (in ha), 1990–2005. (Source: Columbian government with support from the United Nations Office of Drugs and Crime.) ILLUSTRATION BY GGS INFORMATION SERVICES. GALE, CENGAGE LEARNING

Cannabis use is traditional in Asia, and many Asian countries produce considerable quantities of cannabis: Lebanon, Turkey, Kazakhstan, Kyrgyzstan, Afghanistan, Pakistan, India, Sri Lanka, Myanmar, Cambodia, Thailand, and the Philippines are major Asian markets which produce annually between 300 and 1,500 metric tons of cannabis.

Cannabis Resin (Hashish). Three subregions accounted for 99 percent of global cannabis resin seizures: west and central Europe (74%), near and middle east/southwest Asia (18%), and north Africa (7%). The largest seizures worldwide were reported by Spain (794 metric tons or 54% of the total), followed by Pakistan (135 metric tons or 9%), Morocco (86 metric tons or 6%), and Iran (86 tons or 6%). In Afghanistan, cannabis resin seizures declined by almost half, from 81 tons in 2003 to 41 tons in 2004. In Algeria, seizures of some 12 tons of cannabis resin were reported for 2004, more than double the quantity seized in 2002.

The main destination of cannabis resin is west and central Europe. About 80 percent of the cannabis resin destined for the European market was estimated to originate in Morocco. As of 2008, much of the cannabis resin transited Spain and the Netherlands before being shipped to other countries. The

remainder of the resin supply originated in Afghanistan/Pakistan, central Asia (which mostly supplies the Russian Federation, other CIS states, and some of the Baltic countries), or from within Europe (mainly Albania, supplying the markets of various Balkan countries and Greece).

The second-largest destination of cannabis resin is the near and middle east/southwest Asia region. This region is mainly supplied from cannabis resin produced in Afghanistan and Pakistan and, to a lesser degree, from cannabis resin originating in Lebanon. Some of the cannabis resin from Afghanistan/Pakistan was as of 2008 also being shipped to Canada and to countries in eastern Africa. North Africa makes up the third-largest market and is predominantly supplied by cannabis resin produced in Morocco. The importance of other markets is limited. Nepal is a source country for cannabis resin exports to India and to some other countries, and Jamaica is a source country for cannabis resin exports to some other countries in the Americas.

COCA/COCAINE

All of the cocaine consumed in the world is grown and processed in the Andean countries of Peru, Bolivia, and Colombia. In 2005, an estimated 160,000 hectares of coca was under cultivation in these three countries. Most coca was cultivated in Colombia (54%), followed by Peru (30%) and Bolivia (16%). Much of this crop was smuggled across the Caribbean Sea or the Mexican border into the United States, though increasing amounts were transshipped to Europe via Africa.

Colombia. Vast tracts of uncontrollable land, a seemingly endless civil war, powerful criminal organizations, and a long tradition of smuggling, all helped Colombia become the center of the cocaine trade. Although other Andean countries have sometimes produced more coca, Colombia's proximity to the U.S. marketplace has meant that Colombia's drug cartels are the world's leading producers of both cocaine HCL (which is sniffed or snorted) and *crack* (which is smoked).

As of 2008, Colombian cocaine-trafficking organizations were sophisticated and well-organized industries, which derived their strength from control of cocaine laboratories and the smuggling routes to Europe and North America. They sometimes financed the cultivation of coca plants in Bolivia, Peru, and Colombia, often overseeing the processing of the leaves into coca paste and sometimes base, which may then be shipped to laboratories in Colombia where the traffickers refine the coca paste, first into coca base and then into cocaine by the ton.

The Office of National Drug Control Policy estimated the 2006 coca cultivation in Colombia was stable at between 125,800 and 179,500 hectares. After losing one-third of the estimated coca cultivation to herbicidal spraying between 2001 and 2004, traffickers and growers implemented the widespread use of techniques such as radical pruning, replanting from seedlings, and a move to smaller plots. Such countermeasures made it impossible for forecasters to know with certainty whether a field was a mature, productive field or a field that had been sprayed with glyphosate and then pruned or replanted. Moreover, farmers have expanded cultivation into areas off-limits to the spray program, such as national parks and the area along the border with Ecuador, where Colombia suspended spraying in 2006 due to protests from the Ecuadorian government.

Colombia's antidrug efforts also affected the Fuerzas Armadas Revolucionarias de Colombia (FARC).

The governments of Colombia, the United States, Canada, and the European Union describe the FARC as a terrorist organization. Those of Cuba and Venezuela call it a rebel insurgency. As of 2008 the organization depended on drug trafficking, kidnapping, and theft to sustain itself. FARC rebels trained and equipped to shoot down unarmed spray planes have required the deployment of armed security helicopters and search-and-rescue aircraft in the vicinity of spray operations. FARC leaders protect growers who cooperate with them and force others to grow; strengthening their control over the population through economic dependency. The U.S. Government, working with Colombia, shifted the focus of its aerial eradication to target the areas of most intensive coca cultivation.

Peru. Peru is the world's second-largest cocaine producer. The Office of National Drug Control Policy (ONDCP) estimated that Peru's coca cultivation in 2006 ranged from 31,000 and 42,800 hectares and estimated potential cocaine production was 245 metric tons. Considerable political controversy has erupted in both Peru and Bolivia over U.S. backed counternarcotics strategies, particularly coca eradication. Coca leaf (but not cocaine) is a traditional medicine and is legal in Peru and Bolivia. The growers of coca (who are called *cocaleros*) oppose coca eradication and the election of several new cocalero members to Peru's Congress raised the profile of the debate surrounding coca cultivation and amplified the voice of organized, politically active cocalero groups working to stop eradication. Although the attempts by the Peruvian National Police to eradicate coca cultivation in the valleys were disrupted by growers who resisted programmed eradication, the government of Peru exceeded its 10,000-hectare eradication goal: It eradicated 12,688 hectares of coca in 2006 and interdicted over 19 metric tons of cocaine.

Bolivia. Bolivia is the world's third-largest cocaine producer and is a country of concern for U.S. policy makers because coca farmers (cocaleros) led by President Evo Morales have called for an end to forced eradication and other antinarcotic measures. Morales rose to national attention by leading the political opposition to eradication, and his opposition was a central reason for his election to the Bolivian Congress. His association with anti-eradication forces caused his expulsion from Congress in 2002 and led to his presidential campaign. Upon entering office in January 2006, President Evo Morales advocated a counternarcotics policy of *zero cocaine*, *revalidation* of the coca leaf, and repeatedly called for legalization and industrialization of the coca leaf in international forums. While Bolivia met its self-established coca eradication goal of 5,000 hectares in 2005, the 2006 effort represented the lowest level of eradication in more than ten years. Bolivia failed to conduct a study to determine licit demand for coca and rejected the European Union offer to provide full funding support for such a study. President Morales announced his intention to increase the amount of hectarage allowed for legal coca cultivation from 12,000 to 20,000. The government of Bolivia announced it would permit 8,000 hectares of coca in the Chapare region, an increase of about 17 percent, consistent with President Morales's move to permit 20,000 hectares of cultivation.

Although there is much disagreement between Morales's administration and the United States regarding antidrug laws and cooperation between the countries, officials from both countries have expressed a desire to work against drug trafficking with Morales calling for zero cocaine and zero drug trafficking. The government of Bolivia interdicted more than 14 metric tons of cocaine base and HCl in 2006, up from 11.5 metric tons in 2005. The Office of National Drug Control Policy (ONDCP) estimated Bolivia's coca cultivation at between 21,000 and 32,500 hectares. Cocaine potential production remained unchanged at 115 metric tons from 2005 to 2006.

AMPHETAMINE-TYPE STIMULANTS (ATS)

The group of amphetamine-type stimulants (ATS) encompasses amphetamines (amphetamine, methamphetamine), Ecstasy (MDMA and related substances), and other synthetic stimulants (e.g., methcathinone, phentermine, fenetylline). The *World Drug Report 2006* estimated total ATS production at about 480 tons: 290 tons of methamphetamine, 63 tons of amphetamine, and about 126 metric tons of Ecstasy (MDMA). Most of the amphetamine production took place in Europe; most of the methamphetamine production occurred in North America and east and southeast Asia, and most Ecstasy was produced in Europe and in North America.

The number of globally dismantled ATS laboratories, as reported to UNODC, increased from 547 in 1990 to 7,028 in 2000 and to a record high of 18,532 in 2004. The increase was a reflection of the growth in ATS production globally since the 1990s: Methamphetamines and Ecstasy were the most recent drug epidemics. The overwhelming majority of dismantled ATS laboratories were producing methamphetamine, but 86 Ecstasy laboratories were seized, up from 64 in 2000 and 15 in 1999.

The overwhelming majority of the methamphetamine laboratories (97%) were dismantled in North America, mainly the United States, and, to a lesser extent, Mexico. Methamphetamine laboratories were also dismantled in Oceania, in east and southeast Asia, in Europe (mainly Czech Republic, followed by Slovak Republic and Republic of Moldova) and in South Africa (which appeared as of 2008 to be emerging as an important local production center). In Asia, most methamphetamine laboratories seized over the 2002–2004 period were reported from China, Philippines, Taiwan Province of China, Myanmar, Hong Kong SAR of China, and Malaysia. Many of the chemical precursors for ATS production originate in east and southeast Asia, and the switch away from heroin to ATS production by southeast Asian gangs in the 1990s was one of the motors of the methamphetamine epidemic.

Europe's position as the world's main Ecstasy production center appeared to be on the decline, with production shifting to North America (mainly United States and Canada): 48 percent of all Ecstasy laboratories were seized in North America (United States and Canada), and only 23 percent in Europe (mainly Netherlands, followed by Belgium and Estonia), down from 75 percent in 2000. Over the 2002–2004 period, Ecstasy laboratories were dismantled in southeast Asia (Indonesia, China, Hong Kong SAR of China, Malaysia), in Oceania (Australia and New Zealand), in Africa (South Africa and Egypt), and in some South American countries (Argentina in 2003 and Colombia in 2001).

Methamphetamine. The main countries of origin for methamphetamine production in Asia continue to be China, Myanmar, and Philippines. Most of the methamphetamine production in China was located in southeastern China, in Guangdong

Province (which surrounds Hong Kong SAR of China), and, to a lesser extent, in neighboring Fujian province, located off the coast of Taiwan Province of China. China, together with India, is also one of the main source countries of ephedrine and pseudoephedrine, the main precursor chemicals used to manufacture methamphetamine. Significant quantities of methamphetamine were manufactured in Taiwan and the Philippines. Myanmar also continued to play an important role as a production site for methamphetamine. Illicit markets in Thailand were supplied by methamphetamine produced in Myanmar, and important parts of the Chinese market (20%) were also supplied by methamphetamine produced in Myanmar. ATS production in Myanmar was mainly encountered in the Shan state (notably in the Wa region) bordering China, though production was also taking place in areas controlled by the ethnic Chinese Kokang, the Shan State Army-South, and the Kachin Defense Army (KDA). Production was sometimes co-located with heroin refineries. According to the government of Thailand, methamphetamine production largely ceased to exist in Thailand following the crackdown on the market in 2003. Most southeast Asian methamphetamine was trafficked toward Oceania, notably Australia and New Zealand, and North America. The Philippines and China have been identified as other source countries for southeast Asian methamphetamine found on North American markets. Southeast Asian methamphetamine, from Myanmar and the Philippines, crossed Thailand before it was trafficked to European destinations, mainly the United Kingdom, Netherlands, France, and Switzerland.

Large-scale methamphetamine production and consumption had as of 2008 not occurred in Europe where Ecstasy dominated the ATS market. European methamphetamine production continued to be largely limited to the Czech Republic and, to a lesser extent, the neighboring Slovak Republic, some of the Baltic states, and Moldova. Limited imports of methamphetamine from southeast Asia (Thailand and Philippines) were reported in the late 1990s and early twenty-first century.

The main countries of methamphetamine production in the Americas are the United States, followed by Mexico and Canada. U.S. authorities dismantled the largest numbers of methamphetamine laboratories worldwide in 2004 (97%). Methamphetamine production in the United States was once concentrated in California and several neighboring states, but it spread to most states. Most of the *super-labs*, that is, laboratories capable of manufacturing more than 5 kg of methamphetamine in 24 hours, continue to be located in California. In Mexico, which reported the dismantling of 18 laboratories to UNODC in 2004, most methamphetamine production took place in the northern part.

Overall production of ATS was limited in South America (where coca and cocaine dominated the stimulant market) and in central and northern Africa, where *khat* had a similar dominance. (Khat [*Catha edulis*], a flowering plant native to east Africa and the Arabian Peninsula, contains the alkaloid cathinine, an amphetamine-like stimulant.) The main exception was South Africa where ATS production, notably production of methamphetamine and methcathinone, increased substantially.

Ecstasy. Over the 2002–2004 period a total of 33 Ecstasy-producing countries were identified by UNODC member states. The Netherlands and Belgium were the main countries of origin for Ecstasy imports over the 2002–2004 period. But their importance as the main source countries for Ecstasy was declining. The decline of Ecstasy production in eastern Europe, however, appeared to have been offset by increasing levels of Ecstasy produced in other countries, including other European countries, countries in North America (United States and Canada), in the Oceania region, and in east and southeast Asia, indicating that a shift toward Ecstasy production outside the so-called traditional production centers in Europe was gaining momentum. Though production may have well declined in the largest Ecstasy-producing center (Netherlands) and consumption fell in the world's single largest Ecstasy market (United States), the overall trend in global Ecstasy production was upward.

The increasing number of countries where clandestine ATS laboratories were dismantled indicated that ATS production was spreading in geographical terms. Nonetheless, there remained clear concentrations of ATS production in North America, east and southeast Asia, and in Europe.

See also **Afghanistan; Amphetamine Epidemics, International; Bolivia; China; Coca/Cocaine, International; Colombia; Drug Interdiction; European Union; Golden Triangle as Drug Source; Mexico; Middle East; Money Laundering; Operation Intercept; Opium: International Overview; Peru; Terrorism and Drugs; U.S. Government Agencies; U.S. Government; World Health Organization Expert Committee on Drug Dependence.**

BIBLIOGRAPHY

Chouvy, P., & Meissonnier, J. (2004) *Yaa baa: Production, traffic, and consumption of methamphetamine in mainland Southeast Asia.* Singapore: Irasec.

McCoy, A. W., & Block, A. A. (1992). *War on drugs: Studies in the failure of U.S. narcotics programs.* Boulder, CO: Westview Press.

Meyer, K. (2002). *Webs of smoke: Smugglers, warlords, spies, and the history of the international drug trade.* Lanham, MD: Rowman & Littlefield Publishers Inc.

Trocki, C. A. (1999). *Opium, empire, and the global economy: A study of the Asian opium trade, 1750–1950* (Asia's Transformations series). London: Routledge.

United Nations Office on Drugs and Crime. (2006). *2006 World Drug Report.* Available from http://www.unodc.org/.

JOHN JIGGENS

INTERNET: IMPACT ON DRUG AND ALCOHOL USE.

The impact of the Internet on drug and alcohol use has been both positive and negative. On the one hand, it has been the vehicle for important, accurate information on the effects and impact of drugs, including alcohol; has provided the conduit for community organization around drug and alcohol prevention issues; and has served as a virtual training platform for professionals and others involved in drug abuse prevention, rehabilitation, and treatment. On the other hand, it has been the vehicle for directly or indirectly persuading others to experiment with new substances or modifications; has provided explicit information regarding how to grow marijuana and make synthetic drugs, crack cocaine, and various combinations of synthetic and naturally derived drugs; and has been the commercial vehicle for the selling of illegal drugs.

INTERNET SOURCES FOR POSITIVE INFORMATION ON DRUGS

For a concerned parent, teacher, community leader, health professional, drug user, or potential drug user, there is a wealth of factual, scientifically based information available regarding the general nature and extent of drug and alcohol use; information on specific drugs, including alcohol; and guidance for families, and the vulnerable populations of teens, women, seniors, and others. Among other organizations, the federal government's Substance Abuse and Mental Health Services Administration (SAMHSA), a division of the Department of Health and Human Services, provides the broadest range of current research and other information. This administration maintains a number of websites. For the individual interested in or concerned about the effects of a particular drug, current and timely information available on the Internet indicates the short-term, carryover, and long-term effects of the drug. For families that are concerned about their children's vulnerability to drugs, there are guides for parents and children, as well as community organization information for those with a shared interest in drug and alcohol prevention. The information is free. Either online or in printed copy through the National Clearinghouse for Drug and Alcohol Information at the website maintained by SAMHSA or from a steadily growing number of resource sites sponsored by state and local governments and by volunteer and advocacy groups that focus on one or more aspects of drug and alcohol prevention.

INTERNET USES FOR COMMUNITY ORGANIZATIONS

Communities and other groups use the Internet to facilitate their drug and alcohol prevention efforts. There are literally hundreds of websites that provide information regarding drug and alcohol prevention. Many target teens in general, but there are also sites for specific groups, such as Hispanic and Asian families, pregnant women, youth in high-risk neighborhoods, rural youth, and Native Americans. Families or individuals who need help can find a wealth of information regarding treatment and other helping programs that are available in any given location.

Physicians and other health practitioners also use the internet to obtain information. Online journals, legacy medical and professional journals from which articles can be downloaded, and recent studies published by the National Institute on Drug Abuse (NIDA), a part of the National Institutes of Health (NIH), and SAMHSA, are all available online.

The Internet has provided the basis for comprehensive workplace drug and alcohol testing because of its ease of access and the application of proprietary security programs as a part of employer efforts. From government mandated drug and alcohol testing programs, such as those required by the Department of Transportation for safety-sensitive positions in the airline, railroad, mass transit, pipeline, trucking and busing, and maritime industries, the internet permits flexible scheduling for testing at any location, ease of transmission of test results from the drug testing laboratory to the employer, the ability to rapidly organize and transmit drug testing information to those physicians responsible for their review (medical review officers). As of 2008, over 8 million workplace drug tests were performed annually (Quest Diagnostics, 2008). Most of these are managed through an interactive Internet process that involves selection of people for random testing, where applicable; the scheduling of testing; laboratory results; and where not negative, a report from the medical review officer to the employer regarding the disposition of the test.

TWO APPROACHES TO PREVENTION
The internet plays a pivotal role in helping prevention groups mobilize. As of 2008, within the United States and internationally, there are two major approaches to drug abuse prevention. One approach favors a no-tolerance policy that promotes abstinence for the non-user through family, school, and other prevention efforts (e.g., information, education and drug and alcohol testing programs, and treatment and counseling for those who are using drugs). This approach encompasses empowering families and communities to reach out to their stakeholders through informal and formal education and intervention efforts but also includes legal and other tripwire efforts to identify the regular users through random drug testing programs in the schools, law enforcement referrals of drug offenders to treatment, and the use of drug courts and other approaches designed to identify and refer users to programs whose goals are abstinence recovery.

The second approach supports the concept of *harm reduction*, the major premise of which is that the prohibition of drug use is discriminatory, ineffective, and counter-productive. This approach asserts that rather than stigmatize a person for drug use, programs should be established that reduce the harm caused by the drug use and hence reduce the stigma attached to that drug use. People who believe in harm reduction often support some or all of the following: needle exchange; safe shooting houses; other safer-use techniques; heroin maintenance; drug legalization; and the use of street marijuana in certain medical situations. They believe these strategies mitigate public health costs of drug use. Critics call this approach *harm promotion*, asserting that while harm reduction attempts to reduce the physical consequences of drug use it does not reduce the use of legal and illegal drugs.

While harm reduction groups receive significant funding from wealthy libertarians and others, the opposition groups are largely spontaneously formed organizations that have a local or regional interest or are established by volunteers who have lost family members because of drug use. Both sides use the internet aggressively to support or oppose legislation at the local, state, and national level that would support harm education efforts, especially legislation that supports the use of street marijuana for medical purposes, which the harm reduction supporters see as a form of compassionate care for the severely or terminally ill, while prohibitionists see it as a move that may lead to legalization of marijuana. Both sides use the internet to alert their supporters of proposed or pending legislation, mobilize email and other campaigns to inform legislators of their positions, and contact media, especially newspapers, to provide substantiation of their position. The factors stated above that make the internet ideal for commerce also apply here. Hundreds of emails a day can be generated on any issue and disseminated to thousands of people. The consequence is that robustly funded harm-reduction initiatives are often thwarted by aggressive grassroots messages aimed at legislators and other policy makers by the abstinence community.

INTERNET INFORMATION LEADING TO ILLEGAL ACTIVITIES
The availability of information cuts two ways. While the internet provides helpful information

for those wanting to prevent drug and alcohol use, it also provides information that tempts some people to use drugs or continue using them. As of 2008 websites promoting drug use were on the decline; however, individuals could still locate so-called friendly blogs, forums, and news group that provide anecdotal information about the effects of old or new street drugs. Recipes for making a range of drugs from gamma hydroxybutyric acid (GHB, a synthetic depressant) and lysergic acid diethylamide (LSD, a semisynthetic psychedelic) to methamphetamine were also available online. Websites for the purchase of marijuana seeds and accoutrements for a successful harvest abound.

The internet has been a viable method of selling illegal drugs. It is always accessible and affordable; anyone can tap on from anywhere in the world, and one can hide activities with ease. The Wide World Web also lowers transaction costs dramatically. Until 2003, it was exceptionally easy to purchase illicit pharmaceuticals on the internet. Dozens of sales sites existed, some of them legitimate (such as Internet Pharmacies), but many of them sham fronts for illegal sales. While many purported to require a physician's approval, most off-shore sites only required some general health information and a self-certification of need or a brief medical questionnaire filled out. By 2004, the federal government recognized the significance of Internet-selling and began an intensive program to reduce these U.S. rogue sites. As of 2008 there were still a few rogue sites in the United States. However, no websites had been found selling illegal drugs such as heroin, or illegal amphetamine derivatives.

RESEARCH OF THE INTERNET

One study concluded that Web-based data on psychoactive substances seem to influence a broad range of drug-use behaviors in adolescents (Quest Diagnostics, 2008). The study stated:

> participants . . . adopted new behaviors such as modifications in the use of preferred drugs, the cessation of psychoactive substance abuse, and the use of new drugs and drug combinations. The striking finding from [this] study, therefore, is that all respondents in [the] cohort modified their drug use after reviewing online drug information. This observation suggests that the Internet has a profound ability to affect decisions related to psychoactive substance use in a cohort of innovative

> drug users. Interestingly, [two-thirds of the] participants adopted behaviors intended to minimize the risks associated with drug use, a finding that suggests that attempts to reduce the harm associated with psychoactive substances are fostered by online information.

Another study documented the fact that teens use the internet to share drug stories. A study commissioned by the Caron Treatment Foundation on teenage messages about drug use written on the internet establishes that young people regularly chat about drinking alcohol, smoking pot, partying, and hooking up (Boyer et al., 2005). The major conclusions of the study are as follows:

1. Teens focus their discussion of alcohol and drug use on message boards, rather than on blogs or online groups—due in part to privacy concerns. Young adults, however, discuss drugs and alcohol use on their blogs. Older teens and college students post anecdotes, memories, and plans about recreational drinking in their online journals.

2. When teens do post about drugs or alcohol on their blogs, it is usually in the form of a quiz about past experiences. These quizzes usually ask participants to check off drug-use experiences they have had.

3. Many teen messages about drugs and alcohol overlap. Many teenagers discuss topics such as getting together with friends to drink and smoke marijuana, or they share their experiences of getting drunk and/or high.

4. Certain topical themes recur across each subject (alcohol, marijuana, other drugs). Whether discussing alcohol, marijuana, or other drug use, teens express concern for their friends/significant others, discuss their parents' opinions on drugs and alcohol, and warn each other about the dangers of substance abuse.

5. Teens ask more questions about other drugs than they do about alcohol or marijuana. While they were curious about experimenting with alcohol and marijuana, they seek information about other recreational drugs, such as Ecstasy, dextromethorphan (DXM), and shrooms (mushrooms). Teenagers ask other teens about the drugs' effects, sensations of being high, and dosage levels.

The 2005 Partnership for a Drug-Free America teen attitude survey of over 7,000 teens nationwide indicated that almost one-third of the teens responding said that drugs were easy to purchase on the internet (Caron Treatment Centers, 2007).

In a 2002 *Evaluation of the National Youth Anti-Drug Media Campaign* approximately 10 percent of surveyed youth ages 12 to 18 visited anti-drug internet sites while approximately 5 percent of that same cohort visited pro-drug Internet sites. While both males and females visited the anti-drug sites at about the same rate, males were almost twice as likely to visit pro-drug sites. African American youth were most likely to visit antidrug sites, though whites and Hispanics also visited them to a significant degree. However, whites and Hispanics were almost twice as likely to visit pro-drug sites as African Americans (Partnership for a Drug-Free America, 2006). A similar study suggested that women are more likely to procure information from face-to-face encounters, whereas men prefer using online information outlets (Westat & Annenberg School for Communication).

SMOKING CESSATION RESEARCH VIA THE INTERNET: A FEASIBILITY STUDY

The Smoking Cessation Research via the Internet Study demonstrated the feasibility of conducting a brief, self-help smoking cessation intervention over the internet, using a one-group, pre-post design. The website was constructed to recruit participants, obtain informed consent, collect assessment data, provide a brief educational intervention, and obtain 1-month follow-up data, all without human contact. Of the 538 participants who signed the consent form, 230 returned to complete the one-month follow up assessment. Among these individuals, 92 made a serious attempt to quit smoking and 19 reported seven-day abstinence. Intention to quit smoking increased by 67 percent from baseline while 75 percent reported that they found the site helpful for quitting goals. The findings suggest that the Web is a practical environment for delivering and evaluating smoking cessation interventions. More research is needed on internet interventions, particularly on procedures to retain users for treatment and follow-up assessment. Internet interventions have the ability to treat large segments of the smoking population in a cost-effective manner (Stoddard et al., 2005).

See also **Media; Movies; Music.**

BIBLIOGRAPHY

Boyer, W., Shannon, M., & Hibberd, P. L. (2005). The Internet and psychoactive substance use among innovative drug users. *Pediatrics, 115*(2), 302–305.

Caron Treatment Centers. (2007, April 20). A qualitative study of online discussions about teen alcohol and drug use: A word-of-mouth audit. Available from http://www.caron. org/.

Center for Substance Abuse Prevention. (2004). *Tips for teens: The truth about marijuana.* Rockville, MD: Author.

Center for Substance Abuse Treatment (CSAT). For information on drug and alcohol treatment. Available from http://csat.samhsa.gov/.

Partnership for a Drug-Free America. (2006). *The Attitude Tracking Study (PATS): Teens in grades 7 through 12.* Available from http://www.drugfree.org/.

Quest Diagnostics. (2008, March 8). *Drug testing index.* Available from http://www.questdiagnostics.com/.

Substance Abuse and Mental Health Services Administration. *Know what your child is doing on the Internet.* Available from http://www.enotalone.com/.

Substance Abuse and Mental Health Services Administration, Center for Substance Abuse Prevention. For information on prevention of abuse regarding alcohol and other drugs. Available from http://prevention. samhsa.gov/.

Substance Abuse and Mental Health Services Administration, National Clearinghouse for Alcohol and Drug Information. (2004). *Tips for teens: The truth about marijuana.* Available from http://www.mamkschools. org/.

Substance Abuse and Mental Health Services Administration, Office of Applied Studies. For research information and national data on alcohol, tobacco, marijuana and other drug abuse, emergency room reporting on drugs and alcohol, and information on treatment facilities in the United States. Available from http://oas.-samhsa.gov/.

Stoddard, J. L., Delucchi, K. L., Munoz, R. F., Collins, N. M., Pérez-Stable, E. J., Auguston, E., et al. (2005). Smoking cessation research via the Internet: A feasibility study. *Journal of Health Communication, 10*(1), 27–41.

Tackett-Gibson, M. (2006, October). *Reputation matters: Drugs, drug use, and online credibility.* Paper presented at the annual meeting of the American Society of Criminology (ASC), Los Angeles, CA. Available from http://www.allacademic.com/.

Tackett-Gibson, M. (2007, November). *Gender difference in drug information procurement: Findings from an online survey of drug users.* Paper presented at the annual meeting of the American Society of Criminology, Atlanta, Georgia. Available from http://www. allacademic.com/.

United Nations, Office of the Commissioner for Human Rights. (2003). *Internet: Using the Internet for drug abuse prevention*. New York: Author.

U.S. Department of Justice, Federal Bureau of Investigation. A parent's guide to Internet safety. Available from http://www.fbi.gov/.

Westat & the Annenberg School for Communication. *Evaluation of the National Youth Anti-Drug Media Campaign*, Tables 3–38 and 3–39. Available from http://www.mediacampaign.org/.

RICHARD BUCHER

INTIMATE PARTNER VIOLENCE AND ALCOHOL/SUBSTANCE USE.

The potential links between psychoactive substances and violent behavior, and specifically violence against a spouse or intimate partner, have long been recognized. Historically, much of the focus has been on alcoholic beverages, rather than other psychoactive substances. For example, Netzahualcoyotl, king of a small city-state called Texcoco in Pre-Conquest Mexico c.1472 CE, stated "It [alcohol] is like a tornado that destroys everything in its path. It is like a hellish tempest that brings with it all evils. Drunkenness...causes violence among kinfolks" (Soustelle, 1955; cited in Paredes, 1975). In the United States, early temperance tracts emphasized the deleterious impact of alcohol on the family. The Fifth Report of the American Temperance Society states that "in the State of New York alone, in the course of a few weeks, not less than four men, under the influence of ardent spirits, murdered their wives." The 1843 *Temperance Tales, or, Six Nights with the Washingtonians* by Timothy Shay Arthur describes alcohol as a cause of moral decay and presents the final step in this decline with an illustration with the caption "the Husband, in a fit of furious drunkenness, kills his wife." Historical references linking other psychoactive substances to violence generally, or intimate partner violence more specifically, are few. However, in the twentieth century and continuing into the twenty-first century, substances, including cocaine and amphetamines, hallucinogens, and occasionally marijuana and opiates, have been anecdotally linked to violence, although few have been as consistently linked to violence as alcohol.

DEFINITION, PREVALENCE, AND EPIDEMIOLOGY OF INTIMATE PARTNER VIOLENCE

The broadest definition of violence is provided by the World Health Organization (1996) as "the intentional use of physical force or power, threatened or actual, against oneself, another person, or against a group or community, that either results or has a high likelihood of resulting in injury, death, psychological harm, maldevelopment, or deprivation." A similar term, aggression, reflects "any behavior directed toward another individual that is carried out with the...[immediate] intent to cause harm" (Anderson & Bushman 2002, p. 28) with violence being viewed as "aggression that has extreme harm at its goal" (p. 29). While these definitions can include verbal or psychological aggression as well as sexual aggression, intimate partner violence most typically refers to behaviors that have the potential to physically harm or injure one's partner.

Intimate partner violence (IPV) encompasses behaviors ranging in severity from those that result in no discernible injury to those that result in the need for medical attention or result in death. According to the Department of Justice, there are 1,500 instances of homicide and manslaughter between intimate partners each year with more than 1,200 of these involving women as victims (BJS, 1998). Annually, approximately 200,000 women and 39,000 men are seen at an emergency room for injuries resulting from partner violence (National Electronic Injury Surveillance). The National Crime Victimization Survey estimated that nearly 600,000 women and more than 150,000 men were victims of intimate violence in 2001. The 1985 National Family Violence Resurvey of a representative sample of couples—which include less severe instances of aggression, such as single occurrences of pushing or slapping one's partner—reported an annual rate of husband to wife violence of 11.6 percent with rates of wife to husband violence at 12.4 percent (Straus & Gelles, 1990), which suggests that approximately 6.2 million women had been assaulted by their husbands; about 6.6 million men by their wives.

Many couples report that both the man and woman have engaged in partner violence. While there is considerable controversy regarding the meaning of these findings, it is generally recognized that some couples are characterized by mutual husband and wife partner violence, whereas in other couples, partner violence is primarily displayed by either the husband or the wife, with the other person refraining from violence, engaging in substantially less violence, or using violent behaviors only in defense.

Several important risk factors for partner violence exist other than alcohol and drugs. For example, partner violence rates are highest among individuals under thirty years of age (McLaughlin, Leonard, & Senchak, 1992) and decline throughout the lifespan of the individuals (Suiter, Pillemer, & Straus, 1990). In addition, most aggression in marriage has an early onset, often prior to or in the first year of marriage. Couples who do not display aggression during this time are not likely to display aggression subsequently. In contrast, among couples who behave aggressively early in marriage, a large percentage display aggression at some time later in their marriage. Relatively few initially aggressive couples are consistently aggressive throughout the early years of marriage, though the degree of consistency is greater among individuals who have displayed severe levels of aggression. Finally, although there may be some decreases in marital aggression over the early years of marriage, the extent of these decrements is modest (Leonard, 2001). In addition to these factors, many sociodemographic and individual difference factors have been explored as potential risk factors for intimate partner violence (Schumacher, Feldbau-Kohn, Slep, & Heyman, 2001). Factors that have been consistently linked to partner violence by men include socioeconomic status, experiencing or witnessing family violence as a child, hostility, psychological (verbal) aggression, aggression-supportive attitudes, and a variety of different types of psychopathology. In addition, stress, jealousy, and relationship power have also been linked to partner violence. Many of these factors are associated both with partner violence and with alcohol and substance use.

CRITICAL ISSUES IN ALCOHOL/ SUBSTANCE USE
Alcohol and other substances may affect intimate partner violence either through their acute psychological and psychopharmacological impact, or they may have an effect only in the context of the chronic pattern of use (e.g., average daily use, typical use). Acute effects refer to the impacts of the substances only when they are present and

pharmacologically active in the user. Although one may consider the short-term psychophysiological state that occurs after the substance is no longer present (i.e., hangover, withdrawal) an acute effect, little research has focused on how this state affects partner violence or violence more generally. Chronic effects occur as a result of the pattern of use. For example, excessive use may lead to increased marital conflict and, through this conflict, increase the probability of intimate partner violence. These chronic effects may include the long-term chronic impact of substances. Among those who chronically use alcohol or other substances excessively, there may be considerable amounts of time when they are free from the acute effects of the substances.

Another issue is the considerable overlap between the use of alcohol and the use of other substances, both at acute and chronic levels. This overlap is important, particularly in clinical or especially severe samples. For example, an individual with very heavy alcohol use may also use marijuana and cocaine. Similarly, some individuals mix substances or use one substance to ease the effects or withdrawal of another substance. Disentangling the effects of these different substances can be challenging. Small samples of individuals who use only a single substance can suggest the acute or chronic effects of that single substance, but these inferences may not be generalizable to samples that use multiple substances.

EXPLANATIONS OF THE RELATIONSHIPS BETWEEN ALCOHOL OR SUBSTANCE USE AND PARTNER VIOLENCE
There are four broad explanations of the impact of substances on intimate partner violence, one which argues that the relationship is spurious, one that focuses on chronic aspects of alcohol/substance use, and two which focus on the acute impact of alcohol/substance use.

Spurious Association. One explanation argues that the association is spurious, with both alcohol/substance use and partner violence being associated with a third variable that is, in fact, the most critical factor. In this regard, the critical variable is often viewed as hostile and/or antisocial personality traits. Evidence links hostile, antisocial traits to partner violence, and these factors contribute to the association between alcohol/substance use and partner violence. However, some studies of excessive alcohol use have taken these factors into account and have found a relationship between excessive drinking and partner violence occurrence or severity. As of 2008 findings from studies on substance use that have controlled for hostile, antisocial traits have not been entirely consistent.

Chronic Use Explanation. One explanation is that chronic use can adversely impact social/interpersonal relationships. Goldstein's 1985 tripartite model of drugs and violence included two aspects that relate to the social/interpersonal context of use or acquisition. First, the economic compulsive model reflected criminal violence that drug users perpetrate in order to obtain money to acquire drugs. Second, the systemic violence model encompassed violence that was part of the distribution of illegal drugs, including behavior such as turf wars and retribution for inferior drugs or for informing to the police. While such models do not specifically apply to partner violence, the social/interpersonal context of use may be relevant. For example, certain patterns of use may affect interpersonal conflict and thereby increase the probability of partner violence. Homish and Leonard (2006) found that discrepant patterns of heavy alcohol use were longitudinally predictive of declines in marital satisfaction. In addition, they found (2005) that couples that drank heavily apart from each other had lower marital satisfaction than those who drank heavily together. Similar findings have been reported for substance use (Fals-Stewart, Birchler, & O'Farrell, 1999). Also partner violence may be affected by exposure to violent models of behavior. The acquisition and use of alcohol/substances most likely brings an individual in touch with violent individuals, and possibly this exposure reinforces normative acceptance of violent behavior and reduces inhibitions against behaving aggressively. Although the theoretical foundation for this possibility is very strong, research had not addressed it as of 2008.

Acute Use Explanations
Substance Expectancies. One general explanation linking alcohol and violence invokes the idea of alcohol expectancies, suggesting that individuals become aggressive while drinking because they expect that aggression is an outcome of drinking. One theme common in the literature is that alcohol results in violence because individuals believe that they can use it as an excuse to behave aggressively and to mitigate their responsibility and punishment. Quigley and Leonard (2006) described three basic questions arising from this approach. The first question is: "Do individuals believe alcohol causes people to become aggressive?" The evidence indicates that individuals do believe alcohol causes people to become aggressive, and they believe it has that effect on others much more so than on themselves (Paglia & Room, 1999).

The second basic question is: "Do people view intoxication as a mitigating circumstance in blame and responsibility attributions for partner violence?" While Richardson and Campbell (1980) found that an intoxicated man was assigned less blame than a sober man, Leigh and Aramburu (1994) reported that the intoxicated man received more blame, and Dent and Arias (1990) found no effect of intoxication on the blame assigned to the man. While these studies have focused on college students, other studies of social workers (Home, 1994), police officers (Stewart & Maddren, 1997), and couples who have experienced domestic violence suggest that alcohol does not serve as a mitigating factor. Moreover, in the area of domestic violence, evidence with respect to actual behaviors suggests that alcohol does not usually mitigate responsibility or the likelihood or severity of punishment for violent behavior. Thompson and Kingree (2006) found that alcohol use in a violent event was associated with an increased likelihood of reporting the event to the police. Other studies have found that intoxicated aggressors are more likely to be arrested than sober aggressors (Hoyle, 1998), although some studies have not found any impact of alcohol involvement on the likelihood of arrest (Robinson & Chandek, 2000). Finally, with respect to actual punishment, Harrel (1981) used characteristics of 628 pre-sentence reports to predict severity of sentence received by the offender. Alcohol use resulted in a less severe sentence for the low severity crimes but was associated with a more severe sentence for high severity crime.

The third question is: "Does possession of an alcohol-aggression expectancy predict the occurrence of partner violence?" Although some surveys have found this relationship (Barnwell et al., 2006), the one longitudinal study (Leonard & Quigley, 1999) did not find that expectancies regarding alcohol and aggression were predictive of later partner violence. One implication of the excuse position is a placebo beverage should result in increased aggression. The two studies assessing the effect of a placebo on marital behaviors found that whereas alcohol reliably increased verbalizations that might lead to partner violence, the placebo beverage did not, a finding that is consistent with the meta-analyses of laboratory studies of alcohol and aggression conducted by Bushman and Cooper (1990).

Psychopharmacological Effects. The second broad class of models focuses on the psychopharmacological impact of the various substances. While studies of illicit drugs and violence often invoke such explanation, focusing on arousal, reduced anxiety, or altered perceptions, research has not systematically examined these explanations. Regarding alcohol, as of 2008 the focus has been on alcohol's ability to disrupt cognitive processes (e.g., Taylor & Leonard 1983; Steele & Josephs, 1990). Alcohol is generally believed to impair cognitive processes that under normal circumstances would inhibit aggressive responding. Alcohol weakens inhibitions and allows for dominant cues and dominant response options to those cues to determine behavior. Accordingly, alcohol should have more effect on individuals with already somewhat compromised attentional and appraisal abilities and on individuals with aggressive perceptual and behavioral propensities. Much research on the alcohol/aggression relationship agrees. Specifically, evidence suggests that individuals with attentional/behavioral tendencies that are facilitative of aggression are more aggressive with alcohol, whereas individuals with tendencies that are not facilitative of aggression are not more aggressive with alcohol (or are less so).

ASSOCIATION BETWEEN CHRONIC SUBSTANCE USE/ABUSE AND INTIMATE PARTNER VIOLENCE

Cross-sectional Studies. Although there are occasional disconfirming reports, excessive alcohol use by men is consistently associated with partner violence by men, including several studies of nationally representative samples. For example,

the 1975 and 1985 National Family Violence Surveys found that drinking patterns in men were consistently related to marital violence (Kaufman Kantor & Straus, 1989). With over two thousand men in this study, this was one of the largest, most comprehensive studies of the issue. Studies designed to examine the association between alcohol and partner violence in nationally representative samples of specific ethnic subgroups have found some variation in the strength of the association among European Americans, African Americans, and Hispanic Americans (Caetano et al., 2001). Similarly, diversity in the strength of the alcohol/violence relationship exists among Hispanic Americans from different countries of origin (Kaufman Kantor, 1997).

In addition to general population samples, research has documented the alcohol/violence relationship in a variety of more select populations. For example, Leonard and associates (1985) evaluated 352 married, blue-collar workers, and found that men with a current diagnosis of alcohol abuse or dependence had higher rates of marital aggression (50% and 39%, respectively) than men with no diagnosis (15%) or a past diagnosis of abuse (8%) or dependence (18%), suggesting the importance of current alcohol use. Among samples seeking health care, a relationship between partner drinking and partner violence has been observed in samples based in emergency rooms (Kyriacou et al., 1998), primary health care settings (McCauley et al., 1995), family practice clinics (Oriel & Fleming, 1998), prenatal clinics (Muhajarine & D'Arcy, 1999), and rural health clinics (Van Hightower & Gorton, 1998).

Studies of samples selected specifically because of violent behavior or heavy drinking have also generally supported a relationship between heavy alcohol use and violence. For example, with few exceptions, men in treatment for partner abuse have higher rates of alcohol problems in contrast to appropriate comparison samples (e.g., Barnett & Fagan, 1993). Similarly, men seeking treatment for alcoholism manifest higher rates of domestic violence than do comparison groups drawn from the general population (O'Farrell & Murphy, 1995).

While studies focused on partner violence by males have consistently found that excessive drinking is associated with partner violence, the situation is more complex with respect to women's drinking. Early research focused on whether female victims of domestic violence manifest patterns of heavy and problem drinking. For example, the association has been observed among women in primary care settings (McCauley et al., 1995), prenatal clinics (Stewart & Cecutti, 1993), emergency rooms (Roberts et al., 1997), alcohol treatment (Miller et al., 1989), and in the general population (Kaufman Kantor & Asdigian, 1997). These findings are complicated by two factors. First, given the association between women and men's drinking, studies that control for men's drinking are the most pertinent. Across community samples, several studies failed to find a relationship between women's drinking and IPV after controlling for men's drinking (Kaufman Kantor & Asdigian, 1997; Leonard & Senchak, 1996) possibly because of the small number of very heavy-drinking women. Other studies found a relationship (Schafer et al., 2004). Second, given the many couples in which both members of the couple are aggressive, this finding might reflect an association between the woman's alcohol use and her own aggression. For example, Schafer and associates (2004) interviewed approximately 1,600 European American, African American, and Hispanic couples in 1995 and interviewed them again in 2000. For both European American and African American couples, men's alcohol problems were associated with male-to-female violence, and female alcohol problems were associated with female-to-male violence. Studies of clinical samples of alcoholic or violent women are strongly supportive of a relationship. Similar to the findings of Schafer and associates (2004), Stuart and colleagues (2006) studied men and women arrested for IPV and found that perpetrators' alcohol problems were associated with their frequency of IPV, and the partners' alcohol problems were associated with the frequency of their IPV toward the identified perpetrator, for both male and female perpetrators.

Although research addressing women's drinking has usually controlled for the effects of partner's drinking, two studies suggested that the configuration of couple's drinking patterns may be important predictors of IPV. Quigley and Leonard (2000) found that husband and wife excessive drinking in the first year of marriage interacted to prospectively predict violence over the subsequent two years. The interaction indicated that IPV was more likely for excessive-drinking husbands with light-drinking wives. Leadley and associates (2000) found that discrepant drinking patterns were associated with IPV after controlling for heavy drinking. Perhaps excessive drinking is not as contentious when both partners are heavy drinkers as it is when only one partner is.

Fewer studies have focused on chronic drug use than on chronic alcohol use. In general, findings from both clinical samples (e.g., Moore & Stuart, 2004) and epidemiological samples (e.g., Cunradi et al., 2002) have found a relationship between drug use and intimate partner violence. However, many individuals who use illicit drugs also use alcohol excessively and have partners who do likewise. These individuals are more likely to display other characteristics of antisocial personality. When these factors are controlled in multivariate analyses, the relationship between an individual's illicit drug use and partner violence is not uniformly significant, which may reflect issues of statistical power. In a study with a larger sample of abused women (N=427) (Walton-Moss et al., 2005), neither women's alcohol nor drug use differed significantly between abused women and controls in multivariate analyses. However, there was more male drug and alcohol use among the partners of these abused women than the control women in these analyses.

Meta-analyses. The results of these case-control and cross-sectional studies are consistent. Lipsey and associates (1997) conducted a meta-analysis examining thirty-four studies of chronic alcohol use and domestic violence. These meta-analyses studies combine information from many studies to provide a statistical summary of a key set of results that may not be able to be assessed in any single study. Overall, the results showed a significant association between chronic alcohol use and domestic violence. Additionally, Stith and colleagues (2004) conducted a meta-analysis and found that both alcohol use and illicit drug use were predictors of male violence toward partners. Women's alcohol use was a significant predictor of female violence toward their partners; however, there were an insufficient number of studies that assessed women's illicit drug use to examine this issue in the meta-analysis.

Longitudinal Studies. Finally, some longitudinal evidence exists for a relationship between alcohol/substance use and intimate partner violence, although most of the research has focused on alcohol, and on male partner violence. Two of these studies focused on newlywed couples. Heyman and associates (1995) assessed couples prior to marriage and found that scores on the Michigan Alcoholism Screening Test were associated with serious aggression at the six-month assessment, but not at the eighteen- or thirty-month assessment. Leonard and Senchak (1996) also assessed couples at the time of marriage and found that scores on the Alcohol Dependence Scale were predictive of the frequency of marital aggression reported at the first anniversary after controlling for premarital aggression, perceived relationship power, perceived conflict behavior, hostility, gender identity, and history of family violence. Quigley and Leonard (1999) extended this follow-up to the third anniversary and found that husband's alcohol use was predictive of subsequent marital aggression, but only among couples in which the wife was a light drinker.

Two longitudinal studies have examined alcohol use/problems and intimate partner violence over longer time frames, such as three to six years (Caetano et al., 2005; Mihalic & Elliot, 1997). The findings from these studies support a univariate relationship between alcohol problems and partner violence, but when other factors are controlled in the analysis, the relationship is less consistent.

International Studies. A growing international literature documents that individuals who have engaged in intimate partner violence are more likely to use alcohol and other substances or to use them excessively than are individuals who have not engaged in partner violence. Much of this research focused on men's violence against women and did not examine women's violence. A 2002 WHO Report of Violence (Krug et al., 2002) notes that "population-based surveys from Brazil, Cambodia, Canada, Chile, Colombia, Costa Rica, El Salvador, India, Indonesia, South Africa, Spain, and Venezuela also found a relationship between a woman's risk of suffering violence and her partner's drinking habits" (p. 98). In 2004, Kishor and Johnson reported a multi-country study based on the Demographic and Health Surveys program, a nationally representative survey of households. By 2003, eleven countries had collected data from women with respect to domestic violence, although not all of these countries collected data concerning the husband's or partner's alcohol use. In every country in which both domestic violence and partner alcohol use were assessed, there was a significant relationship. These countries were Cambodia, Colombia, Dominican Republic, Haiti, Nicaragua, and Peru. Other studies reported the association among 170 women in poor villages in rural India (Rao, 1997), approximately 1,100 women in northwest Ethiopia (Yigzaw et al., 2004), and among 1,300 randomly selected women in three provinces in South Africa (Jewkes et al., 2002). None of these studies assessed substance use other than alcohol.

Moderators of the Chronic Association. Clearly, no one-to-one relationship exists between chronic heavy drinking or substance use and intimate partner violence. Instead, association is limited to certain people under certain circumstances. Only a few studies have provided evidence addressing this issue, and these are exclusively focused on alcohol use and male partner violence. The most consistent moderator appears to be the presence of other factors that are causally implicated in partner violence. For example, several studies found that heavy drinking is associated with marital violence only among hostile (Leonard & Blane, 1992) or discordant married couples (Leonard & Blane, 1992; Margolin et al., 1998). Evidence shows that alcohol is associated with marital violence in the presence of high levels of negative affect (Leonard & Blane, 1992) and stressful life events (Margolin et al., 1998). Factors that moderate the longitudinal relationship between heavy drinking and marital violence were examined by Quigley and Leonard (1999). This analysis focused on verbally aggressive conflict, a variable that reflects hostility and marital dissatisfaction. This study demonstrated that heavy drinking predicted subsequent aggression only among couples high in verbally aggressive conflict styles.

ASSOCIATION BETWEEN ACUTE ALCOHOL/SUBSTANCE USE AND INTIMATE PARTNER VIOLENCE

It is important to distinguish between alcohol and substance use as chronic variables describing an individuals' usual use and acute substance use that occurs in temporal proximity and prior to the occurrence of partner violence. A number of studies have focused on acute consumption as a predictor of partner violence. The vast majority of this research is concerned with alcohol use.

Event-based Survey Research. Studies of violent events involving intimate partners often report that one or both members of the couple were using substances (usually alcohol) prior to the occurrence of violence. However, these reports, by themselves, are not informative regarding the potential causal role of alcohol or other substances on the occurrence of violence. They become informative when comparisons can be made to the presence of these substances in control events. To this end, researchers have adopted one of two basic strategies, a between-subjects approach and a within-subjects approach.

In the between-subjects approach, individuals who experienced a violent event are compared to different individuals who experienced only a control event, such as verbal conflict, with respect to the characteristics of the event. Several studies in community samples have compared violent events with control events and found that heavy drinking, at least by the male, was more common in violent than in control events (Leonard & Quigley, 1999). McClelland and Teplin (2001) reported on over 1,200 police-citizen encounters and using a validated observational checklist of alcohol found spousal assault encounters were more than twice as likely to involve alcohol as nonviolent encounters. Campbell and associates (2003), in univariate analyses, found a higher incidence of alcohol and drug use prior to femicide in contrast with non-lethal abuse of women. However, this effect was not significant in the multivariate analyses, possibly because it was mediated by other event-level characteristics, such as using a gun.

The second approach to event-level studies, the within-subjects approach, focuses on individuals who have experienced both a violent event and a control event or events, and compares the characteristics of the two. Several studies using this within-subjects approach suggest that acute alcohol use is associated with the occurrence (Leonard & Quigley, 1999) or severity of partner aggression (Wells & Graham, 2003). Studies of couples in treatment for alcoholism (Murphy et al., 2005) and domestic violence (Fals-Stewart, 2003) have reported similar findings.

Only two studies as of 2008 have used an event-based approach to examine the impact of illicit substances of the occurrence of partner violence. Murphy and associates (2005) found that violent events were more likely to involve heavy drinking by both husbands and wives than were control conflict events but that the use of other drugs was comparable across the two events. In contrast, Fals-Stewart and colleagues (2003) collected daily diary data concerning partner violence and substance use from men entering substance abuse treatment and from their partner for fifteen months. Controlling for marital adjustment and antisocial personality, the use of either alcohol or cocaine on a given day significantly increased the likelihood of severe violence on that day.

Experimental Studies of Alcohol and Aversive Verbal Behaviors. In various experimental studies, primarily focused on young men, participants were randomly assigned to receive alcohol or to receive no alcohol or a placebo and then given the opportunity to administer an aversive stimulus to another person usually another male. Several meta-analytic studies (Bushman & Cooper, 1990; Lipsey et al., 1997) confirmed that participants who received alcohol selected more aggressive responses than participants who received either no alcohol or a placebo. However, the relevance of these findings to partner violence was uncertain.

Other experimental studies have examined whether alcohol consumption affects verbal behaviors that might be related to the occurrence of partner violence, particularly within the context of relationships. In these studies, couples were asked to discuss and attempt to resolve potential or actual relationship conflicts. The interactions were videotaped and rated with respect to the behaviors displayed, including verbally aggressive behaviors. Two major projects used the conflict resolution paradigm to study the impact of alcohol on negative verbal behaviors. The first of these, conducted by Jacob and colleagues (Haber & Jacob, 1997; Jacob & Krahn, 1988) involved couples in which the husband or wife was alcoholic or depressed or had no diagnosis. These couples and a teenage child participated in a series of family interactions on two nights, one in which the adults were provided access to their usual alcoholic beverages (alcohol session), and one in which the adults were provided nonalcoholic beverages (no alcohol session). Jacob and Krahn (1988) found that only couples in which the husband was alcoholic tended to display higher levels of negativity during the alcohol session versus the no alcohol session. Haber and Jacob (1997) used the same sample but included couples in which the wife was alcoholic. They specifically compared couples in which husband, wife, both, or neither was alcoholic and found a general increase in negativity from no alcohol to alcohol sessions, except among couples in which only the wife was alcoholic. In the second research project, Leonard and Roberts (1998) allowed couples to discuss a marital conflict under a baseline condition. They were then randomly assigned to one of three conditions: no alcohol, husband placebo, or husband alcohol. Men who received alcohol displayed higher levels of negativity than men in the placebo or no alcohol condition, as did their wives who did not receive alcohol. Although couples that had experienced husband-to-wife aggression engaged in higher levels of negativity, they were not differentially impacted by the alcohol administration. Thus, these two studies demonstrate that alcohol can increase negative relationship behaviors, although whether this increase is specific to alcoholic couples or is applicable to other types of couples is uncertain.

The role of alcohol in aversive verbal expressions was examined by Eckhardt (2007). In this study, maritally violent and nonviolent men were randomly assigned to receive alcohol, placebo, or no alcohol. They then heard brief descriptions of anger-arousing situations, imagined that they were in the situation, and spoke out loud about their thoughts and feelings. They were tape-recorded and their thoughts and feelings were coded. Although ratings of anger were not affected by alcohol, alcohol led to an increase in aggressive verbalizations for maritally violent men, but not for nonaggressive men. Similarly to Leonard and Roberts (1998), the placebo did not influence anger or aversive verbalizations for either group.

Some evidence indicates that individuals with hostile/antisocial tendencies are most responsive to alcohol. In studies described above by Jacob and colleagues, Jacob, Leonard, and Haber (2001) found that among couples with an alcoholic husband, the increase in negativity from the no alcohol to alcohol session was only observed in couples in which the husband was also antisocial. In Eckhardt's 2007 study, alcohol administration resulted in the highest level of aggressive verbal statements among men who scored high with respect to their typical level of anger. Finally, at the daily level, Fals-Stewart and colleagues (2005) found that alcohol use on a specific day increased the probability that severe aggression would also occur on that day and that this effect was the strongest among men with an antisocial personality disorder.

IMPACT OF ALCOHOL/SUBSTANCE ABUSE TREATMENT ON PARTNER VIOLENCE

If substance use, particularly acute substance use, is causally related to the occurrence of partner violence, the cessation of substance use should lead to reductions in partner violence, which is particularly relevant for individuals in treatment for substance abuse. Several studies have found that individual treatment of alcoholism leads to reductions in partner violence (Stuart et al., 2003), an effect that is observed among those alcoholics who have not relapsed (O'Farrell et al., 2003).

Although marital therapy is often viewed as inappropriate for couples in which the husband has engaged in violence, combined behavior marital therapy and alcoholism treatment developed as an efficacious treatment for alcoholism prior to recognition that many of the alcoholics had engaged in partner violence. As a result, considerable research demonstrates that alcoholic behavioral couples' therapy results in reduced alcohol involvement and in reductions in partner violence, that this reduction is also apparent for verbal aggression, and that this reduction is observable up to two years post-treatment (O'Farrell et al., 2003). In addition, O'Farrell and associates (2004) found that the extent to which a couple was actively engaged in behavioral couples' treatment (BCT) was predictive of post-treatment partner violence in alcoholic men, and mediation analyses suggested this occurred because treatment involvement led to improved relationship functioning and reduced drinking.

Although evidence shows that the successful treatment of men seeking alcoholism treatment is associated with reductions in marital violence, it is unclear whether alcoholism or substance abuse treatment of violent men identified in the criminal justice system would have the same effect. Murphy and associates (1998) contrasted partner violent recidivists with nonrecidivists with respect to the different judicial and other interventions to which they were mandated. These groups did not differ with respect to referral to alcohol/drug counseling; however, it is unclear whether all of the participants needed alcohol/drug counseling. A similar analysis was undertaken by Babcock and Steiner (1999). In this study, successful completion of a chemical dependency program was associated with a reduced risk of recidivism, but this was not significant when the analyses controlled for previous criminal record and the number of domestic violence treatment sessions attended. However, neither of these studies was a randomized clinical trial that examined adding alcohol treatment to the other treatments administered to batterers, and neither assessed whether the offender remained in remission, a critical issue in the alcoholism treatment literature. As of 2008, it remained unclear whether treatment for substance abuse among men in the criminal justice system has any added impact on domestic violence beyond the other conditions imposed in that system.

See also **Alcohol; Child Abuse and Drugs; Cocaine; Treatment, Behavioral Approaches to: Couples and Family Therapy.**

BIBLIOGRAPHY

Anderson C. A., & Bushman, B. J. (2002). Human aggression. *Annual Review of Psychology, 53,* 27–51.

Arthur, T. S. (1843). *Six Nights with the Washingtonians: A series of temperance tales.* Philadelphia: Godey & M'Michael Publishers Hall.

Babcock, J. C., & Steiner, R. (1999). The relationship between treatment, incarceration, and recidivism of battering: A program evaluation of Seattle's coordinated community response to domestic violence. *Journal of Family Psychology, 13,* 46–59.

Barnett, O. W., & Fagan, R. W. (1993). Alcohol use in male spouse abusers and their female partners. *Journal of Family Violence, 8*(1), 1–25.

Barnwell, S. S., Borders, A., & Earleywine, M. (2006). Alcohol-aggression expectancies and dispositional aggression moderate the relationship between alcohol consumption and alcohol-related violence. *Aggressive Behavior, 32*(6), 517–525.

Bureau of Justice Statistics (BJS). (1998). *Violence by intimates.* (NCJ Publication No-167237). Washington, DC: U.S. Department of Justice.

Bushman, B. J., & Cooper, H. M. (1990). Effects of alcohol on human aggression: An integrative research review. *Psychological Bulletin, 107,* 341–354.

Caetano, R., McGrath, C., Ramisetty-Mikler, S., & Field, C. A. (2005). Drinking, alcohol problems and the five-year recurrence and incidence of male to female and female to male partner violence. *Alcoholism: Clinical & Experimental Research, 29*(1), 98–106.

Caetano, R., Schafer, J., & Cunradi, C. B. (2001). Alcohol-related intimate partner violence among white, black, and Hispanic couples in the United States. *Alcohol Research & Health: The Journal of the National Institute on Alcohol Abuse & Alcoholism, 25*(1), 58–65.

Campbell, J. C., Webster, D., Koziol-McLain, J., Block, C., Campbell, D., Curry, M. A., et al. (2003). Risk factors for femicide in abusive relationships: Results from a multi-site case control study. *American Journal of Public Health, 93,* 1089–1097.

Cunradi, C. B., Caetano, R., & Schafer, J. (2002). Alcohol-related problems, drug use, and male intimate partner violence severity among U.S. couples. *Alcoholism: Clinical & Experimental Research, 26*(4), 493–500.

Dent, D. Z., & Arias, I. (1990). Effects of alcohol, gender, and role of spouses on attributions and evaluations of marital violence scenarios. *Violence & Victims, 5*(3), 185–193.

Eckhardt, C. I. (2007). Effects of alcohol intoxication on anger experience and expression among partner assaultive men. *Journal of Consulting & Clinical Psychology, 75*(1), 61–71.

Fals-Stewart, W. (2003). The occurrence of partner physical aggression on days of alcohol consumption: A longitudinal diary study. *Journal of Consulting & Clinical Psychology, 71,* 41–52.

Fals-Stewart, W., Birchler, G. R., & O'Farrell, T. J. (1999). Drug-abusing patients and their intimate partners: Dyadic adjustment, relationship stability, and substance use. *Journal of Abnormal Psychology, 108,* 11–23.

Fals-Stewart, W., Golden, J., & Schumacher, J. A. (2003). Intimate partner violence and substance use: A longitudinal day-to-day examination. *Addictive Behaviors, 28,* 1555–1574.

Fals-Stewart, W., Leonard, K. E., & Birchler, G. R. (2005). The occurrence of male-to-female intimate partner violence on days of men's drinking: The moderating effects of antisocial personality disorder. *Journal of Consulting & Clinical Psychology, 73*(2), 239–248.

Goldstein, P. J. (1985). The drugs/violence nexus: A tripartite conceptual framework. *Journal of Drug Issues, 15*(4), 493–506.

Haber, J. R., & Jacob, T. (1997). Marital interactions of male versus female alcoholics. *Family Process, 36,* 385–402.

Harrel, W. A. (1981). The effects of alcohol use and offender remorsefulness on sentencing decisions. *Journal of Applied Social Psychology, 11,* 83–91.

Heyman, R. E., O'Leary, K. D., & Jouriles, E. N. (1995). Alcohol and aggressive personality styles: Potentiators of serious physical aggression against wives. *Journal of Family Psychology, 9,* 44–57.

Home, A. M. (1994). Attributing responsibility and assessing gravity in wife abuse situations: A comparative study of police and social workers. *Journal of Social Service Research, 19*(1–2), 67–84.

Homish, G. G., & Leonard, K. E. (2005). Marital quality and congruent drinking. *Journal of Studies on Alcohol, 66*(4), 488–496.

Homish, G. G., & Leonard, K. E. (2006). The drinking partnership and marital satisfaction: The longitudinal influence of discrepant drinking. *Journal of Consulting & Clinical Psychology, 75*(1), 43–51.

Hoyle, C. (1998). *Negotiating domestic violence: Police, criminal justice, and victims.* Oxford, England: Clarendon Press.

Jacob, T., & Krahn, G. L. (1988). Marital interactions of alcoholic couples: Comparison with depressed and nondistressed couples. *Journal of Consulting & Clinical Psychology, 56*(1), 73–79.

Jacob, T., Leonard, K. E., & Haber, J. R. (2001). Family interactions of alcoholics as related to alcoholism. *Alcoholism: Clinical & Experimental Research, 25,* 834–843.

Jewkes, R., Levin, J., & Penn-Kekana, L. (2002). Risk factors for domestic violence: Findings from a South African cross-sectional study. *Social Science & Medicine, 55*(9), 1485–1692.

Kaufman Kantor, G. (1997). Alcohol and spouse abuse: Ethnic differences. In M. Galanter (Ed.), *Recent developments in alcoholism: Vol. 13. Alcohol and violence* (pp. 57–75). New York: Plenum Press.

Kaufman Kantor, G., & Asdigian, N. (1997). When women are under the influence: Does drinking or drug abuse by women provoke beatings by men? In M. Galanter (Ed.), *Recent developments in alcoholism, Vol. 13: Alcoholism and violence* (pp. 315–336). New York: Plenum Press.

Kaufman Kantor, G., & Straus, M. A. (1989). Substance abuse as a precipitant of wife abuse victimizations. *American Journal of Drug & Alcohol Abuse, 15,* 173–189.

Kishor, S., & Johnson, K. (2004). *Profiling Domestic Violence: A multi-country study.* Columbia, MD: ORC Macro.

Krug, E. G., Dahlberg, L. L., Mercy, J. A., Zwi, A. B., & Lozano, R. (2002). *World report on violence and health.* Geneva: World Health Organization.

Kyriacou, D. N., McCabe, F., Anglin, D., Lapesarde, K., & Winer, M. R. (1998). Emergency department-based study of risk factors for acute injury from domestic violence against women. *Annals of Emergency Medicine, 31,* 502–506.

Leadley, K., Clark, C. L., & Caetano, R. (2000). Couples' drinking patterns, intimate partner violence, and alcohol-related partnership problems. *Journal of Substance Abuse, 11*(3), 253–263.

Leigh, B. C., & Aramburu, B. (1994). Responsibility attributions for drunken behavior: The role of expectancy violation. *Journal of Applied Social Psychology, 24,* 115–135.

Leonard, K. E. (2001). Domestic violence and alcohol: What is known and what do we need to know to encourage environmental interventions. *Journal of Substance Use, 6,* 235–247.

Leonard, K. E., & Blane, H. T. (1992). Alcohol and marital aggression in a national sample of young men. *Journal of Interpersonal Violence, 7*(1), 19–30.

Leonard, K. E., Bromet, E. J., Parkinson, D. K., Day, N. L., & Ryan, C. M. (1985). Patterns of alcohol use and physically aggressive behavior in men. *Journal of Studies on Alcohol, 46,* 279–282.

Leonard, K. E., & Quigley, B. M. (1999). Drinking and marital aggression in newlyweds: An event-based analysis of drinking and the occurrence of husband marital aggression. *Journal of Studies on Alcohol, 60,* 537–545.

Leonard, K. E., & Roberts, L. J. (1998). The effects of alcohol on the marital interactions of aggressive and nonaggressive husbands and their wives. *Journal of Abnormal Psychology, 107*(4), 602–615.

Leonard, K. E., & Senchak, M. (1996). Prospective prediction of husband marital aggression among newlywed couples. *Journal of Abnormal Psychology, 105,* 369–380.

Lipsey, M. W., Wilson, D. B., Cohen, M.A., & Derzon, J. H. (1997). Is there a causal relationship between alcohol use and violence? A synthesis of evidence. *Recent Developments in Alcoholism, 13,* 245–282.

Margolin, G., John, R. S., & Foo, L. (1998). Interactive and unique risk factors for husbands' emotional and physical abuse of their wives. *Journal of Family Violence, 13*(4), 315–344.

McCauley, J., Kern, D. E., Kolodner, K., Dill, L., Schroeder, A. F., Dechant, H. K., et al. (1995). The battering syndrome: Prevalence and clinical characteristics of domestic violence in primary care internal medicine practices. *Annals of Internal Medicine, 123,* 737–746.

McClelland, G. M., & Teplin, L. A. (2001). Alcohol intoxication and violent crime: Implications for public health policy. *American Journal on Addictions, 10,* 70–85.

McLaughlin, I. G., Leonard, K. E., & Senchak, M. (1992). Prevalence and distribution of premarital aggression among couples applying for a marriage license. *Journal of Family Violence, 7,* 309–319.

Mihalic, S. W., & Elliott, D. (1997). If violence is domestic, does it really count? *Journal of Family Violence, 12*(3), 293–311.

Miller, B. A., Downs, W. R., & Gondoli, D. M. (1989). Spousal violence among alcoholic women as compared to a random household sample of women. *Journal of Studies on Alcohol, 50,* 533–540.

Moore, M., & Stuart, G. L. (2004). Illicit substance use and intimate partner violence among men in batterers' intervention. *Psychology of Addictive Behaviors, 18*(4), 385–389.

Muhajarine, N., & D'arcy, C. (1999). Physical abuse during pregnancy: Prevalence and risk factors. *Canadian Medical Association Journal, 160,* 1007–1011.

Murphy, C. M., Musser, P. H., & Maton, K. I. (1998). Coordinated community intervention for domestic abusers: Intervention system involvement and criminal recidivism. *Journal of Family Violence, 13,* 263–284.

Murphy, C. M., Winters, J., O'Farrell, T. J., Fals-Stewart, W., & Murphy, M. (2005). Alcohol consumption and intimate partner violence by alcoholic men: Comparing violent and nonviolent conflicts. *Psychology of Addictive Behaviors, 19*(1), 35–42.

O'Farrell, T. J., Fals-Stewart, W., Murphy, M., & Murphy, C. M. (2003). Partner violence before and after individually based alcoholism treatment for male alcoholic patients. *Journal of Consulting & Clinical Psychology, 71,* 92–102.

O'Farrell, T. J., & Murphy, C. M. (1995). Marital violence before and after alcoholism treatment. *Journal of Consulting & Clinical Psychology, 63,* 256–262.

O'Farrell, T. J., Murphy, C. M., Stephan, S. H., Fals-Stewart, W., & Murphy, M. (2004). Partner violence before and after couples-based alcoholism treatment for male alcoholic patients: The role of treatment involvement and abstinence. *Journal of Consulting & Clinical Psychology, 72*(2), 202–217.

Oriel, K. A., & Fleming, M. F. (1998). Screening men for partner violence in a primary care setting: A new strategy for detecting domestic violence. *Journal of Family Practice, 46,* 493–498.

Paglia, A., & Room, R. (1999). Expectancies about the effects of alcohol on the self and on others as determinants of alcohol policy attitudes. *Journal of Applied Social Psychology, 29,* 2632–2651.

Paredes, A. (1975). Social control of drinking among the Aztec Indians of Mesoamerica. *Journal of Studies on Alcohol, 36*(9), 1139–1153.

Quigley, B. M., & Leonard, K. E. (1999). Husband alcohol expectancies, drinking, and marital conflict styles as predictors of severe marital violence among newlywed couples. *Psychology of Addictive Behaviors, 13,* 49–59.

Quigley, B. M., & Leonard, K. E. (2000). Alcohol and the continuation of early marital aggression. *Alcoholism: Clinical & Experimental Research, 24*(7), 1003–1010.

Quigley, B. M., & Leonard, K. E. (2006). Alcohol expectancies and intoxicated aggression. *Aggression & Violent Behavior, 11*(5), 484–496.

Rao, V. (1997). Wife-beating in rural South India: A qualitative and econometric analysis. *Social Science & Medicine, 44*(8), 1169–1180.

Richardson, D., & Campbell, J. (1980). Alcohol and wife abuse: The effect of alcohol on attributions of blame for wife abuse. *Personality & Social Psychology Bulletin, 6,* 51–56.

Roberts, G. L., Lawrence, J. M., O'Toole, B. I., & Raphael, B. (1997). Domestic violence in the emergency department: 1. Two case control studies of victims. *General Hospital Psychiatry, 19,* 5–11.

Robinson, A. L., & Chandek, M. S. (2000). Philosophy into practice? Community policing units and domestic violence victim participation. *Policing: An International Journal of Police Strategies & Management, 23*(3), 280–302.

Schafer, J., Caetano, R., & Cunradi, C. B. (2004). A path model of risk factors for intimate partner violence among couples in the United States. *Journal of Interpersonal Violence, 19*(2), 127–142.

Schumacher, J. A., Feldbau-Kohn, S., Slep, A. M. S., & Heyman, R. E. (2001). Risk factors for male-to-female partner physical abuse. *Aggression & Violent Behavior, 6,* 281–352.

Steele, C. M., & Josephs, R. A. (1990). Alcohol myopia: Its prized and dangerous effects. *American Psychologist, 45*(8), 921–933.

Stewart, A., & Maddren, K. (1997). Police officers' judgments of blame in family violence: The impact of gender and alcohol. *Sex Roles, 37*(11/12), 921–933.

Stewart, D. E., & Cecutti, A. (1993). Physical abuse in pregnancy. *Canadian Medical Association Journal, 149*(9), 1257–1263.

Stith, S. M., Smith, D. B., Penn, C. E., Ward, D. B., & Tritt, D. (2004). Intimate partner physical abuse perpetration and victimization risk factors: A meta-analytic review. *Aggression & Violent Behavior, 10,* 65–98.

Straus, M. A., & Gelles, R. J. (Eds.). (1990). *Physical violence in American families: Risk factors and adaptations to violence in 8,145 families.* New Brunswick, NJ: Transaction Publishers.

Stuart, G. L., Moore, T. M., Gordon, K. C., Ramsey, S. E., & Kahler, C. W. (2006). Psychopathology in women arrested for domestic violence. *Journal of Interpersonal Violence, 21*(3), 376–389.

Stuart, G. L., Ramsey, S. E., Moore, T. M., Kahler, C. W., Farrell, L. E., Recuperol, P. R., et al. (2003). Reductions in marital violence following treatment for alcohol dependence. *Journal of Interpersonal Violence, 18,* 1113–1131.

Suiter, J. J., Pillemer, K., & Straus, M. A. (1990). Marital violence in a life course perspective. In M. A. Straus & R. J. Gelles (Eds.), *Physical violence in American families: Risk factors and adaptations to violence in 8,145 families* (pp. 305–317). New Brunswick, NJ: Transaction Publishers.

Taylor, S. P., & Leonard, K. E. (1983). Alcohol and human physical aggression. In R.G. Geen & E.I. Donnerstein (Eds.), *Aggression: Theoretical and empirical reviews* (pp. 77–101). New York: Academic Press.

Thompson, M. P., & Kingree, J. B. (2006). The roles of victim and perpetrator alcohol use in intimate partner violence outcomes. *Journal of interpersonal violence, 21*(2), 163–177.

Van Hightower, N., & Gorton, J. (1998). Domestic violence among patients at two rural health care clinics: Prevalence and social correlates. *Public Health Nursing, 15*(4), 355–362.

Walton-Moss, B. J., Manganello, J., Frye, V., & Campbell, J. C. (2005). 10–11 Risk factors for intimate partner violence and associated injury among urban women. *Journal of Community Health, 30*(5), 377–389.

Wells, S., & Graham, K. (2003). Aggression involving alcohol: Relationship to drinking patterns and social context. *Addiction, 98,* 33–42.

WHO Global Consultation on Violence and Health. (1996). *Violence: A public health priority.* Geneva: World Health Organization.

Yigzaw, T., Yibrie, A., & Kebede, Y. (2004). Domestic violence around Gondar in Northwest Ethiopia. *Ethiopia Journal of Health Development, 18*(3), 133–140.

KENNETH E. LEONARD

IRELAND, REPUBLIC OF.

Stereotypes of the Irish as heavy drinkers have had international currency for centuries, but the main aim of this entry is to review drinking habits in the Republic of Ireland against the more recent historic background of economic affluence. In addition to this focus on alcohol, the entry will also look at the relatively new phenomenon of illicit drug use, as well as at policy attempts to reduce the harm associated with tobacco use in this country.

ALCOHOL

The Irish, it would appear, have always enjoyed alcohol, and the coming of Christianity to Ireland in the fifth century did not alter attitudes toward a substance regarded as one of life's great boons. A poem attributed to Saint Bridget, an early Christian saint, describes heaven as a lake of beer around which the heavenly family sits drinking for all eternity. Following the introduction of distillation to Ireland (probably in the fourteenth century), it is possible to trace the emergence of a somewhat different discourse, one that views alcohol consumption as problematic and suggests that the Irish are distinguished by an inability to control their drinking. However, historic portrayals of the "drunken Irish" must be interpreted cautiously, because from the 16th century onward, when the English colonization of Ireland became more systematic, such portrayals formed part of a wider English critique of the Irish, as well as serving as a legitimation of the "civilizing" role of the English in this subject nation.

Early Temperance Efforts. Concerns about excessive drinking came to a head immediately before the catastrophic potato famine of the 1840s, when a Catholic priest, Father Theobald Mathew, initiated a religious temperance movement that persuaded about half of the adult population to take a pledge of total abstinence. A detailed study of this movement titled *Ireland Sober, Ireland Free* (1986), Elizabeth Malcolm reveals that there was a wide range of motivations on the part of those who espoused temperance. Malcolm also highlights the ambivalence of the Catholic bishops toward a movement that was suspiciously Protestant in its denunciation of alcohol.

After the death of Father Mathew—whose leadership was charismatic in style, and who left behind no organizational structures to continue his work—the Irish population appears to have drifted back to its previous drinking habits, and it was not until 1898 that the Pioneer Total Abstinence Association of the Sacred Heart was established under the control of the Catholic hierarchy in Ireland. This mainstream Catholic movement, which still survives (albeit with a limited membership), was more moderate ideologically than Father Mathew, in that it did not view alcohol as inherently evil, but merely regarded abstinence as a voluntary sacrifice that some Catholics might undertake for religious motives.

In 1922, twenty-six of the country's thirty-two counties achieved self-government, and in 1949 they left the British Commonwealth and declared a republic. In 1973 the Republic of Ireland joined what is now the European Union (EU). Although there were periodic expressions of concern at the damage that alcohol consumption was causing to Irish society, it is clear in retrospect that consumption levels were low for the first forty years of self-government, as was the prevalence of alcohol-related problems. In 1950, for example, annual alcohol consumption per adult (age 15 and over) was just 4.67 liters, and this figure rose only slightly (to 4.80 liters) over the next 10 years (Walsh, 1983).

During this period, Catholic temperance was still strong and the influence of the Catholic Church on public alcohol policy was evident in the restricted opening hours of pubs and the policy of no "Sunday opening" in most parts of the country. Following a liberalization of opening hours in 1960 and a marked decline in temperance sentiment, consumption levels crept up gradually, but the most dramatic increases in Irish alcohol consumption have occurred during the years of economic affluence, which began in the early 1990s and are known colloquially as the "Celtic Tiger" era.

A Growing Problem and New Strategies. Changes in drinking levels, patterns, and related problems were documented in a 2002 report of the Department of Health and Children titled *Strategic Task Force on Alcohol: Interim Report* According to this report, "between 1989 and 1999, alcohol consumption per capita in Ireland increased by 41 percent while ten of the European Union Member States showed a decrease and three other countries showed a modest increase during the same period." More recent comparative data for the year 2003 show that, at 13.4 liters per year, adult alcohol consumption in Ireland was third highest for the enlarged EU, which now consists of 26 countries (Hope, 2007). Researchers have also gathered detailed epidemiological data showing that Irish drinking patterns are distinctively problematic—specifically the habit of heavy episodic, or "binge," drinking—and that there have been increases in a range of health and social problems associated with alcohol consumption.

Since the mid-1990s, there has been an almost continuous policy debate on the topic of alcohol and its negative impact on Irish society. Public policy on this issue, however, continues to be marked by ideological conflict and administrative fragmentation. In 1946, Ireland was the first European country to have a branch of Alcoholics Anonymous, and over the next twenty years—largely through the promotional work of the World Health Organization (WHO)—the disease concept of alcoholism gained official acceptance within Irish health policy. The WHO did an about-face on this matter during the 1970s, and a public health, or "total consumption," model of alcohol problems emerged. Unlike the disease concept, which largely attributed alcohol-related problems to the vulnerabilities of a small minority of "diseased" consumers, the public health model emphasized the negative features of alcohol per se, and argued that the prevalence of alcohol-related problems would only be reduced by control policies aimed at reducing societal consumption levels. Since then, public health researchers and advocates have repeatedly recommended that this model should underpin public policy on alcohol in Ireland. Specifically, they argue there should be an integrated national alcohol policy based on the use of evidence-based prevention strategies.

The *Strategic Task Force on Alcohol: Second Report*, released in 2004, recommended that the first objective of such a national alcohol policy should be to reduce Irish consumption to the EU average of 9 liters per annum. In pursuit of this objective, the report recommended that the state should increase the excise duty on alcohol and restrict its physical availability by reducing both the number of retail outlets and the hours of sale. It also suggested that the government control the ways that the drinks industry advertises and promotes its products. These recommendations reflect the new WHO position that alcohol is "no ordinary commodity," but they are in ideological conflict with the neoliberal values currently dominant in Ireland. To date, therefore, the government has been reluctant to implement strategies that would both bring it into direct conflict with the drinks industry and be electorally unpopular.

ILLICIT DRUG USE

In Ireland, public concern and policy in relation to illicit psychoactive drugs dates back to the mid-1960s. The first modern antidrug legislation in the country was the 1977 Misuse of Drugs Act. In retrospect, these early concerns appear exaggerated, for the prevalence of illicit drug use was low, the drugs being used were relatively "soft," and there was little or no injecting of these drugs. Things changed in 1979, when—in what came to be known as the "opiate epidemic"—working-class areas of Dublin experienced a dramatic and sustained wave of injecting heroin use. This upsurge was accompanied by the usual range of health consequences—dependency, overdoses, and the physical complications of sharing needles—as well as increases in acquisitive crime and other social problems in the affected areas (Butler, 2002).

Public policy and service provision struggled to adapt to the opiate epidemic, a task that was further complicated by the advent of HIV/AIDS and the early recognition of the fact that needle-sharing among injecting drug users played a major role in the transmission of this new virus. Prior to the coming of HIV/AIDS, it had been assumed axiomatically that all health-service responses to illicit drug use would have abstinence as their goal, thereby ensuring that treatment and rehabilitation professionals worked collaboratively with colleagues from the criminal justice system in common pursuit of the ideal of a "drug-free" society. In fact, from the late 1980s onward, both statutory and voluntary treatment agencies shifted incrementally to the use of harm-reduction models of service provision, which included methadone maintenance, needle and syringe exchange, the use of mobile clinics, and the introduction of "low-threshold" agencies and outreach work for problem drug users who were uncommitted to any major lifestyle change.

The adoption of such harm-reduction strategies clearly marked a decline in the influence of American methods. Instead, Irish policymakers and service providers drew on the experiences of countries such as Holland, which had previously adopted a more pragmatic approach to managing drug problems, and which clearly had no faith in the approach being used in the so-called War on Drugs in the United States (Butler and Mayock,

2005). In 1993 the EU-established European Monitoring Centre for Drugs and Drug Addiction (EMCDDA) and Ireland's Health Research Board became a national data-gathering "focal point" for this effort. This development further reinforced the tendency for Irish policymakers to look to Europe rather than the United States for guiding influences.

A New Approach. Following recommendations made in the *First Report of the Ministerial Task Force on Measures to Reduce the Demand for Drugs*, issued by the Department of the Taoiseach (prime minister) in 1996, a new managerial approach was taken to drug policymaking. This effort involved the creation of a system of a multilayered policy and administrative structures, including both top-down and bottom-up initiatives. An explicit aim of this effort has been to create a "cross-cutting" response to illicit drugs, in which all central government departments and agencies coordinate their activities to ensure that, as far as possible, there are no philosophical or practical conflicts between different sectors of government. This approach to policymaking was formalized in a policy review titled *Building on Experience: National Drugs Strategy 2001–2008*, which was based on four "pillars": supply reduction, prevention (i.e., education and awareness raising), treatment, and research. It also laid out detailed objectives, as well as specified actions deemed necessary to attain these objectives, and it identified the agencies that would be accountable for these actions.

There is no simple way to determine whether the National Drugs Strategy has been a success. The primary impetus for the creation of the strategy was the necessity to respond to heroin problems in readily identifiable urban areas. Through its community-based structures, the effort could be deemed to be successful in this sphere. However, on the broader front of preventing recreational drug use among adolescents and young adults, the strategy has clearly not made much impact. For instance, the 2003 report of the European School Survey Project on Alcohol and Other Drugs (ESPAD), a comparative study of drug and alcohol use among 16-year-olds in 35 European countries, showed the Irish sharing third place for lifetime prevalence of cannabis use. It was also the leading nation in binge drinking.

One of the unanticipated consequences of the creation of the National Drugs Strategy has been the way in which it has highlighted the absence of any similar strategy to deal with alcohol, prompting suggestions both from community groups and political leaders that the existing strategy should be expanded to include alcohol. In management terms, this is commonly spoken of as creating "synergies," but in political terms it is obviously a move that would be resisted strongly by the country's powerful drinks industry.

TOBACCO

Given the tendency of the Irish to indulge heavily in the use of psychoactive substances, it might come as a surprise that Ireland has led the EU in tobacco control efforts. Public health advocates had conducted a long campaign for legislative control of smoking in public places, culminating in the Public Health (Tobacco) Act of 2002, which established an Office of Tobacco Control (OTC). Despite intensive lobbying from the tobacco and hospitality industries, the OTC persuaded the Minister for Health and Children to introduce national regulations prohibiting smoking in all workplaces, and these regulations came into effect in March 2004. Much of the publicity surrounding this development focused on the fact that smoking was being banned in pubs, and it was commonly predicted that such a ban would be unenforceable. In fact, the ban was publicly accepted and has been successfully enforced, thereby offering protection from secondhand smoke to workers and demonstrating that public health activists could successfully counter the influence of powerful commercial interests.

See also **Alcohol: History of Drinking; Crime and Alcohol; Crime and Drugs; European Union; Foreign Policy and Drugs, United States; Harm Reduction; International Drug Supply Systems; Needle and Syringe Exchanges and HIV/AIDS; Tobacco: An International Overview.**

BIBLIOGRAPHY

Butler, S. (2002). *Alcohol, drugs, and health promotion in modern Ireland*. Dublin: Institute of Public Administration.

Butler, S., & Mayock, P. (2005). 'An Irish solution to an Irish problem': Harm reduction and ambiguity in the drug policy of the Republic of Ireland. *International Journal of Drug Policy, 16(6)*, 415–422.

European Monitoring Centre for Drugs and Drug Addiction (EMCDDA). Available from http://www.emcdda. europa.eu.

Hibell, B., Anderson, B., Bjarnson, et al. (2004). *The ESPAD Report 2003: Alcohol and other drug use among students in 35 European countries*. Stockholm: Swedish Council for Information on Alcohol and Other Drugs. Available from http://www.espad.org/.

Hope, A. (2007). *Alcohol consumption in Ireland 1986–2006*. Dublin: Health Service Executive, Alcohol Implementation Group.

Ireland Department of Community, Rural and Gaeltacht Affairs. (2001). *Building on experience: eational drugs strategy 2001–2008*. Dublin: Stationery Office. Available from http://www.pobail.ie/en/NationalDrugsStrategy.

Ireland Department of Health and Children. (2002). *Strategic Task Force on Alcohol: Interim report*. Dublin: Author.

Ireland Department of Health and Children. (2004). *Strategic Task Force on Alcohol: Second report*. Dublin: Author. Available from http://meas.ie/.

Oireachtas Joint Committee on Arts, Sport, Tourism, Community, Rural, and Gaeltacht Affairs. (2006). *The inclusion of alcohol in a national substance misuse strategy*. Dublin: Houses of the Oireachtas.

Walsh, D. (1983). Alcohol problems and alcohol control in Ireland. In P. Davies and D. Walsh (Eds.), *Alcohol problems and alcohol control in Europe*. London: Croom Helm.

SHANE BUTLER

ITALY. The European Addiction Monitoring Centre has estimated that in the European Union approximately 50 million people out of the total European population of 490,426,060 have tried an illegal substance in their lifetime, and at least 7 percent of these subjects, ranging from 15 to 64 years of age, have done so recently. According to a 2004 report on drug addiction prepared by the Italian Parliament, at least 20 percent of the Italian population ranging from 15 to 54 years of age have tried an illegal substance at least once in their lives and this percentage is even higher, 30 percent, for those 15 to 34 years old. A distinction must be made between recreational drug users and drug addicts, who are estimated to represent less than 1 percent of the total Italian population and the majority of whom are assisted by public health and welfare services.

EPIDEMIOLOGY

In Italy, the impact of illicit drugs was first felt on a broad scale during the mid-1960s. The patterns in Italy were similar to those observed in other European nations. These models seemed to be associated with young people's rejection of the existing political and social order. Opioids, especially heroin, began to be used illicitly, and by the 1970s serious consequences ensued. By then, the countercultural movement and its abuse of illicit drugs had veered from most of its original idealistic principles. Abusers were simply in search of ever more and ever stronger psychotropic effects. Moreover, criminal organizations took charge of the illicit drug trade, not only to increase their profits but also to control and direct the political and social development of the youth of Italy. For the most part, users became abusers who were physically dependent on their drug of choice, so their behavior could be controlled by suppliers.

In the 1980s the drug scene changed, with various control measures enacted by the government and less heroin available on the street. In addition, with less heroin being sold, longer intervals occurred between drug doses for many users. Such modified habits led to decreased tolerance and increased overdosing, with many deaths resulting. For these reasons, the number of heroin addicts in Italy decreased, but in the mid-1980s the illicit use of cocaine emerged as the new drug problem. Its crack and freebase forms were especially harmful among young adolescents. After a modest decrease in heroin consumption in the late 1990s, its further increase was recorded in the early twenty-first century, with cocaine use steadily increasing during the 1990s and first few years of the new millennium. The mode of administration of these drugs also varied—although injection rather than smoking and snorting became common for both heroin and cocaine. In particular, approximately 70 percent of patients treated in the Centers for Addiction Treatment (CATs) admitted heroin use (70% injected it) and 16 percent cocaine use (8% injected it) as the primary substance of abuse.

One interesting study (Zuccato et al., 2005) has also shown that cocaine is present and measurable in surface waters of populated areas. The largest Italian river, the Po, with a 5-million-people catchment's basin, steadily carries the equivalent of about 4 kilograms of cocaine per day. This implies the average daily use of at least 27 +/- 5 doses, of 100 milligrams each, for every 1,000 young adults, an estimate that greatly exceeds official national figures. In this same study, the researchers used the environmental cocaine levels for estimating collective consumption of the drug, an approach with the unique potential ability to monitor local drug abuse trends in real time, while preserving the anonymity of individuals.

In recent years approximately 10 percent of patients seen at CATs identified cannabis as their primary substance of abuse and, compared to other addicted patients, these individuals presented a lower mean age, 19 years.

Another recent survey (Pavarin, 2006), this one conducted in the northern part of Italy, investigated drug use among more than 2,000 youngsters attending open-air musical events—so-called street raves. It confirmed the high prevalence of hashish, marijuana, and cocaine use and a drop in the average age of first-time use, 16 years. In addition, in the years since 2001 several new drugs emerged as specifically consumed by young people. The most commonly used new substances were first salvia divinorum—a psychedelic drug—followed by hallucinogenic mushrooms and 3,4-methylenedioxymethamphetamine (MDMA), commonly known as Ecstasy, poppers, and ketamine. Clear evidence also emerged regarding the potential risks associated with current changes in drinking patterns among youth who are decidedly *buzz-oriented* as well as the high prevalence of risk behaviors, such as the use of mixtures of drugs on the same evening, combining of alcohol consumption with drugs, and driving after drinking.

In regard to the so-called legal drugs, alcohol, and tobacco, in 2007 the Institute of Health estimated that approximately 30 percent of the Italian population—mostly men—smoke tobacco on a daily basis. About 20 percent of these smokers are very young—from 15 to 24 years old—and 8 percent smoke more than 25 cigarettes per day. However, there is evidence that tobacco consumption progressively decreased from 1957 to 2007; in particular, a relevant reduction of 0.8 percent occurred from 2001 to 2007 and the mean number of cigarettes consumed also declined from 16.8 per day in 2001 to 14.1 per day in 2007.

Alcohol use in Italy strongly differs from drug use for historical, traditional, behavioral, and cultural reasons; supply and distribution are also different, because alcohol is free from legal restrictions. Wine is the most frequently used alcoholic beverage. Although wine consumption was gradually displaced during the 1980s with the substitution of other liquors and beers, the total amount of alcohol consumed remained almost constant. Among the 70 percent of Italians who admit consuming alcohol, not quite 70 percent of them consume one or more standard drinks occasionally—one standard drink corresponds to about 14 grams of pure alcohol—and approximately 30 percent report daily alcohol intake.

In addition, from 1995 to 2007 drinking habits also changed; this phenomenon was particularly evident among the young. The so-called Mediterranean habit of drinking alcohol or wine during meals acquired by older generations of farmers has became less popular; conversely, the so-called Anglo-Saxon practice of *binge drinking*—drinking spirits and beer outside meal times to get high or to achieve a state of drunkenness—has been progressively favored by the younger segment of the population. About 8 percent of them describe themselves as binge drinkers. Indeed, in Italy this phenomenon is on the rise. In addition, the age of first-time drinkers has declined to 11 years, and beer and alcoholic soda pop or wine coolers—carbonated fruit-juice-flavored beverages with a concentration of 3 to 5 percent alcohol—have become the most popular beverages among youth. An important related development is the association of illicit drug use and binge drinking with high-risk sexual behaviors. A recent multicenter survey (Bellis et al., 2008) in the city of Venice reported that recreational drug use, particularly cocaine and Ecstasy, in combination with binge drinking altered the sexual decision making of its subjects and increased their chances of engaging in unsafe and later regretted sexual activities. Substance use also appears to be an integral part of strategies for engaging in sex.

Researchers Adamo and Orsini (2007) have calculated that around 7 percent of Italians have alcohol-related problems involving high-risk use or abuse, and 3 percent are affected by alcohol dependence, which appears to be mainly a problem of chronic abuse by adults over the age of 40. However, since the mid-1980s alcohol dependence in Italy has come to include a greater number of women and young people. In same cases, alcoholism has also been complicated by the regular combining of alcohol with psychotropic drugs—that is, tranquilizers—and other substances—that is, cocaine and amphetamines—as demonstrated by the greater number of patients affected by polysubstance dependence treated in CATs.

DEATHS RELATED TO DRUG, ALCOHOL, AND TOBACCO USE

Drug-abuse-related deaths show irregular trends. Most deaths, however, may be attributed to heroin overdoses or to accidents while injecting it. After 1980 two large increases in the death rate occurred, first in 1982 and then in 1984, followed by a steady rise into 1986. From 1986 to 1988 the mortality rate nearly doubled; it subsequently remained steady until 1991 and then dropped until 1994, except among the elderly, for whom the rate increased. Since the mid-1990s the mortality rate has continued to decline. Indeed, from 1993 to 2006 the number of addicts treated in CATs increased—from 109,000 subjects in 1993 to 176,000 in 2006—and a reduction in the number of deaths from overdose was recorded—from 888 subjects in 1993 to 517 in 2006—with a corresponding drop in the mortality rate, from 0.8 to 0.3 percent. Some important factors, such as the administration of agonist or partial agonist drugs in association with counseling sessions and the distribution of informative materials in CATs, have contributed to this important result. Because intravenous drug use is a primary transmission route for HIV and other blood-borne diseases, such as Hepatitis B and C infections, prevention campaigns have also been developed. In particular, in the early twenty-first century CATs have actively distributed sterile needles and condoms, and information regarding the risky behaviors of drug addicts. As of 2008, 44 percent of the CATs in Italy distributed sterile needles and condoms, and more than 90 percent of CATs supplied information regarding the risk of infections associated with the use of illicit drugs. Moreover, CATs have devised vaccination strategies for Hepatitis B: In recent years some 15.8 percent of patients enrolled in a rehabilitation program have been vaccinated (Ministry of Health, 2006; Ministry of Social Affairs, 2006).

It is worth noting that alcohol-impaired driving is a serious threat to the nation's health as well. Driving license regulations have, since 1988, included a test that measures the breath concentration of alcohol in drivers' blood, which must not be over 5 grams per liter (g/l), approximately that of other countries in the European community. In Italy, 30 to 50 percent of traffic accidents are related to alcohol intake, and 50 percent of those subjects who die during such crashes are under 30 years of age. The accidents may be correlated with alcohol use and abuse. In particular, one prospective study (Fabbri et al., 2002) that enrolled more than 2,000 patients admitted to an Italian emergency room for an injury sustained during a traffic accident has shown that the patient's blood alcohol concentration (BAC) was above the legal limit in 25.7 percent of the cases. Also, the number of BAC positive patients increased progressively—from 14.4 to 30.8 percent—with trauma severity, and almost 30 percent of polytraumatized patients were BAC positive. Another Italian study (Giovanardi et al., 2005) confirmed that a significant percentage of injury-producing traffic accidents involve drivers who are under the influence of drugs of abuse, alcohol, or other drugs affecting the central nervous system. Indeed, 40 percent of the study's subjects tested positive for at least one drug and/or alcohol—66 percent tested positive for a single drug, 25 percent for two drugs, and 9 percent for three or more drugs. The recent use of marijuana was determined most frequently—accounting for 19 percent of the 115 total—well surpassing alcohol (10%), amphetamines (7%), and cocaine (6%). It is worth pointing out that most of the drivers who tested positive for alcohol or other drugs were between the ages of 21 and 40.

In Italy, 80,000 subjects die every year as a consequence of tobacco smoking. From 2000 to 2007 the number of Centers for the Treatment of Tobacco Dependence increased: As of 2008, 346 such centers existed. This development is partially attributable to (1) increased awareness of the risky medical consequences of tobacco use among the population of current smokers; (2) preventive campaigns aiming to stop smoking; (3) the warning about the fatal consequences of smoking that is printed on cigarette packaging; and (4) current legislation that prohibits smoking in workplaces and public recreational spaces—that is, cafés, discotheques, pubs, and restaurants.

TREATMENT FACILITIES

As the use of illicit drugs became an ever more serious problem, the emerging need for adequate political and social interventions aimed at preventing this expanding phenomenon and treating drug-dependent individuals became urgent. In accordance with national policy guidelines, a network of facilities was established, as were various links between rehabilitation programs, law enforcement agencies, and judicial structures. This approach was worked out with overwhelming public support, the aim being to sustain every initiative to reduce the availability of and demand for drugs. Many CATs were established throughout all of Italy's regions. In the early twenty-first century a wide range of resources were available: 544 CATs and 575 residential communities and socio-rehabilitative structures—public, private, and voluntary—with most of them situated in northern Italy. Voluntary services continue to increase in importance, both in number and in regional distribution. Of the addicts served by such facilities, almost all are heroin abusers, some not yet physically dependent on the drug. The facilities provide integrated and custom-designed programs based mainly on pharmacological support. Sixty-eight percent of patients are treated with methadone, 20 percent with buprenorphine, 7 percent with naltrexone, and 2.3 percent with clonidine, in association with psycho-social supports (38%), mostly counseling (42%), and social services (41%). Although methadone remains the most frequently used drug in CATs for the treatment of heroin addiction, one contemporary Italian study showed statistically significant improvements in the rate of heroin use, psychiatric status, and quality of life between the 3rd and 12th month of treatment with both methadone and buprenorphine medications, suggesting the long-term efficacy of both these drugs in treating the symptoms of opioid addiction and improving addicts' quality of life.

In the early twenty-first century a multidisciplinary approach to the treatment of alcohol dependence, which is a combination of pharmacological treatment, psycho-social supports, self-help groups, and family interventions, has been embraced.

Because the use of gamma-hydroxybutyric acid (GHB) as a recreational drug has not spread in Italy, it is currently employed in treating alcohol dependence with encouraging results. Indeed, GHB, due to its GABA-ergic activity (which increases the available amount of GABA and typically has anti-anxiety and anti-convulsive effects) is currently used in suppressing the symptoms of alcohol withdrawal syndrome and, alone or in combination with naltrexone, it is used as an anti-craving medication in the maintenance of alcohol abstinence. With the increased use of the above-mentioned drugs, disulfiram has become less popular among physicians. Moreover, counseling and cognitive-behavioral therapy (CBT), alone or in association with the support of self-help groups such as Alcoholics Anonymous (AA), continue to play a relevant role in the treatment of alcoholism. In fact, since the mid-1990s the number of AA groups throughout Italy has risen to over 500. In addition, throughout Italy another type of self-help group, the so-called Club System for Treated Alcoholics (CTA), also exists. It was inspired by Vladimir Hudolin, a Croatian psychiatrist who, in 1960, organized rehabilitation programs for alcoholics and their families in the city of Zagreb with subsequent extensions to other parts of the former Yugoslavia. In 1992 before the start of the Balkan War, some 1,200 Clubs had been established. Afterward the phenomenon of Clubs expanded to the nearer territories of eastern and central Europe. As of 2008, there were more than 2,300 Clubs in Italy.

LEGISLATION

When drug abuse spiraled in Italy during the 1960s, the legislation in force proved to be insufficient to cope with emerging conditions; it did not take into consideration the latest political-cultural trends, scientific knowledge of the day, or the increasingly important role of public health. In 1954 the law dictated that those defendants who produced, used, or sold illicit substances had to be punished with sentences of 6 months to 7 years in jail and additional fines. New legislation in 1975 mandated increased jail time—from 1 to a maximum of 15 years—and higher fines. However, innovative elements such as no punishment for addicts found to be in possession of a moderate quantity of illicit drugs, considered to be for personal use, characterized that legislation; in addition, therapeutic interventions in specialized centers servicing those with certified illicit drug dependence were offered. The confiscated narcotics were to be carefully examined and quantified, and that information was to be considered by the courts in relationship to the physical and psychological needs of the addict. Unfortunately, this individualistic approach was poorly applied, which made the law useless. Regulations approved in 1990 improved the state's power to both take repressive action and mandate intervention, and it defined a daily mean dose to separate administrative offenses from more serious drug-related crimes. The objective was to recover and rehabilitate drug addicts. A 1993 referendum, however, repealed the prohibition on personal drug use and canceled the regulations on a daily mean dose.

In 2006 a new revision of the law was approved by the Italian Parliament. In particular, the current law clearly specifies the maximum misdemeanor amount of individual possession for each illegal drug: for example, 1 g of cannabis, 750 mg of cocaine, 1/2 g of heroin, 750 mg of Ecstasy, 500 mg of amphetamine, and 150 mg of d-lysergic acid diethylamide (LSD). Those defendants found to be in possession of the above-defined amounts are punished with *administrative sanctions*—that is, withholding of a driver's license or gun permit, or official permission to live in Italy if the individual is not an Italian citizen; these defendants may only obtain an end to such sanctions when a CAT officially certifies that they have dutifully followed a therapeutic program with positive results. Those defendants whose possession exceeds the above-mentioned quantity of illicit drugs are considered pushers and punished as criminals with *legal sanctions* from 1 to 20 years of imprisonment.

In October 2007 the law regarding alcohol and driving was modified. In fact, a suspended license for 3 to 6 months and fine from 500 to 2,000 euros are now levied on those defendants found to be driving with a BAC ranging from 0.5 to 0.8 g/l; a suspended license for 6 months to 1 year, fine from 800 to 3,200 euros, and up to 3 months of imprisonment are imposed on those defendants found to be driving with a BAC ranging from 0.9 to 1.5 g/l; a suspended license for 1 to 2 years, fine from 1,500 to 6,000 euros, and up to 6 months of imprisonment are also applied to those defendants found to be driving with a BAC greater than 1.5 g/l. In addition, if a defendant causes a traffic accident resulting in physical injuries to others, the administrative and penal sanctions double; with the previous law, sanctions did not differ if a traffic accident had occurred. In any case, within 60 days of having a driver's license suspended and before re-obtaining it, a subject apprehended for drunk driving must undergo a medical examination that tests for the biochemical markers of alcohol abuse and a consistently positive attitude toward the responsibilities of driving. When the subject presents behavioral modification and/or alterations of biochemical parameters of alcohol abuse sufficient to arouse suspicion of alcohol-related problems, the medical commission may request a further and more specific evaluation in a CAT by a medical doctor who specializes in treating alcohol abuse.

In January 2005 the existing legislation regarding tobacco smoking was modified. The previous law of 1962 prohibited smoking in public places (that is, hospitals, cinemas, theaters). The revised law expanded the same restrictions to all closed spaces (those offering public services, workplaces, and jails) except for those not open to the public. However, with adequate ventilation and separation from nonsmokers, specific areas for smokers are permitted in public places. Smokers violating the law are subject to fines of 27.5 to 275 euros, and inspectors are assigned to enforce it; and owners of public venues found to not uphold the statute may be fined 200 to 2,000 euros. Finally, any form of advertising related to tobacco products and their sale to those younger than 16 years of age is also forbidden.

See also **Britain; European Union; France; Nordic Countries (Denmark, Finland, Iceland, Norway, and Sweden); Spain.**

BIBLIOGRAPHY

Adamo, D., & Orsini, S. (2007). *Use and abuse of alcohol in Italy.* Annual Report of the National Institute of Statistic, Rome.

Bellis, M. A., et al. (2008). Sexual uses of alcohol and drugs and the associated health risks: A cross-sectional study of young people in nine European cities. *BMC Public Health, 8,* 155.

Caputo, F., et al. (2005). Gamma-hydroxybutyrate as a treatment for alcoholism. *Lancet, 366,* 981–982.

Caputo, F., et al. (2007a). Comparing and combining gamma-hydroxybutyric acid (GHB) and naltrexone in maintaining abstinence from alcohol: An open randomized comparative study. *European Neuropsychopharmacology, 17,* 781–789.

Caputo, F., et al. (2007b). Alcohol misuse and traffic crashes. *Lancet, 369,* 463–464.

European Monitoring Centre for Drugs and Drug Addiction. (2005). Difference in patterns of drug use between women and men. European drug situation-Technical data sheet 2005. Available from http://www.emcdda.eu.int/.

Fabbri, A., et al. (2002). Positive blood alcohol concentration and road accidents. A prospective study in an Italian emergency department. *Emergency Medicine Journal, 19,* 210–214.

Giovanardi, D., et al. (2005). Prevalence of abuse of alcohol and other drugs among injured drivers presenting to the emergency department of the University Hospital of Modena, Italy. *Drug and Alcohol Dependence, 80,* 135–138.

Legislation on Alcohol-Related Problems in Italy. (2001). Official Bulletin No. 90.

Legislation on Illicit Drugs, Italian Law No. 1041/54. (1954). *Discipline of traffic, production and use of illicit drugs.*

Legislation on Illicit Drugs, Italian Law No. 685/75. (1975). *Discipline of illicit and psychotropic drugs.*

Legislation on Illicit Drugs, Italian Law No. 49/06. (2006). *Disposition to facilitate the recovery of illicit drugs addicts and modification of the previous discipline of traffic, production and use of illicit drugs.*

Maremmani, I., et al. (2007). Substance use and quality of life over 12 months among buprenorphine maintenance-treated and methadone maintenance-treated heroin-addicted patients. *Journal of Substance Abuse Treatment, 33,* 91–98.

Ministry of Work Social Affairs. (2004). *Drug addiction in Italy.* Annual Report at the Italian Parliament, Rome.

Ministry of Health. (2006). *Smoking, alcohol and drugs.* Annual Report of the Institute of Health, Rome.

Ministry of Social Affairs. (2006). *Drug addiction in Italy.* Annual Report of Institute of Social Affairs, Rome.

Pavarin, R. M. (2006). Substance use and related problems: A study on the abuse of recreational and not recreational drugs in Northern Italy. *Annali dell'Istituto Superiore di Sanita, 42,* 477–484.

Zuccato, E., et al. (2005). Cocaine in surface waters: A new evidence-based tool to monitor community drug abuse. *Environmental Health, 5,* 4–14.

USTIK AVICO
FABIO CAPUTO (2009)

JAPAN. Japan's involvement with global narcotics traffic follows its remarkable emergence from isolated warrior society to modern world power like a secret shadow. In 1868, when Japan formally opened its doors to world trade and diplomacy, it was with the understanding that opium would not be tolerated within its borders. After 1895, as its territories expanded into the Asian continent, the problem of narcotics addiction became a burden of empire. During the 1930s and 1940s, as the nation turned to military adventure in China and the Pacific, opium, morphine, and heroin sales financed espionage and dirty tricks in an all-out war. After surrender in 1945 and continuing into the twenty-first century, Japan has reestablished its reputation for a tough, no tolerance drug policy, and yet amphetamine abuse fueled postwar economic growth. Methamphetamine use remains a problem, although it is dwarfed by the legal drugs tobacco and alcohol.

HISTORICAL BACKGROUND

According to tradition, the poppy flowers dotting fields in the countryside came to Japan with Buddhism. During the Tokugawa era (1600–1868) opium harvests sold to medicine shops provided extra income for peasants in the Osaka region. Opium remained a pharmaceutical, while Japanese—both rich and poor, male and female—enjoyed smoking tobacco from *kiseru* (long-stemmed pipes) and drinking locally brewed sake. Later, when Japan entered the narcotics trade, officials assured each other that the Japanese temperament preferred sake, unlike Chinese people who craved opium. Similar expressions of racial exclusivity marked the general Japanese attitude toward its Asian neighbors as well as their nefarious habit.

In the 1800s, as Western European nations expanded into Asia seeking markets for manufactured goods, Japan remained a closed country, proudly standing aloof from the dangers associated with foreign commerce, trading only with the Dutch at Nagasaki. The Japanese government, under control of the Tokugawa Shogun, denied foreign ships entry to its ports until 1853 when the American Commodore Matthew Perry (1794–1858) backed his entreaty with the threat of force. Within fifteen years new leaders replaced the old samurai regime. Using the authority of the young Meiji emperor (1852–1912), they were determined to create a modern nation with a strong military to guard it.

The closed-country policy of the old order did not mean Japan's governing officials remained unaware of the outside world. They knew that China had fought and lost a war with Great Britain over the opium issue in 1840 and 1842. When Japan finally did open its doors to foreign trade, Article IV of the Treaty of Amity and Commerce of 1858, like those that followed, forbade opium sales. As Japanese trade with Asia expanded, however, Chinese merchants arrived in Japanese ports, bringing their habit with them. In cities such as Osaka or Yokohama, the Chinese enjoyed opium, resulting in periodic police raids on their homes and businesses.

The motivation for opening the nation to foreign trade was the modernization of Japan for protection in a dangerous world. Modernization in the nineteenth century meant expanding the military, producing goods for export, and acquiring colonies. The new Japanese Meiji government excelled in all three areas. In 1894 and 1895 Japan fought and won a war with China, gaining the island of Taiwan off the southern Chinese coast as its first colony. In 1904 and 1905 Japan defeated Russia. As a result, by 1910 Japan owned Korea as a colony and acquired from China the right to build railways and exploit mineral wealth in Manchuria, China's three northeast provinces.

Acquiring Asian colonies forced Japanese government policymakers to reconsider opium. In 1895 the Japanese military prepared to occupy Taiwan, which harbored a Chinese population hostile to the new regime. Taiwan had a substantial population of Chinese opium smokers who acquired their supplies on the open market as the habit was legal in China from 1842 to 1906. As the Japanese Imperial Army faced sporadic warfare against its occupation, the government at home debated extending their opium ban to Taiwan, forcing an already hostile population into opium withdrawal. Many in the government supported a draconian ban on the drug, fearing that opium use in Taiwan would find its way to the home islands.

Gotō Shimpei (1857–1929), a Japanese leader who specialized in public health, offered an alternative. Gotō proposed a colonial monopoly supporting gradual opium withdrawal. His program registered addicts, providing them with legal opium to avoid illicit markets. Complimentary rehabilitation programs weaned addicts away from their habit. Gotō's program granted lucrative opium sales licenses to those Taiwanese who worked with the Japanese government to end anti-Japanese insurrection.

The Taiwan Opium Monopoly system worked well. When combined with parallel monopolies in sugar, camphor, and salt, the colony earned money for the Japanese empire. Addiction rates fell from 169,000 licensed addicts in 1900 to 7,560 in 1941. As Japan's territory expanded—first into Korea, which became a colony in 1910, and then to Manchuria, which became an economic sphere of interest in 1907 and a notorious puppet state under military control in 1932—Gotō's monopoly system followed the spread of empire.

Establishing a functioning government narcotics monopoly created the problem of opium supply. In the beginning Taiwan authorities turned to British Hong Kong for their drugs. In their quest for self-sufficiency, two remarkable men, both with connections to Gotō Shimpei, established careers tied to the monopoly. Nitan'osa Otozō (1875–1950) was a farmer from the Kansai countryside near Osaka. Learning about the opium monopoly, he approached Gotō Shimpei in 1896 with a plan to grow poppies in Japan, releasing the nation from its dependence on British suppliers. With government support, Nitan'osa became an expert on poppies, learning to crossbreed the plant to increase its morphia content. Nitan'osa supplied the Japanese monopoly in Taiwan. As the empire spread to Manchukuo, an elderly Nitan'osa traveled to the puppet state to oversee poppy cultivation in the rich soils of northeast China. He is remembered as Japan's opium king, yet he lived the sedate life of a gentleman farmer.

Hoshi Hajime (1873–1951) specialized in morphine. Hoshi studied business in the United States but returned to Japan where he founded Hoshi Pharmaceuticals in 1910. Japanese morphine came from Germany. Hoshi approached Gotō Shimpei with a plan to manufacture the drug at home from Taiwan opium. As the scheme coincided with World War I, Hoshi's company prospered. Hoshi entered politics and hoped to profit from a stockpiled opium supply he had purchased cheaply from Turkey. His plans failed when political rivals publicly linked his company to a Taiwan bribery scandal. His name suffered further when a British consul determined that the stockpiled opium in Hoshi's bonded warehouses slipped out at night onto the Asian black market.

Hoshi's career exposes a reality that blackened the reputation of the Japanese colonial opium monopolies. On the surface, men who hoped to create a model for addict reform ran the monopolies. Yet the geopolitical climate from the 1910s to the 1930s created temptations and opportunities when China fell into a state of chronic civil war after its 1911 revolution brought an end to the last dynasty. At the same time, Japan's thirty-year expansion into Asia created an empire including colonies, extensive rail and mining rights in Manchuria, and a commercial presence in major Chinese cities.

In spite of the ensuing chaos, opium became illegal once again in China after 1906, yet the appetite for the drug continued among a significant percentage of the population. Given the unstable situation, the money that could be made satisfying an illicit craving tempted Japanese subjects protected by treaties from Chinese jurisdiction. Korean and Japanese traffickers sold morphine from so-called drug shops in the north. Taiwanese gangsters set up shops along the southern coast, while Japanese soldiers of fortune assisted with both drug trafficking and production. Given opium's illegality, morphine and heroin use increased, especially among China's urban poor. Japanese freebooters specialized in providing a cheaper, high-grade product to this illicit Chinese market.

A business that was lucrative in the 1920s became strategic in the next decade when Japanese militarists created the puppet state of Manchukuo in 1932, and expanded the conflict to an outright war with China in 1937 and into the Pacific in December 1941. In Manchukuo an opium suppression program progressed sporadically, but the number of registered addicts remained static while recovery programs showed high rates of recidivism. Opium from Korea and Manchuria supplied the programs (by 1941 Korea had 8,462 hectares in poppies). Unofficially, narcotics continued to be trafficked into China. The profits went into the secret coffers funding Japanese espionage and such dirty tricks as flooding China with counterfeit currency to ruin the enemy's economy.

CONTEMPORARY USE

The Japanese opium monopoly ended with Japan's surrender to the Allies in August 1945. Records of the bureau, along with eyewitness accounts of illicit activities, entered the files of the International Military Tribunal (1946–1948), adding to the reams of damning evidence against the Japanese military government during the Tokyo war crimes trials.

World War II's end also proved that the sake-loving Japanese would indeed fall victim to drug abuse as addicted soldiers returned home. The most famous addict appears in the novel *Shayo* (The Setting Sun) by Dazai Osamu (Tsushima Shuji, 1909–1948), the bad boy of Japanese literature. Dazai's main character, a drug user, heavy drinker, and womanizer, much like the author, became an icon for dispirited postwar youth.

Japan's connection to morphine ended with its empire, and yet many in the defeated army returned home amphetamine-dependent. During the waning years of the war, the military distributed amphetamines to soldiers and support staff alike. At the war's end the drug proved to be a boon to the home population short on food and desperate to rebuild a war-ravaged homeland. A high level of addiction forced officials to address the effects of easy access to the drug in the 1950s, when a zero tolerance policy reminiscent of the 1868 treaty stipulation became law.

In the economic boom years of the 1980s, however, recreational drug use reappeared. Cocaine, marijuana, and assorted psychedelics all became available, but their use was overshadowed by methamphetamine. Called *shabu* in local slang, meth appeals to the workaholic culture of Japan. Its most vulnerable and loyal cohorts are long-distance truckers working grueling schedules, students cramming for exams, and businessmen (salarymen) also keeping long hours, perhaps remaining awake late into the early morning hours over a game of mahjong or poker. Adolescents who abuse solvents often turn to methamphetamine later in their lives. Japanese organized crime (*yakuza*) supplies the illicit market, obtaining its drugs from Thailand, China, Myanmar (the former Burma), or Taiwan. The official approach to addiction is the imprisonment or institutionalization of addicts. One nongovernmental group, the Maryknoll Alcoholic Center/Drug Addiction Recovery Center, treats addiction through self-help. Created by two former addicts who began to hold meetings in places where addicts gather, the organization had grown to 70 facilities by 2006.

Alcohol and tobacco remain the primary addictions in Japan. Japan has a long tradition of brewing sake and distilling *shochu*. The opening of its doors to the West added beer to the national offering. It was only after World War II that a wide range of foreign alcohol became available and popular. Drinking in Japan is a social activity, especially for the workforce for whom after-hours socializing in bars is sometimes typical. Strict traffic laws, an available and extensive public transit system, and the social tolerance of late-night drunks, sometimes intoxicated drinkers help to reduce the fatalities often associated with after-hours drinking. The social nature of drinking, however, means that as the population demographics age, the percentage of drinkers is declining. In the same way, during periods of national stress, such as the Hanshin Earthquake of 1995, alcohol consumption unexpectedly decreased.

Tobacco use began in the 1600s and quickly spread throughout Japanese society, in spite of early government bans. Ornate, small-bowled pipes with long stems adorn woodblock portraits of famous actors and geisha of the Tokugawa period. After Japan was opened to foreign trade, new types of tobacco and methods of smoking were introduced. By 1904 the Japanese government taxed and controlled tobacco products. During the postwar period tobacco products produced via the government monopoly dominated the home market as high tariff barriers made foreign cigarettes a luxury. Under foreign pressure, tariffs eased in 1986, at which time advertising increased the popularity of smoking. Once a government monopoly, in 2000 the Japanese Ministry of Finance owned 67 percent of Japan Tobacco Inc., which controls cigarette production and distribution throughout the nation.

Public awareness of the health risks of cigarettes lowered the number of smokers throughout the 1990s. Once rare, smoke-free areas are sporadically available in the early twenty-first century. Evidence of such changing attitudes may be observed in the glowing cigarettes of the firefly tribe (*hotaru zoku*), those smokers whose wives or colleagues force them to smoke outside. Nevertheless, with male smokers estimated at 52.8 percent in 1999, Japan still has the largest smoking population in the developed world. And, the percentage of female smokers is on the rise. The sale of alcohol and tobacco to youth under the age of 20 is legally banned, but the law has little tangible effect in a nation where open-air vending machines offering both commodities may be found everywhere.

ASSESSMENT

Japan's history of monopoly regulation of addictive substances is bipolar at best. The colonial experience with narcotics demonstrates that an addict population may be reduced as the result of implementing such a system, as was the case in Taiwan, but the potential for easy and large profits can create dangerous failures within it. In the twenty-first century the Japanese government's continued involvement in the tobacco industry hampers the aggressive kind of anti-tobacco campaign that has proven so effective in other developed nations.

See also **Foreign Policy and Drugs, United States; International Drug Supply Systems.**

BIBLIOGRAPHY

Dazai, Osamu. (1956). *The setting sun* (D. Keene, Trans.). Norfolk, CT: J. Laughlin.

Feldman, E. A. (2001). The landscape of Japanese tobacco policy: Law, smoking and social change. *American Journal of Comparative Law, 49,* 679–706.

Higuchi, S. (2007). Japan: Alcohol today. *Addiction, 102,* 1849–1862.

Jennings, J. M. (1997). *The opium empire: Japanese imperialism and drug trafficking in Asia, 1895–1945.* Westport, CT: Praeger.

Journeyman Pictures. (2008). *Japan on speed.* Available from http://www.youtube.com/.

Meyer, K., & Parssinen, T. (2002). *Webs of smoke: Smugglers, warlords, spies and the history of the international drug trade.* Lanham, MD: Rowman & Littlefield.

Reid, R. (2005). Japan: In the shadow of colonialism and Japan Tobacco. In *Globalizing tobacco control: Anti-smoking campaigns in California, France, and Japan* (pp. 201–240). Bloomington: Indiana University Press.

Shimizu, S., Aso, K., Noda, T., Ryukei, S., Kochi, Y., & Yamamoto, N. (2000). Natural disasters and alcohol consumption in a cultural context: The Great Hanshin Earthquake in Japan. *Addiction, 95,* 529–536.

Tobacco and Salt Museum Web site. Available from http://www.jti.co.jp/.

KATHRYN MEYER

JARGON. *See* **Slang Terms in U.S. Drug Cultures.**

JELLINEK MEMORIAL FUND. In 1955 the Jellinek Memorial Fund was established to commemorate E. M. Jellinek (1890–1963) and his great contribution to the field of alcohol studies. A capital fund was developed, and the interest from this fund has been used to provide an annual cash award to a scientist who has made an outstanding contribution to the advancement of knowledge in the alcohol/alcoholism field. The first award was presented in 1968.

Each year the board of directors of the Jellinek Memorial Fund designates the specific area of research for which the award will be made and appoints an Expert Selection Committee to review candidates and recommend an appropriate awardee. The awardee may be selected from any country, the sole criterion being the scientific contribution that the person has made within the selected category. The award is traditionally presented at a major international conference, and, if necessary, travel and accommodation expenses are provided to permit the winner to attend the conference for the presentation.

The following general criteria have been accepted by the board and by previous selection committees as guidelines:

1. The award is to be given to the person deemed to have made, during the preceding years, the greatest scholarly contribution to human knowledge of problems relating to alcohol, in the designated research area.

2. The person selected for the award should be someone who would provide an example and serve as a model for others who might be attracted to work in the field.

3. Only living scientists should be considered for the award.

4. Advanced age or impending retirement would not disqualify someone from candidacy. However, if two or more scientists were considered approximately equal, the one more likely to continue longer in the field would be favored.

5. If the outstanding contribution of a candidate was made more than ten years earlier, consideration for the award would require evidence of the candidate's continuing interest and active participation in alcohol research.

6. Other factors being equal, the person would be favored whose primary identification continued to be in the field.

7. If a member of the Expert Selection Committee is deemed eligible for the Jellinek Award, the chair of the selection committee should consult with the president and request the resignation of the committee member.

8. If a previous award winner becomes a candidate and appears equal to or above all other candidates on the basis of unique new achievements, he or she should not be ruled ineligible. The chair of the selection committee should consult with the president to ensure that the award is for new achievement and determine if he or she is eligible.

9. The award will normally be made to an individual researcher most highly recommended by the selection committee. In special circumstances, if the selection committee recommends two persons of equal and outstanding merit, a joint award may be made to the two.

In 2007, the award was given in the category of epidemiology and population studies to Bridget F. Grant, Ph.D., Chief, Laboratory of Epidemiology and Biometry, Division of Intramural Clinical and Biological Research, at the National Institute on Alcohol Abuse and Alcoholism, National Institutes of Health. Grant received the award for demonstrating leadership in the design, implementation, and analysis of major epidemiologic surveys focused on alcohol and drug use disorders and their relationship to other psychiatric disorders. Other winners have worked in the areas of biological and medical research (2004); social, cultural, and population studies (2005); and behavioral studies (2006).

BIBLIOGRAPHY

Jellinek Memorial Awards. Retrieved April 30, 2008, from http://www.jellinekaward.org.

U.S. Department of Health and Human Services. (2007). *Grant Receives Jellinek Award. NIAAA Newsletter* (NIH Publication No. 07-5346, 2).

H. DAVID ARCHIBALD
REVISED BY LEAH R. ZINDEL (2009)

JEWS AND ALCOHOL. Compared with other religious and ethnic groups, Jewish Americans have an unusual pattern of involvement with alcohol. Studies in the United States consistently find that across religious groups, Jews report the lowest rate of abstinence, with only 6–13 percent being lifetime abstainers (Beigel & Ghertner, 1977; Calahan, 1978; Cochran et al., 1988). Even so, Jews have lower rates of alcohol use disorders. Lifetime rates of alcohol abuse and dependence are approximately 11 percent for Jewish males, compared to 29 percent for non-Jewish males, and 3 percent for Jewish females, compared to 9 percent for non-Jewish females (Levav et al., 1997). Research in the United States and in Israel has found that Jews are less likely to engage in heavy drinking episodes (also known as binge drinking), compared with non-Jews (Luczak et al., 2002; Monteiro & Schuckit, 1989; Neumark et al., 2003).

The etiologic basis is unclear, but researchers hypothesize that these differences result from both psychosocial and biological factors. Early theories concentrated on religious and cultural explanations for the lower levels of alcohol use disorders among Jews; more recent studies have focused on possible biological and genetic influences.

INFLUENCE OF RELIGION

Early theories on the low rates of alcohol use disorders among Jews focused on the symbolic importance of alcohol in the religious (Orthodox) Jewish community. Through the study of Judaism and participation in religious ceremonies, Robert Bales conducted research (1946) that suggested that Jews learn to drink in moderation, and use alcohol primarily for ritualistic purposes. Building on Bales's theory of ritualized drinking, Charles Snyder (1958) hypothesized that as Jews integrated into greater society and became less religious (moved away from or left Orthodoxy), heavy drinking and related problems would increase. To test his ingroup-outgroup theory, Snyder studied nominal religious affiliation and lifetime rates of drinking to intoxication in male Jewish college students and adults. He found the rate of reported intoxication significantly increased with decreased Orthodoxy. Additional support for Snyder's hypothesis comes from a survey of Jewish adults living in Israel. A higher proportion of Orthodox Jews reported being current drinkers, but they drank less frequently and more often for ritualistic purposes than secular Jews (Kandel & Sudit, 1982).

Methodological and interpretive concerns have been raised in reference to these early studies (see Flasher & Maisto, 1984, for a review), and some reports have not found significant relationships between Jewish denomination and drinking variables (Bar-Lev, 1985; Kumpfer & Room, 1967). However, more recent research on college students and general samples continues to support the notion that individuals from more religious denominations report lower rates of intoxication and heavy drinking compared with those from less religious denominations and those who are not Jewish (Hasin et al., 1999; Luczak et al., 2002; Neumark et al., 2001).

Specific religious variables also have been tested in relation to alcohol involvement behaviors. In Jewish American college students, low strength of religious commitment has been linked to heavy alcohol use and negative consequences (Perkins, 1985). In Israel, adherence to Jewish religious requirements was inversely related to frequency of drinking and drunkenness (Aharonovich et al., 2001; Hasin et al., 1999; Rahav et al., 1999). However, religious service attendance did not relate to binge drinking in Jewish American college students (Luczak et al., 2002), nor has it been associated with alcohol use and perceived misuse in Jewish American adults (Cochran et al., 1988). It is possible that some measures (such as service attendance) have more or less salience across religions and thus relate to alcohol variables differently across groups.

INFLUENCE OF CULTURE

It has been hypothesized that Jews are not just a religious group; they are also an ethnic minority with a set of cultural values. Common practices such as eating traditional foods, feeling connected to Israel, engaging in certain customs, singing Jewish songs, and feeling a bond to the Jewish community can be considered components of "Jewish" culture (Langman, 1995). This affiliation also may include religious practices, but it focuses primarily on the solidarity and norms set out by the group. As early as 1947, Donald Glad attempted to summarize this "cultural" view of Jews in relation to alcohol involvement. Although he agreed with Bales (1946) that moderate alcohol use may be learned in the Jewish community through conformity to certain religious customs, he also asserted that other factors, such as group norms, may have a more global influence on alcohol use. He cited factors such as family permissiveness and the strong Jewish sanction against drunkenness as being learned through the affiliation with the group as a whole. He argued that the stigmatization of public inebriety among Jews is captured by the Yiddish expression, "Shikker iz a Goy" (The drunkard is a non-Jew).

In his study of Jewish, Irish, and Protestant male adolescents, Glad (1947) found Jewish adolescents had fewer feelings of guilt regarding drinking, had a younger mean age when they felt permitted to drink, and were more likely to report drinking with their parents. More recent research also has supported the distinction between religious and cultural influences. In a study of drinking patterns among different religious groups in the United States, Freund (1985) found that a liberal family attitude toward moderate drinking was associated with low rates of inebriety regardless of the ritual (religious) reinforcement of sobriety. Greater Jewish cultural identity also has been related to moderate alcohol consumption in young adults (Bar-Lev, 1985), but cultural identity was not associated with binge drinking in college students (Luczak et al., 2002). Taken together, these studies suggest that being a member of the Jewish community and identifying with Jewish culture may protect against heavy alcohol involvement separate from the religious aspects of Judaism.

INFLUENCE OF BIOLOGY AND GENETICS

Along with psychosocial theories, biological explanations have been hypothesized to explain the low level of alcohol problems in Jews. Most self-identified Jews in the United States originate from common eastern European backgrounds (i.e., Ashkenazic Jews) and tend to marry within their religion. Thus, the group is relatively homogeneous and may possess genetic traits that could influence risk for various disorders. In support of this hypothesis, Jews have a significantly lower rate of family history of alcoholism (Monteiro & Schuckit, 1989), one of the strongest and most consistent risk factors for this disorder. The increased risk for alcohol use disorders in people with a family history of alcoholism is mediated by both biological and environmental factors. One important biological factor associated with both family history of alcoholism and vulnerability to alcohol use disorders is an

individual's sensitivity to alcohol (Schuckit, 2000). A low level of response to alcohol has been related to increased risk, and a heightened response has been associated with relative protection from alcohol dependence. In support of a biological theory for the lower rates of alcohol use disorders in Jews, Jewish American male college students were shown to experience more intense reactions to a moderate dose of alcohol than non-Jewish American male college students (Monteiro et al., 1991).

Polymorphisms in several genes encoding isoenzymes involved in alcohol metabolism have been associated with enhanced sensitivity to alcohol and protection against alcohol use disorders (Li, 2000). One such polymorphism of the alcohol dehydrogenase gene *ADH1B*2* has been found in higher prevalence in Jews (32–49%) compared with non-Jewish Caucasians (2–8%). The highest rates of the *ADH1B*2* allele are found in northeast Asians (90–92%), another group with relatively lower rates of alcohol use disorders (Goedde et al., 1992; Neumark et al., 1998; Shea et al., 2001).

Possession of *ADH1B*2* in relation to a variety of drinking variables has been studied in Jews. Jewish men with *ADH1B*2* report more unpleasant alcohol symptoms, such as flushing, nausea, and headaches, compared with men without the allele (Carr et al., 2002). *ADH1B*2* has also been associated with less frequent drinking (including heavy drinking) in college and adult samples of Jewish Americans and in Israeli general and treatment samples (Carr et al., 2002; Hasin et al., 2002a; Luczak et al., 2002; Neumark et al., 1998; Shea et al., 2001; Spivak et al., 2007). Finally, *ADH1B*2* has been related to lower lifetime alcohol dependence severity in a community sample of Israelis (Hasin et al., 2002b). Taken together, these findings suggest the *ADH1B*2* allele has a protective effect on a range of alcohol involvement variables in Jews.

The extant research suggests religious, cultural, and biological factors all contribute to explaining the unusual pattern of alcohol involvement found in Jews. Their relatively low rates of abstinence and alcohol use disorders are likely due to a confluence of factors. How these factors combine and interact should continue to be explored in prospective studies that incorporate biopsychosocial models. Such research will provide important insights into the relationship between Jews and alcohol. However, the research should be tested for generalizability to enable better understanding of the mechanisms by which some individuals might be protected from developing alcohol problems.

See also **Risk Factors for Substance Use, Abuse, and Dependence: Race/Ethnicity; Religion and Drug Use.**

BIBLIOGRAPHY

Aharonovich, E., Hasin, D., Rahav, G., Meydan, J., & Neumark, Y. (2001). Differences in drinking patterns among Ashkenazic and Sephardic Israeli adults. *Journal of Studies on Alcohol, 62,* 301–305.

Bales, R. F. (1946). Cultural differences in rates of alcoholism. *Quarterly Journal of Studies on Alcohol, 6,* 480–499.

Bar-Lev, B. (1985). *A multigenerational study of alcohol behaviors and attitudes among Jews.* Unpublished doctoral dissertation, California School for Professional Psychology, Berkeley.

Beigel, A., & Ghertner, S. (1977). Toward a social model: An assessment of social factors which influence problem drinking and its treatment. In B. Kissin & H. Begleiter (Eds.), *Treatment and rehabilitation of the chronic alcoholic* (pp. 197–233). New York: Plenum Press.

Cahalan, D. (1978). Subcultural differences in drinking behavior in the U.S. national survey and selected European studies. In P. E. Nathan, G. A. Marlatt, & T. Lorberg (Eds.), *Alcoholism: New directions in behavioral research and treatment* (pp. 235–253). New York: Plenum Press.

Carr, L. G., Foroud, T., Stewart, T., Castellucio, P., Edenberg, H. J., & Li, T.-K. (2002). Influence of ADH1B polymorphism on alcohol use and its subjective effects in a Jewish population. *American Journal of Medical Genetics, 112,* 138–143.

Cochran, J. K., Beeghley, L., & Bock, E. W. (1988). Religiosity and alcohol behavior: An exploration of reference group theory. *Sociological Forum, 3*(2), 257–277.

Flasher, L. V., & Maisto, S. A. (1984). A review of theory and research on drinking patterns among Jews. *The Journal of Nervous and Mental Disease, 172*(10), 596–603.

Freund, P. J. (1985). Polish-American drinking: Continuity and change. In L. A. Bennett & G. M. Ames (Eds.), *The American experience with alcohol: Contrasting cultural perspectives* (pp. 77–92). New York: Plenum Press.

Glad, D. D. (1947). Attitudes and experiences of American-Jewish and American-Irish male youth as related to differences in adult rates of inebriety. *Journal of Studies on Alcohol, 8,* 406–472.

Goedde, H. W., Agarwal, D. P., Fritze, G., Meier-Tackmann, D., Singh, S., Beckmann, G., et al. (1992). Distribution of ADH2 and ALDH2 genotypes in different populations. *Human Genetics, 88,* 344–346.

Hasin, D., Rahav, G., Meydan, J., & Neumark, Y. (1999). The drinking of earlier and more recent Russian immigrants to Israel: Comparison to other Israelis. *Journal of Substance Abuse, 10*(4), 341–353.

Hasin, D., Aharonovich, E., Liu, X., Mamman, Z., Matseoane, K., Carr, L., et al. (2002a). Alcohol and ADH2 in Israel: Ashkenazis, Sephardics, and recent Russian immigrants. *American Journal of Psychiatry, 159*(8), 1432–1434.

Hasin, D., Aharonovich, E., Liu, X., Mamman, Z., Matseoane, K., Carr, L., et al. (2002b). Alcohol dependence symptoms and alcohol dehydrogenase 2 polymorphisms: Israeli Ashkenazis, Sephardics, and recent Russian immigrants. *Alcoholism: Clinical and Experimental Research, 26*(9), 1315–1321.

Kandel, D. B., & Sudit, M. (1982). Drinking practices among urban adults in Israel. *Journal of Studies on Alcohol, 43*(1), 1–16.

Kumpfer, G., & Room, R. (1967). Drinking patterns and attitudes of Irish, Jewish and white Protestant American men. *Quarterly Journal of Studies on Alcohol, 19,* 676–699.

Langman, P. F. (1995). Including Jews in multiculturalism. *Journal of Multicultural Counseling and Development, 23,* 222–236.

Levav, I., Kohn, R., Golding, J. M., & Weissman, M. M. (1997). Vulnerability of Jews to affective disorders. *American Journal of Psychiatry, 154*(7), 941–947.

Li, T.-K. (2000). Pharmacogenetics of responses to alcohol and genes that influence alcohol drinking. *Journal of Studies on Alcohol, 61,* 5–12.

Luczak, S. E., Shea, S. H., Carr, L. G., Li, T.-K., & Wall, T. L. (2002). Binge drinking in Jewish and non-Jewish white college students. *Alcoholism: Clinical and Experimental Research, 12,* 1773–1778.

Monteiro, M. G., & Schuckit, M. A. (1989). Alcohol, drug, and mental health problems among Jewish and Christian men at a university. *American Journal of Drug & Alcohol Abuse, 15*(4), 403–412.

Monteiro, M. G., Klein, J. L., & Schuckit, M. A. (1991). High levels of sensitivity to alcohol in young adult Jewish men: A pilot study. *Journal of Studies on Alcohol, 52*(5), 464–469.

Neumark, Y. D., Friedlander, Y., Thomasson, H. R., & Li, T.-K. (1998). Association of the ADH2*2 allele with reduced ethanol consumption in Jewish men in Israel. *Journal of Studies on Alcohol, 59,* 133–139.

Neumark, Y. D., Rahav, G., Teichman, M., & Hasin, D. (2001). Alcohol drinking patterns among Jewish and

Arab men and women in Israel. *Journal of Studies on Alcohol, 62,* 443–447.

Neumark, Y. D., Rahav, G., & Jaffe, D. H. (2003). Socio-economic status and binge drinking in Israel. *Drug and Alcohol Dependence, 69*(1), 15–21.

Perkins, H. W. (1985). Religious traditions, parents, and peers as determinants of alcohol and drug use among college students. *Review of Religious Research, 27,* 15–31.

Rahav, G., Hasin, D., & Paykin, A. (1999). Drinking patterns of recent Russian immigrants and other Israelis: 1995 national survey results. *American Journal of Public Health, 89*(8), 1212–1216.

Schuckit, M. A. (2000). Biological phenotypes associated with individuals at high risk for developing alcohol-related disorders: Part 2. *Addiction Biology, 5,* 23–36.

Shea, S. H., Wall, T. L., Carr, L. G., & Li, T.-K. (2001). ADH2 and alcohol-related phenotypes in Ashkenazic Jewish American college students. *Behavior Genetics, 31*(2), 231–239.

Snyder, C. R. (1958). *Alcohol and the Jews: A cultural study of drinking and sobriety.* Glencoe, IL: The Free Press.

Spivak, B., Frisch, A., Maman, Z., Aharonovich, E., Alderson, D., Carr, L. G., et al. (2007). Effect of ADH1B genotype on alcohol consumption in young Israeli Jews. *Alcoholism: Clinical and Experimental Research, 31*(8), 1297–1301.

Shoshana H. Shea
Susan E. Luczak
Tamara L. Wall

Figure 1. Jimsonweed. Illustration by GGS Information Services. Gale, Cengage Learning

JIMSONWEED. Jimsonweed is a tall, coarse, poisonous plant that flowers, produces seed, and dies in one year. It belongs to the nightshade family (Solanaceae), and has foul-smelling leaves and large white or violet trumpet-shaped flowers. It produces round, prickly fruits. Jimsonweed (*Datura stramonium*) grows in several parts of the world. A strong intoxicant made from this plant was used by the woodland tribes of eastern North America. The plant was also used as an ingredient of wysoccan, an intoxicant employed in the puberty rites of Native Americans in what is now Virginia. Indeed, the name Jimson is another form of Jamestown, the English colony founded in Virginia in 1607.

Smoke from burning jimsonweed was inhaled to relieve symptoms of asthma in India, and cigarettes containing jimsonweed have also been used for the same purpose.

As in other members of the Solanaceae family, the mind-altering substances are tropane alkaloids, and the seeds and leaves contain up to 0.4 percent of these compounds. The principal alkaloid found in jimsonweed (also found in belladonna) is atropine. Atropine widens the pupils of the eyes, helps stop muscular spasms, lessens pain, and reduces bodily secretions. Large to toxic doses of atropine result in restlessness, irritability, disorientation, hallucinations, and delirium.

See also **Plants, Drugs From.**

BIBLIOGRAPHY

Hanson, G. R., Venturelli, P. J., & Fleckenstein, A. E. (2005). CNS depressants: Sedative-hypnotics. In *Drugs and Society.* Sudbury, MA: Jones & Bartlett Publishers.

Houghton, P. J., & Bisset, N. G. (1985). Drugs of ethno-origin. In D. C. Howell (Ed.), *Drugs in central nervous system disorders.* New York: Marcel Dekker.

Lewis, W. H. (2005). *Medical botany: Plants affecting human health.* Hoboken, NJ: John Wiley & Sons.

Robert Zaczek
Revised by James T. McDonough Jr. (2001)

KAVA. Kava is a drink prepared from the root of the Australasian pepper shrub *Piper methysticum*. The word *kava*, which is Polynesian for bitter, pungent, is given to the drink because of its strong peppery taste. Several variations of this drink were once used widely as social intoxicants in the islands of the South Pacific, particularly Fiji. The quality of the drink improves with the age of the root, and the roots are generally at least four years old before they are used. After the root is cut and crushed or grated, the active components are extracted by soaking the preparation in water.

Common effects of kava include general muscular relaxation, euphoria, and loss of fatigue. Visual and auditory effects are also common. In large quantities kava can induce muscular incoordination and ultimately stupor.

While no alkaloids or glycosides have been found in kava, several aromatically substituted α-pyrones, including kawain, dihydrokawain, methysticin, and yangonin, have been isolated from the extracted root. Other as-yet-unidentified components of kava may also be important in the effects of the drink.

See also **Plants, Drugs From.**

BIBLIOGRAPHY

Houghton, P. J., & Bisset, N. G. (1985). Drugs of ethno-origin. In D. C. Howell (Ed.), *Drugs in central nervous system disorders*. New York: Marcel Dekker.

Singh, Y. N. (2007). *Kava: From ethnology to pharmacology*. New York: Taylor & Francis.

ROBERT ZACZEK

KENYA. Psychoactive substances in Kenya are a source of concern both nationally, due to a perceived rise in consumption levels, and internationally, as Kenya has become a significant entrepôt, or distribution center, in global trafficking networks (International Narcotics Control Board, 2007). Kenyan psychoactive substances include fermented beverages, khat (known as *miraa* in Kenya), cannabis, and tobacco (whose usage can be traced back centuries), as well as distilled spirits, heroin, cocaine, solvents, and Mandrax (methaqualone), introduced much more recently. These substances are considered in this essay; tea and coffee—while stimulants and of great economic importance to the country—are beyond the present entry's scope.

ALCOHOLIC DRINKS

By far the most commonly consumed substances in Kenya are alcoholic drinks—brews made from grains, fruits, and honey are as widely consumed as ever, especially in rural regions. Age-old drinks include those brewed from millet, sorghum, honey, and sugarcane as well as palm wine (made from fermented palm sap), a popular beverage on the coast. Idealized accounts of traditional consumption report that such drinks were restricted to male elders who would gather round the communal beer pot each with their own straw. Such accounts of past drinking as socially integrative are compared with a perceived lack of control in present day drinking practices (Willis, 2002).

341

During much of the colonial era, bottled beer and spirits were legally restricted to Europeans. Such restrictions lasted until 1947, after which consumption of bottled beer by the African population grew massively, along with the East African brewery industry. While traditional brews became the drink of the rural areas, bottled beers were associated with urban sophistication and modernity. Post-independence, advertisers even marketed bottled beer as the drink of a successful nation. Opposition and ambivalence to all types of alcohol exists in the early twenty-first century, but the greatest concern is for *chang'aa*, an illicitly distilled spirit available cheaply in most towns and villages. This drink, distilled using homemade equipment, is reportedly often adulterated with pure ethanol to strengthen the already heady liquor.

KHAT

Khat consists of the stimulant stems and leaves of *Catha edulis*, a tree indigenous to forests throughout Kenya but is also cultivated in several areas, the most important being the Nyambene Hills district northeast of Mount Kenya (Carrier, 2007). This mountain range is home to the Meru, whose economy is greatly dependent upon khat. Explorers in the late nineteenth century reported the keen chewing of khat by Meru elders (Neumann, 1898), and by that time the crop was already cultivated and exchanged. The growth of nearby Isiolo, with its khat-chewing Somali residents, spurred on farming and trade and, by the mid-twentieth century, khat was sold as far afield as Nairobi and the coast, despite attempts by the British to restrict it.

Khat is incorporated into many local ceremonies—for example, in the Nyambenes a specially packaged bundle of khat is used in brideprice negotiations—and is now intertwined with Meru and Somali identity. Its consumption is also associated with coastal Swahili, Muslims more generally, and has been absorbed into a pan-ethnic youth culture. Much khat chewing takes place in leisure contexts, but its stimulating properties—its main active constituent, *cathinone*, has the effect of a mild amphetamine—are also used by nightwatchmen, drivers, and students in work contexts (Zaghloul, Abdalla, El Gammal, & Moselhy, 2003). Consumption is linked to insomnia, and sedatives such as *rohypnol* and *piriton* are used by some to counter its effects; others claim drinking milk or beer is effective in inducing sleep.

Khat is exported, much of it being flown to Somalia, Europe, or North America for consumers among the Somali diaspora. This international trade flourishes despite its illegal status in many countries. There is vigorous debate in Kenya as to the social and health impacts of the substance and if it should be banned. However, such is its economic importance for farmers and traders throughout the country as well as its value as a foreign exchange earner that it seems immune to legal restriction.

TOBACCO

While not indigenous to East Africa, tobacco smoking, chewing, and sniffing had already penetrated the interior of the region long before British rule was established, most likely brought by Spanish and Portuguese sailors in the late sixteenth or early seventeenth centuries. Certainly by the late nineteenth century, explorers, such as Neumann (1898), were often offered tobacco by groups encountered far from the coast. The crop became highly commercialized during the twentieth century, and today smallholders in several regions of the country supply British American tobacco with sufficient quantities to satisfy the Kenyan demand for cigarettes, and for export. Growing tobacco has been profitable for some farmers (see Heald, 1991 and 1999 on tobacco farmers in Kuria district), but there is much ambivalence about the crop and its consumption. Antismoking campaigns have begun in earnest, and in 2007 Parliament passed a Tobacco Control Act regulating manufacture and sale. It is also raising awareness of tobacco's dangers through explicit health warnings on packets. In addition, in Nairobi, Mombasa, and Nakuru local bylaws now restrict smoking in public places. Evidence shows that annual per capita cigarette consumption has fallen since the late 1980s, although prevalence is still high according to an online report by the World Health Organization (2003). As antismoking campaigns intensify, there are concerns that falling sales might affect thousands of farmers reliant on tobacco unless they receive support to grow alternative crops.

CANNABIS

Cannabis in East Africa has not yet been studied as thoroughly as alcohol or khat, but even so it has a long history in the area. Cannabis is called *bangi* and may have been introduced through centuries-old Indian Ocean trade links. Like khat, cannabis is consumed both in leisure and work contexts; people believe it is useful when working at arduous physical tasks. Unlike khat, cannabis is illegal; possession and supply are subject to prison terms and hefty fines, so cultivation is hidden. Often the crop is grown among sugarcane in Western Kenya or deep within the forests on Mount Kenya. Indeed, there is concern at the destruction of forest to make way for cannabis. The coast also has a significant number of plantations. Cannabis is inexpensive in Kenya and has become a commercially significant crop with a large local market. Profit can be made on the coast where there is much demand for cannabis from Western tourists. Regarding exports, the United Nations Office of Drug Control and Crime Prevention (UNODCCP) reported in 1999 that up to 50 percent of Kenyan-produced cannabis is exported to neighboring countries and Europe.

HEROIN

Heroin use in Kenya first became apparent in the 1980s, especially in Nairobi and on the coast (Beckerleg, Telfer, & Sadiq, 2006). Some connect its spread to tourism, especially in towns such as Malindi, where a tourist boom in the 1980s increased the number of European visitors requesting the drug and brought locals into contact with it. Originally heroin was consumed by inhaling the vapor of "brown sugar," but in the late 1990s "white crest" appeared on the market, a variety from Thailand that is injected. Thus injecting became more common, a practice especially dangerous given the prevalence of HIV. A 2005 survey of 336 heroin users in Nairobi found "that 44.9% were, or had been, injectors" and that over half the current injectors were HIV positive (Beckerleg, Telfer, & Hundt, 2005, p. 1).

The growth of heroin use on the coast has been alarming and has spurred the creation of the Omari project in Watamu to provide support for those wishing to give up heroin. Much outside attention has focused on Kenya and heroin not because of consumption within the country, but more for its role as an entrepôt in transnational trafficking networks. Traffickers taking Southeast- and Southwest-Asian heroin to Europe have targeted the Mombasa port and the Nairobi international airport as relatively safe nodes in such networks. There have been some attempts to cultivate opium

poppies in Kenya, and in October 1989 police destroyed a plantation of 30,000 plants (United Nations Office of Drug Control and Crime Prevention, 1999, p. 21).

OTHER SUBSTANCES

As with heroin, Kenya serves as an entrepôt for cocaine and methaqualone (Mandrax), a sedative popular in South Africa. There are reports that cocaine is used by wealthy students in large Kenyan towns and that Mandrax is also used by Kenyan students; however, these two substances seem to pass through Kenya en route to Europe, in the case of cocaine (smuggled initially from South America), and to South Africa, in the case of Mandrax (smuggled initially from India). Some laboratories have started producing the substance in Kenya for sale in South Africa. One such factory was discovered in 2007, according to a report by the Kenya Broadcasting Corporation.

Of great concern is the inhalation of solvents by street children, and the sight of young children clutching plastic bottles containing glue is tragically common in urban areas. Of less concern is the consumption of betel leaf/areca nut. This chewable combination has been produced on the coast for centuries and, although still mostly consumed by Asians and Arabs, its use has spread to the African population—it is sold in large towns throughout the country. It is often consumed in combination with tobacco paste, so betel/areca nut use is linked to oral cancer (Warnakulasiriya, Trivedy, & Peters, 2002). Small sachets of Indian-produced *gutka* (containing areca nut, chewing tobacco, and flavoring) are also available. In 1999 UNODCCP reported amphetamine usage in Kenya, although it is hard to gauge the scale of its trade and use.

DRUGS REGULATIONS, POLICIES, AND FEARS

The legal status of the above substances in Kenya varies. Khat is available without restrictions, while alcohol in the form of *chang'aa* is illegal, although its trade still flourishes. Cannabis, heroin, cocaine, and Mandrax are illegal and subject to severe penalties introduced by the Narcotic Drugs and Psychotic Substances (Control) Act of 1994. There is an Anti-Narcotics Unit within the police force to enforce current legislation. Cannabis-related arrests are by far the most prosecuted offenses, and often number around 4,000 annually (UNODCCP, 1999, p. 98). The media have reported a number of highly publicized seizures of heroin and cocaine since the late 1990s, but high levels of corruption are frustrating the fight against trafficking (Mgendi, 1998).

The 1994 act also provided for the establishment of treatment and rehabilitation centers. While nongovernmental organizations run such programs as the Omari Project on the coast, the Kenyan government itself has established a drug rehabilitation unit in Mathari Hospital, Nairobi. Also, a parastatal organization called *The National Campaign Against Drug Abuse* (NACADA) leads educational initiatives in schools and universities and voices concerns over drug use through the Kenyan media. The greatest worry is a rise in consumption by Kenyan youth, and a 2003 NACADA report is titled "Youth in Peril."

The notion that youth are especially at risk from substance use is not new in Kenya and reflects the concern that younger generations are badly affected by rises in poverty, unemployment, HIV, and other pressing factors: The UNODCCP report of 1999 links drug use by Kenyan youth to these socioeconomic factors. Many health workers, religious leaders, teachers, and community leaders express strong fears that drug use will continue to worsen (UNODCCP 1999, p. 35). However, much commentary on substance use in Kenya is perforce rather impressionistic given that scant research—quantitative or qualitative—has been conducted so far. It is hoped that future research will elucidate the situation further and assist in developing policies and treatment facilities sensitive to Kenya's needs.

See also **Africa; Foreign Policy and Drugs, United States; International Drug Supply Systems; Nigeria; South Africa.**

BIBLIOGRAPHY

Acholla, S. (2007, October 4). *Police release identities of Mandrax suspects.* Kenya Broadcasting Corporation. Available from http://www.kbc.co.ke/.

Beckerleg, S., Telfer, M., & Hundt, G. L. (2005). The rise of injecting drug use in East Africa: A case study from Kenya. *Harm Reduction Journal 2*(12). Available from http://www.harmreductionjournal.com/.

Beckerleg, S., Telfer, M., & Sadiq, A. (2006). A rapid assessment of heroin use in Mombasa, Kenya. *Substance Use and Misuse 41*(6–7), 1029–1044.

Carrier, N. (2007). *Kenyan khat: The social life of a stimulant.* Leiden, The Netherlands: Brill.

Heald, S. (1991). Tobacco, time, and the household economy in two Kenyan societies: The Teso and the Kuria. *Comparative Studies in Society and History, 33*(1), 130–157.

Heald, S. (1999). Agricultural intensification and the decline of pastoralism: A Kenyan case study. *Africa, 69*(2), 213–237.

International Narcotics Control Board. (2007). *Annual Report.* Vienna: United Nations Information Service.

Mgendi, C. (1998). Corruption and drugs in Kenya. In United Nations, *Africa Recovery* (vol. 12, no. 1; p. 9). New York: Author.

Neumann, A. H. (1898). *Elephant hunting in East Equatorial Africa.* London: Rowland Ward.

United Nations Office of Drug Control and Crime Prevention. (1999). *The drug nexus in Africa.* Studies on Drugs and Crime. (monograph series issue number 1). New York: United Nations.

Waranakulasiriya, S., Trivedy, C., & Peters, T. J. (2002). Areca nut use: An independent risk factor for oral cancer. *British Medical Journal, 324*(7341), 799–800.

Willis, J. (2002). *Potent brews: A social history of alcohol in East Africa 1850–1999.* Oxford: James Currey.

World Health Organization. (2003). *Tobacco control country profiles.* Available from http://www.who.int/.

Zaghloul, A., Abdalla, A., El Gammal, H., & Moselhy, H. (2003). The consequences of khat use: A review of literature. *European Journal of Psychiatry, 17*(2), 77–86.

NEIL CARRIER

KHAT. *Catha edulis*, commonly known as khat, qat, chat, or miraa, is a tree or shrub that grows wild across highland areas of much of Africa and Western Asia, at altitudes of between 5,000 and 6,500 feet above sea level. Wild khat trees can grow as high as eighty feet in an equatorial climate, although the farmed variety is kept at around twenty feet with constant pruning. Cultivation and use of khat go back for centuries, and its use is deeply embedded in the cultures of Yemen, Ethiopia, and parts of Kenya.

The harvested commodity varies from region to region as to what is considered edible and how it is presented. Either the leaves or tender stems from the khat shrub are worked into a wad in the cheek

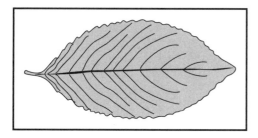

Figure 1. Khat leaf. ILLUSTRATION BY GGS INFORMATION SERVICES. GALE, CENGAGE LEARNING

of the consumer. These are masticated over the course of the khat session, lasting between two and eight hours depending on context and occasion. To neutralize the bitter taste of khat, sweet drinks are imbibed, traditionally tea, but increasingly carbonated drinks. In most settings in Ethiopia, Somalia, and Kenya, khat chewing has become associated with nicotine consumption either with cigarettes or by using hubbly bubblies (a colloquial name for hookah).

The legal status of khat varies around the world and is subject to review and revision by the governments often acting on the advice of the World Health Organization and the UN Office on Drugs and Crime. Khat is a legal substance in Yemen, Ethiopia, Djibouti, Kenya, and Uganda, but it is illegal in Tanzania and Rwanda. It is imported into Somalia daily but has been blamed for fueling the war and chaos that bedevils that country. It is legal in the U.K. and the Netherlands but is an illicit substance in the United States and Canada.

HISTORY

The first known reference to khat in Ethiopia is in the fourteenth-century chronicle of the Ethiopian emperor Amde Zion, in which the Sultan of Ifat is quoted as saying: "I will take up my residence at Mar'ade, the capital of his [Amde Zion's] kingdom and I will plant chat [khat] there because the Muslims love the plant" (Gebissa, 2004). Since about 1400 CE in the city of Harar, the capital of the Hararge region of Ethiopia, Islamic leaders have consumed khat leaves to stay awake during Ramadan. Merchants used it to facilitate long-distance travel, and farmers chewed it regularly throughout the day. Production and consumption were originally limited to Muslims, but over the centuries khat gained an important place in rituals of piety

in Islamic observance, particularly in the Hararge region. For centuries it has been a standard practice for those who participated in religious ceremonies held at the Muslim shrines to spend long hours of the day and night chewing khat while reciting passages from the Holy Qur'an and praying. In Ethiopia some devout Muslims even consider khat holy, refer to it as the flower of paradise, and often offer prayers before they begin to chew it. Although the origins of khat consumption are sometimes linked to the need for Islamic scholars in the Hararge region of Ethiopia to stay awake, the use of khat by Muslims is a source of controversy.

Linguistic evidence points to Yemen as the earliest region to use *Catha edulis* (Ethiopian *chat* is derived from Yemeni *qat*), although Ethiopian documents record dates for khat being sent from Harar between the thirteenth and fifteenth centuries, and the Yemeni records indicate a later introduction. Khat is mentioned by al-Miswari of Ta'izz in the thirteenth century, but he may have been referring to a tea made from khat leaves. Khat is absent from a plant register drawn up for the king of Yemen in about 1271, and Ibn Ibn Battuta, the great traveler, failed to spot it in 1330. It is most likely that khat was introduced to Yemen by Sufi travelers in the late fourteenth century or the early fifteenth century. By the sixteenth century khat was well established in Yemeni religious and legal texts. The theological debate dates from the fifteenth and sixteenth centuries, when arguments focused on the degree to which the plant could be considered an intoxicant and should be placed in the category of *haram* (forbidden) substances, along with alcohol and hashish. Some scholars argued that analogous to wine, khat has consciousness-altering properties, and because it is on the basis of such properties that alcohol was forbidden by the prophet, khat too should be forbidden. However, the prevailing legal ruling in Yemen in modern times has been the more literal Islamic interpretation, that because it was not explicitly mentioned in the Qur'an it should not be forbidden.

Khat, more often known as miraa in Kenya, has been used for centuries in part of the Nyambene Hills within the Meru district. Khat from particularly old trees has long been used by the Meru clans of Igembe and Tigania for ceremonial presentation in brideprice negotiations, requests to elders for

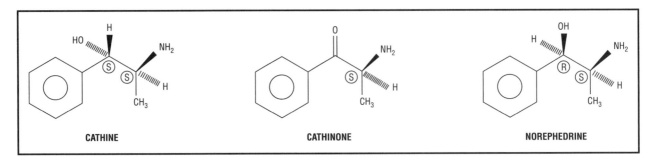

Figure 2. Structure of khatamines. Cathine (S,S(+)phenylpropanolamine or (+)norpseudoephedrine), cathinone (S(−)alphaaminopropiophenone) and norephedrine (R,S(−)phenylpropanolamine). In an analysis of twenty-two khat samples of different origin, the average concentration of these alkaloids in 100 grams of fresh khat were found to be 120 milligrams, 36 milligrams, and 8 milligrams, respectively. (Geisshüsler & Brenneisen, 1987). Illustration by GGS Information Services. Gale, Cengage Learning

circumcision to proceed, and in peacemaking. Farmers also chew a few stems as they work, but most still do not indulge in heavy khat consumption. Most substance-related problems are only indirectly related to khat, in that the farmers and merchants profiting from this lucrative export often convert a good part of their earnings into excessive alcohol consumption.

A mixed agricultural system that now has khat as its main cash crop was developed by the Igembe and Tigania clans who, from the nineteenth century, marketed and distributed khat to an ever widening market, first within Kenya and then beyond. From the mid-twentieth century, Yemeni and Somali Kenya citizens scattered throughout the country provided a ready market for khat from the Nyambene Hills. As consumption spread to different districts and ethnic groups, a khat subculture and associated language to describe khat and its effects developed. Khat has come to dominate daily life among many Somalis living in cities, rural areas, and refugee camps. As chewing spread, local names for khat such as murungi, veve, and gomba emerged. At the coast Yemenis introduced miraa-chewing to the Swahili whom they lived among and intermarried with. Yet, as khat consumption spreads, controversy about its use continues to grow. Many Kenyan government and civil society organizations consider khat to be a harmful substance and claim that it exacerbated the civil war of the 1990s in Somalia and impedes development in the ethnic-Somali dominated area of North Eastern Province.

PHARMACOLOGY

Khat has been known in the West for over two hundred years after samples of the plant were collected in Yemen by the Swedish botanist, Pehr Forsskal (1732–1763). Forsskal identified and classified khat as *Catha edulis* and made the first detailed botanical description of this evergreen shrub of the Celastraceae family.

The pharmacological study of the properties of *Catha edulis* dates back to 1887 when the alkaloid cathine, or d-norpseudoephedrine, was identified as the first active ingredient. The main active ingredient, cathinone, was not isolated until the 1970s. In fresh leaves cathinone combines with a second alkaloid of cathine, norpseudoephedrine, and several other alkaloids, tannins, and other ingredients. Cathinone is highly volatile and breaks down rapidly in leaves and stems once twigs are cut from the live plant.

The constituent mainly responsible for the stimulant qualities and the dependence-producing effects of khat is cathinone. This alkaloid must be considered a natural amphetamine, as the two substances have the same mechanism of action. However, cathinone has a half-life of only one and a half hours, whereas amphetamine is much longer. Because cathinone is absorbed gradually from the leaves during chewing and is inactivated in the body rather rapidly, the pharmacological effects of khat are usually limited.

EFFECTS

Khat stimulates the central nervous system, resulting in a state of mild euphoria and excitement, often accompanied by talkativeness. Chewers report an immediate emotional effect of euphoria, which increases the sense of well-being and can facilitate social interaction. This initial euphoria is followed by a quieter, more introspective mood. This is the phase celebrated in Arabic poetry, and the period when musicians receive their inspiration. Contemplation often turns melancholy. It is at this point that a communal khat-chewing session usually breaks up as the chewers disperse. Experienced chewers know that the melancholic phase is typical and are able to adjust their mood so that negative thoughts and feelings are minimized or eliminated. Some chronic users have been found to carry on chewing in order to postpone the comedown. There are suggestions that the effect of khat is largely conditioned by the context, the company, and the expectations of the user, known among drug researchers as the *set* and *setting*.

Chewing khat tends to cause insomnia. Sleeplessness is sometimes the desired effect, for example, in Ethiopia for staying awake and reading the Qur'an. Across East Africa it is used as a concentration aid by university students, truck drivers, and night watchmen. Africans chew to remain alert; in Uganda night-clubbers use khat to help them dance all night. Those khat consumers who want to sleep may resort to other substances to counter the stimulant properties of khat. Hence, many consumers in Uganda choose alcohol after chewing, whereas many Somalis resort to Valium, which is cheap and easily available on the black market in many East African countries.

Like all stimulants, khat disrupts sleep patterns and proves exhausting after repeated use. The disturbances of natural bodily, as well as social, rhythms can cause disturbances in the mental well-being and social adjustment of some users. For most users, the recovery phase is fairly benign, particularly when compared to that of other drugs. Individual chewers learn to identify the specific effects khat has on them, and they regulate their use to achieve the desired effects. Nevertheless, the pleasurable effects of chewing appear to be broadly similar among chewers regardless of location or culture. Hence, the term *kayf* expresses the experience of the khat-high in Yemen, while in Kenya, Somalia, and Uganda the term *handas* with the same meaning is widely used to describe similar effects. These pleasurable effects are not generally considered by researchers to lead to physical dependence, although there is some evidence

of the problems typically associated with drug addiction; for example, general malaise, trembling, and bad dreams appear to be physiological responses to drug deprivation. These symptoms suggest that a mild form of physiological dependence does result from extremely heavy use.

Nevertheless, most khat users can come off the substance and find relief from unpleasant side effects after short periods of abstinence. In Yemen, Ethiopia, and parts of Kenya, traditional cultures of consumption have set parameters for safe and moderate use. These checks on harmful consumption patterns are absent in settings in which new consumers have taken up recreational chewing and often mix khat with alcohol or cannabis. In areas in which khat use is newer, for example, in East Africa or in the wider Somali diaspora, rituals and customs associated with chewing have not as of 2008 been elaborated and established. The pattern of khat use in most parts of Kenya and Uganda is similar to that in the U.K., in that it is an entirely secular form of recreation with no root in local culture. Language and ceremony are borrowed from older cultures of use and evoke, in the case of Somalis, a tradition that is in fact very recent. There is no religious or ritual dimension to use, and the khat chewing session is not integrated into social life but a semi-clandestine addition to it. It is possible that without such culturally embedded controls on consumption as were developed in Yemen and Ethiopia centuries ago, excessive use might trigger a range of psychiatric conditions.

Chronic khat use can lead to high levels of intoxication that may trigger disorders. These include observed loss of appetite, mood swings, anxiety, insomnia, irritability, and depression. Links between khat use and paranoid psychosis and hypomanic illness with grandiose delusions have been reported from case studies in the United Kingdom as well as Somalia and Kenya. International research on the implications of khat use for mental health was ongoing as of 2008. Studies abound linking khat use with a range of adverse conditions, yet none has been based on sufficiently large sample populations or has been able to discount confounding factors, such as post-traumatic shock and cultural dislocation among Somali refugees, to allow for firm conclusions to be drawn either way. Many psychiatrists and mental health

Khat is said to produce a feeling of euphoria when chewed. AP Images.

practitioners working in the field agree, however, that khat is a powerful trigger for a range of conditions. What remains to be determined are dosage, usage patterns, contributing factors, and individual predisposition.

The most harmful effects of khat chewing are related to the budgets of poor people who cannot afford to buy the substance as well as care properly for their families. The point that khat use is detrimental to family life and finances is emphasized by Somali groups living in the diaspora. In addition, detractors of khat attribute its use to increases in idleness, a decline in morals, female prostitution, criminality among male youth, and the erosion of the family.

KHAT USE IN EUROPE AND NORTH AMERICA
One striking aspect of the khat industry that developed in the twentieth century is its remarkable

distribution system that links producer and consumer. The need for speed arises because cathinone degrades within forty-eight hours of being picked from the tree or bush. This volatility is well known to producers and consumers and has shaped the development of the trade, so that rapid transportation has defined the geographical spread of markets. Khat must and does reach consumers rapidly and is transported by road and air to East African and Yemeni cities and remote hamlets. Hence, during the late twentieth century and into the new millennium khat use continued to spread throughout East Africa, in Kenya, Uganda, Rwanda, and Tanzania, where it is the drug of choice for many youth.

Somalis live all over East Africa as long-term migrants and as refugees since the war of the early 1990s. However, since that war and continuing civil unrest and the resulting dispersal of Somalis across the world, khat has been thrust into the limelight. Khat is popularly portrayed as a dangerous substance in films such as *Blackhawk Down* (2001) and is decried, particularly by the U.S. authorities, as destructive of the Somali social fabric. Yet, khat consumption is a relatively recent cultural phenomenon for most Somalis.

Khat is also exported from Kenya, Ethiopia, and Yemen to migrants living in Europe and in North America. Hence, between 1988 and 2008 khat became a global commodity, openly on sale in London, Manchester, and Amsterdam, and covertly in New York, Toronto, Chicago, and Sydney. The development of these markets has occurred concurrently with the influx of large numbers of Somali refugees.

See also **Amphetamine.**

BIBLIOGRAPHY

Advisory Council on the Misuse of Drugs. (2005). *Khat (Qat): Assessment of risk to individuals and communities in the UK*. London: Author.

Anderson D. M., Beckerleg, S., Hailu, D., & Klein, A. (2007). *The khat controversy: Stimulating the drugs debate*. Oxford: Berg.

Beckerleg, S. (2006). What harm? East African perspectives on Khat. *African Affairs, 105*(419), 219–241.

Carothers, J. C. (1945). Miraa as a cause of insanity. *East African Medical Journal, 22,* 4–6.

Carrier, N. (2005). Miraa is cool: The cultural importance of miraa (khat) for Tigania and Igembe youth in Kenya. *Journal of African Cultural Studies, 17*(2), 201–218.

Carrier, N. (2005b). The need for speed: Contrasting time-frames in the social life of Kenyan miraa. *Africa, 75*(4), 539–558.

Gebissa, E. (2004). *Leaf of Allah: Khat & agricultural transformation in Harerge, Ethiopia, 1875–1991*. Oxford: James Currey.

Goldsmith, P. (1994). *Symbiosis and transformation in Kenya's Mere district*. Unpublished doctoral dissertation, University of Florida at Gainesville.

Goldsmith, P. (1997) The Somali Impact on Kenya, 1990–1993: The view from the camps. In H. M. Adam & R. Ford (Eds.), *Mending rips in the sky: Options for Somali communities in the 21st century* (pp. 461–483). Lawrenceville, NJ, and Asmara, Eritrea: Red Sea Press.

Griffiths, P. (1998). *Qat use in London: A study of qat use among a sample of Somalis living in London*. London: Drugs Prevention Initiative, Home Office.

Kalix, P. (1987). Khat: Scientific knowledge and policy issues. *British Journal of Addiction, 82,* 47–53.

Kalix, P. (1990). Pharmacological properties of the stimulant khat. *Pharmacology and Therapeutics, 48,* 397–416.

Kalix, P. (1992). Cathinone, a natural amphetamine. *Pharmacology and Toxicology, 70,* 77–86.

Kennedy, J. G., (1987). *The flower of paradise: The institutionalized use of the drug qat in North Yemen*. Dordrecht and Boston: Kluwer/Reidel.

Klein, A., & Beckerleg, S. (2007). Building castles of spit: The role of khat chewing in worship, work, and leisure. In J. Goodman, P. Lovejoy, & A. Sherrat (Eds.), *Consuming habits* (pp. 238–254). London: Routledge .

Odenwald, M. (2007). Chronic khat use and psychotic disorders: A review of the literature and future prospects. *SUCHT 53*(1), 9–22.

Randall, T. (1993). Khat abuse fuels Somali conflict. *Journal of American Medical Association, 269*(1), 12–15.

Rushby, K. (1999). *Eating the flowers of paradise: A journey through the drug fields of Ethiopia and Yemen*. London: Constable.

Utteh, H. A. (1997). The plight of Somali refugees in Europe, with particular reference to Germany (1993). In H. M. Adam & R. Ford (Eds.), *Mending rips in the sky: Options for Somali communities in the 21st century* (pp. 449–460). Lawrenceville, NJ, and Asmara, Eritrea: Red Sea Press.

Varisco, D. M. (2004). The elixir of life or the devil's cud? The debate over qat (Catha edulis) in Yemeni culture. In R. Coomber & N. South (Eds.), *Drug use and cultural contexts: Beyond the West* (pp. 101–118). London: Free Association Books.

SUSAN BECKERLEG

L

L-ALPHA-ACETYLMETHADOL (LAAM).

Acetylmethadol (also referred to as *l*-alpha-acetylmethadol, methadyl acetate, LAAM or L-AAM) is structurally related to methadone. LAAM is a potent opioid agonist with properties similar to methadone, except for its prolonged half-life. This slow elimination can be useful clinically, since 50–80 milligram doses of LAAM given three times a week are equivalent to daily doses of 50–100 milligrams of methadone in preventing the symptoms of opioid withdrawal. Thus, addicts on maintenance treatment would need to come to a clinic only three times a week for LAAM instead of daily for methadone. Since the early 1970s, methadone has been the only agent approved for use in maintenance-treatment programs for heroin addicts, but research has shown that LAAM can be a useful alternative. In 1993, the U.S. Food and Drug Administration (FDA) initiated the legal changes needed to make LAAM available for clinical use.

See also **Treatment, Pharmacological Approaches to: An Overview.**

BIBLIOGRAPHY

Gilman, A. G., et al. (Eds.). (1990). *Goodman and Gilman's the pharmacological basis of therapeutics* (8th ed.). New York: Pergamon. (2005, 11th ed.). New York: McGraw-Hill Medical.

Greenstein, R. A., Fudala, P. J., & O'Brien, C. P. (1992). Alternative pharmacotherapies for opiate addiction. In J. H. Lowinson, P. Ruiz, & R. B. Millman (Eds.), *Substance abuse: A comprehensive textbook* (2nd ed.). Baltimore: Williams & Wilkins. (2004, 4th ed.)

Sadock, B. J., & Sadock, V. A. (2007). Opioid-related disorders. In *Kaplan and Sadock's synopsis of psychiatry: Behavioral sciences/clinical psychiatry* (10th ed.). Philadelphia: Lippincott Williams & Wilkins.

GAVRIL W. PASTERNAK

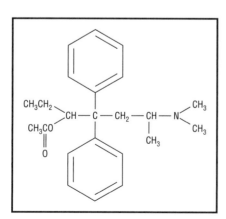

Figure 1. Chemical structure of LAAM. ILLUSTRATION BY GGS INFORMATION SERVICES. GALE, CENGAGE LEARNING

LAUDANUM.

Laudanum refers to a mixture of alcohol and opium. The opium was commonly mixed with different wines or spirits and a variety of other ingredients to disguise its bitter taste. Generally, alcohol accounted for about 20 percent of the preparation. Ancient cultures made use of alcohol-based extracts of opium, and it is not uncommon to find references to such concoctions in the writings of Hippocrates, Pliny, or Dioscorides (Tainter, 1948, p. 4).

However, scholars generally agree that Paracelsus (1493–1541), a Swiss contemporary of Copernicus, Luther, and da Vinci, with knowledge of both alchemy and medicine, can be credited with the creation of laudanum. At the time of Paracelsus, many different preparations existed with varying amounts of opium and other ingredients such as gold, pearls, and a substance called laudanum (Norton, 2005, p. 147).

The final ingredient refers to a gummy plant resin that was commonly used in these medicinal preparations. Whether the resin of the rock rose (*Cistus ladanifer*) gave laudanum, the alcoholic extract of opium, its name, or whether the word *laudanum* comes from the Latin word *laudare*, to praise, is of some dispute among historians (Van Ree et al., 1999, p. 342). However, from the sixteenth century onward, the name *laudanum* was attached to mixtures containing opium (Norton, 2005, p. 147).

Different competing preparations of laudanum existed in the seventeenth century. Yet, around 1670 one of the most popular laudanum preparations was created by Thomas Sydenham (1624–1689), a British physician. Sydenham's laudanum, a liquid, is said to have replaced the solid form used before that time. Aside from opium, the laudanum pill often contained substances such as saffron, castor, ambergris, musk and nutmeg (Hodgson, 2001). From his publications, scholars learned that Sydenham used sherry wine, opium, saffron, as well as powders of cinnamon and cloves in his particular version of the preparation which he administered to treat a variety of diseases such as smallpox, gout, and dysentery (Latham, 1979; Payne, 1900, p. 182). Given the sleep-inducing qualities of opium, the mixture was also prescribed to calm patients.

While other laudanum compounds were available, Sydenham's laudanum was one of the most common forms in which opium was consumed from the eighteenth until the early twentieth century in both Europe and the United States. The substance was widely offered to the public and sold at markets and shops, through mail order and by physicians. In the United Kingdom, the use of laudanum cut across different social classes. Wealthy gentlemen and their wives as well as the working class poor consumed it (Berridge, 1978, pp. 108–109). In the United States, however,

Thomas Sydenham. ENGRAVED BY EDWARD SCRIVEN. THE LIBRARY OF CONGRESS.

historians suggest laudanum use was more an upper and middle class phenomenon with women using the substance disproportionately in comparison to their male counterparts (Courtwright, 2001, pp. 36–37).

In many ways, laudanum was the cure-all medicine of the practicing physician in the eighteenth and nineteenth century who had limited remedies available for prescription. All types of diarrheal diseases were treated with laudanum because of opium's antiperistaltic, constipating effect. Laudanum was also administered to treat cholera, rheumatism, and tuberculosis; to suppress coughing; and to alleviate respiratory diseases. For individuals with sleep disorders, laudanum was a standard part of any treatment regimen (Duffy, 1993, pp. 180–181). Medical journals of the mid-nineteenth century report that laudanum was also used to fight alcohol-induced delirium tremens and as an antidote to arsenic poisoning (Ryan, 1845).

During the Seminole Indian Wars (1817–1818; 1835–1842; 1855–1858) as well as during the American Civil War (1861–1865) laudanum was given to wounded soldiers before they underwent amputations and to alleviate pain in general. It was also used to treat fevers and was given in large doses to cure diarrheal diseases. Both fever and dysentery were common afflictions of soldiers due to the state of their living conditions and frequent malnutrition (Straight, 1978, p. 633; Courtwright, 2001, p. 54).

Laudanum was so readily available throughout the eighteenth and nineteenth century that Americans as well as Europeans used the substance not only to treat their ailments but also to commit suicide (Clarke, 1985, p. 238). If shop owners were not willing to sell large quantities of laudanum, people would go to several sellers to procure a sufficient amount or invent convincing stories that would sway the shop owner. Pretending that the laudanum was for external applications or claiming that the preparation would be used for animals were successful ways to obtain large quantities. Stories of accidental poisoning were equally common, and children often suffered the consequences of an overzealous caregiver who sought to quiet a restless child or treat some other childhood disease by administering laudanum (Everest, 1842; Herapath, 1852; 1853). Overuse and abuse of laudanum and similar preparations was common.

According to the American Pharmacists Association, opium mixtures are controlled substances in the United States and only used to treat severe diarrheal diseases. Present-day compounds contain approximately 10 milligrams of anhydrous morphine per milliliter. Additionally, diluted opium mixtures are used to treat and alleviate withdrawal symptoms in neonates whose mothers were addicted to opioids during their pregnancies. Having recognized the abuse potential and risk of opioids, the Federal Drug Enforcement Administration rated laudanum a Schedule II drug. Laudanum has been tested as an alternative to methadone maintenance and the results from France were encouraging (Auriacombe et al., 1994 p. 567).

Laudanum should not be mistaken for its much weaker cousin, paregoric. Paregoric is a camphorated opium preparation, widely used in the eighteenth and nineteenth century to alleviate diarrheal diseases and infant colic. The mixture contains approximately 4 milligrams anhydrous morphine per 10 milliliters (Loyd, 1997, pp. 428–429). In the twenty-first century, paregoric is rated a Schedule III drug with medicinal use and less abuse potential than laudanum.

See also **Morphine; Nutmeg; Opiates/Opioids; Opioid Complications and Withdrawal; Pain, Drugs Used for; Paregoric.**

BIBLIOGRAPHY

Auriacombe, M., Grabot, D., Daulouede, J. P., Vergnolle, J. P., O'Brien, C., & Tignol, J. (1994). A naturalistic follow-up study of French-speaking opiate-maintained heroin-addicted patients: Effect on biopsychosocial status. *Journal of Substance Abuse Treatment, 6,* 565–568.

Berridge, V. (1978). Opium eating and the working class in the nineteenth century: The public and official reaction. *British Journal of Addiction, 73,* 107–112.

Berridge, V., & Edwards, G. (1981). *Opium and the people: Opiate use in nineteenth-century England.* New York: St. Martin's Press.

Churchill, J. M. Laudanum an antidote to arsenic (1857, April 18). *The Lancet, 69*(1755), 415–416.

Clarke, M. (1985). Suicides by opium and its derivatives, in England and Wales, 1850–1950. *Psychological Medicine, 15,* 237–242.

Courtwright, D. (2001). *Dark paradise: A history of opiate addiction in America.* Cambridge, MA: Harvard University Press.

Dewhurst, K. (1966). *Dr. Thomas Sydenham (1624–1689): His life and original writings.* Berkeley: University of California Press.

Duffy, J. (1993). *From humors to medical science: A history of American medicine.* Chicago: University of Illinois Press.

Everest, G. Poisoning with a minim and a half of laudanum (1842, February 26). *The Lancet, 37*(965), 758.

Herapath, W. B. Case of poisoning by laudanum in infancy. (1852, March 27). *The Lancet, 59*(1491). 303–305).

Heymans, C. (1967). Pharmacology in old and modern medicine. *Annual Review of Pharmacology, 7,* 1–15.

Hodgson, B. (2001). *In the arms of Morpheus: The tragic history of laudanum, morphine, and patent medicines.* Buffalo, NY: Firefly Books.

Kamenka, C. (2001). Laudanum to lignocaine: History of pain management. *Australian Journal of Pharmacy, 82,* 952–956.

Kirk, G. Poisoning by laudanum in an infant; effects of Galvanism (1853, January 22). *The Lancet, 61*(1534), 80.

Latham, R. (1979). *The works of Thomas Sydenham, M.D., translated from the Latin edition of Dr. Greenhill, with a life of the author.* Birmingham, AL: Leslie B. Adams Jr. (Original work published 1801)

Lessenger, J., & Feinberg, S. D. (2008). Abuse of prescription and over-the-counter medications. *Journal of the American Board of Family Medicine, 21,* 45–54.

Loyd, A. (1997). Laudanum and paregoric: History and compounding considerations. *International Journal of Pharmaceutical Compounding, 1,* 428–429.

Miller, R., & Tran, P. (2000). More mysteries of opium reveal'd: 300 years of opiates. *Trends in Pharmacological Sciences, 21,* 299–304.

Norton, S. (2005). The origins of pharmacology in the 16th century. *Molecular Interventions 5,* 144–149.

Payne, J. (1900). *Thomas Sydenham.* New York: Longmans, Green.

Ryan, W. (1845, November 1). Delirium tremens; poisoning by laudanum; erysipelas; recovery. *The Lancet, 46*(1157), 475–477.

Sigerist, H. (1941). Laudanum in the works of Paracelsus. *Bulletin of the History of Medicine, 9,* 530–544.

Straight, W. (1978). Calomel, quinine and laudanum: Army medicine in the Seminole Wars. *Journal of the Florida Medical Association, 65,* 627–644.

Tainter, M. (1948). Pain. *Annals of the New York Academy of Sciences, 51,* 3–11.

Van Ree, J., Gerrits, M., & L. Vanderschurer. (1999). Opioids, reward and addiction: An encounter of biology, psychology, and medicine. *Pharmcological Review, 51*(2), 341–396.

AUKJE KLUGE

LD50.

In preclinical studies, the LD50 is the median lethal dose—the dose of a drug that produces death in 50 percent of the experimental animals tested. The LD50 can be estimated from a dose-effect curve, where the concentration of the drug is plotted against the percentage of animals that die. The ratio of the LD50 to the ED50 (the median effective dose) indicates the therapeutic index of a drug for that effect and suggests how selective the drug is in producing its desired effects. In clinical studies, the concentration of the drug required to produce toxic effects can be compared to the concentration required for therapeutic effects in the population to estimate the clinical therapeutic index.

See also **Research, Animal Model: An Overview of Drug Abuse.**

BIBLIOGRAPHY

Gilman, A. G., et al. (Eds.). (1990). *Goodman and Gilman's the pharmacological basis of therapeutics* (8th ed.). New York: Pergamon. (2005, 11th ed. New York: McGraw-Hill Medical.)

Hollinger, M. A. (2003). *Introduction to pharmacology.* Boca Raton, FL: CRC Press.

NICK E. GOEDERS

LEDERMANN MODEL OF ALCOHOL CONSUMPTION. *See* **Prevention of Alcohol Related Harm: The Total Consumption Model.**

LEGAL REGULATION OF DRUGS AND ALCOHOL.

Legal regulation can be used in four general ways to influence the incidence, prevalence, patterns, and circumstances of consumption of potentially harmful substances, including alcohol, tobacco, and other drugs. The most direct mode of legal intervention is to establish the conditions under which a potentially harmful substance is available. In doing so, the law can employ either a *prohibitory scheme* that prohibits the production or distribution of the substance for nonmedical or self-defined uses, or a *regulatory regime* that permits the substance to be lawfully available for nonmedical or self-defined uses but that may regulate the product, its price, and the conditions under which it is accessible.

A completely successful prohibition would prevent any nonmedical consumption of the proscribed substance; however, the more likely consequence of a prohibitory scheme is that an illicit distribution system will arise to respond to whatever demand exists for the substance. In that case, the manner in which the prohibition is enforced can also influence the product, its price, and the conditions under which it is available.

A second mode of legal regulation is to regulate the flow of information and messages regarding use of the particular substance. The government may initiate its own informational efforts to influence attitudes, beliefs, and behavior. Government may also attempt to influence private communications, either by proscribing certain messages altogether or by regulating or restricting their content. Such restrictions have generally taken two forms: mandatory warnings and proscriptions of certain types of messages.

A third mode of legal control is the direct regulation of consumption, either by proscribing and imposing sanctions for undesired behavior or by withholding benefits or privileges to which the individual would otherwise be entitled. Thus, the law may proscribe use of a substance altogether, or it may prohibit such behavior in certain specified circumstances. Examples of total bans include unauthorized possession and consumption of controlled substances and consumption of alcohol by persons under the minimum age. Situational prohibitions include laws against consuming alcohol or smoking tobacco in public areas. Laws that require drug testing of workers and that permit job termination or discipline as a consequence of a positive test illustrate less coercive measures of deterrence.

A fourth use of the law emphasizes its declarative aspects. Whether a legal control has a direct impact on the marketplace or on the prevalence of the disapproved behavior, it may symbolize and express the official government view of the behavior and may generate derivative effects on behavioral patterns by influencing attitudes and beliefs. To the extent that citizens customarily defer to and respect the law or are influenced by messages of official approval or disapproval, a declaration of illegality may serve an educative, or didactic, role. Specification of a minimum drinking age, regulation of the availability of drug paraphernalia, and sanctions for possession of illicit drugs may all generate these symbolic effects, even if the direct effects tend to be modest.

AVAILABILITY

The National Commission on Marihuana and Drug Abuse identified four models of availability for psychoactive substances: The first involves no special controls at all; the substance is treated in the same way as other unregulated market commodities. Under the second approach, the substance is subject to special controls but remains lawfully

available for self-defined or nonmedical purposes. The third model limits availability to specific purposes, generally to medical and research uses only. Under the fourth approach, the substance is not legally available at all except perhaps for narrowly circumscribed use in research. The first two models can be characterized as regulatory approaches (because the substance is legitimately available for nonmedical or self-defined purposes) and the second two as prohibitory approaches (because the substance is not available for self-defined or nonmedical purposes). Tobacco and alcohol are lawfully available for nonmedical uses, but they are subject to variable regulatory controls designed to affect the product, place, and conditions of consumption. (Only the solvents and inhalants—glue, lacquer, thinner, ether, gasoline, nitrous oxide— are essentially uncontrolled.) However, most psychoactive substances (legally denominated controlled substances) are subject to prohibitory controls, which means their availability is limited by law to medical and research uses. One minor exception among psychoactive substances is peyote, which is available to members of the Native American Church for sacramental uses.

Alcohol. The availability of alcohol is governed by alcoholic beverage controls (ABC) that vary from state to state. ABC agencies view their primary responsibilities as providing an orderly market for the distribution of alcoholic beverages, controlling criminal involvement in the market, and generating tax revenues. Since the 1960s, the trend has been to liberalize restrictions on access to, and availability of, alcohol in order to facilitate private choice, to protect commercial interests, and to raise revenue. Only since the late 1980s have some ABC agencies shown any inclination to use their regulatory authority to influence the prevalence pattern and circumstances of consumption. Relevant aspects of ABC regulation include pricing and/or taxation policies, zoning, and rules regarding hours and days of sale.

Direct regulation, under the authority of ABC boards, is not the only method by which the law can influence the conditions under which alcohol is available. For example, one way to discourage retail sellers of alcohol from selling the substance to a person already intoxicated is to hold them legally liable for injuries subsequently caused by the intoxicated consumer, even after the consumer leaves the premises. Although the legal theory has changed over the years, the risk of liability for commercial suppliers under so-called dramshop liability laws is relatively well established. Moreover, the courts of several states have extended liability to the hosts of social events who served alcohol to obviously intoxicated guests who then cause injuries in their intoxicated condition.

Tobacco. For the most part, the public health dimensions of tobacco regulation have been reflected only in product, package, and advertising requirements designed to facilitate informed consumer choice. Only since the late 1980s has the federal government moved toward a policy that unequivocally establishes reduced consumption as its goal. Although a national prohibition is unlikely in the foreseeable future, several regulatory initiatives are being undertaken at all levels of government. For example, states will not receive federal money for mental health and substance-abuse services, unless they implement a plan for enforcing bans against the distribution of tobacco products to minors. Many localities have banned tobacco product vending machines. In addition, several states have raised cigarette excise taxes with the aim of reducing consumption, and the federal excise tax has been increased by a substantial amount, with the dual aims of reducing smoking and raising revenue.

In 1996, the U.S. Food and Drug Administration (FDA) asserted jurisdiction over traditional tobacco products under the Food, Drug, and Cosmetic Act, on the theory that tobacco products are intentionally marketed to satisfy consumers' addiction to nicotine. Based on this interpretation of the act, the FDA adopted regulations prohibiting the distribution of tobacco products to minors and, as discussed below, restricting the marketing of tobacco products to youths. However, the U.S. Supreme Court ruled in 2000 that the FDA did not have jurisdiction over traditional tobacco products under existing law and Congress had declined to confer such authority as of 2008.

In addition, smokers or their survivors have sued tobacco companies, with mixed success, seeking damages for smoking-induced disease or death. In 1998 the major tobacco companies entered into a Master Settlement Agreement with the state attorneys general, agreeing to pay $246 billion to the states over the duration of twenty-five years to settle lawsuits seeking to recover the states' costs of treating smoking-related diseases. Obviously, imposing liability on manufacturers for the adverse health consequences of smoking can have a major impact on the economics of the industry. In this instance, the indirect regulation of tobacco by the tort system has exerted a more potent influence on industry behavior than many direct regulatory alternatives, such as pricing policies, outlet limitations, or tar and nicotine limitations.

Controlled Substances. The manufacture and distribution of opiates, cocaine, cannabis (marijuana), stimulants, depressants, and hallucinogenic substances outside medical and scientific channels are unlawful under both federal and state controlled substance laws. The production and distribution of these substances within medical and scientific channels are subject to varied levels of restrictions based on their potential for abuse and their level of accepted medical use under the Controlled Substances Act of 1970. The wisdom of these prohibitions, especially in relation to cannabis, has been questioned by some on the grounds that the suppression of nonmedical use is not a legitimate governmental objective, and if it is, then the costs of the prohibitions exceed the benefits of the reduced consumption they achieve.

A particularly controversial aspect of cannabis regulation has been its classification as a Schedule I drug under the Federal Controlled Substances Act and its state counterparts. Schedule I is the most restrictive classification, reserved for drugs without any accepted medical use. Critics of the law have argued that marijuana is medically useful to treat glaucoma, AIDS wasting syndromes, and other conditions. Eleven states have adopted laws that legitimize bonafide medical uses under state law. These laws have created the unusual situation in which any effort to make marijuana available for medical uses could be prosecuted as a violation of federal law. The Supreme Court ruled in 2001 that anyone distributing medical marijuana could be prosecuted under the Federal Controlled Substances Act, and in 2005 extended this ruling further by holding that users of medical marijuana could be prosecuted under the act. However, the federal government has not moved aggressively to initiate such prosecutions. The

Institute of Medicine of the National Academy of Sciences has identified promising avenues of therapeutic use for the active constituents of cannabis and has recommended further research.

INFORMATION REGULATION

A government aiming to discourage what it perceives as unhealthy or unsafe behavior is not likely to be satisfied with the influence of its own messages and may seek to regulate communication by others within the bounds of the First Amendment, which protects freedom of speech. This can be done in two ways. First, the government may require individuals or organizations to convey the government's desired message. Laws requiring product manufacturers to include information on or with their products have become a standard feature of health and safety regulation. Mandatory package warnings have been used as a means of informing consumers about the dangers of tobacco and, more recently, of alcohol use. Second, government may ban communication of messages that it regards as undesirable. For example, laws banning false or misleading advertising are common, but government may choose to go a step further and suppress a message because it is thought to encourage unhealthy or socially disapproved drug, alcohol, or tobacco-using behaviors. Examples include the federal ban on broadcast advertising of cigarettes and state laws that ban alcohol advertising. Public-health advocates have urged the federal government to prohibit all forms of tobacco advertising. Whether such prohibitions actually affect the level of consumption (as opposed to product choice) remains controversial. The FDA 1996 Tobacco Rule, which was invalidated by the Supreme Court in 2000, would have restricted the advertising of tobacco products to a text-only format and would also have banned other forms of promotional activity that are thought to make use of tobacco products attractive to children and adolescents. The tobacco companies agreed to abide by some of these marketing restrictions in the Master Settlement Agreement executed in connection with the suit brought by the attorney generals of these states.

Proposals have also been made to move beyond advertising into the area of entertainment programming, eliminating messages that portray smoking and drinking in an attractive way. Clearly, such initiatives would raise serious constitutional questions concerning free speech.

Governments have also occasionally attempted to purge the environment of messages that are thought to encourage illicit drug use. For example, one provision of the Model Drug Paraphernalia Act (drafted by the federal Drug Enforcement Administration as a model for states to enact) specifically bans paraphernalia advertising. In 1973, the Federal Communications Commission (FCC) threatened to revoke the licenses of radio stations whose lyrics were thought to encourage illicit drug use.

DIRECT REGULATION OF CONSUMER BEHAVIOR

A decision to discourage nonmedical drug use—and to proscribe transactions outside medical channels in order to restrict availability for such use—does not necessarily entail a decision to proscribe and punish unauthorized consumption. Values of individual freedom weigh very differently in the two contexts.

From the perspective of libertarian philosophy, it has been argued that the criminalization of private use (and possession for such use) of drugs is categorically illegitimate, and the criminal prohibition should be limited to behavior that endangers others. This position leads to a discussion of the ways in which drug use might affect others. Even if criminalization is not categorically objectionable, the costs of it may exceed the benefits. The National Commission on Marihuana and Drug Abuse relied on such a cost-benefit assessment in 1972 when it recommended the decriminalization of possession of marijuana for personal use. A few states have decriminalized the possession of marijuana, although they have usually substituted a civil fine. Some of the states that took this action subsequently recriminalized the possession. Aside from marijuana, possession of all other controlled substances is a criminal offense in all states as well as under federal law. In addition, the possession of alcohol by underage consumers is an offense in most states. Even if the possession or use of a substance is not categorically proscribed, prohibitions can be used to deter and punish socially harmful behavior or to provide leverage to coerce individuals into treatment. Public smoking laws and laws prohibiting driving while intoxicated (or while having a

Under the Federal Controlled Substances Act, marijuana is categorized as a Schedule I drug, the most restrictive classification. Opponents of its labeling maintain that marijuana is effective in managing some medical conditions. CANADIAN PRESS/PHOTOTAKE

certain level of blood alcohol content) provide the prime examples.

DECLARATION ASPECTS OF LEGAL REGULATION

Government sends messages by its actions as well as its words. By declaring conduct illegal or by using any of the other instruments of legal intervention described above, the government expresses and formalizes social norms. However, knowledge of the official preferences may actually encourage the disapproved behavior among disaffected, outsider groups. Measuring such symbolic effects is difficult because of the need to isolate these hypothesized effects from other influences on attitudes and beliefs.

Arguments drawing on the declarative aspects of legal regulation are routinely employed by proponents of restrictive controls over the availability and consumption of alcohol, tobacco, and other drugs. Criminal sanctions against the simple possession of controlled substances are frequently regarded as indispensable symbols of social disapproval. Such arguments have been prominent in debates concerning the decriminalization of marijuana possession. Moreover, graded or stratified penalty schemes, which punish the possession of more harmful drugs more severely than that of less harmful drugs, may be favored because they denote the relative seriousness of these transgressions. Public smoking bans and antiparaphernalia laws seem to be particularly designed to reinforce attitudes unfavorable to smoking and recreational drug use.

Statements of legal rules can serve an educational role even if they do not penalize the undesired behavior. Minimum-drinking-age laws (which prohibit the distribution of alcohol to youth) provide a good example because they denote the norm even if the youthful drinker is not punished. Similarly, bans on alcohol or tobacco advertising might be enacted to erase a possible symbol of social approval, even if the proponents did not believe that such bans would directly reduce consumption.

See also **Advertising and the Alcohol Industry; Advertising and the Pharmaceutical Industry; Alcohol: History of Drinking in the United States; Dramshop Liability Laws; Legalization vs. Prohibition of Drugs: Policy Analysis; Minimum Drinking Age Laws; Opiates/Opioids; Parent Movement, The; Tobacco, Advertising and.**

BIBLIOGRAPHY

Babor, T. (2003). *Alcohol and public policy: No ordinary commodity.* New York: Oxford University Press.

Bonnie, R. J. (1986). The efficacy of law as a paternalistic instrument. In G. B. Melton (Ed.), *The law as a behavioral instrument.* Lincoln: University of Nebraska Press.

Brandt, A. M. (2007). *The cigarette century: The rise, fall, and deadly persistence of the product that defined America.* New York: Basic Books.

Cook, P. J. (2007). *Paying the tab: The costs and benefits of alcohol control.* Princeton, NJ: Princeton University Press.

Earleywine, M. (Ed.). (2006). *Pot politics: Marijuana and the costs of prohibition.* New York: Oxford University Press.

Husak, D. N. (2002). *Legalize this! The case for decriminalizing drugs.* New York: Verso Press.

Joy, J., Watson, S. J., & Benson, J. A. (Eds.). (1999). *Marijuana and medicine: Assessing the science base.* Washington, DC: National Academy Press.

Rabin, R. L., & Sugarman, S. D. (Eds.). (2000). *Regulating tobacco: Premises and policy options.* New York: Oxford University Press.

RICHARD J. BONNIE
REVISED BY FREDERICK K. GRITTNER (2009)

LEGALIZATION VS. PROHIBITION OF DRUGS: HISTORICAL PERSPECTIVE. The history of U.S. social and legal policy in regard to psychoactive and intoxicating drug use has been characterized by periodic shifts, strong ideological presuppositions, and deep disappointment. Any analysis of current policy and the debate about drug legalization must recognize the historical roots of current policy that affect the various positions in the debate.

A brief historical note may help place the current discussion of drug policy in the United States in perspective. To borrow a phrase from Ecclesiastes, there is nothing new under the sun. Those engaged in the current, often heated, discussions about national drug policy often act as if their concerns, insights, and positions about intoxication, drug use, and society are unique to the twenty-first century. A cursory review of history indicates that the debate on the meaning and effects of alcohol and other drug use on morals, public safety, productivity, and health is at least as old as written language. Some of the earliest recorded civilizations struggled with the issue and often adopted laws and policies that attempted to regulate strictly or prohibit the use of alcohol and other drugs.

Often these laws were based on a culture's perspective on the will of the divine or combined with basic civil codes. For example, the Torah appears to be very concerned with excessive alcohol use. It was seen as leading to gross immorality. The Christian New Testament holds similar views, particularly on the excess use of alcohol. The theme seems to be one of avoiding all things that harm the body or one's relationship with God, and moderation even in all things that are good. The Qur'an takes a very strong prohibition stand against alcohol and all intoxicating substances. Since much of modern Western civilization derives from these religious traditions, they continue to influence public thinking and policy. From a less theocentric perspective, many ancient civil codes also struggled with the regulation or prohibition of intoxicating chemicals. For example, the Romans seemed especially concerned that slaves and women not use alcohol and forbade its use by them. The concern appeared to be that alcohol would make slaves less productive and more difficult to control and that it would also lead to female sexual impurity. Chinese emperors prohibited the use of opium among their subjects. In addition, during the sixteenth and seventeenth centuries, when tobacco use began to spread around the world, many societies, including the Ottoman Empire, Great Britain, Russia, and Japan, initially tried prohibiting the substance.

These ancient and more recent laws and codes show that the regulation or prohibition of socially perceived harmful substances is not new to the twenty-first century, nor is the range of views on the negative consequences of regulation or prohibition and what would constitute a more effective, less harmful policy.

PHILOSOPHICAL AND CULTURAL TRADITIONS

Among the many legacies that underpin the present discussion of drug policy in contemporary society are four at times overlapping and sometimes contradicting philosophical and cultural traditions. The first is the basic American heritage of individual liberty and limited government interference with any variety of human choice, even if that choice is harmful to the individual making the decision and morally repugnant to the majority of society. This position was eloquently argued by British philosopher and economist John Stuart Mill (1806–1873) in his essay *On Liberty* (1859).

A second major social tradition is rooted in the moral utilitarian view of government that is also a part of the nation's heritage. The utilitarian perspective, also argued by Mill in his book *Utilitarianism* (1863), emphasized that government has a legitimate right to prohibit the behaviors that actually cause real harm to others. From this viewpoint, government has the right and responsibility to protect the common welfare by legally prohibiting individuals from engaging in behavior that is demonstrably harmful, not to themselves (which would have been an interference with liberty), but to other citizens.

The moral utilitarian perspective was an important underlying element in many of the late nineteenth- and early twentieth-century social-reform movements that culminated in the many state laws prohibiting narcotics and other drug use, the national Harrison Narcotics Act of 1914 and the Volstead Alcohol Prohibition Act of 1920. The utilitarian perspective was that narcotics and alcohol use caused real harm to others and society in general in the form of family poverty, crime, violence, and health-care costs.

A third social tradition that has influenced U.S. drug policy is commercialism (Courtwright, 2001). There is ample evidence that through the nineteenth century, U.S. society had a strong commercial attitude toward alcohol use and the use of a variety of powerful drugs. As has been documented by historians, merchandise catalogs and traveling entrepreneurs legally distributed opium, barbiturates, and cocaine as wonderful cure-alls for the ills of the human condition (e.g., Spillane, 2000). These merchants were an organized, respected part of the commercial establishment. Perhaps based on British narcotics commercialism, there has always been a commercial attitude toward alcohol and drug distribution in the United States. From the commercial perspective, alcohol and drugs are a wonderful commodity. They are often rapidly metabolized, highly addictive, and easily distributed. However, by the end of the nineteenth century, this rather freewheeling distribution of drugs caused a widespread public reaction that became incorporated into a variety of health- and social-reform movements.

A fourth significant element in the development of national alcohol and drug policy is a public health perspective. As was noted, at the turn of the twentieth century the United States was in the midst of major social and health reforms. After the passage of the 1906 Pure Food and Drug Act, a host of public-health-based government bureaus and regulations emerged, focusing on improving the quality of meats and other foods and requiring the accurate labeling of drugs. In addition, the American Medical Association initiated major reforms in the medical profession, eliminating over-the-counter narcotic drug advertisements in their journal and supporting the licensing of physicians as the only legitimate prescribers of many drugs. The public-health reform movements attempted to de-commercialize drug distribution and make drug use a medical, not commercial, decision. The passage of the Harrison and Volstead Acts probably represented a significant triumph of the moral utilitarian and public-health perspectives.

Following the Harrison Act and further legislation, the U.S. government instituted various bureaus and departments to carry out law enforcement and antidrug educational programs. Any review of the education programs of the Bureau of Narcotics would tend to conclude that they primarily constituted a heavy dose of propaganda with little basis in scientific fact. The federal proclivity for restricting the availability of drugs and arresting users and dealers continued strongly through the 1960s. During the decades following the Harrison Act and until the 1960s, the media and government were fairly united in their opposition to drug use, and there were few questions about the efficacy of drug laws or the social policy on which those laws were based.

THE 1960S AND 1970S
In the 1960s, U.S. society experienced the coming of age of the first of the baby boomers—those born between 1946 and 1960. By their sheer numbers, a proportion of this generation challenged the traditional socialization mechanisms of society and significantly questioned traditional assumptions, rationales, explanations, and authority. In a drive for generational self-discovery, drug use, particularly as a means to alter consciousness, became a part of the youth movement of the late 1960s and the 1970s. Most of the baby boomers who used drugs explored the use of marijuana and hallucinogens, but over the same years heroin use was increasing in inner cities across the country; crime, too, was increasing. Despite the declaration of a "war on drugs" by the Nixon administration from 1970 through 1971, national surveys conducted during the 1970s and early 1980s showed annual increases in almost all types of drug use among high school seniors, household residents, and criminal justice populations. The one exception was heroin, the major target of the Nixon drug war. Heroin use levels declined and then remained stable, but cocaine use rose dramatically during the 1970s and early 1980s, as did marijuana use among young people. By 1985, more than 20 percent of U.S. adults had taken drugs illegally, and for persons aged eighteen to thirty-four more than 50 percent had done so.

Perhaps because of the fundamental changes in national drug-using behavior that occurred during this period, the modern movement to legalize drugs began. The basis of the argument was that (1) many of the drugs that were then illegal were not as harmful as government and media propaganda portrayed them to be, (2) marijuana in particular was argued to be relatively less harmful than

alcohol and tobacco, and (3) the use of marijuana was a generational choice. In fact, the 1978 National High School Senior Survey showed that in the prior thirty days, a higher proportion of seniors had smoked marijuana than had smoked tobacco. By 1979, the media and American households were holding serious discussion about the legalization of marijuana, moving toward the British System of heroin maintenance, and considering the legalization of cocaine as a nonaddictive stimulant. Social political movements such as NORML were organized to achieve passage of laws decriminalizing marijuana use. With the tacit support of the Carter administration, there were eleven states, including Alaska, that decriminalized the possession of small amounts of marijuana for personal use. Even the director of the National Institute on Drug Abuse in the late 1970s, Robert Dupont, appeared to accept the likelihood that marijuana would be decriminalized. However, in 1977, in reaction to growing marijuana use by young people and a perception that government itself was being tolerant of drug use, groups of parents organized a grassroots campaign to buttress the resistance to drug law liberalization. By 1978, the Parents Movement had become a force to be considered, and their views had ready access to the White House policy office. The apparently about-to-be-successful national movement to legalize many drugs in the 1970s came to an abrupt end with the 1980 election of President Ronald W. Reagan.

THE 1980S
Corresponding with the election of President Reagan, there was a general conservative shift in national consciousness. First Lady Nancy Reagan, who made drug use among young people one of her prime topics of concern, was a welcome speaker at annual national meetings of the parents' groups. The public debate on legalization during the early 1980s was also affected by increasing evidence of the physical and psychological consequences of drug use, declining illegal drug use among high school students, decreasing use among household members, and, maybe, the initiation of maturation among the baby boomers. During the 1980s, U.S. policy was characterized by the increasing intolerance of drug addiction or even recreational drug use. On an official level, this came to be called *zero tolerance*.

According to the official federal policy of the 1980s, the assumption was that to a large extent drug use was an individual choice that could be affected by raising the cost of drug use to the users. It was believed that if enforcement reduced the availability of drugs, thus raising their prices, and increased the consequences of use by increasing the severity and certainty of punishment, individuals would choose to say no to illegal drug use. During the 1980s, the proportion of federal drug control spending allocated to treatment fell from 33 percent in 1981 to just 17 percent in 1992, with increasing shares going to prevention (up from 8% to 14%) and law enforcement (up from 59% to 69%). The increase in the overall size of the federal budget was even more dramatic. The total federal budget for all demand-side and supply-control activities was just $1.9 billion in 1981. This amount escalated sharply when President Reagan redeclared a war on drugs. By 1989, the total had reached $6.7 billion. The resources escalated still further during the Bush Sr. and Clinton administrations, reaching $12.2 billion in fiscal year 1993 and $18.1 billion in fiscal year 2001. (Direct comparisons with more recent budgets are complicated by definitional changes, but federal drug spending during the George W. Bush administrations has grown by an average of only 2 percent per year in real terms.)

By the end of the 1980s, the national drug-abuse policy of zero tolerance with a heavy focus on enforcement began receiving critical reviews from policymakers, public administrators, clinicians, and academic researchers. These critical reviews were generally based on civil libertarian and public health harm-reduction perspectives. The key points made by national policy critics were:

1. About two-thirds of all felony arrestees in major metropolitan areas were currently using cocaine.

2. A large proportion of all criminal charges were drug charges. This had resulted in a significant expansion of prisons and the proportion of the population incarcerated. All this had occurred at a very high economic cost.

3. The high profits from the drug trade were funding international terrorism and resulting in a rapidly increasing rate of violence in American urban areas.

4. Because of the vast amount of cash generated in the drug trade, there was great potential for corruption of government.

5. In an attempt to reduce illegal drug use, draconian laws focusing on search and property seizures had been passed.

6. Treatment availability for the poor had been reduced, with many cities reporting month-long waiting lists for publicly funded treatment slots.

CALLS FOR DECRIMINALIZATION

These consequences resulted in a major reinvigoration of the interest in legalizing or decriminalizing drug use. Those who argue for legalization come from a wide variety of professions and ideological positions, but they all essentially believe that U.S. society has reached the point where it can no longer afford to enforce existing law. There simply are not enough police, courts, prosecutors, or jail cells, nor is there the sense of justice that will allow U.S. society to enforce laws that have been broken by more than 20 percent of U.S. citizens.

In summary, the zero-tolerance, just-say-no policy of the 1980s had come to be viewed by critics as resulting in a virtual saturation of the criminal justice and prison system with drug law offenders, the undermining of crucial civil rights, and the decreasing availability of drug treatment for the poor accompanied by increasing violence in high drug-trafficking areas and large-scale public corruption. Many critics came to view drug laws as contrary to the very basis of a libertarian civil government. These critics saw the war on drugs declared in the 1980s and continued to the present as inimical to civil liberty. In addition to the civil libertarian perspective, there are many critics of current drug-prohibition policy who focus on a public-health harm-reduction perspective. From this perspective, current policy is not reducing the public-health harm caused by drug use. The public-health-reduction model emphasizes that drug abuse and addiction are the product of a complex set of psychological, sociological, and economic variables that are very little affected by the threat of prison. This perspective argues that the best way to reduce the personal and public-health harm of drug use would be to increase drug education and prevention, increase drug-treatment availability, and reduce the harm caused by drug abuse by providing clean needles and, perhaps, decriminalizing use—thus significantly reducing the cost of drugs and the associated crime.

Although there are very few detailed legalization proposals, those who advocate decriminalization generally argue that national policy should move toward an approach in which the distribution of drugs such as marijuana, cocaine, and heroin would not be governed by criminal law but by governmental regulations that controlled the manufacture, distribution, and use of these substances so that they would go only to those already addicted or be dispensed under very regulated conditions. Advocates of this policy believe that the movement of drug policy from criminal law to regulatory restrictions would result in the relatively easy availability of drugs and inexpensive access to them for those who are addicted, thus resulting in a significant reduction in corruption and violence as well as an increasing willingness on the part of addicts to enter treatment. This, it is asserted, would relieve the severe overcrowding of the criminal justice system. At the same time, it is argued, because of strict regulation, this policy change would more effectively protect young people as well as public health and safety than the current policy (Nadelmann, 1988; Wisotsky, 1991).

OPPOSITION TO LEGALIZATION

Critics of the legalization perspective do not question many of the basic judgments of the consequences of the 1980s national policy, but they do severely question the assumptions on which legalization is based. Those who are opposed to drug legalization often draw on the moral utilitarian and public-health perspectives. They make the following arguments:

1. During the 1980s and continuing into the 2000s, drug use, by all measures, significantly decreased among high school and college students as well as in the general population.

2. It is naive to assume that increasing availability, lowering cost, and reducing legal consequences will have no effect on the incidence and prevalence of marijuana, cocaine, and heroin use.

From this perspective, it is argued that once these drugs are legalized, even though regulated, they will enter the arena of advocacy through free speech and thus the realm of market creation and expansion through advertising. Alcohol use, which is severely regulated and illegal for those under twenty-one years of age, is initiated in junior high school. In addition, about one-third of high school seniors report being drunk each month. In most states, tobacco cannot be sold to minors, but smoking among junior high school students is common. These facts imply that regulation to make a drug available to one age group actually makes it available to all age groups.

3. The resulting increase in use in society and broadening of the societal base of use will result in detrimental health, behavioral, and economic consequences that will far outweigh any proposed benefit of legalization.

4. There is no broad societal base for legalizing drugs. Surveys among high school seniors clearly show that a large majority oppose the legalization of drugs—even the legalization of marijuana. Traditionally liberal countries such as Switzerland and Sweden have tried relaxing drug laws and were forced to modify their positions by their citizens, who daily had to experience the consequences of wide drug availability. Additionally, in a referendum in November 1991, Alaskans voted to rescind a marijuana legalization law passed in the 1970s and recriminalized marijuana possession. In a democracy, governmental policy cannot ignore the voice of the public. Dr. Joycelyn Elders, the first Surgeon General in the Clinton administration, was criticized for merely suggesting that the issue of legalization should be debated.

5. Although the costs of drug law enforcement and incarceration of offenders may seem high, it is a misconception to assume that those incarcerated are all petty first-time violators of the drug laws. DiIulio (1993) asserts that "in 1991 more than 93 percent of all state prisoners were violent offenders, repeat offenders (one or more prior felony convictions) or violent repeat offenders." Likewise, most drug-related violators in prison are not just users

but played some (perhaps minor) role in drug distribution. For many the official conviction charge is "possession," but that includes possession with intent to distribute, those who pled down from a trafficking charge, and couriers who possessed very large quantities.

Many of those opposed to legalizing drugs, such as former Secretary of Health, Education and Welfare Joseph A. Califano, Jr., and Mathea Falco, a former Carter administration official, argue that the existing policy should be drastically modified to increase the availability of treatment and educational and economic opportunities in societal groups with high drug-use rates. Specifically, what is called for is an increase in treatment availability in the criminal justice system, either through diversion or probation to treatment or through the provision of therapeutic services in jails and prisons, as well as a major increase in the availability of publicly funded treatment slots in the United States. Policy analysis studies began to conclude that every dollar invested in treatment results in several dollars saved in terms of other social costs, including crime (e.g., Rydell and Everingham, 1995; Gerstein et al., 1994).

Some who oppose drug legalization believe that the current discussion has subtly eroded the public's will to fight illegal drug use. From this perspective, the only way to retain the reduction in general societal drug use that occurred during the 1980s is to retain a vigorous enforcement of drug laws. The advocates of strict law enforcement believe that weakening the war on drugs would be a kind of backdoor legitimization, a demoralizing discussion of the failure of drug policy. Previous drug policy leaders such as William J. Bennett argue that national drug policy during the 1980s was effective in reducing drug use in the general youth and adult population by making use morally, socially, and legally unacceptable and that the drug policy reform debate of the 1990s made drug use more acceptable, resulting in subsequent increases in use (Bennett & Walters, 1995a, 1995b; Rosenthal, 1995).

THE 1990S AND BEYOND
In the mid-1990s it was very difficult to reconcile the extremes of the drug legalization debate, beyond some shared belief in the need for increasing drug education, prevention, and treatment availability. However, as drug problems in the U.S. stabilized and in some cases began to ebb, the stridency of the debate has eased. Drug law reform groups have focused attention on medical marijuana, not across the board legalization, and even the famously severe federal mandatory minimum cocaine sentences and notorious New York State Rockefeller drug laws have been modified. Local drug enforcement has put greater emphasis on controlling drug-related firearms, violence, and disorder through specific deterrence and focused crackdowns, rather than trying to suppress all forms of drug selling and use (e.g., Braga et al., 2001). In many jurisdictions, law enforcement has pushed back underground, for example, to discrete sales arranged by cell phone, resulting in greatly improved quality of life in surrounding communities. Also promising are partnership efforts such as drug courts, drug offender diversion programs including California's Proposition 36, and Hawaii's very successful Opportunities for Probation with Enforcement (HOPE) coerced abstinence program (Belenko, 1999; Hawken, 2006; Kleiman, 1997). These developments might give an optimist hope that, freed to some extent from the distraction of unrealistic "silver bullet" solutions ("create a drug-free America" or "just legalize drugs"), there is potential for a more constructive period of improving drug policy bit by bit through the hard work of pragmatic policy analysis and good governance.

See also **Anslinger, Harry Jacob, and U.S. Drug Policy; Crime and Drugs; Harm Reduction; Legalization vs. Prohibition of Drugs: Policy Analysis; Opiates/Opioids; Prevention, Education and; Prohibition of Alcohol; Switzerland; Temperance Movement; U.S. Government Agencies; Zero Tolerance.**

BIBLIOGRAPHY

Belenko, S. (1999). Research on drug courts: A critical review. *National Drug Court Institute Review, 2,* 1–58.

Bennett, W. J., & Walters, J. P. (1995a, February 10). Renewing the war on drugs. *Washington Times.*

Bennett, W. J., & Walters, J. P. (1995b, February 9). Why aren't we attacking the supply of drugs? *Washington Times.*

Braga, A. A., Kennedy, D. M., Waring, E. J., & Piehl, A. M. (2001). Problem-oriented policing, deterrence, and youth violence. An evaluation of Boston's Operation Ceasefire. *Journal of Research in Crime and Delinquency, 38* (3), 195–225.

Brecher, E. M. (1972). *Licit and illicit drugs.* Boston: Little, Brown.

Califano, J. A., Jr. (1995, January 29). It's drugs, stupid. *New York Times Magazine.*

Courtwright, D. (2001). *Forces of habit: Drugs and the making of the modern world.* Cambridge, MA: Harvard University Press.

DiIulio, J. J., Jr. (1993, May 10). Cracking down. *New Republic.*

Dupont, R. S. (1979). *Marihuana*: A review of the issues regarding decriminalization and legalization. In G. M. Beschner & A. S. Friedman (Eds.), *Youth drug abuse.* Lexington, MA: Lexington Books.

Gerstein, D. R., Johnson, R. A., Harwood, H. J., Fontain, D., Suter, N., & Malloy, K. (1994). *Evaluating recovery services: The California drug and alcohol treatment assessment.* Chicago: National Opinion Research Center and Fairfax: Lewin-VHI.

Hawken, A. (2006). *The economics of alternative sentencing: Assessing the Substance Abuse and Crime Prevention Act.* Doctoral dissertation, RAND Graduate School, Santa Monica, CA.

Inciardi, J. A. (1992). *The war on drugs II.* Mountain View, CA: Mayfield.

Inciardi, J. A., & McBride, D. C. (1991). The case against legalization. In J. A. Inciardi (Ed.), *The drug legalization debate* (pp. 45–79). Newbury Park, CA: Sage.

Johnston, L. D., O'Malley, P. M., & Bachman, G. (1988). *Illicit drug use, smoking, and drinking by America's high school students, college students, and young adults 1975–1987* (National Institute on Drug Abuse, DHHS 89-1602). Washington, DC: U.S. Government Printing Office.

Kleiman, M. A. R. (1997). Coerced abstinence: A neo-paternalistic drug policy initiative. In L. A. Mead (Ed.), *The new paternalism* (pp. 182–219). Washington, DC: Brookings Institution Press.

Mill, J. S. (1921). *On liberty.* Boston: Atlantic Monthly Press. (Original work published 1859).

Mill, J. S. (1863). *Utilitarianism* (Frazer's Magazine). London: Parker, Son and Bourn.

Nadelmann, E. A. (1988). The case for legalization. *Public Interest, 92,* 3–31.

Reuter, P. (1992). *Hawks ascendant: The punitive trend of American drug policy.* Santa Monica, CA: RAND.

Rosenthal, A. M. (1995, January 3). The cruelest hoax. *New York Times.*

Rydell, C. P., & Everingham, S. S. (1994). *Controlling cocaine: Supply versus demand programs.* Santa Monica, CA: RAND.

Spillane, J. (2000). *Cocaine: From medical marvel to modern menace in the United States, 1884–1920.* Baltimore: Johns Hopkins University Press.

Trebach, A. S., & Inciardi, J. A. (1993). *Legalize it? Debating American drug policy.* Washington, DC: American University Press.

Wisotsky, S. (1991). Beyond the war on drugs. In J. A. Inciardi (Ed.), *The drug legalization debate* (pp. 103–129). Newbury Park, CA: Sage.

Young, J. H. (1961). *The toadstool millionaires: A social history of patent medicines in America before federal regulation.* Princeton, NJ: Princeton University Press.

DUANE C. MCBRIDE
REVISED BY JONATHAN P. CAULKINS (2009)

LEGALIZATION VS. PROHIBITION OF DRUGS: POLICY ANALYSIS.

Whether a drug should be prohibited or legalized is perhaps the most fundamental question in drug policy. It is a moderately complex question and most who write about the issue do so from an advocacy perspective, so the debate is even more confusing than it needs to be. It is important to start with a clear definition of what is meant by legalization versus prohibition. There is a spectrum of policy positions. Some drugs can be used for medical but not recreational purposes (e.g., cocaine), whereas others cannot even be used for medical purposes (e.g., heroin). Some drugs cannot be used recreationally but are legal with a prescription (Valium) or when taken under medical supervision (methadone). Some drugs are legal only for adults (alcohol); others are legal for all ages (e.g., the caffeine in soda).

DIFFERENTIATING LEGALIZATION FROM PROHIBITION

When a sharp line needs to be drawn between legalization and prohibition, it is useful to say that a drug is legal if it is legal for that substance to be produced and distributed for unsupervised consumption by a significant portion of the population (e.g., all adults). By this definition making marijuana available for medical use is not legalization if prescriptions are restricted to those experiencing specific, medically diagnosed conditions (e.g., glaucoma), but it would be if any individual could write his or her own prescription. Likewise by this definition the Netherlands has legalized retail distribution, and use of marijuana, although wholesale (large-volume) marijuana production and distribution is still prohibited. Most other drugs in most countries are either clearly legal or clearly prohibited by this definition.

DIFFERENT CRITERIA

Having defined prohibition as compared to legalization, the next important observation is that different people use different criteria for deciding what policy should be. Some people are implicitly if not explicitly consequentialists. They think the right policy is the policy that leads to the fewest problems. Others believe that there is a moral imperative to make substances legal (e.g., libertarians who believe people should be free to consume anything, even if it hurts them) or prohibited (e.g., people who believe the substance is evil for religious reasons) regardless of the consequences.

The challenge for the moral prohibitionists is defending to others why they favor prohibiting some drugs but not others. There are defensible positions predicated on consistent principles ("all intoxication is immoral" or "being physically dependent on a drug is idolatry"), but it is hard to articulate such a defense for U.S. policy. Cigarettes are highly addictive, and alcohol is clearly an intoxicant, but they are both legal. In 1930, alcohol was prohibited, but marijuana was not. Ten years later, marijuana was prohibited, but alcohol was not. One does not have to be very cynical to believe that the moral distinctions enshrined in public policy are just the legal formalization of arbitrary popular prejudices.

The challenge for the libertarian view is less simplistic but no less compelling (at least for those who recognize homo economicus as an ideal type, not a descriptively accurate model of human behavior).

The basic idea is that at least some addictive, mind-altering substances may merit an exception to the general rule that a liberal society should not interfere in the private consumption decisions of its citizens. Mark Kleiman, a drug policy scholar and professor at UCLA, eloquently makes the case in his 1992 book *Against Excess*. The distinguishing characteristics are a combination of factors such as in the following examples: Drugs are intoxicating,

so consumption decisions are often made "under the influence"; for some, drugs cessation is physically painful; drugs offer immediate pleasures and the possibility, but not guarantee, of delayed pain; drug initiation occurs primarily among minors; social influences play a prominent role in initiation decisions. That skepticism of government regulations is healthy for a liberal democracy does not imply that prohibiting a drug is necessarily a bad idea. Liberal democracies tolerate other paternalistic infringements on freedom of behavior (e.g., a minimum wage, motorcycle helmet laws, and prohibitions against swimming where there are dangerous rip tides).

Furthermore, few want minors to have ready access to drugs, but legalizing use by adults inevitably makes a drug readily available to minors because every adult is a potential supplier, whether consciously (e.g., adults buying alcohol for minors) or unconsciously (e.g., minors stealing cigarettes from adults). Legalizers sometimes deny this connection, asserting that cocaine is more readily available to minors than alcohol is, but those assertions are contradicted by minors' self-reports (e.g., in the Monitoring the Future surveys). The moral arguments for or against prohibition are in one sense unassailable. Individuals are entitled to their separate values. But at the same time those values are not likely to be persuasive to people who do not hold them.

For consequentialists, opinions about legalization tend to depend on two factors: (1) how people trade off or value the problems associated with drug use and those associated with prohibition and black markets and (2) on predictions about how legalization would affect those outcomes. Prohibiting a drug will generally reduce but not eliminate its use. The use that persists despite prohibition supports a black market, which generates problems of its own. Indeed, the social cost per gram or per ounce consumed will typically be greater than would be the case if the drug were legally available. So prohibition typically reduces use but increases harm per unit of use.

Those who favor legalization tend to believe that a drug's legal status has little impact on its use. They also tend to be very mindful of the problems associated with black markets (stereotyped as drug dealers shooting people in battles over competing territories), drug enforcement (e.g., racially biased enforcement tactics), and prohibition's increasing the damage per episode of use (e.g., restricting needle availability, increasing spread of HIV by needle sharing). Those who favor prohibition tend to believe that prohibition substantially suppresses use (tobacco and alcohol are used far more than cocaine or heroin) and that many problems stem directly from drug use (e.g., the damage addiction can do to familial relations) not primarily from the drug's illegal status. To them, legalization is tantamount to making a bad situation worse. It might eliminate the black market and associated crime, but if legalization led to a tenfold increase in the number of addicts, the country could still be worse off.

Unfortunately, the public debate about the consequences of legalization is clouded with specious arguments. For example, prohibitionists argue that drugs should be illegal because they are associated with so much crime. Indeed, the majority of arrestees in many U.S. cities test positive for illegal drugs; association does not imply causality, but a reasonable guess is that something on the order of one-fourth of crime in the United States is caused by illegal drugs. Legalizers counter that most of the drug-related crime is attributable to the illegality, not the drugs per se. Only about one-sixth of drug-related crime is psychopharmacological in nature (i.e., driven directly by intoxication or withdrawal). Conflicts between market participants turn violent in part because they cannot resort to the court system to resolve disputes, and one reason addicts commit robberies is to get money to buy drugs that would cost far less if they were legal. Ironically, alcohol is one of the most violence-promoting substances per se, and it is legal.

To give an example from the other side, legalizers cite statistics showing that illegal drugs such as cocaine and heroin kill only thousands of people per year, whereas alcohol and cigarettes kill hundreds of thousands. What they neglect to point out is that far more people use cigarettes and alcohol, so the death statistics per user are not so different. Furthermore, the death statistics for illicit drugs are restricted to acute effects (e.g., overdose deaths), whereas the cigarette and alcohol figures include indirect effects (e.g., deaths caused by intoxicated drivers) and delayed or chronic effects (e.g., from

lung cancer). Focusing on overdose deaths would make cigarettes seem safe, whereas the expansive definition suggests that they kill more people than all other drugs combined, including alcohol.

Both sides lend a patina of scientific rigor to their arguments by citing trends in data, but the divergent trends of different indicators makes it easy to tell statistical lies. An advocate of prohibition might point out that the number of drug users fell dramatically during the 1980s when enforcement expanded rapidly. A legalizer could counter that emergency room mentions of drug use rose as fast as prevalence fell. What is lost in such bickering is the observation that the legal status of the major drugs has been stable in the United States for many decades. Looking at contemporary trends might indicate the wisdom of a more or less stringent prohibition, but there is no direct experience with legal cocaine, heroin, marijuana, or methamphetamines in recent U.S. history. Many seek to draw lessons from other times (e.g., when cocaine was legal in the United States in the late nineteenth century) or places (e.g., Europe), but casual comparisons can be misleading and careful study of those analogies does not give definitive guidance (MacCoun & Reuter, 2001).

Even anecdotal evidence can be spun in different ways. Occasionally, there are accounts of a mother selling her baby for crack. Some argue this kind of action proves drugs should be legalized. If they were cheap enough, addicts would not have to resort to such extreme measures. Others counter that the fundamental problem is that the drug is so powerful that it becomes more important to a mother than her own child; therefore, everyone should be protected in whatever ways possible from exposure to such temptations that can erode basic human values and worth.

The next important observation is that different drugs are different, and it may well make sense to prohibit some but not others because they have different properties (e.g., some drugs can trigger violent outbursts [PCP]; others tend to sedate [heroin]). It is by no means the case, however, that one can unambiguously rank substances from the most to the least dangerous because a substance can be very threatening in one respect but not in others. Cigarettes are highly addictive, but they are not intoxicating. Heroin can be deadly

	Caffeine	Tobacco	Alcohol	Marijuana	Heroin	Cocaine
Acute health risk	None	None	High	Minimal	High	Moderately High
Chronic health risk	None	Huge	High	Some	Minimal	Some
Use affects health of others	No	Yes	Fetuses	Possibly	No*	Fetuses
Problems caused by withdrawal	Minimal	Unpleasant	Physical risk	Minimal	Physical risk	Extremely unpleasant
Intoxication leads to accidents	No	No	Yes	Some	Moderate	Unclear
Intoxication leads to violence	No	No	Yes	No	No	Some
Likelihood of addiction given use (as observed in the U.S. in last 30 years)	Minimal	High	Moderate	Moderate	High	High
Addiction disruptive to daily functioning	No	No	Yes	Somewhat	Yes	Yes

*Injection drug use can spread blood-borne diseases (BBDs), including HIV/AIDS and hepatitis, but it is injecting with shared equipment, not the heroin use per se, that is the proximate source of the spread of BBDs.

Table 1. Substances and their risks. ILLUSTRATION BY GGS INFORMATION SERVICES. GALE, CENGAGE LEARNING

(overdose deaths are not uncommon) but in and of itself creates almost no chronic health damage. Heroin addicts are usually in poor health because they are poor, spend money on heroin rather than on food or shelter, and inject with dirty needles, but the heroin per se does not degrade organs the way alcohol destroys the liver or smoking causes emphysema. Table 1 illustrates the concept.

The table divides the substances by legal status. The legalization question asks whether any substances on one side of the line should be moved to the other. It does not address changes in laws, programs, or policies that do not move a substance across the line. It might or might not be a good idea to repeal mandatory minimum sentences, cut the number of drug arrests in half, expand treatment and prevention programs, approve marijuana for medical use, eliminate profiling as an enforcement tactic, reduce the military's role in drug control, and repeal drug-related civil forfeiture statutes. Doing so would blunt many of the criticisms of prohibition, but it would not constitute legalization. Conversely, one could raise the legal smoking age, require people to pass a drinker's test to get an alcohol consumption license, or ban smoking from all public spaces,

but none of those would extend prohibition to a new substance.

There is no constituency for prohibiting caffeine, and prohibition of alcohol is perceived to have failed so badly in the last century that there is little interest for trying it again. There is some discussion of banning tobacco use, but such proposals are probably political non-starters.

The more seriously debated proposals would legalize one or more of the substances prohibited as of 2008. For discussion purposes, it is convenient to differentiate three groups of substances: (1) cocaine, heroin, and methamphetamines, (2) marijuana, and (3) all other illicit substances.

Cocaine, heroin, and methamphetamine are not similar pharmacologically, but they have key commonalities. They are expensive, are subject to stringent enforcement, can dominate the life of an abuser, and have large, established black markets. These are the substances whose use can most confidently be predicted to rise substantially and to be problematic if they were legalized. These substances are very simple to produce, but sell for many times their weight in gold because they are prohibited and subject to severe sanctions. They are also the source of most of the corruption, violence, and disorder associated with drug markets, so legalization would bring many benefits. Most observers, though, believe this would be an example of making a bad situation worse. At a minimum, legalizing these substances is a high stakes gamble that is only partially reversible. There are other, safer alternatives to exhaust first (e.g., mending rather than ending prohibition) and more information that should be gathered about how legalization would affect use before seriously contemplating such a radical change.

Marijuana presents quite a different situation. Prohibition makes marijuana more expensive than it otherwise would be, but a daily habit is no more expensive than a two-pack a day cigarette habit. Likewise, daily marijuana use is not a recipe for enhancing performance, but it does not preclude most daily functions (e.g., personal hygiene, holding down a job). So a tenfold increase in use is a less likely outcome of legalizing marijuana than for cocaine, and even if it did happen, that outcome would be less catastrophic. However, the benefits of legalizing marijuana are also far smaller than the benefits of legalizing cocaine, heroin, and methamphetamines because marijuana markets are less violent and marijuana users generally do not resort to crime to support their habit. Likewise, marijuana offenders account for only about 10 percent of those in prison for drug law violations. There is no consensus about whether legalizing marijuana is wise. Some say yes. Many say no. What is clear, though, is that the risks, uncertainties, and potential benefits are all much smaller when considering legalizing marijuana than when considering legalizing cocaine, heroin, and methamphetamines.

The last category is diverse, so general statements are difficult. It includes drugs that can be used as a weapon in sexual assault (e.g., GHB) and drugs used not for their mind or mood altering properties but to enhance athletic performance (e.g., anabolic steroids). Two general observations are possible, however. First, prohibitions are relatively more effective and relatively less costly when preventing the spread of substances that are not commonly used than they are at reducing the use of an established drug. Second, by definition, there is more to lose in terms of increased availability and use when altering the status of drugs that are now rare. By those principles, it would be easier to make a case for legalizing XTC (Ecstasy) or LSD, for example, than for PCP, but they are not frequently the focus of legalization proposals, which typically address just marijuana or all drugs collectively.

See also **Cocaine; Heroin; Legal Regulation of Drugs and Alcohol; Legalization vs. Prohibition of Drugs: Historical Perspective; Marijuana (Cannabis).**

BIBLIOGRAPHY

Kleiman, M. A. R. (1992). *Against excess: Drug policy for results.* New York: Basic Books.

MacCoun, R. J., & Reuter, P. (2001). *Drug war heresies: Learning from other times, places, and vices.* New York: Cambridge University Press.

JONATHAN P. CAULKINS

LIMBIC SYSTEM. The limbic system is a group of brain structures organized into a functional unit that is important in the expression of emotion and mood states. The term *limbic lobe* and associated terminology can be traced to the French neuroanatomist Paul Broca (1824–1880), who used it first to describe the forebrain structures that encircle the brain stem. The *limbic system* is a broader classification, composed of brain structures that form an integrated circuit surrounding the thalamus—an important relay station between higher brain centers and the hind brain and spinal cord.

The limbic system is thought to be important in emotional behaviors. This was hypothesized on the basis of neuropathological investigations of the brains of individuals displaying bizarre emotional disturbances. These initial clinical observations were followed by animal studies, in which the loss of these structures produced significant changes in emotional responsiveness. As research techniques and methodologies were refined, it became clear that limbic structures had an important and complex role in the expression of behavior. It is now believed that these structures are involved in a number of significant behavioral processes. In particular, the limbic system and related structures are thought to be important in the expression of emotion related to euphoria and feelings of well-being. For these reasons, the limbic system may have an important role in drug abuse.

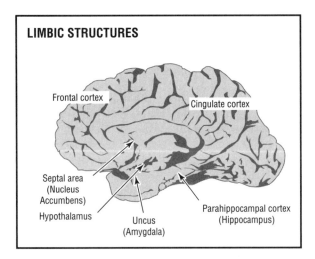

LIMBIC STRUCTURES

Frontal cortex

Cingulate cortex

Septal area
(Nucleus
Accumbens)

Hypothalamus

Uncus
(Amygdala)

Parahippocampal cortex
(Hippocampus)

Figure 1. The limbic system—composed of structures generally located between the brain stem and higher cortical structures. Some of these components are labeled in the sagittal section of the brain. The structures in parentheses lie behind the structures listed above them. The hypothalamus, hippocampus, septal nuclei, nucleus accumbens, amygdala, cingulate cortex, and frontal cortex are components of the limbic system that may have an important role in drug abuse. ILLUSTRATION BY GGS INFORMATION SERVICES. GALE, CENGAGE LEARNING

LIMBIC SYSTEM COMPONENTS

The limbic system that surrounds the thalamus provides an interface between the midbrain and higher cortical structures. The general structure and components of the limbic system are shown in Figure 1. These include the amygdala, the nucleus accumbens, the olfactory tubercle, the septal nuclei, the hippocampus, the hypothalamus, the cingulate cortex, and the frontal cortex. As can be seen in the figure, these structures are positioned between the brain's major relay station—the thalamus—and higher cortical structures. The separate components of the limbic system are interconnected such that activity initiated in one structure affects other components. One of the hypotheses about the basis of emotion speculated that reverberating neuronal activity in this system was responsible for affective behaviors. Initial animal studies using either direct electrical stimulation or lesions (loss) of various components of the limbic system substantiated the important role of this system in behavior.

THE ROLE OF THE LIMBIC SYSTEM IN BEHAVIOR

Electrical stimulation or the destruction (lesions) of components of the limbic system alter behavioral

processes. Lesions of the hippocampus disrupt memory processes, whereas lesions or stimulation of the amygdala affect emotional behavior and feeding in a manner similar to manipulations of the medial and lateral hypothalamus. Stimulation of the lateral hypothalamus produces aggressive responses, whereas lesions of this area produce a placid behavioral profile. In contrast, lesions of the medial hypothalamus produce a highly excitable and aggressive pattern of behavior, whereas lesions of the amygdala result in placid and nonaggressive behavior. Early studies found that lesions of the lateral hypothalamus can decrease feeding, whereas lesions of the ventromedial region produce excessive levels of feeding resulting in obesity. Recent experimental studies have demonstrated the complex nature of the involvement of hypothalamic cells in feeding and drinking; however, like most complex behaviors, the mechanisms that control hunger and satiety are not simply located in a single brain center.

Some structures of the limbic system are important in reinforcement processes. The term *reinforcement* applies to processes perceived as rewarding or good, which therefore are repeated, such as electrical self-stimulation. For example, animals will repeatedly emit a response that leads to the delivery of brief electrical stimulation of small electrodes that are implanted in selected brain structures. Humans will also choose to stimulate many of these same brain regions and report positive feelings of well-being and euphoria. The limbic system sites that produce these effects in animals include the lateral hypothalamus, nucleus accumbens, frontal cortex, cingulate cortex, and the brain-stem nuclei believed to be part of the limbic system—these include the substantia nigra and ventral tegmental area, which both contain dopamine neurons that send inputs to many limbic-system components. Measures of brain-glucose metabolism, which directly reflect brain-cell activity, have been used to determine the involvement of specific brain regions in animals electrically self-stimulating three of these brain regions. The stimulation of each of these regions produced significant activation of several limbic-system structures that included the nucleus accumbens, amygdala, hippocampus, and the frontal and cingulate cortices. This area of investigation has led neuroscientists to propose that there are brain circuits dedicated to the behavioral processes related to reinforcement. Drugs of abuse likely produce their positive effects through the activation of these brain circuits.

THE ROLE OF THE LIMBIC SYSTEM IN DRUG ABUSE

A large number of experiments have focused on identifying the brain circuits that mediate the reinforcing effects of abused drugs, because the reinforcing effects are responsible for drug abuse. These experiments have included the use of drug self-administration techniques and sophisticated neurochemical procedures to measure the involvement of specific neurotransmitter systems. As of 2008, evidence indicates that limbic structures and brain cells that project to limbic structures play an important role in these processes. It is clear that dopamine-containing neurons that project from the ventral tegmental area to the nucleus accumbens have a critical role in the reinforcing actions of cocaine and amphetamine. Removal of these inputs with toxic agents that selectively destroy dopamine-releasing brain cells disrupts intravenous self-administration of these drugs. Additional evidence of the importance of this region in drug abuse comes from glucoseutilization studies. The levels of glucose metabolism are significantly elevated in a number of limbic structures in animals self-administering cocaine intravenously. Other experiments have directly shown dopamine levels in the nucleus accumbens to be increased in animals intravenously self-administering cocaine. Collectively, these data imply an important role for the limbic system in general and specifically for dopamine neurons in the limbic system tied to the brain processes involved in stimulant abuse.

The brain circuits involved in opiate reinforcement appear to be very similar to those mediating cocaine self-administration. Limbic structures are clearly implicated in opiate reinforcement, but a central role for dopamine is less obvious. Significant changes in the utilization of some chemicals (neurotransmitters) involved in transmission between brain cells have been shown in the nucleus accumbens, amygdala, and the frontal and cingulate cortices of animals intravenously self-administering morphine. However, loss of dopaminergic inputs to the nucleus accumbens does not affect drug intake, whereas a similar loss of serotonergic inputs does. Similarly, nucleus-accumbens dopamine does not appear to be elevated in animals self-administering heroin as it is in animals self-administering cocaine. However, evidence does indicate an important role for limbic structures and chemicals used to communicate between cells of the limbic system in opiate reinforcement. Limbic structures also appear to be important for ethanol (drinking alcohol) reinforcement. The levels of dopamine appear to be elevated in the nucleus accumbens of rats orally self-administering alcohol. Injections of drugs that antagonize dopamine directly into the nucleus accumbens decrease alcohol self-administration, whereas drugs that enhance dopamine action increase alcohol intake. In addition, animals will self-administer alcohol directly into the ventral tegmental area—an area that contains the cell bodies for the dopamine cells that send inputs to the nucleus accumbens. These data collectively indicate that the nucleus accumbens and dopamine-releasing inputs to the nucleus accumbens are important to alcohol reinforcement.

CONCLUSION

The limbic system plays an important role in behavior. These brain structures appear to be central to the processes that mediate the reinforcing effects of electrical-brain stimulation and of several highly abused drugs. The nucleus accumbens appears to be a structure central to the reinforcing properties of cocaine and amphetamine, but it appears less important to opiate and alcohol reinforcement. A more exact definition of specific neurochemicals and brain-cell pathways in the limbic system that are involved in drug abuse will become clearer as new methodologies are developed.

See also **Neuron; Neurotransmission.**

BIBLIOGRAPHY

Koob, G. F. (1992). Drugs of abuse: Anatomy, pharmacology and function of reward pathways. *Trends in Pharmacological Sciences, 13*, 177–184.

Koob, G. F., & Bloom, F. E. (1991). Cellular and molecular mechanisms of drug dependence. *Science, 242*, 715–723.

Lowinson, J. H. (2005). *Substance abuse: A comprehensive textbook.* Philadelphia, PA: Lippincott Williams & Wilkins.

Sadock, B. J., & Sadock, V. A. (2007). Functional and behavioral neuroanatomy. In *Kaplan and Sadock's synopsis of psychiatry: Behavioral sciences/clinical psychiatry* (10th ed.). Philadelphia: Lippincott Williams & Wilkins.

Wyss, J. M., van Groen, T., & Canning, K. J. (2003). The limbic system. In P. M. Conn (Ed.), *Neuroscience in medicine* (2nd ed.). Totowa, NJ: Humana Press.

JAMES E. SMITH
STEVEN I. DWORKIN

LYSERGIC ACID DIETHYLAMIDE (LSD) AND PSYCHEDELICS.

LSD is the abbreviation for lysergic acid diethylamide. It is the most potent member of a group of hallucinogenic substances called the indole-type hallucinogens. These drugs have structural similarities to another indole, the neurotransmitter serotonin.

HISTORY

LSD was originally synthesized at the Sandoz Pharmaceutical Company in Switzerland as part of a long project begun in the 1930s. The aim was to develop useful medications that were derived from ergot, a fungus (*Claviceps purpurea*) that infects such grasses as rye. Some of these compounds were found to be useful in medicine—such as methysergide, for the treatment of migraine headaches, and ergotamine, which is widely used in obstetrics to induce contractions of the uterus and stop bleeding after the delivery of a baby. These medications do not have hallucinogenic properties.

The chemist in charge of this drug development project was Albert Hofmann. In 1943, he synthesized a compound he called LSD-25 because it was the twenty-fifth compound made in this series of ergot derivatives. He accidentally ingested some of it and within forty minutes had the first LSD "trip." He told his colleagues he was not feeling quite right and got on his bicycle to go home. Later, he carefully described the vividly clear flood of perceptions that are characteristic of the "mind manifesting" or psychedelic drug. This, then, was a complete surprise. Thereafter, the drug and various substitutions of different atoms on the basic molecule were extensively tested for medical uses in the late 1940s and in the 1950s. No specific medical use of LSD or its psychedelic variants has been found.

Because of its potency and the extensive reports of laboratory studies in animals and in the clinic, LSD has become the prototypical hallucinogen, or psychedelic drug. It also became the emblem of a social movement—which, in fact, was a confluence of various movements that had begun in the early 1960s; they peaked in the late 1960s. By 1973, the "acid culture" had subsided into a small but still active subculture of various psychedelic drug devotees seeking meaning and profound insights. The feeling of a "great discovery" about such drugs and the human mind had occurred as early as the nineteenth century; artists and writers, such as Baudelaire and Rimbaud in Paris, had discovered hashish and the altered, somewhat dreamy, states of consciousness and euphoria produced by this potent form of marijuana—the active ingredient of which is tetrahydrocannabinol (THC). For a period, they became absorbed with hashish and wrote about its alluring effects. The drug scene evoked the promise that the human mind must contain remarkable powers. Toward the beginning of the twentieth century, mescaline, the active hallucinogenic compound in the peyote cactus, similarly was tried by a few explorers in medicine and in the arts. In New York City, during the early part of World War I, many influential people and intellectuals took either peyote "buttons" (the dried tops of the peyote cactus) or mescaline (the synthesized active ingredient of the buttons) and called it a "dry drunk." Similarly, after World War II, LSD caused a flurry of excitement among some professionals, and its medical value was tested in psychiatric patients. Writers such as Aldous Huxley wrote exciting books about the effects of mescaline and, later, LSD—yet there was still no widely popular movement until 1960.

Then Timothy Leary, a young psychology instructor at Harvard, explored the Mexican or "magic" mushroom, *Psilocybe mexicana*, and its active ingredient, psilocybin—and later LSD— claiming criminals became loving and peaceful and others more creative. He popularized this on campus and, when he was not reappointed to the faculty, proclaimed himself to be a martyr to his

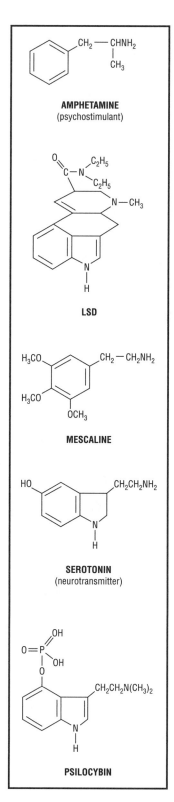

Figure 1. Chemical structures of amphetamine, LSD, mescaline, serotonin, and psilocybin.
ILLUSTRATION BY GGS INFORMATION SERVICES. GALE, CENGAGE LEARNING

cause. Between 1960 and 1966, the media repeatedly "discovered" LSD—in effect, advertising it. As publicity increased, subcultures experimenting with mushrooms and LSD grew up in the East and West Coast cities. Musicians, rock music, the hippie lifestyle, "flower children," and many in the various protest movements against the Establishment and the Vietnam War were loosely joined to Leary's attempt to lead affluent and middle-class youth. Well-publicized festivals celebrated LSD and marijuana, such as the Summer of Love in the Haight-Ashbury section of San Francisco. Leary's challenge was for youth to "turn on, tune in and drop out" with acid. As more and more youth were curious to try experiences their parents had never dreamed of, rebellion led not only to acid experiments but to extensive polydrug abuse—the extensive use of marijuana and various street substances. Either LSD or some variant and even heroin were tried. In addition, the search for new drugs with different and improved characteristics (more or less euphoria, hallucinogenic activity, or stimulant properties), literally hundreds of so-called designer drugs were synthesized (DOM, MDMA, DMT, etc.). Because any drug can have bad effects, the unsupervised use of all of these compounds led to frequent "bad trips" (which fundamentally were panic reactions) that brought people to emergency rooms. This generated widespread concern that all American youth (and, later, those in Europe) would become dreamy and "way-out acid heads." In 1966, the Sandoz Laboratories ceased distribution of the drug because of the often-exaggerated bad reactions and the public concern. As the claims for enduring LSD insights proved transient, research with LSD in humans essentially stopped.

Thus, one of the ways people use the effects of drugs that seem to enhance the clarity of mentation (mental activity) and perception (while not producing confusion, dreamy-euphoria, or oversedation) is to become absorbed in periods of intense exploration with a few others "in the know." Those with such inside information form a kind of cult and then advertise, but they eventually see some bad effects (the wrong people taking the drug in the wrong circumstance with unfortunate consequences) and sooner or later see little real use for the drugs. The minor or major epidemics then die down, only to recur as later generations rediscover the compounds.

Dr. Timothy Leary, center, in custody, being led to U.S. Customs House at La Guardia Airport, 1966. © BETTMANN/CORBIS.

EFFECTS

LSD is one of the most potent hallucinogens known; one-billionth of a gram of LSD per gram of brain produces profound mental changes. Although subjective effects occur in some individuals after doses as low as 50 micrograms, typical street doses range from 10 to 300 micrograms—street dosages vary widely. Misrepresentation also frequently occurs; someone will try to purchase synthetic tetrahydrocannabinol (THC), the active ingredient of marijuana, and receive LSD. Thus, the intake of LSD can be accidental as well as intentional, and the lack of quality control in illicit supplies is a hazard. Because of its high potency, LSD can be applied to paper blotters or the backs of postage stamps from which it is dissolved for consumption. Unsubstantiated reports of LSD added to stick-on tattoos for young children have

caused alarm, even though absorption through skin would be far too slow to deliver enough drug to the brain to produce and sustain a trip.

The absorption of LSD from the gastrointestinal tract and other mucous membranes occurs rapidly, with drug diffusion to all tissues, including brain. The onset of psychological and behavioral effects occurs approximately 30 minutes after oral administration, peaks in the next 2 to 4 hours, depending on the dose, with gradual return to normal by 10 to 12 hours. The first 4 hours after a 200-microgram dose are called a trip. In the next 4 to 8 hours, when over half the drug has left the brain, the "TV show in the head" has stopped. At this point subjects think the drug is no longer active, but later they recognize that they, in fact, had paranoid thoughts and "ideas of reference" in the last 4 to 8 hours of the trip. This simply means that there is the feeling of being at the center of things, being hyperalert, and having a conviction that everything going on refers to oneself. This is a regular but little-publicized aftereffect, which finally dissipates 10 to 12 hours after the dose.

From 12 to 24 hours after the trip, there may be some slight letdown or feeling of fatigue—as if one had been on a long, steep roller coaster ride. After these intense and even frightening moments, the ordinary world might for a time seem drab. There is no craving to take more LSD to relieve this boredom; one trip usually produces satiation for a time, although some may want to repeat the experience. Memory for the events during the trip is quite clear. Those who revisit the experience sooner or later decide they have learned what they can and go on with the practical, daily affairs of living. In one experiment on creativity, subjects received either LSD or the stimulant amphetamine during a period of pleasant surroundings and music. The only difference between the two groups six months later was a slight tendency for those who had received LSD to buy more recordings! So the promise of lasting insight or creativity was not kept.

Drugs that make one feel different—alcohol being typical—can signal a "holiday from daily reality." The way the effects of such drugs are interpreted is critical. Beer at the Super Bowl means "loudly letting go" and champagne at the White House means a time for graceful speech and feelings. Thus personal and social expectations (called *set*—or how one is set to go) and the surroundings (called *setting*) have much to do with the ultimate effects of drugs. This is distinctively and especially the case with psychedelics. Thus when the chemist Albert Hofmann first ingested the active ingredient of the Mexican mushroom psilocybin, the perceptions capturing his attention were related to Aztec symbols and art! For some, therefore, the trip may simply be funny and odd—for others it will have special meanings. Set and setting partially determine the character of such trips.

Fundamentally, LSD produces a heightened clarity and awareness of sensory signals—of sights, sounds, touch, lights, and colors. Similarly there is special significance given to thoughts, memories, or verbal interchanges. For example, gestures or

inflections of speech or many cues that are normally in the background are felt to be more important than what is being said or usually meant—and in looking at a picture, the central figures may take on a life of their own, the small background details that are normally ignored emerging, capturing attention.

While awareness is strikingly increased, control over what is being attended to is weakened. For all these reasons, unstable surroundings or confused motives at the time of drug ingestion may lead to a less-controlled trip or even a panic-generating trip. Many are aware that the trip is not quite real and fundamentally feel as if they are "spectators" of what they are so intensely experiencing. Many rely on guides, a group, or the rhythm of music to carry them through this period of altered perceptions in which control is diminished. Thus, personal intent and reliable surroundings are major factors affecting the different kinds of experiences that people will have.

While every trip has an individual characteristic, there are regularities in the trips. This has been called a "march of effects" following drug ingestion. Thus, observers note, the first sign of feeling different is like "butterflies in the stomach" or a slight nausea and feeling of "whoops, here we go" as if on a roller coaster. Parts of the body simultaneously feel strange or different. At about the same time (30–40 minutes after drug ingestion), the cheeks are slightly flushed and pupil size begins to increase, maximizing within an hour or two. These changes are due to the effects of LSD on the sympathetic and parasympathetic nervous systems. The pupils react normally but are enlarged. After 4 hours they slowly begin to return to normal size, which finally is achieved at 10 to 12 hours after taking LSD. At the beginning of the trip, all soon note that what is at the periphery of their vision suddenly seems as clear as what is normally at the center of vision. Over the next 90 minutes, there is a feeling that tension is welling up. Laughing or crying will relieve the tension. Often subjects say they are laughing because of what they see or crying because of their feelings. But this is simply based on a need to relieve the fluctuating rise of tension. The trip moves on into the second and third hours when perceptual fluctuations and intensities are mainly noted. People also report perceiving several feelings simultaneously. A common observation is, "I don't know if I'm anxious, thrilled, or terrified." Just as perceptions are in flux, so are feelings, and these feelings and emotions may capture center stage in the second and third hours. Throughout the trip, people feel as if they are on the brink of an exhilarating but also dangerous experience. This intensity dies down about 4 hours after the usual dosage. If very large doses of LSD (500–1,000 micrograms) are taken, there is less capacity to be a spectator and far more intense self-absorption and fear. Some call this "dying of the ego" and relate the experience to mystical versions of death and rebirth.

Because the familiar seems novel and is seen in a different way, specialists in perception have been interested in what is called the "breakdown of constancies" that occurs with the drug. Normally we correct for what the retina sees by putting the world into order. We usually suppress the nonessential and focus on what we need to do to get about during the day. Just as with a camera, the retina sees the hand placed 6 to 8 inches in front of the eye as large. But the brain corrects for it and keeps size constant. Under LSD, corrections for constancy do not seem to happen. Many sensations that are normally dampened can thus have free play under the drug and the world will seem far less regular than it does in daily life.

One of the aftereffects in some—clearly not all—people is called "flashbacks." Days, months, or years after tripping, with no particular trigger or with an intense sensation, there may be a sudden few minutes in which subjects feel like they are back under the drug. They also may see flashing lights and other optical illusions. These flashbacks may be very disturbing. Flashbacks can occur after only a single drug experience and unpredictably. There has been no explanation as to why or how flashbacks occur. Scientists cannot predict (by observing a trip) if flashbacks will later occur or who is vulnerable. While these aftereffects are upsetting to some, most people do not experience them or those that do are not bothered. Others simply observe that their dreams may be more intense for a time after the drug experiences. One scientist noted that riding on a train to work, he was distracted from focusing on his newspaper for several months by the telephone poles whizzing by. These were normally at the periphery of his

attention as he was reading, but after LSD, he could no longer suppress this irrelevant detail. There were more reports of such phenomena after publicity about them; given the millions of trips with LSD, these aftereffects are certainly infrequent but not rare.

Perhaps the most alarming bad effects of the drug have been the panic states occurring during a trip. Native Americans note that if one is in conflict, the effects of mescaline during religious ceremonies are unpleasant and can evoke terror. They then pray with the panicked person and "talk him down." One cannot predict whether a panic experience will occur. "One good trip does not predict a second one" is the general wisdom concerning this risk. Higher doses lead to less control and more intense effects, but panic states can occur at doses as low as 75 to 100 micrograms. For those who might be at risk for other mental disorders, hallucinogenic experiences may often destabilize them and precipitate some form of mental illness. For others, the experience may lead to a subsequent absorption with the unreal ("dropping out"), rather than coping with the challenges that the tasks of the ordinary world present. Occasional suicides or rare impulsive acting out of odd ideas arising during a trip have led some to loss of control and tragedy.

For most, the experiences have few negative or positive aftereffects. Although it has often been suspected, no permanent change to the cells of the brain (brain damage) has ever been scientifically established. There is no generally accepted evidence that the drug produces chromosomal abnormalities or damage to a developing fetus (although no nonprescription drugs during pregnancy is the only safe rule to follow). The bad effects of a period of diminished control are unpredictable, and in that fact lies the real risk. Thus, it is the intensity of the experience and how well or poorly it can be managed, the unpredictable flashbacks, and how this "TV show in the head" or this "waking dream" gets woven into one's subsequent life that are at issue when hazards are considered.

TOLERANCE

One striking feature of LSD, mescaline, and related psychedelic drugs is tolerance, which is a loss of typical drug effects after repeated doses. In brief, with daily doses the duration and intensity of effects rapidly diminish to the point where no subjective effects are perceived. After 200 micrograms per day of LSD, there is simply no detectable drug effect on the third or fourth day. After three or four days without LSD, the full initial effects can be triggered by the same dose that has been "tolerated." Thus tolerance develops and dissipates rapidly. When subjects are tolerant to LSD, the usual dose of mescaline required for a trip is also no longer effective. This is called cross-tolerance. It is readily seen with similar dosage schedules of psilocybin, LSD, and mescaline. There is no cross-tolerance with the nonhallucinogenic stimulant drug amphetamine. Thus, there must be some common mechanism of action among the psychedelic drugs beyond their structure and similar array of mental effects.

Tolerance is seen both in humans and laboratory animals. The lack of pupil enlargement is a common sign of tolerance. In animals, some drug effects show tolerance and some do not. For example, a heightened sensitivity of rats to mild electric shock persists after daily doses and does not show tolerance. Such persisting drug effects during periods of tolerance have not been studied in humans. How and why a psychedelic drug loses and regains its potency in this fashion is not yet understood, but there is no withdrawal discomfort after stopping a psychedelic drug when it has been taken over several days. This differs from the classic effects described for opioid drugs, where an uncomfortable withdrawal with drug cessation requires more drug for relief. Such physical drug withdrawal phenomena are not found with psychedelics.

LSD AND SEROTONIN
LSD is known to affect many places in the brain where the body's neurotransmitter serotonin naturally has actions and effects, and the biochemical effects of LSD in the brain are mostly linked to those sites related to serotonin. LSD acts as a kind of impostor at receptors that recognize serotonin. LSD is like serotonin but different. Thus with LSD, the receptor signals other parts of the brain that there is too much serotonin, and these parts of the brain respond by tuning down cells that make serotonin. Yet, in fact, the chief effect of LSD is to cause *less* serotonin to be released in the neighborhood of the receptor—rather than too much,

there is too little. This is one example of how LSD miscues the systems governing the flow of information between various brain neurons. In fact, overloading the brain with serotonin can reduce the LSD effect, and diminishing brain supplies of serotonin will increase LSD effects. Yet serotonin itself does not cause the scrambled perceptions that LSD does. How this miscue by LSD leads to the vivid effects is still unknown.

LSD, other indole-type psychedelics, and many hallucinogens related to mescaline (but surprisingly not mescaline itself) are known to act especially at a subtype of the serotonin receptor called the $5HT_2$ receptor. In laboratory animals, daily doses of LSD or psilocybin lead to fewer of these receptors, an effect that would be expected to produce tolerance; however, with 3 or 4 days off the drug, the number of $5HT_2$ receptors returns to normal. Both LSD and mescaline act at certain brain neurons, such as the locus coeruleus, and make it more responsive to inputs from the environment—such as a pinch. Researchers speak of such effects as lowering the gates to sensory input. We know the ways by which LSD affects certain brain systems but still far less than we need to know to explain the full panoply of effects.

Although many of the psychedelic drugs are known to interact with serotonergic $5HT_2$ receptors, and this interaction appears to be of critical importance in producing their hallucinogenic effects, the hallucinogenic drugs can bind to a subtype of serotonin receptors that is located on serotonin nerve-cell bodies and on their terminals (which release serotonin that goes to the adjacent nerves with $5HT_2$ receptors). Interactions with these various receptors can lead to changes in the firing rate of such cells. The designer drugs MDMA and MDA cause the release of both dopamine and serotonin, effects that might contribute to their psychostimulant properties. The differential interactions of the various hallucinogens with multiple sites and systems may underlie the qualitative differences in the experience they produce.

See also **Cults and Drug Use; Hallucinogenic Plants; Monitoring the Future; Plants, Drugs From.**

BIBLIOGRAPHY

Freedman, D. X. (1986). Hallucinogenic drug research—if so, so what?: Symposium summary and commentary.

Pharmacology, Biochemistry and Behavior, 24, 407–415.

Glennon, R. A. (1987). Psychoactive phenylisopropylamines. In H. Y. Meltzer (Ed.), *Psychopharmacology: The third generation of progress.* New York: Raven Press.

Grinspoon, L., & Bakalar, J. B. (1979). *Psychedelic drugs reconsidered.* New York: Basic Books.

Grob, C. S. (2002). *Hallucinogens: A reader.* New York: J. P. Tarcher.

Hanson, G. R., Venturelli, P. J., & Fleckenstein, A. E. (2005). Hallucinogens (Psychedelics). In *Drugs and Society.* Sudbury, MA: Jones & Bartlett Publishers.

Jacobs, B. L. (1987). How hallucinogenic drugs work. *American Scientist, 75,* 386–392.

Jacobs, B. L. (Ed.). (1984). *Hallucinogens: Neurochemical, behavioral and clinical perspectives.* New York: Raven Press.

Jaffe, J. H. (1990). Drug addiction and drug abuse. In A. G. Gilman et al. (Eds.), *Goodman and Gilman's the pharmacological basis of therapeutics.* New York: McGraw-Hill Medical. (2005, 11th ed.)

Lewis, W. H. (2005). Hallucinogens. In *Medical botany: Plants affecting human health.* Hoboken, NJ: John Wiley & Sons.

Masters, R., & Houston, J. (2000). *The varieties of psychedelic experience: The classic guide to the effects of LSD on the human psyche.* Rochester, VT: Park Street Press.

Shulgin, A., & Shulgin, A. (1991). *PIHKAL: A chemical love story.* Berkeley, CA: Transform Press.

Siegel, R. K., & West, L. J., Eds. (1975). *Hallucinations: Behavior, experience and theory.* New York: Wiley.

Weil, A. (1972). *The natural mind.* Boston: Houghton Mifflin.

DANIEL X. FREEDMAN
R. N. PECHNICK